THE NEW GLÉNANS SAILING MANUAL

THE NEW GLÉNANS SAILING MANUAL

Translated by
James MacGibbon and
Stanley Caldwell

Boston, Massachusetts

Nouveau Cours de Navigation des Glénans
First published © 1972
Editions du Seuil
Reprinted 1973, 1975, 1976

Translation © James MacGibbon 1978

U.S. Edition published by
SAIL BOOKS, INC.
38 Commercial Wharf
Boston MA 02110

Distributed to bookstores by
W. W. Norton & Co., Inc., New York

Printed in the United States by
R. R. Donnelley & Sons Company

ISBN 0-914814-10-9

Introduction

This new Glénans Sailing Manual, following on the sailing courses we brought out over ten years ago, is a collective work produced by instructors and skippers at Les Glénans. Each chapter is the result of much critical discussion and careful checking. Some have contributed more than others, but no one wished to be singled out from the name which unites us all – Glénans.

The course is a synthesis, neither an encyclopedia, nor a mere compilation. We have only included what seems to be essential in the experience of succeeding generations of sailors and instructors – during more than a quarter of a century at Glénans.

Our aim is to enable the beginner virtually to learn on his own. Les Glénans only claims to offer the right background to those who really want to learn how to sail, and is no narrowly structured school with examinations and diplomas. By the same token our manual aims to give friendly encouragement and allay your anxieties without, we hope, forgetting to warn you of the dangers. The approach, at least in the beginning, applies equally to someone working alone and to a crew of two, and that is why, for instance, there is no mention of that maid-of-all-work at sailing schools, the Caravelle, because it is not a boat for a beginner on his own.

We hope too that the manual will be useful to those who have already done some sailing as a means of checking and extending their knowledge, and getting real feeling for the whole business. It is in fact quite a comprehensive work. The experience of many seas – from the North Cape to the Canaries, from Ireland to the coast of Poland, from Gibraltar to Turkey – has enabled Glénans skippers to broaden their knowledge and pass it on. But certain subjects, like astro-navigation for instance, are not covered since we consider that there are already excellent books on that subject and we have nothing to add. In such cases we merely refer you to the relevant sources.

The book can be read in two ways: sticking to the text or just following the photographs and diagrams with their captions – one complements the other. A detailed index allows immediate reference to terms and all other information.

Thanks to all concerned with it, the New Glénans Sailing Manual, although it is a recognised authority, can be easily understood by everyone. We hope that, even more than its predecessor, it will play its part in spreading the comradeship of the sea throughout the world.

Glénans Sea Centre

Introduction to the U.S. Edition

There is no doubt that this is the most monumental sailing instruction work ever printed—nearly 800 pages' worth of teaching technique from small dinghies to offshore cruisers as developed by the staff of the world-renowned Sea Center in the Glénans Islands off the coast of France.

And therein lay SAIL's dilemma for its U.S. edition. In so large and definitive an undertaking, should we attempt to "Americanize" the efforts of Glénans' instructors by adding approaches to sailing that are peculiarly ours? Certain spinnaker-launching procedures, for example, or maybe domestic types of cooking stoves? Should we put in our own navigational chart samples and buoyage systems rather than theirs? Should we retire the venerable Arpège 30-footer and illustrate a more up-to-date U.S. cruising design?

Clearly we could scrape together dozens of points in which we might override the choices and authority of the Glénans staff. But we would have created some hybrid—part Continental, part American, part personal preference—and to what purpose? If the language of sailing were indeed universal as presumed, then surely it would survive meters instead of feet, "anti-cyclone" rather than "high-pressure area," and the Caravelle over, say, a Bantam.

And so we decided against intruding on the work of 30 years of expert teaching. In the end, we feel, American readers will have little difficulty in assimilating the European material, and in fact will be well exercised by it. More importantly, SAIL will have presented the Glénans course from beginning to end in the painstaking detail that, after all, is exactly how it is taught on that rugged Brittany shore. And Glénans hasn't lost a student yet.

SAIL Books, Inc.

Translator's Introduction

This *New Glénans Sailing Manual* is an entirely new book not to be confused with the one they published some fifteen years ago. It is based on the instructional methods used with notable success at Glénans for over thirty years. This means a certain amount of repetition, something at first I considered might be modified. I soon realised however that this is one of the classic approaches to teaching – as anyone who has served in the armed forces will recall. It is undeniably effective. For instance, every opportunity is taken to ram home the importance of safety precautions at sea. In any case, few readers will read the manual right through from the first page to the last. It is not that kind of book, for each part, each chapter, is a complete handbook on its particular subject, to be studied or referred to according to need. Such repetition therefore serves to stress the importance of certain basic methods allied to a degree of discipline and, what is particularly characteristic of Glénans, a total commitment, an attitude of mind which all seasoned yachtsmen will recognise.

We discussed the possibility of including British and American classes of boats but as the Glénans boats have some special characteristics, it seemed sensible to keep to them in the knowledge that they have at least approximate counterparts in most countries. Indeed it is interesting to know the types of craft this famous sailing centre regard as most suitable for instruction.

Although every effort has been made to render all the facts and theories faithfully in English, certain liberties have been taken with the style to achieve what Glénans wanted – an accurate English *version*. It would have been impossible to write this English version without assistance from the Glénans Sea Centre itself and I owe a special debt of gratitude to Mr Royston Raymond who checked and corrected my draft: he too, with his extensive knowledge of the French language and greater understanding of the particular philosophy on which the epilogue is based, is solely responsible for that section. I also wish to thank Mr F. J. Burton, until lately Chief Meteorological Officer at the Plymouth Meteorological Office, RAF Mountbatten, Plymouth for checking the terms in the long chapter on his subject. It was particularly fitting that he should do this for he is one of those who contribute to the BBC Shipping Forecasts that are appreciated at Glénans quite as much as they are by British yachtsmen.

The diagrams being a special feature of the book, I am specially indebted to Mr Victor Welch for his tireless expertise in modifying many of them for black and white reproduction and overlaying the translated terms on nearly all of them.

Like the original French book, this translation is also a team effort but as one person must be responsible for any shortcomings in the English text I felt bound to have my name on the title page for any errors and infelicities are my responsibility and mine alone.

Finally, should any readers find the text didactic or doctrinaire, a visit to the Glénans Islands would dispel any such impression. I went there myself on a cruise and my visit was as memorable for the practical and understanding approach to instruction in sailing as for the friendliness of the instructors and those attending the courses, and the beauty of the archipelogo with its fine white coral beaches.

James MacGibbon
November 1977

Contents

1. Starting sailing

When you decide to take up sailing, don't get bogged down in theories and instruction. Learn to swim, get yourself a boat and take it out on the water.

Sailing is not one of those natural sports, like football, which you can begin to play instinctively. Sailing doesn't come naturally; you will have to adapt body and mind to new ways of moving and thinking, sometimes in a way that will seem contrary to your instincts. This is why you can't learn it all from a book, even this one.

At first you will feel alarmingly ill-at-ease, inept, apparently quite incapable of coping with the unexpected. Without losing your sense of self-preservation, you simply have to gain confidence, developing reactions that cannot immediately come naturally. In brief, have your wits about you.

This chapter is intended to ease you into your new way of life, picking up the essential but initially formidable terms as we go along, as if you, the beginner, were in our company while you got the boat ready. Then, together, we shall go on board and box the compass and see how the boat behaves in the wind round all 360 degrees.

This may sound confusing for we are going to lay down the course to be followed having just said that you ought to find your own. But the truth is that what follows won't help the novice much before he goes for a trial trip. It should though help him a little to know what he has to do to come to terms with his boat. And when he is back on shore he may be helped to understand what went on – or wrong. And if you have already crewed for an experienced helmsman you will be the better able to understand what he was up to. Lastly we hope that instructors will see the point of allowing beginners to come to terms on their own with the elements and that does not preclude discreetly giving them confidence. The time for passing on knowledge will come soon enough – as soon as they come back from that first sail, when there will be a flood of questions, all sharpened by a real sense of urgency. Theories following a little practical experience can be immediately assimilated, not something to learn by rote but as a key to progress. We mean this sailing course to be as different as possible from learning your tables.

The choice of a boat for beginners

Whatever plans you have, it seems sensible at the start to go for a small, light dinghy with a centreboard of a type to be found everywhere – on lakes, rivers, at the seaside. The centreboard is of course just a movable keel that can be drawn up and let down as required. 'Light' boats have only their crew as ballast – something to forget to your cost!

There are two other categories of sailing boats which are for cruising: displacement yachts with fixed keels and boats of intermediate type, ballasted with a shallow keel *and* centreboard.

A centreboard dinghy is not necessarily any simpler to handle

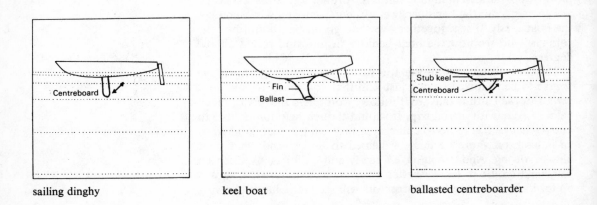

sailing dinghy   keel boat   ballasted centreboarder

An Optimist

than a ballasted yacht, but it has the advantage of getting you down immediately to the basics: you are in close contact with the water, the reactions of the boat are felt at once, sometimes forcefully; you suffer for your mistakes immediately but without serious consequences. It is ideal for developing natural reflexes and familiarity with wind and sea.

The first beginner's centreboard dinghy that comes to mind is probably the 'Optimist'. It is difficult to imagine anything simpler than this tub with one sail – almost too simple to be true. However, the Optimist sails very well, but its size confines its use to children who scarcely need any lessons because they learn on their own. But if you are older don't try to squeeze into an Optimist, unless you are wanting to learn yoga!

So go for a bigger boat where movement on board is not only

possible but necessary for the best handling of the craft. A feeling for this balance must be acquired early on. By the same token it is better to choose a boat with two sails – a sloop. Contrary to what you would expect, it handles more easily and the principle of balance under sail is soon made clear. Paradoxically, one might very well say that the single sail dinghy or 'cat boat', is for children and champions and, on occasion, for hardened single-handers.

Dinghies with two sails are best handled by a crew of two. A beginner on his own is unlikely to be able to cope or to get the best out of the boat. He may only torture himself. A dual apprentice-ship is infinitely preferable; and particularly in adolescence when the idea of team or crew spirit is consciously felt, for the delights of this new-found comradeship cannot be appreciated so distinctly in any other activity. For two people to handle a boat well is not only 'sharing out the work' but being constantly alive to the rela-tionship between a couple who are re-acting instinctively to each other to the point where what each contributes is no longer discern-ible from the whole. Bawling each other out, too, is exciting, and making fools of yourselves in concert is also a basic experience. Anyway capsizing on your own is depressing!

A two-man dinghy is the most popular type today – from 12ft to 20ft and almost any length between. The choice is not an easy one. Beginners should obviously avoid trendy beach toys and advanced racing dinghies – sophisticated machines for trapping wind are anyway outside the normal price range. On the whole it is wise to avoid 'tender' boats which capsize at the first careless movement: frequent duckings do not, after all, get you very far.

A good beginner's boat must first and foremost encourage a feel for the sea; it must be simple and yet complete in itself; be stable, reasonably safe and at the same time lively: make no allowances for the crew without expecting them to be as nimble as acrobats; finally it must be as cheap as possible, whilst still being a real boat.

There are a number of boats with those qualities in varying

A Vaurien

degrees. The 'Vaurien', a plywood boat (also built of fibre glass) is the best known of them. Its qualities have made it for some time now internationally popular. Defined by the Larousse Encyclopedia as being 'perfectly suited for beginners and sailing schools', such fame has not spoiled its vitality. You'll find Vauriens on almost any stretch of water, so you can compare your progress with your friends and, when you are ready, take part in racing. In fact it is a boat which will suit you for a long time.

Boats have developed considerably since the Vaurien was introduced, particularly since fibre glass took over with its ease of maintenance. Its use has extended to all kinds of boats, from the small pram for sculling in a harbour, to displacement yachts, as well as racing dinghies. But they are expensive for beginners' use and, that apart, we haven't yet found one sufficiently sturdy to stand up for long to the rigours of a sailing school.

We shall use the Vaurien as our model and get busy now with fitting her out.

Fitting Out

The main components of a dinghy are really quite simple and their assembly is no mystery: the mast is kept upright in the hull by three steel cables, two shrouds and a forestay; each sail has a halyard for hoisting it and another, called a sheet, for controlling it laterally according to the direction of the wind. Finally there is the centreboard helping the boat to move more forward rather than sideways, and a rudder, helping it to keep going in a straight line. Simple as it all may be it has taken centuries to perfect this rig and no doubt it will in its turn prove to be primitive.

When it comes to assembling your dinghy, commonsense and following the instructions will be all you need. Only be sure to do it yourself and make the boat all your own.

At the same time you must begin to learn the terms. Vocabulary is part of the fitting out process and the purpose of using it is not to be 'folksy' or to flummox the landlubber. Most terms are as necessary as the things they designate, born of harsh necessity, by their very nature concrete, full of imagery, as we shall begin to discover in the following pages.

The Vaurien

Designer: J. J. Herbulot
Year launched: 1952
Length: 4.08m
(Beam) Breadth: 1.47m
Weight: 95 kilograms
Sail area: 8.80 square metres

The hull of the Vaurien is *hard chine*. The chine, that is the joint between the bottom and sides of the boat, is at a sharp angle. The centreboard is a simple shaped plank which slips (chamfered side forward) into the centreboard casing as if into a sheath: we call it a *dagger board*.

The *buoyancy tanks* of the plywood Vaurien are inflatable bags. Three are fitted inside the cockpit, each 40 litres capacity. They must be fixed very carefully; if the boat capsizes the bags on the submerged side exert an upward pressure of 120 kilograms: the boat and crew are in a way hanging on to the lashing of the bags.

. . . and Others

Most other dinghies today are made of fibre glass and differ from the Vaurien mainly in the following ways. They have a *moulded* hull: the chine is rounded off. They usually have a *pivoted* *centreboard* (mounted on an *axle*). When it is raised it retracts inside the centreboard case.

Many of them have a *traveller*, a track along which the mainsheet block can slide but first time out it is better to dispense with that and make it fast at the middle of the track. The buoyancy of these boats is usually tanks that are an integral part of the hull. They are partially filled with expanded plastic material. Water does sometimes get into them, but can be emptied out through drain sockets – and always check before going out.

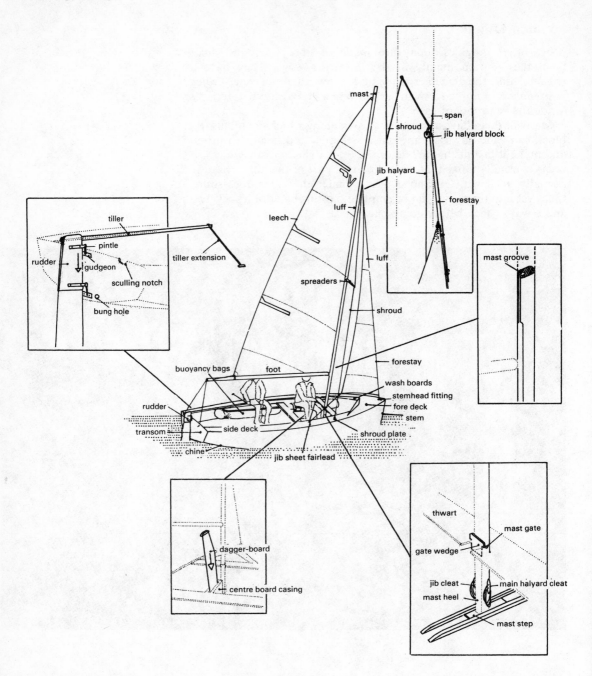

tiller

pintle

rudder

gudgeon

tiller extension

sculling notch

bung hole

mast

span

shroud

jib halyard block

jib halyard

luff

forestay

leech

luff

mast groove

spreaders

shroud

forestay

buoyancy bags

foot

wash boards

stemhead fitting

rudder

fore deck

stem

transom

side deck

shroud plate

chine

jib sheet fairlead

thwart

mast gate

gate wedge

dagger-board

jib cleat

main halyard cleat

centre board casing

mast heel

mast step

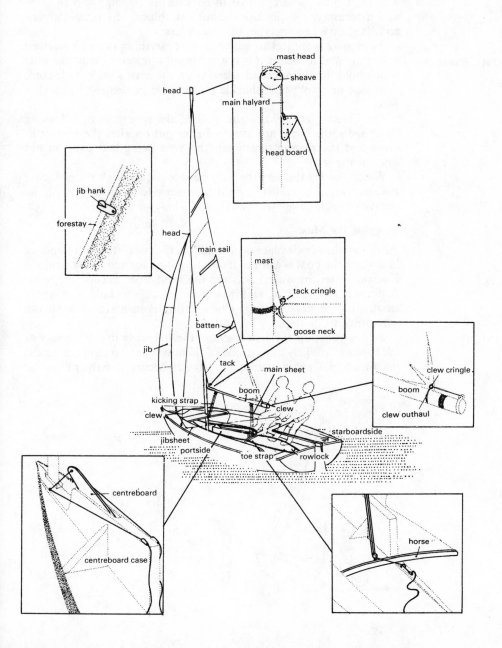

mast head

sheave

main halyard

head board

head

jib hank

forestay

head

main sail

mast

tack cringle

goose neck

batten

jib

tack

main sheet

boom

clew cringle

boom

clew outhaul

kicking strap

clew

clew

jibsheet

portside

toe strap

rowlock

starboardside

centreboard

centreboard case

horse

Mouse everything that can unscrew

Dressing the Mast

The mast must be dressed or fitted with its rigging: two shrouds and a forestay, the jib halyard with its block, the main halyard and its sheave and, maybe, two spreaders.

All rigging is subject to vibration so everything must be screwed up tightly and locked if it is not taken off after every trip: the nuts which hold the shrouds and forestay on the mast should be locked, with glue or a split pin; shackle pins should be secured by locking wire.

The shrouds are held at the ends of the spreaders by a lashing (see page 130). These are usually better put on after the mast is in place and the rigging tensioned (the boat being laid over on her side for the job).

Watch out for the way the halyards are fed through their blocks: the end with an eye must be on the correct side. A drop of oil on the sheave of each pulley will stop it squeaking or binding.

Stepping the Mast

Although the crew's place is normally in the cockpit, avoid standing in it when the boat is ashore. Its bottom is pliant and easily strained if unsupported by water. So, step the mast from outside the boat. A dinghy mast is light, and it is quite possible to hold it at arm's length (if it is not blowing) when setting it in place through the gate down to its step.

Before you step the mast, secure the halyards to their cleats at the foot or, as likely as not, one of them will get entangled near the masthead. To avoid confusion, always secure a halyard to the

same cleat. As a rule, the main halyard is made fast to the *starboard* cleat (right hand facing the bow) and the jib halyard uses the *port* (or left) cleat.

The Vaurien's forestay is attached to the stemhead by a lashing, but other boats have other means.

The rigging should be adjusted so that the mast doesn't bear against the sides of the gate, but just touches the aft end. The tension of the jib luff governs the final set of the rigging.

Bending on the Sails

The two best ways of ruining sails before they are even used is to lay them on the sand (which works its way into the stitching, where it acts as a powerful abrasive) or to smoke while you work.

Bending on the Mainsail. First find the tack: this is the corner at the angle of boom and mast where the *bolt ropes* meet (ropes sewn on the luff and foot) and where the sailmaker usually puts his name.

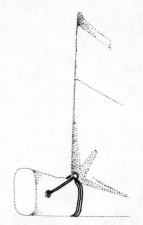

The turns under the boom are as important as the others

When the foot is fed along the boom groove, and the tack fixed to its hook, pull the foot fairly taut and make the clew fast by means of lashing. As this part of the sail is specially vulnerable, a turn of the lashing should be taken round the boom as shown in the drawing.

When the foot has been set up, trace along the luff from tack to head to check that there are no twists.

Before *shackling* the halyard to the headboard of the sail, check that the halyard is free of twists and tangles aloft and drops straight from the masthead sheave and is not round a shroud or the spreaders.

Put the battens gently into their pockets; never force them or they may tear the sail. It is better if they are too short rather than too long (half an inch play is quite acceptable).

The mainsheet is the most difficult rigging job; think carefully about which way it runs. It should run naturally in its blocks, without criss-crossing or the blocks pulling across their axes.

When the sheet is rove, tie a *figure-of-eight knot* in the end to stop it unreeving. Never use any old knot because it pulls tight and can't be undone easily.

Finally, fit the *kicking strap* or boom vang between the boom and the mast. This keeps the boom horizontal and reduces twist in the mainsail.

Bending on the Jib. Starting at the luff, find the tack (this is the wider of the two forward corners, it too carries the sailmaker's mark); make it fast to the stemhead fitting, then fit the jib hanks to the

Figure of eight knot

forestay. Start at the tack and be careful to fit them without twisting the sail, or they won't run on the stay. When the jib is bent on, the plungers are usually to starboard.

Before shackling on the halyard, see that it is clear aloft, so that it isn't wrapped round the forestay or that the *standing part* isn't round the *fall* (that part between the block and the cleat).

Reeve the sheets through the fairleads either side, making figure-of-eight knots at their ends.

Hoisting Sail

The boat must be *head to wind* – its bow pointing into the wind. If the wind is allowed to blow from port or starboard, the mainsail will be blown to leeward as it goes up, the luffrope won't run easily in the groove, the headboard will get caught under a shroud and you will have all sorts of trouble; in a fresh wind the boat might even capsize. Try attaching a strand of wool to each shroud as a simple wind indicator or telltale.

Hoisting the Mainsail. Pull the halyard with one hand and guide the luff of the sail into the mast groove with the other. Take it inch by inch and don't force it. The sail won't go up if something is jammed: the sail may be caught in the groove (only the boltrope should go in): a batten may be trapped under a thwart or a gunwale or caught in a shroud.

When the sail is nearly right up, fit the boom into the gooseneck. Then sweat on the halyard, stretching the luff steadily. Make the halyard *fast* on the starboard cleat. The sail should now flap gently in the breeze with a slack sheet.

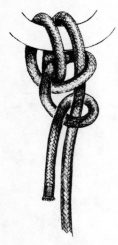

Fisherman's bend

Cleating a halyard: a round turn, a half figure of eight and a half hitch. If the rope jams it is because (1) there is no round turn, (2) more than a half figure of eight or (3) the half hitch is the wrong way round. NB when cleating a sheet, do not use a half hitch but a round turn followed by three or four figures of eight

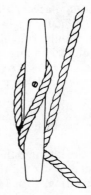

Hoisting the Jib. There should be no difficulty if the jib hanks have been properly clipped on to the forestay. Hoist and tighten the halyard as much as possible before making it fast to the port cleat.

Now check that you have on board the rudder and centreboard and the following gear:

5–10lb anchor, with a line of 100–150 feet made fast to the anchor by a *fisherman's bend*. Don't forget to make the other end fast to the ring provided for this, or to the foot of the mast. The whole affair, anchor and line should be stowed for preference in a special bag in front of the mast.

An oar if you know how to scull, or two paddles.

A *bailer* for emptying water from the boat.

Two lifejackets – not to lie in the bottom of the boat but to be put on by the crew before they set out.

All is now ready and, weather permitting, you can set off (the sails should, however, be lowered while the boat is still on land, and not rehoisted until she is afloat).

If the weather is bad, you can always pass the time learning a few knots.

Conditions for the First Sail

The first sail should be on a safe, uncrowded stretch of water in completely calm conditions, and you must develop as soon as possible a weather sense: you must be able to look at landscape and weather with a new awareness. This calls for alertness, observation and patience. To start with you are bound to doubt your own judgement which has been shaped in landlubber conditions.

The Place

It is not always easy to find the ideal place such as a small lake, a quiet river or an enclosed bay; but it is worth looking for to avoid the risk of straying too far out to sea; and even the most inviting waters can conceal snags, such as strong currents which might sweep you into dangers, be they sluices, waterfalls, or Scylla and Charybdis themselves, apart from gusty winds and rough water. Beware of sailing in crowded channels. There is no provision

Beaufort scale of wind force

Beaufort Number	Description	Speed in knots*	Height of sea in feet†	Deep sea criteria
0	Calm	less than 1	—	Sea mirror-smooth.
1	Light air	1–3	$\frac{1}{4}$	Small wavelets like scales, no crests.
2	Light breeze	4–6	$\frac{1}{2}$	Small wavelets still short but more pronounced. Crests glassy and do not break.
3	Gentle breeze	7–10	2	Large wavelets. Crests begin to break. Foam is glassy.
4	Moderate breeze	11–16	$3\frac{1}{2}$	Small waves becoming longer; more frequent white horses.
5	Fresh breeze	17–21	6	Moderate waves, and longer; many white horses.
6	Strong breeze	22–27	$9\frac{1}{2}$	Large waves begin to form; white crests more extensive.
7	Near gale	28–33	$13\frac{1}{2}$	Sea heaps up; white foam blown in streaks.
8	Gale	34–40	18	Moderately high waves of greater length; crests begin to form spindrift. Foam blown in well-marked streaks.
9	Strong gale	41–47	23	High waves; dense streaks of foam. Crests begin to roll over.
10	Storm	48–55	29	Very high waves with long overhanging crests. Surface of sea becomes white with great patches of foam. Visibility affected.
11	Violent storm	56–63	37	Exceptionally high waves. Sea completely covered with foam.
	Hurricane	64+		The air is filled with spray and visibility seriously affected.

* Measured at a height of 33 feet above sea-level.
† In the open sea remote from land.

aboard a dinghy for hoisting the regulation two black balls to show the vessel is manoeuvring with difficulty!

On the other hand, don't make your maiden voyage in utter isolation. Some sort of company is essential, be it escort by motor-boat at a respectful distance or at least a friend ashore who knows what is happening and who can call help if necessary.

This kind of precaution won't spoil the fun and will give you freedom to manoeuvre when faced with the unexpected. Rest assured the stretch of water you contemplate using won't feel the same once you are afloat. In a boat you'll soon realise that a sea-scape is made up of the elements – that is the ever-changing beauty of it. At first, it will seem that your eye, narrowing as it sweeps the horizon, takes in a precise area with well defined boundaries, unchanging distances, a steady light; but you will be wrong. The boat itself will make you free of this brave new world, showing you that this immense space has meaning and direction, is crowded with different zones; that boundaries alter and distance change with the changing winds. There is much to marvel at. You will soon learn that the world of the seas is but a conjunction of eternal movement and displacement, 'where vacant shuttles weave the wind', combining and dissolving in infinite variety with the chang-ing weather, forever revealing a new face. And that is no mean discovery.

The Weather

When the sun shines and the view is good, it is easy to underesti-mate the strength of the wind. Nobody would recommend starting in dull weather and remember that what we call good weather ashore can be the very devil at sea.

Don't forget that near land, in the shelter of the coast or river bank all may be quiet and safe but, if the wind is blowing off-shore, everything changes in a moment and the boat can be driven out to sea.

For your first sail, therefore, avoid an offshore wind or at least be certain of being able to make for land if the wind takes control.

If the wind is on-shore, your departure is more difficult but your return is inevitable. The ideal is to set out when the wind is blowing along the shoreline gently.

Don't be old-fashioned and imprecise and hold up a wet finger to find the wind's direction; ears are your best indicators. The noise made by the wind changes as you turn your head: when the hum is strongest (and pressure is equal on both ears), you are either head to wind or facing downwind and your nose will tell you which way.

The sooner a sense of wind direction becomes instinctive the better. Winds dominate the sailor's life and you have to accept this as a fact of life. Regard the wind direction as a constant if you can and the coastline as moving in relation to it! When you reach that stage, you will find this all perfectly natural and wonder how you have survived so long without it.

The wind only comes from the points of the compass. Never say, for example, that the wind is blowing straight from auntie's place because, a little further on, without having changed direction, it will be blowing from another relation's house or Mac's bar. But if you say the wind comes from the west, that remains true whatever the boat does.

Having ascertained direction, you must now determine strength. With no wind, you can only learn to row or scull, and when it blows too hard you've had it. The ideal wind for tyros is force 1 or 2 in the Beaufort Scale. A wind of force 2 is a 'light breeze' in official language. Head to wind, the sails will flap quite gently. The jib clew, renowned for its restlessness, fidgets harmlessly and won't hurt you if it catches you on the cheek. The telltales lift, but not quite horizontally; smoke drifts without dispersing, you can feel the wind on your face but you won't bother to turn away. The water is just marked by ripples, or perhaps by small wavelets if the surface is extensive. (You'll notice though that if there is a swell even without wind, waves can break and then it's wiser not to go out.)

The best wind of all is steady, without gusts. Watch out when the sky is black or brightly luminous after bad weather: sunshine and showers will alternate, and it will blow during the showers; this is *squally weather*.

Always remember that the wind is fickle and can shift, and this is a first-class reason for not going far from the shore, even if conditions seem to be perfect. These shifts often follow a known rhythm. In summer, when fine weather is firmly established, the wind tends to follow the course of the sun and at the end of the day, therefore, it goes into the west. Sailing off a south shore therefore gives good conditions. But later in the evening the wind might go suddenly into the north and strengthen. It is then time to go home.

The subject is inexhaustible and it will crop up again more than once.

Clothing

If you decide to wear nothing but a swimsuit to get a good tan you will regret it. It is never too hot on a boat, and after capsizing, it's even cold. Even wet clothes are better than nothing.

Sea boots hinder movement in the boat and in the water. Never wear them. Light sailing shoes or sneakers are the thing; without them you can easily stub your toe, and toe straps are hard on bare feet.

Lifejackets

Capsizing in a dinghy is always a possibility whatever the weather's like. *It is plain common sense always to wear a lifejacket.* Without one, it is difficult to stay long in the water and get the sails down. The water is always colder than you think and you become exhausted more quickly than you'd expect. Proper lifejackets are necessary and if they feel cumbersome, all the more reason for getting used to them. You may not look your best in them: but it's better to survive inelegantly than to drown beautifully.

First Sail

Getting Ready

Fine weather. The boat is at the water's edge. Sails have been bent on, as in the trial rig, and everything is there: rudder, tiller, centreboard, anchor and line, paddles, bailer.

Now it's time to put on personal gear – lifejackets. It's also time to decide who does what: one of you will be *helmsman* and will hold the tiller and mainsheet; the other will be *crew* (or jib sheet hand) and will look after the jib and centreboard.

As it is calm, the boat can be carried into the water before hoisting sail (when there are waves it is often better to hoist on land; and that isn't so easy because, remember, you should not stand in the boat, and you have to hoist from outside).

Carry the boat, don't drag it, for a scratched hull is a sad hull, and the centreboard is liable to jam if the case is blocked with sand or gravel.

Carry the boat right in until it floats. If it is kept half in and half out of the water the hull suffers terribly.

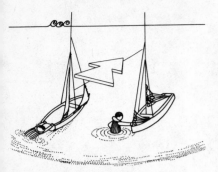

Held by the forestay, the boat comes gently head-to-wind and the sails can be hoisted

Now the helmsman should hold her by the forestay, the bow into the wind – but this time there's no need to consult the burgee: once it's afloat and held bow or stern the boat will swing naturally to the wind. Held by the stern, she will swing so that the wind blows on to her stern, and that makes control more difficult (you don't hold a horse by the tail!), so hold on to the forestay and the bow will swing head to wind and the boat float docilely.

The crew now climbs aboard and starts hoisting sail. Mainsail first (remember to keep the battens clear). When it is tight, pull on the halyard to stretch the luff taut and then make fast on the starboard cleat. After checking that the mainsheet is running free and not pulling on the boom make up the kicking strap (without overdoing it).

The jib comes next, hoisted hard up (don't worry if the forestay slackens slightly; the jib *must* be hard up), and the halyard is cleated to port. A final glance round: all lines, halyards, sheets, and anchor gear should be quite free, no danger of tangles and ready for instant use, each in its proper place.

Lastly the crew fits the rudder and tiller and sits down on the forward thwart (seat), facing the mast. All is ready.

The helmsman pushes the boat out as he climbs aboard. If this first sail is on a small enclosed stretch of water, choose a spot where the wind is blowing off-shore (it's a light breeze, remember); the boat will sail herself into deeper water. If you can't get these conditions, the best plan is to accept a certain disorder until you have paddled out far enough from the land to be able to sort yourself out under sail before being blown back to the shore.

Early Days

Helmsman and crew will have not the slightest doubt about one thing: the boat is unstable. Don't both sit on the same side but crouch in the centre of the dinghy and move circumspectly.

Get used to this narrow, moving shell, the cockpit, even before you turn to the sails. Normally it's easy enough to balance yourself, but reflexes which assure the control and dignity of *homo sapiens* ashore don't work afloat. In this new unstable environment you can only be at ease if you enter into the game: true equilibrium is dynamic and now it will only be achieved when wind fills the sails and the boat gets under way.

Meanwhile keep your cool staying in the middle of the boat while the sails continue to flap gently. This, incidentally, is a basic rule, always to be remembered at such moments: *whenever you find yourself in trouble*, whatever the reason, and feel you are about to 'lose balance', instead of instinctively clutching at anything to hand *let everything go and get in the middle of the boat*. She will calm down immediately, stop sailing and, sails flapping, patiently wait for you to recover.

Now get going. Lower the rudder and centreboard; take hold of the tiller and each to his or her sheet. Let the sails fill with wind and see what happens.

If there is an instructor around, he should look the other way. At all costs he must not shout advice, ill-timed right now and bound to be ill-understood, it will only generate panic (and over-excite the fish). Learn by your own mistakes!

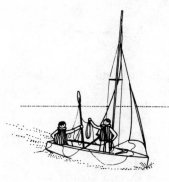

Beginners must learn by their own mistakes

Simple Exercises

This initiation over, you can now perform some tests, putting theory into practice to show you how the boat reacts to different conditions.

First let go the sheets, take out the tiller and raise the rudder and centreboard: everything slack.

Equilibrium

The dinghy is now on her own, and drifts to leeward before the wind, like a toy boat. At the same time, she won't drift any old

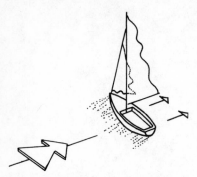

When the sheets are let fly, the boat no longer heels, comes broadside on to the wind and drifts gently

how and quite quickly she will find her natural position, presenting one side or the other of the hull to the wind, drifting at right angles to the wind, or *beam-on*.

Whenever you 'let everything go', the boat will find this beam-on position. This is another basic principle. The sails will billow out to leeward like flags down wind, more or less at right angles to the fore and aft line of the boat.

Everything on the side of the boat (as divided by the centreboard or keel) from which the wind is coming is to *windward*. Everything on the other side is to *leeward*. The keel or centreboard is, so to speak, the dividing line between windward and leeward.

Meanwhile the boat is still drifting down wind making *leeway*.

You can gauge the amount of drift by picking out landmarks ashore in line with the bow and the stern of the boat. This is having marks *in transit*. And if you take other marks on the shoreline as well, you will notice that the boat will be making slight head-way as well as leeway. The reason is simple: the mainsail is not completely at right angles to the centre line of the boat and the boom is pressing on the lee shroud slightly aft of the mast. As it is not completely free, the mainsail catches a very small amount of wind and deflects a few puffs; the infinitesimal energy thus gathered pushes the boat slightly forward.

Lowering the Centreboard

Now lower the centreboard, right down. You will find at once you are making less leeway for the centreboard resists sideways displacement of the boat. There is no mystery here. It's just the same principle that makes it easier to push a plank of wood head-on than sideways in a tank of water. Stopping the boat making leeway is the centreboard's principal function.

This is confirmed when the centreboard is lowered: she turns and *luffs up*, bow to the wind. Then she returns slowly to her original position – with the wind abeam.

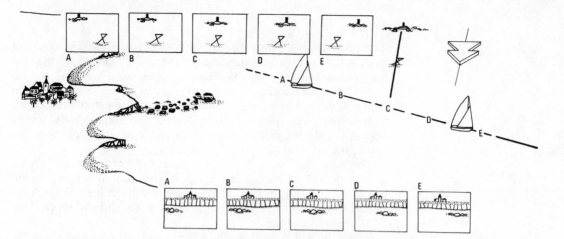

This at least is what happens to a boat with a dagger plate. A boat with a pivoting centreboard may react slightly differently. When a pivoting board is slowly lowered, the boat, instead of luffing up, turns away from the wind at first: she *bears or falls away*. Then, when the board is right down, she luffs up a little as if she had a daggerboard.

You can illustrate the same principle, but more quickly by shifting weight. If both crew move to leeward, the boat will *list* (lean over) to leeward and luff. But if weight is moved to windward, the boat will *list to windward* and fall away.

These reactions can all be easily noticed because the boat is moving forward slightly. They are slow and slight because speed is almost zero, but they show how the boat will behave when sailing properly.

When two fixed landmarks are in line, one behind the other, they are in transit. In diagram C, beacon and buoy are in transit

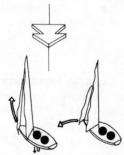

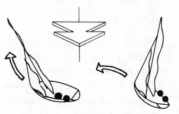

centre board down   centre board up

The boat's tendency to luff up or bear away is affected by the position of the centreboard and where the crew sit

Mainsail Only

The boat has been moving slightly forward because the wind has been getting a little purchase on the mainsail. The greater the surface exposed to the wind, the better you move.

Now pull on the sheet and you *sheet in* to *fill* the sail. It will then flap less, fill and belly, tight, concave – a sight to delight all sailors.

Simultaneously the boat comes to life. She heels slightly, moves forward and straightaway begins to point her bow towards the wind; she luffs up.

The more the boat luffs, the more the wind comes from in front so that the sail offers less and less purchase; soon it will flap again, *lift* as we say, and the boat slows down. To make the sail catch the wind better it must be hardened in a bit more, and still more if the boat continues to luff.

When the sail is hard in, the boom is almost fore and aft in the boat (the sheet is hauled in as much as it will come) and the boat still insists on luffing. Inevitably the sail starts to lift again and now there is nothing to be done. The boat stops, appears to hesitate for a moment and slowly, as though in spite of herself, turns back again, her bow swerving away from the wind as she falls away.

While falling away, the wind fills the sheeted-in mainsail again; the boat heels sharply, moves slowly forward and luffs yet again, only to come to a halt once more *head to wind*. If this is not to continue indefinitely, you must ease the mainsail by giving it more sheet (easing it off). In light winds there is no danger, but in stronger weather a sudden heel after falling away can easily lead to a capsize if you don't ease the sheet smartly.

The lesson is we have just met the *forbidden head-to-wind zone*. It stretches for about 45° either side of the eye of the wind. The boat cannot sail pointing in this quarter, although she is singularly obstinate in turning towards it.

Jib Alone

Sheet eased, mainsail flapping, the boat returns to her natural position, wind on the beam. Now harden the jib alone. The crew pulls on the leeward sheet, just enough to fill the sail. This time the boat moves gently forward and embarks on a turn opposite to the previous one, not moving towards the wind, but turning off it. Instead of luffing she bears away.

The more the boat bears away, the more she slows down. But the jib doesn't lift. On the contrary, it is sheeted too hard. With the wind coming more and more from the stern, the jib should be eased so that it gets as much wind as possible.

The boat has no tendency to heel and all is peaceful. The time comes when she has turned sufficiently for the wind to fill the mainsail, even though this has been eased completely and it is rubbing the lee shroud. It then is between the wind and the jib so that the latter, blanketed, is suffocated.

As we have learned, wind on the mainsail causes the boat to luff and the bow moves slowly the opposite way towards the wind again; and as the mainsail loses its wind, the jib gets it back again, stops the luff and starts to make the boat fall off or bear away once more. It must be possible to create a balance between the action of the two sails, so that the boat might move more or less straight forward.

For the moment, we can draw the first conclusion from these experiments. Broadly speaking, everything happens as though the centreboard were an axis around which the boat pivots one way or the other according to whether you harden the forward or after sail. Neither sail appears capable, by itself, of ensuring a straight course.

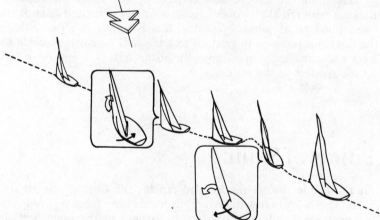

Mainsail acting as a rudder: to stop luffing, let out the sheet, to stop bearing away, pull it in

Both Sails Together

From this position of wind abeam, harden both sails at the same time, hoping that this time the boat will sail straight. Note a mark on the shore line with the bow and sheet in both sails slowly. *For a sail to be properly set the sheet should be as free as possible without the sail actually flapping.*

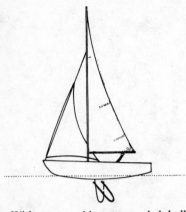

Without a rudder, a rounded hull will only find its balance if the centre-plate is slightly raised

But you will find that nothing turns out as expected. While the mainsail is still lifting, not properly sheeted home, it has an effect on the jib [even though the latter is correctly sheeted]. The boat moves forward and luffs immediately: *the effect of the mainsail on the boat's direction is much greater than that of the jib.*

If you want to sail straight, you must therefore allow the mainsail to flap a lot while keeping the jib properly sheeted; there is a delicate balance to be found. The boat will yaw, but you can try to get rid of the yaw without touching the jib, by playing the mainsail lightly. If the boat luffs, the mainsail is sheeted in too hard and must be eased; if the boat bears away, the mainsheet should be pulled in slightly. To sum up, the jib is driving the boat by itself, while the mainsail acts as a rudder.

This exercise is practised much more easily in a hard chine centreboarder with a hull like the French *Vaurien* class. The Vaurien is better adapted than most dinghies to this kind of manoeuvre. Its hard chine gives it a certain grip on the water that a rounded hull lacks. The latter will not do this unless the centreboard is partially raised: so, by altering the centre of lateral resistance, one can find the best balance between the sails. But even so this mode of progression is patently far from satisfactory. Balance between the two sails remains precarious and cannot be maintained on all *points of sailing*, that is to say in all directions the boat can point to in relation to the wind. Nor is it possible to steer a steady *course* on a transit for instance. It is high time to call on the services of the rudder.

Points of Sailing

Fit the rudder on its pintles and replace the tiller in the rudder head. The helmsman will have both hands busy from now on, not having three hands when he wants to haul in the mainsheet. It requires the kind of co-ordination that only comes with practice, working it out for yourself.

Wind on the Beam

The boat is again in the stable beam to wind position, sails flapping.

Pick a landmark on the shore in line with the bow and sheet in both sails until they stop flapping. The boat moves forward and the helmsman sits on the gunwale to windward, facing the tiller.

He will immediately feel that the tiller is tugging leewards. If he resists the pull just enough to keep the helm amidships, the tendency to luff, already experienced on the same point of sailing (but without the rudder), will reappear. To keep the wind on the beam, the helmsman must pull the tiller slightly towards him if he is to hold the boat on a steady course.

Now the boat picks up speed, both sails are full and *setting* well. Continue sailing with this beam wind for a while to get the feel of the tiller, and to decide on the most efficient position for the crew.

The Working of the Rudder

The first, fairly obvious point is that putting the tiller to the right, turns the boat to the left, and *vice versa*. This ceases to be disconcerting as soon as you see how the water exerts pressure on the rudder blade.

The helmsman, sitting to windward, pulls the tiller towards him to bear away; to luff, he need only allow the tiller to go amidships. Clearly there is a marked imbalance on this point of sailing as the boat generally has a tendency to luff rather than bear away, and this is called *weather helm*. A tendency to bear away, on the other hand, is *lee helm* (it is safer, above all for a beginner, to have a boat with weather helm that reacts surely and consistently).

At first the effect of the rudder may seem so strong that while you are groping about you'll use it out of all proportion to the yawing of the boat; and it must be realised that *the rudder blade, while it is not in the fore and aft axis of the boat, acts like a brake*.

Tiller to the right, the boat turns left. Tiller to the left, the boat turns right

But it is the rudder which keeps the boat on a proper course; and, if it is to work without braking, both sails must be correctly sheeted and the hull balanced because a well-trimmed boat doesn't need a lot of rudder to stay on course.

Hull Trim

The crew is the only ballast in the boat and, as it is mobile, it can be placed to suit trim, lateral or longitudinal.

Lateral Trim

In a beam wind, as soon as it has any strength, both crew should sit on the gunwale to windward to counteract the heel of the boat.

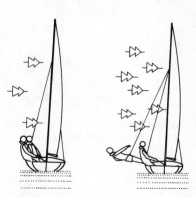

Good lateral trim

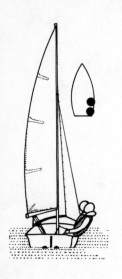

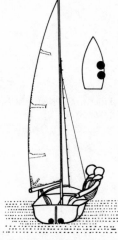

(*above*) Crew too far aft transom too low in water; (*below*) well placed

When the wind grows stronger, you should lean out beyond the gunwale with your feet underneath the toe straps: you are *leaning out*. In racing dinghies, the crew at the foresheets can wind up completely outside the boat, with his toes on the gunwale and his weight slung from the mast harnessed to a *trapeze*.

Leaning out is essential, because excessive heeling is inefficient. The turbulence which appears around the hull may give an impression of speed, but it is, in fact, only produced by the abnormal position of the hull in the water. Heeling also, as we saw in the first chapter, gives the boat weather helm and makes her luff, so that you have to compensate by pulling on the tiller, which once more brakes the boat. *For best results the boat must be kept as upright as possible in the water.*

Longitudinal Trim

It is easy to see how a boat that is heavy in the bow cannot cut through the water properly, but it is equally important for her not to be weighed down too much aft with her transom half-buried in the water – the most common fault with beginners.

It is not easy to check that your trim is right. If you lean over the stern to look at the transom, you will always find that it is too low in the water! So ask a friend to sail alongside and tell you. The amount of wake will also give some indication. And if you want drama, sail with the bung out. If your ballast is correctly spread the water just reaches the rim of the bung hole without coming into the boat. Soon you will learn where to put yourselves instinctively so that the hull slips through the water with minimum resistance.

In carrying out all these tests you can experience not just the straight beam-wind condition, but all the points of sailing covered by *reaching*. A little closer to the wind is called a close reach and a little further off is a broad reach. Close reach and broad reach are not very different from beam-reaching, as far as sail trim and handling are concerned because the boat reacts comparably easily and quickly over this whole range. Now let's examine headwind and following-wind conditions which we have only touched on briefly.

Close Hauled

To sail closer to the wind, let the tiller return to the centre line of the boat and the boat luffs, as she passes the point of close reaching; the sails begin to flap, and they must be sheeted in a little until they just stop flapping.

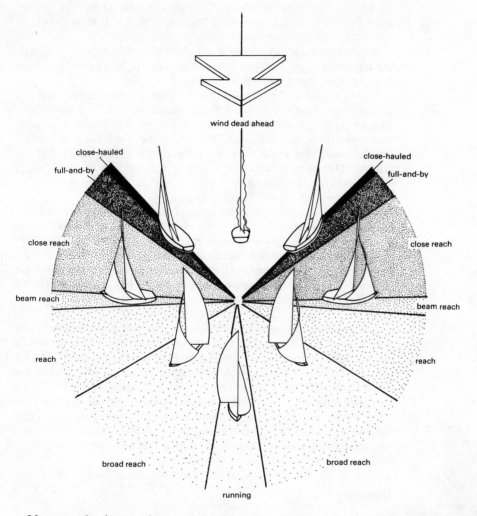

wind dead ahead

close-hauled

full-and-by

close-hauled

full-and-by

close reach

close reach

beam reach

beam reach

reach

reach

broad reach

broad reach

running

Now you begin to gain ground against the wind as you *work to windward*. The wind suddenly seems to have more force than it had on the beam, and once the boat settles on this new point of sailing, she livens up. The tendency to heel increases and, although she seems to settle deeper in the water, she answers quickly to the helm. The hull vibrates slightly with the passage of water and slips easily along with sails nicely rounded. You are *full and by*, eating

Points of sailing: *close-hauled*, the sails are sheeted in hard and flat; *full-and-by* they are still sheeted in but well filled with wind; *reaching* follows by gradually easing the sheets – hence the terms *close reach*, *reach*, *broad reach*. Sheets are eased right off when running up the ground, with good speed and little leeway. Don't spoil it by having the sails too tight. You should ease sheets frequently until they flap slightly, and then harden in again, just to the point where the sail has merely a suggestion of a tremor.

If you point up more, you must sheet right in so that both sails are flat or *hard in*. You are as close as you can be to the forbidden head-to-wind zone, sailing *close hauled*.

This is a point of sailing where the boat travels tensely, and the easy going conditions of the full-and-by course are soon forgotten. The wind stiffens and irons out the sails as the boat heels more and, whenever there is a stronger puff, the crew must hang out energetically and you must keep the tiller up to windward to stay on course. The boat is now making way through the water against some resistance and, if there are small waves, her bow must carve through them. Now the fun has begun.

This is an exciting point of sailing that reveals a boat's ability to combat the elements. The crew must pay unfailing attention to the wind, for it is never completely steady, either in direction or strength. It can *head* you or it can *free* you by blowing more or less directly on the bow; it can also *freshen* (get stronger) or *weaken*. The helmsman must constantly be modifying course to keep sailing efficiently and the crew must move to keep the boat upright.

It takes time to learn to sail well to windward. At first you are apt to steer by a landmark and that is exactly what you must not do. In fact, to windward you are making leeway all the time and you will find that you have to point up more and more to keep on your landmark; and as a result, you fall away increasingly to leeward, making less and less progress. Working to windward is hard work and can be frustrating. Leave it to the wind and keep your sails filled. You will not point up so well but you will go faster and make less leeway. You'll get more fun and satisfaction that way.

Running

Now back to the beam-reach to start examining the downwind sector. To get there you must bear away. The helmsman therefore pulls the tiller towards him – but the boat will resist and will strain to return to the beam reach until you slacken the sheets, so ease them until the sails are almost flapping, as we have seen them do on the other points of sailing.

Running with sails goose-winged

As you bear away, you first pass through the broad reach, where the boat reacts very much as she does on the beam reach. The mainsail can now be eased until it starts to bear on the lee shroud; heeling is slight, speed is high and the boat is comfortable.

If you continue to bear away, conditions change considerably. Everything seems calm and you scarcely feel the wind. Speed seems to drop off (which is partly true), the water is smoother and the hull glides sweetly along. The boat makes no leeway (you can raise the centreboard) and sitting out is no longer necessary, so that the crew can settle down comfortably inside the boat. Wind and boat henceforth go hand in hand and you are *broad reaching*.

You may perhaps already be *running before the wind* because, on this point of sailing it is not always easy to know exactly where the wind is and it sometimes happens that you bear away a little too much without realising it. The burgee is unreliable and the telltales only give a vague indication of wind and there is a feeling of uncertainty about. You can try taking the jib across to the other side from the mainsail (*goosewing the sails*). If it does not fill on the other side, you are not yet running. If it does, you are dead before the wind, and there is no indication that you are not too far over (running by the lee).

But the helmsman must use the tiller with great care. By standing up with the tiller between his legs, he can feel the least reaction of the boat in the soles of his feet.

On this *passive* point of sailing with the wind aft, which seems at first sight much easier than the more *active* point of sailing close-hauled, you are not entirely safe from mishap. If you put the helm slightly too far to leeward, the boat will come up quickly into the wind, and the wind suddenly grows stronger than you thought it was. If you put the helm up to windward, you can pass

As soon as the wind is strong enough, a gybe can mean a capsize

beyond the position of a dead run without knowing it. The boat begins to get the wind from behind her mainsail. When it gets right round on the lee side, the boom suddenly slams across on to the other tack, as quickly and as easily as you turn a page in this book. But the boom is heavy and long and it will bash against the shroud, as likely as not dotting you one on the head en route. This is called a *gybe*. In light conditions it is not serious, but the wind is inconsiderate and the violence of the boom, in passing sharply from one side to the other, can start the boat off on an uncontrolled luff on the new tack, and this sudden change can result in a capsize.

Whatever the consequence is, you have passed a new milestone for up until now the boat, from close hauled to dead run, has always had the wind on the same side. Now, for the first time, she gets it from the other. The leeward side has become the windward side and *vice versa*. Whether on purpose or not, you have changed tacks.

Changing Tacks

There are two ways of changing tacks: by turning so that the wind passes round the stern (gybing), or by turning through the forbidden head-to-wind zone, from one close-hauled tack to the other (going about).

Experience shows that the beginner, left to himself, masters the gybe more quickly than going about, although the latter is far safer.

Gybing

Gybing, such as you have just suffered, is not the best way of going from one tack to another. It is a nasty shock for boat and crew and it is difficult to regain control when it happens without

Gybing: A. get the wind well behind you; B. sheet in the main gradually, using the tiller to prevent the boat luffing up; C. bring the sail over; D. let the sheet right out, again using the tiller to stop the boat luffing up on the new tack; E. bring the jib over

warning. Rather than suffer it in silence, like a necessary evil, when you must change tacks going down wind, it's better to learn how to do it gently, maintaining control throughout. There is all the difference in the world between an involuntary gybe and a controlled gybe. The latter is intentional and organised.

The main difficulty in gybing is in deciding exactly when the wind is dead aft. You look at the burgee, you try to judge by the wind blowing on your ears and when you consider that it is right behind you, you begin gradually hauling on the mainsheet until the sail is hard in. This alters the trim of the boat, which wants to luff up when you begin and you must therefore hold the tiller slightly up to windward to maintain course.

You are sailing on a tightrope. Theoretically, in light winds, when the mainsheet is pulled in, the sail should not want to fill on either side and consequently it is ineffective and the boat continues to sail on under the jib only which, now it is no longer blanketed, fills nicely.

In practice, it is rare to have the wind dead astern or, if you have, it will be difficult to keep it consistently there.

If you are a little *by the lee* (with the wind blowing slightly from the same side as the mainsail), the sail will slam suddenly on to the other tack before it has been fully sheeted home. This is a semi-involuntary gybe, which is much more controllable. Let go the mainsheet at once so that the mainsail doesn't remain hard in on the new tack.

If the wind is not completely aft, the mainsail, although fully sheeted home, does not want to move to the other side. You should therefore pull the tiller slightly up to windward so that the boat bears away a little more. The sail will then move across and you ease the mainsheet quickly and steadily (taking care not to get it round your feet). As soon as the sail is trimmed on the new tack, it is hard to keep the boat with the wind aft, because she has a tendency to luff on the new tack, and the more the mainsail is hauled in, the sharper the luff will be. You should therefore ease the sheet rapidly and guard against luffing by holding the tiller up to the new windward side (but not too much, or you risk gybing back again!). It only now remains to sheet the jib (which has been somewhat neglected during this operation) home on the other side.

To sum up, to be successful, a gybe needs the trim of the boat to be right, a certain finesse in appreciating the wind, and rapid reactions. There's no need to look upon it as a nightmare operation to embark on with teeth clenched. You must though be on your

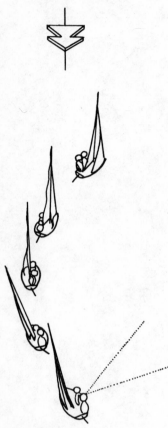

Going about

toes, but not too hasty, treat the sail like the page of a rare book, and handle the tiller with a delicate touch.

Get plenty of practice in fine weather before trying out a gybe in a fresh wind. Until then, it is better to decide to tack through the eye of the wind, even if this means taking more time. Going about may seem more difficult than gybing, but it is really a clear-cut operation.

Going About

We have already decided that a boat that is really close-hauled cannot point further into the wind without coming too near the forbidden zone. Starting from a close-hauled point of sailing, to go about let the bow pass through this forbidden zone, so that the boat comes round still close-hauled, but on the other tack.

As the sails have no thrust while passing through the *eye of the wind*, you must rely on the boat's own momentum, or *way*. You must therefore be sure beforehand that you have reasonable speed.

Begin by deciding the course that you will be sailing when you are close-hauled on the other tack. This is about 90° in the other direction. You should therefore choose a mark ashore, to windward (behind your back), at right angles to the boat.

Sail close-hauled with the sails correctly trimmed, to ensure this speed. At the right moment, the helmsman lets go the tiller and sheets in with both hands. At the same time you both move into the middle to encourage the boat to heel slightly in the new direction. With the heel and the tightly sheeted mainsail, she turns quickly. The crew should watch his jib and not ease it until it has started to flap; as soon as it shakes, he lets the sheet go completely, and grasps the weather sheet without hauling it in. The crew should begin to move to the other side of the boat when the jib clew, shaking in the eye of the wind, moves to the other side of the mast. At this moment the crew sheets home the jib on the new tack. The helmsman, who should have changed hands on the tiller and mainsheet, now finds himself with the mainsail still sheeted in to leeward, with its other surface to the wind. He eases it off a little so that the boat picks up speed and the manoeuvre is complete.

This business of going about will agitate you at first: the sails flap, the boat turns, the wind comes from you-know-not-where, each crew man gropes for his right place under the menace of the boom. Your whole world gyrates but, more likely than not you'll find, more or less in front of the bow, the landmark you chose a little while earlier.

Sometimes, you seem to have succeeded but the boat, although the wind is on the new side, has stopped. So ease sheets to avoid a sudden heel, and allow the boat to run off a little and pick up speed. It's only too easy to fail to go about (it can happen to the best of us), the boat fails to pass through the eye of the wind, stops and falls back again on to the old tack. Here again, ease sheets and bear away to avoid heeling; then start all over again, not forgetting to ask yourself what went wrong.

Were you really close-hauled? Did you have enough speed? Did you keep the mainsail properly sheeted? This last point is important if the boat is to go about properly.

Mishandling the jib is the most common mistake. If you ease the sheet before it shivers, the boat loses speed at the vital moment. But above all, if you sheet the jib home too soon on the new tack, before the boat has turned, it will be back-winded on the original tack, stopping the swing of the bow completely, and forcing it to fall away again. This is the kind of thing that kills confidence between the helmsman and his crew. The crewman must keep his eyes glued on the jib and not rush things and should sheet it home on the new tack only when he sees it clearly flapping on the other side of the mast, on the imaginary line between forestay and lee shroud.

There are other mistakes to be made; if, instead of simply releasing the tiller, you push it vigorously to leeward, the rudder will act as a brake without turning the boat; and if you hold it back a little, the boat will luff too slowly also losing way to your disadvantage. It can also happen that the crew stay too long sitting out to windward or hurl themselves too quickly on to the other side before the sails have filled on the new tack. In such cases keep your cool, and try again, if you have not already capsized.

The right displacement of the crew in the boat is probably the initial key factor. It must be properly synchronized with the movement of the boat, without jerking, and in one smooth action (going about is fast, and lasts between 5 and 10 seconds at the most). Both crewmen should move towards the middle of the boat as the bow comes into the wind; be crouching in the middle as the boat is head-to-wind; and pass to the other side as the boat bears off on the new tack.

A successful tack depends above all initially on the helmsman. Release the tiller and keep the mainsheet right home; and the boat will pivot on her axis almost in spite of herself.

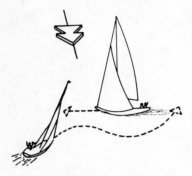

The boat on port tack must give way to the boat on starboard tack

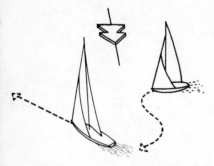

If both are on the same tack, the boat to windward gives way

Port and Starboard Tack

When a boat gets the wind from the right, she is said to be on the *starboard tack*; when she receives it from the left, she is on the *port tack*. Don't confuse this term with the tack that is the lower front corner of any triangular sail.

When you change direction either by going about or by gybing, you are therefore changing tacks. These definitions are used in the rules of the road at sea: when two sailing vessels are sailing on different tacks and their paths cross, the boat on the port tack must give way to the one on the starboard tack.

Working to Windward

If you set out with a wind blowing off the shore, and if it has not changed when you return you will have to work to windward, and you will not be able to get home in a straight line, as the boat is not able to sail closer than 45° to the wind direction. You must therefore sail close-hauled on one tack and then on the other, *working to windward* or *beating*.

Your course will scarcely follow the crow's or the bee's line; the route is much longer and the boat, close-hauled, does not sail at her fastest. But there is no other way and it is conceivable that at the end of this first outing you will decide to buy a motor boat.

However you just have to get back to the shore, although this is easier said than done when the wind is coming exactly from the direction you want go go. And if there is not much water, you'll have to raise the centreboard as you approach the shore, and we know that the boat will then go sideways – you can no longer sail to windward. On their first days out true realists raise the centreboard and rudder well before they are likely to touch bottom, and take out oars or paddles.

When the wind blows along the shore, you can beach without trouble, wind abeam and gradually raising the centreboard and rudder. But take care: ramming beach or bank is not the most sophisticated means of stopping. Just before reaching the shore, you should put the tiller down to luff up into the wind, with all sheets eased. The boat stops and you climb out straight away to hold on to her.

Finally, if the wind blows on shore there is no difficulty. You merely have to put yourself back to the situation we were in early on in this chapter. Let go of everything and raise the centreboard and rudder, whereupon the boat will put herself beam-on to the wind and drift gently to the shore.

Capsizing

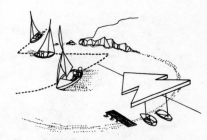

Once the centreboard is up, the boat can no longer sail into the wind. Use the sculls or just step out. If there is not enough water for the centreboard you are bound in be within your depth

The weather having been good up till now, there's been no occasion to capsize but, as we have touched on this eventuality several times, let's look at it now a little more closely.

Usually (but not always) a boat capsizes to leeward, when you haven't enough speed on, the sails are hard in and you're heeling over too far.

The dinghy lies on its side and stays there with the hull supported by its buoyancy and the mast lying along the top of the water. The crew flops gently into the water to leeward.

First point: do not try to hang on to the inside of the boat, or put your weight on the mast or rigging. If you do this, the boat stands a good chance of turning completely upside down. If the mast is submerged and pointing straight down, complications ensue and righting the boat without help becomes very difficult.

Next step (before anything else), get the sails down, a tricky job the first time you do it, but you'll see how the mast will then come upright much more easily.

With the boat lying on her side, one of the crew works his way round to the centreboard. This is the only possible point where weight can be applied to right the boat (if you were sailing down-wind, with the centreboard up, you must therefore first manage to lower it; one pushes, the other pulls and it's a bind). Whoever is in charge of operations puts his feet on the centreboard and, with both hands on top of the gunwale, leans back and, more often than not, the boat will come upright without difficulty. If not or if the boat rolls back on its side, the other crew should hold the bow head-to-wind. This is a great help.

When they have been righted, many boats, even very light dinghies like the French *Vaurien*, are pretty full of water. Stability is thus minimal and there is a danger of capsizing again if you try to get in over the side, or if two of you get aboard and one moves too much to one side. One crewman therefore gets aboard, over the transom, and bales from the broadest part of the hull.

(Use windcheater, shirt or trousers if you have lost your bailer.) He then helps his friend aboard, also by the transom. Everything shipshape, you start sailing again.

With experience you can carry out this exercise quickly, but it takes time to get used to it. It is probably best, by the way, to drop your anchor (which should be placed on board so that it falls freely to the bottom, at least when the boat turns over completely). This is particularly important if the wind is blowing the boat on to a dangerous shore or out to sea.

Another basic rule: if you capsize and can't right yourself *never leave the boat*. The shore is always further off than you think and the hull of a boat is more conspicuous than a swimmer. It is the best marker buoy there is while you are waiting for rescue.

When boats have really extensive built-in buoyancy, when they are righted they are virtually empty and you can start off again at once. This might appear to be an advantage and, indeed it is for an experienced crew, who can get quickly over the side of the boat as it goes over and put their weight on the centreboard, swinging inside the moment the boat rights itself. But this doesn't come easily to beginners. Generally, they fall slap into the water and then their difficulties begin for the hull floats high, the centreboard and gunwale are difficult to reach, the boat is being blown rapidly downwind and can soon drift, out of the crew's reach. The extra security which this built-in buoyancy seemed to offer is suddenly no longer so attractive.

With a dinghy that holds a lot of water after capsizing the difficulties involved in righting it are such that you should think twice before risking it. All the same the beginner will have to tackle the problem, for you must eventually be prepared for a capsize, and it's wise to go in for one, under instruction, so as not to be literally 'at sea' when it happens for real. No matter how good your seamanship may become, it may well happen and you ought to know that you get easily exhausted when righting a boat for the effort involved is considerable. Two capsizes in succession are enough: it would be silly to keep on at it before having a rest. It's silly anyhow to invite capsizing, worse still to be proud of it. You never capsize except through doing something wrong; its not a reason for putting out flags!

Now we must get on to the next stage. Although the principles examined in this chapter are rudimentary, they must be fully absorbed for they are basic.

Certain wrinkles, however useful to start with, must be rethought. For example, you should soon stop taking landmarks on the shore, as we have suggested earlier, and begin to steer the boat purely in relation to the wind and its shifts as it veers and backs.

We need not abide by the basic principles too strongly. It would be wrong, for instance, to believe too firmly in generalisations such as: the jib makes the boat bear away, the mainsail makes her luff – as has been stated up to this point. This was all right in the particular case under review, but the relationship between the sails and the balance of the boat on the move are much more complex (you can find boats which have weather helm under the jib alone!).

Remember, for the moment, that a boat and her crew form an entity, each component reacting in relation to the whole within a complete framework.

Part 1. The Boat

Now we must consider the boat itself. Already it is clear enough that she is no more use on her own than a riderless horse, so it is time to study her, find out what brings her to life and learn the subtleties of tuning her to concert pitch. Really come to terms with her. She has to be treated almost as a human being, not to be enjoyed one day and ignored until you want to sail again. The penalty of such callous treatment will be the reproach of finding her deteriorate and it will be clear that boats and boating are not for you. You and she are a partnership which has to be worked at, hardly less than with love affairs or marriage. So that is why we deal next with practicalities without going quite as far as naval architecture or comparing the pros and cons of dozens of different designs on view at boat shows. The approach is strictly utilitarian: you have a certain boat, so you must know her good and bad points, and what to do to keep her alive and well. This involves practical judgement on a number of levels: choosing the boat, tuning it, general use and maintenance including simple repairs.

This kind of practical knowledge entails more than one advantage. When you are afloat it is essential to be able to carry out running repairs yourself and not always seek help; and this breeds self-confidence and self-reliance. It brings too the added bonus of economy, confirming that sailing is not for millionaires only. At the same time yards will see that you know what you are doing, they will respect you for it and be encouraged to give good workmanship when that becomes necessary.

The points made in this section are numerous and the discussion will be detailed at times and therefore a little heavy-going. Don't try to read and digest it in one sitting. Remember that, like sailing, this book is for pleasure. As a whole, this part of the manual should be regarded as a storehouse of information, to be referred to through the index as need arises. It doesn't pretend to be exhaustive for, in any case, it is quite impossible to make this kind of reference book complete when boats and all their gear are constantly being developed. It should though help to guide you, in place of an experienced friend, through a maze of gimmicks and wrinkles that goes up and down as well as round and round. Or so it will seem at first.

2. What Kind of Boat for What Kind of Sailing?

The notable thing about a sailing boat nowadays is its shameless lack of serious purpose. Gone is its traditional use. The passengers that it welcomes on board have no gainful reason for coming and even the cargo of stores it carries is eaten up during the voyage. And, unlike Columbus, when we go westwards we know where we are going. Where lies the adventure? Privateers are scarce and gunrunners a poor lot.

All that is left is the yen to sail. Yachts are made today only for men and women who feel that urge to sail the seas, purely for pleasure – a strange but stimulating impulse that takes many forms. Some think of it primarily as a sport: be it on river, lake or the sea, all they need is a stretch of water on which to exert their cunning in using wind and the waves to outwit their competitors. For others the water opens up an entirely new scene, pleasant to sail past, while for others still it is for fishing, exploring coves and creeks along the coast and seeing the land from a new viewpoint. Yet more are bent on cruising, learning to live a different kind of life at sea.

No one can say which kind of sailing is best and there is no reason why you should not enjoy more than one aspect of it at the same time. Your choice will depend on how much you care about being self-sufficient at sea, whatever the weather. How far do you want to go, how long do you want to be at sea, how much discomfort and what hazards are you prepared to put up with? The fulfilment of this wish for independence is determined by your capacity, your physical and moral fortitude. It depends, too, on the boat, how well she rides the seas and what sort of amenities she offers. Every boat is designed for a special purpose and she should be kept for that.

In fact, when defining and differentiating between different kinds of sailing and the boats to go with them, it's a case of looking from one to the other, 'tacking' between dream and reality. This is why we shall describe some types of boats suited to their appropriate purposes.

Our choice is limited to our own experience at Glénans, a school for beginners and for those who wish to cruise. We have already dealt with boats for beginners. We shall deal briefly with boats for racing, for day sailing and for fishing. Cruising we shall treat in more detail. Our examples are drawn only from boats we know: obviously there are many other excellent designs. We leave aside multi-hulls – catamarans and trimarans which we have had no opportunity to try out. In the same way, we don't cover really big boats – yawls, ketches, schooners or square riggers – confining ourselves to classic boats useful to the average yachtsman.

Racing

In days gone by yachtsmen raced in straw hats and even fancy waistcoats: today a wet suit is the proper rig. Times have changed, boats have changed, and so has racing. Speed is all. Everything about a racing dinghy is designed to that end.

The lightest possible hull is equipped with a huge driving force – a sizeable sail area. Far from being a resting place, the hull is most likely to be the simplest of perches for the crew to brace themselves on, straining outside the hull – to achieve the balance so cruelly lacking in the boat. But who thinks of complaining about instability? That's exactly what it is all about.

In a racing boat everything can be adjusted under way: mast, rigging and sails. Mastery of this frail, sensitive structure drawing enormous power from the interplay between opposing forces is an enticing objective, something worth working for. And work you must, making yourself familiar with the complexities of racing rules and the complicated gear; practising the adroit movement inboard from the trapeze, mastering the spinnaker, that multicoloured capricious bubble so useful with a following wind, or on a reach.

Racing is an exercise in subtlety. Your dinghy must be sensitive to handle, and have a quick and lively response. In light winds it is not enough to know how to make the most of the wind; you must also be able to steer craftily enough to steal your opponents' wind while keeping yourself clear of others' cunning traps. In fresh winds thinking must be allied to rapid reflexes and an athletic turn of speed. Your chief care is keeping afloat while rushing along

like a fireball. The slightest misjudgement results in immediate punishment – capsizing.

The boat should be unsinkable: you should be able to right her quickly and be off again, or at least hold on while awaiting help.

You depend on others for help; the watch on shore and a swift motorboat. Self-sufficiency doesn't enter into it much and is short-lived: a highly trained crew racing in waters that are well supervised, with first-class rescue services can just about keep going in a Force 6–7 wind, but it is an exercise in virtuosity (and tremendously exciting as well).

Speedy, easily handled and unsinkable, a racing dinghy must also be transportable. On her own she amounts to almost nothing; she is too frail to be moored; she should be easily carried by its crew, though a trolley or helping hands for carrying can come in useful.

Finally, for a racing dinghy to be of any interest she must be a class-boat well represented in your local sailing area.

With a one-off affair one may get fleeting moments of pride, but racing on your own is rather a joyless pastime.

Here are two racing dinghies well known in France and elsewhere: a single-hander, the *Finn*; the other for a two-man crew, the *470*.

Finn
Designer: Richard Scarby
Introduced: 1949
Length: 4.50m
Beam: 1.51m
Sail area: 10sqm
Weight: 150kg

The *Finn* is a prestigious boat that has been popular since its first appearance for single-handed racing in the Olympic Games. She is una rigged with a cold moulded hull (now in fibreglass). It is fairly heavy. Unlike most dinghies she has a metal centreplate which provides some slight ballast. The rigging is simple: it has no shrouds, the boom is slotted into the mast and the whole (mast and boom) pivots as the sail is trimmed.

In spite of its simple design, the *Finn* is a pricy boat because of her very fine construction. Her tuning and handling need the finesse of an experienced helmsman, preferably of athletic build. Anyone weighing less than 80 kilos would have his work cut out to master her. There are other una rigged boats – the *Moth* and the *Laser* for instance, that are cheaper and more suitable for lighter weight single-handers.

470
Designer: Andre Cornu
Introduced: 1965
Length: 4.70m
Beam: 1.68m
Working sail area: 12.70sqm
Spinnaker area: 12.50sqm
Weight: 115kg

The 470 is a two-man sloop with a moulded fibreglass hull, a trapeze, a spinnaker and all the latest go fast gear.

Somewhere between the 420 and the 505 or the Flying Dutchman, the 470 is a racing dinghy in the middle range. It doesn't demand exceptional physical qualities of its crew; even a light crew can survive. It is reasonably priced. The 470 has international standing and the racing is pretty hot!

With advancing years, inclining towards a more stable boat which is still in the top flight of competition, most of us consider buying a keel boat such as a Soling or a 5.5m. With luck you will by that time be able to afford one.

Day-Sailing and Fishing

Day-sailers and fishing boats are very different from racing boats, their chief quality being their stability. Here no-one sets out to pass the day crouched on a plank; they expect to sit down like civilised human beings. Not for them to care about high performance, *haute couture* sails and clever gadgets. Off they go, young and old, fat and thin, supplied with food and drink. They hope for a bit of sunshine, to gaze at the scenery or not to gaze as they please. In short, to be relaxed and comfortable (but are people still capable of even this kind of relaxation?).

These boats should be broad-beamed and have plenty of ballast, and have a shallow draught to allow exploration of coastal inlets. On the other hand they must go well, specially the day-sailers: speed is part of the fun; also it ensures a rapid run home if the weather deteriorates.

Fishing boats should have a deep cockpit, making it possible to stand up, and be roomy for casting the rods. Gunwales should be narrow to facilitate leaning out over the water when hauling in lobster pots, nets or landing a big fellow. It should not rock too much at anchor, and should ideally have a diesel – it is not always possible to troll under sail.

Day-sailers and fishing boats are often open boats; it only takes a wave to fill them. They must therefore have full built-in buoyancy. Should they fill with water it should be possible to empty them, get aboard again and reach home. Such craft should lend themselves to both day-sailing and fishing. The 'Fréhel' is a good example.

Fréhel
Designer: Henri Garetta
Introduced: 1966
Length overall: 5.10m
Length on the waterline: 4.25m
Beam: 2m
Draught: 0.65m
Ballast: 150kg
Total weight: 550kg
Sail area: 17.50sqm
Diesel engine: 7 horsepower

The *Fréhel* is modelled on the traditional Breton fishing boat. Built of fibreglass, it is rigged as a gaff sloop with topsail and

bowsprit. There is also a Bermuda rigged version with a cuddy. With this rig the boat sails closer to the wind. With a gaff rig it is faster in a following wind. Anyway its hull, broad in the beam and sturdily built, is not cut out for speed, and it is not to be expected that such a boat will point up too well: it needs plenty of wind in its sails.

But it is strong and practical. Its long keel ensures easy steering and it takes the ground well. It has full built-in buoyancy.

It would be safe to sail a good mile or so from the shore and to get as far as 'the islands' in really good weather. Its performance as a sailing boat is fairly limited and a diesel is an indispensable auxiliary. All kinds of this sort of boat are being built, often on local lines: the *Pescadou*, for instance, for the Mediterranean.

Maraudeur
Designer: Jean-Jacques Herbulot
Introduced: 1958
Length: 4.86m

Beam: 1.72m
Draught: centreplate up: 0.33m
          centreplate down: 1.13m
Ballast: 70kg
Total weight: 272kg
Sail area: 14.30sqm

The *Maraudeur* is a ballasted centreboard sloop with a moulded fibreglass hull. It is three quarter decked with a cuddy containing two bunks. This is, however, rudimentary and not intended for sleeping in at sea.

Though designed as a day-sailor, you can take short trips along the coast, provided you are not more than an hour or two away from shelter. It is fast, sailing well into the wind, with full buoyancy, and has a self-draining cockpit, but its rig isn't very different from a light dinghy. The weather soon gets too much for it. Once a Force 5 wind gets up you must run for shelter. As it can't be righted it shouldn't roam far afield without other boats around.

This adaptable boat puts you within a wide and varied sailing range to suit your mood and the weather. You can explore small rocky inlets up and down the coast. In calm water a 3hp outboard motor which can be housed in a cockpit locker supplies enough power. You can beach her with the help of inflatable rubber rollers (almost indispensable accessories) and she takes the ground without any problems. Light and uncluttered, she can be towed easily, behind even a small car. She offers an exciting prospect to an active crew not averse to the simple life who can take her where they will; on inland waters or in foreign waters, free to wander like water gypsies.

Cruising

The freedom of cruising is limitless. We begin by day-sailing along the coast in a small boat, leaving in the small hours and entering an unknown harbour at nightfall, a never-to-be-forgotten first day. Later, the time comes when we venture to get under way one fine, clear night, in an area with familiar landmarks. After the first moments of anxiety, the sight of land, picked out by the rhythmic flashings of its lighthouses, is very reassuring. Later on, a coastal cruise in a bigger boat keeps you at sea for two or three days at a time. Appetites grow with experience; and vaulting ambition lands us on the high seas, in a still bigger boat. The sea is for every day, our feeling for complete self-sufficiency is realised in the fullest sense. Life changes its tone, its rhythm, becomes a succession of sense-sharpening watches followed by long lazy spells. Come good weather, bad weather, the open sea, contrary to what you may suppose, is no place to mull over abstract ideas: they get swallowed up. Contentment lies in preoccupation with small details in the midst of boundless space. There are some that have cruised this way right round the world without touching port, and think nothing of it.

Others, less philosophical, prefer ocean racing, straining at all costs to get the utmost out of their boats and themselves, following the tradition of the tea-clippers that raced to be first home.

To say what cruising range can be achieved on this or that cruiser is no simple matter. The size of the boat and of its crew are not decisive factors. The heart of the matter is how well you can adapt to a different time-span lasting longer than a day in which is encompassed the needs of ordinary life: eating, sleeping and conserving your strength which you will need when you run into bad weather. A cruiser must be safe and easy to live in, and really seaworthy as is expected of every boat. All these requirements are part of the whole, but we shall take them one by one.

Living Conditions

For a day or a week the boat is our home. It can be rudimentary, recalling the dens we built as children. But there are certain essentials: a cooking stove, a bunk and protection against damp and cold.

Make no mistake: we are talking about living on a boat at sea. There are floating gin palaces where life in port is a dream. But once clear of the jetty they are rapidly transformed into chaotic heaps and eventually, into sumptuous coffins: a houseboat is not a cruiser.

When sailing one can be content with very little; everyone must have their own bunk and a place to keep their things. There must also be room for cooking and storing provisions, for navigation instruments and the sails and the bosun's locker – not to speak of the guitar or the trombone.

And in addition there must be a degree of comfort; the boat

should be dry and airy; there must be hot food followed by sound sleep. This last is essential, and your self-sufficiency depends on it: with good sleep you can keep going for days.

Safety

Well-slept a man can withstand hard blows, and be of good cheer; the bunk, therefore, is an element of safety.

But there are more fundamental requirements. What matters is not, as was once thought, the size of the boat nor its displacement. We know now that a small boat can withstand bad weather as well as a big one: Jean Lacombe in his 6.50m *Golif* took part in the same race as Tabarly in *Pen Duick II* (13.70m). A recent development too is that a new boat is safer than an old boat of the same size: fifteen years ago a 6.50m boat would have meant an open boat like a Breton *Canot* with a very limited range; now it could be, for example, a *Mousquetaire*.

Similarly a light boat can be quite as seaworthy as a heavy one. In bad weather a heavy boat is difficult to handle. A lighter boat is generally easier to heave to, and rides the waves better than a heavy one. Heavy boats are gradually giving place to lighter ones. The twelve-tonner, *La Sereine* is 12.50m long, whereas *Red Rooster* with the same overall length is only 9.5 tons, and there are yachts of the same length which displace 6 tons and less.

Safety, therefore, is to be looked for elsewhere, namely buoyancy, stability, watertightness, and the quality of the rigging. Added to all this is the ultimate guarantee – full built-in buoyancy. This is

generally attained by filling enclosed areas with enough expanded polystyrene to keep the boat afloat even when it is full of water. Full buoyancy is easy enough in a small boat: a *Mousquetaire* can keep sailing even when holed. This is more difficult to achieve in a big boat because buoyancy compartments take up too much room. But it is well worth trying: if the boat is suddenly and seriously damaged (specially in a collision) it should at least keep afloat for the time it takes the crew to get clear and into the life-raft.

To sum up, a cruiser should afford simple living conditions, and safety to the point of being unsinkable. Comfort is a personal matter; but safety is in everyone's interest.

These essentials are the framework within which there is room to cater for everyone's preferences. This is why there are so many cruising boats, each one more seductive than the last. The search for the ideal boat never ceases.

Day Cruising

When racing you only stay on the water as long as the competition is on.

In a day-boat you only go at the best time of day, but when cruising by day you are out from dawn to twilight. You are equipped to stay out at sea if the wind drops and night overtakes you. But it is better not to overrun the hours of sleep and everyone on board can stay awake from start to finish. In the evening you make for a port or a sheltered creek, leaving it next day fresh for another day's sail.

You will never venture far from the coast, but follow the routes formerly used by working boats, real rock dodgers that always took the 'inner passage', and hardly ever brave the open sea.

The *Corsaire* is specially safe and well adapted to this kind of sailing.

Corsaire
Designer: Jean-Jacques Herbulot
Introduced: 1954
Length: 5.50m
Beam: 1.92m

Draught: with centreplate up: 0.55m
        with centreplate down: 1.00m
Ballast: 150kg
Total weight: 550kg
Sail area: 16sqm

The *Corsaire* is a ballasted centreboard sloop with a hard-chine plywood hull. It has two berths with room for a third.

It is a true cruiser, stable when heeling over, non-capsizeable, with full buoyancy, and a self-draining cockpit.

In the right weather one can live on it for a day – even longer if you have to. It will withstand hours of rough weather, up to Force 6 when close-hauled, Force 7 when sailing with the wind on the beam.

There your self-sufficiency ends: it offers too little in the way of proper eating or sleeping facilities in rough weather. Its rigging will only take a limited strain, and it is unsuitable for cruises of more than twenty-four hours. But its shallow draught allows you to explore narrow creeks for shelter. With such a boat one can ease oneself into cruising by taking short legs of five to ten miles. Later, the more experienced sailor, attuned to the sea and able to interpret the weather, can venture on more ambitious cruises.

The crossing between Penmarc'h and Audierne, for instance, is dangerous in all weathers for the uninitiated and is feasible only for an experienced crew with a well-equipped *Corsaire*.

Cruising in Coastal Waters

Coastal cruising is no longer sailing only by day. Night falls and sailing continues, so you must be able to sleep on board and have good hot soup and not just sandwiches.

From now on you will often stand off to sail in the open sea, out of sight of land. You will begin to feel at home on the high seas.

Coastal cruising, indeed, covers a vast area of sailing; to demonstrate the possibilities, here are three very different boats; on the one hand, the *Mousquetaire*, on the other the *Galiote* and the *Nautile*.

Mousquetaire
Designer: Jean-Jacques Herbulot
Introduced: 1963
Length: 6.48m
Beam: 2.30m
Draught: centreplate up: 0.76m
            centreplate down: 1.34m
Ballast: 450kg of iron
            steel centreplate 50kg
Overall weight: 1,300kg
Sail area: 19.30sqm

The *Mousquetaire* is a ballasted centreboard sloop with a hard-chine ply hull. It has four berths (five at a pinch) and room for a fitted stove. It has all the safety features of the *Corsaire* but to a higher standard. One can live on it, eat and sleep properly even in a Force 5 wind, and cruise for longer than twenty-four hours. It

will take a Force 7 wind easily when close-hauled and a Force 8 when the wind is on the beam. It has a true cruising rig. Though larger than the *Corsaire* it too can easily get into small anchorages – a coastal cruiser on a larger scale. With its extended range it can cruise round all the inlets of a treacherous coast such as we have in Brittany and the more daring sailor with a good meteorological cover can even make the great leap forward as far as the cliffs of perfidious Albion. But that would be a real test.

Galiote and Nautile
Designer: Jean-Marie Finot
Introduced: 1970
Length: 8.30m
Beam: 2.85m
Draught: 1.35m
Ballast: 900kg
Total weight: 2,100kg
Sail area: 39.80sqm

Keelboats with a double chine hull, these two sloops have five to eight berths. They are not two versions of the same boat: the *Galiote* is in aluminium with a doghouse. The *Nautile*, a little longer, is of ply construction with a *flush deck*. These boats, equipped with a galley, a wc and a chart table, are capable of long cruises. They have a high freeboard giving better protection than the *Mousquetaire* and they are more spacious. Below one can stand upright and more than one job, be it cooking or navigation, can be carried on at the same time. There is room for spare dry clothes. It is easy to stand upright on the deck and even stretch one's legs.

Coastal sailing is not much fun on these boats. Because of their draught they cannot get into small anchorages, but need a proper harbour. One can envisage longer cruises, such as Ushant-Cape Finisterre, bearing in mind that one is running the same risks as on an ocean cruiser.

Ocean Cruising

The land disappears, we shall see it again but not in any hurry. The boat's possibilities are almost limitless. One falls to dreaming of everything one could do if only one dared.

Arpège
Designer: Michel Dufour
Introduced: 1967
Length: 9.25m
Beam: 3.00m
Draught: 1.35m
Total weight: 3,300kg
Ballast: 1,200kg
Sail area: 45sqm

The *Arpège* is a sloop with a moulded fibreglass hull designed for a crew of six, and is notable for its comfort. Its cabin is almost a three room suite: the cooking-navigation area can be cut off from the saloon which again can be cut from the wc-sail-locker compartment.

You can stand up in the cabin; and sleepers can cut themselves off from those who are awake, a great advantage during a long haul.

One can live on it for days at sea. But a special authorisation is needed to cross the Atlantic. The *Arpège* has been designed as a cruiser-racer. As this type of boat cannot be given full built-in buoyancy an inflatable life-raft should be carried.

La Sereine
Designer: Eugene Dervin
Introduced: 1952
Length: 12.50m
Beam: 3.40m
Draught: 2.10m
Ballast: 5,300kg
Total weight: 12,000kg
Sail area: 73sqm

The *Sereine* is a bermudan cutter of classic construction in wood. She has accommodation for a crew of ten. Below she is divided into four compartments: navigation area, galley, saloon, wc-cum-sail-locker.

She is a moderate performer, speed being sacrificed for deep sea comfort. Ports are no longer a necessity: you can dry your socks on board, shut yourself off, or walk about on the deck. The duration of your cruise is only limited by the amount of stores you can carry. Its deep draught limits it to deep-water harbours.

Ocean Racing

Theoretically, ocean racers have no special characteristics: they are cruising boats pushed to the limits of their performance.

In fact they are for the most part highly specialised boats in which everything is subordinated to speed. The .choice must be made while the boat is still on the drawing-board for it is essential for it to conform to rating regulations. There is a system of measurement for estimating a boat's sailing performance so that it can be fairly compared with other boats. One tries to make the most of the opportunities allowed within the set limits for it is this that will mainly determine the design of boats built for racing. Different regulations give rise to different types of boat. Cruising yachts benefit from this research for the strict racing regulations stimulate the designer's imagination. Every year sees a new standard of efficiency. Sails become longer, shorter, or two take the place of one. A fashion is started which other boats follow and important modifications result from this competition.

Though the sport is extremely costly – boats must 'adapt or die' every season – ocean racing at one end of the spectrum is one of the most fascinating aspects of sailing and produces wonderful boats.

Red Rooster
Designer: Dick Carter
Introduced: 1969
Length: 12.56m
Beam: 3.69m
Draught: centreplate up: 0.82m
          centreplate down: 2.80m
Centreplate weight: 2.5 tons
Weight overall: 9 tons
Main sail area: 23.50sqm
Headsail area: 41sqm

Unlike the other boats described, *Red Rooster* is not part of the Glénans fleet. We include her because she illustrates strikingly the spirit of research that pervades the world of the ocean racer. Not that one can say for certain that she indicates a new departure. Nothing dates quicker than this kind of boat: built in 1969 and winner of the Fastnet race the same year, *Red Rooster* was beaten the next year and Dick Carter was already on something new.

Red Rooster has the large hull, the clear deck and low super-structure typical of the American designer. Note, too, the almost insolent simplification of the rigging and all the fittings, so very much in the fashion of the day: no kicking strap, a rudimentary mainsheet slider – but enormous winches. And the boat possesses even more curious features: a centreplate weighing 2.5 tons, raised and lowered by a winch. The rudder itself is also movable and can be raised like a dagger-board with hardly any difficulty.

With its centreplate up *Red Rooster* can be sailed in less than a metre of water but can also attain tremendous speeds: in a light breeze, say Force 3, she can clock over 9 knots; in fresh winds, close-hauled, 7 knots like the best of them, and with the wind on the beam, she does easily more than 10 knots and quickly disappears over the horizon.

Choosing a Boat

Not everyone can own a *Red Rooster*, and it would be highly imprudent to begin with one. Before considering buying even the smallest boat, get in as much sailing as possible to make sure you like it enough to take on the responsibilities that go with it. Besides, you can sail all your life without ever owning a boat. There are clubs and places where you can charter a boat; and, since people persist in buying boats too large for themselves, crewing is a job with no risk of unemployment.

However, if you are overcome by the desire to own your own boat, it is as well to sit down and review the situation calmly. This is simple enough if you set your sights on a sailing dinghy. The sum involved won't condemn you to living on ship's biscuits to the end of your days. A dinghy is not expensive to maintain and will last for ten years. In any case the mistake isn't serious since it is easily sold, specially if it is a class boat. Nothing need be said about fishing boats either: fishermen are wise folk who know exactly what they're after, and keep their boats for a long time.

After that the choice becomes more difficult. One may hesitate between a day-sailer and a small cruiser, or between two similar cruisers. Among the different types of boat we have described there may seem to be clear-cut differences, but in fact they are not so obvious. It is not just a question of the size of one boat or another: there is the question of accommodation and what you want to use it for (as we have sketched out). This depends on the crew and resources available. If you can put your boat on a trailer, the expenses are much less.

How to decide? Ask yourself two questions: what exactly are you going to use the boat for? How much money can you set aside not just to buy it but to keep it up from year to year?

What is it For?

We have already said that a day-sailer like the *Maraudeur* and a coastal cruiser like the *Corsaire* don't offer you the same scope of action. And there is an even more fundamental difference: an attitude of mind. A *Maraudeur* is carefree: no need for a high standard of upkeep since you won't be living in it. Nor for elaborate safety precautions since you will never be far from land. Nor even for much sailing expertise. It is a simple way of escape, an agreeable pastime; and, once it is laid up ashore, you can forget it.

A *Corsaire* demands more attention, care and time. You can't be casual about cruising: you must have the will to learn a new technique, and to provide the boat with everything needed for navigation. The boat must play an important part in your life. If you don't accept these premises, owning a *Corsaire* is pointless. With rudimentary equipment and an inexperienced crew one must be content with short day outings: the boat is used like a *Maraudeur* without the advantages of the latter if you capsize. It's a waste of money to own a better boat than you need; you are just not making use of the capability and freedom that you have bought.

On the other hand, if you are prepared to equip the boat completely, with cooking facilities, a complete wardrobe of sails, navigation instruments, charts and reference books, spare anchors, a radio, a pump, a radar reflector, etc, once the crew is well-trained and working together, the *Corsaire* can do better than it was designed for, and serve as a true cruiser even for night sailing. It is then used almost like a *Mousquetaire*.

The same comparisons could be made about other types of boat. To sum up: a boat is as good as its equipment and its crew. Rather than under-employing a boat, it is better to buy one that is rather more modest than you want and that you can occasionally push to do more than it was designed for.

The Price

Once you know what you want it for, the question of cost can be gone into in some detail. No-one would deny that a boat is expensive: first, the price. Don't forget that the yard price doesn't include bunks, cooking stove, safety equipment, navigation instruments, a dinghy, etc. To equip a small cruiser, allow for a surcharge of between 40% and 50% of the basic cost.

These expenses are foreseeable. But you have to remember the annual cost of insurance, harbour dues, mooring charges, storing and upkeep during the close season.

Once the season is over a boat is nothing but an encumbrance. That's something to bear in mind just before you put your money down. The cost of wintering varies according to the boat and where you keep it.

In a well-supervised anchorage a boat can be kept afloat all the year round, thus avoiding the expense of hauling her out of the water and supervision. If the hull needs no attention (fibreglass or unpainted aluminium) that, too, will save money. In this way the out-of-season costs are easy to estimate. But there is an unknown factor: the care of the rigging and the sails, which can mount up alarmingly if you want to 'keep in the race'.

If the harbour is badly equipped or poorly supervised, the boat must be taken out of the water: taking the mast out, slipping her, storage charges and then the whole process in reverse is all very expensive. It is a great economy if the boat can be towed on a trailer to your own place. There is no precise answer to what kind of hull you should choose. If you can leave your boat afloat all the year round, it is an advantage to have a fibreglass hull. On the other hand a plywood hull, generally cheaper to buy, is not hard on the pocket if left in an inexpensive anchorage during the season, and if you can take it home for the winter and paint it yourself.

Naturally all manner of considerations crop up at the moment of decision. Ask yourself if the boat in question is appropriate for the place where it will be sailed. You must be sure, too, of being able to call on a suitable crew, let alone giving the time to it yourself. All that is common sense – and having had some experience.

Having done your sums, you are almost quit of your anxieties. You only have to choose a boat which meets your criteria. This is a question of taste, patience and flair. Prowl around, look in at showrooms, visit yards, exchange views, go home, have another look at the boat, more discussion, read the rest of this book and finally, launch out on the sea.

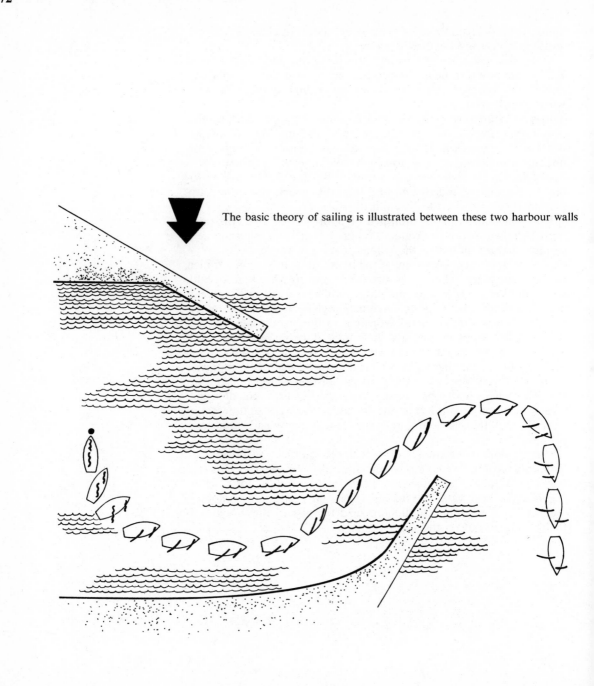

The basic theory of sailing is illustrated between these two harbour walls

3. Theory

You can get a fairly good idea of how a boat works by watching one put to sea from any port. You'll soon see the principal forces that are playing on her and how they interact.

The boat is on her mooring, sails hoisted, all ready. Still tied up at the bow, she faces the wind and the sails flap idly amidships.

The mooring is cast off and she drops astern with the force of the wind which is working on hull, spars, rigging and flapping sails.

The boat quickly falls away beam-on to the wind. When she is almost square on, the crew haul in the sails gently. The bow points steadily now, the boat heels a little and, still making a lot of leeway, pushes gently forward. Another force can now be seen at work, acting on the sails, and it is not driving in the same direction as the wind.

The boat gradually accelerates, still making leeway and drifting towards the quay. On board nobody moves; they wait. The boat accelerates more and suddenly, without apparent reason, everything has changed: she heels a little more, ceases to make leeway and moves forward decisively. Now it becomes clear what this new force is. As wind, course, and sail trim all remain constant, it is the effect of the water acting on the keel which counteracts leeway and enables the boat to pick up speed.

From now on the boat is under control, and everybody appears to wake up. The helmsman luffs up a little, the crew haul in the sheets. The boat works her way to windward, sails close-hauled, to avoid the jetty. On this point of sailing she heels quite a lot, and does not make much speed, and leeway comes into evidence again.

The jetty passed, the boat bears away on to a reach and sheets are eased slowly. She heels less and makes less leeway. Speed picks up rapidly now that the wind appears to work on the sails more efficiently than when the boat was travelling minutes ago to windward.

As the boat bears away still more, the sheets completely eased, the mainsail bears against the lee shroud. The jib is soon blanketed, so it is taken across to the other side of the boat. The boat now heads out to sea with the wind dead aft, her sails goosewinged. Heel and leeway are eliminated but, in spite of the entire sail area being spread before the wind, speed is less than before. The wind force on the sails has weakened.

The theories which have just been put into practice are elementary but important none the less, and worth being summarized:

The force exerted by the wind on the sails varies according to the course and according to the trim of the sails.

The water exerts on the keel a force which, at least to some extent, counters leeway; the intensity of this force is related to boat speed.

These two forces act against each other – one in the air, the other in the water – and make the boat heel.

To sum up, the boat presses against the water by means of her keel in order to draw from the wind the necessary propulsive energy.

Now we must examine these forces – how they come to bear on the craft, whence they come and their strength.

Wind and Sail

When billiard balls collide, they exert an equal force on each other in opposing directions. This is the principle of action and reaction.

In the same way the wind, when it encounters an obstacle, a sail for example, is deflected. The sail exerts a force on the wind in order to deflect it and the wind exerts on the sail an equal and opposite force. This latter force is the one we are interested in.

How the Force Shows Itself

Imagine a large open sea, with a constant wind blowing over it. These airstreams can be shown graphically by parallel lines. If the area is divided in two, the wind blows at the same force between *a* and *b* and between *b* and *c*.

Then a boat arrives and her sail deflects the air-stream but only in the immediate neighbourhood of the sail. Further off, at $c-c^1$

it is unchanged or has resumed its original direction at $a–a^1$.

The air coming up against the sail on the windward side has to change direction, and what air started between a and b escapes through the narrower corridor $a^1–b^1$, getting compressed in the process.

To leeward, if the air continued to flow straight, a vacuum would be created behind the sail and, in order to fill it, the air-stream has to deflect round the sail. The result is that the air that started between b and c has to fill the broader space, $b^1–c^1$, with a correspondingly lower force on the leeward side that creates a forward suction on the sail. This high pressure to windward and low pressure to leeward combine to make up the force exerted by wind on sail, which we shall call *aerodynamic force*.

Direction

The force exercised by a fluid moving over a surface is perpendicular to the surface, regardless of the angle of incidence. By the same token the force applied at each point of a sail is perpendicular to the surface.

In practice, the effects of the high and low pressure forces are more or less perpendicular to the chord of the sail.

Strength

To sum up, aerodynamic force is:

Proportional to the surface of the sail: if you reduce sail by half, the force is reduced by half.

Proportional to the square of the wind speed: if the wind speed is doubled, aerodynamic force is quadrupled.

In accordance with the law of equal and opposite reaction already mentioned, you might think that the greater the angle through which the sail deflects the wind, the greater would be the force exerted on the sail. In practice, this is not quite the case. As you gradually sheet in a sail to bring it closer to the wind, aerodynamic force does increase to start with but, beyond a certain angle of incidence, it decreases sharply and maintains relatively weak, as the angle of impact becomes greater.

This unexpected breakdown suggests a sudden change in the airstream. At low angles of incidence, this flow is undisturbed or *laminar*; but as the angle of incidence increases, turbulence appears, only weak at first without decreasing the aerodynamic force. Then,

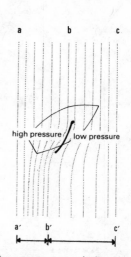

High pressure to windward + low pressure to leeward = aerodynamic force

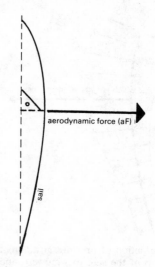

Direction of aerodynamic force

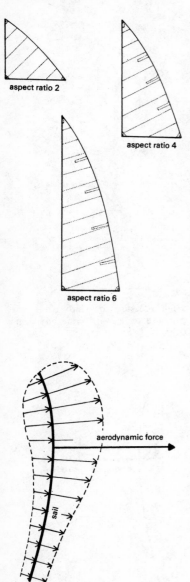

aspect ratio 2

aspect ratio 4

aspect ratio 6

aerodynamic force

sail

Distribution of pressure at different points of the sail, to windward and leeward

suddenly, the sail stalls. The angle of incidence has become too great for the air stream to maintain laminar characteristics, so that it bounces off the sail to windward and it cannot fill the vacuum to leeward. Air eddies are formed and the flow is completely disturbed. These eddies interrupt the high and low pressure system around the sail with bad effects on the force generated.

You can't easily get out of a stall. Easing the sheet a little won't get you back to the lower angle of incidence you had before for the air flow remains turbulent, and aerodynamic force does not increase again. To sort it out, the sail should be eased well beyond the critical angle until it starts to flap. Only then are the eddies dispersed and the air flow settles down again. Now you can begin sheeting in.

This experience proves how closely aerodynamic force is related to the angle of incidence between wind and sail. The wind must be deflected, not broken up. It follows that the shape of the sail itself is important: the cut of its concavity and the aspect ratio of height to its surface area. Worked out mathematically, so as to allow for leech round, aspect ratio is represented by the formula $AR = L^2 + SA:1$, where L is the luff in feet and SA the sail area in square feet. A less precise, but acceptable, formula for triangular sails is $AR = 2L \div F:1$, where L is the luff and F the foot in feet. For the same angle of incidence, sails of different shapes produce different forces and they stall at different angles of incidence. To give you an indication, for a similar camber this angle can be in the order of 15° for a sail with an aspect ratio of 6:1 (high aspect ratio), or of 20° to 25° for a sail of aspect ratio 3:1 (low aspect ratio). We shall examine this in more detail later.

But always remember, whatever sail is being considered, that aerodynamic force is greatest where you can deflect the wind through a large angle without stalling your sails.

All the foregoing relates to the overall strength of the aerodynamic force, but this force is not spread over the whole area of the sail equally. Wind tunnel tests have shown that:

The greatest force is produced in the front third of the sail: a sail is more efficient near the luff than the leach.

The low pressure on the leeward side of the sail has much more influence than the high pressure on the windward side. Perhaps this surprises you at first.

It follows that it is important to avoid disturbing the air-stream close to these areas, doing all you can to keep it smooth flowing.

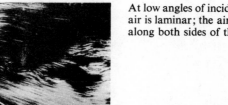

At low angles of incidence the flow of air is laminar; the air flows regularly along both sides of the sail centre

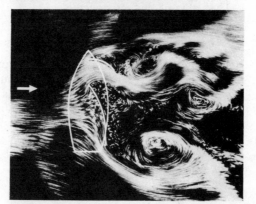

If the sails are sheeted in too hard, the flows becomes turbulent; the boat goes slower

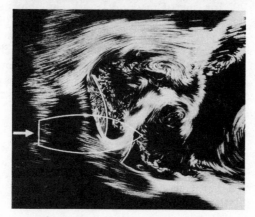

With wind astern the angle of incidence is very unfavourable, the flow is extremely turbulent

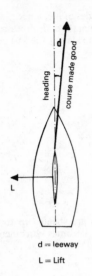

d = leeway

L = Lift

Water and Keel

As the centreboard of a dinghy and the keel of a keel boat both have the same rôle – to stop the boat from making leeway – we shall use the word keel only through this section.

Other things being equal, a keel works in the water as a sail does in the air except that, instead of a fluid flowing over a surface, here it is a surface which is moving in a fluid, but the interaction is exactly the same.

When a boat makes leeway, it moves sideways in the water: the keel resists the water at a certain angle (the angle of leeway) and sets up a force in reaction, perpendicularly to its surface. This force is called *lateral resistance*, which we shall just call the resistance of the keel.

The value of this resistance is:

Proportional to the surface of the keel.
Proportional to the square of the boat's speed.

The angle of leeway functions in the same way: the greater the leeway, the greater the resistance, always supposing that the flow of water is *laminar*. As with the sail, there is a critical angle beyond which it stalls and eddies appear around the keel, resistance decreases sharply and then it is weak in relation to the angle of leeway. The only remedial action is to bear away until the leeway angle is markedly inferior to the critical angle, and the flow of water becomes laminar once again.

The critical angle depends on the aspect ratio of the keel and on its thickness. It can be about 30° for a keel which is thick and short, 20° for one of medium length and thickness, and only 12° for a deep, fine keel. It can also vary according to the camber of the keel (and research is going on to produce a keel which has a camber which can change from side to side on each tack).

The forces acting on a keel are much more distinct than those on a sail: a keel is rigid, and water is 795 times denser than air.

Although the hull also produces some resistance, for simplification we have only considered the keel.

Why a Boat Sails

Having digested these facts of physics, we can now analyse in more detail how the various forces combine to drive a boat forward.

Setting Out

Let us put our boat back on its mooring, and consider the procedure.

After casting off, the boat drops gently astern, then bears away to its position of equilibrium, drifting sideways. The angle of resistance of keel to water is in the region of 90°, water flow is turbulent, and lift (or resistance) from the keel very weak.

The important thing is to gather speed, to create lift and stop the boat moving crabwise towards the quay. So the helmsman bears away and the crew trim the sails, to catch the wind from astern instead of abeam.

To understand how we can profit from the force exerted by the wind on the sails, it is best to look again at the parallelogram of forces used in physics, and to break down aerodynamic force in relation to the two directions which interest us: one along the fore and aft line of the boat, which is the *propulsive component* (or thrust); the other at right angles to this line, which is the *drift component*.

If the crew, instead of allowing the boat to bear away, were to sheet in the sails at once, the wind would be too much abeam and propulsive component would be weak and drift component strong. The boat would continue to make leeway without moving forward, because lift would still be weaker than drift and the vessel would end up against the quay.

But the crew is on the ball, and they only sheet in the sails when the boat has borne away almost on to a reach. From then on the wind is in a favourable direction, providing good thrust with slight drift: the sails have been trimmed to give the most efficient deflection.

The boat, still making leeway, starts to move forward and, as a result, the leeway angle lessens. When this angle eventually becomes considerably lower than the critical angle, water-flow round the keel becomes laminar, so that lift increases suddenly; the boat heels and moves forward decisively. You are now under control, making practically no leeway, so you can luff up without fear.

The fact that the boat heels at the moment that she moves forward is easily explained. Lift and drift form opposing forces which tend to heel the boat. While lift remains weak, the combined force is weak so the boat heels only slightly. As soon as the keel 'bites', lift increases, the combined force becomes stronger and the boat heels more.

To Windward

The boat now works up to windward and the crew has sheeted-in the sails some more – aerodynamic force is now directed sideways. As we saw earlier, it is noticeable that the propulsive component is not so strong as when the wind is abeam, so that the boat goes

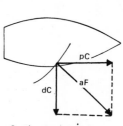

pC = thrust component
dC = Leeway
aF = aerodynamic force

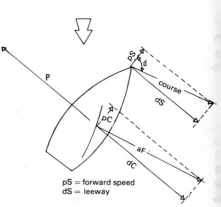

pS = forward speed
dS = leeway

If the sails are sheeted in too soon when the boat is close-hauled, the drift component (or leeway) which is very great needs to be counteracted by a very strong resistance from the keel. This cannot be obtained unless there is a good drift speed. As the propulsive component is weak, forward speed remains low and consequently the angle of drift is enormous and cannot diminish

The play of forces on getting under way

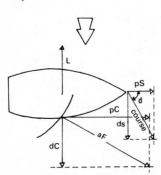

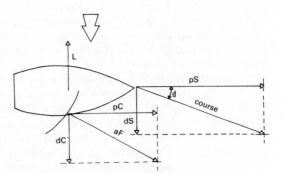

Getting under way: the sails are only sheeted in when the boat has borne away sufficiently: the aerodynamic force is well directed, leeway component is as limited as possible. The resistance needed is low and can only be achieved with excessive leeway because, the flow being turbulent, the keel does not act efficiently

Speed increases: leeway component is the same, so is the resistance. Leeway does not slacken as the flow is still turbulent; but, as the boat is now moving faster, the leeway angle diminishes

more slowly the more she heels. At the same time she makes noticeable leeway.

One way or another, keel resistance and drift components must counterbalance. We have already seen that resistance depends on speed and now our speed has diminished. It also depends on the surface of the keel: but this does not change. Finally, it depends on the angle of leeway. As long as the flow of water is constant, a larger angle of leeway will ensure good resistance, and this now works to our advantage. *To sum up, the boat takes up by herself the appropriate angle of leeway, according to her speed, to let the keel develop sufficient resistance to counterbalance drift.* Less speed means more leeway, and conversely, when speed increases resistance increases and there is less leeway.

Now what happens when you luff too much? Propulsive component decreases and leeway increases; the boat slows down as the angle of leeway gets bigger. Soon this angle becomes too big, and it passes the critical point when the keel loses its power and, at once,

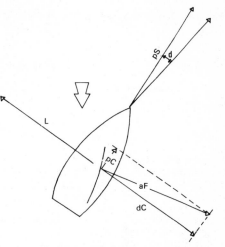

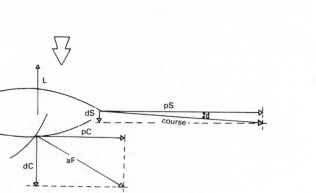

Speed increases more: leeway angle
lessens still further and, suddenly, the
keel 'bites' (the flow has become
laminar). All at once, adequate resistance is achieved with little leeway
and the leeway angle becomes
negligible

Now one can luff up as, with a laminar
flow, the resistance can increase
enough to balance a large leeway
component. Leeway angle increases
only slightly

resistance weakens and the boat moves sideways – as we have
already learned. You must now bear away sharply and start all
over again.

Finally, we should remember that the boat heels more going to
windward than with the wind abeam, because the combined force
of resistance and drift increases.

Reaching

Once past the end of the jetty, everything is easier and the helmsman bears away, while the crew eases sheets bit by bit, always
keeping the sails filled. Aerodynamic force is gradually directed
further forward and the propulsive component increases and the
boat picks up speed. Drift component and keel resistance diminish
and, with greater speed, leeway is virtually zero. The boat hardly
heels at all and the difference between resistance and drift components is small.

The boat continues to bear away and soon passes the position of

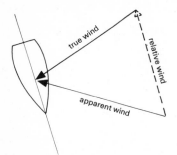

True wind and apparent wind
The wind that a boat gets when under
way has neither the same direction
nor the same strength as the *true
wind*. The wind created by the boat's
speed (*relative wind*) combines with
the true wind to give an *apparent
wind*. It is this apparent wind which
effectively acts on the sails; it is the
wind indicated by the burgee at the
head of the mast and felt by the crew.
The apparent wind is always further
ahead (nearer the bows) than the true
wind. The angle of difference can
be as much as 35° or more on a reach.

It is stronger than the true wind
when close-hauled, weaker when
sailing free when the angle of difference can vary from plus 30° to minus
50°. This can be felt quite distinctly
when the point of sailing is changed

reaching. The mainsail presses against the lee shroud and, as the
sheet can't be eased any more (yet the boat is still bearing away), the
airflow is no longer deflected and becomes turbulent – stalling
occurs.

Broad Reach and Dead Run

The wind now blows virtually from aft, is turbulent and relatively
weak, its strength now varying little while the boat continues to
bear away until she is dead before the wind; there is neither
heeling nor leeway.

It is now clear that of the two principal forces which combine to
drive a boat forward, aerodynamic force is clearly positive, while
resistance from the keel is something you have to put up with. Its
resistance is necessary for the boat to bite on the water, it has its
debit side: when it moves forward through the water at a slight
angle, according to the amount of leeway, the keel works as a brake.

We must now turn to what the crew has been up to while he has
been setting sail. At the start, he knows that the keel is necessary
to drive the boat forward, and that he must make it start working
for him right away; but as soon as it begins to bite he wants it to
fight against the boat as little as possible. To this end, he can only
play with the trim of the sail. Depending on the point of sailing,
the important thing is not always to trim the sails for maximum
aerodynamic force, for if this force is directed athwart ships, its
drift component is large and the keel comes very much into play.
It is better to employ a weaker force but one directed further ahead.
In other words the crew must not only consider the angle of incidence between the wind and the sails (which determines the degree
of aerodynamic force employed) but also the angle between the
sails and the fore-and-aft line of the boat (which determines the
direction of this force). In practice, one must compromise but the
one golden rule is to ease your sheets as much as possible.

Indeed, everything about boats is a compromise at sea and in
their construction. Spars are needed to hold up the sails, but they
should be as unobtrusive as possible because they greatly affect
the strength and direction of aerodynamic force. Even the hull
has its uses: it floats and you can step the mast in it (and, of course,
live aboard), but it too acts like a brake in the water. All these
impedimenta mean you must compromise increasingly on the
problems of stability, accommodation, and safety, to achieve the
best possible overall efficiency. The Eeyores will always point out
that the level of this efficiency is wretched. But happier people will

realise that a sailing boat makes the best of conditions which are unfavourable initially but improve according to the way the boat is handled: helmsmanship and sail trim become absorbingly fascinating and this is what we are going on to now.

Sails

Sail Efficiency

At sea it is no good concentrating on just one sail-efficiency factor at a time or even on the interaction of all of them, good or bad. That is better done by the theorists in wind tunnels with the help of models. Such tests are conducted under conditions which are remote from reality, as we shall see; what is discovered in such places is, nevertheless, interesting in as much as it demonstrates clearly how aerodynamic force developed by one or another sail varies according to its angle in relation to the wind.

The results of this kind of scientific experiment can be very simple and need not daunt the reader who is not familiar with the invisible physical forces that are at work. All the following diagrams are based on the apparent wind direction which comes from the centre of the sail in question for each angle of incidence between wind and sail, an arrow shows the direction of the force in relation to its angle of impact; if the ends of all these arrows are joined, a curve is formed, called a *polar diagram*, which illustrates how the aerodynamic force varies according to the angle of incidence. (For the purist, the arrow does not represent the aerodynamic force itself, but a co-efficient which allows us to compare at similar angles not only sails of different shapes but also, within certain limits, of different areas. But the same reasoning applies.)

The first curve on page 84 shows the efficiency of a bermudan sail with average aspect ratio and draught. We can compare the actual results described earlier in this chapter with those in the diagram. Note that at low angles of incidence (corresponding to sail trim for points of sailing between close-hauled and a broad reach) total aerodynamic force increases steadily with angle, obtains a maximum at 15° and thereafter falls away sharply. For the sail under consideration, therefore, an angle of incidence of 15° is the critical angle beyond which the sail stalls. What has been a steady airflow up to this point, becomes turbulent. For angles

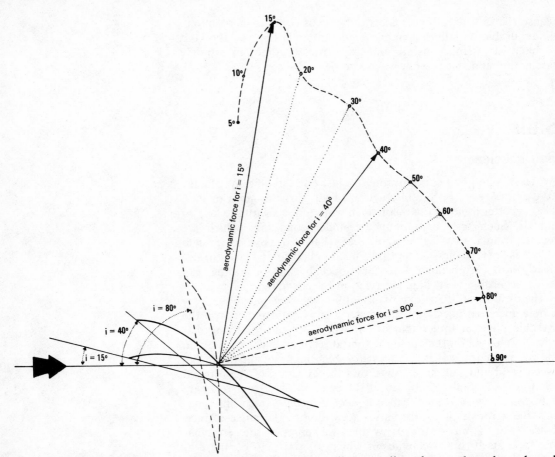

Efficiency of a bermudan (or marconi) sail, of average aspect ratio and belly, set at 15°, 40° and 80° to the wind

greater than 30° (corresponding to sail angle on a broad reach and dead run), the force remains fairly constant but weak.

The acuteness of the curve approaching 15° is worth noting as it shows how a small variation in the angle of incidence causes a large variation in the total aerodynamic force. In practice, this signifies that *sail trim must be precise for all angles where air flow is steady*; beyond that point trim is less critical.

The same curve also shows the direction of the force. We have noted that this is more or less perpendicular to the chord of the sail. If, however, we trace (in dotted line) the different perpendiculars to the sail for the different values of the angle of incidence, it becomes clear that the *aerodynamic force is nearly always directed*

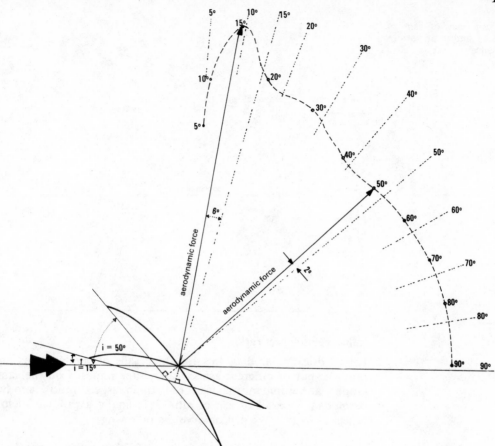

forward at less than right angles to the sail (which is interesting enough for amateur physicists). The difference is particularly noticeable at the critical angle of 15°; beyond this it decreases, reducing an angle of some 90° to zero.

In the case of very acute angles, say 5°, total aerodynamic force is, in fact, directed slightly aft of the perpendicular.

All this only relates to our average bermudan sail. With other sails total aerodynamic force could be directed behind the perpendicular giving very different angles of incidence.

The main interest in discussing these forces is to enable us to compare different shapes of sail. In particular, it allows an assessment of the influence on efficiency of the different shapes of sail.

Difference in efficiency of sails of aspect ratio 6, 3 and 1 at various angles of incidence

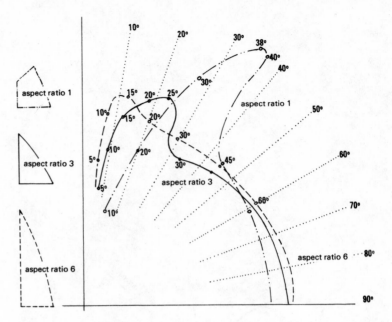

Influence of aspect ratio

Let us draw polar diagrams for three sails of similar areas and draught, but of different aspect ratio, superimposed on the same graph; a bermudan mainsail 6:1 (high aspect ratio), another bermudan mainsail of aspect ratio 3:1, finally a gaff sail of low aspect ratio 1:1. We can observe the following:

● At low angles of incidence, it is this high centre of effort sail which develops the greatest aerodynamic force and at the best angle.
● This same sail stalls at a lower angle of incidence than the others.
● The gaff sail develops a much larger force between 25° and 45° incidence; it does not stall until an angle of 38° (but the fall-off in efficiency is rapid: note the spectacular return of the curve). As they approach 90°, sails with a high aspect ratio regain a slight advantage.

A bermudan sail of high aspect ratio is therefore clearly more efficient to windward. On a reach, a low aspect ratio bermudan sail

can be squared away before the wind further without stalling (a slight advantage). The gaff sail is very powerful on these points of sailing, but close-hauled its efficiency is indifferent. The ability to work to windward, being considered such a desirable quality nowadays, the use of high aspect ratio sails on modern craft is thus at least partly vindicated.

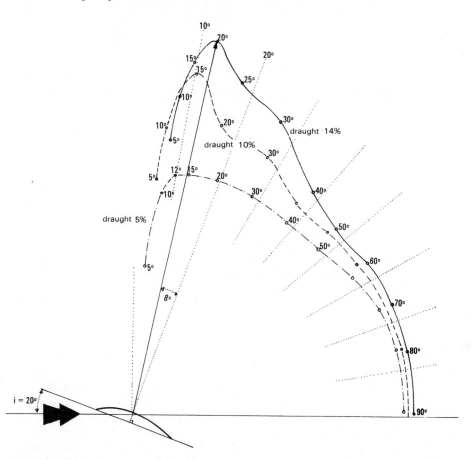

Influence of Draught

The centre of effort of the sail plan is usually decided when the boat first takes shape on paper, and this decision is normally the designer's. But the draught of the sails is another matter. The

Influence of belly (set here at 5%, 10% and 14%) on the power developed by the same sail

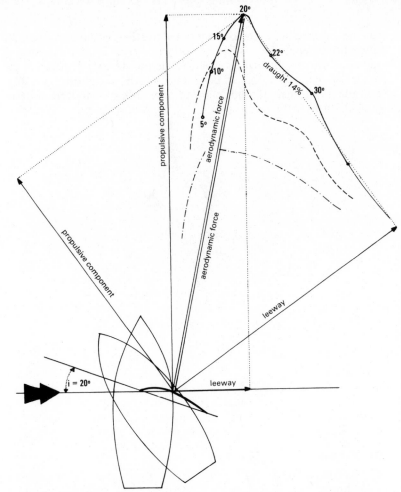

Direction of aerodynamic force with
wind on the beam and close-reaching

draught of modern sails can vary greatly, the same sail being made
at will in a form that can vary from the shape of a plank to a bag –
very nearly. This decision is the crew's and it can have important
consequences on aerodynamic force.

Let us take a single bermudan sail with aspect ratio of 4.6:1.
If we consider, for a given wind strength, three polar diagrams
corresponding to three draught modifications in this sail: 5%,
10% and 14% (these percentages relate the draught to the length
of luff at that point), we can immediately see that the deeper the
draught:

The greater the force developed by the sail, particularly at low angles of incidence.

The more the sail can deflect the wind through a large angle without stalling.

The more aerodynamic force is directed forward. At the critical angle of 20°, the force is directed 8° forward of the perpendicular.

The advantages depend on the strength of the wind for *if the wind is weak, you should increase the draught of your sails as much as possible to generate maximum force; but in high winds, when heeling becomes excessive, the sail should be flattened out so that it develops less force.*

Remember (this is not shown on the graph) that the position of maximum draught in a sail is important. Total aerodynamic force being greatest near the luff, it follows that belly in the forward third of the sail will generate a stronger and better angled force. All great minds don't think alike on this subject so let us accept for the time being that belly in the middle of a sail is not too bad. Everyone agrees though that maximum draught towards the leech is bad, at any rate when you are close-hauled or on a close reach.

Sail Trim and Points of Sailing

This discussion of sails has so far been general and theoretical. What concerns us is not so much the aerodynamic force developed by a sail, as how to exploit this force to propel the boat. So let us go over the foregoing theories, imagining we are at sea and take what advantage we can from our sails on different points of sailing.

Beam Reach to Close Reach

The upright boat in the drawing is on a beam reach and is steering at 90° to the apparent wind. Her sail, which has a maximum draught of 14%, may be trimmed to the optimum angle of incidence of 20°. Aerodynamic force is therefore at a maximum; the normal parallelogram of forces shows that they are nicely balanced: the propulsive component is strong and the drift component and heel are weak. On this point of sailing, even if the wind increases, you can maintain a draught of 14% for a long time.

Now the boat luffs up (the serrated boat in the drawing) until she comes on a close reach. The crew sheets the sails in a little so that the angle of incidence stays the same at 20°. Only the angle between the sail and the fore and aft line of the boat has changed.

You can see that the aerodynamic force, while still good, is not so well directed: the thrust is less than when the wind was abeam, and leeway and heel have increased considerably; and heel increases the harder the wind blows. It is when you are close-hauled that you have to watch out.

Close-hauled

You are now pointing closer and you are sheeting in the sail so as to maintain an angle of incidence of 20°, still with the same draught of 14%. But you are getting less and less for your money: heel and leeway increase at the expense of the propulsive component. Too much in fact, particularly if you have children and the dog as well as a nervous mother-in-law on board.

Let's take a closer look at the 14% curve at low angles of incidence. By easing the sheets slightly so as not to deflect the wind more than 15°, the force is weaker but better directed than before. Thrust is actually slightly better, for leeway and heel have diminished.

If you continue to ease the sail, so as to deflect the wind only 12°, this improvement is confirmed: propulsive component only weakens slightly, but leeway and heel get slighter. The boat is travelling nearly as fast and is behaving altogether better.

This is not the end of it. If you now reduce the draught of the sail from 14% to 10%, still maintaining an angle of incidence of 12°, thrust is held and leeway and heel reduce still further. She now sails fractionally slower on a better and more comfortable course.

To sum up, when going to windward:

> *It is not a question of trimming sails to the optimum angle of wind deflection, but to an angle which reduces leeway and heel to a minimum consistent with reasonable thrust.*
> *There is no point in having a sail with draught greater than 10%: you will only increase leeway and heeling.*

These are the general principles of working to windward in fresh winds. Initially reduce the heel, and then get the best thrust possible. In very strong winds, it may be necessary to flatten and ease the sail, reducing the draught to 5% and only deflecting the wind by 7°. We know that aerodynamic force increases with the square of the wind speed, so that even if the wind is only deflected through a small angle enough power will be generated.

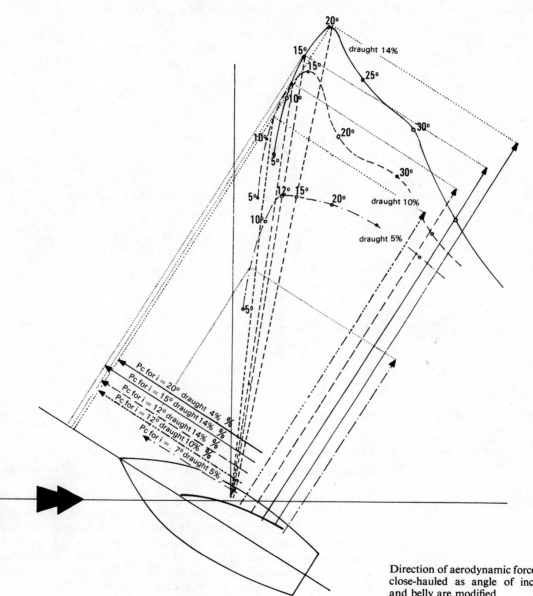

20°

draught 14%

15°
15°
25°

10°
30°

10°
20°

5°
30°

draught 10%

5°
12° 15°
20°

10°
draught 5%

5°

Pc for i = 20° draught 4% %
Pc for i = 15° draught 14% %
Pc for i = 12° draught 14% %
Pc for i = 12° draught 10% %
Pc for i = 7° draught 5%

Direction of aerodynamic force when
close-hauled as angle of incidence
and belly are modified

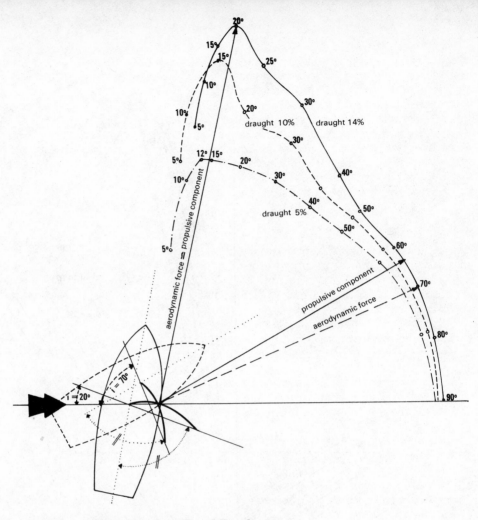

Power and direction of aerodynamic
force on a reach and a broad reach

From Reach to Broad Reach

Between these points of sailing, these foregoing difficulties scarcely
arise. ·

On a reach the sail can be trimmed to its optimum angle, because
force is then at a maximum and directed very near to the fore and
aft line of the boat (black boat in the drawing). Leeway and heel
are negligible and the sail has plenty of draught; the only problem
is the airstream constant; but on this point of sailing speed is good
and the direction of the apparent wind differs appreciably from
the true wind. When the sail presses against the lee shroud, and is

at an angle of incidence of 20° to the apparent wind, it only needs a sudden increase in wind speed or a chance speed decrease for the apparent wind to change and blow more from the direction of the true wind, increasing the angle of incidence and the sails will stall.

You are then on a broad reach (serrated boat in the drawing). Airstream is now turbulent and aerodynamic force is much weaker. Sail trim is not now crucial, nor is the draught going to make much difference. On this point of sailing, as on a dead run, the only way of strengthening aerodynamic force is to increase your sail area. No need to worry about leeway and heel.

Hindrances

Curves and angles have just been examined in terms of creating an ideal aerodynamic force produced in a wind tunnel using a metal sail. Rather academic conditions, but they demonstrate what can be done to improve sail efficiency. In reality, of course, it is not such plain sailing.

To repeat, aerodynamic force is at its best when there is minimal turbulence in the airstream. However, on a real boat, at grips with unpredictable elements, there is plenty of turbulence:

Rigging and spars disturb the wind even before it reaches the sail. The mast in particular, with its sizeable area of resistance, disturbs the flow along the luff just where force is theoretically greatest.

Friction of wind on sail, specially if the latter is not very smooth, creates turbulence over the whole surface. Movement of the boat, on waves for example, causes sudden variations in the force and direction of the apparent wind. Other chance factors can have adverse effects: a crew member standing near the luff, or to leeward of the sail, can spoil things (the more so if the boat is small and the crew member large).

Because of such factors, actual aerodynamic force is found to be less than what is theoretically possible.

Remember that spars, superstructure, hull, deck, and crew are all in varying degrees obstacles in the wind's path. They make up what may be called *windage*, each generating a force of its own directed along the line of the wind, which combines with the force developed by the sail. The upshot of all this is to divert the total aerodynamic force of the boat closer to the wind than would

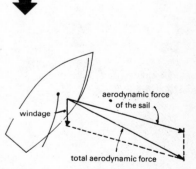

Close-hauled, get the heavy members of the crew into the cabin and the boat's windage will be appreciably reduced

happen if the sails were left to themselves. This windage, while it can be beneficial with the wind aft, is a great handicap with the wind forward of the beam specially while sailing under reduced canvas in bad weather, when, in the worst cases, the boat quite simply fails to go forward.

All this may be remote from the force represented in these graphs but, whether we like it or not, it is *total* aerodynamic force that matters in getting the best out of your boat.

Interaction of Sails

The most obvious way of increasing aerodynamic force is to increase your sail area. But big sails bring their own problems, particularly in supporting the mast. One solution is to use more than one sail of moderate size – this seems a practical way of getting better results. Let's examine here the most usual combination – a mainsail and a head sail, be it jib or spinnaker according to point of sailing.

Setting a jib for'ard immediately gives rise to these points:

The jib is hanked to a stay of a small diameter that does not interfere very much with the airstream at the luff. The jib indeed works under better conditions than the mainsail.
The jib sends to leeward of the mainsail air which it has deflected. As a sail gives its greatest propulsive force from its lee side, it follows that the jib influences the efficiency of the mainsail. Particularly to windward, it is clear that if the slot *between the two sails is correct, the airstream through it will be steady and benefit the effectiveness of main and jib.* Further, the narrower the clearance between the leech of the jib and the mast the more the wind speed accelerates and pressure to leeward of the mainsail will be lowered still more, with increased efficiency there was well.

Now we can examine how this interaction varies on different points of sailing.

Close-hauled

See what is demonstrated in wind tunnel tests. Airstream indicated by the arrows in the drawings is being produced to leeward of the sail.

1 The boat is close hauled under mainsail alone. The mast upsets the airstream considerably and is noticeably turbulent.

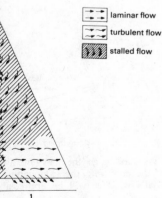

laminar flow

turbulent flow

stalled flow

1

2 Without changing either course or sail trim, a jib is hoisted. We can see that airstream to leeward of the jib is quite regular there, and it has become so to leeward of the main. There is still turbulence, though: at the upper part of the mainsail, where it is not affected by the jib; and at the head of the jib itself where it is very narrow as is the clearance between the sails.

Air can also be detected escaping between the foot of the sail and the deck. This is only harmful if it tends to balance the pressure between the two sail surfaces (in practice, this can be partly eliminated by using a 'deck sweeping' genoa, whose foot lies along the deck).

3 The boat bears away by 5°. Sheets are eased, so that the angle of incidence stays the same. There is no change on the main-sail, but the turbulent zone extends lower down the jib.
4 If the boat bears away a further 5°, with sails eased corres-pondingly, the airstream on the lee side of the jib is hopelessly unstable, or stalled.

As the boat bears away, the slot between the sails is enlarged, because the mainsail pivots on a vertical axis while the jib turns on an oblique one. There is less clearance at the head than at the foot of the sails and more air passes between jib luff and mast. To sum up, the more the boat bears away, the more the slot up aloft closes up with harmful effects on air-stream.

The slot should be kept as open as possible by:
easing the jib sheet – and it helps if the fair leads are fixed as far outboard as possible. Sheet in the mainsail more than the jib – necessary in any case because the mainsail is already getting on the leeward side the wind deflected from the jib.

It is jib trim that is critical. Tests on a boat of about 33ft overall show that a sheet that is one inch too tight means a loss of some 20% efficiency over the whole sail plan.

The effect is equally bad if the jib deflects air on to the main's lee side and back-winds its luff. This can happen if the weather jib sheet is too tight, the mainsail is not sheeted in enough, or the jib is badly cut and its leech curls inward. And of course, smooth airstream through the clearance is not improved if a crew member is hanging around between the sails.

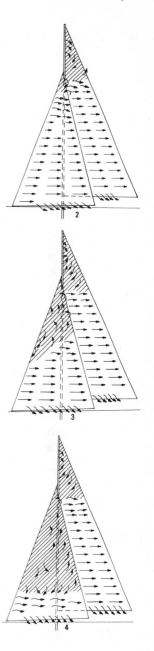

Another factor that does not show up on rigid sails in wind tunnels is twist. The leech of a terylene sail for instance is less taut at its head than near the foot giving some twist because, under wind pressure, the head tends to twist further outboard than the foot. However if this twist is well controlled, it is not a bad thing because, 10–15ft up, the true wind is stronger than it is on the water, and so the apparent wind is blowing more freely in the upper part of

No jib: the air flow to leeward of the main is turbulent, efficiency poor

Jib up: the air flow on the lee side of the main is laminar and efficiency increases considerably

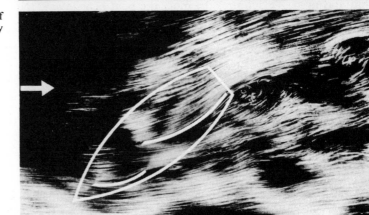

the sail which can after all be pulled in less tightly. We shall come back to this again when it comes to practical sailing. All we are concerned with here is taking care to adjust the two sails so that the slot between them is as correct as possible from top to bottom. We can bring into relief variations in aerodynamic force during the following tests:

When the boat is under mainsail alone, close hauled, total force is weak; the boat lacking power, progresses with difficulty to windward.

When a jib is added, increase in force is out of all proportion to the increase in sail area. The boat really comes to life when there is a regular airstream over the sail plan as a whole.

As soon as the boat bears away a little, airstream to leeward of the jib becomes turbulent, and its force slackens. But, thanks to the jib, airstream to leeward of the main remains consistent and so does the drive of the mainsail.

To repeat, if both sails are eased, total aerodynamic force is weaker but better orientated, and the overall result is better.

Broad Reaching

As the boat bears away, the sails are eased. The jib balloons and, on a close reach, it does not work well, because it no longer smooths out the air along the lee side of the main. You can try to improve its efficiency (and consequently the slot), by booming it out to leeward. In any event, the boat is now sailing well, because the main is now set to the best angle of incidence and total aerodynamic force is working for thrust.

Beyond a beam reach, there is less air passing between mast and forestay. On a very broad reach the jib begins to be blanketed by the mainsail and it becomes virtually useless; it only comes into its own again when the wind goes nearly dead aft and it can be boomed out to windward, on the opposite side to the mainsail – or goose-winged.

But further off the wind than a close reach, if the wind is not too great, it is time to replace the jib with a sail more useful for reaching and running conditions – a spinnaker, with its enormous surface, develops more propulsive force. With the wind anywhere aft, it can be set to attract maximum wind. With a deep draught and low aspect ratio, it also deflects the wind through a large angle without stalling completely. In these conditions, it ensures a steady airstream to leeward of the mainsail up to points when it would

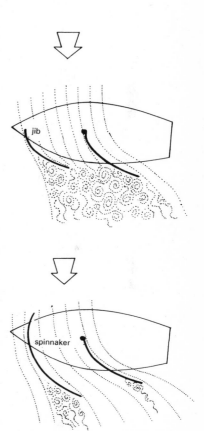

On a reach, the spinnaker laminates the air on the lee of the main up to significant angles of incidence

masthead rigged sloop

Bermudan cutter

Bermudan ketch

otherwise have begun to stall.

Spinnaker trim on a reach is the same as jib trim: the clearance between the sails should be as wide as possible. You should therefore ease the sheet and move its fairlead as far outboard as possible (even passing the sheet over the end of the boom). On this point of sailing, the spinnaker should not have too deep a draught or it will disturb the smooth flow of air across its surface, whereas a flat spinnaker, well trimmed, can maintain a smooth airstream to leeward of the mainsail up to angles of incidence of 30° to 40°.

Running Free

On a broad reach and a free run before the wind the airstream stops. All you can do is to hoist as much sail as possible: use a very full spinnaker for you have to catch all the wind you can.

Different Rigs

In the example showing the interaction of sails, the rig had a jib which did not reach the masthead. Let's analyse briefly several other types of rig and their various sails.

Masthead Sloop. When the jib is carried to the masthead the airstream to windward is steady all over the lee side of the mainsail. The upper part of this sail therefore works at its best on this point of sailing. With the same sail area, the masthead sloop can have a shorter mast than the sloop we have been considering, and heeling will therefore be reduced.

Marconi or Bermudan Cutter. Breaking up the headsail into two, jib and staysail, makes for easier manoeuvring as each is smaller and gives you a variety of trim. According to wind and point of sailing, you can adjust the area and the shape of the two sails, and this makes the cutter rig more adaptable. From an aerodynamic point of view, this rig can be useful provided you know how to take advantage of it, and in light winds, a genoa can transform a cutter into a sloop.

Ketch and Yawl. With this type of two masted rig (main mast and the shorter mizzen at the stern), the mizzen is primarily a balancing sail, but from a close reach to a dead run, it adds to the thrust. A mizzen staysail can also be set and the thrust developed by this sail plan is then considerably greater than with a sloop of the same size.

To windward, on the other hand, with a wind of more than Force 3, the mizzen is not much use – even a hindrance, because it is

Bermudan yawl

Bermudan schooner

working with wind deflected from the mainsail and has to be sheeted closer than the main, increasing heeling. With the mizzen furled, though, ketches and yawls can always be rigged as sloops.

Schooner. Here the shorter foremast is for'ard of the main mast. The flying jib steadies the air for the jib, the jib for the staysail, the staysail for the foresail, the foresail for the mainsail. . . . This type of rig is not common these days, largely because few boats large enough to exploit it are being built.

Obviously, the more sails there are the more difficult it is to control their interaction. If the sails are not well trimmed they end up by blanketing each other, and their very multiplicity is therefore a disadvantage. Whatever the rig, the best trim is only discovered at sea by trial and error.

And this can be said of the simplest boat.

The Hull

Archimedes put it concisely: 'Any body immersed in a liquid is subjected to a pressure equal to the weight of liquid displaced.' And so your boat floats.

'This pressure,' he added, 'is directed vertically upwards through the centre of gravity of the volume of liquid displaced.' And so your boat is more or less stable.

The fact that a boat so often tends to be inhibited about moving forward is a point which Archimedes seems to have overlooked, but then he moved in rather limited circles!

Buoyancy, stability, reluctance to move forward: these are the three factors of our hull study. Plus one more – the rudder.

The weight of the water displaced by the hull is equal to the total weight of the boat and its contents

Buoyancy

The weight of the boat is called *displacement*, on the amount of water displaced when it floats. The *immersed volume*, or the part of the boat that is under water, is governed by its weight and the density of the water. Under the neat and tidy metric system, a boat weighing 1,000kg (about a ton), floating in water of a density of 1, sinks until her immersed volume is 1,000 litres (about 250 gallons); the weight of the water displaced is 1,000kg.

The part of the boat in the water is the *bottom*. The part above

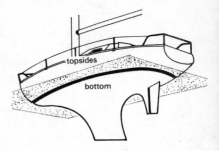

water is the *topsides*, which can be considered as spare buoyancy. If a boat is completely submerged any air left inside will help her to surface again, depending on the volume. The greater the volume in relation to the weight of the boat, the more quickly she will rise to the surface. To put it another way: the greater the volume of the interior in relation to her immersed volume, the safer she is. This relationship, which is called reserve buoyancy, is a safety coefficient.

To give a boat a good buoyancy ratio, the naval architect either increases the volume of the interior or reduces the immersed volume.

The interior volume depends:

on the height of the *freeboard*, or topsides, (a high freeboard has the additional advantage of fending off breaking waves). on the *overhangs*, or the length of the bow and stern sections above the waterline.

But high freeboards and long overhangs mean more windage. Boats are designed with less displacement nowadays; and the more so because it has other advantages. Light boats work better to windward in bad weather than heavy ones, they are not so wet and handle more easily; last but not least, they are less expensive.

Obviously, for a given waterline length, the displacement can only be modified within limits, unless you want bizarre craft, but the limits are reasonably flexible. An average cruising boat of about 15ft on the waterline will have a displacement less than two tons; but there are designs of approximately the same size weighing less and more than that. Boats of about 20ft waterline usually displace about $2\frac{1}{2}$ tons.

Dinghies of course have much lower displacement than cruising boats, principally because they have no ballast – the crew, eschewing ease and comfort, takes its place. They are racing machines, capable of high speeds, and they don't bother too much about the second part of Archimedes's theory of the stability of floating objects. A cruiser is altogether a more serious affair.

Stability

The trim of a boat is the way she balances when motionless on calm water. Stability is defined by her speed in returning to normal trim after it has been disturbed by wave or wind or whatever reason.

This stability depends on: firstly the force of gravity acting vertically through the boat's own centre of gravity. Secondly the force exerted by the water on the hull: 'the resistance of the water is directed upwards through the centre of gravity of the mass of liquid displaced'. The hull's centre of gravity is the *centre of buoyancy*.

As soon as you step aboard a boat, you can see that her lateral stability is much more tender than her fore and aft stability.

Lateral Stability

In fig. 1 of the drawing, G is the centre of gravity, C the centre of buoyancy. When the boat is at rest, G is vertically above C.

If the boat heels (fig. 2) the hull tips and the centre of buoyancy

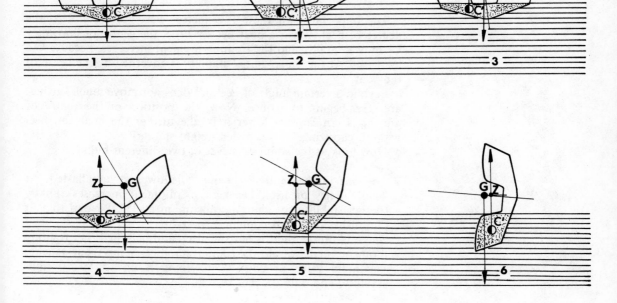

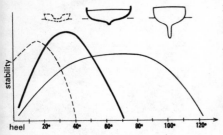

Graph comparing stability of a dinghy (with crew) with a broad, lightly ballasted hull and with a deep, heavily ballasted hull

moves to C^1. Weight and buoyancy counteract to give righting moment and this works to return the boat to her original trim. The extent of this righting moment is governed by the position of the metacentre M (fig. 3) situated at the intersection of a vertical from C^1 and the centreline. So long as it is above the centre of gravity, the righting process is exerted but beyond that point, the two forces combine to make the boat heel still more and, in the end, capsize.

The position of the metacentre is governed by the beam of the boat: the broader the beam, the more the centre of buoyancy moves outwards when the boat heels, and the higher the metacentre.

The value of *righting moment* is defined by the horizontal distance GZ between the centre of gravity (G) and a line dropped vertically from Z to C^1 (figs. 4, 5, 6). The longer GZ is, the greater the righting moment. And the higher the metacentre M is above the centre of gravity G, the greater is the line GZ. It follows that the line MG must be long to ensure the boat's stability:

M is raised by giving the boat a large beam.
G is lowered by keeping weight as low down as possible.

The importance of these two factors varies according to the degree of heel. When a boat heels a little, the centre of buoyancy C^1 moves rapidly and the righting moment increases, because GZ increases. At this stage, initial stability is governed by the beam of the boat.

Beyond a certain angle of heel, C^1 does not move much further, and GZ begins to reduce. Now, the position of the centre of gravity is critical: the lower it is, the further the boat can heel without capsizing. This is called weight stability.

Now look at the stability curves of two different hulls:

The one in the centre is beamy, shallow and unballasted. At small angles of heel, her righting moment increases rapidly (design stability) reaching its maximum at 35°. Beyond that, it diminishes rapidly becoming zero at 70°.

The hull on the right is narrow, deep and ballasted: her righting moment increases slowly (initial stability is low) but reaches maximum value around 40° retaining it up to 80° (weight stability) and only touches zero at 125°.

Stability of a Dinghy

On a light dinghy, the ballast is movable. When the crew sits out, the centre of gravity G moves to windward, to G^1, and the righting level becomes proportional to the line G–G^1. If the boat heels, this level extends further to G^1–Z.

The stability curve of the dinghy on the left has a good righting moment even at a zero angle of heel for the crew can keep the boat completely upright. It increases at small angles of heel, until it obtains its best point around 15°, when it diminishes rapidly to zero at 40°.

Liquid Ballast

Now suppose there is some water in the bottom of the boat. The real immersed volume which is floating the boat is the part not filled with water.

If the boat heels slightly, this volume does not shift very much; the centre of buoyancy hardly changes and the righting moment remains weak – (it can even develop a reverse moment and increase

1. Unstable hull
2. The boat finds its stability when it heels slightly
3. When it heels more, the righting moment comes into play but it is smaller than it would be if there were no water in the bottom

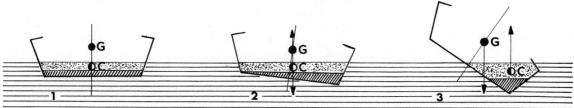

4. Here, water in the bottom only aggravates the position when the boat heels over steeply
5. The water in the bottom has little effect provided it does not reach the turn of the bilge

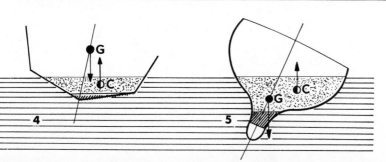

the tendency to heel). Provided there is not too much water, only the initial stability is reduced so far and as soon as the boat heels a little more, the water moves into the chine, remaining fairly static. Then the real immersed volume begins to change normally, and this explains why a flat bottomed boat, with some water aboard, is only stable when she is moderately heeled on a tack.

In a boat with a V-shaped hull, the influence of moving-water ballast is only felt at relatively big angles of heel and the deep keel boat in fig. 5 is only affected when it heels over steeply.

The Role of Stability

Safety. Stability is a primary safety factor, greater or less according to the boat's design and the conditions in which she is sailing.

When sailing on a crowded, well supervised stretch of water you don't have to worry so much. Light dinghies have good initial stability and the crew can do the rest. But as soon as you go sailing further afield, you should have a boat which can cope with mistakes and the unexpected without capsizing: this means a boat with a ballasted keel, which has positive stability up to at least a 90° heel. When you reach the stage of sailing offshore you run the risk of heavy weather so good stability up to 120–140° is essential.

Power. Stability is not just a passive safety factor. It is a significant influence on the power a boat can develop.

We now know that heeling is part and parcel of her ability to move because the sails can only function efficiently when there is a counteracting force at work to keep the boat upright.

A boat's power comes from the aerodynamic force developed by the sails, which depends on the boat's stiffness – its ability to keep as upright as possible. This is where stability comes in. *The greater the stability, the greater power a boat can develop*, particularly when going to windward.

It follows that a dinghy's power is directly related to the crew's ability to lean out. With a fixed keel boat, righting moment depends primarily on the shape of the hull and on distribution of weight: it is a question of placing ballast and any other weight as low as possible and keeping the upperworks such as deck, superstructure and rigging as light as possible. A good hefty crew on the windward side can have a significant stabilising effect even on a fairly heavy boat.

Roll

A boat rolls from side to side on waves, and the movement is accentuated the higher her metacentre and the greater her power are. It is said that 'a boat that rolls a lot, sails fast'. A beamy boat with a flat bottom rolls a lot (certain catamarans – are almost unliveable in). Nevertheless, a sailing boat rolls less than a motor boat, because she is steadied by her sails and keel, at least when the wind is forward of the beam. With the wind aft this advantage is lost and you can expect an uncomfortable passage.

Fore and Aft Stability

When a boat pitches, her centre of buoyancy moves longitudinally. It creates a force which tends to bring the boat back to an even keel, if the centre of gravity is below the longitudinal metacentre, and its height depends on the length of the boat. There is no worry here for longitudinal stability is not a serious factor. On the other hand longitudinal trim of the hull is highly important: *boat speed will be affected far more by faulty fore and aft trim of 5°, for example, than she would be by the same angle of heel.*

The position of the crew in a dinghy is critical to about 6in. If either of them is too far aft or forward, stability, speed and, above all, the way the boat answers the helm can be greatly reduced.

It is worth checking the hull trim of a cruising vessel from time to time, by having a look at the boat on her mooring from a distance. At sea, you should see that the crew does not congregate at one end or the other and the smaller the boat the more important this becomes.

Do not overload a small boat fore or aft

Pitching

A ground swell can make a boat see-saw and that is called *pitching*. This spoils the forward thrust and often has a deplorable effect on stomachs. It gets worse quickly if weight is distributed at bow and stern and the boat will have difficulty in lifting to a sea. To reduce pitching, bring all possible weight to the middle of the boat.

Drag

When a boat sets off under sail, she meets some resistance in the water. She can accelerate until this resistance exactly balances the thrust of the sails and then she settles down. Obviously, if this resistance is reduced by one means or another the result is more speed.

The study of drag is very complex. There have not been enough tests carried out in experimental tanks for it is difficult to recreate exactly the conditions experienced at sea, and only basic principles can be studied in terms of mathematical equations. In striving for the most efficient hull design, therefore, the naval architect's flair plays a big role. But all kinds of factors come to bear in the course of construction, fitting out and tuning. There is always an element of the unknown, and this is all part of the attraction of sailing. One boat is narrow and deep; another is beamy. This one has a bluff bow; another seems to have fat quarters. Some naval architects rely on weight stability others on hull shape, and often the results are not too different. One boat, unsurpassed to windward, mysteriously fails to reach properly, while another which sails happily through a short chop, practically stops in a different sea; and so on.

The principal characteristics of a new boat can be specified and insisted upon but, as with cooking, it does not always turn out as planned. Several boats over the years have had a touch of greatness and will never be forgotten: Surcouf's *La Confiance*, Mrs Pitt-Rovers' *Foxhound*, Slocum's *Spray*, Captain Illingworth's *Myth of Malham* and Dick Carter's *Tina* are some of them and who can say what their secret was? The truth is there is a whole aspect of drag which is the consequence of hull design, that is not fully understood. Some boats just have better thrust and better handling characteristics than others. But some causes of drag can be assessed fairly precisely, such as friction, wave drag and the possible effect of heel and leeway.

Friction Drag (Skin Friction)

Friction caused by water is proportional to the area of the hull under water – the wetted area: it varies according to the condition of the hull's surface and to some extent to the boat's speed.

The water in immediate contact with the hull does not move in relation to the hull, and it follows we are speaking of friction between water and water. The hull takes the water in its immediate area – the boundary layer – along with it and thus adds to the weight of the boat. A rough, dirty hull pulls along much more water than a clean and polished one, so that the surrounding layer is not just thicker, the surface irregularities make their own turbulence, all acting as a brake.

The only ways of limiting friction drag are:

For the designer to reduce the wetted area as much as possible; for the crew to keep the bottom polished, and to scrub it clean frequently.

Wave Drag

As she moves forward, a boat cuts through the water which closes behind her again. As a result, a series of waves is created which uses up much of the boat's drive. Wave drag ultimately determines maximum speed.

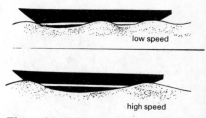

low speed

high speed

The position of the second wave indicates the boat's speed

As the hull moves forward, it sets up a series of waves, the first of which comes slightly aft of the bow. As speed increases, the distance between the waves increases and, when the second wave reaches the after end of the waterline, the boat has attained her *critical speed*. Indeed, if speed increases still more, the wave begins to leave the stern of the boat and creates further turbulence which increases drag appreciably. The energy spent in creating this turbulence is largely wasted, and trim of the boat is spoiled. Forward, the boat rides on the bow wave; aft, the stern sinks into the trough increasing the wetted area aft of the beam. Beyond the critical speed, therefore, even a large increase in thrust results in only a very slight acceleration.

This limitation does not apply however to a light, flat-bottomed boat. When she reaches her critical speed, if there is enough wind and the boat is properly balanced, a force develops that bears her up and makes her *plane* over the surface. In this attitude, the boat can achieve speeds considerably beyond her critical speed, as drag far from increasing can actually decrease.

Planing is the prerogative of dinghies and some light cruising boats. Displacement boats are restricted to their critical speeds which depend on their waterline length and, to a certain degree, on their shape.

The value of this critical speed is given by the equation V (speed in knots) $= 1.34 \sqrt{\text{LWL}}$ (waterline length in feet). This gives critical speeds as follows (for displacement boats):

	LWL	Critical Speed
Small daysailer	16′	5.4 Kts
Family cruiser	25′	6.7 Kts
Large ocean racer	50′	9.5 Kts

In no way can the crew alter wave drag. The designer alone can draw the most effective lines mainly by keeping down the width of the beam.

As critical speed is partly a question of length on the waterline hulls tend to be designed to allow their waterline to increase when the boat is under way and heeling slightly.

Drag Caused by Heel and Leeway

As we already know, heel and leeway, inevitable as they are, detract from the boat's progress. Leeway, since it causes turbulence around the hull, increases friction drag; and heel, because it modifies the waterlines of the hull.

In any event, when heel and leeway are working together (which is generally the case especially when close-hauled), the total result is obviously disastrous. Experiments with a model of a racing yacht have shown that, for a boat with a 30° angle of heel and making 4° of leeway, drag is one and a half times greater than when heel and leeway are absent. These two factors do not always have the same importance. With a heel of 25° and no leeway, drag only increases by 5% but with the same angle of heel and making 5° of leeway it increases by 55%.

Finally, if we estimate the relative importance of the different elements of drag in relation to the speed of the boat, it can be stated that: friction drag increases in proportion to speed, whereas wave drag is practically non-existent when the boat starts to move. Therefore at low speeds it is friction drag which counts. That is why, in light airs, a rough, dirty hull is such a handicap.

As speed increases wave resistance is set up and increases rapidly. At 80 or 90% of critical speed these two elements of drag are more or less equal but beyond this point wave resistance dominates.

It can be noted that in light airs, all things being equal, heavy displacement craft go better than light displacement ones. But, as soon as the wind freshens, the latter take off and quickly reach their critical speed whereas heavy boats take much longer to reach this point.

The Rudder

The rudder blade behaves in the water rather like a sail in the air. When the tiller is moved the rudder swings and the angle of incidence between it and the water flow is modified. This last exerts a force at right angles to the surface of the rudder blade which is thus

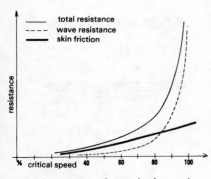

Resistance to forward thrust increases considerably when the boat reaches its critical speed

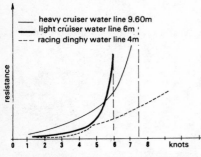

Graph of drag for three different boats. It will be noticed that for the dinghy drag increases quickly before if lifts, then more slowly once it is planing

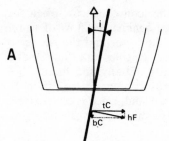

A

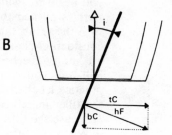

B

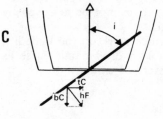

C

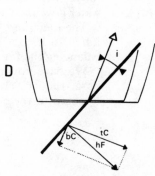

D

pushed sideways. This force is proportional to the area of the rudder blade and the square of the speed of the water (the rudder only works when the boat is in motion) and also to the angle of incidence; it increases as the angle increases but here again a stall can occur if the critical angle is exceeded.

To recap: when the boat is moving directly forwards and you put the tiller to the left, a force is exerted on the right of the rudder. This force pushes the stern of the boat to the left and the bow swings right. Conversely, push the tiller left and the boat turns right.

The force exerted by the water on the rudder has two effects:

It turns the boat to port or starboard.
But it also acts as a brake: the greater the angle of incidence, the greater the braking effect. As we said in Chapter 1, every touch on the tiller is a touch of the brake.

In practice, therefore, avoid excessive action on the tiller because its braking influence can outweigh its directional effect. And when

A. Break-down of the force exerted by the water on the rudder (hydrodynamic force: hF):
turning component (tC);
braking component (bC);
Angle i is the angle of incidence between the rudder blade and the laminar flow
B. As the rudder angle increases, so does the turning component
C. At the beginning of a turn, avoid extreme movement of the tiller: the braking component of the rudder will be greater than its turning component. Hydrodynamic force is weaker than in A because the critical angle of stall has been exceeded and the flow has become turbulent
D. But, in the middle of a turn, the tiller can be pushed further over: the angle of incidence remains weak as the boat is now turning

you begin to swing round there are other consequences: when the stern is pushed to one side, it is angled against the flow of water with the result that the angle between the water and the rudder is considerably less than the angle between the tiller and the fore and aft line of the boat. Use the tiller gently initially and finally, but half-way you can use the rudder hard without risk of stall. In practice let the boat do the turning itself and, once it has started, the tiller merely encourages the boat to move of its own accord. Just ease the tiller across.

When the turn is finished, don't bring the tiller back amidships too quickly, because now it is the angle of incidence between the water flow and the other side of the rudder which can get too wide.

The function of the rudder is not just to turn the boat: its main job is to keep a steady course, when this cannot be achieved by balancing the forces of water and wind.

We have now analysed the forces which work on the hull: lift, drag, rudder. These make up the whole hydrodynamic force as opposed to the aerodynamic forces described earlier.

Stability under way

If anything is to move in a straight line at a constant speed, the forces which propel it and those which hold it back must come to terms. When a boat is moving steadily through the water, forward aerodynamic thrust balances drag, lift balances leeway. *The boat has equilibrium when the aerodynamic and hydrodynamic forces are equal, interacting on the same axis.*

When these forces are unbalanced, they make the boat either luff or bear away. If the aerodynamic force is strong enough to leeward of the hydrodynamic force, the boat wants to luff and she is said to have *weather helm*; the other way round, the boat tends to bear away because she then has *lee helm*.

The strength and direction of these forces, and their respective pivotal points must be borne in mind. Aerodynamic force may be taken as acting through a point called the *centre of effort* (*CE*), just as hydrodynamic force acts through the *centre of lateral resistance* (*CLR*).

Movement of CE

The position of the centre of effort depends on a number of factors:

Choice of sails. For example, if you replace the jib by a spinnaker, the CE moves forward; if you take down headsails, it moves aft.
Sail trim. CE moves aft if you ease the jib and keep the mainsail sheeted hard in; it moves forward if the headsail is sheeted in and the mainsail eased out.
Sail shape. When the wind gets up, the belly in the sails tends to move aft and CE shifts likewise.
Heel. When the boat heels, CE moves to leeward.

Movement of CLR

The position of the centre of lateral resistance is determined principally by speed. The greater the speed, the further the CLR moves forward; it moves aft if the boat slows down, and right aft if the boat makes sternway.

CLR can move a lot on a dinghy, as a result of moving the centreboard. If you raise it slightly, you bring it aft and the CLR shifts in the same direction.

Finding the Best Trim

The factors which we have just examined are simple. To balance their boat, the crew can make adjustments, remembering which effect one will have on the other. But it's a delicate business. A shift of the centre of effort is brought about by changing the strength and direction of aerodynamic force and that affects the hydrodynamic force. An ill-considered change of trim can cause a series of repercussions which can just as easily make things worse as improve them. Results can vary widely from one boat to another, so treat all generalisations with profound scepticism. We shall examine a few typical situations in the following pages, to show how the various forces play each other up and what goes on when the boat achieves equilibrium.

Obviously, these examples cannot cover all aspects of the problem for other factors may enter. Heel, for example, not only affects the centre of effort, it also alters the underwater lines of the boat, either accentuating or diminishing a tendency to luff; and the movement of the sea can carry a boat in a direction contrary to her natural inclinations.

Trim

A. The boat is sailing close-hauled, in perfect balance, and aerodynamic force (aF) and hydrodynamic force (hF) are in line. There is nothing more to say.

B. The same boat heels. The centre of effort is carried down to leeward and the two forces are now slightly out of alignment. A torque is set up which tends to make the boat luff, and she carries some weather helm.

C. The boat heels to windward, the torque is reversed and the boat carries lee helm.

D. The jib sheet is eased slightly, in the hope, perhaps, of bringing the centre of effort aft again and thus regaining weather helm. The CE does, indeed, come aft. The jib, however, is too slack so, although aF is directed further forward, it is weaker, speed falls off and the centre of lateral resistance also comes aft. The torque remains weak and the boat recovers weather helm only slightly.

E. The jib is lowered, or *handed*, and CE comes aft a good deal. As airflow to leeward of the mainsail is turbulent, aF is weak and poorly directed. Speed falls off considerably and the CLR comes aft in proportion. The boat has lee helm.

F. The wind freshens, so that the sail fills towards the leech, the CE falls back and aF is poorly directed. Speed drops and CLR falls aft, but not enough to stop the boat carrying a lot of weather helm.

G. The boat is now on a reach. On this point of sailing she usually carries weather helm.

H. On a centreboarder, you can bring the CLR back far enough to balance the boat by raising the centreboard a bit. Obviously, the boat only has to heel a little to regain some of her weather helm.

I. Reaching under spinnaker, aF increases, CE is carried forward and outboard. Speed is high and CLR is well forward. Even raising the centreboard on a dinghy will not bring it far enough aft to ease weather helm completely.

J. Broad reaching under spinnaker and there is something of a sea so that the boat rolls. As the mainsail is not particularly efficient on this point of sailing, CE moves well forward. Depending on the roll of the boat, aF is sometimes to windward and sometimes to leeward of hF so that the boat alternately carries lee and weather helm; this means that the helmsman has plenty to do.

K. Dead run. The spinnaker is to windward so aF is also to windward of hF giving lee helm, the more so since the spinnaker tends to heel the boat to windward.

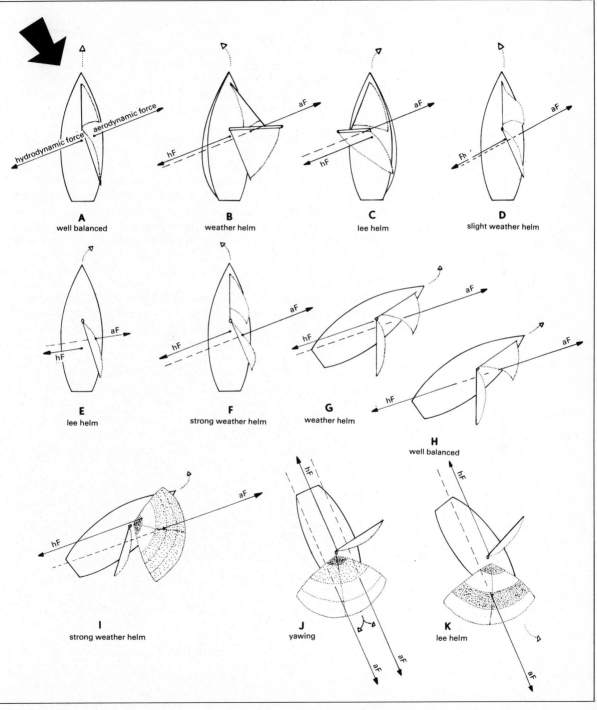

A
well balanced

B
weather helm

C
lee helm

D
slight weather helm

E
lee helm

F
strong weather helm

G
weather helm

H
well balanced

I
strong weather helm

J
yawing

K
lee helm

hydrodynamic force   aerodynamic force

aF   hF

The crew can exert control by means other than sail trim and heel. On small boats, for example, a change of longitudinal trim can influence balance: the boat loses lee helm if you weigh down the bows, and loses weather helm if you bring weight aft. You can also move the mast by raking it forward or aft, and this will move the CE. Balance can be modified in such a way and perhaps improved so it's worth a try, but mind you don't bring the boat to a halt!

To be frank it is not essential for all the forces to be perfect for a boat to sail properly. Indeed it is rare for a boat to keep of her own accord correct balance on all points of sailing and in all wind conditions. That of course, is the job of the rudder, to bring aerodynamic and hydrodynamic forces into harmony. Although the rudder acts as a brake and should not be used excessively (a boat which needs a lot of rudder to maintain a steady course is an unbalanced brute, in any case), but most of the time this braking effect is the lesser of two evils, and the boat's progress will prove to be more efficient that way than if everything is sacrificed to avoiding weather or lee helm.

Never forget the maxim: all boats differ and you must learn and come to terms with the eccentricities of yours. Theory can only offer the basic principles of the problem. Long experience can bear it out – or just as easily confound it.

4. Rigging

Rigging covers everything to do with the boat's sail power: spars, shrouds, stays, sails and then sheets. Part of the rigging is fixed: the mast and its shrouds, and stays – the *standing rigging*. The rest is the sails and the running rigging: the halyards and sheets, which control them.

This distinction is convenient, but always remember that the best tune and trim of rigging is not necessarily achieved by regulating only one or the other. They are inter-related. The mast and its boom are not an entity set up once and for all, and on which the sails are then spread or bent: these two spars can be out of true, but may be controlled by the crew to get a better set to the sail. It is a question of marrying spars and sails in a harmonious relationship, to cope as effectively as possible with all points of sailing and weather conditions.

Before studying the different parts of rigging, you must understand the function of each and how to adjust them.

Adjusting the Rigging

At the outset it is important to distinguish between the two different rigs. It is the question of height at which the mast is stayed.

When the mast is stayed from the top it is a *masthead rig* – particularly popular with large cruising boats.

Alternatively the mast is stayed at about one-third down from the top – a typical dinghy rig.

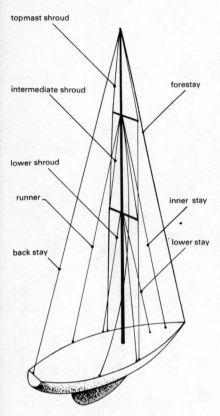

topmast shroud

intermediate shroud

forestay

lower shroud

runner

inner stay

lower stay

back stay

Ballasted centreboarders and small cruisers use either form and we shall see that there are also masts without any shrouds at all. Generally speaking, however, the above distinction is the rule. A mast's action is controlled according to how it is placed and stayed, and this in its turn determines controls on the whole of the rigging plan.

First of all then let's examine the principles behind staying the mast, and then at the role of each part of the rigging and how they work.

Staying the Mast

Principles

Imagine a radio mast held by four stays. The mast is high, but you can make the stays fast as far from the base as you like.

The stays take the strain horizontally and vertically. When the wind blows, the stay to windward takes the horizontal strain which increases vertically at the same time and is absorbed by compression of the mast. Meanwhile the leeward stay has no work to do.

If we anchor the windward stay nearer the mast, the mast/stay angle gets less, the parallelogram of forces therefore alters for the worse; although the horizontal pull remains constant, the strain on the windward stay and the compression of the mast increase. If the angle is reduced too much, the stay snaps or the mast buckles in high winds. Experience shows that the angle of mast to stay on a boat should be in the order of 15°, and never less than 13°.

At rest, the mast is held up by the whole of the standing rigging. When the wind blows, only the rigging to windward is doing the job

The force required to hold up the mast is represented by the vector (a).

As the angle between the mast and the shroud decreases, compression on the mast and traction on the shroud increases. If the angle is reduced too far, something will snap

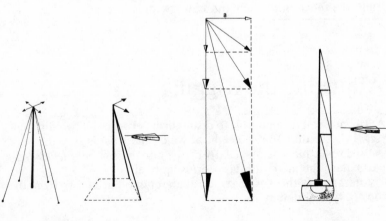

Masthead Rig

Let us now consider longitudinal (fore and aft) and lateral mast support.

Lateral Support. The drawing shows that a stay or shroud at an angle of 15° at the masthead, will fall well outboard of the boat and we therefore have to resort to the use of spreaders. But the shroud, now angled straight down from the spinnaker tip, creates a horizontal strain on one of the spreaders, which is liable to bend the mast at that level, so an extra shroud is required there to keep the mast straight.

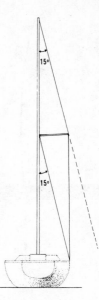

This system may be repeated as often as necessary, each shroud being at the minimum angle to the mast and the number of 'panels' being sufficient to bring the last shrouds down to deck level. The lower the shroud the heavier the loading, so the stronger it must therefore be.

Fore and Aft Support. The strains fore and aft on a mast are much greater than the lateral loads. This support is provided by a forestay (to stop the mast head moving aft) and either by two *running backstays* or a *standing backstay* (to stop the masthead moving forward).

Because the forestay must be extremely tight if it is to remain taut even in strong winds, the mast is subjected to great compression and must, therefore, be kept as straight as possible if it is not to snap. This gave rise to oval masts (with large longitudinal sections, and to supplementary stays for extra support (*inner forestay*, *lower forestay* and running backstays).

Non-masthead Rig

Lateral Support. On a dinghy, the shrouds and forestay are fastened well below the masthead. When the boat is under sail, the mast bows and the upper part, as it is not stayed, falls off to leeward, at the same time the lower part bends to windward.

Longitudinal Support. Since there is no standing backstay, the shrouds are attached to the hull slightly aft of the mast. Their tension keeps the forestay straight, at least while the wind is not strong. As soon as it freshens slightly (force 3), the jib pulls the mast firmly forward and the shrouds are no longer adequate to prevent this. It is only by sheeting the mainsail hard home that the luff of the jib can be kept straight. The lee shroud goes slack.

To sum up: *with a masthead rig, the mast is kept permanently rigid by the standing rigging; with a non-masthead rig, the mast is supported by the standing rigging, the running rigging and the sails.*

To tune the rig, you have to balance standing rigging and sails, to suit all points of sailing and in all wind forces. In the first case, with taut standing rigging, it is the sails which must conform; in the second, the running rigging must be adjusted as much as the sails.

In both cases, the situation has to be watched principally when beating to windward and this point of sailing must be looked at first.

Dinghy Rigging

To begin with, don't forget one of the principles explained in chapter 3. Sails should be flattened as the wind increases to maintain a good thrust without excessive heeling or leeway. A dinghy will capsize in force 4, in spite of the weight of her crew to windward, if her sails are too full. If the sails are properly sheeted in the boat will sail without difficulty in this strength of wind.

As a dinghy's mainsail has a much larger area than her jib, we shall look at the main first.

Mast and Mainsail

To modify the mainsail's shape you can regulate:

The curve of the spars, the mast in particular.
The tautness along the edges of the sail itself.

Curve of Mast

By increasing the curve of the mast, you can not only flatten out the mainsail but, beyond a certain wind force, virtually remove any trace of belly.

Racing helmsmen try to evolve a system of rigging control which, if correctly set up, adjusts itself according to the strength of the wind. The principles are:

A forward bow to the mast flattens the mainsail.
A port or starboard bend spills wind from the sail, which thus eases up the boat.

A forward bow is made by tightening the kicking strap (or American vang) and the mainsheet; this can also be controlled by the mast gate.

Lateral bend is due to the wind. It is limited by the mast gate and the spreaders.

Kicking strap (or vang) and mainsheet can make the boom bend.

Control varies according to the type of rig. Here are three examples:

A mast without spreaders and with only one control point – the mast gate.
A mast with mast gate and spreaders.
An unstayed mast.

Mast without Spreaders

Mast Bend. The extent of bend is regulated by the kicking strap (or vang) and the mainsheet, while its position is controlled by the mast gate.

If there is play between the mast and the forward edge of the mast gate, the mast can be bent along its full length and this gives overall flattening of the mainsail.

But if the mast is tightly wedged against the forward edge of the mast gate, you can only bend the top of the mast, thus only flattening the top of the mainsail.

Sideways Bend. If there is plenty of lateral play in the mast gate the wind can bend the mast from head to foot and the sail spills a lot of wind.

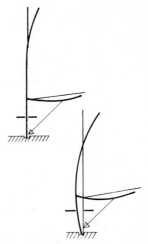

The same kicking strap arrangement will have different effects according to how the mast gate is set up

A heavy crew wedges the mast into its gate and chooses long spreaders.

A light crew allows some play to the mast in its gate and opts for short spreaders

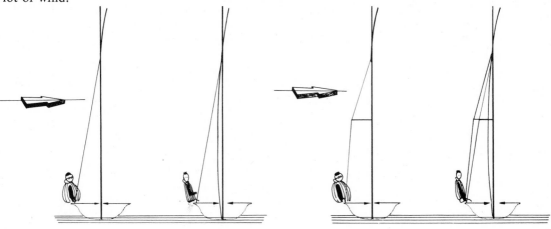

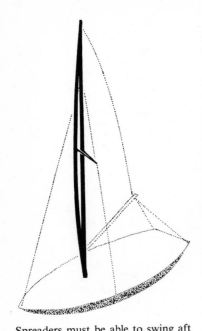

Spreaders must be able to swing aft when the mast bends

If, on the other hand, the mast is firmly fixed laterally in the mast gate, it will flex less, particularly towards its base. The sail will then only spill wind in fresh conditions and that only aloft.

Depending on ballast you can flatten the sail and spill wind within the limits of the adjustment available. In fresh winds, a light crew must bend the mast and allow it to flex more than a heavy crew who can sail with a stiffer mast.

Mast with Spreaders (e.g. 470)

Without spreaders mast bend can only be controlled from low down, but with spreaders you can also control it aloft. It is the width of the spreaders that now counts. The longer they are the sharper the angle of the shroud at the outer end; this means great pressure is exerted by the shroud on the spreader which keeps the mast stiff. It follows that the shorter the spreader, the wider the shroud angle, the shroud exerts less pressure and the mast bends more. A heavy crew normally would like long spreaders, while a light one wants them short.

Spreaders should not be fixed rigidly to the mast for when it bends, the part where the spreaders are fixed moves forward and, unless there is some play in the fitting, it will break. Spreaders are usually fitted with an aftward slant and should not be allowed to move forward very much or else, off the wind, they will allow the mast to bend aft when, for instance, the boat is reaching under spinnaker, and the mast could be in danger of breaking.

Unstayed Mast (e.g. the Finn)

This mast is really like a whip aerial, for it is held up solely by the step and the gate. When sailing to windward and on a close reach, it is therefore the mainsheet alone that bends it. Obviously the thicker the mast the less it bends and the Finn helmsman must choose one which is stiff or flexible according to his own weight, and then work on it. By planing it down where he wishes for flexibility or reinforcing it with wood splints for rigidity.

Here again, the heavier the helmsman is, the stiffer he can afford his mast to be.

Shape of Mast and Mainsail

When the mast or the boom bends some of the sail's curve is lost. Mast and sail must be matched for if their curvatures are not complementary, even a good sail flattens unevenly. With balanced mast and boom but a poorly cut sail the result is the same.

You should try to modify the one or the other but think twice before altering the cut of the sail yourself!

Examples

A. The mast is bent aloft and is almost straight for the lower three-quarters. As a result, the sail is bellied low down and at the leech and, when close-hauled, has a large crease which runs towards the clew from the point where the mast is bent. Mast bend must be corrected.

B. Mast and boom bend are even, but the sail is badly shaped. There is not enough round to the after part of the foot, and the luff is slack half way up. The sail should be recut.

C. The boom is bent too much near its after end; consequently the foot has too little round at this point. This kind of fault makes a crease along the inner end of the battens, which may disappear if the boom is straightened.

D. Spars and sail are perfectly matched, and the result is balanced.

In general:

If there is a crease from the clew towards the luff, mast bend or the shape of the luff should be looked at.

If there is a crease from the head towards the foot, boom bend or the sail's shape at the foot are at fault.

If there is a crease from mid-luff towards the foot, it is usually the sail which is badly cut.

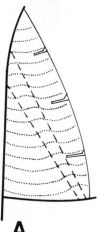
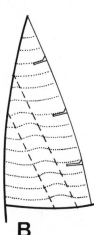
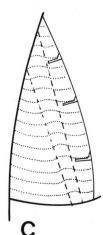
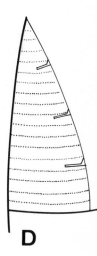

A   **B**   **C**   **D**

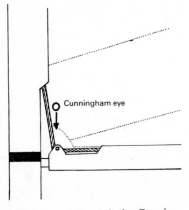

Cunningham eye

A line passed through the Cunningham eye allows the luff to be tightened without lowering the boom

Mainsail Tension

The mainsail can be flattened by other means than bending the spars. You can 'work' on the sail itself.

By stretching the foot you diminish curve and by stretching the luff, you stop the belly shifting towards the leech when the wind freshens.

The foot is stretched by pulling on the clew; the luff, by lowering the boom (the halyard is only used to hoist the sail). On racing boats, the mainsail must be set within precise limits which are marked on the spars, but it must be possible to stretch the sail within these limits. Stretch the foot at the forward end, having fixed the clew at its mark, and stretch the luff by bowsing down on the Cunningham eye without lowering the boom.

Battens

Battens should be carefully polished, and bevelled at the edges and corners. The forward ends should be flexible to allow the sail to take up its natural shape, and they should be stiffer towards their after ends. The object of battens is to hold out the sail where it extends outside a line joining the head to the clew. Without battens, this part of the sail would flap uselessly.

Some dinghy sails have a full-length top batten right up to the mast. This allows the working area there to be increased and its belly aloft to be effectively controlled. The more tension which is put on the batten, the more sail will belly! The weaker the wind, the greater should be the tension. In practice, much trial and error is needed to find out which thickness of batten (and how much tension to put on it).

Forestay and Jib

Forestay Tension

For maximum efficiency, particularly to windward, the luff of the jib must be as straight as possible. The forestay must therefore be well tensioned, as it is the mainspring of the boat. There are two different situations:

The forestay can be part of the boat's standing rigging (the luff of the jib merely has its bolt rope which would stretch under tension). The forestay should therefore be under maximum tension when you set up the rigging.

Or the forestay can be part of the jib (i.e. the wire bolt rope sewn into the luff of the jib or over which the woven luff is sleeved). It is therefore tensioned when the jib halyard is hardened, and this sets up the whole rigging.

In medium or heavy weather, when the lee shroud is slack, it is tension on the mainsheet which keeps the jib and forestay sufficiently tight.

In light weather, the forestay does not have to be under particularly great tension to keep straight. The shrouds stop the mast moving forward and the mainsheet can be eased.

Luff Tension

Even with the forestay well tensioned, the belly in the jib tends to move aft when the wind gets up, due to cloth stretch. It can be kept forward by stretching the luff, which may be done:

The curve in the jib moves further aft the more the wind blows. This must be prevented

If the luff is made of woven material (i.e. there is no luff wire).
If the luff is free to move over a wire.

In the first case, the luff is stretched by pulling on the jib halyard; in the second, by bowsing down the tack downhaul.

Sheet Fairleads

To ease the boat in heavy weather, it is sometimes necessary to spill wind from the jib. This is best done by moving the fairlead aft or up. This slackens the head of the sail and spills wind, so that the boat heels less, wallows less and makes better progress.

On boats with a fixed jib fairlead, the sheet lead can be modified by altering the height of the tack – something to be done before setting sail.

Summary

In light weather, spars are straight, luffs are slack, rigging is not under strain and sails belly nicely.

When the wind freshens, rigging should be stiffened by tightening the jib luff, mainsail bellying is progressively lessened by tightening the luff and foot and by bending the spars.

When the wind strengthens still more, the boat may be eased by feathering the top of the mainsail.

In very heavy weather, the lower luff of the mainsail which has not been flattened is allowed to flap so that only the bottom of the

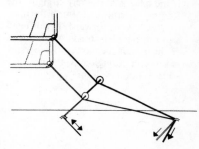

By raising or moving further aft the lead of the jib sheets the head of the jib sags to leeward and the boat heels less

leech area is pulling. Forward progress is now the role of the jib and it too can be feathered aloft if necessary.

Cruiser Rigging

Most modern cruisers have masthead rig. The crew's attention must be focused on the jib, which is the principal sail.

On these boats, the genoa is big and the mast must be a stout one. The mainsail, smaller than the genoa, is mostly operating in a wind stream disturbed by the mast and is that less efficient. With this sort of rig, you should set up the mainsail for average conditions and concentrate on the jib.

Mast Tune

Mast tune is too often thought of in terms of *rake* (sternward tilt) but this is really only of secondary importance, for it is much more important to have a mast which is straight.

If the jib is to set well and work properly to windward, the forestay should be as straight as possible. However if the mast bends the forestay loses tautness.

Mast tune should be undertaken at sea, to windward, because this is the point of sailing where the forestay is liable to sag most to leeward.

Adjust Masthead Rigging in Harbour

First adjust mast rake approximately (exactly, if you have the proper marks for reference). Tighten the forestay to its maximum, without deforming the hull.

Put moderate tension on the shrouds to set the mast laterally perpendicular, to the waterline.

Lock or secure all the bottlescrews to secure forestay, shrouds and backstay, for they will not be touched again.

Adjust the lower shrouds roughly so that the mast is not too much out of alignment.

Tuning the Mast at Sea

Efficient tuning is ideally done under all plain sail on a calm sea in wind Forces 3 to 4.

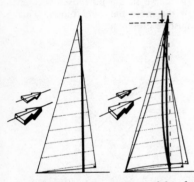

If the mast is absolutely straight, the forestay remains taut. But if the mast is already bent forward, it will bend still more under stress. As the head of the mast is then lower, the forestay is not taut enough and it is not possible to point well up

Tuning is a matter of adjusting the lower shrouds and stays until the mast is quite straight.

Sail, therefore, to windward, with a crew member stationed at the foot of the mast, looking up the groove or track. His job is to call out which shroud should be eased or tightened (by slackening or tightening the bottle screws).

Let us take as example tuning a mast which has one set of spreaders and a lower forestay.

The boat is on the port tack. If the mast bends forward and to starboard, slacken the lower forestay and tighten the port lower shroud. You will find that you usually have to undo and do up each bottle screw several times before finding the correct tension. Note: when you tighten a bottle screw make sure that the rigging to leeward is slack.

When this operation is finished, change tack and do the same thing on the starboard tack. If you manage to straighten the mast on this tack by only regulating the lower shroud, tuning is complete. But if you also have to change the tension on the lower forestay, you must go on changing tack until you strike a satisfactory compromise.

The same method applies for a mast with two sets of spreaders and an inner forestay. Tuning takes longer, but is not more difficult.

Once the mast is tuned like this the boat should be sailing at its best. But if the rake is not quite right you will only then notice it and you'll have to start again from scratch.

Tuning a mast takes at least an hour – often longer, 4 or 5 hours, if it is to be done really well. You should remember several simple rules in the course of your efforts at perfection:

Do not alter masthead rigging.
Pay more attention to easing off than to tightening.
See that the leeward rigging stays slack.
Be tirelessly patient.

If the mast is well tuned for working to windward, but is not quite right on other points of sailing or at anchor, don't worry unduly.

Standing Rigging, Tuning under Way

Forestay tension on certain boats can be altered while under way. This is done by altering the tension on the backstay by means of the backstay adjuster or, if there are two backstays, by bowsing them

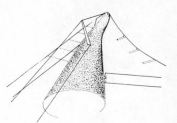

The lower forestay is too taut, and the lower port shroud not taut enough

It is teasingly inconvenient if the bottle screws are not the right way up. They are correctly fitted when the shank which has the right hand thread is underneath. When you turn the bottle screw clockwise it should tighten the shroud

closer together. Initial tune of the mast is effected along the same lines as with ordinary rigging; the forestay should be set up hard. After this, the forestay is adjusted according to the point of sailing and the wind strength, being slackened off as you bear away or as the wind goes light.

Each time you change points of sailing, or the wind strength varies, you should check that the mast is still straight. Small tackles to stiffen the lower forestay or the two forward lower shrouds may be necessary, so that the mast shall not bend too much when reaching.

Jib

As we saw when discussing the dinghy, the belly of a jib shifts aft as the wind gets stronger, because the weave of the cloth is blown slightly out of shape and, at the same time, the forestay sags off to leeward. As you can only alter the cut of a jib within fairly narrow limits, on a large cruising boat the solution lies in changing sails. Choose a jib which is right for the weather, taking care above all that its cut is correct.

Choice

The three genoas in the illustration belong to the same boat, and all three are the same size.

The light weather genoa has a well rounded luff, which results in a deep belly when set on a straight forestay. The medium weather genoa has a straight luff so that, when the forestay sags slightly off to leeward, the belly in the sail is the correct depth and well placed.
The heavy weather genoa has its luff hollowed in order to match the deep sag of the forestay.

Adjustment

Adjustment of the luff depends on the way the sail is made. There are three types of luff:
A. The luff is made of cloth and is seized on to wire. It can't therefore be stretched.
B. and **C.** The luffs are 'soft' rope. The luff is therefore adjustable and you can make them longer by pulling them tight.
D. The cloth luff is sleeved over the luff wire, and runs freely on it. The luff can be stretched independently of the wire.

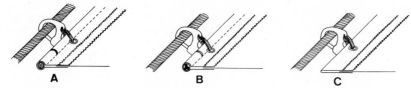

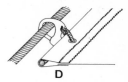

With jib **A**, the sailmaker has already set the tension of the cloth on the wire to a pre-determined extent, according to the wind strength the sail is normally expected to meet. If the wind strength changes, the jib must be changed.

With jibs **B**, **C** and **D**, luff tension can be varied. It is therefore possible, to some extent, to stop the belly being blown too far aft. Each jib is designed for a specific range of wind strengths. When going to windward, logic is taken to its extreme on certain boats by leaving the jib sheet fast and adjusting luff tension only. This tension can vary 4–8in, according to the size of the jib.

When the luff is stretched to its fullest extent and the jib is still too baggy, you must change sail.

If you want to ease the boat for a short while without changing the jib, you can raise the sheet lead, or take it further aft, which makes the head of the sail spill wind. You also limit heel like this, without much loss of speed.

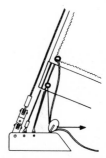

The tension of a jib luff is modified by hauling it down with a line taken to a winch or with block and tackle

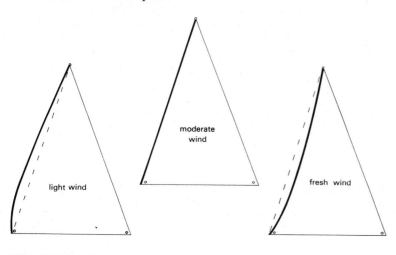

The cut of three genoa luffs to suit different weather conditions

The Mainsail

When the wind gets stronger, begin by lessening belly in the

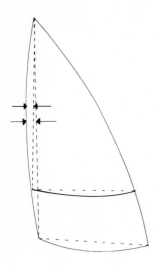

mainsail by stretching the foot, and then by bending the boom. Belly is stopped from moving aft in the sail by stretching the luff.

On boats with a rigid mast, if the wind continues to increase you can only flatten the mainsail further by taking in a reef. A reef will eliminate almost all the bulge at the foot of the luff, and therefore over most of the sail.

If the wind goes on increasing, take in a second reef and even a third. By now it is no longer a question of flattening the sail but simply reducing its area.

Flexible Masts on Larger Boats

Larger boats do not usually carry flexible masts but there are some that do. On such craft the mainsail is usually fairly big, so it is important to get maximum benefit from it. It is not normally cut with a large belly, and the sail can be further flattened by flexing the mast. This does not do the jib any good, but that is of secondary importance in this case because this type of boat is not designed to sail particularly close to the wind, and more than makes up in speed for what she loses by not pointing finely.

Often this kind of mast, by flexing fore and aft, seems to help the boat through a short chop.

The disadvantage of such a mast is that, if it is not tuned correctly, it can break in a fresh wind. And the discomfort and even danger of being in a dismasted boat are only to be experienced once, not to mention the expense of repairs!

Small Non-masthead Cruisers

These small cruisers cannot be classed as large boats, if only because of their slender masts and light rigging.

In the relative sizes of their small jibs and large mainsails they are comparable to dinghies. The crew should therefore pay particular attention to the main.

To tune the rigging, adjust the curve of the spars as on a dinghy. However, the rigging is different and you will almost certainly not be able to adjust the mast 'gate'. Equally, because the mast is stronger, it will not be possible to bend it so easily with the mainsheet and the kicking strap. A change in shroud tension is about as far as you can go.

Frequent turning of the bottle screws is not very practicable and the shrouds are therefore better adjusted through the block and tackle set up, for example:

Between the two forward lower shrouds, or between the inner forestay and the mast, to bend the mast.
Between the two aft lower shrouds to limit bend.
Between lower shrouds on the same side to give the mast a bend that will allow the mainsail to spill wind.

These arrangements give the mast (and consequently the sail) the shape best suited to the weather.

For the same wind strength, rigging adjustment is not constant on all points of sailing, and what has just been suggested applies to beating to windward. When you are sailing a little freer you should let the spars straighten up, and ease luffs in both sails and the foot of the main to increase belly and, it follows, their efficiency.

Standing Rigging

Spars and standing rigging are the framework on which the sails depend. Under spars are included: masts, spreaders, booms, spinnaker poles and so on. Under standing rigging are included: the wire ropes that hold the mast up (stays and shrouds), their adjustable fittings and the ironwork of spreaders and boom.

These must offer the least possible wind resistance which holds back the boat and, if it disturbs airstream too much, the sails are less efficient.
Be light. All weight aloft reduces stability.
Nevertheless, be strong. This requirement limits the other two.

Spar and rigging design have to be a compromise with one or other of the requirements getting priority according to the type of boat. On a dinghy, rigging is made fine and light, sometimes to the detriment of strength because, in the conditions where these boats sail, a failure rarely puts the crew in danger; but on a cruising boat rigging failure can put you in real trouble.

New materials and design now make lighter spars and rigging possible without loss of strength, and they make for the greater safety that is wanted all the more so now that boats sail harder and faster.

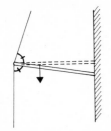

If it is not to slip, a spreader must bisect the angle formed by the turn of the shroud and . . .

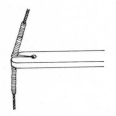

. . . – be firmly fixed to the shroud. It is fastened in the same way as the serving of an eye (cf p 142)

Spars

The Mast

As a mast is under constant pressure it must be rigid. Stout sectioned masts are rigid but heavy, with greater wind resistance and disturbance of the airstream on the mainsail.

Masts can be thinner provided the number of support points is increased, but then it is the shrouds that disturb the airstream and they add a bit of weight. A mast that is designed to bend needs greater strength than a straight one because it obviously is more liable to break.

Masts are best left in the hands of the designer and builder.

Spreaders

A spreader should only work when it is under compression, so there should be some play where it joins the mast to let it swing and take up the correct alignment and not bend; but it should be attached firmly to the shrouds to prevent it slipping up and down or getting detached.

It must also be streamlined to reduce wind resistance and be light because it is high up.

Boom

A boom should be light for two reasons:
It is fairly high in the boat.
When it swings over, particularly in a gybe, it can damage the rigging (and crack the odd head which gets in the way).

The thickness of a boom depends on the flexibility required and on the positioning of the mainsheet fittings. This means thin booms if the main is to be flattened by bending of the boom.

Spinnaker Pole

The spinnaker pole is the spar which holds out the tack of the spinnaker, or the jib clew, to windward when running downwind. The other end is fixed to the mast.

Spinnaker poles are subjected to compression strains which can be very great, particularly in a beam wind, so they must be strong. They must also be light, largely to make them easier to handle, but also for safety's sake because they are often set at head level.

Whatever material is used, wood, metal or plastic, the ideal shape of a spinnaker pole is that of a spindle with tapered ends. The only advantage of untapered poles is that they are easy to make and therefore cheaper.

The length of the pole is usually limited in racing yachts to the length of the base of the foretriangle. Cruising boats may, with advantage, have poles which are 20%–30% longer, and jib or whisker poles twice as long – always provided they can be conveniently stowed.

Materials

Wooden Spars

Traditional wooden spars are now used much less. Maintenance, weight and cost have all combined to lose them popularity in favour of those made of metal and even plastic. It is just as well, however, to know the principles of their construction and how to repair them, for older boats still have them.

Construction. The most common wood used for spars is North American spruce. A spar is made up of several pieces glued together, after being hollowed out as much as possible (the walls are usually between $\frac{1}{2}$in and 1in thick), solid at each end and where the fittings are attached.

Maintenance. Principally for aesthetic reasons, wooden masts are usually varnished and not painted, and every year they must be given 5 to 7 coats to keep water from weakening the glue. The head and the heel must be well impregnated with varnish or else water will be absorbed at the ends, and the result would be rot and glue failure.

An old mast can be made to look better by planing it down slightly, but, obviously this cannot be done more than 2 or 3 times.

Masts and booms should always be stored on a straight rack, dry and airy, so that they never lie out of true. They should rest on their only flat surface, the track.

Fittings. Fittings should be fixed to spars with great care because the wood is soft. There are two ways of doing this:

Wood screws hold well if they are long and thick; they resist a sideways pull better than a straight one.
Bolts hold well under both conditions.

In principle, fittings should be attached at solid points with only

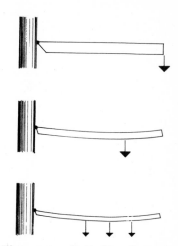

Three ways of attaching the mainsheet to three different boom sections

When spars are hollow, fitments can only be attached where there is reinforcement

shearing strain on screws. Whenever possible bolts should be used to reinforce screws. Bolts are essential when fittings are to be subjected to great strain.

It is a good idea to get into the habit of double-checking where you want to drill a hole in a mast because every hole makes it weaker, and even if an unwanted hole is filled in again, the wood fibres have been cut.

Every hole can let in water, so always varnish the inside of any hole drilled for a bolt, and smear the screws with grease.

Finally, if you have to block up an unwanted hole, don't use too large a dowel as it can swell and split the wood.

Repair. All repairs to wooden spars should be made with spruce. The two pieces meet each other in a scarph joint (a bevelled overlap, with a slope of about 10%, measured along the length of the spar), and use glue; never use screws or nails.

When repairing a groove in a mast or boom which has been damaged:

1. Put a strip of wood (A) in the groove so that the broken piece can be lined up or the split supported.
2. Stick with glue.
3. Hold the repaired section tightly together with a length of sisal, wound at half-inch intervals. When it is in place, damp the cord by dabbing with a sponge well away from the glue; it will shrink and tighten the joint. Use a rapid-setting glue or keep wetting the string until the glue goes off.

Once wet, the line shrinks and tightens

Metal Spars

Metal spars are becoming more and more common. The metal used most often is an alloy of aluminium (A) and magnesium (G) such as AG_4 (4 indicating the percentage of magnesium, in this case 4 per cent). Masts are also made of titanium, which is expensive and its use on boats is still in the experimental stage.

Alloy spars start life as extrusions of regular diameter but can be tapered to obtain less weight aloft, better streamlining and different characteristics of flexibility.

Construction. The original maximum length of a tube in the factory is not usually more than 40ft, owing to handling limitations. A higher mast is made by sleeving or welding two or more tubes.

To sleeve, the two ends are carefully matched and then a slightly smaller section is inserted, half into each end. It is screwed or riveted in place, and then glued, usually with Araldite to make sure that there is no danger of movement, no matter how slight, or else the sail slides or bolt rope would jam on the track or in the groove.

Welding is practised more frequently nowadays, although it needs special equipment, and must be done in an inert gas atmosphere (Argon) to avoid oxydisation while the alloy is warm. Moreover the weld must be 'roasted' in a special furnace so as not to be brittle.

Repair of metal spars requires the same equipment; and it is by no means available at every boatyard.

Maintenance. Light alloy spars do not need much maintenance, especially if they are anodised – as they usually are.

Whenever possible, leave the mast in the boat during the winter lay-up, but remove the running rigging (halyards, sheaves, etc.) which tend to chafe the surface.

If the mast has to come out, an important precaution is to avoid contact with copper, brass or bronze.

Attachment of Fittings. The problem of galvanic action arises with the use of light alloy, and we shall go into this more fully when discussing metal hulls. It need only be said here that you cannot fit any kind of metal to a mast made of aluminium alloy. Copper fittings are out, although stainless steel is all right, provided an insulating pad is inserted – a plastic coating for example.

Attachment of fittings is much easier to metal spars than to wooden ones. Bolts, pop rivets and pre-drilled and tapped backing pieces are used, and here again, galvanic action must be guarded against. Some yards use self-tapping screws which look rather like wood screws, yet grip straight on to a slightly undersize hole in the alloy. It is a cheap system which is not to be trusted (the hole soon gets bigger through galvanic action between the screw and the mast), and such screws usually have soon to be replaced.

Recently, alloy fittings have been welded straight on to the mast. Such welds should be done using the same technique as when jointing two mast sections.

As metal spars are completely hollow, shroud attachments and halyards can be placed inside the mast, thus considerably reducing wind resistance.

Plastic Spars

Not very common, reinforced polyester resin spars appeal to some yachtsmen.

Such masts are in one piece. Their main advantage is that they are impervious to all atmospheric conditions so they are not subject to rot or rust, although they do have their drawbacks. Fitting of attachments is difficult and they cannot be repaired.

To be economic, plastic construction requires mass production and such spars thus seem destined to be restricted to dinghies for a while yet.

Wire Rigging

Composition

There are three different kinds of wire currently used for standing rigging.

Single Rod is the simplest of all, and the newest, but it is really only used on offshore racing yachts at present. It is composed of a cold drawn section, round for a forestay, but often streamlined when used for shrouds, so as to offer less wind resistance. Thin and light, rod rigging has virtually no stretch and will doubtless be used more, despite its drawbacks, which are:

Rigidity. It must be laid out straight or coiled in a large circle (about 10ft diameter).
Brittleness. It loses a lot of its strength at the slightest graze.

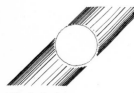

Rod rigging
(round section)

Lenticular rod rigging

1 × 19 wire. Only patent terminals may be used with this wire

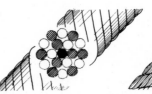

7 × 7 wire rope. This is the only standing rigging wire that can be bent round an eye

Single Strand Wire is usually composed of 19 wires made up as follows: six wires are twisted round a central core, to serve as the first layer; on top of this, either in the same or opposite direction according to the type of wire used, is twisted a second layer of twelve further wires which results in a make-up of $1 + 6 + 12 = 19$ wires, usually known as 1 × 19. Single strand wire, although more flexible than rod, will not bend through a very tight radius, so it cannot be passed round a thimble, but must be swaged or fitted with swageless terminals such as Norseman or Sta-Lok.

Finally comes *wire rope* (7 × 7). Each strand comprises a wire core surrounded by a layer of six further wires; one strand then acts as a core for six other strands. This is more flexible than single strand wire because, for a given diameter, there are more wires which are therefore thinner. It can be bent round a tight radius, so you can splice it round a thimble, coil it, etc.

TABLE OF WIRE BREAKING LOADS
Breaking strains expressed in kilograms

Diameter in mm	3	4	5	6	7	8	9	10
SS rod	850	1,450	2,200	3,050	4,100	5,400	6,700	8,200
SS 7 × 7 ⎫ SS 7 × 19 ⎭	550	950	1,450	2,100	2,800	3,850	4,900	6,200
galv 7 × 7	650	1,100	1,750	2,500	3,450	4,500	5,700	7,000
galv 7 × 19	580	990	1,550	2,250	3,000	4,050	5,200	6,500

SS = stainless steel
galv = galvanised wire

All the above figures for breaking strains are approximate. They can vary appreciably according to the quality of the rope. Precise estimates are only possible by referring to the manufacturers.

Types of Metal

Wire can either be galvanised or stainless steel, each of which has its advantages and disadvantages.

Galvanised Wire rusts and needs maintenance, but it is strong, flexible and initially cheap.

Stainless Steel Wire does not rust and looks good, but it is not so strong as galvanised wire, is weakened by bending and scratching. It is expensive, sometimes very expensive initially, although it lasts so much longer than galvanised that it is cheaper in the long run.

If you sail a lot (more than 100 days a year), it is worth using galvanised wire and changing it every two years; it will be cheaper in the long run than stainless steel rigging. The latter may be better if you don't sail much; in which case make sure that you use the right size and check it frequently.

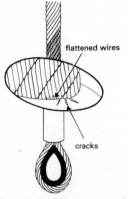

Stainless steel cable tends to break at the collar. When shiny, flattened areas in the strands appear near the collar, it is high time to change a shroud for it is already partially broken. Here, cracks also indicate that the collar itself is breaking

Beware of rusty and/or broken strands! This cable must be renewed at once

Fitting the Rigging to Mast and Hull

There are several ways of fixing wire to mast and hull. These are the most common.

Splicing is the oldest method, not used often these days owing to cost and maintenance (it requires serving, protection against corrosion). In any event, a splice can only be made on 7 × 7 wire rope.

Talurit or Pressed. The system is as follows: the wire passes through a metal band or collar of alloy or copper, around a thimble and back into the collar again where it is crimped home, that is to say that the collar is squeezed round both parts of the wire in a hydraulic press. The strength of this system is excellent providing the collar is properly placed; it must not be cracked (easily visible under a magnifying glass). The collar should not lie hard up against the thimble, or the points of the latter, when they are squeezed into the thimble by the press, may cause a crack to start.

To avoid galvanic action, use light alloy collars on galvanised wire, and copper collars on stainless steel. If by chance you have stainless steel rigging with alloy talurit collars, ensure that they are painted and check closely.

Swaged Terminal. This terminal can only be used with stainless steel wire. It consists of a long sleeved terminal, also in stainless steel, into which the wire is inserted without being bent so it can be used with single strand wire. The terminal is either machine crimped round the end of the wire under great pressure, or else it is hand fitted by means of a special fitting such as Norseman or Sta-Lok. Either method is good, but take care, because there are several other makes and they are not all excellent.

All wire terminal systems cost money, but as with wire itself this is no field for false economy, because a failure will land you in expense out of all proportion to the saving.

Wear and Maintenance

Excessive wear in wire is symptomised by broken strands. Galvanised wire can be tested very simply: bend it and, if it stays bent or only straightens slowly, scrap it.

Galvanised wire can be protected by coating it with a mixture of Stockholm tar and linseed oil, but this is a messy business and bearing in mind the comparative cheapness of galvanised wire, it is better to change it fairly regularly as we have already pointed out.

Although it needs no maintenance, it is not easy to tell when stainless steel rigging needs replacing. If it has been subjected to excessive strain, and lost some of its strength, you can sometimes detect small flat bits on the strands (often round the collar) and that means metal fatigue.

Mast Fittings

All joints in standing rigging should be made by clevis pins or bolts secured by split pins. No other system can be trusted for attaching rigging to masthead fittings, shroud adjuster plates to cables, bottle screws to toggles, toggles to chainplates, gooseneck pins, etc.

The only way to secure a clevis pin or bolt is by means of a split pin, which cannot come out. Rings and other pins can easily be torn out by passing sheets or halyards.

Tape all split pins so that they do not tear sails or running rigging.

Masthead Fittings

Shackles must *not* be used to join the upper ends of wires to masthead fittings because they are not strong enough. A good way is to use a tang where the eye at the end of the wire fits between two straps (which need to have a breaking strain at least equal to that of the wire; see table p. 135).

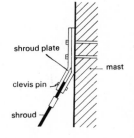

Mast fittings should be inspected regularly and renewed if they show the slightest signs of wear. When checking on strength, always measure the section at the weakest point. Stainless steel fittings are particularly brittle so make sure that there are no cracks. Above all, inspect seizing wire and split pins regularly, i.e. every fortnight.

Bottle Screws or Turnbuckles

Shrouds are made fast to the hull with bottle screws which are fixed to a chainplate. Rigging tension can be adjusted to a fine point by the bottle screws.

There are many types of bottle screws and they are nearly all as good as each other, but remember that they should have the same breaking strain as the wire. Ideally the breaking strain should be indicated when you buy them. One can have a rough idea by calculating the breaking strain of the screw (stainless steel breaks at 60 to 80kg/mm²).

The bottle screw should be fixed to the chainplate with a universal joint, called a *toggle*. Unless it can swivel in all directions it is easily damaged if by bad luck you run into a jetty or the side of a

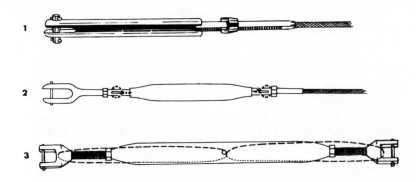

boat with higher freeboards than your own, or if someone climbs on board holding on to a shroud.

Bottle screws should be locked so that they cannot unscrew. Locking nuts (1) are often used, but they are not always completely safe and it is better to have split pins which pass through the stem of the threaded part (2) and are trapped by the barrel. A good alternative is to use seizing wire (3).

Adjustable Straps

On small boats, you often find straps with holes in them for adjustment instead of bottle screws. This is the simplest system and these can take rough treatment over a long period. They do not, of course, allow for fine adjustment to rigging tension, but we have already seen this is taken care of in dinghies by the jib halyard and mainsheet.

Chainplates

Chainplates must be very securely fitted to the hull as we shall see later, and they should be fastened in relation to the angle of pull on them, or they will soon give trouble.

Chainplates are subject to wear, and like bottle screws must be checked at least once a year to ensure that their smallest section is at least as strong as the shroud.

Gooseneck

The gooseneck links the boom to the mast, and allows the boom to move horizontally and vertically. Without straining the gooseneck, the boom should be able to move from deck level to an angle of about 50°, and from side to side as far as the shrouds will let it.

A gooseneck which runs on a track on the mast is now more usual than a fixed one, largely because it makes stretching the luff of the mainsail easier. There are several ways of allowing vertical movement to the gooseneck, but a track is by far the best.

A good gooseneck should have a tack fitting on its centre line, and hooks for reef cringles; if the gooseneck is a sliding one, there should be the same number of hooks as there are reefs.

It is a good idea to have a boom which can rotate because the gooseneck is not then subject to torsion, and you can control luff stretch no matter at what angle the boom may be.

Spinnaker Boom Fittings

On a double-ended spinnaker pole the fittings at the two ends are, as the name implies, absolutely identical.

On a single-ended pole each end of the spinnaker boom has different gear, one fitting to the mast, and the other clipping on to the spinnaker tack.

The mast fitting must allow the pole to move horizontally through 180°, and the outboard end to move from deck to the vertical.

On very small boats – principally dinghies – the spinnaker pole is attached to the mast by a simple hook which fits in a ring. This fulfils the dual function of fixture and universal joint but this would not be strong enough on bigger boats where a true universal fitting is required. The cup system is as good as any to engage the end of the spinnaker pole for there is no risk of torsion.

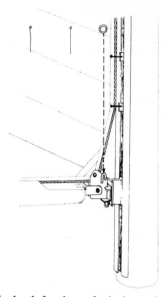

The hook for the reef cringle on the gooseneck must be as far forward as possible. The base of the luff is cut on a slant to accommodate the tack cringle but it is straight at the level of the reef points

Fittings at the outboard end of spinnaker poles are designed to:

Be attachable to the tack by snap shackle, or hook.
Clip on to the wire spinnaker guy, snap shackle or fairlead.
Clip on to an outhaul.

The outhaul is a line for pulling the spinnaker tack to the end of the pole. It too is fixed with a snap hook on the spinnaker tack; it passes round a pulley at the outer end of the spinnaker pole to the inboard end and is made fast on a cleat on the pole itself.

Some spinnaker poles have two outhauls, one for each tack. But outhauls only work on small and medium size boats. On larger craft they can easily break under the strain and you constantly worry about the pole going through the spinnaker.

Running Rigging

Running rigging in this context covers not only lines and ropes such as sheets and halyards, but also the fittings and fixtures which facilitate mobility; pulleys, fairleads, cleats, winches, shackles, snap hooks and piston hanks. While the standing rigging ensures that the mast is held in the ideal position, running rigging hoists, stretches and controls the sails.

All this movement and the friction it creates cause wear and tear or *chafe*: a sheet chafes in its fairlead, a halyard on the sheave, and even the best cordage and fittings suffer.

It is not as unequal a battle these days now that some of the causes of chafe have been reduced through simplification of rigging and improved fittings, which make for easier running; but chafe can never be completely eliminated. Running rigging has the same characteristics and needs as standing rigging, and the quest for thinner and lighter materials to reduce drag and weight aloft is never-ending.

Synthetic Cordage

Most rope these days is made of synthetic materials, which have completely ousted natural fibres such as cotton, hemp and manilla. The chief advantage of synthetics is that they are rot-proof, but they deteriorate in ultra-violet rays, and therefore exposure to the sun.

The best synthetics can result in second-rate cordage. Fibres which have not been stabilised properly, for instance, shrink and go hard with use; it is not the quality of the material which is at fault, but the way in which the rope has been laid. It is therefore worth choosing the different kinds of rope carefully and price is not always the best yardstick. The most common materials are:

Polyamide (nylon): elasticity is low until subjected to 25% of its breaking strain, when it becomes very great. It is extremely susceptible to ultra-violet rays.
Polyester (Terylene, Dacron, etc.): has considerable elasticity in

the initial stages of stretch until 25 % of breaking strain is reached when there is practically no more. It is not particularly susceptible to ultra-violet rays and is the most expensive of the three.
Polypropylene: has very little elasticity, but is extremely susceptible to ultra-violet rays. It floats and is cheap.

TABLE OF BREAKING STRENGTHS OF ROPES
Breaking loads expressed in kilograms

Diameter of the rope in millimetres	6	8	10	12
Laid nylon	810	1,400	2,100	3,000
Plaited nylon	530	1,150	1,750	2,400
Laid Terylene or Dacron	540	930	1,350	2,000
Plaited Terylene or Dacron	500	700	1,200	1,700
Laid Polypropylene	550	950	1,350	2,000

These loads are average. They can vary enormously with the quality of the fibre and the way it is made up.

Laid and Braided Rope

Rope is made in great variety for specific purposes. Twisting or laying the strands together in traditional rope walks seems to be on the way out and plaiting or braiding is now being used more and more.

Hawser laid rope (three strand) has a poor resistance to chafe. When a strand parts, it unravels, unwinding little by little throughout the whole length and the rope is useless. You must whip the ends of a line with twine; even if you burn the ends of the strands of synthetic rope to seal them, they unravel quickly if they are not held by a whipping. The advantage of laid rope is that it is much easier to splice than braided line.

There are very many kinds of braided line. The tendency nowadays is towards composite manufacture – a core (plaited, laid or bunched) of fibres inside the outer layer. This reduces stretch. The skin is usually made of a different material which acts as protection against chafe and ultra-violet rays as well as strengthening the whole rope.

Braided line therefore has an obvious advantage in its resistance to chafe, and a broken strand does not make the whole line unusable. Its disadvantage is that you can't splice it. Manufacturers are trying to resolve the problem of making a braided line which can be easily spliced.

Knotting and splicing synthetic fibres is difficult, particularly when the material is stiff and shiny, for the fibres are then slippery and will not hold. To cope with this matt-finish ropes are being made and they are also softer on the hands.

Synthetic rope can be bent safely only four times its diameter. It can bend more but it will suffer fatigue and weaken if it has to be rove through a very small block. But it stands up to that better than a wire cable under the same conditions.

Knots and Splices

If a rope is to be useful on a boat, you must be able to join it up to other parts of the rigging. This is where the art of knotting and splicing comes in.

Cutting and Whipping Ends

Synthetic ropes are best cut with a hot knife: heat the blade until it is red hot and then cut with the back of the blade; this cuts the line and seals each end.

Sealing by heat is not durable and that is why the ends should be whipped. This has the double advantage of crimping the sleeve and the inner core of composition braided line.

When you cannot cut with a hot knife, whip both sides of the incision before you cut.

Some prefer to heat-seal all the fibres at the end of the line, over a distance equal to approximately twice its diameter instead of whipping; but do it with a hot blade and not with a naked flame. This method is not so secure, and never lasts as long as the rope itself.

Whipping. Use a double thread with a size 5 needle (or a bigger one, 14.5 or 14). Draw it through the rope, wind it tightly together round the rope and pull it through the rope again at the end of the whipping.

Next, make three seizings, pulled very tight over the end of the whipping, by stitching the thread through about a third of the rope. The seizing should be parallel to the lay of the rope and to the strands that compose it, if it is a laid rope.

To finish off, make a half hitch on the last turn of the seizing, and then push the needle through the rope at an angle and cut the thread where it emerges

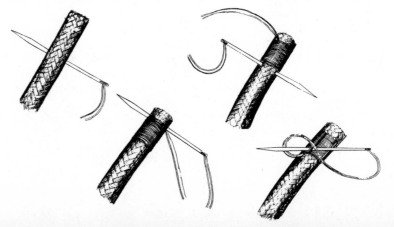

Eye Splices

When a permanent loop is needed at the end of a rope, you should make an eye which is spliced, in the case of laid rope, and sewn for braided line.

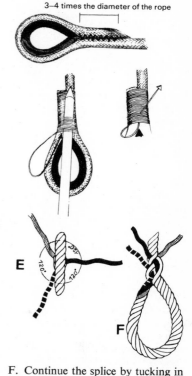

cut at an angle

3–4 times the diameter of the rope

Sewn Eye. Use a double heavy nylon thread and a size 15 needle (or larger). As it is virtually impossible to put the needle right through the rope, sew on one side, only going through about a quarter of it at a time.

If you want to be really meticulous, you can serve the sewn part with a coarser thread as follows: turn the thread round the rope tightly from the end, trapping the end of the thread under the first turns. When you have done about two thirds of the whipping, continue but slip something like a pointed pencil under the turns. Then pull it out and draw the other end of the thread under the turns as shown in the diagram. Then tighten the slack turns hard, one by one. Pull hard on the end that emerges from the serving and cut it off

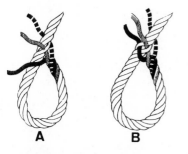

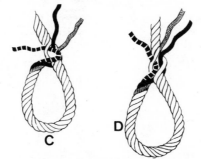

Eye Splice. The eye shown here is as you must face it.

The standing part (the long part of the rope) is held in the left hand, the bight (or loop) in the right hand.
A. Begin by making the bight the size that will fit round the thimble. Be careful to tuck in first the middle strand in the diagram (against the lay)
B. The lowest strand in the diagram is tucked in the next
C. The loop has been turned over.

Now comes the third strand which is tucked from right to left under the free strand (you are not working in the opposite direction to the others, all three are tucked against the lay.)
D. Now is the time to pull the splice gently tight and check that all is going well. The third strand should be parallel with the one on its immediate right
E. The three strands should come out on the same level of the rope, making angles of about 120° to each other

F. Continue the splice by tucking in the ends in the same order. To avoid making mistakes, work systematically, always tucking in the end on the left of the one you have just done. Each time a tuck is made, pull upwards on the strand to tighten it. Four tucks of each strand are enough for a good hold but, for a perfect job, do six tucks, removing some fibres off each strand after the fourth tuck

Knots

There is a great variety of knots and you must learn some of them so that you can make them quickly at the right moment. Some can be tied or untied under tension, others cannot; and some tighten up in use – like a Gordian knot, while others unravel easily.

Let us concentrate here on the more common knots which should be enough for sailing round the world, provided you know them instinctively and can tie them without thinking.

Reef knot. We do not use it at sea and it is only shown here to demonstrate its futility. It either jams tight or slips

Slipped reef knot. Easy to undo but it does not hold very well. Only useful for reefing points

Sheet bend. This is the knot to use instead of the reef knot for joining two ropes. It does not slip and undoes easily enough, but it can only be tied and untied when the ropes are not under tension

Double Sheet bend. Used for joining two ropes of different thickness

Slipped half hitch. A knot of many qualities. The turns allow a rope that is running out to be checked. The half hitch is easily made and undone under tension. Specially useful for towlines and reef pendants

Fisherman's knot. Always difficult to untie, it is used for joining two ropes more or less permanently: two half sheets to a jib clew, for instance, or for joining up that fishing line that could not be disentangled from the log line

Bowline. Can be tied with all types of rope, never slips or jams. It has many uses: mooring, putting a loop on a ladder or round a bollard, attaching a rope to a ring or eye (to a reef cringle for instance) and many others. Its only drawback is it can only be made on a slack line. You should be able to make it quickly, even in the dark. Can be made with the bight towards you or away from you.

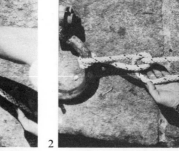

Bight away from you
1. After making a round turn to prevent chafe, make an overhand knot
2. With the right hand, pull the fall towards you while giving some slack to the standing part with the left hand
3. Pass the fall under the standing part and –
4. – bring it back through the bight.

1

2   3

Bight towards you
1. Take the fall in your right hand, take it across the tail end and turn over by moving both hands forward.
2. The basic twist has been made.
3. Pass the fall below the standing part and –
4. – bring it back through the bight

4

Clove hitch. Its great qualities are its speed in making and its holding power. A rope running out can be immediately jammed. Also useful when a bowline might jump off anything like a samson post. It can be slackened without untying but it can slip when not under strain, or tighten very hard when under strain.

1

2

3

4

1. The first half-hitch is made by making a bight over the fall
2. It can now be seen how it can check a rope running out
3. The second half-hitch is made by making a bight over the fall and –
4. – it is finished. But never make a round turn before the first half-hitch is made; it can then turn and the knot quickly jams

The tugman's hitch. The ideal method for tow-ropes, it can be made while the rope is still running out, made and remade under tension; and it does not tighten right up. To prevent slipping, the free end must be at least 1m long or turned round a cleat

1

2

3

4

1. The first round turn stops the rope running freely
2. Five or six more turns and it will not slip
3–4. Make secure by making a bight over the samson post

Coil, Uncoil and Untangle

To prevent your ropes degenerating into a mass of 'spaghetti' (which only ruins them and your own nervous system) you must learn to coil and uncoil properly.

Because of the way it is twisted together, *a laid rope should always be coiled in a clockwise direction*; untwist each coil lightly between the thumb and the index finger so as to have loops and not figures of eight in your hand. At the same time, so that a rope can allow its twists to work out, its end should be free. *Begin each coil at the fixed end* – if the rope is made fast.

Likewise, uncoil by beginning at the fixed end, this time anticlockwise. When you want to uncoil a coil of rope, which is free at both ends, it does not matter whether you start at the inside or the outside of the coil, but always work anti-clockwise.

If, despite these precautions, the line stays kinked and twisted, lay it out and untwist it over its entire length.

Braided rope can be coiled and uncoiled in either direction, but is usually coiled clockwise. In any event start at the fixed end to let out any kinks.

A rope is coiled in the direction of its lay – clockwise. At every loop, give it a quarter turn towards the coil with finger and thumb. This stops the coils becoming eights. To finish the coil off, pass the free end round it three or four times and then take it through the top

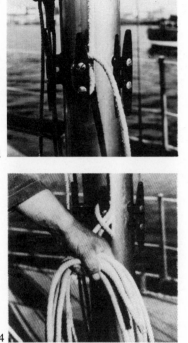

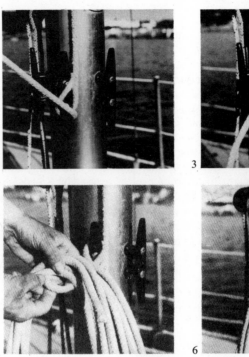

Cleating a halyard and tidying the slack. The halyard is made fast round the cleat in the usual way: (1) a round turn, (2) a half figure of eight, (3) a half hitch. To tidy the slack, (4) coil it, (5) put your hand through the coil, grasp the fall of the halyard near the cleat and pull through making a small loop. (6) Hook the loop over the cleat

To disentangle a rope, pull only through loops

When the rope is tangled, kinks and twists can abound and they can look like knots. Free the loops from each other without working on the ends, because you might make real knots out of the tangle that way.

Wire

Steel wire in running rigging has certain advantages: it does not stretch very much and has high tensile strength and resistance to

chafe, without being too heavy. It has, nevertheless, the same drawbacks as wire used in standing rigging because it can rust and it does not like sharp bends. It is difficult to handle and sometimes dangerous.

Composition

Wire strand for running rigging is made of a large number of thin wires. In practice, the finer the individual wires are the smaller the bend that the made-up wire can take without damage. This is a major consideration when choosing wire that has to pass round a sheave.

Galvanised or stainless steel wire, the two most common types, are made up as follows:

7 × 19, that is to say 6 strands of 19 wires (1 + 6 + 12) each, twisted round a core of one further similar strand. This will accept a bend down to 11 times its own diameter.

7 × 37, or 6 strands, each made up of 37 wires (1 + 6 + 12 + 18), twisted round a core of a similar strand. This is usually only made in sizes larger than 8mm ($\frac{3}{8}$in) diameter, with a 1in circumference and normally has a minimum bend of 8 times its own diameter.

Both these types of wire are made in galvanised form with a textile core which makes them slightly weaker but less vulnerable to bending fatigue and they stretch rather more. If the textile core is impregnated with grease, it helps to prevent corrosion.

Wear

Dread of corrosion makes many yachtsmen insist on stainless steel wire, but this is not necessarily the best choice. The problem is the same as with standing rigging in that stainless steel wire is more expensive, less supple and weaker than galvanised wire of the same diameter. The latter, bearing in mind its cheaper initial cost, can be changed every year or every two years; in this way you ensure against mid-season breakages.

Whatever wire you use, it must be changed at the first sign of broken strands, but you must also find out what is causing such flaws. There are four possibilities:

The stranding occurs at a splice. In this case the wire is too weak and must be replaced by one with a larger diameter.

Stranding appears over a fairly long distance, particularly at half halyard height. Here, the halyard is probably chafing on a fitting.

Stranding appears on the jib halyard, about a foot from the head of the sail: you have probably sailed for a while with the halyard wrapped round the forestay.

The wire has a permanent 'S' deformation. This is a recurring problem with spinnaker sheets and guys, and with wire sheets wound on a winch. The fault stems from the way the wire is handled; if the system is not revised, the malformation will gradually increase and the wire will eventually break.

Broken strands will also appear remorselessly along the full length of any wire that chafes against a sheave in a badly designed block or if the sheave is out of true.

Finally, if you try to make the wire turn through too sharp a bend, when a halyard, for instance, has to pass over a sheave of too small diameter it will tend to spiral. You should immediately either change the sheave, or change to a wire of smaller diameter or greater flexibility.

Maintenance

It is not too difficult to make an eye splice in flexible wire, particularly with a drawing in front of you, or better still the photographs in the following pages.

You should also have a few screwed cable clamps of the right sizes on board, galvanised or well wrapped in grease. The simplest and easiest to use are Bulldog grips and you need at least two if you want to make sure that the wire will not slip. A box spanner of appropriate size is essential when fitting these grips (an adjustable spanner would be useless for this job).

Wire is stored in rolls like garden hose or electric cable. If you cannot roll it, it must be coiled but in a particular way, and you can only coil wire properly (it is just the same with a hose or electric cable) by taking a turn in one direction and then in the other: that is to say a turn, a half hitch, then a turn, a half hitch and so on.

When the wire is needed, if you have rolled it then unroll it; if you have coiled it then uncoil it. Use one system or the other or you will get it kinked and the wire is finished.

A wire rope is coiled in loops and half hitches, alternately, by turning your hand

Cutting Wire

It is an elementary precaution before cutting to put a seizing on the

Eye splice on a wire rope

A. Prepare by whipping the rope where it must not become unlaid. Unlay the rest and cut the core as close as possible to the whipping. Make the loop and place the unlaid strands so that two of them pass on either side of the standing part and the last two strands remain on top

B. Tuck end No 1 under two strands and No 2 on its right under one strand and against the lay (from right to left)

C. Turn the rope round and tuck strand 6 under two strands and strand 5, on its left, under one strand with the lay

D. Check for mistakes: each end should emerge out of the lay separated by only one strand

E. Now tuck in strands 3 and 4, crossing under the lay opposite to which they lie

F. A strand is now coming out of each lay and the first complete tuck has been made

G. Make the next two tucks by by-passing each strand over the one on its left and under the next one. Stretch out the splice by pulling the strands hard upwards and hammer down each tuck

H. Three complete tucks have now been made. Make two more with the even-numbered strands only, each under two strands at a time. Finally cut off all loose strand ends and serve the splice as shown on the opposite page.

Splicing wire to fibre rope (tail splice). Alternate strands must be unlaid for 60cm and 40cm. To do this: tape off at 60cm and pull out 60cm strands preventing the 40cm strands from moving with adhesive tape. Completely unlay the 60cm strands; tape off at 40cm free and unlay remaining strands.

A. Place the wire rope 20cm from the end of the fibre one (the end is just left of the photo). Tuck two long strands under two of the fibre rope strands so that they come out of two different lays. Put the three shorter strands and the core of the wire rope up against the lay which has remained free and lay them into the cantlines of the fibre rope by turning as the strand marked with an arrow on the right of the photograph indicates. Go on until you reach the point where the shorter strands are whipped

B. From the other side (towards the left) roll the fibre rope round the wire rope until the wire is buried in the fibre rope for about 10cm length

C. Repeat the operation described in A with the longer strands and the core of the wire rope which must also be completely buried in the fibre rope

D. Tuck in the three longer strands (if you have a hollow spike, take the wire strands through the fibre strand instead of tucking over and under: this is stronger and more pleasing to the eye); four or five tucks will be enough and make the last tuck under two strands

E. Cut off projecting ends and serve with tape to eliminate any sharp points. Position the tape to allow for a little stretch

Make a palm and needle whipping over the tucked longer strands and do the same with the shorter ones

F. Unlay and thin out evenly the ends of the fibre rope strands and coat them with bees-wax. Fix them to the wire rope with sail thread, using a chain stitch

G. Serve the whole splice with sail thread wound very close and tight. Stretch the splice, using a winch, and make the turns with the help of a serving mallet. The diagram below shows how the thread is arranged round the mallet. Finish off as with a sewn eye (cf page 143)

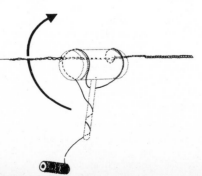

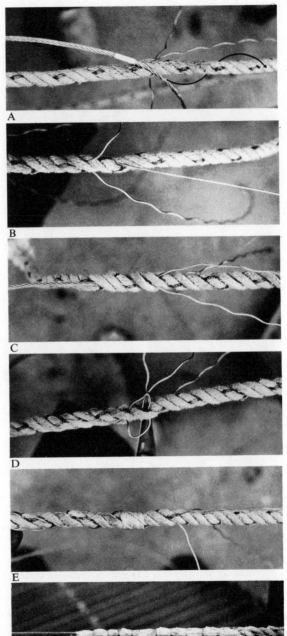

wire, or it will immediately unravel for quite a length as it is cut. Wire can be cut:

With a cold chisel, using the anchor as an anvil.
With wire-cutters (essential equipment on board).

Fittings

There is an infinite variety of fittings and accessories for running rigging. A catalogue would take several pages and would be immediately out of date, because new types and gadgets are always being produced. We live in a world of gadgetry, where fashion plays a large part and a lot of money can be laid out – not always to good purpose.

So we will content ourselves with a brief selection of the principal fittings, and explain their use in the captions.

For simplicity, the items are grouped according to their different functions.

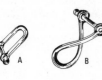

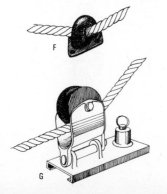

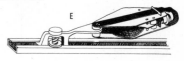

Shackles
A. D shackle
B. half-turn shackle
C. harp shackle
D. joggle shackle
E. snap shackle
F. spinnaker snap shackle

Blocks

A. *Single Block*
B. *Double block*. If it is to work well, the two sheaves must turn in the same direction but the snag is that they are not under the same strain and the block tends to twist
C. *Fiddle block*. As the falls of the tackle are in the same plane, the block does not twist, provided the sheaves are turning in the same direction
D. *Single block with becket and swivel*. The standing part of the tackle is made fast to the becket. If the becket has a swivel (as here) the block can settle in line with the pull.
E. *Ratchet block*. Used for dinghy sheets, it allows the crew a little respite. The sheave acts like a brake with adjustable power
F. *Fairlead*. Not noisy like a block as it does not knock the deck but it does offer more friction
G. *Roller fairlead*. This thumps the deck much less than a normal block and brings the sheet nearer the deck. When this roller fairlead is fitted to its track, the plunger that secures it fast must be on forward side or the sheet will chafe on it

Cleat

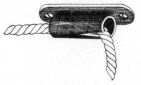

Trumpet cleat. Chews up rope. Seldom used since the invention of the clam cleat

Clam cleat. An inspired invention with no mechanism to go wrong, it holds well and is inexpensive but it has two faults: it gives some 5mm slack to the rope and therefore cannot be used for halyards; it tends to trap every rope that goes near it. To jam well, the rope must be allowed to fall a little as it comes out and there is something to be said therefore for mounting it on a base

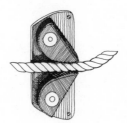

Tackles and winches

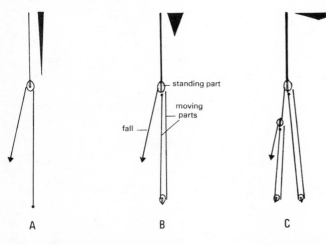

standing part

moving parts

fall

A   B   C

A. The power gained with this runner is double (less friction). The travel is long – by hauling in 1m of rope the tackle is shortened by 50cm
B. With a double whip the power gained is thrice. The travel is less – by hauling in 1m of rope the tackle is shortened by 33cm
C. With this Burton, the power gained is nine times but the haul is long

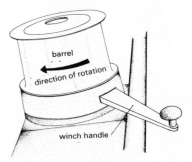

barrel

direction of rotation

winch handle

When a tackle is rigged, it is the standing part that is to be fixed to the becket of the top block which is rove through in clockwise manner

Halyards

A halyard should be:

> Light to reduce weight aloft to a minimum.
> Thin to reduce wind resistance. The drag of a halyard can be considerable especially if it does not lie hard up against the mast (a halyard which is 2in from the mast is tantamount to making the mast 2in wider).
> Subject to as little stretch as possible to keep the tautness of the sail constant.

There is only one textile which does not stretch appreciably: pre-stretched Dacron or Terylene. It tends to be hard, which is inconvenient, but it is lighter than wire and this is a big factor, particularly in small boats.

Generally speaking though, wire is the better answer for it is thin, has a high strength/weight ratio and does not stretch. It is, however, difficult and dangerous to use, and is best left to boats with winches. In some cases only the upper part of the halyard is wire and the fall is in synthetic rope.

Wire to Rope Joint

Wire and rope can be joined in different ways:

> The end of the wire has an eye splice, as does the end of the line or rope, and the two eyes are then joined by a shackle.
> The rope is spliced directly on to the eye of the wire (the join is thus permanent).
> The wire and rope or line are joined with a tail splice.

The last of the three methods above should be used when the length of the wire is limited (to ensure tautness in the sail as we shall see). For example, if the joint will not pass through the block at the masthead, the end of the wire, to which the head of the sail is attached, will not come down low enough to the deck for it to be reached. A thin joint must therefore be made without a shackle or eye.

Lengths

The fibre part of the halyard must be long enough for the end to be made fast to a cleat when the sail is lowered.

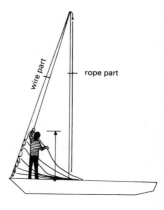

When the jib is handed it must be possible to reach the wire part of the halyard (which is attached to the sail); when it is hoisted the wire part must not reach the cleat

The wire part must come as low as possible so that, when the sail is hoisted, the splice is just above the cleat.

The length of the wire part of the halyard depends on the way the luff of the sail is stretched:

If a tackle is used, the wire should end up high enough to allow the tackle to be fitted between its end and the deck. You can only use a tackle with the first two kinds of joins mentioned above. You must be able to attach it to a shackle and, in the first method, this is already there; in the second a shackle must be fastened to the eye in the wire.

When the join is made with a splice, you must have a winch or some other means of hauling down the tack.

If a winch is used, the wire span must be long enough to enable at least two turns, or better four, to be taken on the drum.

Wear, Change of Halyard

The fibre part of the halyard does not wear evenly. The worst places are where the line bears on the sheave at the masthead or is wound round a winch or cleat. It is good economy to plan from the start to have halyards long enough so that you can shorten them when you have to cut out or shift areas that have worn. You can also reverse halyards end for end, so that the parts which run on the sheave and are cleated are relieved from wear and tear. Shorten or reverse the halyards long before they break. . . .

All wire halyards remain strong as long as they are treated well, but if they get wrapped round the forestay, or are allowed to kink, they will soon let you down.

Have spare halyards on board for a long cruise in one of these ways:

Have a wire a little longer than the longest of wire rope in use, fitted with an eye at one end. When required, it is cut to the correct length and a second eye fitted, either with a clamp or with a splice.

If the blocks are large enough, use a pre-stretched terylene rope temporarily.

Have a complete spare halyard ready for each sail.

Wire stored on board should be lightly greased and wrapped in rag.

Headsail Halyards

Headsail halyards are generally fastened to the sail with a snap shackle rather than an ordinary shackle, for it is well known how easy it is to lose the pin when changing sail. You can use a simple 'S' hook or shackle on dinghies.

Unless they run inside the mast, headsail halyards should be rigged on swivel blocks rather than fixed sheaves, so that they can be put to other uses, be they hoisting gear on board or holding the boat upright against the quay when you dry out. In the latter instance halyard and tackle might get strained if the block were rigid. Headsail halyards must be rigged forward of the spreaders or they can be jammed by the mainsail, especially when it is well out on a run.

Ways of Tightening Jib Halyards

Headsail halyards should nearly always be hoisted tightly. These are the usual ways.

Lever (fig. A). Hoist hard up, hook the end of the wire to the lever which then adds the last bit of tautness. This system is only for light dinghies.

Basic Tackle (fig. B). The rope part of the halyard is fitted with an eye with which you can form a tackle when the sail is hoisted. As soon as the eye can be reached, pass a bight of halyard through it at point P. Hitch the bight of the halyard thus formed round the cleat then bowse it down. When lowering sail, you have to ease the halyard slightly to free it from the cleat; never pass the end of the halyard back through the eye. This system works for jibs up to about 100 square feet.

Tackle (fig. C). Hoist hard up the cleat the halyard. The upper block of the tackle is then hooked into the shackle at the end of the wire part of the halyard, then bowsed down and made fast on the same cleat. Using the same cleat eliminates mistakes when lowering sail. Always make a figure of eight knot in the tackle fall so that it cannot unreeve through the block. This system works for jibs between 100 and 200 square feet.

Winch (fig. D). This is the simplest system to use. There are two types:

The bottom action winch is the simplest. The handle does not get in the way and, as it can stay fitted to the bottom of the winch barrel, there is no risk of losing it.

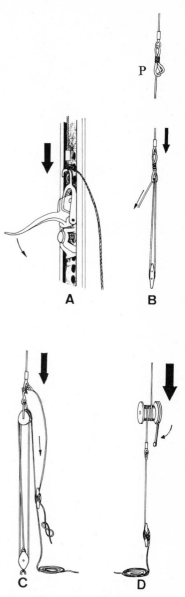

Four systems for sweating up the jib luff

The top action winch is not so convenient; the handle has to be taken off and on, but it can be extremely useful, particularly when a light (5mm) anchor line of about 300ft has to be hauled in.

On balance if you only have one winch, it is preferable to have a top action one. There are winches for all sizes of sail.

Hardening at the Tack

Hoist with an ordinary halyard and make fast on the cleat; then stretch from the tack of the sail with a tackle or a winch. This system has one great disadvantage: you get very wet crouching on the foredeck while trying to harden a number two jib or a storm jib. This method works for jibs up to 300 square feet.

Stretching at the Head and the Tack

When the luff of a jib is sleeved over a wire (or bolt rope), the wire must be hardened from the head, and the luff of the sail itself from the tack.

For complete tautness, the wire of the jib being stretched should reach as near as possible to the cleat and around the winch. Jibs with short luffs should therefore have head and tack pennants so that the snap shackle at the end of the halyard is always at the same point on the forestay.

Main and Mizzen Halyards

The end of the main halyard never has a snap shackle, because it cannot fit over the headboard; use a shackle.

Ways of Tightening Main Halyards

Some racing dinghies and other fast boats have a locking hook at the masthead, which is attached to the headboard by remote control. The halyard can then be extremely thin and light as it only serves to hoist the sail to the hook; the sail is then stretched from its tack. Obviously, with this system you cannot reduce sail by reefing.

On cruisers, as you have to lower sail as you reef, a different system is needed to stretch the luff.

Basic Tackle. This is only used on small boats if you can still reach the eye when the mainsail is *close reefed* (when you are reefed right down).

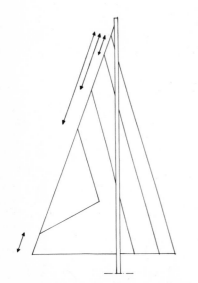

To ensure that the wire part of the halyard is always at the same height in relation to the cleat or winch, a wire extension is fitted to the head (and eventually to the tack also) of each of the small jibs

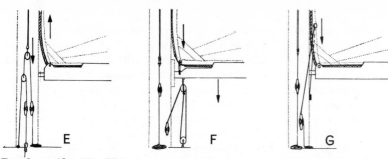

Three systems for sweating up the luff of the mainsail

Purchase (fig. E). This is an ancient system, still used on large boats. The mainsail is hoisted by a simple *purchase* (pulley with standing part and fall) and it is then stretched on a tackle with a block attached to the standing part of the halyard purchase): $2 \times 2 =$ four-fold power.

Winch. Stretching is done in the same way as with headsails, and here again if there is only one winch, it should be a top action one as we have already seen.

Reel Winch. The halyard is all wire, which rules out any possibility of stretch regardless of the number of reefs taken in. The main drawbacks are that it is not always easy to see that the wire rolls on to the drum evenly; the winch itself must be strong for if it breaks down you are in trouble for a wire halyard can only be made taut by a barrel winch).

Stretching at the Tack. The sail is first hoisted hard up and the halyard cleated. You can now stretch the luff in any one of three different ways:

Lower the boom of a small boat by hand and clamp the gooseneck hard on its track.
Lower the boom by pulling on a tackle or a winch (fig. F).
Without lowering the boom, pull down on the Cunningham eye (fig. G).

Sheets

Sheets should be:

Always of rope. They should for preference not be subject to stretch, and above all they should be easy and safe to handle.

Preferably of braided rope. Sheets are the most hard-used parts of the running rigging, and are subject to chafe over a great part of their length against lifelines, shrouds, turn buckles, winches, and even on non-slip deck coverings. Ordinary three-strand laid rope wears quickly and unravels easily; braided line (with its plaited sheath) stands up better to chafe.

Of sufficiently large diameter, because they have to withstand considerable, occasionally excessive strain.

And they must handle comfortably. On a small boat extremely thin sheets may have the necessary strength, but for handling you normally use rope of at least 1in circumference (⅜in diameter).

Headsail Sheets

Length. Each headsail should have two sheets at least as long as the foot of its jib plus the distance from the forestay to the fairlead. If the same sheet is used with several jibs, it must be measured on the largest jib using the furthest aft fairlead.

The two sheets are sometimes one length of line; the centre is attached to the clew and the two ends carried aft to the cockpit.

Continuous Sheet. On dinghies, you sometimes find a continuous sheet, which has its two ends fastened to the clew by bowlines and its whole length passes from one side of the cockpit to the other and back to the sail. The length of this kind of sheet should be measured with the jib boomed out and adding two feet of slack.

Fastening the Sheet to the Clew. The attachment of the sheet to the jib should be light and strong. The simplest method is to splice or knot the end of the sheet in the clew cringle, and this is usually adopted in boats with only one or two jibs, dinghies in particular.

But if the same sheet has to serve several jibs, you must be

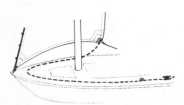

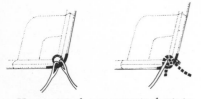

How to measure the length of the jib sheets

How to attach two separate sheets to the jib clew: either splice two eyes on the cringle or make a *fisherman's* knot

A knotted strop is a very good substitute for shackles on the jib clew. See photo 1 above. A loop made with an overhand knot (the simplest of all) and then some 20cm further on a figure of eight knot, in which the line is passed several times through itself.

The strop is seized on to the sheets (using palm and needle (photo 2)). To bend the sheets on to the jib clew (photo 3), the loop is passed through the cringle and then the stop knot through the loop. Obviously the stop knot must be big enough not to slip through the cringle

able to take it off easily. As light a shackle as possible is seized directly to the sheet, without a thimble to save weight. Snap shackles are not recommended, because not many stay closed when the jib clew has flogged from side to side a few times. There is no doubt that the best system is a *knotted strop*.

As on modern boats, the jib clew often almost touches the deck. The sheet attachment must be short enough to allow the clew to come as near as possible to the fairlead.

Chafe Prevention. To stop sheets wearing themselves out too quickly, watch out for chafe when they bear on the lower shrouds and all parts of the rigging. If you cannot remove the cause of chafe (by changing the position of a stanchion, for example), do your best to reduce it by fitting PVC tubes (which turn freely) over shrouds and bottle screws, and by using plastic covered lifelines.

Chafe is inevitable at sheet leads be they blocks or fairleads; but it can be minimised by using the right blocks which lie in the direction of pull, and also by using fairleads which are smooth and properly lined up.

Some non-slip deck coverings are another cause of chafe. You may be able to do without the non-slip surface along the natural line of the sheet.

As we know, like halyards, a sheet does not wear evenly and you can prolong its life by end for ending it in good time.

Rope Ends. It is as well to protect the ends of your sheets by sail-makers' whipping, above all when you are using braided line (the filaments shift easily underneath the sleeve). A figure of eight knot at the end will also help to hold sleeve and filaments together.

Mainsail and Mizzen Sheets

The mainsail sheet must have a powerful purchase to pull the boom in and out and, on small boats, to bend the mast and boom and to tighten the jib luff. It is easy enough to reeve a sheet with enough blocks to ease the strain which in any case is less than the pull of a headsail sheet.

Length. The sheet must be measured on deck. When the boom is eased out against the shroud, you should still have a fair length of sheet to spare.

Layout. The blocks should have large sheaves, and be well apart to allow the sheet to run smoothly and quickly. When it is necessary to have a block with two sheaves, a fiddle block (sheaves one above the other) rather than a sister block (sheaves alongside each other)

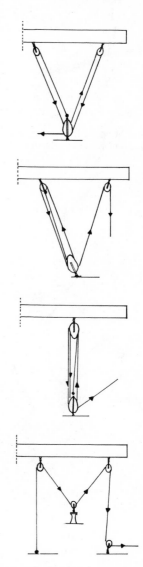

Four methods of setting up the main-sheet

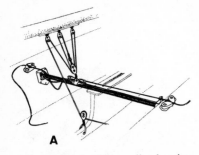

A

A horse fitted with a roller bearing traveller which can be adjusted under tension

is better. The sheaves of any one block should all turn in the same direction. Finally, blocks should swivel to suit the angle of stress wherever the boom may be.

Chafe. A mainsail sheet is most subject to wear when close hauled, and the section nearest to the blocks gives way first. By reversing the ends and later by shortening it, you can triple its life.

Ends. A main sheet should be seized at both ends. There is no need to splice the fixed end: a simple bowline is enough, and that undoes easily when you wish to reverse it.

Horse and Traveller

This fitment, a metal bar, allows the centre lower block of the mainsheet to slide athwartships. The block is attached to a metal traveller which runs on the bar. It permits the mainsail to be kept flat while being feathered in gusts.

There are three common types:

The *roller bearing traveller* slides on the horse even when the sheet is under tension – a desirable attribute. Its position can be controlled by two lines passing through jamming cleats (fig. A). The *sliding traveller* is perhaps better for large boats because of its strength. On certain models movement is improved by Tuphnol bearings. Movement of the traveller is limited on each tack by movable and adjustable lugs, but the lugs are liable to break if you gybe often.

A third is equally suited to small boats with simple rigging and to large craft. Movement of the traveller is limited either by a single line led to a jamming cleat at the centre of the boat (fig. B) or by two single lines taken to the ends of the rail. The drawback of this system is that the traveller cannot move when the sail is sheeted hard and on a large boat the lines wear quickly (though easy to replace).

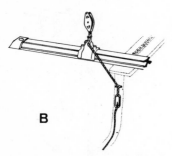

B

Horse with a sliding traveller

Mainsail Controls

Kicking Strap or Vang

To be effective, the kicking strap must be strong and not stretch. On dinghies and small cruisers it is taken from the boom to the base of the mast. As we have seen, it not only serves to keep the boom down on a reach but to some extent to bend the mast and boom. It can be a simple three- or four-part tackle, with synthetic rope, but this is subject to some stretch. It is usually made of wire pulled tight by a rope tackle. If the pull is not strong enough you can rig a second tackle on the fall of the first. A third solution is a small drum winch and the whole strap is then made of wire.

On larger boats the downhaul has to be movable and rigged vertically between the boom and strong points on the deck. It is then only for holding the boom down on a reach, and not for bending the spars.

This type of downhaul can also serve as a boom preventer, but it is risky when sailing downwind when an inadvertent gybe can break the boom. It is as well to rig a proper boom preventer.

Boom Preventer

This is a warp from the bow which, in a heavy sea and a following wind holds the boom out to stop it gybing.

It should be made fast on the boom near the main sheet. This gives it better purchase and lessens the danger of breaking the boom in case of a gybe or if you try to harden in the sheet and forget to release the preventer.

The forward end should be made fast so that it can be released under tension (on the bits use a round turn and a half hitch, or two round turns and a half hitch; on a cleat use figure of eight turns without a half hitch).

Topping Lift

A topping lift is useful on small boats and essential on large boats with heavy booms to allow the crew to lift the boom during operations such as reefing for example.

It also should be strong and without stretch so that the crew can lean hard on the boom without it lowering. It can be a synthetic rope or wire but, if it is wire, the part that touches the headboard must be fibre rope or it will chafe.

An extra advantage of having a stout topping lift is that it can serve as a spare main halyard or for hoisting a man up the mast.

Clew Outhaul

The clew outhaul holds the clew of the mainsail fast to the end of the boom. A simple lashing is adequate for small cruising boats and dinghies, but on larger boats it is convenient to be able to regulate

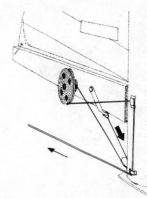

When the rope tail unrolls off the large drum, the wire kicking strap rolls up on the small drum

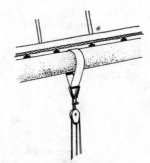

Kicking strap for a large boat

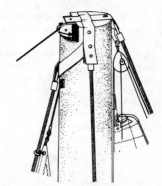

The topping lift (between backstay and mast) is chafing the headboard of the mainsail. All that is needed to stop this is a larger block. Note how the spinnaker halyard block is fitted on the forward edge of the mast to let it swing through 180°

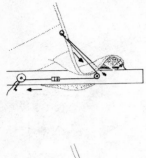

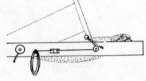

A. (*above*) The standing part of the reef pendant is made fast on the starboard side of the boom, it is rove through the cringle, round a bee-block and through a clam cleat. It is then tightened in on the small winch.

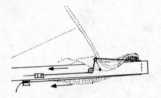

(*below*) Once the reef is taken in, the winch is made free for the next reef.
B. Here the pendant is double. One of the pendants passes round the end of the boom and is used for tightening the foot. The other passes round a beeblock and through a clamcleat. It is used for bringing the clew cringle down to the boom

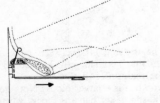

If there is no hook at the tack, a pendant will serve

the tension on the foot of the sail while under way, without having to alter course. One method is to have an outhaul fitting that slides on a short track. This can be moved out or eased by screw adjuster or a rope passing round a sheave at the end of the boom and back to a small tackle or winch also on the boom.

Reef Pendants

Some boats still employ this traditional method of reefing. Reef pendants are the clew outhauls for each reef. While being soft enough to be knotted, these pendants must be hard enough not to stretch; Dacron or Terylene line is the most suitable material.

At the clew various types of pendant may be used.

On small boats by 3 metres (10ft) of line, whipped at each end, and taken directly round the boom. Something more elaborate is needed on larger boats. (In the United States and UK roller or slab reefing is normal.) Much the simplest method is shown in fig. A where the cringle is pulled down to the boom by tightening the reef pendant, stretching the foot at the same time. To make this system work well, the bee-blocks must be positioned precisely for if they are too far forward the foot will not be pulled hard enough; and if they are too far aft, the clew will not be pulled hard down to the boom. If the position of the bee-blocks is adjustable, so much the better.

The system shown in fig. B, which is a little more complicated, has the advantage of tension on the foot being adjustable under sail. Also, even if the reef cringles alter position as the sail grows older, it is still not necessary to move the bee-blocks.

Both systems will only work satisfactorily if the bee-blocks are fixed low on the boom.

Tackles can be used to haul down the tack cringle but this means a tackle for every reef band and consequently the boom gets cluttered up with gear. It is better to use a winch.

The reef pendants can be made fast to standard cleats but they are not very practical as they tend to catch other lines. Jamming cleats or clancleats are preferable and should be placed as near as possible to the clew to cut stretch in the reef pendant to a minimum. Hooks are better than pendants *at the tack*, because the tack cringle is then hooked straight on to one of these; they are essential when the boom is fitted to a sliding gooseneck.

If there are no hooks, you can pass a pendant through the boom (fig. C). There are other ways of doing it depending on the size and shape of the spars, but there is one golden rule: never allow a reef pendant to get caught in the gooseneck, for it will not last long that way.

Reef Points

These light cords fixed permanently to the sail, hold the loose cloth after a reef has been hauled down. Certain fluffy polypropylene lines are excellent for this purpose. A reef point should be long enough to allow the tying of a slip reef knot around the sail. Always pass the reef points between sail and boom if possible.

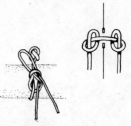

The fastening of a reefing point through the eyelet and round the boom

Spinnaker Gear

Spinnaker Halyards

Stretch in a spinnaker halyard is much less of a headache than in other halyards.

On small boats, a synthetic rope halyard is the norm. It should be rove through a nylon *bullseye fairlead* at the masthead to allow it to take the strain of the sail through 180° and should be of a reasonably large circumference because it wears on the bullseye fairlead; braided line is preferable to three strand cordage, because the lay of the latter can open under tension and twist the head of the spinnaker as it is hoisted.

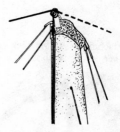

Good: the fairlead is well placed and all runs clear; but this system only works when the halyard is all-fibre

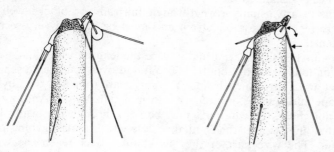

Bad: the crane is not offset to keep the halyard clear and it will chafe against the forestay

The stretch factor cannot be ignored on larger boats: as it stretches, the halyard lets the head of the sail rise and fall with considerable wear on the block. To combat this and minimise chafe, use halyards which are half wire and half synthetic line,

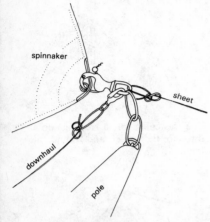

The attachments at the tack of the spinnaker on a large boat

The plunger of the snap shackle is often hard to move specially with cold fingers. Fitted with a short line it is easier to get a grip. The line must be very short and single (a double one catches on everything and is liable to open the shackle). A knot at the free end gives better purchase still

but reeved through a block which can swivel freely without the halyard rubbing on the mast or rigging; it is best to mount it on a crane to keep it free from the mast.

The halyard should be attached to the head of the spinnaker with a swivel to let the head of the sail unwind if the halyard twists during hoisting.

When you hoist a biggish spinnaker of more than 400–500sq ft, be ready to take a turn of the halyard on a winch if the sail fills too soon.

Spinnaker Sheets and Guys

Spinnaker gear includes two sheets. When in use the windward one is called the guy and the one to leeward the sheet.

These ropes are usually synthetic on boats of medium size and under, where the spinnaker is controlled by hand. They should stretch as little as possible and be large enough to handle comfortably; braided line is better than laid rope and use light lines in fair weather.

In dinghies and small daysailers, sheets and guys may be permanently attached to the spinnaker. On larger boats use oval-jawed snap shackles (which can be opened under load). These shackles should be swivelled to prevent kinking in the sheets/guys and have two rings attached which the down haul and spinnaker pole can be hanked on to.

Sheets are usually rove through fairleads or blocks well aft. These blocks take a big strain and must be big and very securely fastened.

Spinnaker sheets are usually twice the length of the boat.

For spinnakers of about 1,000sq ft and over you need a separate sheet and a guy on each side. The sheets are rope and the guys are $\frac{1}{2}$ rope and $\frac{1}{2}$ wire for strength and minimal stretch. And, as they do not chafe, the wire guys may be rove through the piston hank at the outer end of the spinnaker pole which makes gybing much easier. The wire part of the guy should never reach the winch, whatever the position of the spinnaker pole, to avoid difficult handling and damaged fingers.

Spinnaker Pole Downhaul

The downhaul stops the spinnaker pole from skying up.

Depending on the size of spinnaker, there are three different arrangements. On dinghies and with any spinnaker less than about

250sq ft, the downhaul is made fast to the centre of the spinnaker pole and runs by the foot of the mast to the cockpit. With spinnakers between 250–500sq ft, the load is greater and the downhaul is attached to a bridle to ease the pole and lessen the chance of breaking or buckling. These two systems allow the pole to be eased or squared aft without adjusting the downhaul.

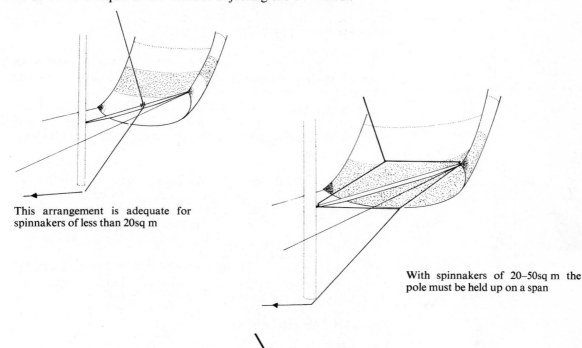

This arrangement is adequate for spinnakers of less than 20sq m

With spinnakers of 20–50sq m the pole must be held up on a span

Spinnakers of more than 50sq m must have a topping lift and a down-haul bent on to the end of the pole

The downhaul in a big boat is made fast to a ring on the guy (at the end of the pole) and then runs back aft via a block at the bow. With this arrangement, as you cannot change the spinnaker pole about without altering the downhaul, you need one for each tack. They are more or less the same length as sheets and of marginally smaller diameter; in practice, old sheets can serve as downhauls.

Spinnaker Pole Topping Lift

The topping lift holds the pole up.

A simple piece of shockcord is good enough for spinnakers up to about 150sq ft (the level of the pole end is controlled by the downhaul).

For spinnakers between 150–300sq ft, obviously stronger elastic must be used, with a check line to stop the pole dropping too low.

For spinnakers bigger than this, use a rope topping lift, large enough to handle well.

Like the downhaul, the topping lift can be rigged in three different ways. In the centre of the pole or on a bridle for small spinnakers – both allow the same topping lift to be used on each tack (provided the pole is symmetrical). When the spinnaker is larger, the topping lift should be made fast to the end of the pole, and this means two topping lifts – all the more necessary as two spinnaker poles are usually carried.

To make it easy to work, the topping lift should be rove through a pulley well up the mast – about two-thirds of the way. On a cutter the block should not be above the lower forestay.

Spinnaker Pole Heel Fitting

On dinghies and small daysailers, the spinnaker pole fitting is fixed on the mast and cannot be adjusted for height. A track is used on slightly larger boats. The track has a slide which is moved by hand and locked by a thumbscrew. Finally, on large boats where the spinnaker pole is too heavy to manhandle a rope hoist is used. This is made fast to the spinnaker pole cup fitting, is rove through a block at the top of the track and returns to the cup fitting; a single control therefore ensures up and down adjustment of the pole on the mast.

There is a still simpler system: a bicycle chain passing over a cogwheel and worked by a handle. The only drawback is that the chain is not stainless but it is not expensive and can always be changed every year or even several times a season.

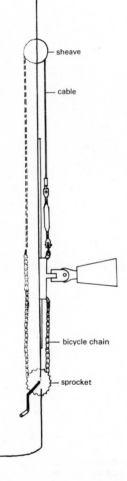

sheave

cable

bicycle chain

sprocket

The only disadvantage is the chain rusts

Sails

The Sail Wardrobe

The number of sails required depends less on the size of boat than on the kind of sailing she has to do. The more ambitious the sailing, the more sails you need; and they are expensive.

There are all kinds of sails for all kinds of rigs and each can be useful as long as you know how to use it. Happily they are not all essential so let us look at the basic ones.

Dinghy Racing. A mainsail, a jib and, usually, a spinnaker. If you have a fat wallet you can have several suits of these three sails of sizes to suit different wind strengths. You have to choose which set to use before setting off from the shore.

Daysailing and Fishing. A mainsail, a jib, a storm jib if you don't have a roller jib.

Local Sailing. A mainsail, a No. 1 jib, a storm jib and a staysail for cutters. Genoa and spinnaker are desirable but not essential.

Coastal Cruising. A mainsail, a genoa, a No. 1 jib, a storm jib; if possible a No. 2 jib, a spinnaker and a trysail. For cutters add one or, better still, two staysails.

Deep Sea Cruising. A mainsail, a trysail, a spinnaker, a genoa, a No. 1 jib, a No. 2 jib, a storm jib; for cutters, two staysails.

Offshore Racing. A mainsail, a trysail and all the jibs and spinnakers required to set all sail the boat can carry in every kind of weather.

We are only speaking here of the simplest rigs and the more usual sails without mention of the mizzen, mizzen staysail and spinnaker staysail.

Sailmaking

Cloth

Sailcloth is made up of two bands of interwoven threads; the longitudinal one called the warp and the transverse one, the weft. Sailcloth must naturally be strong and above all must keep its

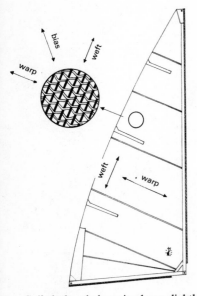

Sail cloth only loses its shape slightly when cut along the weave (warp and weft) but a good deal more if cut on the bias. Every effort is made to arrange the cloths so that they take the strain on the weave

shape. There should be as little distortion as possible either across the warp or across the weft or diagonally along the bias but this last is difficult to obtain.

The weight of the cloth is chosen according to the size of the sail and the use it will be put to; a heavier cloth is used for heavy-weather sails rather than for light-weather sails. Weight of cloth is calculated by ounces per square metre in Great Britain and per yard $\times$ 28½in in the USA; this results in the American weight for a particular cloth being apparently 20% lighter than the British designation for precisely the same cloth.

Until the 1950s sails were made of cotton. Nowadays they are all made of polyamide or polyester.

Polyamide. This is nylon which is both elastic and strong. It is used for downwind and reaching sails (spinnakers, spinnaker staysails).

These are all very light sails; in the seventies they were made of material as light as half an ounce (quarter of an ounce in the US) and they will no doubt be even less in the future. For the moment, at all events, the normal range of cloth weight in nylon is ½–3 ounces.

Polyester. This is used for all other sails. Cloth weight ranges from 2–13 ounces, and it is sold under different trade names, depending on the country where it is made, as follows:

Dacron	USA
Terylene	Great Britain
Tergal	France
Tetoron	Japan
Polyant	Germany
Terital	Italy
Lavsan	Russia, etc.

Some sailmakers weave their own cloth – Hood for example uses Dacron thread, while Ratsey and Lapthorn produce Vectis cloth from Terylene.

Polyester cloths are coated with a finishing agent – well, slightly or hardly at all. Dacron is available in all three finishes; Terylene may be lightly finished or not at all; Tetoron is usually heavily finished and Tergal either heavily or slightly.

The finishing agent prevents the cloth from stretching. A tightly woven one has little need of it, but a slack cloth may need a lot. Thus, certain very light cloths which have been woven loosely are heavily coated with the sort of resinous material. The stiffness

Different weights of cloth in relation to types of sail and use

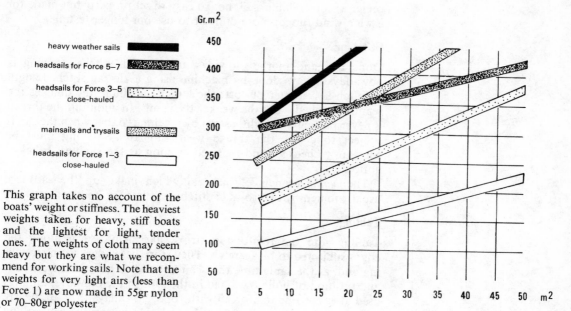

heavy weather sails

headsails for Force 5–7

headsails for Force 3–5
close-hauled

mainsails and trysails

headsails for Force 1–3
close-hauled

Gr.m^2

450
400
350
300
250
200
150
100
50

0   5   10   15   20   25   30   35   40   45   50   m^2

This graph takes no account of the boats' weight or stiffness. The heaviest weights taken for heavy, stiff boats and the lightest for light, tender ones. The weights of cloth may seem heavy but they are what we recommend for working sails. Note that the weights for very light airs (less than Force 1) are now made in 55gr nylon or 70–80gr polyester

of this coating can be felt (only relative, because the layer is obviously extremely thin) as well as its brittleness.

Heavily treated cloth can be recognised by its hard finish; when it is folded, white lines appear at the creases, as the dressing cracks. The finishing material has a low inherent strength of its own and it does not resist weathering well. It is thus pointless to have heavy-weather sails made from thickly dressed cloth.

Heavily finished sails do, however, have their uses if they are only used in light weather and, above all, if they can be stowed without being tightly folded. Such sails are slightly less expensive than others and they hold their shape well when used in the appropriate wind strength. If they are used in heavy weather, the dressing breaks down quickly and the sails pull badly out of shape.

The choice of cloth is so wide it is best left to the sailmaker; but talk things over with him when ordering a sail, for there are some decisions which can only be taken by the owner. Some will ask for a 'moulded' sail, or one that has a tailored shape, easy to set and use in light weather, in the knowledge that it will have to

On the top rows the stitches are small. One keeps the cloths together, the other holds the seam down. On the lower two rows the stitches are large and are all for keeping the cloth together – and there are not over-many of them. The seam is not stitched down and there is every likelihood of the cloth fraying

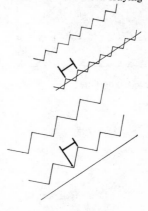

be quickly replaced if it is used in too strong a wind. Another will prefer a 'controllable' sail, not so easy to set properly but made for a wide wind range; more difficult to use but longer-lasting.

Stitching

Done by hand in the old days, using small stitches, sewing is nowadays always done by machine using a zig-zag stitch. Length of stitch is a matter of cost: the larger the stitch, the quicker the seam is finished – but the weaker the result. In addition, the thread is never particularly tightly sewn by machine so that when the sail is subject to chafe, the thread wears quickly. Stitching must be constantly checked, and repaired as soon as the slightest break is noticed.

The *cloths* (panels of material which make up the sail) are usually joined by two rows of stitching; three for boats of any size.

Tablings

Tablings are the reinforcing strips, like hems, sewn along the edges subjected to bias stretch. They stop these edges from stretching and, at the same time they can be used to control the amount and position of hollow wanted in the sail. In the old days, tablings used always to be reinforced with rope; nowadays they are nearly always made of tape or strips of sailcloth sewn on the ways along the edge of the sail. To these tablings is added either a wire (for jib luffs), or rope (for some mainsails). The purpose of wire is to keep the luff straight; that of rope is solely to hold the sail in the mast groove.

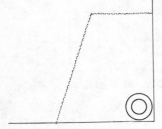

Mainsail tack and cringle

Cringles

There are three kinds of eye: punched, hand sewn and traditional cringles.

Punched Eyes are grommets punched into the sail. They will not withstand much strain because they pull away from the cloth easily.

Handsewn Eyes on the other hand, can withstand considerable strain. Cunningham eyes and reef cringles in particular should certainly be hand sewn. Machine sewing only holds moderately well since the thread is not tight enough; done by hand, sewing is much stronger but obviously costs more.

Traditional Cringles are rope eyes formed on the outside of the bolt rope round a thimble. They are not always used these days, and are being replaced by triangles or rings held by webbing at

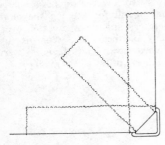

Jib clew (triangular)

the edge or corner of the sail. Cringles, triangles and rings are all stronger than handsewn eyes.

Reinforcing Patches

A sail should be reinforced where it will be subjected to particular strain. As an example, let us examine the clew of a spinnaker.

Suppose that the weight on the clew eye is 1,000lb and that an inch of material can withstand 50lb. If half the circumference of the eye is 2in, ten thicknesses of cloth are needed if the eye is not to tear out.

A bit further into the sail, where a seam 4in long can be sewn, only five thicknesses are needed so that an effective 20in of cloth are available. Where the seam measures 7in, only three thicknesses are needed, and so on until the point is reached where the last two thicknesses are sewn over the arc of a circle 20in in length.

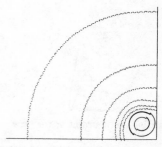

Spinnaker clew

A reinforcing patch is, therefore, more than merely an extra support; it is vital and the slightest piece of stitching which comes undone should be repaired immediately.

Sail Shape

Like a woman's bosom, a sail should:

Have a certain roundness. Flat as a plank, the sail will not deflect the airflow properly.
Keep its shape, whatever the strain on it.

Roundness (or belly) is achieved by shaping the panels by tapering their sides according to the curve required, by taking in tucks or darts at the appropriate places, or by adding curve to the luff or foot. The curve should not, however, be excessive or the leech curls over and does not allow the deflected air to escape.

The shape is kept by laying the cloths in such a manner that the heaviest pull always comes along the weft of the cloth. There are several ways of achieving this as we shall see.

Mainsails

There are two principal problems in making a mainsail:

The first is the leech. This is not supported and yet it must not curl over. It is nevertheless subject to considerable stress, particularly when closehauled.

If it is to keep its shape, it should be cut on the weft. The cut of the seams make this feasible. The other problem is matching curved sails to straight spars.

Sail Cutting

The most usual cuts are as follows:

Sail A. This is the traditional cut: the seams run at right angles to the leech (not allowing for the round at the roach), letting the weft take most of the strain. This is the cheapest cut and the most common.

With this type of sail, the foot is made to fit the boom by sewing darts into the seams. These, even though they may be large, sometimes do not give enough draught and it is sometimes better to shape the foot panels by, for example, cutting the two bottom seams on the twist; these are then sewn together along their rounded edges, which gives all the hollow you want.

Sail B. With this cut you have seams cut at right angles to the foot as well as to the leech. Bending the sail to the boom is a little tricky as it is designed to be loose footed along the boom allowing the belly to be easily controlled. The bottom of the sail is of very light cloth, loosely stitched, and prevents air from escaping between sail and boom.

Sail C. Here also the foot is cut on the straight along the foot and this helps the sail to keep its shape. The drawback is that these sails are expensive, because cutting the cloths needs skilled and meticulous workmanship and entails wasting a lot of material.

Distribution of strains at the clew

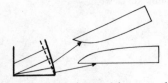

How darts are inserted between the cloths

Cutting for fullness at the foot

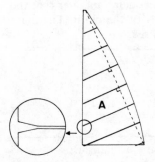

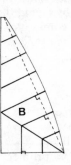

The Luff

Darts and tapered cloths alone cannot ensure good draught in a mainsail. The luff must also be curved.

With the mainsail which is designed to set on a rigid mast, this curve of the luff must run the whole length. Large near the foot, because the sail is biggest there, reaching its maximum one-fifth of the way up. Very reduced near the head, it must nevertheless still be enough for the sail to have some belly when it is reefed.

The curve of the luff on a mainsail designed for a flexible mast must allow for the maximum mast bend. The shape of the luff then requires nice judgement, because the mast does not bend evenly over its full height:

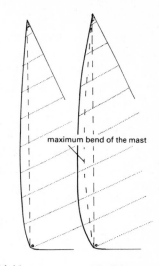

maximum bend of the mast

Rigid mast   Flexible mast

Mast bend is even as far as the forestay. The curve in the luff varies according to the size of sail, being large near the foot and reducing evenly upwards.
At about the hounds, mast bend is more pronounced, so the curve in the luff should begin to increase again.
The masthead bends little, so luff curve here is much reduced, particularly because the head of the sail should be completely flat in heavy weather.

The Leech

Reinforcement is reduced at the leech, as we have seen, to keep it from curling over. At the most, a light tabling is sewn on, not too tightly.

Battens hold-up the roach, where the sail lies outside a straight line from the head to the clew. The battens should be very flexible at their inner ends to allow the sail to take up its shape; they should be progressively stiffer towards the leech.

The top batten is sometimes taken right across the sail to press against the mast. This is called a full length batten. It augments roach at the leech and consequently affects the sail area. A full length batten must be flexible, so that it does not stop the sail taking up its natural shape, and the inner end of its pocket must be reinforced. When the wind is weak the stiffness of a full-length batten gives the sail that extra bit of curve which a light wind cannot give unaided.

Battens are made of wood or plastic (nylon or polyester). Wooden ones are cheap but break easily if they are thin enough to bend sufficiently or, if you want them to be strong, they are too stiff. Nylon battens are more expensive, but they are flexible and

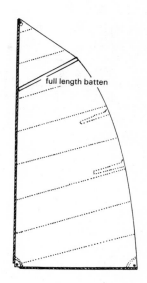

full length batten

strong; you can alter their thickness, and thus their flexibility, with a hot iron.

The Foot and Reefs

Shape is not quite so tricky at the foot as it is at the luff. It has an even curve of between 1.5% to 10% at the foot length. This curve dictates, to some extent, the fullness of the sail.

When sail is reduced, it is one of the rows of reef points which becomes the foot. There should therefore be a small amount of curve along each line of reef points but less than on the normal foot because it is a flat sail that is now wanted. The luff and leech reef cringles should have the same reinforcing patches as the tack and clew.

The Three Corners of the Sail

The Tack, which is not subjected to very heavy stresses, is not particularly strongly reinforced.

The Clew takes heavy strains (which run parallel to the leech), so the clew cringle must be worked on several thicknesses of cloth. When the foot rope runs in a boom groove, the canvas tends to tear between the clew cringle and the bolt rope, so you should always lash the clew round the boom as well as out to the end.

The Head chafes first between the headboard and the luff rope when the sail runs in a mast groove. Keep an eye on it, and have it repaired immediately if it shows signs of wear.

Vertical strain, which is considerable, is taken by the headboard. The tendency to pull away from the mast at the head is relatively slight but nevertheless, if the luff runs with slides on a track, ensure that the top slide is particularly strong (made fast with a shackle, for example). When the bolt rope runs in a luff groove, a slug slide may be placed on the halyard itself.

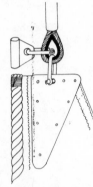

A slide attached to the halyard prevents the head board pulling away

Jibs and Staysails

Sail Cutting

In jibs as in mainsails, the seams can be cut in different ways. Jibs have two free edges, which should both be cut on the straight. The most usual cuts are as follows:

Sail A. This cut is suitable for small jibs, provided that the clew angle is near to 90° and that the seams strike the leech at right angles. This cut gives only a moderately good sail.

Sail B. The cloths are at right angles to the leech for most of the way, and the bottom cloth is parallel to the foot. Resistance to stretch is improved.

Sails C and D. When the sail is too big for any foot bias to be accepted, the seams are laid at right angles to the foot and leech, and meet at the seam which bisects the angle of the clew. This cut is used for yankees (sail D) and most genoas.

Sail E. The seams radiate from the clew, and the weft of the cloth is always on the line of strain. This is wasteful in labour and material.

The Luff

If the jib is to match the sag of its stay properly, the luff must be shaped differently in light and heavy weather sails.

While the stay is straight – in light weather – there is merit in having a jib with a rounded luff, so that the sail has belly in spite of the straightness of the stay. On the other hand, when the forestay bends to leeward as the wind gets up, curve in the luff becomes an embarrassment, because the belly in the sail made by the curve in the stay exaggerates what has already been produced by the curve in the luff. You should then use a jib with a straight luff. If the wind goes on increasing, the forestay bends even more and you must change jibs again, this time choosing one with a hollow luff.

Some sailmakers cut the luff of genoas in an S form, to shape the sail to best advantage: this gives it luff curve low down (when the genoa is broad and needs considerable belly – not so much aloft where the sail is narrow and needs to be relatively flat). The same result can be achieved with larger darts lower down than higher up.

Darts are essential in heavy weather sails with hollowed luffs. Without them, these sails would be completely flat and have too little power.

The Leech

The leech is not reinforced, usually having a strip of material sewn on as a light tabling or hem. As it is not easy to fit battens to a jib, it has no roach: the leech is straight on light weather jibs and hollow on heavy weather sails.

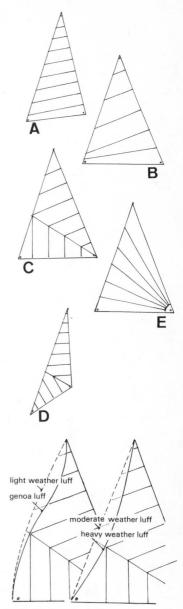

Each jib has its luff cut to suit the weather it is designed for

The Foot

The foot of a jib is generally straight or slightly hollow. A light weather sail can be given a little curve – sometimes even a lot when the extra depth acts as a kind of skirt which touches the deck and stops air currents passing under the sail and equalising pressure on both sides.

The foot of a large or Yankee jib is made like its leech.

The Three Corners of the Foresail

The luff of a jib should always be set up hard and so at the head and the tack it must be strong.

The jib also stretches tautly between its luff and the clew. The latter is the most abused single point of the whole sailplan; it is subject to the heaviest strain of all and it chafes against the rigging and is always being flogged by the wind. It needs to be particularly well made.

Although the tack and head suffer less strain they should nevertheless also be reinforced. If the jib is to be well set, the top and bottom hanks should be close to the head and tack respectively. As they work harder than the rest, these two fittings should be resewn frequently.

Spinnakers

Cloth

All spinnakers are made of nylon, light or not so light according to the size of the sail and the force of wind it is designed to meet. It follows that reaching spinnakers are of slightly heavier cloth than running spinnakers so that they do not too readily lose their shape.

Cloth Weight (French)	Size of Spinnaker all sizes	Max. Wind Force
$\frac{1}{2}$–$\frac{3}{4}$ oz	all sizes	force 1
1oz	100–500 sq ft	force 5
	500–750 sq ft	force 3
1$\frac{1}{2}$–2oz	500–750 sq ft	force 7
	750–1,500 sq ft	force 4
3oz	650–1,500 sq ft	force 7

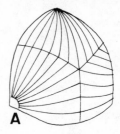

Sail cutting

Spinnaker designs are numerous (you only have to watch the start of a race downwind to see this). In general, the aim is to lay the cloths so that the sail will take up good shape and not be too easily stretched, particularly at the leeches. Sailmakers thus tend to cut the cloth to run parallel to the edges; some of them, however, prefer to keep the leeches slightly on the bias for reasons of shape and sewing.

The most usual patterns are as follows:

Sail A. Seams radiate from the three corners (star-cut) and is good for keeping the sail's shape.

Sail B. Seams are at right angles to the leeches. These sails have two distinct sections: the upper cloths, separated by a seam down the middle, are placed at right angles to the leeches, while the lower cloths are horizontal.

Sail C. The middle of the sail is cut on the straight of the fabric. The sailmaker accepts some bias on the upper and lower leech (the leech seams at the mid-way point lie parallel to each other).

Sail D. A composite style with a radial cut at the head and horizontal cloths in the lower half.

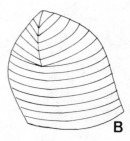

All these solutions have their advantages and drawbacks. The present tendency seems to be to avoid patterns that have bias on the leeches, because poor shape there stops a smooth flow of air across the spinnaker.

Spinnaker Shape

To set well, a spinnaker should be shaped more or less like a half-cylinder, capped by quarter of a sphere. The head of the sail should lie almost horizontally, for the deeper the bulge of the sail at the head, the greater is its lift. The shape of the head affects the set of the whole sail: when the middle part does not look well, the fault often lies in the cut of the head area.

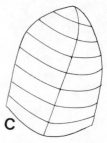

Spinnakers have many shapes, like other sails. As you sail ever closer to the wind, or as the wind freshens, so you should use flatter and flatter spinnakers which have the advantage of spilling wind more quickly if you broach to.

Certain spinnakers are specialist sails and are particularly efficient under precise conditions of wind force and direction. When cruising, it is better to use a general purpose sail, whose efficiency is average on all points of sailing.

Edges

The three corners of a spinnaker have to be well reinforced, because

all the strains are concentrated at those points.

The leeches are usually only reinforced with tape which must stretch equally with the sail, or leech curl will result.

Although the foot often chafes on the pulpit and forestay, it has little protection, for to build in reinforcement would create a 'hard' area in an essentially 'soft' sail. It is therefore generally here that the first repair patches appear.

Repair and Maintenance

Wear and Tear

If you want to keep your sails for a long time, you must be constantly on the watch for chafe, which is inevitable no matter how well you treat them. Whatever the sails rub on should be as smooth as possible and all sharp snags must certainly be removed. Encase the lower ends of shrouds with rollers or plastic tubing, wrap split pins with adhesive tape, parcel spreader ends or fit anti-chafe discs or other protectors.

You can also reduce sail-chafe by taking sailing precautions: keep the jib off liferails, the mainsail from between the boom and the lower shrouds, the spinnaker clew off the forestay – to mention only three.

Finally, remember that the boat moves, even when it is moored. A jib left on the forestay and not lashed tight, a mainsail caught between the boom and the crutch – all such instances cause damage. It is therefore better always to take sails off in harbour, as in particular this will reduce their exposure to ultra-violet rays which make the fabric deteriorate after a time.

Drying and Storing

Although they are virtually rot-proof, synthetic sails should be dried and stowed carefully.

A wet sail can quite well stay one or two days in a sailbag, but it should be dried out as soon as possible, or it will eventually produce a rash of black spots.

It is a good idea to rinse your sails occasionally in fresh water; when a sail dries after being soaked in seawater, salt crystals remain behind in the weave where they get to work like an abrasive quite as harmful as sand.

How to Rinse Sails. By working them in a tub preferably of fresh water, but even a salt-water rinse, after a day's outing in fresh sunny conditions gets the worst of the saline crystals out.

How to Dry Sails. Ashore, you can hang up or spread them on the grass (never on sand, cement or asphalt which can abrade them). Avoid all unnecessary exposure to the sun.

On the mooring, you can hoist them aloft by the tack, but only in little or no wind, because a sail will suffer ten times more from thrashing about in the wind than from being stowed wet in a bag.

At sea, when you have wet sails in the locker (usually small, heavy weather sails) you wait for the moment when you can set them, either in their usual place or else decoratively with other sails when the wind is free.

How to Store Sails. When sails are stored for any length of time, they should be folded loosely, put in a dry place, and protected from light and the attention of rats. And make sure that the family realises that sails must not be ironed or folded neatly, in squares.

Repairs to Stitching

As soon as the first stitches of a seam begin to go, you should get out the needle and thread because repairs will be easy while it is only a question of fixing a few stitches, and much more of a job when the seams themselves begin to move.

Depending on the weight of cloth, you can re-sew a sail with a domestic sewing machine using a zig-zag stitch. This usually works up to about 6oz cloth; above that weight you will have to sew by hand.

At sea, rather than take a sewing machine, it is better to have a member of the crew who is handy with needle and palm. He only needs minimal gear: needles, cotton thread, beeswax and a palm.

Use No. 17 sailmakers' needles for cloth heavier than 7oz, No. 18 needles for cloth between about 4–7oz and a No. 19 or a domestic needle for anything lighter.

Cotton thread is easier to use than synthetic. Wax is used on the thread not to protect it, but to stop it snarling up in the sewing. *Always sew with the thread doubled to fill up the holes made by the needle.*

Sticking a Patch

It is hard for an amateur to sew a patch over a large tear as expertly as a sailmaker. Sticking is much easier and, if the sail is going to

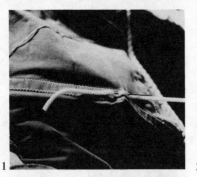

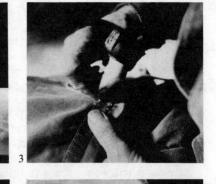

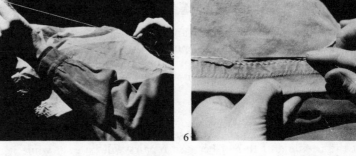

1. When repairing a seam you sit down with the sail placed double on your knees. Above, the sail has been fastened to a point on the right to enable the cloth to be pulled out tight as you work. Sewing is done from right to left, with an oversewn slanting stitch (round seaming), at an angle of some 30° to the edge of the cloth

2. A sailmaker's palm enables the needle to be pushed through the cloth without hurting the hand. The needle must be held as shown in the photograph

3. You begin your stitch just outside the part of the seam that has parted. Shove the needle through the sail. Then lift the needle gently up to free it from the under layer of cloth (you must hear its scrape at each stitch)

4. Push the needle with the palm until you can pull it from the other side of the seam

5. Once the needle is right out, pull hard on the thread with the left hand. Then start again

6. Make twelve stitches per needle length

At the first opportunity have your handiwork admired or criticised by a sailmaker

be subjected to heavy wear, the patch can then be strengthened with a few stitches.

Adhesive plaster from the first aid box can serve as an emergency patch, but there is special adhesive tape made for the purpose. At a pinch ordinary sail cloth can be made to stick if you use any appropriate adhesive.

Whatever you use, the patch will not stick to the sail unless both sail and patch are clean and dry. The surface can be dried quickly by wrapping it round a bottle of boiling water.

Spread the sail flat, with the two halves of the tear fitting together. The patch is then laid on the sail with the lines of the weave of each matched up. If you warm the patch (with the same hot bottle), it will stick better.

It goes without saying that this kind of repair is only temporary.

Stitching on a Hank

 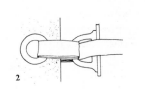

Use double nylon thread. Make eight loops on one side of the luff wire, then four on the other. Serve the eight loops against chafe

Stitching on a Slide

1   2   3

Fastening a slide with webbing: 1. Attach the webbing with a running stitch. 2. Pass the webbing through both eyes three or four times. 3. Finish off with a running stitch

It is easier with thread but not so strong

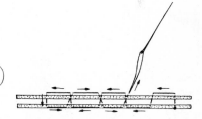

A running stitch

Darning

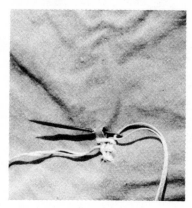 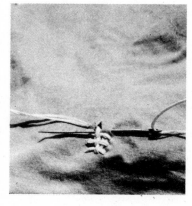

A darn can be used for small tears of not more than 3–4cm. Sew from right to left as follows: the needle is passed down through the tear up through the cloth on the left. It is passed back over the tear and stabbed through again on the right, and comes up through the tear and behind the previous stitch. The latter is therefore secured under the next stitch. The darn is begun and finished a little before the start and end of the tear. Two or three stitches are made to the centimetre. Each stitch is 1–1.5cm wide

Sails or Tarpaulins?

The best sails will soon become shapeless and only good for keeping the rain off the hay:

> If you do not make the adjustments they require to fit the rig properly without delay.
> If you set them badly.
> If you set them in winds too strong or on the wrong point of sailing.
> If you let them chafe.
> If you do not get your sailmaker to check over temporary repairs at the earliest possible moment.
> If you store them in bad conditions.

5. The Hull

We have dwelt at length on rigs and rigging because the yachtsman often has a choice when it comes to the gear he wants for his boat, and how to install and maintain it. There is obviously less freedom of choice with the hull of the boat but a little background knowledge does not come amiss. You don't need to know exactly how a hull is made to be a good skipper, but you must know its weak points, which you should inspect when you buy the boat and then regularly throughout the season. It is equally important to know how to do routine maintenance, how to fix snags as they occur at sea and to be able to undertake running repairs that do not require the help of a specialist. This chapter covers some of the basics, and the only assumption is that you know how to use a hammer or screwdriver.

Weak Points in a Hull

Generally speaking, regardless of the material used, the points to watch are all joints and reinforcements, together with the super-structure. That sly process, galvanic action, must also be guarded against at the ends of fastenings and in the hull itself.

Joints. The components of a hull are joined by various agents which may be nails, glue, bolts or welding. Each and every joint can become the weak link in the chain, and one faulty joint can put the whole boat in danger.

Reinforcements. Reinforcements are used to strengthen the hull wherever it is subject to particular stress, such as at chainplate fastenings, the mast step, etc. Proper strengthening should spread the strain over a wide surface, and the particular area should always be in first class repair. If you want to add a fitting which will be subject to heavy use, make sure that it is mounted on a good

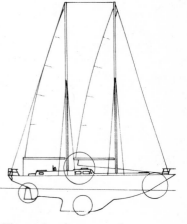

The weak points to watch

When added fittings, be sure to use a reinforcing backing pad

anchorage. For instance, if you want to fit another cleat on the deck, see that it has a backing plate fixed below it underneath the deck.

Superstructure. There are strong hulls with superstructures of alarming fragility. In some cases the shape of the cabin top has been designed more for sunbathing amenities than for withstanding the impact of a heavy sea shipped green; or solidity has been sacrificed for economy or lightness. We have already seen that a stout cabin top is essential; and it should not only be stout, but also fastened securely to the deck.

Galvanic Action. Between two different metals, the introduction of a conductor (usually salt water, or the layer of salt which it deposits) provokes electrolytic action, and a positive current flows from the less electro-positive of the two, which is slowly corroded.

On a boat, therefore, certain combinations of metals are to be avoided at all costs. Cadmium plated or galvanised steel or light alloy must not be mixed with cupro-metals (a bronze rigging screw on a galvanised chainplate, for example); the steel or alloy fittings won't last long. Some combinations (stainless steel on light alloy for example) can be accepted provided there is an insulating pad between them. Other marriages are safe without this precaution: alloy on galvanised steel is all right (but remember that galvanising has a limited life).

In practice, fittings in light alloy are fitted to a light alloy hull as much as possible; alternatively stainless steel fittings (appropriately protected) can be used, or else a non conducting material such as one of the plastics (nylon, Tuphnol, etc.).

The possibility of galvanic action must always be borne in mind when you carry out repairs or improvements. If, for instance, you fit stainless steel chainplates to a hull with galvanised fastenings, you should ensure that the two metals are separated with a strip of plastic or a pad, for otherwise the galvanised fastenings near the chainplates will be eaten away.

This type of protection cannot always be used on the hull itself, where a simple and effective solution consists of fitting *sacrificial anodes*. These are plates of zinc fitted to the hull so that galvanic action takes place on them and virtually nowhere else. This method is used when a bronze propeller is mounted on a hull with galvanised fastenings. The anodes must, of course, be replaced well before they have perished.

Types of Construction

In chapter 2 we mentioned the different materials actually used in boat construction: the classic work of *La Sereine*, the Mousquetaire in marine plywood, the Finn and Arpège in plastics, and the metal-hulled Red Rooster and Galiote. Yachts are also built in ferro-cement. Each of these materials has its pros and cons, all worth examining particularly with regard to maintenance.

Wooden Hulls

Wood is of course the traditional material and up to about 1950 nearly all yachts and dinghies were made of it. There are still some very beautiful wooden boats sailing but not many are built nowadays.

Wooden hulls are usually round bilged. They have good buoyancy, at least in the smaller sizes; but they are relatively heavy and not all that rigid. Wood construction does not lend itself to mass production or rather the mass production of boats built of wood does not lower the price appreciably. Their maintenance, too, takes time and money and this is why wood is being replaced by the new materials.

Carvel construction: many timbers, many joints and many worries

The owner of a boat built of wood on classical lines has a lot to worry about, principally because it is made of a large number of individual pieces.

Strength. There are numerous joints, not always easy to check, and they tend to weaken little by little as the boat 'works'.

Leaks. These are difficult to eliminate completely because of the many joints with relatively small surfaces.

The caulking of the garboard seams between keel and planking is one of the points to watch. If it needs replacing, it is a job for the yard. The owner who tries caulking seams himself stands in danger of doing more harm than good. (Caulking cotton is driven into the seams dry.)

The deck, because the wood swells when wet and contracts when it is dry, tends to leak, as it is made of individual planks. The best way round this is to use P.R.C. caulking that has some elasticity and will adhere to the wood when it 'works'. The same mastic should be used for the joint between the coach roof and the deck and for the joint between the deck and the hull – two places renowned for making water.

Durability. Wood can rot. Apart from anything else, it is impossible to paint in certain places (where planks meet, for example).

Wood has one deadly enemy: the gribble. This mollusc, common in warm and temperate climates. attacks wood under water. It cannot be seen, and it cannot be heard. To kill it, the boat must be dried out for a month (although it is not good for boats to be dried out too much), or left in fresh water for three months (difficult to arrange).

There are two tests for assessing the condition of a wooden hull. Ashore you can stick the point of a knife into the planking, both inside and outside, principally down near the keel and also near the joint of the deck and hull. On the water you can test the boat by sailing her hard in brisk weather; if there is any play in the joints, the hull will take in water (but remember a good boat *can* make water simply because her topsides have been dried out and a good wet sail puts that right). A leak below the waterline or a loose piece of caulking is often due to a poor joint.

Maintenance. Haul the boat out of the water and paint it every year; check on watertightness at regular intervals; keep air circulating when she is afloat. These routine measures alone show that maintenance can be a problem.

Repairs. It is risky to undertake repairs to a wooden hull yourself, and even small jobs should be undertaken by a yard. A hard knock, like a collision or taking the ground too hard, can strain such hulls beyond the point of repair.

Glued Wooden Hulls

One of the disadvantages of traditional wood construction is that there is less strength across the grain than along it. Glued construction is equally strong in all directions because it is made of 5, 7 or 9 thin layers laminated and glued with the grains running at various angles.

When the plywood panels are mounted flat on the boat's timbers it is called chine construction. When each layer of the plywood is bent and glued over the shape of the hull, the process is known as cold-moulded construction. In both cases, the skin is glued to the main structure (keel, floors, ribs . . .) and this union aids rigidity.

Plywood construction is well suited to mass production, giving a

Cold moulded hull

particularly cheap chine built hull. Cold-moulded construction lends itself to building one-offs and suits the DIY man. This type of hull is round bilged and it is reasonably priced. Plywood and cold-moulded hulls are light, strong and are easily made to be unsinkable.

Strength, Leaks. Strength and watertightness are provided by the glue; but if the boat leaks, you have a problem on your hands because this means the gluing is bad, and the hull is weak.

To judge the condition of a glued hull, you must inspect every joint. If you can see cracked paint or lumps at the joints the gluing is poor, even if the boat is not yet leaking.

Durability. Plywood does not rot as long as water cannot seep into the edges of the ply. But the boat will soon deteriorate once water starts to enter between the filet and the end grain ply. Gribble does not cause much trouble because it is stopped by the first layer of glue.

Maintenance. Although not so onerous as with classic wooden hull maintenance of a plywood or cold-moulded boat has still to be done: the hull must be dried out from time to time and repainted.

Repairs. Certain small repairs are within the limits of the average owner, as we shall see at the end of this chapter. Larger repairs and general maintenance must be entrusted to a yard where the boat can be dried out and the work done in a controlled temperature (otherwise the glue will not set). A well glued hull can withstand severe damage (skin stove in for instance) and still be fairly easily repaired.

Frame of a hull in marine ply, hard chined

Fibreglass

Fibreglass is the most commonly used material for boats these days. It is not unlike reinforced concrete; the glass element is the equivalent of the steel rods and the resin does the same job as cement.

It is most suitable for round-bilged boats and for mass production, it is much cheaper than wood and there are signs of it coming down in price – or at least not increasing as fast as other materials.

Untreated fibreglass burns much more readily than wood and gasoline or petrol is a much greater danger than on wooden craft.

Strength, Leaks. The problem of joints is reduced to a minimum on most fibreglass boats, because the hull-to-deck joint is the only weak point; but that has proved to be a considerable source of trouble on many boats. A poor joint can be irreparable and the boat gives up the ghost long before its time.

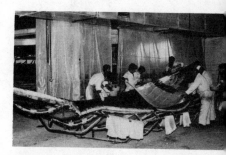

GRP hull. The fibreglass is being put on the mould

Other places to watch are the superstructure where weaknesses, such as flexible decks, hatches and coach roofs which bend under the weight of a crew member can be disquieting. There are also the places where rigging is secured and other points of strain. If the hull shows signs of cracking at any of these, there is little doubt that it is the beginning of the end.

As long as the hull retains its strength it is watertight.

Maintenance. The great advantage of fibreglass hulls is that maintenance can be cut to the minimum, without damage to anything but smartness. Boats made of it can stay several years in the water without seriously deteriorating.

If you want to keep the boat looking smart, however, you must polish her regularly, and if this does not do the job then she must be painted. In fact, at the end of several years the outer protective coating (the gel-coat) wears thin, and you should use polyurethane or other special formula paints which have good adhesive qualities. Even this work can be reduced if the hull, or at least the first layer of resin, is of the same colour as the gel-coat. This is all too seldom the case.

Repairs. A good fibreglass hull is stronger than a wooden one and it is not so easily holed. Small repairs can be undertaken by the owner, but major repairs are not for the amateur, although new techniques to help him may evolve.

Steel Hulls

Steel hulls are only worthwhile with boats having an overall length of about 40ft or more. The hull would be too heavy with less length than that; but for boats of 60ft and more, steel is actually one of the best materials, but you can't expect steel hulls to be unsinkable, given their size and the greater density of steel.

Steel is suited to round bilge and hard chine hulls (the latter are cheaper), but it has its own problems: the compass must be carefully swung and compensated, while a hand bearing compass is out of the question and you have to use a pelorus. Nor is it possible to take radio bearings inside the boat, because the hull shields the receiver.

Strength, Leaks. As a steel hull is all one piece, the plates being welded to each other, the boat is resistant to shock because the plates bend but do not break and watertightness is excellent.

Durability, Maintenance. Rust and corrosion are the number one enemies of steel hulls, and are worst naturally enough in the most inaccessible places, and continual war must be waged against them. As soon as rust appears, you must chip it away with a pointed hammer, and then repaint carefully. This is a job without end. You must be at it constantly and, of course, over the years the hull will gradually become thinner as it grows older. The only satisfactory solution to the rust problem is to have the entire hull cold galvanised, but this is a major undertaking.

Finally, we must mention the recent introduction of Corten steel, which has the same properties as copper or light alloy, in that its surface oxydisation serves as a protective shield over the whole hull.

Repairs. Both small and large repairs can only be undertaken by a boatyard.

Alloy Hulls

Aluminium (aluminum) or light alloy is the latest material for yacht building. It is expensive and therefore not very widespread at present. It can, however, be competitive for hulls between 25 and 50ft overall. Smaller boats would be too heavy and larger ones too expensive.

For economy reasons, most designs in this material are hard chine. Sufficient buoyancy can be built in when they are not too big.

Aluminium or light alloy does not affect the compass, but it is not possible to take radio bearings inside the boat.

As with steel hulls, alloy boats are strong and completely watertight.

Durability, Maintenance. Oxydisation is almost non-existent. On the other hand, galvanic action is a constant worry. The hull can be eaten away even by a paint which contains a pigment based on copper, and even a small coin lying in the bilge can work its way slowly through the hull over a long period. Problems are many and unexpected. You must even take care not to moor for too long beside boats with hulls painted with bronze or copper-based paint or, worse still, copper-sheathed.

But the main advantage of light alloy is that there is no maintenance needed at all, because its own superficial oxydisation affords the hull complete protection. It is positively better not to paint it because if the smallest piece of paint is chipped away, galvanic action would concentrate on the bare spot instead of being spread over the whole hull.

Aluminium hull. The deck is laid before the topsides

Putting the mesh in place for a concrete hull

Ferro-cement Hulls

Cement is not yet common, but it has already undergone tests (ferro-cement craft have sailed round the world) and it is being used in several countries. China has adopted the material for one class of boat. It is a form of construction particularly suited to the amateur, because it needs neither a mould, no special conditions, nor a lot of tools.

The principles are similar to those for fibreglass: a skeleton of steel replaces the glass fibre, and the cement takes the place of the resin.

The hulls are very strong: only a major collision can spring a leak, but the surface tends to flake a little. Repair is easy: after having got rid of the broken cement by chipping, the hole or crack is simply filled with fresh cement. Attachment of fittings is also simple because you can put a bolt through the hull as you would in a house.

If cement is painted, it is only for looks and not for protection and this kind of hull needs no maintenance for years.

Compass and radio, though, are up against the same problems as in a steel hull.

Maintenance

To make a good job of rubbing down, fold a sheet of glass paper three times. If you fold it only twice the smooth undersides of the paper slip on each-other. Not folded at all, the hand has no grip

Painting

Many boats still have to be painted for it protects the hull and makes it look smart.

Several coats, usually of different paints, are needed to do this efficiently, since each of the several paints has its specific purpose.

First of all you apply primer which protects the surface, sticks well to it and is a good base for the next coat. Manufacturers state what is suitable for each job. The main purpose of the topcoat (often called enamel) is to protect the surface against knocks, scratches, the weather, water and sun.

Between these two coats you lay on an undercoat. Its job is to hide defects in the surface of the primer, but it is never very sound and is only useful if you want a perfectly finished hull.

How to Repaint the Hull. The secret of success is the preparation of the surface. This takes three-quarters of the time spent on the work. It needs great patience and care.

Paint must be applied on a clean and matt surface if it is to stick well. This means the hull must be scrubbed to get rid of all dirt and grease, then it must be rubbed down with glass paper to make the surface even and matt, and to take off the old damaged paint, revealing the sound paint layer beneath. If the rubbing down is well done, water does not collect on the surface and drops but just wets it evenly.

Washing and rubbing down can be done simultaneously with 'wet and dry'. Take a brush to rough surfaces, or places that are difficult to get at, using a mild scratchless scouring powder.

While the rubbing down goes on you can assess the state of the old paint. If it holds well, it is the best of undercoats, but unfortunately that is not always the case. You can easily see if the coat is not holding well when you come to an indented spoiled part and you can clearly see where the coat ends. Everything that doesn't hold must be stripped off.

If the old coats are more than 2mm thick, you must rub the surface down to the wood, removing the paint with a blowlamp (or US torch) or a paint-stripper. Then you will have to clean the surface very thoroughly.

After you have rubbed down and cleaned, rinse the surface with fresh water. Hosing is not enough: you must rub energetically with a sponge. When the hull is dry, you should be able to rub your fingers without tracing a grain of dust. Now the hard work is done and painting can begin.

If you have gone down to the bare wood, you have to start from scratch, coat by coat, and each must be completely dry before the next is applied. The primer does not need rubbing down but each successive undercoat must be rubbed down after it is dry until it is absolutely smooth. If you are putting on more than one coat of enamel, each must be lightly rubbed down after it is dry so that the next sticks properly.

If the hull has not been stripped to the wood, start by making good: where the paint is completely or partly missing, you must repaint it coat by coat. Here too you must rub down each coat but not the primer.

Each coat must be thin and evenly spread and the same colour as the rest of the hull. Never change paints when applying top coat.

What Paints to Use

There are many makes of paint and you must use compatible types

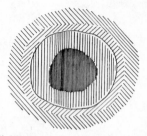

A dividing mark between the first and second coats is clearly visible and that means the second coat is not sticking well to the first coat

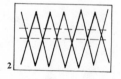

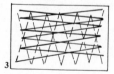

Painting: 1. Lay the paint in the middle of the surface to be covered; 2. brush out one way; 3. then the other way; 4. finish off by brushing in one direction only towards a surface that has already painted

on the one job. The commonest types used for yachts are:

Enamels. They are easy to apply but not very durable. They can be put on in temperatures of 5–25°C even when humidity is up to 90%. The surface ought to be dry and never paint in strong sunlight. Some enamel paints can be applied even when it is raining.

Alkidurethanes. They are moderately durable but should not be applied when it is either too cold or too damp (less than 10°C and not more than 70% humidity). Only use on a very dry surface.

Polyurethanes. They have two constituents which must be well mixed. They are the most durable but difficult to use (never in temperatures below 18–25°C) and the relative humidity must be below 60%. The surface just be scrupulously dry and grease-free.

These polyurethane paints have several characteristics: on wood the same paint can be used as a primer (diluted), and for all the succeeding coats, including the top coat; and you do not have to wait for a coat to dry before applying the next—it can be tacky but as long as it does not come off on your finger you can start on the next coat. This tackiness means you do not have to rub it down. Lastly, polyurethanes don't adhere to any other types of paint.

Special Paints

You can buy non-slip paints but you can make them yourself, as we do at Glénans, as follows:

Apply a fairly thick coat of polyurethane.
Sprinkle it with fine clean sand immediately.
When it is hard sweep off the loose sand lightly.
Then apply one or two more coats of polyurethane.

Varnish. Varnish needs constant care, for although it looks very smart it is not very durable. The wood darkens at the slightest crack and it is already too late to revarnish. Unlike old paint which can be rubbed down, old varnish must be completely stripped even if it is not badly blemished.

If the wood is to be adequately protected, it must have five to seven coats of varnish a year and that is a chore. Some yachtsmen, especially the British, are for ever rubbing down and varnishing, seldom being without a piece of glass paper and a tin of varnish in their hands. They are to be seen bending over a rubbing-strake, working away, and their varnish is impeccable.

Bottom Paints

'Bronze bottom' (a hand-finished copper based underwater paint).

These cover all paints made of powdered copper suspended in varnish. Most of them are glycerophaltic and they are applied in the same manner.

Its action is simple: the top coat oxidises and as copper-oxide is poisonous it keeps the bottom weed-free for a time. When you rub down, use a very fine abrasive (400 to 600) and the oxidising will start afresh. After ten to fifteen coats have been applied further application would be superfluous for by that time the coats of paint will be so thick that it is as if the bottom is copper-sheathed.

Anti-fouling Paints

They are much more poisonous but not so durable. Most of them won't stand exposure to air and they must be applied just before you re-launch.

At Glénans, after we have applied about ten coats of Bronze bottom, we put on a coat of anti-fouling on top of that which cuts down the work and avoids our having to haul out so often.

Special Precautions. If there is anything like galvanised nails in the hull you must fill in the heads carefully otherwise copper-based paint will corrode them.

Only recommended paints can be used on aluminium hulls, and it is better to use none.

Galvanising

The moment a spot of rust appears in steel it can be regalvanised, but not any old how. There are three ways of doing it.

Hot Galvanisation. Soak the piece of metal in a bath of zinc oxide solution. It gives excellent protection.

Spraying. The zinc solution is sprayed on. This method is the only one possible on large areas, particularly hulls. It is often used on smaller areas and this is a pity because the process is not so effective as steeping in a zinc solution.

Electrolytic Galvanising. A very inadequate method. Proscribed in the best circles except for screws, which can't otherwise be done.

Running Repairs

Stopping Leaks

You have to spend time and take trouble making and keeping a

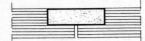

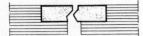

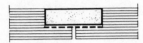

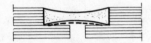

When an elastic sealer is stuck to the bottom of a joint, it cracks when the joint plays. Mask the joint to prevent this happening

boat watertight. This is one of the principle concerns of the skipper, be it the hull or the deck, the hatch covers or the hatches. Each is a problem of its own.

Permanent Joints

To make watertight joints which are normally fixed (rabbets, covering board, coach roof/deck joint, port holes), elastic sealants are particularly useful, because they hold even when there is a certain amount of play in the joint. When they are applied at the point to be made watertight, they turn into a rubberised joint, either as the result of humidity in the air or with the addition of a catalyst.

Joints should be of a width so that the sealant does not have to stretch more than 100%. It follows that the sealant must not stick near where the two pieces are to be jointed because, if they should open up, stretch at this point becomes excessive and the rubber will tear. To prevent the sealant sticking at these joins, cover them with a strip of paper or a piece of cotton cloth.

Sealants should be applied on a well prepared surface. It is as well to apply a primer to the appropriate points to ensure complete adhesion. Naturally you should follow the maker's instructions precisely.

Moving Joints

The problem is very different when it comes to making hinged port holes watertight. Leaks can be stopped by using a tight fitting rubber gasket. Main hatches and the like must have some kind of protection – coaming and scuppers. The first acts as a break to the main onslaught of water (in particular when it runs along the deck), and the second restricts the entry of water. A third is a space which acts as a kind of expansion chamber where any water that has seeped in loses all its impact before being drained to the outside again; a fourth and last is foam rubber which mops up any drops.

Major Openings

A hatch, almost inevitably, may be left open occasionally. There are few things more unpleasant than water splashing on a bunk, or

Making a watertight hatch

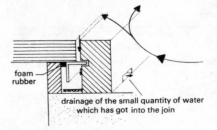

foam rubber

drainage of the small quantity of water which has got into the join

dripping on to the chart table. Splash barriers and other deflectors can be fitted to channel the water into the bilges.

Attachment of Fittings

Method of Fixing

Nails. Only to be used for fastening one piece of wood to another, nails must be galvanised, stainless steel or copper.

Your hammer must be quite free of grease if you are to knock in a nail without bending it. Tools are often greasy and if this applies to your hammer you may not strike a clean blow and the nail will bend.

So start by cleaning your hammer. Then choose the right size of nail, not so small it won't hold, not so large that it splits the wood.

The following tips will help you to avoid splitting the wood:

Select a nail of a length equal at the most to four times the thickness of the piece of wood to be nailed.
Do not place the nail too close to the edge or the end.
Always nail a thinner piece on to a thicker piece of wood, and not the other way round.
If the point is very fine it may be as well to blunt it with a file.

Hammering in really large nails is not easy. The hammer is often too light to make a good job of it. It is better to make a pilot-hole (all the more so because the nail will hold better and will not split the wood), using a nail a bit smaller than the one you wish to insert. Cut off the head and put it in a drill as a bit. This works surprisingly well and it does not matter that the pilot-hole is a little short. The join will obviously hold better if the two pieces are glued as well.
Wood Screws. A screw is used normally to fix anything you may wish to dismantle later, or to fix metal or plastic to wood.

Screws can be stainless steel, galvanised or cadmium plated steel, or brass (this last should be avoided outside because it gradually disintegrates). When you are choosing screws always think of any possible galvanic effects they might have.

The screw should be long enough to ensure that the threaded end is well embedded in the wood.

To attach a fitting with screws:

A. Thread diameter
B. Shank diameter
C. Head = shank diameter × 2

Place it in position.

Drill a shallow hole through one of the screw holes of the fitting, with a bit of the same diameter as the screw hole in the fitting. Then bore further with a bit of the same diameter as the core of the screw making a pilot-hole as deep as the screw will finally penetrate.

Insert the screw; mark the other holes and so on for the remaining screws.

In soft wood, you can make pilot-holes with a nail or bradawl. Even in soft wood, you should never fit a screw without a pilot-hole, for the screw can be deflected by hard grain in the wood.

Finally don't forget to wipe all screws with tallow before inserting them (if you have no tallow, cooking fat will do).

Neoprene Dowel (Rawl Nut). This type of fastening holds very fast in all materials. The plug is threaded at one end and, when a screw is inserted, it retracts and swells out. If the wood you are working on is thin, the dowel expands behind it; if it is thick, the dowel swells in the hole until it blocks it completely. It holds almost as well as a bolt.

It is the cheapest and the safest method (in the absence of a backing piece) of fixing anything to plastic. As the hole drilled to take the dowel is necessarily fairly large, the load is spread over a wide area.

When a rawl nut is used in metal, it is important to smooth off the hole on both sides so that the dowel is not cut.

Used on wood these plugs have several advantages: you can use old screw holes, which have enlarged so that they will no longer take a screw; you can also attach small fittings on plywood without a backing piece.

The only drawback is that a neoprene dowel can move slightly.

Rivets. There are many kinds of rivets, but in general their use is best left to professionals. There is, in fact, only one type of riveting which can be undertaken by the average owner: clenched nails, used in the way that we shall discuss when looking at repairs to plywood hulls.

Glue. Glue is a first-class way of fitting attachments, and it is often stronger than the material it is joining. If you try, for example, to separate two pieces of wood which have been well glued together, the wood will break but not the joint.

In this case, however, it is only the two surfaces that are firmly attached to each other. If the materials are relatively weak (ply-

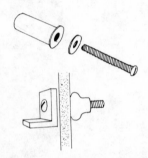

Neoprene plugs have excellent holding properties and ensure water-tightness

wood, for example, has very little strength in shear), the glue should be reinforced with nails or rivets.

There is a huge variety of glues on the market. Almost everything can be stuck together and each has its appropriate glue.

Every glue has its own instructions for use, and it is wise to take heed. Generally speaking:

Glues do not like humidity (either in the material or the atmosphere).

They adhere badly or not at all when it is cold: most glues operate at temperatures between 18°–25°C.

The thinner the layer of glue, the better it holds; it is therefore a basic requirement to clamp the two pieces firmly together after gluing.

Many glues have two constituents: the glue proper and a hardener. You must keep the two pieces from moving until the glue is quite hard, otherwise it will not hold. Use clamps whenever you can.

Cleats

There are seldom enough cleats on a boat, they are often badly placed and sometimes poorly fixed. You should know how to fit and to move them and where new ones should be added.

A cleat must obviously be fitted to a solid part of the boat (and be solid itself). To make it hold well, the ideal is to bolt and glue it; it is then completely secured. When you cannot bolt it, it must be screwed on but then glue is indispensible, otherwise the screws will start working and the cleat will end up by tearing away.

The best attached cleat will not last long if it is not placed at the right angle of pull. It must always lie longitudinally in the direction of pull. You can offset it about 10° from this direction, to ease making fast, but never beyond that.

Never forget that cleats should be perfectly smooth or they will chafe any line attached to them. A little work with a file or glass paper can make ropes last longer.

Jam and clam-cleats are easy to fix because their mountings are large enough not to need glue. When a clam-cleat is working properly, the rope should be able to hang down from its after end; you can sometimes use a wedge to raise the after end, but it is also important to site this without there being any danger of the line jamming again when it is eased away.

Clamcleat correctly fixed: the rope can fall as it comes out

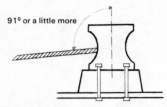

91° or a little more

If the turns are not to ride over one another, the angle between rope and winch barrel axis must be slightly more than 90°

Winches

A winch takes great strains and it must be strongly bolted on a firm base. Above all, it must be properly aligned to take the rope at right angles to the axis of the drum or, better still, at just above 90°. Otherwise the turns will pile up on each other on the winch (in what is known as *riding turns*), the line jams and cannot be eased off.

If the same winch has to serve several sheets, each one must still reach the drum at the correct angle. To this end, a common fairlead can be fitted for all sheets.

Stanchions and Guard-rails

Stanchions bend easily, but this does not matter too much. A stanchion is not a safety factor in itself because it is the guardrails which do the job. Indeed, it is even not particularly wise to fix a stanchion so firmly that it cannot move or bend at all, because then it may be torn off its base. It is better to have stanchions that can be easily lifted off and thus easily straightened.

Guard-rails should not be too tight, because they have greater strength if they are given a little play. The fixtures on the pulpit and stern rail, to which the lines are attached, must, of course, be very strongly secured; and the pulpits above all must be made very fast.

Lifelines

Lifelines or jackstay wires should be stretched fore and aft to which the crew can hank themselves and yet be able to move from one end of the boat to the other without ever having to unhook their harness.

The wires are fitted flat along the deck, one on each side, mounted on very solid fixtures. To lessen the load which they have to withstand (about one ton), they should be given plenty of slack. If this slack hinders movement along the deck, the lifelines can be stiffened by rigging shock cord.

Built-in Buoyancy

A boat can be made unsinkable in two ways: by inflatable buoyancy or by compartments filled with closed cell foam (expanded polystyrene) which should be able to float the boat when she is full of water. When buoyancy is installed, it must be remembered that its effort will always be upwards. Two or three hundred pounds of thrust should make you careful about the way you fix it to the boat. For instance, when a block of foam is placed under a bunk, the bunk itself should be made strongly enough to withstand the thrust which might be put under it.

Buoyancy should be carefully placed: too low and a boat that fills will be in danger of capsizing and floating keel upwards; too high and the deck will never come out of the water; too far aft and the boat puts her nose down.

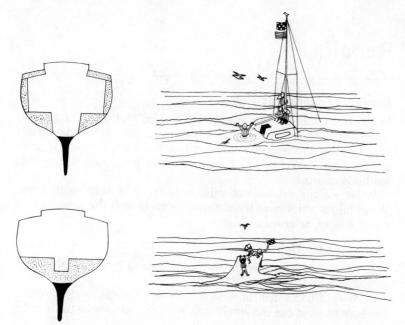

Distribution of buoyancy reserves should be neither too high nor too low

Centreboard and Rudder

When checking on the weak points in a boat, remember to look underwater at the pivot of the centreboard and the hinges of the rudder in particular.

On a ballasted centreboarder, when the plate starts to have a little play in it (owing to pivot wear or wear in the hole it pivots on), trouble can arise. To check whether the centreboard has got too much play you must, at least once a year, move it by hand from below. This can be done either by lifting the boat out on a crane or by turning her over on her side on the shore and lowering the centreboard horizontally.

It is deeply mortifying to lose your rudder, but it happens. As it is always being moved, screws and bolts come undone easily, work loose or wear, so they should be frequently looked at. You can reduce rudder trouble if all nuts are secured with a locking fluid (a cement which fixes the bolt and the nut).

Repairs

Repairing a Marine-ply Hull

In most cases, a hole in a marine-ply hull isn't a tragedy; the repair is well within the capabilities of a reasonable handyman. Only cutting tools are needed: chisel, plane and saw. Rasps and glass paper must never be used because they encourage the wrong methods of work.

What we suggest here is valid only for relatively small holes. When larger holes have to be done, the method is the same but the repair has to be glued as well.

To Cut out the Hole

1. Mark out a trapezoidal 'window' taking in the whole of the damaged wood.
2. With a hand drill bore two holes in opposite angles. With a key hole saw cut out the window about 2 or 3mm inside the marked lines.
3. With three fine nails which aren't fully driven home, fix a batten, very straight, along the mark of one of the sides.
4. With a well sharpened wood chisel, cut out the wood lying outside the batten. The chisel must be held as in the photo and care taken not to cut into the batten. The edge of the cut must be straight, at right angles to the planking and true.
5. Do the same for the other three sides.

How to hold a chisel

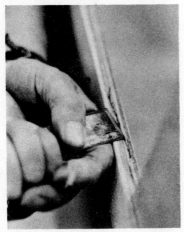

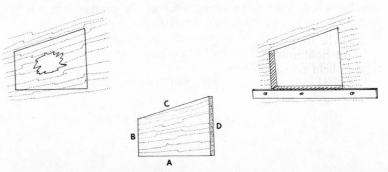

To Prepare the Piece of Wood

1. In ply of the same thickness as the planking, cut out roughly a board of the same shape as the hole but several centimetres larger.

2. Plane up the longest edge, really straight and true. The photo shows how to hold the plane; you lean on the forward end of the plane at the beginning of each stroke, on the back at the finish.

3. By applying the board to the hole, mark out side B then square up its edge. Put the board in place and check from the inside that it is even along both edges. Adjust if need be.

4. Do the same for side C. If a little too much is planed off on this third side it is still possible to save the board by nibbling away at side B (this is the advantage of a trapezoidal board over a rectangular one).

5. Square up the last side. This time, be very careful: if you plane too much away, everything has to be done all over again.

How to hold a plane

To Make the Backing

Make a backing plate in ply of the same thickness as the planking, or a little thinner. This backing must be bigger than the filling piece, some 3cm all round (the sides are therefore 6cm larger than those of the filling piece). Make a good bevelled edge.

To Fix the Backing

1. Paint the side which will be applied to the planking with thick paint. This protects the wood and ensures watertightness.

2. Nail on the backing, with a nail every 3 or 4cm, following the lozenge shape of the hole.

3. Clench the nails.

To Fix the Filling Piece

1. Paint the innerside and the edges, not too thick, it won't be able to squeeze out because you will have fitted it so well!

2. Nail it on with a few nails in the middle, then all round as for the backing.

3. Clench the nails in the same sequence.

How to Nail

1. Use fine galvanised nails.

2. Drive in from outside to inside with a light hammer, an assistant holding the 'dolly' (a heavy object) on the inside. The dolly is held firmly up against the backing, without moving, and free from the point of each nail.

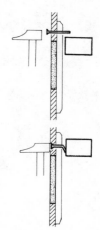

Hammering in and clinching a tingle

How to Clench

1. Cut off the points on the inside so that they don't stick out more than 3mm and bend them over.

2. Make sure they are tight, by tapping with a light hammer on the head of the nail whilst a helper holds the dolly against the bent-over tip of the nail.

Special Cases

If the hole is close to a frame, the window must be cut out up to the middle of this frame, but without damaging it. The ticklish bit is to get all the ply out without taking away any of the heavy timber. It is advisable to begin the work with an old chisel. This saves damaging the good one on the nails driven in during building.

If the ply is only stove in slightly, it isn't always necessary to cut out the damaged part: you can make do with putting a backing on the inside.

Repairing a Plastic Hull

In spite of appearances, repairing a plastic hull hardly presents any difficulties. The technique to use is much simpler than for ply. The number of tools is smaller: rasp, saw, brush, scissors.

Care however must be taken over atmospheric conditions, specially temperature and humidity, before undertaking a repair. It must be recognised too that this repair, whatever is done, will not be able to stand up to everything: in fact the very structure of the hull (fibreglass cloth) is cut, and the resin put in its place never sticks perfectly to the old resin.

For slight damage the 'replastering' we are going to undertake is nevertheless adequate.

Requirements

1. Minimum temperature: 18°C.
2. Relative maximum humidity: 60%.
3. The fibreglass must be very dry, which is difficult to achieve since it is hydroscopic.
4. The edges of the hole must also be very dry.
5. The resin must be fresh (less than four months old).

Cutting Out the Hole

1. Get rid of all the damaged part of the hull. The shape of the hole is not important.

2. Chamfer off very broadly the edges of the hole: the slope must be about 10%.

Backing and Support

Since the material used to stop up the hole is fluid, it must be given a temporary support, and the area to be remade must be backed. The backing, whatever material it is made of, must be covered with cellophane so that the resin doesn't stick to it.

Preparing the Resin

So that the resin should polymerise (harden), a hardener (1% generally), often wrongly called a catalyst, must be added. For the polymerisation to take place at the required speed, an accelerator in the proportions of 0:5 to 4% is used (1% if the temperature is 18°C). Finally the resin may be coloured.

Be careful while handling: the hardener must never come into direct contact with the accelerator; the reaction gives off a great deal of heat and can result in an explosion. Anyway, repair materials containing accelerated resins can be bought commercially.

Soaking the Matt

For repairs, the fibreglass is used in the form of *matt* which is cut with scissors according to the shape of the hole.

The cloth can be impregnated with resin either *in situ* or before being applied, but it must be completely soaked, and there must be no air bubbles. To get rid of the latter, dab carefully with a brush.

Stopping the Hole

1. Coat the edges of the hole with resin.
2. Make up the whole thickness of the hull by putting one on top of the other for as many layers of matt as necessary.
3. Cover the repair with cellophane, which both prevents the resin from running if the repair is being made on a surface other than horizontal, but also allows the surface to be shaped, with a rubber roller or one's fingers.

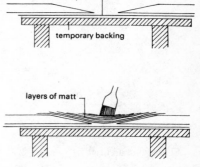

Finish

1. Wait until the resin has begun to set but is not yet very hard.
2. Take off the cellophane and smooth down the surface with a rasp or glass paper.
3. 'Paint' with a gel-coat.

4. Take away the backing support, if it is still accessible.

Sharpening Tools

To carry out these few jobs correctly, a very small number of tools is needed. But it is essential that these tools are in good condition, well looked after and used properly. We thought a few hints would not come amiss.

The Screwdriver

The screwdriver must fit as perfectly as possible into the head of the screw: its blade must have true, even sides, a thickness corresponding to the groove of the screw, a width equal to the diameter of the head of the screw.

The surface edges of a screwdriver are corrected with the help of a grinding wheel. So that the two faces of the blade should be truly even in the working part, they must be ground hollow, therefore on the round edge of the wheel. Be careful not to lean too heavily on them: if steel heats too much it loses its temper. At 200°C it turns the colour of straw, at 600°C it turns blue and becomes worthless. A temperature of 200°C therefore must not be exceeded, and these 200°C are quickly reached, especially if the end of the screwdriver is thin. In all cases, you must have a jug of water by the side of the wheel and dip the screwdriver in it frequently (about every ten seconds, say).

Obviously the same angle of presentation of the blade to the wheel must be kept all the time, so you must not take your hand off it from the moment the operation is begun; hold it always by the blade at the same place and support the index finger on the fitting of the wheel.

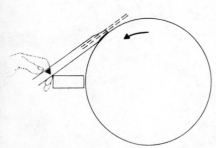

Sharpening a screwdriver: position of blade and direction of the grindstone's rotation

Wood Chisel and Plane Blade

A first principle: if a wood chisel or a plane blade is to cut well, the back of the blade must be perfectly flat right to the cutting edge. There must only be a bevel on one side and it is this side only that must be sharpened. The angle of the cutting edge must be between 20° and 30°.

To grind, proceed as for the screwdriver. A slightly concave surface is therefore obtained. On the cutting edge of the blade appears a scarf, or wide edge.

To polish the chamfered edge of the blade, rub on a very flat oil stone (respecting the angle of the chamfer), until you have

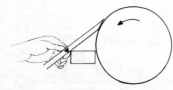

Sharpening a chisel

obtained a small shining part all along the cutting edge.

To hone, the chamfer and the back of the blade are alternately rubbed on the stone. Take care not to lift the handle of the tool while rubbing the back; take care over the angle when rubbing the chamfered edge. Let us repeat that it is very important not to make a false bevel on the back of the blade; if you do, the tool is done for.

The cutting edge of these tools is very fragile, and a few precautions are to be taken not to blunt it too fast. When you put down a chisel, be careful always to put it down on wood, cutting edge uppermost; a plane is turned on its side. When the tools are put away, wrap the blade of the chisel in a greasy rag; withdraw the blade into the plane.

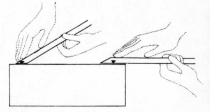

Rubbing off the wire edge on an oil stone.

Seaman's Knife

This is the all-purpose tool *par excellence* without which a sailor is but a shadow of himself. It doesn't need to have lots of accessories. A good blade can fill all the roles: marlin spike, cork screw, can opener, bottle opener, nail cutter or tooth pick.

A regular steel blade always cuts better than a stainless steel one, but it is best to have it fixed into the handle with stainless rivets.

The knife is not sharpened on a grinding wheel. You can on occasion thin down a new blade on a grinding wheel, but the sharpening itself is to be done only on a stone. Both sides of the blade must be rubbed on the stone, cutting edge forward, otherwise you create a wire edge, only fit for cutting butter – in summer!

The bevelled edge after the wire edge has been rubbed off

6. Gear

By gear we mean the equipment that is not built into the boat but is obviously essential: anchors, chain and mooring lines, the auxiliary engine (not essential, but usually fitted) navigation instruments; and many small items such as oars, boathooks, fenders, legs (to keep the boat upright when it dries out) and the humble bailer. Other items are treated elsewhere, in their proper context, such as safety equipment in the chapter on safety or household items in the chapter on life on board. These are described in no particular order and are the things which have proved to us to be of practical use.

Mooring Gear

Anchors and Chain

What sort of anchors and anchor chains and line should a given boat have?

Experience is the best criterion, and before even explaining our choice, here is what more than twenty years of experience at Glénans have shown to be the right ground tackle for certain of our boats. The range should be wide enough for everyone to be able to place his own craft in the correct bracket.

See table opposite

As a general principle never be tempted to choose lighter ground tackle than what is shown in the table because it is cheaper and easier to handle. That is poor economy and if the ground tackle seems to be too heavy for the crew, it is really the crew who are too light to handle it.

TABLE OF GROUND TACKLE

Light Dinghies (Vaurien)	1 Danforth type 5lb 30 fathoms braided nylon $\frac{3}{4}$″ circ. ($\frac{1}{4}$″ or 5mm dia.) 1 fathom chain $\frac{1}{4}$″
Daysailers 400–650lb (Caravelle)	1 CQR type 10lb 15 fathoms chain $\frac{1}{4}$″ or 15 fathoms braided nylon $1\frac{1}{4}$″ circ. ($\frac{3}{8}$″ dia.) and 1 fathom chain $\frac{1}{4}$″
Daysailers 900–1,200lb (Cavale, Corsaire)	1 CQR 15lb 15 fathoms chain $\frac{1}{4}$″ or 30 fathoms braided nylon $1\frac{1}{4}$″ circ. ($\frac{3}{8}$″ dia.) and 2–3 fathoms chain $\frac{1}{4}$″
Trailerboats 1–1$\frac{1}{2}$ tons (Mousquetaire)	1 CQR 15lb 1 CQR 10lb 15 fathoms chain $\frac{1}{4}$″ 30 fathoms braided nylon $1\frac{1}{4}$″ circ. ($\frac{3}{8}$″ dia.) 3 fathoms chain $\frac{1}{4}$″
Cruisers 2–3 tons (Dogre, Nautile)	1 CQR 35lb 1 CQR 25lb 20 fathoms chain $\frac{3}{8}$″ 50 fathoms braided polypropylene 3″ circ. (1″ dia.) 3 fathoms chain $\frac{3}{8}$″
Cruisers 3$\frac{1}{2}$ tons (Frégate)	1 CQR 35lb 1 CQR 25lb 1 CQR 10lb 20 fathoms chain $\frac{3}{8}$″ (tested) 50 fathoms braided polypropylene 3″ circ. (1″ dia.) 3 fathoms chain $\frac{3}{8}$″ 50 fathoms braided nylon $\frac{3}{4}$″ circ. ($\frac{1}{4}$″ dia.)
Cruisers 9–13 tons (Sereine, Iroise)	1 CQR 45lb 1 CQR 35lb 1 CQR 10lb 20 fathoms chain $\frac{1}{2}$″ 30 fathoms chain $\frac{3}{8}$″ 60 fathoms braided polypropylene 3″ circ. (1″ dia.) 3 fathoms chain $\frac{3}{8}$″ 80 fathoms braided nylon $\frac{3}{4}$″ circ. ($\frac{1}{4}$″ dia.)

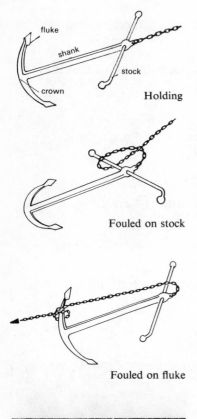

Holding

Fouled on stock

Fouled on fluke

Grapnel

Anchors

As the table shows, an anchor is described by its weight and its shape. We speak about a fisherman anchor of 30lb. The shape is often patented the Danforth anchor and the F.O.B. anchor; both have pivoting flukes, but not the same holding characteristics.

They all have their advantages and disadvantages.

The Fisherman

This is the oldest form of anchor and it is one of the safest. It holds on any bottom where anchoring is possible at all: sand, mud, gravel, weed and even rock (but sometimes it is difficult to break it out there). Its holding powers are not exceptional, but they are sound. Even if it *drags*, pulling through the seabed like a plough cutting a furrow, it continues to offer steady resistance.

Fisherman anchors vary somewhat in shape. Some are thick-set and very strong; their wide flukes hold extremely well in mud but may not dig into a hard bottom, particularly if there is any weed on top. The long and slim types are not so strong but their flukes sink more readily into a hard bottom.

A fisherman anchor has its disadvantages, being a bit clumsy and, particularly on a small boat, cumbersome to handle. Setting up the stock is just one more thing to do (its pin should be secured with a line; metal fastenings, particularly those with flat pins, won't stay in). If it is not used properly, the anchor can get fouled if the mooring line gets a turn either around the stock or the fluke; then it will drag.

The Grapnel

This is another traditional type of anchor. It has four or five flukes and its holding power is slightly less than that of a fisherman anchor, but it is particularly effective in weed. Rather like the fisherman anchor, it is cumbersome and unhandy.

Pivoting Fluke Anchor or 'Danforth'

A fairly recent design of intentionally lightweight, this anchor does not have the drawbacks of the fisherman type in that it cannot get fouled by the stock for the very good reason that it has none and seldom gets fouled by the fluke. It is easy to handle and to stow.

Holding power is good in sand and in mud, reasonable in shingle, uncertain in rocks, and bad in sea grass or weed. Movement of the flukes is often jammed by shells or small stones, and it easily becomes clogged by weed. When it begins to drag, its holding power falls off rapidly.

The different types of this anchor vary widely in efficiency. Some, indeed, will only hold in a very good conditions. Among the best on the market are the Colin, F.O.B. and Danforth.

Plough or CQR Anchor

This is certainly one of the best of all modern anchors. Its holding power is at least double that of the fisherman and it holds well on all bottoms, except in very dense seaweed. It is very difficult for it to be fouled by the fluke.

Even if it drags, it still has the same resistance and it has the additional advantages of being less cumbersome and easier to handle than the others.

The CQR has many imitations, some poor, some very bad.

How Many Anchors?

Dinghies need only one anchor but daysailers and fishing boats should have a second.

All cruising boats should have at least two to allow you to put out a kedge for extra hold, to anchor fore and aft, or to kedge off. Also, if the main anchor is lost, you are not completely helpless.

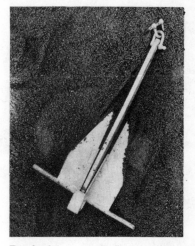

Danforth

Chain

The first advantage of chain is its weight, which holds it on the bottom making the pull on the anchor as horizontal as possible. The chain also serves as a shock absorber, because the boat does not, of course, exercise a steady pull on its anchor, but jerks on it; the weight of the chain damps down the shock.

Its second advantage is resistance to chafe, because it does not wear on the bottom, on the sides of the *hawse-holes* or in the fairleads in the gunwale or sternhead roller. But weight has its inconveniences for it is hard work pulling it in, it weighs down the boat and, as it is inevitably stowed forward, it encourages pitching.

At Glénans, we use standard chain. *Tested* or *proofed* chain may be used instead, and its strength is over half as much again, size for size, as standard chain. Thus a standard chain of $\frac{3}{8}$in may be replaced by a tested chain of $\frac{1}{4}$in. The advantage of this is debatable, for a light chain will not have as good shock-absorbing properties and you must let out a greater length to achieve the same result. When you weigh anchor you have to haul it all in again.

CQR

In practice, small chains should not be trusted and we advise against anything less than ¼in.

The length of chain to let out is generally three times the depth of water. The depth of your anchorages will vary according to your cruising grounds and this will more or less decide the amount of chain you should have on board. In any case, you should never have less than 15 fathoms.

To buy too light or too short a chain is just as dangerous as having too light an anchor and when the boat is pounding to pieces on rocks, it is too late to regret the three or four extra fathoms that you left at the chandler's.

Making the Chain Fast

The chain should be joined to the anchor with shackles, which must be as strong as the rest of the ground tackle. For a given size, a shackle is weaker than chain so you should always have one size larger (¼in chain, ⅜in shackle). Shackles must always be moused, even if you are only anchoring for ten minutes.

The end of the chain (the *bitter end*) should be made fast to the ring in the chain locker with a number of turns of rope with a total breaking strain equal to that of the chain (four parts of ¾in circ (¼in dia) nylon = a ⅜in chain). The whole lashing should be at least four inches long so that it can be easily cut. Wire and shackles must be avoided, because it takes too long to release them if you need to slip your cable or load in an emergency.

Maintenance

The fine coating of zinc which covers galvanised chain gradually breaks down bit by bit, and rust appears. As soon as this happens, the chain begins to wear quickly, as rust is a strong abrasive. Rust can be kept in check if, when laying up each year, you spray the chain with motor oil (which will have dried out by the following spring and the chain will not dirty the boat).

When rust appears, you can have the chain re-galvanised. Left to itself, a chain will last for five years on average; re-galvanised twice, it can last for eight to twelve years. Two re-galvanisings will together cost about half the price of a new chain.

A chain will, of course, wear even if it is well looked after. The part which wears most quickly is the bit most often at water level. To distribute this wear, the chain should be end for ended every year.

As a rule, chains should be replaced as soon as the weakest link

Seizing of the bitter end to ring in chain locker

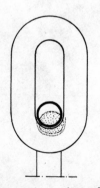

Wear takes place where the links rub on each other

is reduced to 75% of its original thickness.

Warps

Every boat should have at least one big warp for anchoring or towing. It should be two or three times as strong as the anchor chain, or it will quickly become too weak with age, and it should be at least 30 fathoms long.

On long cruises it is very useful to have two of these lines:

One should be heavy, with a breaking strain equal to the weight of the boat (at least up to three tons). This main warp can serve as a tow rope, mooring line, anchor line or trailing warp. It can be in polypropylene, which is a light and bulky textile (which is useful for trailing). This is the general purpose warp which everyone should have.

The second should be two or three times as strong as the chain because it will frequently be used for anchoring. Nylon is best because, contrary to polypropylene, it sinks and thus stands less risk of being cut by the boat's propeller. Use braided nylon because it has better resistance to chafe.

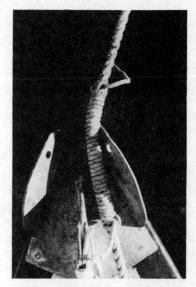

A warp is expensive and wears out quickly. It can be protected at spots likely to chafe if it is parcelled with a lighter line: start with a clove hitch, then a series of tight round turns and finish with a clove hitch

Anchor and Line for the Ship's Tender

The boat's tender should have ground tackle of about 75 fathoms (this may seem excessive to some) of fine line and a 5lb anchor.

This tackle has several uses: as well as serving to anchor the tender it can be used to anchor the yacht herself, regardless of her weight, in a flat calm against a head current that is not too strong (it is convenient then to have a top-action halyard winch available for hauling up the anchor). The line can also serve as a trip-line for the main anchor and, on occasions, as a lead line for sounding.

Fixed Moorings

When you want to moor regularly in the same place, like your home port, you obviously do not want to drop the anchor every time; so you install a permanent mooring, where the anchor is replaced by a slab of concrete or other device. You almost invariably have to get permission from the local harbour master.

Mooring Block

Ideally this reinforced concrete block should be as thin as possible, and concave underneath. Its weight should equal the breaking strain of the yacht's normal anchor chain. For a Mousquetaire we use a block weighing 500kg as her 7mm main chain has a breaking strain of roughly 580kg.

Chain

To reduce the radius of swing, and for economy, a chain shorter than the anchor's can be used (one and a half times the maximum depth of water); but it should be stronger ($\frac{3}{8}$ for a Mousquetaire) to take the bigger strain when you lay or take up the mooring. As it is heavier, it absorbs the pull as the boat snubs the chain which should be attached to the concrete slab with as strong a shackle as possible: $\frac{1}{2}$in for a $\frac{3}{8}$in chain, or even $\frac{5}{8}$in if it will fit. The shackle should be moused with wire, thick enough so that rust does not eat through it too quickly.

A fixed mooring chain does not need to be galvanised because, as it is always immersed in water, it does not rust. On the other hand, as opposed to an anchor chain, it is near to the bottom that this chain will wear most quickly, and its condition must be inspected annually by taking up the mooring at a low spring tide or by divers.

On some moorings, the boat always swings in the same direction and the chain twists. You can cope with this by fitting a swivel. The swivel may get jammed and you should look at it every three months and untwist the chain by hand if necessary.

A chain without a swivel must be untwisted every six weeks.

The Buoy

The chain can be joined to the buoy on the surface in different ways. To clarify these explanations, it is convenient to call the buoy on to which the rising chain is shackled directly a *mooring buoy*, and the buoy which is linked by a line to the chain is a *pick up buoy*.

Mooring Buoy. It should be filled with flotation material so that it will not sink even if it is punctured. Its buoyancy should be equal to twice the weight of the length of chain clear of the bottom at high tide.

You have to remember that the chain of a fixed mooring is always on the move and it wears because the links are continually rubbing on each other, even when no boat is moored on it.

Pick-up Buoy. In this case the mooring chain lies on the bottom, when no boat is moored, and the pick-up buoy is attached to nylon line one and a half times the depth of high water. A light chain is fitted between the main chain and the line, and this is the one which is made fast on board. It should be small enough to pass through the bow fairlead (same size as the anchor chain) and long enough to stretch from the surface to the samson post. A caveat is that the nylon line can entangle or be cut by a propeller. To reduce this risk, you can weight the line by adding a weight of 5 or 6lb, some 5 or 6ft from the surface, by a lead-weighted line.

Permanent moorings for boats of some 1,200kg. Pick-up buoy on left, mooring buoy on right

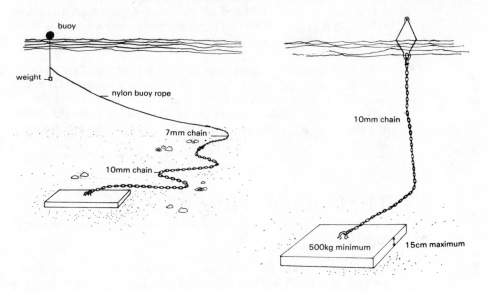

Auxiliary Engine

Purists recoil from running their engine at all but, unfortunately, it deteriorates rapidly when it is not being used. It is usually enough to turn it over regularly and to give it minimum maintenance to keep it running well. But breakdowns can happen and it is useful to know how to cope with them.

When the boat is used by different people, such as co-owners, you must keep a proper check list on board, as is done on aircraft, to show new-comers what is necessary to do and not to do.

Choosing the Engine

In our opinion the choice lies between a petrol/gasoline outboard motor or a diesel inboard engine. We cannot emphasise enough the constant danger of having a petrol or gasoline inboard engine on a sailing boat: even if the installation is perfect, it is still risky because the danger lies in the fuel being extremely volatile and inflammable. In spite of the advantages of being cheaper in some areas and lighter it is never the only choice, and is always the least safe.

The choice of outboard or diesel inboard is made according to the type of boat and the power that you require.

It is always easier to have an outboard engine than to install a diesel; but beyond 20hp fuel consumption of an outboard is high, and above 25hp it is extremely heavy and not very practical on a sailing boat.

A diesel positively enjoys running for long periods, fast or slow, whether you are becalmed, fishing or recharging batteries. It needs space and the boat must be able to carry the additional weight.

If the diesel outboard is ever perfected, we shall naturally prefer it to the petrol or gasoline motor. The Americans believe Volvo have done it.

The Outboard Engine

Safety

An outboard motor with a fuel tank incorporated in it is dangerous for two reasons. When it is laid on its side, fuel can escape through the air valves on the tank. Secondly, you may one day inevitably succumb to the temptation to refuel while running, and this is a grave fire danger.

If the tank is separate from the engine, there is not so much risk. When you lie the engine down there is little hazard because the tank is some way from the engine and its sparks; and since the fuel capacity of the tank is larger, there is less temptation to refuel on the move. As the fuel has to be sucked along the fuel pipe by the engine, the risks of a leak in the pipe are almost nil.

Another danger factor is an engine which has no fairing or is not housed in: you can burn yourself on it and also hurt yourself on the fly wheel.

Installation

The great advantage of an outboard is its extraordinary convenience: installation aboard and removal ashore is a simple matter; and it can be easily taken to a mechanic or a yard for repairs or winter storage, which is less expensive and easier than having an expert come to the boat.

When an outboard engine is fitted, follow one fundamental rule: the propeller and the water cooling intake must always be properly submerged when the engine is running (even in a seaway or when the boat heels). Equally important: when the motor is not being used the propeller should be raised right out of the water. You should therefore be able to raise or lower the engine without having to take it off the bracket.

The best solution is to have an outboard well, preferably one which can be blocked off when the motor is raised. In default of a well, the motor should be fixed on the transom or on a removable bracket, although it is then exposed to weather and other damage; also, if it is heavy, its weight at the stern of the boat increases pitching. If it is not possible to raise the motor completely out of the way under sail you should take it off its bracket and stow it, either in a locker set aside for this purpose (which should not allow fuel vapour to pass inside the boat), or else fix it vertically to the stern pulpit, or lay it on deck, protected by a cover which should be taken off in fine weather to let it dry out. Taken carefully down to the shelter of the cabin, it is the bane of weak stomachs and a gratuitous fire risk.

It is obviously a wise precaution to make outboard motors fast with a line to the boat while they are being handed off their brackets.

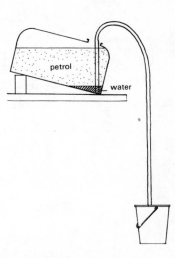

Operation

Modern outboard engines work well as long as they are given care. Most faults stem from neglect rather than from true mechanical faults.

Fuel Supply

If the fuel pipe or line is not connected properly, the motor will not work; this is obvious, but fuel starvation is nevertheless the most frequent cause of breakdown. Always think of this first if the motor stops running.

There can be water in the fuel. You should therefore:

Water in a fuel tank can be syphoned out by using a rubber tube that ends in a length of pipe which can reach the bottom of the tank

Empty the carburettor bowl (a special tool is often necessary). Clean out the fuel tank, either by draining it as well or, still better, by syphoning from the bottom.

The best way to stop an outboard motor is to disconnect the fuel pipe. This empties the carburetor and the motor does not leak fuel when laid on its side.

Spark

Plugs soot up and wear out in use. They should be cleaned from time to time and the gap reset (the gap should be about .02in, or three thicknesses of the average chart). In any case they are not indestructible and should be changed at the end of about 100 hours' running. Other spark problems are better left to a mechanic unless you have special knowledge.

Cooling

A cooling failure, brought on by a breakdown in the cooling system, is extremely bad for the engine for it can overheat and seize up in less than a minute if the water circulation fails. The amount of water in the circuit is extremely small, so rapid and continuous circulation is essential to keep the engine cool. Don't forget that the water inlet must be below the surface; and it will come above it if, for example, the whole crew go forward to pick up the mooring.

It is equally important to check that the inlet is not blocked by weed, plastic bags or other flotsam.

Most of its workings such as mending a faulty water pump needs an expert mechanic.

Lubrication

The engine is lubricated with the oil that is mixed with the fuel. Always ensure that the percentage of this mixture is correct: not too much, not too little. It is also important to mix the oil and fuel properly by vigorous shaking; or you can buy it ready-mixed from a fitting station.

There is secondary greasing which is often neglected: the various engine accessories such as throttle, gear control, shaft pivot, fixing bolts, etc.

Running Speed

Outboard motors are designed for fast running, and they can work for several hours continuously at 90% of full throttle without harm.

When it runs for any length of time at low throttle, it is liable to carbon or soot up and will be difficult to start again. For easier starting it is as well to run the motor for several seconds at high speed before shutting off the fuel.

Broken Starter

It is always possible to start the engine, even when the normal electric starter is broken by simply winding a cord round the fly wheel head. With some engines you first of all have to take off the starter with a screwdriver (don't forget to take one with you when you fit the outboard on the ship's dinghy).

Engine Overboard

If the engine falls in the water, it must be quickly overhauled by a mechanic. If this cannot be done immediately, it is better to immerse the engine in fresh water rather than leave it in the open air without doing anything.

General

Finally, if you have an outboard motor, you should also have on board at least two spare plugs and the appropriate tools for removing them, the carburetor bowl and the starter. The best possible winter lay-up is with your local outboard agent.

The Diesel Engine

This is altogether a larger and more complex piece of machinery than the outboard motor. To get the best out of it, you must acquire a smattering of mechanical knowledge: you should know how to bleed the fuel system, replace hoses, adjust the tension of the dynamo belt, do an oil change and grease generally.

Installation

There would be no need for this paragraph if engines were always installed expertly but, alas! you cannot take this for granted. You might be able to superintend the installation yourself and, if necessary, have it modified.

You don't have to turn the cabin into a workshop littered with greasy and evil smelling bits of machinery. There should be a drip-tray underneath the engine to catch dripping oil and diesel fuel. Otherwise the bilges get filthy and the cabin smells. This drip-tray should be placed well down and be easily emptied with a syringe. The engine should be installed in a closed compartment that allows it to draw its air from outside. Otherwise the greasy smell of diesel fuel invades the cabin.

A diesel engine vibrates and is noisy, but this can be kept to a minimum if it is mounted on a rubber shock-absorber. If this plan is adopted, all other joints between the hull and the engine must also be flexible, or they will break. It follows that the propeller shaft coupling must also be flexible and so must all connecting pipes and the exhaust. All these connections are subject to wear. Rubber shock-absorbers and flexible couplings don't like diesel oil and the flexible section of an exhaust pipe rusts quickly, and all of them need to be renewed every year or two.

The position of the fuel tank deserves special mention. It ought to be lower than the engine. This means that a leak in the fuel pipe makes the pump suck air and the engine stops, but at least fuel does not escape into the bilges.

Petty engine troubles are bound to arise, the worst being lubrication faults and cooling defects. In a car these failures are signalled by lights or dials which the driver has constantly before his eyes. On a boat, however, the dash is not always in your view and a good refinement is to duplicate warning lights with an alarm signal, which goes off whenever there is either a lubrication or a cooling breakdown. As soon as the signal is heard, you should stop the engine, after looking at the control panel to find out what is causing the trouble. If it has been well installed, the sound signal should go off whenever the engine is stopped or started, in the same way that the oil warning lamp lights up on the dashboard of a car.

The salt water inlet cock should be mounted where it can be got at easily, and everybody on board should know where it is; it should have its own handle, permanently fitted, to allow it to be shut off immediately in case of trouble.

Finally, you should have a good set of tools and equipment for running repairs and normal maintenance. Naturally enough, you only need the equipment for the jobs that you know how to do. If you are a hopelessly poor mechanic, at the first sign of trouble, turn off the engine and carry on as though you had never had one!

Operation

Fuel Supply

If there are air bubbles in the fuel pipe (always the case when you run out of fuel) the engine will stop for the slightest air bubble blocks the fuel injection pump.

To bleed the circuit:

1. Unscrew the fuel supply line at the injection pump (when there is no bleed tap). Allow the fuel to run or pump it by hand until no further air bubbles appear, then refix the fuel pipe.
2. Undo the nut holding the fuel lines onto the injectors, one turn of the nut only. Open the throttle and turn the engine if possible by hand, until all air is also ejected from this part of the circuit, then tighten the nut and start the engine.

This is an extremely simple operation when you have done it once; get a mechanic to show you.

Cooling

Most modern diesels have two cooling circuits: the engines are cooled by fresh water which, in turn, is cooled by salt water.

The fresh water is contained in a closed circuit system, identical to that of some cars. It should always be kept topped up and a supply of fresh water for this purpose should be kept on board. It is dangerous to put salt water into the system, even for emergency purposes, because the metal liners will not stand up to it.

The salt water system is an open circuit. Water is pumped through a strainer below the water line, passes through a heat exchanger where it cools the fresh water, and is then ejected through an outlet and often through the exhaust pipe.

If a warning light indicates that the engine is over-heating, it should be stopped immediately, and the water level in the fresh water system checked.

If there is a shortage of water, the system should be filled up after the motor has had a chance to cool off a little and after having repaired any leaks.

If there is plenty of water, the engine should still be allowed to cool off a little and started again to check the salt water circulation. If this is normal, it is probably the fresh water pump which has broken down; there is no chance of repairing this yourself.

If the water circulation is weak or not working at all, there are several possible reasons:

The salt water inlet seacock may be closed.

The strainer may be blocked. This can be checked by closing the seacock, taking off the inlet pipe, opening the seacock again to see if water flows in.

If neither the seacock nor the strainer is at fault, the situation is more serious: either the circuit is blocked or the pump has failed. Again the mechanic must be consulted.

Lubrication

Always use the type and grade of oil recommended by the engine manufacturer, keeping to the same brand in the correct quantities; too much is just as bad as too little.

Change the oil too often rather than too little. Even if the engine has not been run a great deal, do not run her on oil which is more than 3 months old.

When the oil warning light comes on because oil pressure is low the engine should be stopped and the oil level checked. If it is low, it is merely a question of filling up. Otherwise, get back under sail because the breakdown is serious and impossible to repair at sea.

If the gear box has a separate sump from the engine, its oil level should be checked every two weeks and changed at least once a year.

Ancillary items should not be forgotten. Fresh water and salt water pumps, stern gland, remote controls (gear and throttle) and dynamo should be greased or lubricated at least on every oil change and more often if the engine is used a lot.

Electrics

As soon as the engine starts, the dynamo or the alternator should charge the battery, and this can be checked by the gauge or warning light. After the engine has been running for a time (five minutes to two hours) the charge will slacken but the meter should never drop to zero. If the dynamo is not charging, it is often because its driving belt has stretched, and that is easily tightened.

If the battery is to work and last long, it should be kept topped up about a $\frac{1}{4}$in above the plates. This level should be checked once a month and topped up as required with pure water (distilled water or rain water). If there is a general impression of lack of electricity (weak lighting even when the engine has just been running) it is often due to the battery cells not being fully topped up.

Starting, Running, Stopping

Before starting, check:

The levels of fuel, fresh water and oil.
That the salt water inlet cock is open.
That the engine is out of gear. If the engine has an electric starter, avoid running it for too long or you will quickly drain the battery; after two failures to start, it is better to check that everything is in order than to keep on pushing the button.

Once the engine has started, check:

That the salt water cooling system is circulating.
That there is sufficient oil pressure.

It is best to allow an engine a short while to warm up before putting a load on it. Run it for a few minutes at low revs and then, once in gear, keep to half-speed for the first five minutes.

A diesel engine can be run at approximately 80% of its maximum power for indefinite periods.

If you want to be able to run for long periods at low revolutions, if you are fishing perhaps, you should choose an engine designed with this ability and have it tuned accordingly.

Finally, to stop the engine, decelerate and then switch off and that is all. If the engine has been properly fitted there is no need to close the sea water inlet valve or the fuel tap (the latter can cause an air block in the fuel pipe).

Laying-up

If you want to find your engine in good condition in the spring, there are several things to do.

Fill the lubricating system with inhibiting oil, and put a little in each cylinder. Choose a type of oil recommended by the engine manufacturer.
Empty the fresh water system to avoid freezing.
Remove the battery, the generator and the self starter, and take them to a garage.
Clean the outside of the engine, and wipe over lightly with oil.
Turn the engine by hand for several revolutions once or twice a month to stop the piston gumming up and thus damaging the liners and piston rings.

Navigation Instruments

Navigation instruments all measure something and they are therefore generally fragile and expensive. You should think carefully about where to stow them. The ones that are frequently used should be in well protected places and be easily accessible, so that they can be always put back in place when not in use. The ones that are fixed should be protected from knocks and also, of course, from water.

Compass

A compass gives direction in relation to magnetic North.

It comprises one or more magnets fixed to the compass card, a circular plate graduated from 0°–360°, mounted on a pivot and operating in a liquid inside a closed bowl. Depending on the brand of compass, the liquid may be white spirit, glycerine, petroleum spirit or a mixture of water and alcohol.

The magnets line up in the direction of the earth's magnetic field and the card is graduated so that zero always points to magnetic north.

Steering Compass

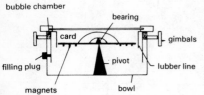

The centreline of the boat is shown on a steering compass by a mark, the *lubberline*, which allows the helmsman to read directly on the card the course which he is steering. The compass is gimballed so that it always stays horizontal irrespective of the boat's movement.

There are several types of steering compass.

Traditional Compass. This is a simple instrument and therefore fairly cheap. The ship's course can be read from it at all times, but it is not very convenient for the helmsman because he has to keep a rather small graduation mark in line with the lubberline. This type is really only practical if the thirty-two divisions of the standard compass card (North by East, etc.) are marked on it, thus making them easy to see.

Domed Compass. This is the same type of instrument as the traditional compass, but the glass that covers the bowl is domed and acts as a magnifying glass on the graduation marks. To bring out the magnifying effect, the helmsman should place himself either in line with the principal lubberline or else directly to one side, because the compass has two auxiliary lubberlines at right angles to the axis. This compass is suitable for boats with wheel steering, but it is not so convenient if you steer with a tiller. It is fragile and really only comes into its own on larger boats.

Grid Steering Compass. To maintain a course by following the markings of a compass is a tiring and demanding business. With this type of compass it is much easier to maintain course because you merely have to keep easily seen lines parallel. This means the compass can be fitted anywhere – provided that you can see it!

This type is produced in two forms. In the first, the compass is fairly ordinary but the card has conspicuous markings, usually a thick line running north to south. The lubberline is continued over to the outside of the compass bowl. The glass has a grid superimposed with a transparent card, graduated from 0°–360° and having two parallel lines running north to south; this grid may be rotated and then locked in position. To set the course for the helmsman, the grid is turned so that the course selected coincides with the lubberline on the compass. The helmsman then merely has to align the north–south line on the compass card down the middle of the grid lines. It is still possible to read the course being steered against the lubberline inside the compass bowl. The only drawback of this fitting is that condensation or water can get between the rotating grid and the glass underneath it, making it difficult to read the compass card.

Compass set for a course of 244° magnetic. The boat is on course when North on the card coincides with North on the grid

The other version of this type has an identical card but no transparent grid. In this one, the north–south lines are marked on the compass glass, and it is the rim of the bowl which is marked, so that the entire compass turns in a framework which has its own lubberline. While it eliminates the drawback of the first compass, you cannot however read your course without lining up the zero mark of the compass bowl with the lubberline of the azimuth ring.

Vertical Reading Compass. This compass is not often seen in cruising yachts, because it is difficult to site it conveniently. As the lubberline is behind the card, the helmsman has to reverse his reactions at the helm.

There are also many simplified compasses without gimbals and smaller, which are perfectly satisfactory for small boats.

Installation

When a compass is installed it should be placed as far as possible from anything metal on the boat. If you are not able to eliminate completely the magnetic influences of metal, the compass will not point accurately north; it will have a *deviation*. It can, however, be *compensated*. This operation, which should be carried out by a specialist, consists of placing near the compass magnets designed to counter the electrical and magnetic influences on board.

A grid steering compass can be placed either in front or behind the helmsman; it need not be very near to him because it should be easily readable a few feet away. A domed compass should be just in front of the helmsman so that it can be read perpendicularly to its axis. A traditional compass should also be in front of the helmsman but its position is slightly less critical. To keep the cockpit clear, you should have two domed compasses, or else two vertical reading compasses on the aft bulkhead on the coach roof, or else a single vertical reading compass on the coach roof itself. The snag of this kind of lay-out is the risk of interference between the compasses: steering, hand bearing and radio direction finding. The steering compass is often blocked from the helmsman's view by crew who sit between him and the coach roof. Whatever position is finally chosen, the compass should be firmly mounted and shielded from knocks.

Lighting

Compass lighting should be efficient but not so strong as to blind the helmsman. Low voltage bulbs should be used, preferably coloured red (you can colour them yourself with nail varnish).

Some compasses, unfortunately usually extremely expensive, have properly fitted built-in lighting; others are more simply luminous (usually course keeping compasses), which is good but the luminosity only lasts for a year or two. In practice compass lighting is usually installed by the owner. A simple and effective method is soldering directly onto a bulb a wire which is then joined to the ship's electrical supply or to batteries. The bulb is attached to the compass glass with modelling plasticine, which also acts as a form of shade. Lighting the compass by a flashlight is not advised for dry batteries which are not always anti-magnetic (even if they appear to be cased in plastic). The reading given by a compass lit in this way can be false and it only becomes true when it is once again plunged into darkness . . .

Maintenance

A compass needs little maintenance, but do not forget to lubricate the joints of the gimbal, or the azimuth ring of certain course-keeping compasses.

If a bubble appears in the liquid, it can be got rid of by up-ending the compass for a moment and then slowly turning it back again. If it does not disappear, more liquid must be added by an expert. Compass liquid is usually a 50/50 mixture of pure alcohol and distilled water; if this does not work, consult the manufacturer.

Hand-Bearing Compass

This is an ordinary compass which can be held in the hand, and which has a prism allowing the holder to view horizontally while still being able to read the compass card.

Although it is portable, this compass must be treated with care. It should either be kept in its case or held in the hand; never put it down 'for a moment' in a corner nor hang round the neck.

If it is lit by batteries, make sure that these are anti-magnetic. To check whether they are, put them on top of the compass and watch its reactions as you move them about. Make sure to check each battery because, although of the same type, individual ones may not be absolutely anti-magnetic.

Because it is portable, the hand bearing compass is not compensated like a steering compass, compensation being only valid for one particular position. In steel boats or those made of ferro-cement (which is reinforced by magnetic metal) it is better to rely on a fixed steering compass only. Alternatively, it is possible to use an azimuth bearing ring, with which the angle off from the centreline of the boat to a particular landmark is taken and not the actual compass bearing.

The Log

To measure the speed and the distance made good by a boat, mechanical logs are used and, more frequently than ever now, electronic logs. It is also very easy to make for oneself the traditional 'ship log'.

Ship Log

The ship log is a small, flat piece of wood, ballasted so as to float vertically and attached to the log line by a span (see the illustration on the following page). Along the line put knots 25ft 4in apart (i.e. 1/240 of a nautical mile). Drop the 'log' in the water and pay out the line as it drops astern. Then, after the first knot, count the number of knots that slip through your hands inside 15 seconds (i.e. 1/240 of an hour). This is why speed is given in 'knots', so 8 knots is 8 nautical miles per hour.

Also, instead of measuring the distance run in a given time, one can measure the time necessary to run a given distance. In this case two knots are made 100ft apart, the first one 15 to 20ft from the 'log'. As a boat travels 100ft in one minute at 1 knot the remaining calculation is simple: $\frac{1}{2}$ minute = 2 knots, $\frac{1}{3}$ minute = 3 knots, $\frac{1}{4}$ minute = 4 knots and so on.

The ship log is not only easy to make but it is accurate at all speeds, which cannot be said for other logs.

The Mechanical or Patent Log

This is a meter that counts nautical miles. It is turned by a rotator which is pulled behind the boat. The meter registers the distance travelled through the water but it does not indicate speed directly.

Streaming and recovering the log line requires some elementary know-how. Since the rotator turns as soon as it is put in the water, the line twists if it is not able to turn the instrument. When you stream the log, therefore, the end is made fast to the governor and the line is paid out in a bight before throwing out the rotator. When you take in the log, detach the line from the instrument and let it trail in the water while you pull in the rotator; this allows the line to untwist. To avoid the risk of losing the whole assembly overboard, pass the bight round the rail. When the rotator comes to hand, the whole of the line is then trailing in the water and has untwisted itself. It can then be drawn in and coiled as it comes.

This instrument is simple and strong, but it has its faults for it does not register well below speeds of two knots and it can be jammed by seaweed without being noticed. The rotator has been known to be taken by a large fish and, if you are fishing yourself, it can happen that the rotator makes your first catch.

The mechanical log requires a little maintenance. The meter should be oiled every five hundred miles and the line should be changed as soon as it shows signs of wear near the rotator.

Making a ship's log

The float. Use a piece of 8mm plywood, a small wedge of timber and a piece of lead sheeting for making the float illustrated in the diagram. The lead weight must be just heavy enough to make it float upright, just breaking the surface.

The span consists of two lengths of line, 3–4mm in diameter and 80cm long and a clothes peg. Tie a figure of eight knot in the middle of one length and a loop at one end. Tie the other end to the hole in the piece of wood at the upper corner of the float. Fix the other length of line in the spring of the clothes peg with figure of eight knots on either side of the spring. Attach the other ends of this line to the lower corners of the float. All you have to do now is to clip the peg to the upper line in front of the figure of eight knot (to stop it slipping back). You now have a detachable span. Its three lines should be of equal length. This is a convenient arrangement when the log is pulled in: just shake the line, the peg opens, the float turns edge-on to the water and offers no resistance.

The Line. Use a plaited line 2–3mm in diameter and at least 70m long (if you expect to make 8 knots). To attach the line to the span, make a large loop at the end, big enough to go over the float. Pass it through the small loop at the end of the span, drop it over the float and pull tight.

Tie a series of figure of eight knots along the line, the first about 10m from the float. Theoretically the interval between knots should be 7.71, but in practice, as the boat is slowed a little by the log, 7.50m is more practical. Tie small pieces of different coloured materials in the figure of eight knots that can be easily recognised. Flake the line into a bucket attached to the stern.

If you have no such materials, the log can be made even more simply by attaching a bottle to the lead line, filled with just enough water to let it just float. In this case the knots should be spaced at 7m intervals to allow for the drag of the bottle

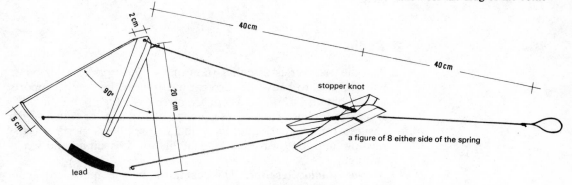

The Electronic Log

It works on the same principle: the number of turns of a rotator (or of a paddle wheel) are counted. The rotator is more like a propeller and is extremely small (approximately $\frac{1}{2}$in in diameter) and is fitted underneath the hull; counting is registered electronically and the instrument shows both the distance travelled and your current speed. A repeater dial can be placed close to the helmsman to show the boat's speed at all times.

The electronic log is more delicate than its mechanical counterpart, but it is more sensitive for it reads down to half a knot. If seaweed catches on the propeller the helmsman usually notices immediately thanks to the repeater dial. The rotator is retractable and can be withdrawn for cleaning at all times.

Barometer

'Do not tap my glass, I am doing my best. Do not fasten me to the main bulkhead, the pounding of the boat upsets me,' implores the barometer.

The barometer is for showing the actual atmospheric pressure, so that it can be compared with the forecast given by meteoroligical stations. To calibrate the instrument note the reading at 06.00 hrs or at 18.00 hrs GMT and then compare it with the pressure given for these times in the local newspaper the following day. Alter the needle of the barometer (by means of the small screw at the back) to correct any over- or under-reading. Check again the following day.

Radio

A radio receiver is essential (nowadays obligatory) on all boats which cruise, to know the correct time, to hear the weather reports and to obtain D/F fixes. There are three basic types.

Domestic Radio. This is the universal transistor radio which ensures time signals and reception of weather reports on the medium and long wave-bands. Suitable for day sailing and week-ending.

Marine Radio Receiver. This operates on the high frequency, medium, long and trawler bands used by coastal radio stations.

D/F Radio. This receives signals from radio beacons in the HF band and can give bearings by means of a sensitive aerial which can be rotated to minimum signal, thus showing the bearing of the particular beacon relative either to north or to the ship's head. Some aerials can be mounted on a hand bearing compass, or have a compass incorporated.

Radio receivers should be carefully stowed on board, well out of the way of damage and spray. Keep away from compasses, because loud speakers incorporate fairly powerful magnets. The D/F aerial is even more fragile than the H/B compass and should be stowed immediately after use.

Leadline and Echo Sounder

Leadline

A full length leadline consists of a line some 125ft long, fitted with a lead weight of 6–8lb spliced to one end. The weight should have a hollow in its base which can be filled with tallow (or even soap) to collect a sample of the bottom, either to identify the area or merely to verify that it has, in fact, touched bottom.

The leadline can be marked off using indelible marker pens. One colour for the tens of fathoms (1 mark at 10, 2 marks at 20) and another colour for the fives (1 mark at 15, 2 marks at 25). Mark individual feet over the first 2 fathoms and individual fathoms for the first 5.

Don't forget that the line will be stretched by the lead so mark accordingly.

A leadline is best stowed in a bucket, a bag or a basket. Tie its free end into the container and then flake the line down keeping the lead on top (if you coil it, you are sure to get it tangled).

A leadline is an adequate depth finder for most boats, and is essential even if you have an echo sounder.

The Echo Sounder

This is an electronic device which shows continually the depth of water under you and to considerable depths, thus enabling a *sounding* to be followed easily (a contour line on a chart showing the relief of the sea bed).

The echo sounder consists of an ultrasonic transmitter/receiver working through a transducer fitted to the ship's bottom. Because she heels, a sailing yacht often has a transducer fitted on each side, with a mercury operated change-over switch to ensure that the leeward unit is always in operation. The transducer head should be kept clean, or its readings will be suspect. For offshore use the echo sounder should work to at least 50 fathoms (100m).

Wind Vane and Anemometer

These two units are generally interconnected and mounted at the masthead, their readings being transmitted electronically to dials in the cockpit. They are only found on well equipped boats because they are expensive and are only really needed for racing yachts. Since they record wind which is not interrupted by the rigging, the readings they give are accurate and valuable, at least while the wind is steady and the sea calm. But in very light winds and a choppy sea their readings are too variable to be reliable.

The Sextant

The sextant is an optical instrument allowing angles to be measured with great accuracy and particularly the angle between a heavenly body and the horizon.

Principle

On a framework made in the form of an arc, a telescope and a small mirror (the horizon mirror) are firmly mounted. The *arc* is toothed and graduated from 0° to 120°. A large mirror moved by an arm or *index* (and therefore called the *index mirror*) pivots on the axis of this arc. The index has a micrometer screw engaging in the teeth of the arc and graduated in minutes and tenths of a minute of arc. The horizon mirror is of transparent glass which has a high coefficient of reflection.

By looking through the telescope, the horizon is seen through the horizon mirror and, superimposed upon it, the image of the heavenly body is reflected by both the index and horizon mirrors. By pivoting the index mirror the two points, between which the angle is to be measured, are brought together: in this case the lower edge of the sun and the horizon. To know the degree of the angle, the degrees are read off on the arc, the minutes and tenths of a minute on the drum of the micrometer.

On old sextants, the horizon mirror has its left half transparent and its right half silvered. The edge of the reflecting part and the transparent part is in the line of sight. There is no micrometer: the arc is graduated in degrees and tens of minutes. The minutes and tenths of minutes are read on the vernier of the index.

Micrometer Sextant

Adjustments

The sextant is a very exact instrument, but easily goes out of adjustment. It must be periodically checked:

Before each season, check the alignment of the mirrors.
Before each observation, measure the index error.

Perpendicularity of the Index Mirror to the Arc. With the sextant two clips can be supplied which are used for this adjustment. The sextant having been laid down flat, a clip is placed on each end of the arc.

You must look through it as shown in diagram A. The perpendicularity is correct (photo B) when the edge of the clip, which is seen directly, is in prolongation of the edge of the clip reflected by the mirror (the latter has adjusting screws on its back).

Perpendicularity of the Horizontal Mirror to the Arc. The sextant is held flat. The arm is set to zero. Through the telescope a horizontal line some way off is sighted (the ridge of a roof for instance or a calm horizon). The adjusting screw is turned if necessary until the direct image and the reflected image of this line are superimposed exactly (diagram C).

Index Error. The sextant is held vertical. The direct and the reflected image of the horizon are brought together. The angle read on the sextant ought to be zero; if it is not, the difference from zero gives the index error (diagram D). It must be known so as to add it to or take it away from any angles subsequently read: it is added if it has been read to the right of the zero on the arc, it is taken away if it has been read on the left.

Upkeep

The sextant is fragile, it must not be subjected to the slightest shock. Upkeep consists of regularly coating the instrument with a thin layer of vaseline (with the help of cotton wool). It must be kept in its box, protected from water. The arcs of old sextants have such fine graduations on them that it is better not to touch them.

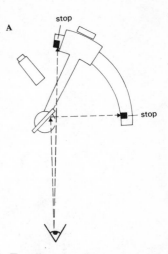

A. To adjust the mirrors, the sextant is placed flat on a table and you take a sight as illustrated above. B. The index mirror is at right angles to the arc. 1. The right hand stop is seen in the large mirror. 2. The left hand stop is seen direct. 3. The edges of the stops are in line. C. The horizon mirror is not yet perpendicular to the arc. D. The index error is here +5′

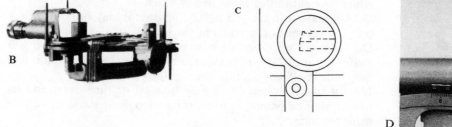

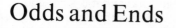

Odds and Ends

There is still a whole range of small items on board a boat, and only the phrase odds and ends can cover all of them. As you may imagine, the odds and ends are all important, but we shall only deal here with the more usual ones.

Boat's Tender

This is the largest accessory and the most abused. When it comes to a tender or dinghy, the yachtsman has many conflicting stipulations: since it is only an auxiliary it should be cheap; as it must be lifted on board, stowed and carried on shore, it must be light and not bulky. Ideally it should be able to take the whole crew ashore at one time, along with their equipment and food; thus, it should be large, well built and stable – a proper boat. We also consider that it should be unsinkable.

It is impossible to meet all these conditions, or at least most of them, and there is only one answer: an inflatable dinghy. In spite of its defects when it comes to rowing in strong wind, it is the only type we are going to consider here.

Precautions. An inflatable dinghy is nearly perfect apart from its excessive windage. It is tough and only deflates or gets punctured if it is carelessly treated. To keep it in good condition, several elementary precautions must be taken.

Do not step on it when it is deflated or folded.

When approaching the shore, get out before it touches the bottom.

Do not let it chafe on the beach, at the water's edge: it should either be right out of the water or afloat.

Do not leave it in the sun tightly inflated: it may burst if the air pressure increases too much in the heat.

Do not moor up alongside a harbour wall or slip because it will chafe; but it can be safely moored alongside the boat, and it will not chafe itself nor damage the topsides.

Do not tow it at sea, for it may take off or turn over; and its towing ring or painter is not strong enough to stand this treatment for long.

The valves are the most usual cause of air leak, and it is a good idea to put a drop of mineral oil on these every month or so.

Propulsion. As it is so light, an inflatable boat needs efficient propulsion to make way against the wind and the waves. Sculling is rather ineffectual even with a proper notch in the transom. Rowing is much easier, but the boat must have proper rowlocks and oars (collapsible oars are often not solid enough). You must be able to sit reasonably high up on a jerrican for instance. In addition to the oars, a good pair of paddles will also come in useful. An outboard motor is the best propulsion but you must first make sure that the transom is strong enough to take it.

Repairs. Don't wait till a rubber dinghy bursts before taking action. Trouble can be avoided by sticking patches over places that are beginning to wear. Strips of reinforcing material can be bought to stick over places most likely to show signs of wear through first. Keep an eye on weak spots such as where the wooden transom slots in and reinforce them before they actually become unstuck.

To repair a punctured rubber dinghy:

Find the leak. Blow up the dinghy then wipe it with a well-soaped sponge and see where it bubbles.

Carefully rub down all round the hole with a file or glass-paper. Be sure to remove all the top surface of the rubber which is specially treated so that it won't stick. Rub down the patch as well.

Apply the first coat of rubber solution on the two surfaces that are to be stuck. Wait for at least a quarter of an hour to give time for the solution to dry.

Apply a second coat, and wait again. When the solution is tacky (it may stick to your finger, but not much), put the patch on.

For the repair to stick properly the temperature of the air and the two surfaces must be at least 20°C.

Laying Up. Before putting an inflatable boat away for the winter, it should be hosed down with fresh water and then stowed half inflated, away from light and heat. If you must leave it folded, make sure that it is dry and dusted with French chalk.

The Scull and its Rowlock ('crutch' to the purist)

On modern boats, which often have a high freeboard, the scull has to be very long: the entire blade must be under water and the sculler should be comfortably placed. There is hardly ever room for the scull in the cabin: it must be kept on deck, easily accessible and well secured. Its chocks should hold it straight, otherwise it may warp. It is best placed on the same side as the rowlock.

The rowlock is on the port side for right-handers. It should be held at an angle of 30° for the sculler to get the right purchase. On some cruising boats this rowlock may be fixed. On some boats however you must be able to remove it as it can be a snag for the mainsheet or whatever. In which case, make sure it is tied on.

When the transom board is higher than the deck it is better to cut a sculling notch reinforced with brass or copper.

Rowlock and or notch must be perfectly smooth to prevent wear on the scull.

Mooring Lines

At least two mooring lines of 70–700ft are needed on a cruising boat, and three or four are infinitely preferable.

As long as they are strong they do not need to be the best quality for you may need to cut them and, in any case, they will wear out quickly. At Glénans we use polypropylene of $1\frac{1}{4}$in circumference for day sailers and up to $2\frac{1}{2}$in circumference for bigger boats.

In relatively tideless waters like the Mediterranean it is useful to have a number of steel cables with an eye spliced in either end for mooring directly to the rocks in narrow creeks and inlets where there is no holding ground. The cables can be passed around rocks on either side of the creek and the boat attached to them by nylon warps. If it blows up a bit one can, with this method, keep the boat steady in the middle of the creek.

Fenders

Fenders are to protect the boat's topsides against harbour walls or other boats. There are many types made of a wide variety of materials. Ideally they should not move once they have been made fast, and only flat fenders have this quality, but there are not many on the market at the moment. Old car tyres are the most efficient; but they are awkward to stow and make black marks on white topsides unless they are covered with canvas.

As well as ordinary fenders, it is useful to have two or three large inflatable buoy-type fenders, which are extremely practical when there is a lot of movement.

Fenders should always be hung vertically, or they will ride up. To be really effective you should have three or four on each side, the smallest in the middle and the largest towards each end.

Legs

Legs are lengths of wood or metal which keep the boat upright when she dries out. They should be three or four inches shorter than the keel when in position to avoid the whole weight of the boat resting on them when the keel settles into the sea-bed.

The base of each leg should be dimensioned in relation to the size of the boat. If the base is too narrow, the leg will sink into the ground, be liable to strain out of true and break; but if it is too broad, it may not bed sufficiently into hard ground to line up with the keel. Our experience shows that surfaces of 8 square inches for a $2\frac{1}{2}$ tonner, 12 square inches for a 6 tonner and 16 square inches for a 9 tonner are about right. But do not have 16 square inches for a $2\frac{1}{2}$ tonner.

Legs are usually bolted, into the bulwarks if there are any or, if not, into the hull itself (do not forget in this case to bung the holes when you take off the legs). These points must obviously be reinforced.

Even on a small boat, leg bolts should be strong or they will quickly bend. To give an idea of size, we suggest bolts of $\frac{1}{2}$in diameter for a Mousquetaire, $\frac{3}{4}$in diameter for a 2 tonner and 1in for a 10 tonner.

Finally, so that the legs shall be absolutely vertical, they should be rigged with the aid of guys run from the foot of the leg and made fast on board near the bow and transom. The guys should preferably be of polypropylene line which does not stretch too much.

Pump, Bucket, Bailer

A bailer or a pump are the best means of getting a small amount of water out of the boat. But when there is a lot of water, the pump is usually not fast enough and there is nothing so efficient as a good bucket. It is exhausting to use in all senses of the word, but it is efficient at least until the water level is down to a few inches. At this point the pump or the bailer can take over again.

The Heads

There are many sorts of heads: the most commonly used at the moment is the marine head. The essential part of this equipment is a hand pump allowing the contents to be emptied straight out into the sea. So, in principle, it offers the same guarantees of comfort as your land installation. In fact, the pump often turns out to be far too fragile. It must be used carefully, and yet with firmness. It blocks up easily, only accepting the thinnest of papers, and sometimes even no paper at all. It can cause a leak, and you mustn't forget to shut off the stopcocks in the hull every time it is used. It needs a certain amount of upkeep; cocks and plunger have to be greased at least once a year. Finally, this apparatus shouldn't be used in crowded harbours, or in tideless basins, which will gradually be turned into cesspools.

Chemical WCs have certain advantages: if we overlook some very advanced systems, usually they do not cost a lot, and you have no mechanical troubles. It is a clean system and doesn't pollute harbours. Clearly there are some chores to be done: they must be emptied regularly and the correct chemicals put in; if you spill the latter in the boat, they attack wood and metal hulls.

The mere bucket, however, remains a very reasonable solution, which only makes the tactless blush. It has the advantage of being cheap, not leaking, and there is no danger. It can't be used however in harbours, but they usually have lavatories.

Finally, on boats where civilisation has not yet made its inroads, there are people who go for a stroll – in the absence of all these systems – as far as the pulpit, and find there total comfort.

Lighting

On board a boat, lighting is either by electricity or paraffin.

Electricity. As you only have a weak current, losses must be kept to a minimum. It is therefore advisable to use large diameter cable. As contacts oxydise quickly (which increases the losses) it is better to solder joints rather than fit watertight junction boxes (which in fact let in water, and retain it), and use switches with silver contacts rather than brass.

Fluorescent tubes consume less current than ordinary bulbs. As for the number of bulbs to put in, everything depends on how well you tolerate the noise of an engine recharging batteries.

Two independent circuits should be fitted for preference: one for navigation (navigation lights, compass light, chart table), one for living accommodation (galley, saloon, bunks).

Paraffin. Huddled in the hut we call the cabin, sheltered from wind and wave, many yachtsmen marvel at the discovery of the quality of paraffin lighting. The lamp gives a soft, sensitive light, and recreates a long forgotten atmosphere. It only smells bad if the wick is badly trimmed.

There are some handsome paraffin lamps swung in gimbals, but you can also make do with hurricane lamps. These must have sound fixings in well chosen spots.

To put out a hurricane lamp, blow on it; if you lower the wick too far it falls into the paraffin container – anyway that is one way of keeping a supply of spare wicks.

Even if you have electric fitments, you must have at least one hurricane lamp on board, in case of breakdown, and to serve as a mooring light.

When you haven't electricity, nevertheless you must have a fixed lamp available supplied from a number of batteries (the sort used for lighting caravans). It is useful when you need to have light quickly – or to look for the matches. . .

Tools

A certain minimum number of tools are indispensible on board any boat which cruises overnight, and the following are essential:

An adjustable spanner (able to grip the largest bolt on board)
A pair of pliers
1 medium screw driver
1 small electrician's screw driver
1 hammer
1 marlin spike
1 pair of bolt croppers or wire cutters (to cut away shrouds if dismasted)
1 sailmaker's palm and assorted needles

Finally, if the boat has an auxiliary engine, tools for simple repairs and maintenance.

This list is the minimum, and we recommend adding the following which have proved themselves invaluable from time to time:

1 small saw
A hacksaw with spare blades
1 cold chisel (the anchor serves as an anvil)
1 hand drill and bits
1 wood chisel
1 oilstone
1 small vice (if it can be fixed on an edge)
Spanners, pliers and screw drivers of various sizes and a corkscrew!

Spare Parts

Here it is impossible to give a typical list as everything depends on the boat, and the skipper must just ensure that he has a wide range.

When talking of the hull, the rigging and the sails, we have frequently mentioned spare items which have seemed to us necessary. We would add here:

Spare line or rope for all sizes used on board, and as long as the longest of them. For example, if the boat is only equipped with one kind of line (same material, same diameter) it is only necessary to have one line as long as the main sheet to cover all eventualities (nevertheless, its as well to have one or two spare reef points, which are probably not of the same size).

Sailcloth of the same weight as the principal sails and some sail thread: cotton for stitches and hemp or nylon for whippings.

Some wire, galvanised, stainless and brass.

Stainless steel split pins, of all sizes used on board (in order not to lose them, they should be stuck between two strips of adhesive transparent tape).

One or two blocks.

Some shackles.

Several pieces of plywood, to close a broken porthole, make an improvised water barrier, or merely to make small repairs.

One or two sail battens of the largest size.

Some tallow for shackles and screws; oil for blocks and sheaves; grease for winches; a bottle of Scotch in case the other one breaks, etc, etc.

7. Laying-up and Fitting Out

As it sails a boat knows no rest. The sea and the wind subject it to continual strain. Salt water and sea air gnaw away at it. A ceaseless battle has to be fought against wear and corrosion; inspect, repair, maintain in every corner. Even the running maintenance, as we have outlined it in the preceding chapters, in the long run proves inadequate. There comes a day when it is not enough, and a serious general overhaul is needed.

For a yacht, the opportunity for this overhaul is the end-of-season laying-up (until the golden age of all-the-year-round sailing). Laying-up gives you a chance to look into details, to ferret out signs of wear, of hull, rigging and equipment. It is also the time to think of the future: if the work of laying-up is conscientiously done, the next fitting-out will be simple.

Since the days spent on laying-up and fitting-out are days lost for sailing, it is in the owner's interest so to organise things that the work is reduced to a minimum. In fact, preparations for laying-up can begin a long way ahead – throughout the whole season, specially during the last days of cruising. A good way of not finding oneself up to the eyes in work at the last moment is to keep a notebook on board in which anything that goes wrong is noted daily. This notebook isn't only used at laying-up time but all the time: in it are noted all the little repairs you can do yourself in port and ticked off as they are done. But in the notebook also are the repairs that can wait until the end of the season, renewals of equipment that must be made, and desirable improvements. We recommend having a thick book which will last several years; it will become a real 'health record' of the boat. It enables you to make an instant appraisal of the state of things and have a long term view. It is also the link between the day you lay-up and the day you come to fit-out, reminding you of what can so easily be forgotten during the dark winter months.

Laying-up

Common gossip has it that a good sailor is lazy by nature. Let us understand by that that he is a wise man, anxious to avoid unnecessary chores. In laying-up a modern yacht, this attitude is reasonable enough. This type of boat is in fact made of durable, easily maintained materials; moreover, it usually sails little, and is not very worn at the end of the season. It seems therefore that a good job of laying-up can be done by sticking to the following principles: repair everything which has to be repaired, but take as little apart as possible ensuring the maintenance of the equipment in its normal place.

Of course, there is no law against completely unrigging your boat and having the pleasure of going over it with a fine toothcomb during the winter. But this means that the boat must be near home, and that you have time to spare. And that usually is not the case. In fact, the way you lay-up depends to a great extent on where and how you keep the boat over winter.

Methods of Laying-up

A dinghy doesn't get in the way much; it can winter anywhere, the hull simply turned over on the ground, the mast if possible under cover somewhere, and all the equipment carried away in the car. But the bigger the boat is, the more equipment it contains and the more complicated things become. We have already called attention to this when discussing the choice of boat: if it is transportable and can be stowed at home, it is all quite simple; if it cannot be transported you must plan according to the type of yards in your area and, naturally, your financial resources. There are several ways and means.

Wintering Afloat. This is the simplest solution: you hardly lay-up at all and the boat is there ready for use anytime; but this can

Dinghies can survive the winter quite happily if they are turned upside down and raised above the ground to allow air to circulate. They must be secured fast if they are not to be blown about by the wind

only be considered if the boat lies in a perfectly sheltered harbour, well equipped and under constant supervision, even at night. There must be a reliable watchman to air and dry the boat regularly; to keep an eye on the warps and to renew them, if need be, without waiting for them to break; to put the fenders back in place, change them, and, eventually, to warn off squatters and pilferers.

The laying-up berth itself does not cost very much out of season, but the price of looking after the boat is often high. You should allow for one or two careenings in the course of the winter, even if you do not use the boat. Paint- and varnish-work deteriorate quickly.

A boat's tolerance of wintering afloat depends on how it is built. It is valid for boats of the vintage class for they benefit from being kept in the water although, sooner or later, they ought to be dried out and inspected for rot or gribble. Plywood hulls tend to get a little heavier and, if not well built, deteriorate more quickly in the water than slipped. But a fibreglass boat survives perfectly; all you need to supply is elbow grease in the spring to restore the hull to its original gloss. A metal boat does not suffer either, unless it is moored side by side with another, or too near a hull covered with copper based paints.

Wintering on the Beach or in a Mud Berth

You must moor the boat high enough for it only to be reached by the water at spring tides. This is the traditional way of wintering in areas with a big tidal range; it is particularly suitable for wooden boats, which dry out just enough for the gribble to die and for the hull not to become heavy. It also has the great advantage of being cheap (there are often no harbour dues) provided that you can do the beaching and floating off yourself. You must therefore be able to lay it up at the September equinox and put it back afloat during the spring equinox. Between times, a certain amount of supervision is necessary, at least at high spring tides. In any case the boat must be completely emptied as it is unlikely to be in anyone's charge.

You are perfectly safe until the next equinoctial spring tide

Wintering on a mud berth, without legs, is also first class, especially for vintage boats, which neither dry nor work. Here too the boat must be boarded from time to time and pumped out and moorings checked.

To sum up, these two methods of wintering are worth considering by owners who can visit their boats fairly often.

Slipped in the Open

We have already mentioned that if you have a garden, laying your boat up there on its trailer or legs is an ideal solution and the cheapest.

Boats too big to be towed can be stored in the same way in a boat park or a harbour parking lot – somewhat more costly. If the boat is out of reach of itchy fingers, almost all the equipment can be left on board, only perishable equipment (electronic equipment, navigational instruments) being taken out. The paintwork does not deteriorate much.

An old boat that winters in this way must be put back in the water as soon as spring comes.

The best way to lay-up if you want to do odd jobs over the winter

Wintering under Cover

This is obviously the way to avoid headaches, but is also the most expensive. It need not be considered unless there is a lot of work to be done on the hull. It is most suitable for wooden racing boats, which must dry out so as not to get heavy (they are so well constructed that the seams don't work). This is the preserve of the gleaming topsides specialist.

Under cover, mildew is no threat and all the equipment can stay on board, even the radio.

Detailed Survey

We must now proceed to serious laying-up, whatever method is adopted.

Insofar as it is possible, this laying-up must take place without delay, immediately after the last cruise. At that moment you know all the weak spots on the boat and you are still very much involved. Later, interest wanes, you forget what needs to be done and become involved in other activities.

We shall consider the attention to be paid to the hull, rigging, sails, then to the fitting-out gear – in that order.

The Hull

The interior of the boat must be scrupulously cleaned out. All nooks and crannies must be explored, the bilges left absolutely clean, to eliminate dampness, the risk of rot and to avoid being confronted six months later with remarkably tenacious and depressing smells. Preferably, rinse out the whole interior of the boat with fresh water and it will be far less damp.

This cleaning is a good opportunity for inspecting the hull along all its seams. Examine particularly the spots which have a reputation for weakness in any particular type of design: rabbets, deck line, all metal fittings, rudder and centreboard fittings – everything.

Next grease all mechanical parts; winches, tracks, blocks, windlass. Wipe all aluminium and chrome parts with a greasy rag.

Finally, it is vital that air circulates throughout the interior. Take all precautions: locker covers should have holes or be left open, fix all doors ajar, hatches open, etc. Inside, leave all cupboards open, lift up the floorboards. Let the air circulate everywhere.

If the boat is to be in the open, put a cover over the hull (still allowing air to circulate), but this protection is only indispensible for old boats with narrow deck planks.

The business of painting the hull arises less and less now as only wooden boats still need it. A boat which sails all the year round must be repainted at least every two years; a boat which sails only in summer, not necessarily so often.

Don't forget that painting must be finished at least a week before fitting out to give it time to dry completely.

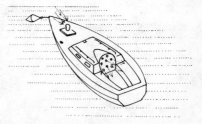

However you decide to lay-up, the cabin must be well ventilated

Rigging

Leaving the Mast up. If the boat winters afloat or beached, the mast and the whole of the rigging can for most of the time be left up, provided that you know the exact state of every piece of rigging. You should have adopted the habit of making frequent inspections. You do not need to take the mast out unless there is an important repair to be done, or if you have one you can't climb easily.

When the mast and spars are left up you must pay them the honours, armed with a long nozzled oil can and a greasy rag, to oil blocks, sheaves, grease halyards and all wire and metal parts. Care must next be taken to tie up any running rigging firmly so that it doesn't flog against the mast. If the halyards are worn and do not look as if they will last the winter, replace them with reeving lines, light lines which will allow the new halyards to be rove in a moment in the spring (particularly convenient with halyards passing up inside the mast). You will hardly wish to install anything when laying-up, for it will only deteriorate during the winter; but take a careful note of what must be replaced in the spring.

Mast Laid on Trestles Fully Rigged. An important precaution when you are taking the mast out: release the bottle screws first from the shrouds and not from the chainplates; if you do not, there is a grave risk of losing bits and pieces from them (and you can't buy bits of bottle screws any more than you can buy pins for shackles). By the same token, when you step the mast, put the bottle screws first onto the chain plates and not onto the shrouds.

The mast can be laid down fully rigged, preferably under cover for water can collect when it is left flat. A wooden mast must be laid very flat and on the only straight side: its groove. With an aluminium mast, the possibility of galvanic action must also be remembered: remove or insulate from the mast all parts in brass. Also remove stainless steel rigging if the mast is not under cover.

Always lay the mast on its track

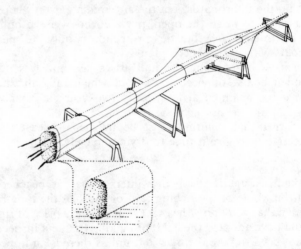

Unrigged Mast. To unrig a mast completely involves much work, and it is another good opportunity to lose something. It is only really necessary when it needs repairing or revarnishing, and even then with a little juggling it can be avoided!

Sails

Rinse the sails carefully in fresh water to get rid of the salt, then dry them. Inspect each sail minutely. Small repairs which must be done are done straight-away (or in any case written down). Sails needing the sailmaker's attention are sent straight off to the sail loft.

If the boat is wintering afloat, is very dry, and you intend to use it during the winter, the terylene sails can stay on board. Don't leave them in their bags but lay them out loosely on the bunks to let them air.

Otherwise, they are stored in a dry place. So that they do not take up too much space they can be folded along the foot, then rolled up.

Fitting out Equipment

While you are cleaning out the cabin, you must be ruthless and not yield to sentimentality: get rid of the trusted but filthy frying pan, the cheese grater which is already a bit rusty, the little bits of rotten line and tatty ends of string which 'might still come in handy', the ashtray fashioned out of a corned beef tin, the ball point pen which only works if you wedge it with a match, the pretty flowers from the Isles of Scilly rotting in a jam jar. Better to commit them mournfully to the deep right away, than have to throw them away with disgust six months later.

For the remainder of the gear, the principle is still the same: if your wintering plan allows it, the greatest possible number of things are left on board. It's the best way not to lose anything.

Everything you take off must be carefully noted in the notebook. The obsessionally orderly owner leaves labels stuck in the places where gear has been removed and indicating where it has been stored on land. This precaution is not to be laughed at if you are not sure of fitting-out the boat yourself.

Certain categories of gear must be stored on land in any case; others on the contrary are only to be taken off if the boat remains open to the four winds.

Electronics, Electricity, Engine. The electronic equipment (echo, sounder, log etc.) can only be left on board if the boat is wintering in a locked compound; otherwise store them at home. All terminals, those on the pieces of equipment and on the fixed installations on board, must be coated with vaseline. Treat in the same way terminals on the lighting circuit: switches, bulb holders, fuses, battery terminals.

The batteries themselves, the alternator and the self starter are stored in the garage. For the inboard engine, refer to the advice on wintering given in the preceding chapter. An outboard engine is best entrusted to the agent for that make, who will check it over and carry out any repairs.

Navigation Equipment. Compass, sextant, glasses will be better on land; smear their joints with vaseline. Take out charts and navigation books to repair them, bring them up to date and to plan next year's cruises.

Safety Equipment. Store the life rafts with the appropriate agent for their compulsory annual check. Rinse with fresh water and carefully dry life jackets, harness, buoys; hang them up inside the boat. Grease the snap hooks. Take apart waterproof torches, throw away the batteries, smear the terminals with vaseline. The out-of-date or merely suspect flares, must be dumped far offshore.

Textile Material. Rinse all textiles in fresh water and dry them; hang up the lines and canvas leeboards inside the boat; turn the mattresses at least on their sides if you cannot possibly store them at home.

Galley Equipment. Clean all the galley utensils carefully (as usual); grease the aluminium ones. Here too pay attention to galvanic action: don't leave a stainless steel gadget in an aluminium pot. Clean the stove thoroughly (as usual), and grease it carefully. A gas stove burner, suspected of leaking, must be ruthlessly thrown away. Grease the pumps, taps, empty the water tank, wash out water containers with bleaching fluid. Do not forget the washing up. Take off all food stuffs, even canned food.

Odds and Ends. Stow the anchor and chain somewhere other than in the bilges, where there is always a risk of water during the winter. Immerse the tools in diesel (in the plastic bucket for instance). The sculling oar can be hung up from the coach roof, from at least three points so it does not go out of shape. Grease the working parts of the wc; the simplest thing if you have the boat on land is to pump into it one or two litres of engine oil (even used oil).

At the end of the laying-up process, the notes which haven't been ticked off in the notebook have to be dealt with: draw up a detailed list of the repairs to be carried out and get into contact with the people who are going to do this work. You must be ready to give precise details of what needs to be done; particularly if there is a leak to be stopped, its exact location must have been ascertained whilst cruising, since it isn't necessarily easy to see when the boat is at rest.

Draw up also a list of equipment to be ordered, and put the orders in immediately if possible, that is if laying-up doesn't coincide with a low spring tide of your finances. At least put the notebook in a safe spot, while you await sunnier days.

Fitting out

If the laying-up has been well done, fitting-out is child's play. All that need be done is to put back in place everything you have taken out, fit the new equipment and check that the whole thing works. It's simple. Of course in fact it's very seldom as simple as that for there is always something that has been forgotten and means lost time, all the greater because you are a bit out of touch and it is probably splendid sailing weather already. You must keep your cool and don't rage and go through the notebook to find what you haven't written in the first place. The least you can do is to note in capital letters the firm decision you have taken to pay more attention next time – a resolution still easily forgotten.

When you have found the missing bottlescrew, changed the block which has gone sick during the winter, paid a fortune to the local blacksmith for him to repair the rudder right away, sent a member of the crew for the tenth time to the garage for news of the battery; when you have checked, with the help of the fitting-out list, that all the equipment is in its place and in good condition, only then can you think you are ready. But that is improbable.

The boat may seem complete, the crew too, but is there proof that everything is really shipshape? Rather than setting off immediately on a cruise, it is prudent to be patient a little longer; just long enough to take a trial trip and spend a night on board.

First Sail of the Season

Before going on board, you check from the quay that the trim of the boat is correct. Then you get ready to make sail and ensure that all the rigging is running correctly by hoisting and dropping sails, running out the sheets, trying the winches. You try out the engine, the sculling oar too (sometimes the rowlock is jammed in its socket).

You linger a little longer over the matter of safety. Everyone makes sure he has his own equipment: lifejacket, harness and snaphook, waterproof torch. All this reassures you that everything is in good condition, working well and that everyone knows how to equip himself. Everyone too must know how to release the life-

A final inspection of the boat's trim

buoy and its marker, and know where the flares, all torches and smoke flares are stowed. Finally, you check the lashings of the life-raft and rehearse releasing it.

Getting Under Way. Rather laboured at first. Getting out of harbour. The boat wakes up – so do the crew. At sea, the first task is to adjust the standing rigging (see chapter 4). Then you embark on a systematic exploration: go through all the essential manoeuvres, try all the sails, take in all the reefs. Be sure the sheets are long enough; that all the jib hanks are well sewn on, that all the reefing pendants are there.

When you have the boat well under control, the skipper has the 'man overboard' drill rehearsed to perfection, to ensure that his crew are at least capable of fishing him out. Only then will he consent to go home, with peace of mind.

During the course of this outing, it is very rare for some deficiencies not to be noticed. Everything has been noted down as it arose and, once back on the moorings, you find yourself faced once again with an impressive list of things to do.

First Night

Lastly it is important to settle down on board in real cruising conditions. Have at least one meal and sleep one night on board before the great departure. The meal must be a real feast for this isn't the time to be stingy. You are celebrating the opening of the season and at the same time checking that all the galley equipment is there, that there is enough crockery, that the stove works well, that there is salt and pepper; that the lighting is functioning and that the radio works – on all its frequencies. After that everyone to his bunk – if it is there. And you will not be setting off at crack of dawn for there is another urgent shopping list. Don't forget the oilskins. Nor the ball point. Nor the dinghy. Now let's chance it. Let's go!

Part 2. Boat Handling

When you begin boat handling it is possible to use a copy book method, but you cannot go on that way for long. As soon as you and your boat have come to terms on the route to be taken, you will find a whole gamut of new experiences in seamanship to be explored. Totally unforeseen situations will arise; some you will cope with first time, others will confuse you and will only be resolved with time and experience. You are bound to make some monumental mistakes and remember that the school of trial and error is still not completely outmoded.

In an attempt to analyse seamanship in some detail, we are not going to marshal the facts in any set order for such a theoretical approach would not bear any relation to practice. We shall put to sea again to study how the boat behaves on different points of sailing. Mastery of the ship's tender, putting to sea, anchoring, sail changing, and manoeuvring the ship in the close confines of a port – all come from practical experience of boat handling and that cannot be acquired at a stroke.

The same basic principles of boat handling apply to all sailing boats, so we shall discuss dinghies and cruising boats in the same chapter. There will inevitably be differences to be pointed out for all boats are not handled in the same way nor in the same spirit. A racing dinghy is an athlete's machine, over-canvassed and unstable and you are normally aboard for only a few hours; your only concern is sailing, driving the boat to her limits and taking every risk for you are bound to be in supervised waters. It is quite different with a cruising boat: you are living aboard, eating and sleeping, so that handling is not your sole preoccupation; there is the safety of ship and crew and you must be ready for bad weather: you are sailing a less extreme craft.

As for handling, we shall first distinguish between light and heavier boats. A light dinghy can slow down quickly and can pick up way again equally quickly, so she can manoeuvre easily. The heavier cruiser carries her way for some distance and reacts more slowly to wind changes, the effects of waves and her rudder. In a dinghy the crew are mobile ballast and their distribution in the boat directly affects her progress. They are already less effective on a day boat or a light cruiser and become of relatively minor importance aboard a heavy cruiser.

It is difficult to put the boats in precise categories: a fairly large boat, which is light, may have the reactions of a dinghy, while a small heavy vessel will more nearly approach the characteristics of an offshore cruising yacht. Each boat has her own idiosyncracies which you only discover through experience. There are no hard and fast rules and that is how we like it!

8. Control

Good boat handling depends above all on a proper appreciation of importance of the wind. Like all basic themes, this one will be repeated at regular intervals: you will never do any good in sailing until you have a deep feeling for the ways of the wind, your only valid reference point.

Unfortunately this reference point changes constantly and, if you want to get the most out of your boat, you must never forget that no situation ever lasts long and that, no matter how carefully you have trimmed to a particular wind, everything may have to be re-adjusted at any moment. A good helmsman is quick to observe a change of wind direction or strength and is quick to adapt to it. There is nothing more important than this: it is always necessary to watch the set of the sails, trim of the boat and feel of the helm.

In this chapter we shall examine these three factors in succession – for each point of sailing and for different strengths. The experienced yachtsman, in practice, has them all in mind at the same time, for it is their interrelation that is important. Changing the set of the sails usually means attention to the boat's trim and the tiller and *vice versa* all round for the boat's progress depends on the balance of all three.

While it is impossible to give detailed advice for every situation we can indicate a general line of suitable action. There are no precise indications to show when (and for how long) a boat has perfect trim. That is why, even if you have reached the stage of true understanding with your boat, it is always worth keeping an eye on how others are faring; in that way you will improve the handling of your vessel even if you don't wish to get involved in racing.

First of all, we shall examine sailing close-hauled for it is when beating to windward that the trim of a boat is of paramount importance. And it is on this point of sailing that the effect of wind change must be fully understood. Here precision is all-important.

Close-Hauled

Best Course to Windward

The Ideal Close-Hauled Course

A boat working to windward is said to be sailing close-hauled, but the degree of closeness to the wind is seldom the same. As we have already seen in the first chapter, when a boat luffs up from a beam-wind position, she first of all passes through close-reaching as she slowly points towards the wind; she then passes successively through *full-and-by*, *close-hauled*, to the point of *pinching* or sailing just too close to the wind. Beyond this, she enters the forbidden head-to-wind zone, when the sails begin to flap.

A boat which has to work her way to windward to reach a point that lies exactly where the wind is blowing from, must just sail as close-hauled as she can. There is one exception: you can also sail close-hauled to reach a point outside the head-to-wind zone because you may want to steer slightly further up to windward of your objective to allow for leeway. When you have to tack, the problem is different because the course is not chosen in relation to a fixed point, but purely in relation to the wind itself. Then your course will change frequently and you must be continually taking advantage of shifts in the wind to gain ground to windward, without losing speed; you can creep up, in this way, reducing effectively the angle between tacks.

Your success in 'cheating' the wind like this depends on its strength and the state of the sea, as well as on the boat and the way she is handled. Generally speaking, a boat which makes good an angle of 45° to the wind, while maintaining reasonable speed, is said to point 'well'. A slim racing vessel can reduce the angle between tacks to 85°, but the angle between tacks can widen to as much as 110° for the same boat when the wind is fresh or, the reverse, very light, for a boat points up best in medium weather.

Sailing close to the wind has to balance against keeping up reasonable speed. The force of the wind on the sails when they are close-hauled is badly orientated for the thrust component is limited and heel is intensified; and it is only the boat's speed that stops leeway becoming extreme. It follows that if you are to maintain speed you cannot point too high up into the wind. *So the best course to windward has to be a compromise between course and speed, leeway being the common enemy of both.* You opt for better direction or more knots according to the strength of the wind and the state of the sea, pointing up to shorten the distance, thereby accepting a reduction in speed and an increase in leeway, or keeping the sails comfortably full, which will increase speed and reduce leeway but lengthen the distance to be run. For example, by sailing

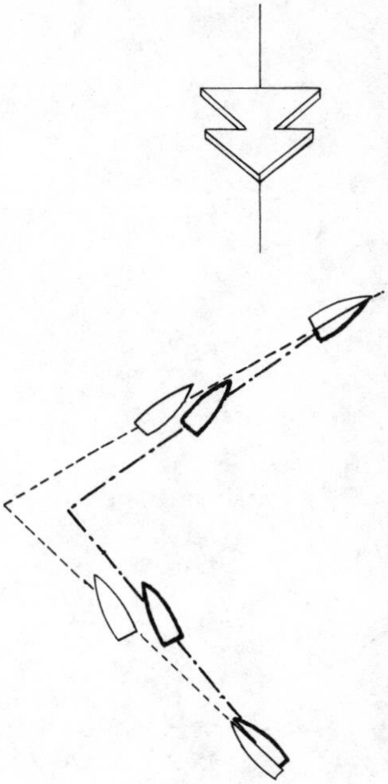

Close-hauled, the wind force exerted on the sails (the aerodynamic force) is badly orientated. Drift and heel components are much stronger than the propulsive component

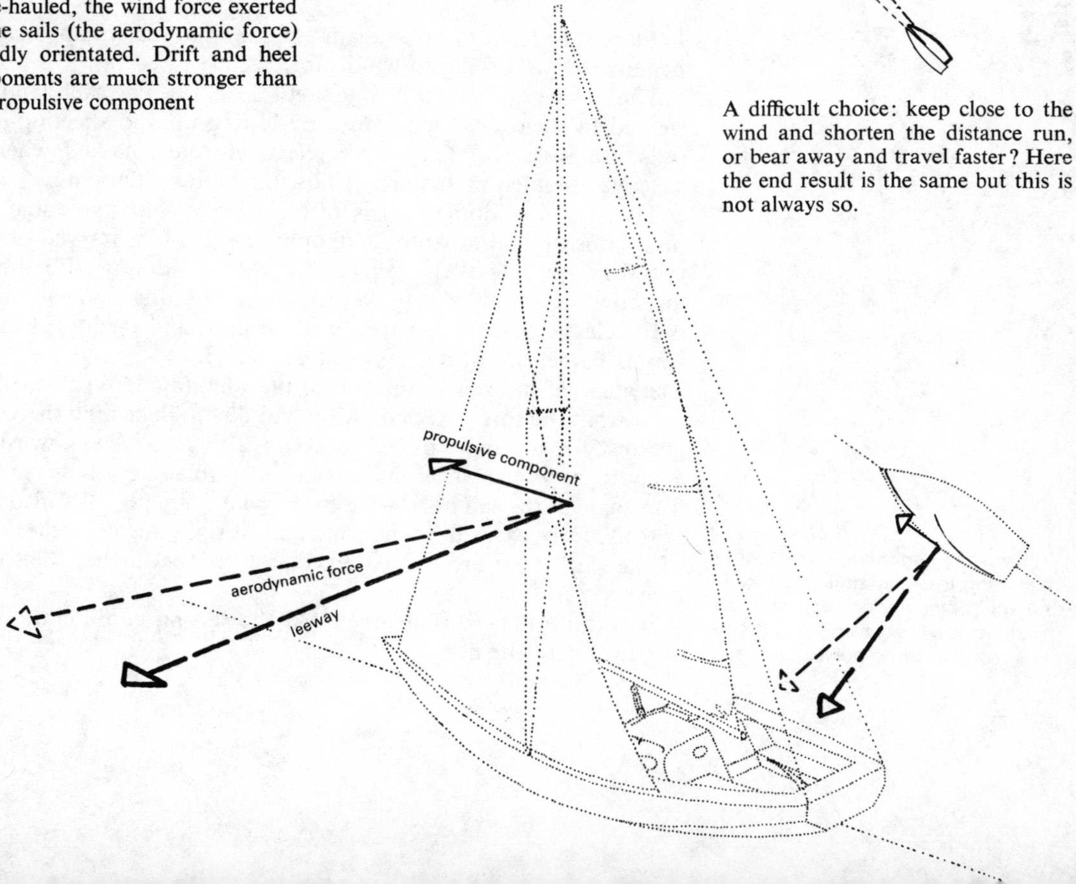

A difficult choice: keep close to the wind and shorten the distance run, or bear away and travel faster? Here the end result is the same but this is not always so.

propulsive component

aerodynamic force

leeway

a course of 45° from the wind, speed is five knots with 5° of leeway; with a course of 49°, speed is 5.25 knots and leeway is reduced to 3°. By bearing away 4°, the course made good is only reduced, in fact, by 2°. Will the gain to windward make this up? If you decide to bear away a bit more on a freer course, the problem is to know how much to free off and when your increased speed no longer compensates for the longer course you have to cover. You can only learn the answer by sailing alongside another boat, or by having sophisticated navigation instruments that calculate the speed made good to windward. When you are racing it is usually only at the end of a beat to windward that you know if you have made the right decision.

However, there is no point in trying to lay down general rules for each case is different and needs its individual answer. The balance between your course and speed made good is never the same, because conditions are always changing and the best course to windward is the ideal that the helmsman seeks tirelessly.

Trial and Error

Let us come down to earth again and see what really happens when beginners try working to windward.

The novice in the first chapter set off on a beam reach, and then steered to a close-hauled course by luffing up and sheeting in the sails progressively. They were effectively close-hauled when the sails were hauled in as hard as possible without flapping.

The result of doing this is often disconcerting: you find your boat bobs up and down on a choppy sea, held in, starved of effective wind, pulling at the reins and crabbing sideways, for the sails are now too tightly sheeted and you are pointing up too much. It is the classic beginner's experience (in light and medium winds at least). To get out of it, you must consider:

The angle of the sail in relation to the wind (angle A). We already know that the force exerted on the sail due to deflecting the wind is greatest for an angle of deflection of 20°–25°; to windward, this encourages you to sheet in the sail to try to achieve that angle.

The angle of the sail in relation to the boat (angle B). We also know that the force exerted by the wind acts at right angles to the surface of the sail: the more it is eased, therefore, the further the force is directed forward.

It is important to remember that the second consideration is at variance with the first.

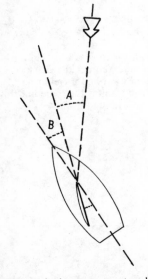

Which is the better course to adopt? By sheeting in the sail angle A increases and you get greater power; by easing the sheets angle B increases and you get a better directed power

What, then, is to be done?

First of all, ease the sheets a little. Immediately you will find that the boat 'breathes' a little more easily and makes less leeway, but she is still not travelling very fast. Once the boat has slowed down, for whatever reason, it is extremely difficult to pick up speed again when close-hauled, even if the sails are correctly trimmed.

You should therefore bear away; acceleration usually increases immediately.

When you have regained speed, luff up once more little by little and try to find a good compromise between speed and angle off the wind.

This compromise is only found by successive trial and error: trim sails for the course to be made good, but the course made good by the boat depends on the trim of the sails...

Trim of Sails

The diagram shows three different trims for the same sail, together with their corresponding efficiency.

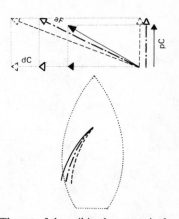

The sail on the right, trimmed well inboard, is in no danger of lifting and is getting plenty of thrust. But the trim is not really right because the thrust is poorly directed: heel and leeway are too great in relation to progress forward. The sail on the left which is eased well off has less wind force on it, but it is better orientated so that, although forward progress is less, so is the leeway. The luff of the sail tends to lift, so this is not the ideal trim; we shall see later, however, that it sometimes has to be adopted in a strong wind, when heeling becomes too much for the boat and the crew to manage.

The best trim is obviously the middle sail, where movement forward is good and the degree of heeling is acceptable. Under these conditions the sail trembles slightly at the luff, so it is sheeted within the limits of lifting.

The set of the sail in the centre is the best compromise: the propulsive component (pC) is quite good, the leeway (or drift) component (dC) is slight. The aerodynamic force (aF) is both strong and well directed

Sailing a Better Course

We are of course trimming sails in relation to a constant heading. We must now see whether this heading cannot be improved.

When we consider the graph of a sailing boat's speed on different headings we can see straight away that there is a certain latitude. Track OM represents the ideal close-hauled position, but tracks OM′ and OM″ make little difference to ground made good to windward (OX′ is not much different from OX). You can thus

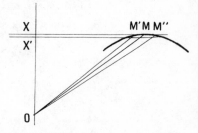

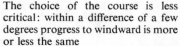

The choice of the course is less critical: within a difference of a few degrees progress to windward is more or less the same

vary the angle a little to suit your tactics or sea conditions. But this latitude is not more than a few degrees even under the best conditions and diminishes rapidly as the wind increases or if the boat is not properly trimmed.

Even when you have settled on the right compromise between heading and boat speed, it is not yet time for self congratulation. Even in a steady medium wind, many factors combine to alter things. Beginners are inevitably liable to commit errors of helmsmanship that destroy good balance:

If You Point to High, you repeat your recent mistakes and retribution comes at once: speed drops off, so leeway increases with greater resistance to progress and speed slackens still more. . . This is a chain reaction which soon makes a small boat lose all its way.

If You Bear Away too Much, on the other hand, the situation is quite different. The boat starts by accelerating and then suddenly sits upright and slows. You have stalled, and the flow of air over the sail and of water over the keel gets turbulent. This phenomenon was explained in the third chapter and we shall come across it again when we discuss reaching. You have to accept that you are now in a difficult situation. You are in a bit of a mess without knowing the reason. Urgent action is called for: ease sheets generously to clear the sails of air turbulence, and bear well away so that the broken water round the keel is left behind.

Now it only remains to return slowly to a close-hauled position, picking up speed as you go; that's what it's all about.

To avoid this kind of mistake it is important, particularly for beginners, to luff up gently and briefly. This is getting the *feel of the wind* to see if it has freed (which will allow a better course), or to be certain that you are not bearing away more than is necessary.

Only by trial and error can you learn to sail properly to windward, and it takes time. On the other points of sailing, the consequences of bad judgement are not so serious and there is less difference between one boat and another: on a windward leg you can often see gaps opening between boats of the same type on the same course without the reason being apparent. The right, almost instinctive, touch of sail trim and balance of the boat play their part as well as finesse at the helm. Now we'll look at the whys and wherefores in detail.

Tuning

Sail Shape

We already know that when you are beating to windward the sails should be trimmed so that they are nearly on the point of lifting. We can go further and say: *sails are properly trimmed when they lift all along the luff*.

To achieve this the angle which the sails make with the wind has to be considered but, quite as importantly, their shape has to be considered because it is closely linked with the angle.

Curve

The curve or belly of the sail is of the first importance in beating to windward. As a general rule you cannot point so high with sails with a deep curve as you can with flat ones, for, even when they are sheeted close, full sails lift earlier.

But it is also important to remember that the curve of your sails should be regulated in relation to the strength of the wind. To tune in this way you have to watch:

Position of the Curve. The curve should always be in the same place – roughly in the middle of the sail. When the wind increases, the curve tends to move aft towards the leech, and it must be brought back to the middle again by tightening the luff still more.

Amount of Curve. The more the wind increases, the more the sails should be flattened to deflect the air at a smaller angle. It is important to note here that *the mainsail is flattened in heavy weather not to enable it to be sheeted closer but, on the contrary, to enable it to ease just a little without lifting*.

Variation in Sail Curve

A sail always tends to take up, to a greater or lesser degree, a helicoid shape, with the head of the sail (where movement is less restricted than at the foot) tending to fall away into line with the wind direction. This must be controlled, although it is not necessarily detrimental in itself as the wind is stronger near the top of the mast than at boom level (there is a difference of 10% at 30ft); the apparent wind therefore comes less from ahead at the top of the mast than near the boom, and the head of the sail need not be so closely pulled in as the foot. Aerodynamic force is better

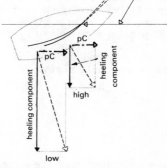

apparent wind at the top of the sail
apparent wind at the bottom of the sail

pC

pC

heeling component

heeling component

high

low

The apparent wind is less sharply directed at head of the sail and a certain amount of twist makes for a better directed aerodynamic force

The part played by the mainsheet traveller

The traveller only comes into play when the main is close-hauled and is much more effective than the kicking strap. It enables the sail to be flattened by bending boom and mast, controls the twist of the sail and modifies its orientation. It makes it possible to let the mainsail in or out without touching the sheet itself: only the traveller has to be moved in- or outboard. This is called opening or closing the slot

The kicking strap

Close-hauled, it modifies the curvature of the sail by bending the boom and mast; and it allows the twist of the sail to be controlled when there is no traveller. On other points of sailing, it makes it possible to control the shape of the sail when it has been eased out beyond the point where the traveller can be effective

orientated aloft, with the same thrust but a weaker element of heel. In fresh winds, this variation can be a positive advantage, because the head of the sail falls off more to leeward and, as a result, the boat is less hardpressed.

This curve variation is often more noticeable on a sloop than on a cat-rigged boat, which has no headsail, specially when the jib of the sloop does not reach to the masthead. This is because the jib, wider at its foot than at its head, deflects more wind lower down and, to prevent backwinding, the mainsail has to be sheeted closer.

It follows that the mainsheet traveller should be kept near the centre line of the boat in light winds; if it is allowed to remain to leeward, the sail will not be drawn in close enough to the wind at the foot and will be too close higher up.

Control of sail shape has been discussed in the fourth chapter and need only be briefly recalled here.

Jib Control

Curve in a jib is not controllable if the sail has a wire luff so it must be changed when the wind changes; but if the jib has a rope or a taped luff, it is possible to control draught by stretching the luff as you do with a mainsail.

Twist in the Leech can be controlled by altering the sheetlead. This is done either by moving the fairlead forward or aft on the deck, or by raising or lowering the jib tack.

Mainsail Control

Position of the curve is regulated by tension on the luff. The degree of curve is affected both by luff tension, and by the degree of bend which the kicking strap and the mainsheet traveller can bring to bear on the mast and boom; these last two also control *twist*.

Sail Trim

Bearing in mind these last factors, we can now consider sail trim to windward more precisely.

The jib should be sheeted in as reasonably close as possible. It is this sail that determines how the boat is to point, so luff up until it trembles all along its luff and then bear away 2 or 3 degrees.

The mainsail should be hauled in as little as possible, only enough to ensure it is not back-winded by the jib.

The sails are in ideal trim when the luffs of the two sails lift simultaneously along their entire length.

When the sea is choppy, the pitching of the boat offers a useful check on trim. If the sails are properly sheeted, they will lift slightly when the boat rolls forward over the top of the waves. The faster movement of the masthead means, in effect, that there is an

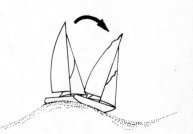

When the boat pitches forward on a wave crest the top of the sail moves faster than the bottom

increase in the relative wind strength there because it comes from slightly more ahead up aloft. This helps you to determine whether you are steering too close or too far off the wind.

Boat Trim

Beating to windward is a vexatious business. The boat is fighting against wind and sea, and needs help. Problems of rudder balance and of fore and aft and lateral trim become important.

Rudder Balance

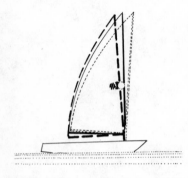

Raking the mast aft will (probably) increase weather helm

When a boat with sails properly trimmed and its tiller amidships has a tendency to luff, she is said to carry weather helm; but if she bears away, she has lee helm. No well-designed boat has a lee helm, but you have to counteract either tendency by holding the tiller to one side or the other to steer a straight course, and that is obviously not going to help your speed; every touch on the tiller is a touch on the brakes. It is when you beat to windward that rudder balance is particularly important, and that is when you must get it right – remember that all rudder movement has a braking effect. Usually a boat that works well to windward is equally good on all the other points of sailing.

Mast. Giving the mast a forward rake reduces weather helm; raking it aft increases it. But any alteration to the mast upsets the boat's whole trim to an unpredictable degree, and it is even possible that you will end up with just the opposite of what you had wanted. You should therefore go about that very gingerly.

Centreboard. Generally speaking a centreboard should be right down when you sail to windward, as it is on this point of sailing that the leeway is at its strongest. However, a pivoting centreboard can be slightly raised on occasion; this does not reduce the immersed area but merely brings it aft, thus altering the CLR and giving the boat's trim a fine adjustment.

Should a boat be perfectly balanced, or should she carry slight weather helm? There are helmsmen who like lee helm, but they are rare. In any event, too much helm imbalance either way is wrong and there is no doubt that it is best to have a little weather helm, because the boat is more alive and the helmsman gets the feel of the tiller more quickly, whereas a boat which is perfectly balanced demands great concentration and much finesse. To sum up, while it may be legitimate for each helmsman to tune his dinghy as he wants her, there is no doubt at all that a cruising yacht should have slight weather helm if only because helmsmen perform at their best when they feel its gentle pressure.

Fore and Aft Trim

No boat will sail as well as she can unless she is floating to her designed waterlines – neither too low or too high in the water, nor down by the bow or the stern.

Weight should be concentrated, as a general rule, at the middle of the boat for, if the bow or stern is too heavy, pitching is accentuated on a rough sea.

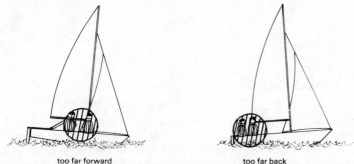

too far forward   too far back

Fore and aft trim is important for all boats, and most of all in a dinghy. As a rule the crew should sit slightly forward when going to windward. In practice this, like all forms of balance, is not a set rule and in fresh winds the crew have to move their weight constantly to give the boat maximum drive to cleave its way through broken water.

A light cruiser or dayboat is easily unbalanced if, for instance, one person goes forward to change jibs, or fishes over the stern. In larger boats it is where gear is stowed that affects fore and aft trim, and it is wise to keep heavy pieces as low down in, and as near, the middle of the boat as you can.

Lateral Trim

If it is to give of its best *a boat should heel as little as possible.* When it heels sharply, the hull is not in the position for which it was designed and is held back. Heeling also gives a boat more weather helm.

To minimise heeling, you obviously trim the sails so as to reduce the heel component of the wind, but you should also get the crew on the windward side. There are two rules for this.

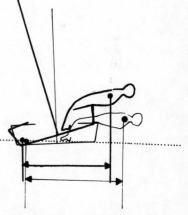

The flatter the boat lies on the water, the stronger is the righting moment

Sitting out is most effective when the boat is still nearly upright; it is much less so when the boat is already well over. In light weather, though, a little heel is sometimes wanted because it helps to hold the sails to leeward; it also reduces the wetted area, particularly in dinghies. Some boats with long overhangs (Dragon, Soling, etc.) are designed to sail heeled, as the angle lengthens their waterline length and increases speed.

Leaning out is more efficient the nearer you are to the waterline, and especially so in chine-built boats; you can sometimes be of more use in a light cruiser's weather berth than hanging onto the weather rail.

How to Steer

The basic principle, which holds good on all points of sailing but particularly to windward, is to avoid putting the tiller over too hard or too briskly. Remember that speed is precious, quickly lost and only slowly regained, and that every turn of the rudder loses some of it. It should be amidships as much as possible.

This is a fundamental rule but good helmsmanship is above all a matter of intuition and close attention to all that is going on. An alert helmsman feels the life in a boat through the rudder, especially when she carries a little weather helm. When you are going fairly fast to windward, a gentle resistance is felt on the tiller and, with experience, this tells you as well as anything how the boat is going. The slightest loss of speed lessens this resistance and the tiller seems less alive, so something is wrong.

In some ways the tiller plays the same role as the reins of a horse and it should not be used to hold the boat in check but to hold her just right, letting her give of her best. A well trimmed boat almost knows herself what she has to do and the helmsman must learn to recognise what is natural movement and when he should intervene. With practice, the tiller serves less as a means of correcting your course and more as a means of preventing you going off it.

The way in which one steers is a reflection of the helmsman's character and, among all the other factors, age counts for a lot!

Maximum boat tune is not achieved in a day. It is best done in

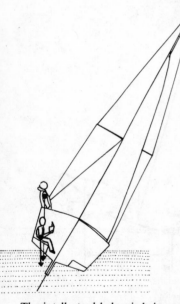

The intellectual below is being more effective than the worker on deck

medium, steady weather, although that does not admittedly mean very much because medium weather for one is heavy weather for another. It is somewhere between the moment when you no longer have to look for your wind and the time when heeling begins to be acute.

Indeed the very idea of a steady wind is expecting too much for we already know about its inconstancy. To be realistic, we now come to the well known wind which is 'variable'. We shall then go onto heavy and light weather.

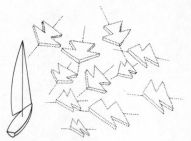

Wind is rarely consistent in strength and direction

Variable Winds and Squalls

A sudden, momentary increase in wind strength in medium and light weather is a gust; in heavy weather we talk of a squall. The dividing line between the two depends not only on the size of the boat but also (need it be said?) on the nerve of the crew.

What Happens in a Gust?

We know that the apparent wind (which is what matters as far as sail trim is concerned) is a combination of the true and relative winds brought about by the speed of the boat, and its direction lies between the two. Close-hauled, it always comes from more ahead, nearer the bow than the true wind. The important point is that every change in strength of true and relative wind brings about a change in the strength and direction of the apparent wind.

1. The gust arrives and the true wind increases in strength, but the boat does not react straight away, therefore the relative wind stays the same. The direction of the apparent wind approaches that of the true wind and it frees.

2. The boat, trimmed as necessary, picks up speed, so the relative wind increases in strength. The direction of the apparent wind moves away from that of the true wind and it heads you.

3. The gust is past, so the true wind slackens but the boat does not slow down at once and the relative wind therefore remains strong. The direction of the apparent wind moves further towards the latter and it heads you still more.

4. The boat slows and the apparent wind comes from the same direction as it did before the gust.

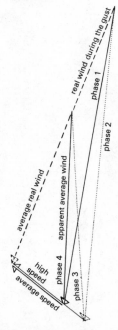

How the apparent wind modifies in a light squall
Phase 1: it freshens and frees;
Phase 2: it continues to freshen but heads you;
Phase 3: it slackens and heads you more;
Phase 4: it drops back to its original strength and direction

What to Do?

Particularly when beating to windward, a gust is an advantage, because it gives you an opportunity to work higher to windward than the true wind would otherwise allow. To take full advantage, you should be able to see it coming and manoeuvre accordingly.

In a dinghy that answers quickly you should luff up a little and trim sails closer; as far as the mainsail is concerned, this can be done simply by shifting the mainsheet traveller.

On a cruising boat, when the sheets are made fast, you will hardly have time to retrim sails and you merely alter course, luffing up as the gust arrives, so that the sails are kept at an efficient angle to the wind.

As soon as the apparent wind heads you, bear away again to keep the sails from lifting and to maintain the increased speed acquired in the gust for as long as you can.

Obviously, wind changes cannot always be anticipated, but the principle remains valid and you must keep your eyes open for such 'wind falls'.

Fresh Winds

Fresh conditions usually mean you cannot relax comfortably. Whenever the boat tends to heel well over, or becomes difficult to control, or movement through the water is not steady, and some people on board wish to take to their bunks, the weather can be said to be fresh.

You cannot hold a perfect windward course under such conditions because drag and the waves act as a brake; you must ease sail. To keep going well you must learn to maintain a forward thrust without excessive heeling.

Easing Sail

As the wind increases, and the boat's natural ability to right itself and the weight of the crew to windward can no longer maintain an efficient lateral trim, you must flatten or 'open' the sails.

Because the wind is increasing, you only have to deflect it less (at least, in the first instance) and the power exerted on the sails becomes less; because the sails are eased off, this power is also better directed and progression forward is greater.

Mainsail Trim

The belly should be kept well positioned on the sail (which should be flattened) as described above. The sail is then trimmed until it is just not lifting, with the mainsheet traveller eased as much as possible. Curve variation may be increased until the upper third of the sail (which exerts the strongest effect on heeling) 'feathers' completely.

Jib Trim

Trimming begins by making the right choice of sail. You must have the jib for the wind you expect. Some jibs can be adjusted by tightening the luff wire (see chapter 4) and the belly of the sail can be flattened and stopped from moving aft.

To stop the jib losing its shape, it must, for sure, be very tight on the forestay for, if it bends, the curve of the jib is accentuated and moves aft. The jib itself balloons outwards and closes in at the leech. All it is doing now is to increase heel without driving the boat forward.

The head of the jib can also be spilled, if conditions demand it, by moving the clew aft or up. This makes the foot of the sail stiffer and the leech easier.

Sail Interaction

The jib may tend to back-wind the mainsail. This usually means that the former is too full so try to adjust its trim and, if you cannot succeed, change jibs.

When you have done all you can with the jib trim and it is still back-winding the mainsail, it is better to let the latter lift all up the mast rather than sheet it too tightly; whatever you do, you must not curb the boat too tightly.

Best trim is obtained in fresh winds when both sails lift at the same time, but only towards the head and you can ease the boat by luffing up slightly to spill wind.

Reducing Sail

If the wind continues to freshen, what you have done up to now won't be enough. Dinghies should now make for the shore (it would be foolhardy to stay out). Cruisers should start thinking about reducing canvas, and whether it is done at once or later depends on how much the boat can take.

First Steps

In the first place, make quite sure that all sails are flattened as much as possible.

Taking in the first reef reduces area but it reduces the curve at the luff and the foot and removes a good deal of its belly.
The first jib change does not necessarily mean putting on a smaller jib, but a flatter one.

Second Step

When flattening the sails is no longer adequate, the time has come to reduce sail. Take in two or three reefs in the mainsail and put on a smaller jib; its flat cut helps to keep a reasonable airflow going despite some inevitable sag in the forestay. If the jib is still not small enough, change down again.

Sail Balance

As it is important not to upset the balance of the sailplan, you must reduce sail forward and aft. As sharp heeling increases weather helm, there is a temptation to keep plenty of sail on forward but that is a mistake, and here is a typical example.

Two five-tonners, which have a lot of weather helm when they heel, are sailing thirty miles off shore in a wind which is freshening to force 8. On one, the skipper orders a progressive reduction of sail both forward and aft of the mast as the wind gets up, until the boat has a flat storm jib and a close-reefed mainsail. Sails sheeted well home and mainsheet traveller right down to leeward, the boat handles nicely, full-and-by.

The second skipper, anxious lest his boat should carry too much weather helm, holds onto his large jib as long as possible. As the wind increases, he changes jib later than the first boat: No. 1 when the other has No. 2, No. 2 when the other has her storm jib up. On the other hand, he has taken in one more mainsail reef than his rival. In the end, as nothing seems to hold her, he takes off the mainsail altogether and tries to sail under No. 2 jib alone. The boat heels alarmingly, and quite inevitably, develops horrible weather helm because she has too full a jib for the wind and a forestay which is probably sagging badly to leeward; she has no hope of sailing well.

It is only too clear you must choose the rights sails in fresh winds: *to keep the boat properly balanced, pay as much attention to the curve of your sails as their area.*

Balance of the Boat

The boat can still heel a lot, even under reduced canvas, and you must try to sail as upright as you can. Mini cruisers like the Mousquetaire which have stable hull forms can hold their own up to force 8 if heeling is kept to a minimum, the sails flattened and sheets freed as necessary.

Fore and aft trim is also important, even if it may not seem to matter so much as lateral trim. If weight is not concentrated in the middle, the boat will lose speed as she pitches and slams into every wave.

In a dinghy the crew shifts weight to help the boat ride the waves. In a cruising boat you may not be able to do more than shift heavy gear like the anchor and chain into the middle of the boat.

Working the Waves

Even with good longitudinal trim, a boat will soon be impeded by waves, especially if she is light, but once again everything is relative and a slight swell to the heavy cruiser can be heavy weather for the dinghy. This is the difference.

The Dinghy

Getting through the waves is a major impediment for a dinghy: she is light, quickly loses speed if she slams into a wave, and all the more so if her sails are not driving. You have to work your way over the waves by keeping your sails full, as follows:

When the boat is balanced on the back of a wave and the relative wind increases, the apparent wind comes ahead; you must therefore bear away to keep the sails driving. When the relative wind slackens and the apparent wind frees in the troughs, you can luff.

This only holds good while the sea is starting to get up, and only for certain wind strengths. When the sea gets rougher and the wind really gets going, different factors come into play and a dinghy, being low in the water, gets the lower part of her sails suddenly blanketed from the wind in the trough between two big waves. To make best progress you should:

> Bear away in the troughs, to keep the head of each sail (the only part getting any thrust) full.
> Luff sharply on the crests, to avoid heeling over suddenly.

These two solutions cannot always apply; circumstances will soon show what you should do. The basic principle is always keep the sails full to give the boat maximum forward thrust and keep it from stopping. At the same time, the helmsman must make sure that his crew can keep his weight well out, on the trapeze if appropriate, without being forced to get back into the boat at every wave. . .

The Cruising Boat

A heavy boat keeps her way on so the problem here is less urgent. There are two solutions.

> Take the waves on the weather bow by approaching each one at a slight angle and then luff as soon as you pass over the crest; when the waves roll in the same direction as the wind, you will find that a good boat has a natural tendency to do this of her own accord.
> Take each wave plumb on the nose by luffing to reduce the impact, and then bear away over the crest to pick up speed again; when the waves are not in the same direction as the wind and are approaching head on, there is little else you can do.

In breaking seas you must make yourself take them bow on even if it means losing way. This action is somewhat theoretical, because it is difficult to luff sufficiently in winds strong enough to break the wave crests.

Even with heavy displacement craft, it is an important safety factor not to lose speed in such conditions. As soon as you think

Waves and wind in the same direction: bear away before the crests, luff up afterwards

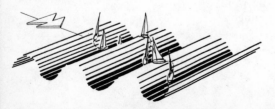

Waves head on: luff up before the crests, bear away afterwards

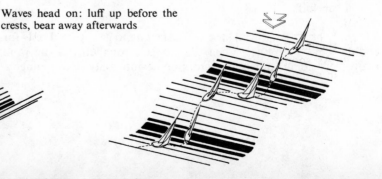

you are getting too slow, regain your speed by bearing away as speed is more important than maintaining a course.

Strong and Squally Winds

The Dinghy

Sailing a dinghy in squally conditions is extremely testing and the helmsman has to have his wits about him all the time if the boat is to be kept moving.

One school of thought believes that, as a squall hits the boat, the jib should be kept cleated home to maintain drive, and the mainsail eased just enough to keep a constant angle of heel (the crew sitting out as far as possible).

Easing the mainsheet however can often tend to increase the belly in the mainsail and even in the jib (because the forestay slackens); and, instead of easing the boat, you press her more. There are two ways of overcoming this problem.

Leave the mainsheet as it is but luff up in the squall, letting the mainsail tremble in the eye of the wind.
This needs some expertise, for the boat must be handled with finesse in the squall to maintain lateral balance and speed at the same time.
Without easing the mainsheet, free traveller right down to leeward to let the mainsail out a trifle. In this way the boom is held down but eased to leeward, thus assuring forward thrust without too much heeling.

In practice, you usually take both actions, at the same time.

Cruising Boats

On larger boats you should choose the sails that suit the weather, in size and fullness, allowing the boat to pass through the squall without lying on her ear and to keep up speed whenever the wind lightens. A reasonable compromise is to have a flat jib, which is right for strong winds, and a mainsail with some shape to it which, although possibly a bit full for the squalls, keeps the boat moving well as soon as they are past. The jib is kept sheeted home in squalls, the mainsail is eased if necessary and you luff up to reduce heeling. As soon as the wind eases off, the mainsail should be sheeted in again and you bear away to pick up speed.

Light Weather

Weather is light when the breeze is gentle and only just to be felt. It is not always easy to decide exactly where the wind is coming from and cigarette smoke is a good indicator or take off your shirt and watch for goose pimples! It is always possible that, although the sea may be completely calm, a very slight breeze may be passing over you nine or ten feet up. Tell-tales on the shrouds or a wind vane may let you know.

You cannot in these conditions hold a close-hauled course, because resistance on the hull is too great for the very weak forward thrust; and you have to bear away a little to gather momentum.

Sail Trim

As the wind is so weak, it must be deflected as much as possible by having the sails very full. They should be eased out so that what force they exert is used to the best advantage.

In this kind of weather although the sea is calm, there may be a swell. The sails, flapping at each roll, can give you some way on but on the whole it is a trying time for boat and crew.

Hull Balance

A dinghy crew tries to sit inboard to reduce wind resistance. If weight is moved forward, the transom is lifted from the water which can give the boat a little more weather helm. Heeling the boat slightly reduces the wet surface and allows the sails to hang correctly. Sudden movements and redistribution of hull trim must be avoided. Any way the boat has is priceless and it is at the mercy of the slightest involuntary movement.

Steering

The tiller must be treated with the utmost finesse and yawing is not to be forgiven. If you point too high you will slow down and the apparent wind speed will fall away sharply, because it is made up almost entirely of relative wind. If this happens, ease sheets and bear away to get moving again.

If you bear away too much, airflow over the sails becomes turbulent, the boat slows and seems to lose the wind. You have then to luff up slowly and sheet in gently to get back on course. It takes time to correct every error and every movement should be made slowly.

Light and Variable Winds

The slightest puff is worth its weight in gold and you must never miss a chance of using one but do not rush at it. When you feel a puff you must sheet in and luff up at the same time and work up to windward and increase speed. But do not hold your new course too long. As soon as the wind drops again, bear away and ease sheets in order to keep a good relative wind for as long as possible, for it is this paradoxically that keeps the boat moving.

You need a fine sense of touch in light breezes and to remain alert to the presence and direction of the wind. This is the only way to keep way on and to stay close to the wind.

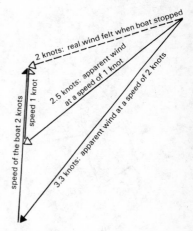

The strength and direction of apparent wind depend a good deal on the boat's speed

On the Wind: Full-and-By

The expression 'full-and-by' means you are not pointing quite as high as close-hauled, and the sails are nicely filled.

The difference in trim between close-hauled and full-and-by is minimal, but the situation is very different. When you sail full-and-by there is no more need to point up very finely, as if you were on a knife edge, to reach your landmark in the head-to-wind zone or even on the edge of it. You can now sail straight towards your goal without further luffing up and bearing away.

Sail Trim

The sails are not so closely sheeted and not so flat as when you were close-hauled; but, although you can deflect the wind now through a larger angle without so much heeling, be careful not to ease the sails quite as much as your freer course might suggest.

When the wind increases, you do not necessarily have to flatten the sails, though this naturally varies from boat to boat. A dinghy always well canvassed, may find difficulty in sailing full-and-by with sails which have a lot of belly; it may even be necessary to reduce sail in a heavy cruiser when changing from close-hauled to full-and-by.

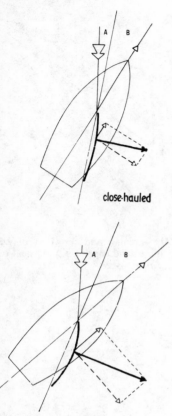

close-hauled

full-and-by

Steering

Now you must keep strictly on course, because variations in strength and direction of wind are met by trimming the sails and not moving the tiller.

It should not be difficult to hold a course on this point of sailing as the boat is well balanced and should respond easily to the helm. Full-and-by is a good point of sailing when you have to steer the boat within confined areas, such as narrow channels, crowded ports, or coming alongside.

Having defined the best close-hauled course as a compromise between pointing high and speed, it must still be emphasised that without speed you have not got a course. This is what should always be uppermost in your mind when sailing to windward. The boat must maintain power and ease of movement, and she must be allowed some flexibility still if you want her to sail effectively along the narrow margin between close-hauled and full-and-by.

Running Before

Running Before

A dead run is easy to define; with your back turned towards the wind, you sail on course directly opposite to head-to-wind; and it is not all that easy to hold the boat steady. We shall therefore also include here the broad reach, which point of sailing involves the wind coming from up to 30° on either quarter.

In medium conditions, downwind sailing is comfortable and easy. Theory, with all its complications, is no longer a problem because the wind pushes the boat and the boat moves forwards, even with badly trimmed sails, or even without sails. Good speed through the water is not essential to maintain a course as there is no leeway, and no heeling. You can play about with all sorts of fancy sails and life is pleasant, for the boat does not slam into the waves, but seems rather to run with them. The apparent wind is less than on any other point of sailing. At last you have comfort!

A following wind is treacherous for it is easy to misjudge its true force. As soon as the wind rises all those factors that made life easy, now begin to cause anxiety. The boat, with little to hold her back, is inclined to yaw from side to side, and needs the helmsman's full attention if she is to be controlled properly and avoid the twin dangers which lie in wait: gybing and broaching-to.

Sail Trim

Carry all available sail: mainsail, spinnaker, spinnaker staysail (if you have one) – all you have that will work for you provided you are not expecting to change course.

On cruising boats the jib is handed; on dinghies, roll it up in light weather, otherwise sheet it loosely to leeward.

Mainsail

Air flows turbulently on this point of sailing and the efficiency of the mainsail is indifferent. You must give it as much belly as possible, keep the twist to a minimum and present the largest surface to the wind that you can to get the maximum thrust.

Curve or Belly and Twist

Ease the luff and foot to increase belly, and use the kicking strap to cut down twist. Downwind there is no need to feather the head of the sail. Also, a sail with twist makes the boat luff and heel to windward, compelling you to be bearing away time and again, and thus creating a disagreeable roll that makes the boat become difficult to hold on course.

Sail Trim

The mainsail should be at right-angles to the wind downwind, with the sheet paid out and the boom resting against the shrouds. A roll starts up very easily when there is no athwart ships pressure on the sail to keep the boat steady. Also, a well eased mainsail can interfere with the spinnaker's air flow, so in practice it is better to sheet the boom in a little.

Spinnaker

The spinnaker is hoisted on this point of sailing (the sail and its

With a following wind twist can be dangerous: the downhaul must be tightened

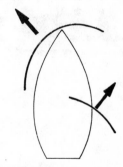

Sheet in the mainsail gently to reduce rolling and improve air flow round the spinnaker

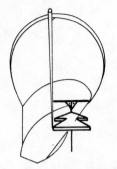

The spinnaker pole should be at right
angles to the apparent wind and –

use are described in pages 165 *et seq*).

Like all sails, the spinnaker should deflect the wind. Its deep
concave shape means that it can turn it through a particularly large
angle, and its cut is designed to catch as much wind as possible. It
is therefore important:

To open the spinnaker as fully as possible to windward with the
spinnaker boom, which should be at right-angles to the apparent
wind.

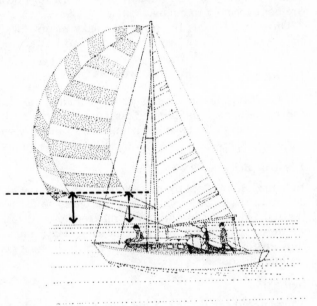

Tack and clew must be at the same
level

to the mast

To hollow the spinnaker, by raising the spinnaker boom provided
tack and clew can both rise with it. The foot of the sail should
remain horizontal, always remaining parallel to the horizon. If
it is possible to adjust the height of the spinnaker boom attachment on the mast, the spinnaker boom should also be kept
at right angles to the mast or else it will put too much strain on its
heel fittings and risk shipping up or down its track. On dinghies
and small cruisers where this kind of adjustment is not possible,
the spinnaker boom end should be allowed to rise slightly.

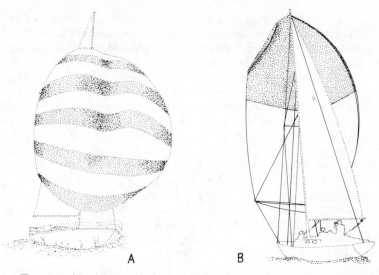

A   B

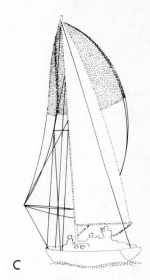

C

To ease the sheet as much as possible. This is a general rule for all sail trimming, but it is specially important here because, if the spinnaker is to maintain balance, its air flow must escape quickly. A spinnaker, too tightly sheeted, which does not let the wind circulate freely, is liable to collapse in the middle and wrap itself round the forestay. A mortifying experience for the crew.

Spinnaker work without tears I
A. Sheeted in too hard: it is going to furl itself round the forestay
B. Well freed off: slight furl at the top of the luff
C. Sheet eased out too much: it is about to collapse

As with other sails, the spinnaker should be eased to the limit. If it is eased too much, you will see the top of the luff fold slightly inwards; this fold is not necessarily bad in itself, but it indicates that you have reached optimum trim and are near to the critical point. If you ease a little more, the spinnaker will collapse not in the middle this time but by suddenly collapsing on the luff, shaking the whole rigging.

The ideal therefore is to trim in until the luff is slightly shivering but with no trace of a fold appearing.

It would, of course, be naive to expect the spinnaker could keep its trim for any length of time. Its balance is precarious and easily upset by rolling, or even by the wind shadow set up by the passage of another boat. One member of the crew should keep constant watch on the luff, and be ready to sheet in as soon as a fold threatens. You can haul in the sheet by hand, even on large boats, from in front of the fairlead, and you can do this briskly, hand over hand,

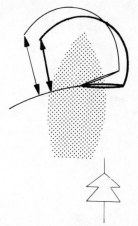

It is better to have the guy eased off a bit too much than too little: the air then circulates more easily

for you are really only turning the spinnaker around the wind inside it to help it get back into shape; but as soon as you have done this, ease out as much as you dare again. It is only when the spinnaker continually drops at its head that you should sheet in and keep it in; even then, as soon as the luff stops shivering, or the head of the sail no longer falls in at all, you can ease out the sheet a little.

Generally speaking, any change in the sheet needs a corresponding change to the guy, although it cannot be adjusted as easily because it is under strong tension. It is preferable to have a guy eased too much rather than not enough, because in the former case, although the amount of air picked up by the sail is a little reduced, the slot between the mainsail and the spinnaker leech is broader, improving air flow; with the guy not eased enough, the spinnaker will be very full and will tend to hold its wind and it is only a matter of time before it becomes twisted round the forestay.

The principle to remember is that *a spinnaker will only fill well if the wind is allowed to circulate round it.*

Jib

If you have no spinnaker or if it is damaged, or if perhaps your crew are not up to hoisting it above a certain wind strength, you have to resort to a jib which has a good belly and can deflect a lot of wind.

Boom it out to windward (goosewinged). If you have a spinnaker pole, use it with the working jib to windward and perhaps with the genoa to leeward where the sheet may be led to the end of the main boom; this rig can be carried with the wind 15–20° off the dead aft position. But if you have a jib pole (considerably longer than a spinnaker pole), you can carry the genoa to windward when the wind is 30°–40° from dead aft.

The jib sheet is liable to chafe quickly where it runs through the end of the spinnaker pole, so it is better to use a spinnaker guy,

ing do without a spinnaker . . .

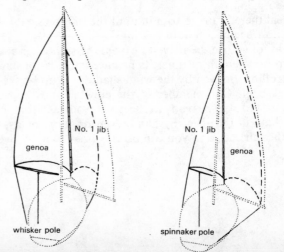

which has a snap shackle or hook for fixing to the end of the pole (don't forget to rig another guy to leeward, in case you have to gybe).

Boat Trim

With the wind aft, the way the boat reacts on the helm is partly governed by the balance of the sails:

Under fully eased mainsail alone, the boat tends to turn up to windward for she carries weather helm.

When a jib is boomed out to windward, you can reduce weather helm by heeling the boat to windward.

When a spinnaker is set, the effect of the mainsail is largely compensated and the boat is balanced; however, a spinnaker often makes the boat heel to windward, giving her an unpleasant amount of lee helm.

Spinnaker work without tears II
A. The helmsman has borne away too much –
B. – which gives this situation
C. But gybe the main over to the same side as the spinnaker pole and –
D. – it will sort itself out. The main is then gybed back in the proper manner. All is well

In fine weather, the sea does not roll her about and it is relatively easy to hold her on course. Broaching to is easily kept in check, because you get plenty of warning by the luff of the spinnaker falling in, but any tendency to bear away is, as always, more troublesome.

If you bear away a little beyond the point of the wind being dead aft, or when you are sailing *by the lee*, the spinnaker will be masked by the mainsail and is then liable to collapse and wrap itself round the forestay: one turn round the stay and you will for sure not be able to stop it twisting more; luffing will only make things worse. The only way to unwrap it is to change course, gybe, and then sail by the lee on the other gybe. The spinnaker may then sort itself out.

As a general rule, when sailing under spinnaker with the wind aft, as soon as anything goes wrong the helmsman should luff rather than bear away, because once a spinnaker has collapsed it is easier to set it to rights than when it gets wrapped round the stay.

The Centreboard

A dinghy with the wind aft is being thrust forwards only and the centreboard is doing nothing for you and raising it right up reduces wetted area. This is all right in light weather, but in fresh conditions it is better to leave it lowered a bit because, without any centreboard at all, the boat is not so easy to control as soon as the wind is not dead aft. Then she is liable to yaw, skid sideways, and roll, making it difficult to keep a straight course. And how will you right after a capsize without a little centreboard?

Equally, if the centreboard is too low, the boat cannot slide sideways at all if she starts to broach and the result is also a capsize. A great dinghy sailor has described this as the centreboard 'tripping up' the boat.

It is worth recalling that the hydrodynamic effect of the centreboard increases with the square of the speed. When you are moving fast and you don't need much centreboard, only let it down a little.

It is better to keep the centre plate slightly down if only to help you right the boat

Fresh Winds

Difficulties begin to multiply downwind as the weather becomes brisker. The slope that you are sliding down becomes steeper and you don't have good brakes. A well canvassed boat, sailing at high speed in a sea which has started to get up, needs expertise at the helm.

It is not easy to discuss light dinghies and cruising boats at the same time under these conditions. Downwind in heavy weather, a dinghy turns into a wild thing, with little or no stability, and you must react quickly, have eyes in the back of your head and maintain a precarious balance by shifting your weight in the boat. Under jib and mainsail an ill-judged sail trim makes you capsize without warning, to windward as well as to leeward, and most of the time you hardly know what is happening. A spinnaker, which should be slightly more tightly sheeted than in medium weather, makes the boat more stable, but you must have to be able to set it and tame it. All this can be exhilarating, without risk of dire consequences for a good crew in supervised waters, but it is then more like gymnastics than sailing.

It is altogether different in a cruising boat where considerations of safety take precedence over all others. You cannot slow up easily sailing before the wind and a spinnaker makes everything more complicated: you cannot, for instance, gybe round and go to the rescue quickly if anyone falls overboard.

The first and most important rule to observe, for all points of sailing but particularly downwind, is to put on harnesses in plenty of time – as soon as the wind begins to blow. Then you must be able to see at once when it is time to take down your spinnaker. Poor seamanship makes different boats react in different ways. Dinghies capsize, either by broaching to or by gybing, but we have already seen that their problem is special; others, particularly ballasted centreboarders drawing little water, are merely blown over on their side without necessarily breaking anything, but probably tipping their crews into the water; heavier, deep-keel boats cannot tip over and lose their masts under the strain.

Spinnakers can be kept up for as long as you are master of the situation; everything therefore depends on the ability of the crew. Spinnaker drill is only perfected slowly, by carrying the sail each time in a slightly stronger wind (provided experience is gained in waters where accidents will not bring serious consequences). We shall learn later about when to take the decision to take down a spinnaker.

The main problem of downwind sailing in heavy weather is maintaining course, for the boat is more liable to yaw (with all the attendant complications) than on any other point of sailing. Rather than sail straight downwind, it is wiser to keep the wind 10° or 15° on the weather quarter as a precaution against gybing.

Rudder Balance

Instability Caused by the Sails

A spinnaker makes the boat pitch in heavy weather because it tends to lift the stern of the boat while pulling the masthead forward. As the boat is held back by the water, this tendency makes the boat bury her bows, making steering difficult. You should bring all possible weight aft to keep the bows up.

Take care not to allow any play in the spinnaker, so hoist it to the masthead, see that the spinnaker pole is well braced, and even lead the sheet by the end of the main boom. If you are sailing under spinnaker for any length of time, it is wise alternately to ease and hoist a few inches of halyard every two or three hours to avoid constant chafe at the same point on the masthead sheave.

If you are sailing with the jib boomed out, using the spinnaker gear will enable you to keep the clew of the sail in position.

Finally, cut down twist as much as possible by using the downhaul.

Instability Caused by the Sea

Waves roll the boat and help to throw her off course. A following sea tends to make the boat luff if it strikes the hull on the weather quarter, or to bear away if it comes from the leeward. This is aggravated if the particular wave catches the boat as she heels to windward or leeward respectively, increasing yawing beyond a regular swinging movement.

This is when judicious use of the tiller comes in. You must anticipate the action of the waves because, once yawing gets going, the rudder has little effect. When the swell is coming from windward, bear away before the wave arrives and it will then merely

Under spinnakers keep her down by the stern

Take action before the wave reaches you if you are not to gybe or luff

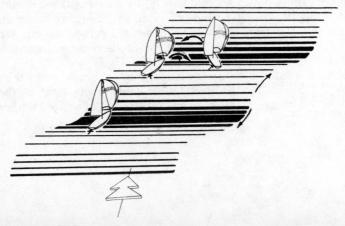

bring the boat back on course. On the other hand, luff in advance of waves coming from leeward, to avoid the danger of an unintentional gybe 'down the hill'.

This requires finesse and firmness at the same time. The braking effect of the rudder can be ignored now because the important thing is to stay on course. Steering under these conditions tests your stamina.

aerodynamic force

Spinnaker work without tears III
The consequence of luffing: the boat comes to a halt and heels violently. Have you a downhaul on the leeward side?

Broaching to

Even if the helmsman is constantly alert the boat can still take charge and start luffing uncontrollably. If the spinnaker is up, complications can set in: the boat lies over, slows up and soon virtually stops with the wind on the beam. She tends to stay on her side because the spinnaker is working more or less in reverse: wind is entering at the foot and escaping where it can at the side.

If you react quickly enough, while the boat is still moving through the water, you can control the situation by letting the spinnaker sheet run out and bringing the tiller right up to windward. But if the boat has already slowed down too much for the rudder to be effective, you will stay beam on, spinnaker flogging violently and shaking the entire rig. You have to act quickly. One solution is to carry the spinnaker clew to the bow. Not being able to fill, the spinnaker is obliged to give up and collapses in the middle. The boat immediately stops heeling so much and you can then carry on. In order to be able to do this, you must obviously have a downhaul leading from the end of the spinnaker pole to the bows. This downhaul, which is usually taken off in light weather so as not to weigh down the clew, should always be attached in fresh weather, readily available for this emergency drill.

Spinnaker work with tears IV
The picture is too horrible to show

Bearing Away

If broaching to is troublesome, bearing away can be much more serious because it can lead to a gybe and then broaching to on the other tack. If a main boom preventer has been rigged, the sight is spectacular and the boat gets into horrible confusion, which does not last long because something usually breaks quickly.

In an unsettled sea, a main boom preventer is needed. You must settle for a course 10° or 15° off the wind because, all things considered, it is safer to risk broaching to than a sudden bearing away.

Reducing Sail

Getting a spinnaker down in heavy weather is clearly no simple matter, and you must learn to anticipate and get the washing in in good time.

Beyond a Force 5 the difficulties increase with compound interest. The instability, caused in part by the rhythmic rolling set up by the swinging spinnaker, is more or less constant. There is a real danger of sailing under the waves, even with the large boat and, if the mast doesn't break, the whole boat could, theoretically, go under.

Mental and physical fatigue is sometimes a reason in itself for lowering the spinnaker. You must be fit and fresh to carry one in heavy weather. It is almost impossible to relieve the man at the helm and whoever is in charge, when the wind gets up, has to settle down to the job. He begins to get the feel of the boat and becomes one with her, reacting as required. Any replacement, thrown in as it were at the deep end, needs time to adapt himself and is liable to make a misjudgement which can often cost a blown spinnaker or even a broken mast.

Running for a long time under spinnaker in a heavy sea strains the nerves of any crew, because they can never relax. A tired skipper or helmsman can make the wrong decision, and there is no need even to speak of the problems of picking up a man who falls overboard.

'Get it down in time' is the watch word for spinnaker drill under these conditions, and even a smaller spinnaker is not often the right answer. It is not so much a question of sail area as stability because, as the sail is only fixed at three points, the hard tugging puts great strain on the rigging. It is better to change to a genoa or a boomed-out jib, loss of speed being compensated for by extra stability. It removes that anxious look on crew's faces.

It is also usually wise to reef the mainsail. This affects speed hardly at all in fresh weather and it will then interfere less with the spinnaker. Above all, should any rapid change of course be necessary, the boat answers more readily and handles generally more easily under shortened sail.

Light Weather

Running dead before the wind on a swell in very light weather is as testing as in heavy conditions, and you find yourself almost regretting the excess of wind which was recently causing so much fuss. Now there is plenty of time to play with the spinnaker, which does little good, and to think up gimmicks to make the boat go. Roll becomes enemy number one and on a heavy boat when you are not racing and have been sailing like this for two or three hours, it is sometimes worth dropping all sails to rest the crew and the rig.

Nevertheless it is important to know how to keep the boat moving in light weather, whether you are negotiating a difficult channel or trying to gain several miles to avoid a foul tide, or simply to make port on time.

Sail trim becomes important again.

As soon as you start moving, the apparent wind is less than the true wind and ceases to be of much help.

A light spinnaker of (26gm^2) cloth, with light sheets, (4mm for 100m^2) might just fill. You can try 'working' the sails by sheeting in gently to fill them, and then holding them as soon as they are reasonably set. If there is practically no wind, they must be kept out by hand.

The sails must, somehow, be kept as full as possible. Even in a swell, the boat may move forward slightly.

Heel the boat slightly so that the sails can take up their natural shape, if only by gravity. The crew should move about as little as possible. There is no need for extreme action like going down below because wind resistance downwind is, if anything, beneficial. In a dinghy raise the centreboard right up.

Whistling for the wind works – they say.

As soon as the wind gets up a bit, downwind sailing is fast and pleasant, and is fairly trouble free, unlike running free in heavy weather. In a way it is as demanding downwind as to windward, although the problems are different. To windward, you must maintain speed at all costs, while downwind it is a question of anticipating the vagaries of the boat caused by wind variations and the state of the sea and mainly maintaining course.

Some helmsmen prefer windward work, others downwind. It depends on your temperament.

Reaching

Between downwind and windward courses there is the wide and more comfortable sector of reaching. The word itself is indicative: you reach out for your destination with the ease of a rider at the gallop.

This is the best point of sailing which the boat takes to naturally. She travels fast and it is easy to get the best out of the wind. When it rises, instead of shortening sail as you do to windward, you hang onto it and all that happens is that you go faster. There is less need to trim sails to the point where they begin to lift. You only want to deflect the wind through the best angle for maximum thrust. If she is well trimmed on this point of sailing, a dinghy seems to leap forward: she planes.

All goes well until suddenly, for no apparent reason, the boat slows, swings upright and the crew have to sit inboard. The wind seems to have disappeared and, after all your efforts, you have fallen into the trap of stalling.

Stalling

We discussed this phenomenon at length in Chapter 3: as a sail is sheeted home more and more, the thrust it generates increases steadily until the crucial point beyond which it falls away rapidly. This crucial point occurs when the sail becomes an obstacle to the wind rather than an airfoil. Air flow, laminar and regular until this moment, suddenly becomes turbulent, and wind pressure on the sail drops quickly.

The breakdown is disconcerting and it is difficult for an inexperienced crew to know what to do. To windward, poor sail trim was shown up by the luff lifting, and it was enough to sheet in a little to put things right. You get no warning of stalling and it is not easy to get out of it. You should either ease the sheets well out, or luff sharply, to get rid of the turbulence in the sails before getting going again and re-trimming the sails.

True Wind, Apparent Wind

Stalling can be caused by a sudden variation of wind, yawing or the boat slowing-up by chance, but the reason invariably is that the angle of maximum deflection has been passed and consequently the sails are sheeted in too tightly in relation to the apparent wind.

On a reach, with the wind roughly abeam, the difference in direction of the true wind and the apparent wind is greater than at any other point of sailing. The apparent wind comes from much further ahead than the true wind and, the faster you go, the greater this difference becomes (it can be as much as 30°). It is important to realise that the slightest change in speed brings about a material change in the direction of the apparent wind. When the boat slows down, whatever the reason may be, the apparent wind can blow more free and the sails are, in a moment, much too closely sheeted; air flow, laminar up to this point, becomes turbulent. That is stalling. Loss of speed, not very marked at first, becomes very noticeable even though you have made no change in the trim of the sails, the trim of the boat or the course.

Different Reaches

The situation changes entirely the moment an air flow, that has been steady over the sails, becomes turbulent. This stall is the dividing line between a reach and a broad reach, the latter being very close to a dead run as we have already seen.

The reaching sector is so broad that it is usually divided into two: reaching and close reaching. First of all we shall look at the sail trim that is common to both the divisions, and then consider control of the boat. First of all this control is largely a matter of the skill and keenness of the crew, and close reaching and reaching can either be the points of sailing which make for enjoyment or anxiety. We have laid some stress on stalling but it is not a necessary evil, and need never arise on a reach provided you don't sheet in the sails too closely. The boat will, in any case, travel very nearly as fast. But when you want to extract the last ounce from your craft, sails should be trimmed to perfection and *best trim is just*

On a reach, variations of the apparent wind can be quite large

short of the stall. Under that trim the boat comes to life, specially in a fresh wind. The speed can be exhilarating and the experience is all the more exciting because you are never sure when you may overdo it and make a mess of things.

Sail Trim

Sails should have plenty of belly on a reach. The more they have, the more they deflect the wind through a large angle without stalling. They then give maximum thrust and, at the same time, you will get early warning of the trim not being quite right, for very full sails are properly trimmed for reaching just after trembling as the luff is ironed out. If it returns, bear away a trifle.

The set of the sail should be watched all the time when you are sailing at speed. The faster you go, the more the apparent wind comes ahead and the more you should sheet the sails in to go on deflecting the wind through the optimum angle.

You must also keep an eye cocked on the interaction of your sails. On the reach the foresail, spinnaker or jib, tends to curve inwards at the leech. The air stream is compressed in the slot between the two sails which must be avoided at all costs. Easing the headsail sheet is not always the best remedy because the sail then bellies; you are better off if you hold out the clew by reeving the sheets to the end of the main boom.

Sails do not need to be flattened on a reach in heavy weather. It is enough to ease sheets a little to make deflection less. The thrust exerted by the wind is not less and, because it is better orientated, the power of the boat is further increased.

Hull Trim

Many boats have a strong weather helm when close-reaching and reaching, because the centre of effort is carried well to leeward, and this is difficult to counter. It can be reduced on dinghies with a pivoting centreboard if this is partly raised. In any case, heel over as little as possible because heeling aggravates weather helm.

Whatever kind of centreboard you have, it should be lifted at least half way when you are travelling fast, because the heeling component is relatively weak compared with the thrust. The keel can be raised completely on ballasted centreboarders.

As soon as there is a good breeze, a light dinghy can easily plane if you move aft and lean out as much as necessary to main-

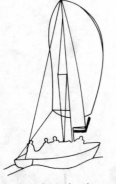

A spinnaker sheet that is rove round the end of the boom should be cleated on the mast and not taken aft or else it becomes a mainsheet

tain stability. When the wind is very light, avoid jerky movements in the boat because one sudden movement can make you stall, and you will lose time in re-establishing a steady air flow over the sails. This is particularly important in a race in light weather: the crews who sit tight move fastest.

Close Reaching

A close reach is the fastest point of sailing because air flow over the sails is laminar, and the aerodynamic force is strong and very well orientated. In fresh winds dinghies will heel over unless you sit out energetically to keep your sails trimmed to the optimum angle of deflection. It is rugged work but it gets results and, if you are agile enough, fabulous results! It is also fun!

This point of sailing is more or less half way between close-hauled and a beam reach: you have a wide range of trim to play with. The set of the sails can, in practice, vary between the point of stall and complete lifting of the luff of the sail. The beginning of a stall can be quickly countered by easing sheets a lot to avoid turbulence; then sheet in progressively until the air flow becomes laminar again.

Gusts are coped with either by luffing up as you would when going to windward, or bearing away and easing sheets – it depends on the circumstances: if someone is out on the trapeze and you are planing, it is better to bear away, easing sheets, to reduce heeling and so increase speed still more.

The important question is now, should you change to the spinnaker or genoa? It is not easy to decide which of the two will be the more efficient, and the drawing opposite shows a situation where, theoretically, spinnaker and genoa with appropriately trimmed mainsail will give the same speed. If it is to stay full, the spinnaker has to be sheeted fairly hard, and so the large amount of wind that it gathers does not work to the best advantage; the genoa collects less wind but is better orientated. The advantage may seem to be with the spinnaker but, under genoa, the mainsail can be eased more than under spinnaker. It follows that the better orientation of the mainsail and genoa compensates for the greater amount of wind that flows over the combination of mainsail and spinnaker.

It is difficult to decide exactly when the spinnaker ceases to be more efficient. When it is hoisted, you can look at the direction of pull on the halyard at the masthead, which shows the direction in

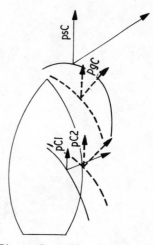

$pC1 + psC = pC2 + pgC$. In other words in this case, spinnaker and genoa have the same efficiency

which the sail is pulling, although this is only a rough and ready guide. In practice, on this point of sailing, the spinnaker usually only pays off in light weather. In strong winds the extra speed it gives will probably not make up for the extra distance travelled owing to the almost inevitable occasional broachings to, and you also have to take account of the time required to change sail. Is it worth it? Usually, yes!

Reaching

On a reach there should be no hesitation: if the wind is not too strong you have to fly the spinnaker.

Remember, though, that it is on a reach that the sharpest stalls occur. As you bear away from a close reach, ease sheets gradually, keeping the sails properly trimmed in relation to the wind. The moment comes when the mainsail is pressing against the shroud, but you cannot bear away any more without stalling. Even if you stop bearing away the situation is precarious, for the slightest drop in speed caused by the slam of a wave on the hull, for example, can produce a stall. When it happens, it can no longer be overcome by easing sheets because they are already fully eased. You must luff up sharply until the sails shiver, then bear away again gently to get back on course.

It is easy to observe the difference in behaviour of different boats by watching the air flow over their sails. It can happen that two boats, steering the same course with the same sail trim, maintain entirely different speeds, because one of them, having borne away onto this course, has maintained laminar flow and thus plenty of speed, while the other, which has luffed on to the course from the dead aft situation, is still suffering from turbulent air flow and is lagging behind. If she wants to keep up with the first boat, the second should luff up sharply for a moment and, until she does, the two boats are really in two entirely different worlds.

On a reach in variable winds, there is little point in cogitating on what to do: if you luff in a gust, you can only overpress the boat still further, so always bear away and ease sheets. When the gust is very strong, you can even exploit the stall by bearing away sharply to produce it intentionally and, as the air flow becomes turbulent, the aerodynamic force on the sails will diminish. In the final analysis therefore the stalling becomes a kind of safety measure.

Planing

A boat is planing when she suddenly takes off at great speed, the bottom seeming just to brush the surface of the water.

Under certain conditions of wind and course, a dinghy will plane spontaneously. It is even difficult to stop her sometimes and you may be led to think that it is the easiest trick in the world; but to continue planing for a long time, in varying winds and on different points of sailing, is an art which takes some acquiring.

Planing Defined

The hull of a boat moves through the water at a certain angle of trim, and sustains a force directed upwards, *lift*, and a force directed aft, *drag*.

When the lift becomes superior to gravity, the hull emerges from her own wave formation onto the surface and, as its wetted area decreases, drag decreases correspondingly. Speed increases in proportion to the reduction in the forces which militate against forward movement: skin friction, suction, drag. The hull behaves more and more like a water ski, and the boat mounts onto its own bow wave which then shifts aft towards the middle of the hull. The after end of the hull then becomes the lifting surface. You are planing.

To plane, you have to have:

A light boat with a hull that is broad and flat aft.
High speed (which requires enough wind and large sails, well set).
A favourable angle of trim (which must stay favourable even when you are planing through waves).

Boat Control

The best conditions for planing are a close reach in a Force 3 wind and slightly broken water.

The apparent wind is slightly forward of abeam and, as the air flow is laminar, aerodynamic force is good; heel can easily be kept in check.

In a steady wind, you start planing by tugging on the jib sheet several times to ease the bow, while you move gently aft; in variable winds, it is easier to wait for a gust then bear away slightly and sheet in the mainsail, and the boat will leap forward.

The difficulty is to continue planing for any length of time when the force or direction of the wind is never completely steady.

To start with, do all you can to keep the boat upright. This is in any case one of the basic rules of dinghy sailing. It demands meticulous attention: shifting your weight in and out tirelessly or by sitting out and adjusting sail trim and course.

The height of the centreboard must be carefully watched. You do not need to lower it much, because you are travelling fast, but its position has to be adjusted to suit the sail plan and the wind. It will vary, for example, according to whether or not you are carrying a spinnaker. Only practical experience can enable you to know how much to raise or lower it. It is worthwhile to mark it when you have found what height works best in certain conditions.

When bearing away or luffing you should remember the effect of centrifugal force, which will tend to tip the masthead outboard if you turn sharply.

In strong or variable winds, you must continually be changing the trim of the boat. Bear away and ease sheets in the gusts, never forgetting that heeling component will not increase when the sail is eased and the boat will accelerate without heeling over. Luff and sheet in during lulls and the sheeted-in sails will maintain the same angle of heel preventing windward heel. If the lull is sudden, luff sharply and centrifugal force will keep the boat upright long enough to allow the crew on the trapeze to come in without a ducking.

It is obvious that you will go better if you can keep the boat upright without forever changing course at the whim of the wind, so you must learn how to alter weight trim quickly. Start by practising when the wind is not too strong, and you can sit out and get back into the boat easily. Helmsman and crew must work in close co-ordination, and both have to be very fit. A well practised crew can achieve marvellous results.

Conditions for Planing

Planing is only possible under certain winds and points of sailing.

To windward, the force exerted by the wind is badly orientated, the heeling component is large and the thrust component is weak, so a monohull dinghy cannot lift from the water. (Multihulls can do it.)

It is possible to plane sailing full-and-by if you are able to sit out sufficiently to keep the boat upright (with crew and helmsman both out on a trapeze).

Close-reaching is the ideal point of sailing. You can plane in a lighter wind than is necessary on other points of sailing.

On a beam reach you need a little more wind. Sailing on a broad reach or with the wind nearly dead aft requires a good wind and an experienced crew.

Generally speaking, it is not possible to plane in light winds. The ideal is medium weather. Planing in heavy weather, specially for any length of time, is a sport for experts because the boat reacts more quickly than the crew. The problem is to remain in the boat while the boat remains on the water, and the exercise is the acme of the excitement of sailing. The boat seems to be breaking all the rules which generally govern her conduct. She is inspired with a new animation and you feel that at any moment she will take wing. But when the sea is choppy, it nearly always ends in the same way: you come up against a wave, the angle of trim is thrown out, turning into an angle of dive, and the boat puts her nose under and literally corkscrews herself into the water.

Although it is a bit special, planing is excellent training in all round control of the boat. When everything is well set up, properly regulated and trimmed, she seems to know what to do. This may not always be so obvious to you, but keep in the back of your mind this idea: sailing a boat well is largely a question of allowing her to express herself. Boats have some affinity with horses.

This is not to rule out firm, sometimes harsh control, but this control has only one aim: to overcome obstacles and to deal with situations that sometimes seem to defy solution.

The moral is, never maltreat a boat by trying to get out of her more than she can give.

Whipping a horse turns it into a mule and at sea some booms hit back with justification.

9. Going About and Gybing

Changing tack is a basic manoeuvre in boat control: either with the wind ahead or astern, the boat turns on its axis through the eye of the wind as you change from one course to the other. On any one tack, the sails can only be subjected to progressive changes of trim, but now they pass either quickly or slowly from one side of the boat to the other. In either case there is a pause, a moment of uncertainty, and it must not be allowed to last too long and get out of control.

The eye of the wind is a kind of wall. Beating is a progress to windward from one side of this wall to the other; tacking is to have the impetus to leap over the wall and, when you are sailing close-hauled, maintenance of speed is the essence of the manoeuvre.

When you change tack with the wind aft by gybing, speed is not so important, and you must concentrate on where you are going, because yawing can ruin everything. Downwind the boat is balanced on the top of the wall, so to speak, and you must not fall down on one side or the other.

The two operations are just about as different as they can be.

Going About

There is no great drama in going about: with the boat close-hauled on one tack, you luff up through the eye of the wind and soon find yourself close-hauled on the other tack.

During this operation the sails will shiver when they are dead

into the wind. The boat passes through an angle of about 90°
without help of the sails, depending on her momentum, or *way*. That
is the essence of the whole exercise: if way is feeble or is allowed to
fall off, the boat may refuse to pass through the eye of the wind,
and the tack fails; you *miss stays*.

To come about properly you must observe these basic rules:

Start from the close-hauled position.
Have enough speed.
Use your sails to advantage, at the start and the finish of the
manoeuvre.
Use the tiller gently to avoid the braking effect of the rudder.

The first two rules, which are preparatory, are just as important as
the last two, which control the manoeuvre as it takes place.

Principles

Preparation

Close-hauled. If you start from any other point of sailing than
close-hauled, the dead zone which the boat must pass through
without propulsive force is much too wide and you are liable to
lose way before you even reach the point of head-to-wind.

It is important, therefore, at least for beginners, to get close-
hauled and to sail for a moment like that to ensure that you are
properly trimmed and are going well.

It is now possible to come about successfully provided that the
sails are well trimmed throughout for the points of sailing you are
passing through, for they must play their part to the end.

You can learn fairly quickly to synchronise the movement of a
dinghy and its sails. It can be more difficult on a cruising boat
owing to its bigger sails, and sometimes to the gadgets used for
trimming them.

Speed. When sailing fully close-hauled, the dead zone you have to
pass through is as small as it will ever be. But if the boat is not
making much headway and seems reluctant to pick up speed, the
angle will feel even wider and the boat may not make it. So never
hold her back. You only need to trim sails for an ordinary close-
hauled course and the boat will sail as though nothing was afoot:
she does not need any warning that you are going to tack.

You must try to start the turn at a point when the boat is nicely

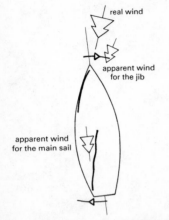

real wind

apparent wind
for the jib

apparent wind
for the main sail

When going about, the jib must be kept sheeted in as late as possible, particularly if the sea is rough. It continues to drive the boat forward after the mainsail has ceased to be effective

settled. But never forget that speed is essential and if, for instance, you have just struck a wave and lost speed, delay coming about for a moment or two.

The Sails

The sails lose their drive as the boat passes through the eye of the wind, it loses way and the flogging sails hold the boat back. In fact, a flogging sail presents more wind-resistance than one sheeted in too hard or even slightly backed.

It cannot be over-emphasised that the sails should be kept filled for as long as possible during the first part of the turn and that they should be sheeted in to pick up the wind again as soon as possible on the new tack.

Point one. Coming about starts with the help of the mainsail. We already know that it has a big influence and that when you sheet the main in, the boat luffs up. Sheet it hard in therefore and, if the boat heels more, it will only help.

Then tighten the jib progressively (if it is not already fully home), leaving it full for as long as possible while you turn. Remember that the rotation of the boat has an odd effect on the sails, the apparent wind freeing the jib but heading the mainsail. So the main lifts fairly soon while the jib remains full for longer. This is only noticeable on a slow boat, but it is something to remember: keep the jib sheeted in to the last moment.

Point two. Eventually, of course, when the jib empties and lifts suddenly. Let its sheet fly, at the same time, easing the main sheet slightly to have it correctly trimmed on the new tack. The boat's way keeps it turning until it passes through the eye of the wind and bears away on the other tack. The sails still shudder on the new tack. Now comes the moment of the classic mistake, the most frequent cause of missing stays: trimming the jib as soon as you see its clew move to the other side of the mast. If you do trim in then, the jib will pick up the wind on the wrong side, backing, and stopping the boat dead in her tracks. This is simply because you have forgotten that the sheeting point of the jib is not on the centre line of the boat but right out to one side. Before sheeting hard home, you must wait until the imaginary line joining the jib's tack and clew has passed through the eye of the wind; in practice this happens when its clew is shaking fairly near the shrouds.

The mainsail is not the cause of the trouble: it fills happily on the new tack. If the boat has lost speed, just bear away a little and ease sheets before trimming into the wind once more.

The Tiller

A violent movement on the tiller punches the breath out of the boat making the rudder act as a brake and making the turn more acute. As a result, speed is lost. Too gentle a tiller can also lead to too slow a tack, which also dissipates speed. You must choose a mean between the two.

In practice good boats come about without much work on the tiller. *It should be enough to leave the tiller while you sheet in the mainsail, and the boat will turn of her own accord.*

The real task of the helmsman is to watch the tiller move over and merely to round off the manoeuvre, exerting any necessary control when the sails start shaking.

Going About in a Dinghy

To go about neatly in a dinghy, you must remember two main points:

The boat is light and loses way very quickly but, equally, it picks it up again quickly: it is therefore important to pass through the dead zone with all speed.

The boat is unstable, so you must maintain constant trim.

Speed

As the boat loses way quickly, get up extra speed at the start. From the close-hauled position, bear away slightly (3° or 4°) without easing sheets. The boat will pick up speed, heeling slightly; coming about will then start spontaneously but you can help it by sheeting the mainsail hard in. Release the tiller and the boat will pivot round at once.

If you have someone on the trapeze, you must give him time to get into the boat, unhook, move under the boom and set himself up again on the other side! In this case you must keep your hand on the tiller so as not to come about too quickly for him.

After coming round the boat will have lost speed, so bear away slightly, but further off the wind than when you started the turn 5° or 10°), and pick up speed before coming back on the close-hauled position.

1. The boat is close-hauled, nicely trimmed, travelling at a good speed
2. The sheets are clear

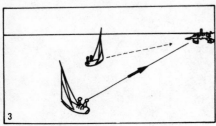

5. The crew watches the jib which must remain sheeted in
6. The boat has luffed up, the tiller following the movement. The main flaps but the jib is still sheeted in. One of the crew comes inboard

3. The tyro helmsman looks over his shoulder and notes the heading he should make after going about
4. He begins to go about: sheets in hard and allows the boat to heel a little, following the movement with the tiller or letting it go

7. Luffing up continues. The jib flaps and its sheet is let fly. The crew is now in the middle of the boat and the helmsman comes in

8. The boat is head-to-wind. The helmsman changes hands on the tiller at the same time letting out the amount of sheet taken in at the beginning of the manoeuvre. The crew are now on opposite sides of the boat's axis
9. The boat bears away on the new tack. The main is already drawing. The jib has passed in front of the mast and the crew begins to sheet it in, not too hard. The crew sits out on the weather gunwale, the helmsman is amidships
10 The boat has borne away enough for the jib to be sheeted in

11. Crew and helmsman sit out. The sails are filled. When the boat has borne away enough for it to accelerate briskly, the helmsman brings the tiller amidships

Balance

The boat has been suddenly released from the pressure of the wind, coming upright as she turns and then leans over heavily on the new tack. While this is happening the crew must follow the boats movement to ensure uninterrupted balance. When you start to change tack, move towards the middle of the boat while she still heels slightly, be right in the middle while she passes through the eye of the wind, and move onto the opposite gunwale when the sails fill again and the boat starts to heel over on the new tack.

All this would be easy enough if you had nothing else to think about; but while going from one side to the other, the helmsman has to transfer the tiller and the sheet from one hand to the other. When the main sheet traveller is in the middle of the boat, he can move across facing forward without any particular difficulty; but when it is on the transom he is obliged to cross over facing aft if he is to change hands easily, and for that one moment he cannot see what is happening.

The crew has to face aft when moving across because of the kicking strap. As he steps over the centreboard case, he picks up the new sheet and slackens the sheet he has just released, by pulling it forward in front of the fairlead.

What with the boom, the tiller and its extension, the three sheets and the kicking strap, both crew are in a confined space, where movement is restricted, although they must always be in control and not get tangled up while doing everything at the right time. A certain amount of chaos is inevitable while you are learning, and it sometimes helps if one of the crew moves across before the other to avoid getting in each other's way. Coordination is the key word, and successful coming about should give the impression of a well oiled machine, as sails and crew switch sides, smoothly bringing their forces to bear on the new tack in one synchronised movement.

Going About in a Cruising Boat

When a heavy boat is moving steadily through the water she carries a good way; but if it is lost it is difficult to get it back.

The boat's way dictates when and how you change tack. A steady turn, which keeps her moving, will take her round satisfactorily in a fairly wide sweep which gives the crew time to attend to their duties smoothly and with good timing.

Procedure

The boat is moving fast close-hauled. You luff up gently, sheeting in the sails harder at the same time, first the mainsail and then the jib. In this case, the sheets are made fast and this is not the time to let them go; the mainsail is sheeted even harder by swigging on its purchase, the jib by swigging on the sheet between the fairlead and the cleat, or by using the winch. If the rigging includes runners, you should first look to the one which will be to windward when you are on the new tack. What is then the lee runner is not released until the manoeuvre has been completed.

When the mainsail luff shakes, release the running part of the sheet on which you have been swigging. Because it is sheeted absolutely flat, the jib will still keep full until you are almost head-to-wind; it should only be released when the clew shakes.

As soon as the boat has passed through the eye of the wind and begins to bear away on the new tack, the slack of the leeward jib sheet should be pulled steadily in but without actually sheeting the sail home. If the headsail is a genoa, the foredeck hand will help the sail round the mast.

Do not sheet in the headsail too soon, but when you do so waste no time over it. The idea being to sheet it home just before it begins to fill on the new tack. This operation has to be nicely timed and you will only master it with practice. If you are too slow, aching muscles will be the penalty you pay.

If you have no winches, you may have to luff up off your close-hauled course momentarily on the new tack to pull in the jib more when it has much less weight in it. This is really a confession of failure, but it is much better than carrying on with a poor trim.

If your boat is a cutter, and you do not have enough crew to work the two headsail sheets at the same time, you should deal with the jib first and then the staysail; if you do it the other way round the jib clew will thrash furiously against the staysail luff, with all the attendant risk of chafe. Also, if the jib is sheeted first, sheeting the staysail is easy; it is only when the order is reversed that troubles occur.

Words of Command

Coming about in a cruising yacht calls for good crew work, because everybody has a job to do and a particular time to do it. The skipper must achieve this coordination by giving his orders loud and clear. The cry 'helm's a-lee!' is now only heard on TV as the reconstructed square-riggers go through their ponderous studio movements. There is nothing to stop a skipper working out his own system, but this is standard practice these days.

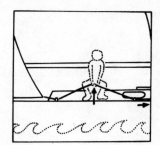

The skipper calls 'ready about!' and the crew, when they are ready, reply 'jib ready' or 'staysail ready'.

If it is near meal time, it is also wise to make sure that all is secure in the galley.

The executive order for the operation is 'Lee-oh!' The helmsman puts down the helm, but the headsail sheets are not released until the order is given to let go.

Some skippers make their orders more salty by using carefully selected swear words, but these are not guaranteed to speed up the operation.

Handling Characteristics

A heavy cruising boat manoeuvres slowly but powerfully, giving you time to correct any slight mistakes while changing tacks; but if it does miss stays you lose a lot of time.

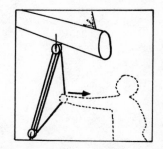

'He who knows the right way to tackle work is a strong man.' — old Turkish proverb

It is not possible to describe precisely the handling of smaller boats such as light cruisers or ballasted centreboarders. A boat's behaviour when it comes about, just as on other points of sailing, depends much more on her weight than on her size. A light boat carries little way but comes about quickly, while a heavy boat, even a small one, has good way and turns more slowly.

According to their hull and balance, some boats turn more easily than others even though their weights may be approximately the same. Older boats, on the whole, are more reluctant to go about than modern boats. The important thing is to know the limitations as well as the qualities of your own boat and not try to make her turn faster than she wants to.

Going About in Heavy Weather

As the wind increases, it becomes increasingly difficult to go about without a hitch. This is due either to the force of the wind itself or the state of the sea; or it may be the crew's inefficiency.

The Wind

Beyond a certain wind strength, windage can be a major obstacle, making a boat that will go about easily in a Force 3 wind impossible to turn in Force 7. She no longer amasses sufficient energy to beat the opposition.

The reason is often that the boat is not carrying canvas suitable for the weather: an under-canvassed boat has not enough power; a boat with sails too full or poorly trimmed cannot sail close enough to the wind, heels a lot and is held back. Finally, if the boat is over-canvassed it is also more difficult to sheet the sails hard, they lose a lot of their pulling power and the boat heels and wallows. This can put you in a nasty predicament. When you decide which sails to hoist, ask yourself which ones will enable the boat to go about easily.

The Sea

When the sea begins to get up, the waves have a habit of taking way off the boat at just the wrong moment and of pushing her back onto her original tack. If you watch their rhythm, and only start coming about after the last large wave of a series (usually about 5–9 waves), you should be all right.

A dinghy, which can so easily lose way even in medium weather, stands the best chance of success in large seas if you act quickly, starting to come about just over the crest of one wave in order to pass through the eye of the wind when you are in a trough. If all goes well, you will be helped round by the next wave. In these circumstances, brisk, strong work at the tiller is justified, because it is more important to achieve the turn than to maintain speed, which may well be out of the question in any case.

This method is also effective for cruising boats in very steep seas.

The Crew

Going about successfully depends largely on the crew. When the weather is deteriorating, control is lost by precipitate action or by indecisiveness. In dinghies, for instance, fear of a capsize often results in sails not being sheeted hard enough home. In cruising yachts, the crew can fail to sheet home the headsail adequately either owing to sea-sickness, the difficulties caused by excessive heeling or just because it is felt that a sheet will have to be eased again almost immediately.

Full preparation for the manoeuvre is important so that everyone is alerted for success: speed, sail trim, efficient sheet handling. It is better to take your time and be certain than to rush in only to make a hash of things.

Ensuring Success Going About

When it looks as though things might go wrong there are one or two tips which might help.

You can come round without touching the jib. As soon as the boat passes through the eye of the wind, the jib will fill with the sheet to windward and thus forces the bow off onto the new tack, the jib sheet only being released and re-cleated on the leeward side when you are safely round. As you can well imagine, this entails loss of almost all speed and you have to bear away sharply to pick it up again.

If, as the result of some false move or having inadequate way on at the start of the turn, the boat gets into irons, head-to-wind with sails flapping, quick action may still save the day.

If this happens when you are trying to get onto the starboard tack for example, hold the jib clew out to starboard, so that the sail fills aback; push the mainsail out to port and hold the boom down to reduce twist; reverse the tiller, putting it to port so that, as the boat gathers sternway, the action of the water passing over the rudder will help to shove the stern round to starboard.

As soon as the boat is pointing well away from the wind, release the boom, let draw the headsail, and then pick up speed with wind on the beam before returning to the close-hauled position steadily sheeting home the sails.

If this is not done quickly, the boat will slowly fall back on her original tack and that is, of course, complete failure. You will have to pick up speed on a reach before starting all over again. This is done by easing all sheets and waiting for the boat to bear away herself. But you can speed things up by adopting the plan that is basically what has just been done, but in reverse: jib sheeted to windward on the port side, mainsail pushed out to starboard, helm to starboard.

Even an old salt can miss stays. In fine weather and with plenty of water under your lee there is little to worry about; you merely have to start again, as long as you realise what has gone wrong. In practice it isn't always necessary to follow all the above instructions. It is, for example, possible to tack without much speed if helm and

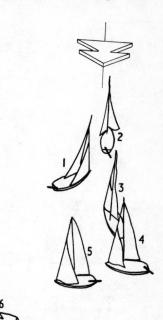

1. The boat luffs up slowly
2. Jib and main are backed and the tiller reversed
3. The jib is kept aback
4. When it is certain you can go about, the jib is brought over and the tiller to windward
5. You pick up speed with the wind on the beam
6. Now you can return to the close-hauled position

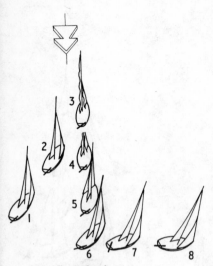

1. Luff up slowly
2. Go on luffing
3. The boat stops even before coming head-to-wind
4. The boat makes stern way, the tiller to leeward
5. The jib is sheeted in to port, the boat bears away
6. Jib is let fly and sheeted in on the lee side
7. The tiller is moved to windward
8. Pick up speed with the wind abeam before trying again

sheets are properly coordinated and controlled. Equally, a headsail which lifts too soon doesn't necessarily mean that the boat will miss stays provided you have enough way on. But going about well is what matters and in bad weather you can't cut corners if you want the best performance, and that only comes with practice. With modern boats you can grow so used to seeing the boat do most of the work on her own that there is a danger of paying too little attention. You may end up by becoming inexpert at controlling coming about and you may fail, just when you have to do the job meticulously. In bad weather, as long as you have allowed sufficient margin for error and there is a hitch, don't be afraid to start again.

In the event, if you can't get it right, as a last resort there is always the alternative of gybing round (wearing ship).

The Intentional Gybe

Gybing intentionally is changing tacks with the wind aft, without necessarily altering course to any marked degree. The mainsail is freed right off and swings from one side to the other through 180°. If the spinnaker is up, this also has to be moved to the new windward side, and that means reversing the spinnaker pole.

Of all manoeuvres under sail to be mastered, this is probably the most delicate, particularly when there is any wind about. The danger of yawing, always a liability downwind, is accentuated by any changes in trim and balance as a result of shifting sails. At any moment the boat, if not watched carefully by the helmsman, can broach to, get out of control or bear away too soon until she is by the lee; then she will experience an uncontrolled gybe, when the boom slams violently across from one side to the other, potentially cracking the skulls of anyone in its way and leading to a broach to on the new tack (with spinnaker confusion as a bonus).

The gybe must only be carried out under certain specific conditions.

The boat should be dead before the wind and should not change course during the manoeuvre.
The boat should be kept upright. This is particularly important

for a dinghy, as a sudden heel may carry the boat off tempestuously on an unintended course.

More than ever, *everything on board must run free*. All sheets, and particularly the main sheet, must be free to run out, and the boom must be clear to move across freely (release any boom preventer which may have been rigged).

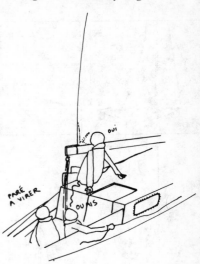

There is no need to hurry. Unlike coming about, a gybe need not be done at speed and slowing down won't impede its execution; nor is it necessary to change over the sheets of both sails simultaneously.

Now we can consider the control of each sail in turn: the mainsail, which provides most excitement, then the jib and finally the whims of the spinnaker.

Mainsail

The action needed for moving the main from one side of the boat to the other is unusual in that when you go about, the sail lifts as you come up into the eye of the wind and loses all its thrust for as short a time as you can manage. A gybe is exactly the opposite. As the mainsail leech nears the eye of the wind as you haul it in, the sail doesn't lift and it never empties the wind off its surface. The leech is now the 'leading edge' of the sail, and it is neither fixed nor will it remain on the centreline of the boat; it only stops being subjected to wind pressure on one side as soon as it starts getting it on the other.

At least, when the mainsail is sheeted right home to the middle of the boat, wind pressure in it is minimal. It is therefore helpful, as a first step, to bring it hard in so that you can ease it gently at the critical moment – as soon as the wind has changed from one side to the other.

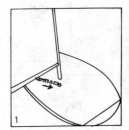

As we shall see, it is perfectly possible to let the sail move across without all this ceremony, but in fresh winds or when you are not quite sure of yourself, the classic way is best.

Traditional Method

1 *The kicking straps should be tightened to cut down twist and avoid the danger of a chinese gybe.*
2 *The mainsheet traveller should be blocked in the middle of the horse, so that the boom can be pulled hard in and doesn't slam across when the boom moves over.*

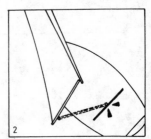

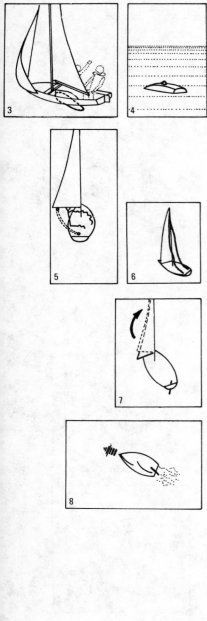

3 *In a dinghy, the centreboard should be raised two thirds, particularly in fresh winds, so that the boat does not 'trip over' if she broaches to after the gybe.*

4 If the boat has a daggerboard, take care that the raised part of the board does not block the passage of the boom or, indeed, interfere with the kicking strap. If it does, you are doomed to capsize.

5 The boat is placed square before the wind, properly trimmed and with her sheets free to run.

6 If you have runners (adjustable backstays), you will probably be able to slack them both off on this point of sailing.

7 Sheet home the mainsail steadily. This will make the boat want to luff up towards the wind, but this must be counteracted by the tiller.

8 As you continue sheeting home, the boat will settle down and the tendency to luff will lessen, while the speed falls off. The sail is now sheeted hard in, but it is still full of wind from the same side (starboard in the diagram). You now need only to alter course very slightly to leeward to make the sail gybe.

9 The wind suddenly fills the sail now from the port side. The helmsman should immediately let the mainsheet run right out steadily, at the same time firmly checking with the tiller any sign of luffing on the new tack. The boom's movement will be slowed by the friction of the sheet on the blocks.

10 *The figure of eight knot at the end of the sheet stops it unreeving itself through the block. Now the sail is properly set again.*

11 *Trim is re-established on the new tack and the boat has not changed course.*

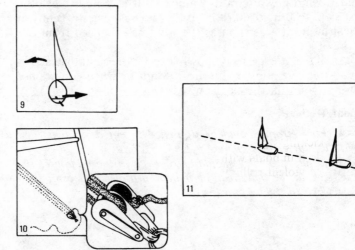

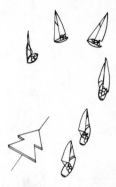

Classic Mistakes

Broaching to before the turn. The boat was not running with the wind right astern. When the sail is sheeted in the boat's very strong tendency to luff up is difficult to control with the helm

Chinese Gybe. The kicking strap was not pulled tight, the boom lifted and the lower part of the sail went over while the upper part was held back by a batten or a spreader. The sail may be torn. The only way is to gybe back again at once so that the whole sail is out to one side

Broaching to after the turn. This happens after a bad gybe but also after a correct gybe if the mainsheet catches somewhere (under a foot for instance) and if the helmsman does not counteract the boat's movement in time. It can also be caused by a wave

Another Common Method

In light winds you can gybe more quickly if you know what you are doing.

The boom is moved across, without pulling in the sheet, but only bunching it up and pulling the sail across in one firm movement. In boats that have kicking straps, this can be done by the crew and it works very well in dinghies, but can be a bit dangerous in cruising boats and you should be careful not to do it without weighing up the forces involved. It is not always possible to bring the boom across the centreline or, if it is, to stop it taking charge as it fills away after the gybe. Look out too for the slack bight of mainsheet that can ensnare the incautious and propel him overboard.

This quick method is not, of course, suited to all rigs. It cannot safely be used above Force 2 with gaff or gunter rigs, although you can employ it in fresher winds with a bermudan rig provided you have a good kicking strap to prevent a chinese gybe.

But do not do it in boats with poor initial stability, because there is then a risk of violent rolling which can throw the unwary overboard.

It should never be used on any boat in strong winds, because the

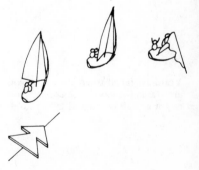

Accidental gybe. The boat has passed from the position of wind astern, unnoticed, and it is sailing by the lee. The sail slams over unexpectedly. This kind of gybe can be violent, breaking something or, quite simply, making the boat capsize

The starboard sheet has been released without the port sheet being pulled in: the clew of the jib catches on the forestay

You have failed to go about. As you are falling away to leeward, you might as well go on and gybe round

action of the mainsail slamming across subjects the rigging to unacceptable shock and something may give.

Jib

Running downwind, the headsails pose few problems on the foredeck. About the only point to watch is not to ease the lee sheet right off before hauling in the other; otherwise the headsail will ride forward of the forestay which might snag the clew as you finally try to pull it in on the new tack.

If the headsail is boomed out, you must of course take off the boom, move the sail across to the other tack and set it up again on the other side.

Action After Failing to Go About

Going about can misfire and it is awkward if either you do not have enough sea room to leeward for another attempt or else you feel that you will only miss again and prefer not to try. In which case you are in trouble and you will have to gybe quickly.

If the boat has missed stays she will be in irons, wallowing with flapping sails, and the wind will be on the beam. Even if you have borne away quickly to this position (by backing the jib), you won't get any further without getting some way on the boat, so sheet in the sail for reaching (with the jib a little harder in than the mainsail), then bear away further, ease the sails as you go, and pick up speed.

As you bring the wind dead aft, sheet the mainsail hard in. If the boat is turning quickly you probably won't be able to get the sheet right home – but the more you can, the better everything will work.

As soon as the boom goes across, ease the mainsheet right out and, even if you reckon on coming hard on the wind right away, it is best to check her on the tiller for a moment to ensure you are under control, or you may find yourself luffing rather faster than you had expected. The jib is, of course, sheeted on the new tack as soon as possible.

Any sudden luff (or bearing away) is usually accompanied by an equally sudden heel. Bring this under control before you start sheeting in the sails to come back hard on the wind.

The Spinnaker

The spinnaker is the only sail which can remain full through the gybe. Its movement from one side of the boat to the other is not so marked as with the other sails, but it is no less delicate an exercise for all that.

When there is only one spinnaker boom (as is usual), it must be taken off the spinnaker and set up on the other side. The sail is thus not very well set just when you want to shift it. The trick is to keep the spinnaker well filled during the entire manoeuvre and this can only be done by keeping the wind dead aft.

On Dinghies

Start by gybing the mainsail and jib, for the crew must be able to work the spinnaker without being under pressure. Each man then has his part to play.

The helmsman must ensure that the boat is well balanced. He stands, tiller between his legs, far enough aft to compensate for the weight of the crew who will be up near the mast. He must not only keep good fore-and-aft trim, but must see to it that rolling is not set up. As soon as all is ready he should cleat the mainsheet and take the spinnaker sheet and guy in hand, for he it is who will be responsible for spinnaker trim, easing out or hardening in sheet or guy as required.

The crew, standing near the mast, should grasp the spinnaker clew in one hand, unhook the pole from the mast with the other and snap it onto the clew. He must then work hand over hand on the

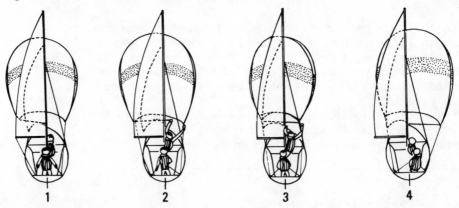

1   2   3   4

1. After main and jib have been passed over, the helmsman takes hold of spinnaker sheet and guy and keeps the boat balanced

2. The crew unhooks the spinnaker pole from the mast . . .

3. . . . . and fixes it to the new tack of the sail

4. He then frees the old tack of the sail and hooks the pole on to the mast

pole to get to the other end, which he takes off the spinnaker and clips onto the mast.

The helmsman trims the spinnaker until his crew gets back to his station and takes over the sheet and guy.

The crucial moment is obviously when the pole is off the mast and each end is clipped to a corner of the spinnaker. The sail is rather too tightly held in at this point but it must somehow be kept filled, particularly in fresh winds, to avoid any violent movement which can lead to capsizing through accidental gybing or broaching to.

On Cruisers

Spinnaker gear in cruising yachts is of many kinds, and gybing must be performed accordingly. We shall look first at general principles and then examine specific examples.

General Principles

1 To make things simpler, the spinnaker staysail or the jib should be handed, and the spinnaker pole downhaul should be slackened off.

2 The helmsman should steer dead downwind and the spinnaker will tend to shift over to windward, if anything. This sail will set happily without its pole which, under these conditions, only holds the tack in more than it helps to spread the foot.

3 The operation can either be carried out with one or two poles.
One pole. The pole is unhooked from the tack and hooked straight away onto the *clew.*
Two poles. The second pole is attached to the clew.

4 The spinnaker, either completely free at the foot, or else held

in by one or two poles, is shifted to the opposite side of the boat by sheeting in one side and easing off the other. This is the critical moment because, if you either don't ease enough on one side or pull hard enough on the other, the sail will flap. If you harden more on one side than you ease on the other the sail will be restricted, may collapse in the middle and wrap itself round the forestay. Coordination is therefore very important.

This is the moment to push the mainsail across the other way.

5 The spinnaker is now trimmed (with two poles, the one to leeward must now be taken off).

Depending on whether the boat has an inner forestay, the gybe can now take several forms as we shall see.

One Pole: no inner stay

If the boat has no inner forestay, the pole can hinge on its mast fitting and pass in front of the mast inside the forestay. This is a simple matter, as it only involves unhooking the pole from the spinnaker clew, handing it round in front of the mast and hooking it onto the new clew while it is still close in on the foredeck. The spinnaker and mainsail can then be trimmed on the new lee side.

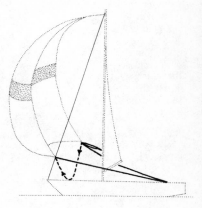

One Pole: an inner stay

If the boat has an inner forestay, the pole cannot swing from one side to the other while it is still fixed to the mast. In this case, as with dinghies, the pole must be symmetrical so that both ends can each be fixed to the mast or to the sail. When the pole is free at both ends, not attached to the sail or the mast, it is the spinnaker pole topping lift that supports the spar as it is switched from one side to the other.

When the spinnaker pole topping lift is attached to the middle of the pole, there is no great problem.

When it is fixed at the outer end of the pole, a second topping lift is required. The first part of the drill is to rig this to the heel while the pole is still in place. The correct length of this second topping lift has to be learned with experience so that the pole will be at the right height after the gybe.

The sequence is then as follows:

1 The heel is unclipped from the mast.
2 The outer end is taken off the spinnaker tack. The pole is then supported by its topping lift or lifts and the spinnaker is completely free to float (the sequence should be carried out in the above order; if the outer end is taken off the tack first, the pole sticks forward from the mast like a spear pointing at the spinnaker and can pierce it).
3 The mainsail is gybed across and the spinnaker floated to the new windward side. The pole is moved across and clipped on, first to the new spinnaker tack then to the mast.

This operation is easy enough in fine weather, but it can be like a circus act in fresh winds and lumpy seas and needs several crew to carry it out.

If the mast has an inner forestay, two spinnaker poles make life much easier. These poles can be single-ended, but there is an extra benefit if they are double-ended: if you lose or break one, you can always carry on with the other.

Twin Poles

When the boat has twin poles, it makes no difference if the boat has an inner forestay or not.

1 The second pole is rigged to leeward, clipped to the mast and the spinnaker clew.
2 The spinnaker, with a pole on each lower corner, is moved from one side to the other as the mainsail is gybed across.
3 The leeward pole is eased forward and, as soon as the outer end is to hand, it is unclipped from the spinnaker and eased down to the deck by its own topping lift.

Twin Poles, Twin Sheets, Twin Guys

This rig is only used on large boats. There is a sheet and guy on each side, the former of rope and the latter of wire with a rope tail. The jaws at the outer end of the spinnaker pole run freely along the guy, so that the pole is never fixed to the spinnaker itself and therefore does not have to be clipped or unclipped from the sail at any time, and you only have to slacken off the guy and topping lift right off to bring the pole down to the deck. On each side there is a pole, a sheet, a guy, a topping lift and a downhaul.

In the diagram the boat is on the starboard tack, just before the gybe.

To starboard the guy is tight and the lazy sheet slack (the sheet can be cleated in readiness for the gybe).
To port, the lazy guy is slack and the sheet is doing its job.

The manoeuvre goes as follows:

1 The port pole is rigged and topped up, and the guy is pulled in so that the clew of the sail is drawn down to the end of the pole.
2 The mainboom crosses to starboard and the spinnaker is moved over to the port side;
   by easing the starboard guy (the starboard sheet now comes into action);
   by pulling in the port guy (the port sheet goes slack).
3 The starboard topping lift and guy are eased right away so that the end of the pole is lowered to the deck.

With the spinnaker up, gybing is more complicated than going about. It is especially dangerous in heavy weather, because the boat has no lateral pressure on her to keep her steady and may suddenly start rolling wildly with unforeseen consequences.

We said above that you can gybe instead of going about if you miss stays while trying the latter; but here again a gybe is not recommended in heavy weather (even without a spinnaker) unless you are in full control of your boat, and it is wiser to persevere with going about even if it takes time.

If you give up going about there is only one answer: lower the mainsail and gybe in comfort under the jib.

The boat is on starboard tack and you are getting ready to gybe: topping lift has been hoisted to bring the pole level with the spinnaker clew. When the main has been swung over the spinnaker will be changed by letting the starboard sheet fly and harden-in the port sheet. All that remains to be done is to drop the starboard topping lift and bring the starboard pole on to the deck. Then trim the spinnaker

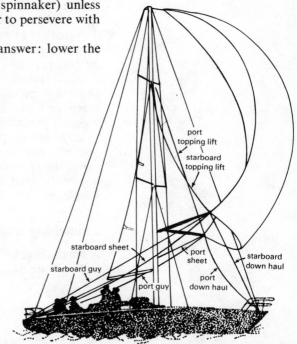

10. Arrival and Departure

Boat handling when you leave or reach port, be it a beach or a harbour, can be tense and even spectacular. The ability, experience and coolness of the crew are put to the test. An unpremeditated landing on the beach in disorder, or wild gyrating round a mooring buoy are meat and drink to experienced lookers-on who savour every last morsel of the muddle. It also hurts the pride of the skipper, but if that is the only damage suffered he has been lucky.

These manoeuvres make demands on the boat's ability to turn quickly, and the basic principle is that she can only do so if she is moving. On getting under way, see to it that you pick up speed as soon as possible. When beaching or approaching a mooring, keep speed on the boat long enough to maintain control, and then lose it as quickly as possible. In both cases, the few moments when the boat has not enough way to answer the helm must be kept to a minimum.

When you get under way it is best to move off, when you can, with the wind aft, or at least on a reach, for the boat can pick up speed and can sail decisively in some direction. Mooring is a question of reaching your berth just when the boat has lost its way, either head to wind or as close as possible to that point (you cannot possibly stop with the wind aft of the beam).

But the restrictions of the coastline or of the harbour, the direction of the wind and the state of the sea often militate against these simple requirements.

Launching from a Beach

A dinghy is got ready on the beach, with the sails bent on the spars and all equipment on board. We saw in Chapter 1 that it is always best when the sea is calm not to hoist the sails until the boat is on the water, because you can then climb aboard to do the job, which is never to be done when the boat is on shore.

Remember too that the boat should always be carried to the water and not dragged to it. This is not only a question of conserving the hull, but also of avoiding sand and gravel being forced up into the centreboard case.

Humping the boat can be a chore, so the tendency is naturally to aim at the nearest navigable water, but that is not always ideal for launching. Before deciding, take into consideration the wind, slope of the beach and state of the sea.

Wind direction. Whatever the wind direction, you should avoid launching too near obstacles such as a rocky headland or a moored boat, even if you are to leeward of them; your boat may well not be under full control for the first few seconds after the launch, and you should beware of any wild manoeuvres.

If the wind is blowing on shore, and you have to launch to windward or even a beam reach, it is best to set out from the most windward part of your beach. Then you will have maximum sea room to leeward which is always a wise precaution that can yield dividends. The sea too is usually calmest at that point.

To get it to your chosen stretch of beach, the boat should be walked through the water towed by the forestay, making sure that the surf does not pound her on the bottom.

Slope of the Beach. On arriving at the chosen spot, the helmsman turns the boat head-to-wind and holds onto the forestay. The beach may be steep-to and you may well have to stand in water up to your waist. This is not entirely satisfactory, even when the water is warm. It can also make getting aboard difficult. In such a case hold the gunwale between the forestay and the windward weather shroud.

Launching from a steep beach has, however, one advantage: you can lower the centreboard at least partly; but you may still not be able to fit the rudder (even if it lifts) because the stern will almost certainly be too near the bottom. If the slope is gentle, the helmsman can make his way far enough out to install a lifting rudder even if he cannot lower much centreboard. The best beach is one where the helmsman can stand with water at mid-thigh level when he is holding on to the bow of the boat, which should be well afloat.

Rollers. The nature of the beach takes on increased importance when waves are breaking. On a steep beach, the rollers will break near to the water's edge and you are soon beyond them once you

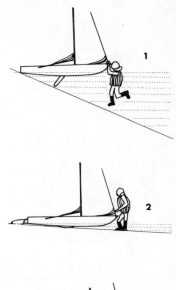

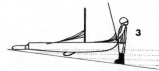

Gradient problems: 1. water enough for the centreplate but a little too much for the helmsman; 2. the helmsman is all right and the rudder is fitted but the centreplate cannot be lowered; 3. the gradient is just right

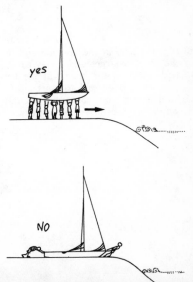

yes

NO

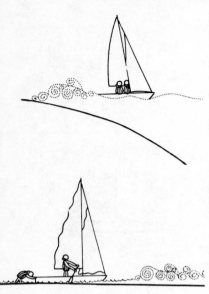

launch; but on shallow coast the waves break far out and the helmsman must tow the boat beyond them or paddle out.

Whatever the conditions are, choose the calmest spot, usually at the windward end of the beach. You can also help yourself by picking your moment, watching the sequence of the waves which usually establish a pattern of large and small ones in succession, and the smallest waves often come after the third big one.

There will be times when it is too rough to get through the surf at all and you may be wise to take a walk in the country.

Launching on a Reach

Importance of Wind Direction

A beam reach is, as we already know, the easiest as well as the fastest point of sailing. With the wind on the beam a boat almost settles down on her own and, once under way, she quickly begins to make good headway without much leeway. It follows that it is ideal for launching. You do not need much centreboard, sail trim does not have to be precise and it also allows you time to correct mistakes for the boat will not suddenly turn head-to-wind or gybe. Take stock of the wind before you put the boat in the water and see if you cannot set off on a reach no matter what direction it takes you on at the start.

It is also a convenient point of sailing when you have to move off without your rudder in position, whether it is a fixed or lifting one. With the latter type, if there is much sea running, remember it is easily damaged.

Not all boats are easy to control without a rudder, so complete

If you set off at the up-wind end of the beach you get under way easily with wind on the beam; at the lee end you are obliged to start close-hauled and you never get enough water for lowering the centreplate

tyros should refer back to early parts of this book to ensure they are familiar with the technique of doing so. It is in any case good practice for understanding how a boat behaves, how it is influenced by using the sheets only and, lastly, useful in an emergency should you break or lose the rudder.

Boat Trim

There are several ways of making a boat luff up or bear away without a rudder, which can either be adopted at one and the same time or separately. They have already been explained, but they are worth repeating here. *A boat luffs up when she heels, when the mainsail is sheeted in, when the centreboard is fully lowered or when she is down by the head.*

A boat bears away when she heels to windward, when the mainsail is eased, when the centreboard is raised, even partially, or when she is down by the stern.

Speed is an influential factor. The faster a boat goes the more weather helm she carries. If she is going slowly, she may develop some lee helm (more likely still if she goes astern).

With no rudder you have to rely on the mainsail for steering, forward speed being provided largely by the jib. As speed creates weather helm, the role of the jib becomes more important than revealed in the early part of this book. A jib that is too tightly sheeted will tend to make the boat bear away without contributing much to the forward thrust. Sheeted correctly, it gives speed and, although the boat still has weather helm she is manoeuvrable.

These basic principles only outline sketchily the action and reactions of boat and sails. In practice, considerable ability, self-confidence and even flair are needed to co-ordinate successfully the various forces acting on the boat. To produce the best performance, imagination and a sensitive hand on the tiller are required.

Teamwork is essential for the crew must know exactly what his helmsman proposes to do. If balance is to be maintained, each must play his part. Usually it is best for the crew to remain in one spot slightly countering heel, while the helmsman takes responsibility for the boat's trim. Excessive movement should be avoided by both of them and if only one has the prime responsibility for trim there is no danger of their taking contrary action. The helmsman should make his intentions quite clear, preferably before a manoeuvre than *during* it and never *afterwards*.

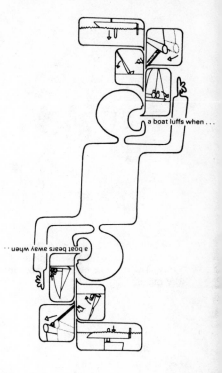

a boat luffs when . . .

. . . a boat bears away when . . .

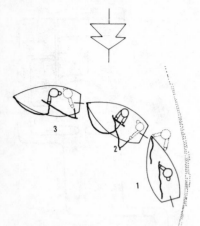

1. Ready to go. 2. Begin to sheet in the jib and lower the centreplate. 3. Only now do you begin to sheet in the main

Setting off Without Rudder

The helmsman holds the boat by the forestay either head to wind or slightly inclined on the tack he wishes to follow. The sails are fluttering and all is clear inboard. The crew gets on board and checks that the sheets are freed. He lets down the centreplate a little, depending on the depth of water. He grasps the jib sheet in one hand and the mainsheet in the other, ready to hand it to the helmsman.

The helmsman, without moving from where he is standing, hauls the boat out on the chosen tack, leaping aboard as he comes abeam of it and grasping the mainsheet. The crew hardens in the jib so as to get some way on. He can also lower the centreplate a bit more if possible but this is much less important than looking after the jib.

The boat is now sailing under jib alone, the mainsail only being sheeted home enough to clear it of the lee shroud. If the jib is kept properly trimmed (just on the point of lifting), if the wind is steady and not too fresh and, if the helmsman keeps proper trim, then the trip starts without mishap and the boat rapidly picks up speed making little leeway. It sounds easy, but it is more difficult than that in practice.

Steering Without the Rudder

When the boat starts off slowly, it will bear away. Let us see what happens if the crew takes no action. As the boat bears away, the mainsail begins to fill and speed picks up, but the boat starts to luff up. She soon luffs too much, and first the mainsail, and then the jib flap; speed slackens and she bears away once again (if she has not already come about as she will do if the mainsail was not eased enough at the start) and the cycle starts again.

Left to herself, the boat tends to follow a drunken, zig-zag course which must be checked by correct distribution of ballast and by modifying sail trim. It must all be done smoothly, little by little, or the whole pantomime starts up again, the boat bearing away, the crew allowing her to heel to leeward and the helmsman sheeting in the mainsail, with the result that the boat luffs up sharply. The mainsail is eased once more, the boat straightaway heels to windward, and so bears away yet again. Two or three sequences like this and you are on a crazier course than ever, probably eventually finishing up with a nasty gybe and an undignified return to the shore amid shouting and swearing.

It all comes down to a question of crew technique, of working the mainsail carefully so that you check by anticipation the boat's tendency to turn one way or the other and avoid going in the opposite direction. Don't take extreme action: don't let the boat heel too much, don't sheet the sails too tightly and don't worry too much about leeway.

The situation is similar in strong winds, but the boat carries more weather helm. Things are difficult when the wind is not steady: keep alert and don't jerk from one side of the boat to the other if you want to stay upright, particularly if the wind gusts or, as suddenly, drops.

It is always better to wait until you are well away from the shore before fitting the rudder. While the helmsman is doing this (and it is not easy in a choppy sea) the crew should hold both sheets and keep the boat sailing on a steady course.

To sum up, boat control under these conditions only comes with practice. It is an art not learned overnight and, when you see a boat carrying out this drill smoothly and without fuss, you can be quite sure that the crew are expert.

If you are able to lower the centreboard and fit the rudder right away, a beam wind makes your departure dead easy.

On a weather shore

Launching with the Wind Aft

A gentle offshore wind is an invitation to set out: the boat is eager to go, the sea is calm and the wind blows like a zephyr across the beach. Nevertheless, prudence is the watchword. The boat will sail away easily enough, even without the crew aboard if they are too casual; and the calm sea and light wind can suddenly change as soon as you have passed out of the lee of the land. The weather forecast is more rewarding listening than pop programmes when the wind is offshore. A quick walk up to the headland before you leave will show you what is really going on out to sea.

The easiest way to set sail now is to hoist the jib only; provided, of course, the mainsail can be easily hoisted while under way which is not always the case with all boats.

It is usually the best plan to hoist both sails. The helmsman holds the boat head-to-wind, the bow turned towards the shore this time. If he can wade in deep enough, he should put in the rudder; if not, he will have to use a paddle because you don't want to sail downwind without the rudder unless the weather is very light.

The crew should check that the jib sheets are eased right off and free to run, and he should overhaul the mainsheet so that the boom can swing freely against the shrouds while the bow turns away from the beach. There is no need for any centreboard, but lower it a little bit all the same to give the boat a little lee helm.

When all is ready, the helmsman should haul the boat past him, standing firm, and turn her so that she is facing out to sea. Then he climbs in over the transom. In fresh conditions he must move quickly, because it is extremely difficult to hold the boat as soon as she is beam-on to the wind. Unless he is agile and brisk he may literally miss the boat. Once he is in he takes the tiller or paddle sitting to windward right in the stern so as to maintain a little lee helm.

If the rudder has not yet been fitted, he should now slowly turn across wind or onto a close reach before trying to put it on.

If you have left a well sheltered beach, try to avoid having the wind dead aft the moment you sail out of the lee of the land. The wind may gust suddenly and from a slightly different direction and you may broach to or gybe.

Launching with a Head Wind

Obviously you cannot set out straight away with a head-on wind, not even close-hauled because, on leaving the beach you are without a rudder and have very little centreboard. You cannot hope to lie closer to the wind than about 70°. If the wind happens to be blowing exactly at right angles to a beach and moreover rollers are breaking, you are unlikely to get off under sail.

But this does not often happen for the wind will not be blowing

Speed is all. By keeping too close to the wind you drift and cannot clear the shore. Bear away boldly and you pick up speed, leeway is reduced and then you can gradually luff up

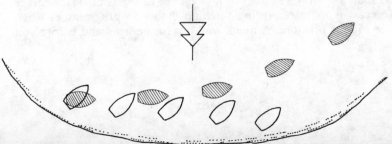

directly on shore or the shore line will be curved. As likely as not you can manage to get a free wind by starting from a point well up to windward.

You will not have much sea room to leeward. In your impatience to get out as quickly as possible you may be tempted to try to sail too close to the wind too soon; this is a good way of making a quick return, because lack of speed will make a lot of leeway and you will never get far enough out to lower enough centreboard. So keep the wind as free as possible, keeping the sails full. The crew should take particular care not to sheet his jib in too hard. Speed is essential. Luff up gradually, lowering the centreboard little by little until you can get onto a close-hauled course.

This calls for some finesse, but you can take comfort in the thought that you are at least in no danger because you can always return to the shore – which you could not do so easily as with an offshore wind. Never forget this safety advantage.

You have forgotten it again!

Returning to Shore

This poses the same kind of problems you faced on setting out, particularly as far as the landing place is concerned. If the wind is ahead (offshore) choose for preference a fairly steep beach to allow you to keep centreboard and rudder down as long as possible. If waves are breaking on the beach, land as far up to windward as possible where there will be less surf.

Generally speaking, a breaking sea makes beaching more difficult than setting out. The boat is going with the waves and is liable to pick up speed at the wrong moment; and she is less able to cope with waves at the stern than at the bow; when the stern lifts, she will tend to swing to one side and present her beam to the wind; in practice, it is often necessary, when the wind is free, to turn a half circle on arriving and take the waves on the bow; but it is not easy.

At the earliest moment the crew should step into the water to lighten the boat and keep her head or stern onto the waves. This is the moment to keep the hull under control.

Don't forget to raise centreboard and rudder before they hit the bottom. After the panic of getting them down on leaving you tend to forget about taking them up.

Coming in on a beam wind
1. Smooth sea: approach with the wind on the beam, luff up and drift in full-and-by

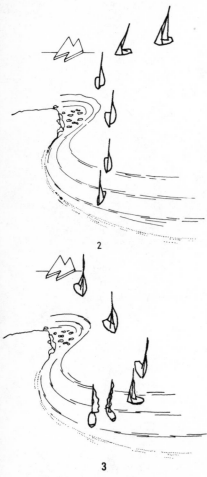

2

3

2. Rough sea: drop the main when full-and-by and come in on jib only
3. If you can't drop the main you must head up into the breakers at the last moment

You want to have very little way on when you approach the shore: ideally, hardly any at all. At all costs never run straight for the beach with the wind aft and sails goosewinged, no matter how much you enjoy planing like a surf board. It will be an aquatic show for the spectators and the boat could be a write-off.

Beaching on a Reach

This makes everything easy because you have a choice of coming in close-hauled or on a reach.

In fine weather you point straight at the shore with the wind on the beam, then luff up a little to come closer to the wind, then raise centreboard and rudder, and the wind will drift the boat gently in.

If there is sea at all, the boat should be steered across the waves, either taking them on the bow or the stern.

The best way of all is to sail well up to windward of the point where you want to land, lower the mainsail and then run in under the jib alone, still keeping at right angles to the breakers.

When you take down the mainsail you should be full-and-by and not bow into the wind because, as soon as you lose way, the boat will only bear away and the sail will fill again before it has been handed.

Especially when the sea is breaking very white, aim at the beach well up to windward; centreboard and rudder should be raised (pivoting centreboards too if the rollers are large) and the helmsman should use a paddle to steer with on the final run in. The crew steps out as soon as he is in his depth, not letting the boat turn across the waves, and pull her well up as soon as possible.

Halyards can sometimes jam and the mainsail will not come down; in that case you must round up head to the waves. Aim for the shore with the wind on the beam. Raise rudder and centreboard fairly soon and, at the last moment luff up sharply, preferably on the back of a wave. Head-to-wind the boat will more or less stop, if both sheets are eased, and the helmsman gets out quickly and seizes the bow to keep the boat's bow towards the next wave. Always jump out to windward in these conditions, in case the boat runs you down.

If you have no stomach for acrobatic exercises, a less hazardous system is to ask your crew (it always falls to him!) to get out as soon as the waves break, he holds onto the bow and turns the boat into the wind. He cannot do this in a heavy surf.

Landing with the Wind Aft

You must sail in under jib only or under bare poles. In very light weather it may be possible to keep all sail on, coming onto a reach at the last moment; then raise centreboard and rudder and sheet the sails fairly close; the boat should then gently drift in sideways to the shore.

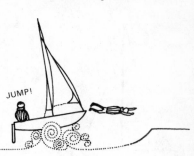

JUMP!

If the waves are running high and you cannot lower the mainsail, drop the anchor outside the surf and then let the boat full astern towards the beach. You then lower all sails before hauling out to get the anchor up.

Landing Head-to-Wind

When the wind blows offshore there will not be a large sea running and the wind will become lighter as you approach. An uneventful landing under these conditions is very nearly guaranteed.

However, there are some things to remember. You want to arrive close-hauled, but you cannot do it all the way because the centreboard must be raised as you approach.

One way round the difficulty is to try to find a good sloping shore; or a small inlet may enable you to approach at least some of the way with the wind on the beam. The wind even may not be blowing directly offshore. Aim always at the part of the shore up to windward, get close-hauled and don't forget to keep an eye on the depth of water under you. The crew gradually raises the centreboard while the helmsman bears away little by little, easing sheets so that the boat picks up speed. Even if you do not have all the centreboard down, it will be enough to keep up some speed, stop leeway and the boat will not drift sideways. At the last moment a sharp luff should take the boat to the shore under her own way with centreboard and rudder completely raised. If you know the beach, you obviously choose the steepest part which lets you keep

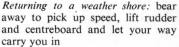

Returning to a weather shore: bear away to pick up speed, lift rudder and centreboard and let your way carry you in

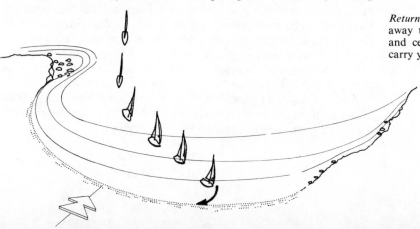

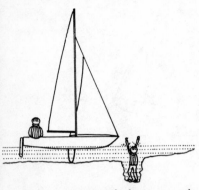

Unless you are unlucky you are in your depth when you have to raise the centreplate

the centreboard down longer and sail to windward for longer.

This is not always easy, but when you have to start raising the centreboard, you are usually within your depth and can step over the gunwale and hold on. If you have not reached the stage of landing under sail, it's wiser to step out soon than to keep the centreboard down too long. If it should touch the bottom hard, a pivoting centreboard can easily bend and a dagger plate can easily jam in its case. If this happens, attempts to free it will only be abortive and strain the case and fittings still more. The only course is to get out, to lighten the boat, and lay her on her side to ease the centreboard from the bottom. You will at least by now have made your landing.

Manoeuvring in Harbour

Deck Drill

As you approach harbour after cruising for some days, the skipper should be seeing that everything has been prepared. The crew have probably grown used to comfortably long tacks, unimpeded by shallows or headlands, with plenty of time to carry out orders. Mooring gear, warps and fenders easily get shoved away into the inner recesses of the boat or lost underneath a pile of gear that was more immediately important. Now is the time to get it all out and put it back where it belongs, check that warps, lines and fenders are handy and that the anchor chain is not jammed by a mass of sail bags. Have the boat hook and sculling oar on deck.

Clear the deck, see that sheets and halyards are free to run and that you have neither too much nor too little sail up. You must have enough sail for good manoeuvrability for the wind can be flukey in harbour. Equally, you must not be carrying too much sail: a genoa, for instance, may be inconvenient as it takes time to sheet it home, it can get caught aback, and it blocks the helmsman's view; a working jib is much more convenient. In short, the sails must be well balanced and the decks cleared for action.

And get ready in plenty of time. There is nothing worse than 'panic stations' at the eleventh hour, particularly if you are entering a strange port. It is no time to be doing the washing up.

Nearing Land

Consult tide tables, the list of lights, the pilot book, chart and harbour plan to know what to expect. Check your notional plan of operations from the cockpit for it may have to be modified. When you first see the features of the coastline they do not always seem to match the descriptions given in the books. Making landfall is a solemn moment and can be confusing. It is only too easy to make assumptions and you can only be certain when you can put a name to all the features. It is satisfying to pick them out as you approach. The whole crew can participate in this visual exploration of the coastline as it looms up and the approach always takes longer than you expected.

As you get nearer landmarks stand out, transits come into line and the whole coastline sorts itself out. Sailing instructions have to be followed according to the time of day, the wind and tide and visibility, not to mention the presence of other boats. All these factors will affect your plan of action. If you decide to choose an open anchorage in a creek or in a bay, the size of any boats already there will indicate depth, and the way they are lying will tell you something about wind and current. The number of masts behind the harbour wall as you approach a port will give an idea of how crowded it is and whether there is a lot of movement. Smoke and flags are a useful guide to wind direction near port and again the size of boats moored or dried out on legs and where they are lying are all guides to where you can go. That first drink on land is not far off.

Where to Moor

The skipper must have a clear all-round view during the approach. It is often better for him not to take the tiller, leaving him free to concentrate on where to go and directing operations. He will have explained his general plan and delegated the crew their respective duties. For their part, the crew should always be ready to accept

A natural harbour: the Fazzio inlet near Bonifacio, Corsica

St Malo harbour at the end of the
Cowes-Dinard race

unexpected, even contradictory instructions. The skipper may
decide to anchor instead of tying up alongside, or to pick up a
mooring buoy, or even to sail out again; you have to take what
comes – it's all in the day's work.

The ideal situation on entering a strange port is to be able to sail
round inside looking for the best place. Mooring places can be
vacant for good reasons: they may hide underwater obstructions,
be reserved for the harbour master or fishing boats. You should also
be careful not to settle on a spot which is difficult to leave. If in
doubt it is sensible to tie up temporarily to a jetty, buoy or another
boat while you make inquiries. Marinas and other well organised
harbours often have a visitor's berth which you can sail onto at
once and then report to the harbourmaster for instructions.

When you go into a commercial port, remember that you are not
usually allowed to tack back and forth in the main channel, which
is used by large boats unable to change speed or direction in confined waters. If you have to use the fairway, it is best to put on the
engine (and let us hope that it doesn't choose this moment to fail
you).

Berthing charges are high in the middle of the season whether
you anchor or tie up. If you don't want to pay, anchor outside,
choose a sheltered spot and be sure you know the nature of the
bottom and the flow of tides and currents. The length of your stay,
as well as the weather forecast, can influence your decision and
other boats will show you where to go. It is wise to join them,
allowing plenty of room because two boats will not necessarily
behave in the same way; and it is safer to moor to windward of a
large boat in case she starts to drag anchor if it starts to blow.

Anchoring

It is really only outside the harbour proper that you can drop anchor without worrying about fouling it but you will not be in such good shelter as inside and your ground tackle has to be good. A small centreboarder only needs one anchor; a cruising boat must have at least two together with appropriate mooring lines and, of course, chain.

If the crew is staying aboard you can use a light anchor for a short stop in fine weather. If you mean to go ashore the main anchor must be used and if bad weather threatens, both anchors should be put out.

Three types of anchor cables are required: chain, a warp and a light line.

The anchor chain is the main standby and it has great advantages. Its weight makes it lie along the bottom and helps the anchor to dig in well; it is also strong enough to withstand chafe on a rough bottom. With a chain equal to three times the depth at high water, you have good holding power and a reasonably restricted swing. Don't forget however that three times the depth (measured from the waterline) is the absolute minimum and you may need more for large boats in less water; 45 metres of chain for 75m of depth is all right, but in 2 metres it is better to put out at least 20 metres.

If you moor in very deep water, the weight of a heavy chain can pose a problem for it can be difficult, even impossible, to haul it in without a windlass or capstan unless you have a very strong crew – or are content to spend the rest of your cruise there. Beyond five fathoms you can use a warp, which will give holding power provided you let out at least five times the depth of the water. But it is not so strong as a chain and can wear and chafe, either in the fairlead or on the bottom, so it is best to parcel it where it passes through the fairlead and you should have three or four fathoms of chain between the anchor and the end of the rope.

Finally, a long, light line can be extremely convenient for anchoring temporarily or in deep water when there is no wind and a current.

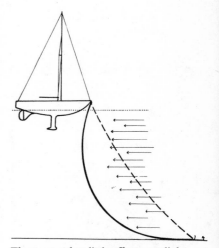

The current has little effect on a light line but a great deal on a heavy one, so much so that it can be impossible to break out the anchor until the tide slackens

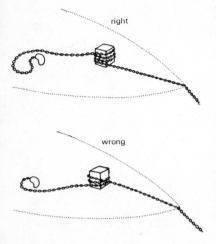

right

wrong

The well-ordered heap-of-chain method

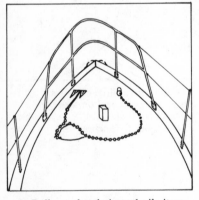

A. Pull out the chain and pile it up
B. Take a turn round the samson post

Preparing to Anchor

The Chain

It is worth recalling at the outset that the chain should be made fast inside the boat by lashing and not with a shackle to allow it to be quickly cut if you have to slip your anchor in an emergency; and, unlike a shackle, it cannot rust.

You should start your preparations for anchoring by pulling out onto the deck a length of chain equal to at least three times the maximum depth you are expecting. Now take three round turns on the bitts with the uppermost turn leading the chain straight into the navel pipe; in this way, whatever the ultimate strain on the chain, you will always be able to let out a little more slack, which is not possible if the turns are made the other way up. Never put a half hitch on the bitts for it will tighten up and you will have to use hammer and cold chisel to clear it.

A pile of chain on deck gets in the way and there is always a risk that it will fall overboard if the boat suddenly heels. It should be got out as late as possible and to be sure that it can run free have the anchor end on top.

Start by piling the chain onto the deck as it comes out of the navel pipe, until you have the right amount. If the chain is not marked in fathoms or if the paint has worn off, you should pull it out, yard by yard, to estimate fairly accurately the amount you have on deck. Having taken a round turn on the bitts or capstan, the anchor end of the chain is now jammed underneath, and it will carry the whole lot into the water in a lump if you leave it like this. The next step is to turn the pile by flaking it down again, starting with the end made fast to the bitts. As the top of the pile leads directly to the anchor it will run freely. This method allows you to get the chain on deck at the last moment, because it does not take long and anyone can do it.

In heavy weather a pile of chain might easily fall over the side, so flake it down a little earlier on deck in lengths. If the weather is really bad, the bights of chain can be lashed with a couple of sail ti-ers.

If you are going to be completely ready to drop anchor, the chain must be lead through the fairlead or roller and back on deck to the anchor. It should be cleared from its chocks and check that it is clear of the pulpit or rail and that it will swing down free from the roller. Leave a little slack chain between the anchor and the roller or it may jump out with a jerk when the anchor is dropped.

Anchoring with a Warp

You can sometimes see a worried yachtsman carrying an anchor warp with almost maternal care in a coil. This is nearly always a waste of effort. *A coiled warp becomes a tangled warp*, for carrying a rope in this way makes it get into a mass of knots when it is moved. It is better to uncoil it straight out of its locker and recoil it down on deck where you want to use it.

This takes a little time. In practice, if an anchor warp is properly stowed in a locker, all you have to do is to take the end, which has to be made fast to the anchor, forward (underneath the sheets) to the foredeck. When you lower the anchor the warp will uncoil from the locker quite happily. If you cannot do this, then you have to coil it down again properly on the foredeck. A rope coils in a clockwise direction, flat on the deck, in an oval shape. This should be done in several steps, starting at the outside and coiling towards the middle, otherwise all of it will be dragged into the water in one lot as soon as the first coils are pulled away.

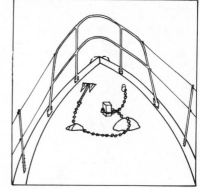

C. Reverse the pile of chain

The other end should be made fast to the inside of the locker with a lashing or by a bowline round the mast. The anchor end should be made fast with a fisherman's bend or by a round turn and a bowline. Like the chain, the anchor warp should be placed in the fairlead or on the roller before dropping the hook.

When there is a length of chain between the anchor and the end of the warp, the join must be businesslike. A bight of chain should be closed with a shackle or two half hitches and a lashing and the bight of rope which passes through the loop should be fastened with a bowline. In this case, it is the line and not the chain that is placed in the roller, otherwise the knot or shackle will jam just when you wish everything to run smoothly.

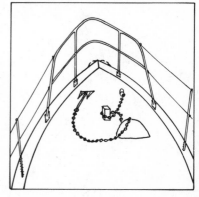

D. Anchor's ready

Anchoring with a Light Line

Here again the line should be flaked or piled and turned. To ensure it is ready for instant use, the line can be kept in a bucket or bag,

Ready to let go

Another system: flake out the chain

A light line has two bad habits: 1. it tangles easily; 2. it all runs out into the water if not made fast. Remedy: 1. don't coil it but flake it into a bucket or a bag; 2. leave the first metre out and make it fast to the mast

The tripping line on the left is too short and the anchor is being pulled the wrong way round. All is in order on the right

Two methods of attaching tripping line

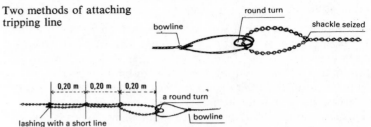

but with enough hanging free from the bottom of the pile to make it fast to the mast. It should be flaked down into the container like a chain in its locker.

Tripping Line

It is well known that an anchor can get fouled in all sorts of snags on the bottom – something to remember before you let it go. The safeguard is to tie a thin line to the crown of the anchor. You can then pull it out by its arms which will be dug in, if it is caught in a snag.

What should be done with the other end of this line? One convenient way is to tie it to a small buoy, but it is then at the mercy of the propeller of a passing boat; and when you weigh anchor with contrary wind and current, you have to get hold of it with the dinghy. Alternatively, it can be tied to the chain itself, but this is not satisfactory because the tripping line can tangle round the chain. If the line is too short too it can prevent the anchor digging in. If there is any sort of current, a long tripping line of robust dimensions, offers considerable resistance and can loosen the anchor. The best answer is to have a thin tripping line which is long enough to bring it back on board: the tender's anchor line, or even the lead line, are just about right for the job.

Like all safety equipment, the tripping line is an encumbrance when it is not in use, but it is worth having when you anchor when you suspect that the bottom is foul. It is always better to be safe than sorry.

Anchoring Head-to-Wind

This is the classic way. Get sailing fairly fast to leeward of the chosen spot, preferably with the wind on the beam. Lower the jib as soon as possible to clear the foredeck; but keep it ready to re-hoist in a hurry. If the boat does not balance too well under mainsail alone, keep the jib up a little longer but not too long for it gets in the way of the foredeck crew when the boat luffs up. And, if it partly fills on either tack, the bow will bear sharply away at precisely the wrong moment.

Close to leeward of the anchorage, luff up quickly and pull in the mainsheet to keep up speed. The boat moves ahead with way on while the helmsman holds her head-to-wind; he can tell that he is doing this if the boom flops from side to side over the cockpit and he has to mind his head.

Meanwhile the skipper checks speed over the ground by a convenient transit on the beam. He should not order 'anchor away' until the boat has come to a stop, otherwise the anchor will be overtaken by the chain and risks getting fouled on itself instead of digging in.

The crew should let the anchor go quickly but only letting chain equal to the depth of water, not more, or it may fall in a pile on the anchor and foul it that way.

If you are using a standard fisherman's anchor with a stock, there are certain special precautions to take not to foul it by the stock or the fluke.

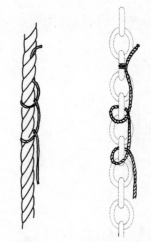

Methods of making fast the tripping line to the anchor chain or warp

Hang the anchor over the bow by its chain and lower it gently with the chain under tension.
Never throw the anchor over the side.
Only anchor when the boat is falling astern (or moving ahead if anchoring with the wind astern).

While this is going on, another member of the crew should lower the mainsail, but also be ready to hoist again quickly if the anchor

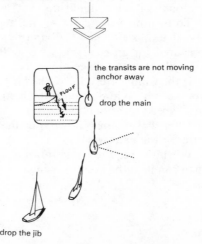

the transits are not moving
anchor away

drop the main

drop the jib

drags. The boat starts to fall astern; the crew on the bow lets the chain play out slowly so that its braking effect holds the bow and doesn't allow it to pay off while the boat slips backwards. The anchor chain can be snubbed with the foot, but to make sure it does not trap your toes, wear boots.

When the anchor is down, skipper checks, by picking out shore transits, that the anchor is holding.

Anchoring with the Wind Astern

There may be several reasons for anchoring with the wind astern.

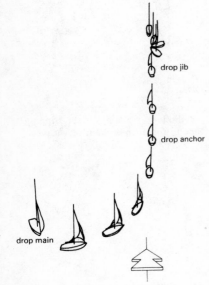

drop jib

drop anchor

drop main

In very light winds, if you anchor head-to-wind the boat is slow in falling astern and the chain will pay out sluggishly. By anchoring downwind you can keep up enough movement for the chain to pay out quickly, letting the anchor bite on the bottom with minimum delay.

Whatever the wind, this method is quite practical if the bottom is covered with seaweed. Modern stockless anchors (plough or balanced fluke types) don't always hold well on this kind of bottom and the sharper tug provided by anchoring downwind gives them a better chance to dig in.

If you drop anchor quickly you will know straight away whether it is holding. When the chain goes taut the boat should swing round on it fairly sharply. If the swing is gentle, the anchor is not holding and you must start over again.

When anchoring downwind, you must ensure that the chain is clear to run quite freely. A chain is best for this and don't forget to take a couple of turns on the bitts for when the slack has been paid out the boat will be brought up short with a jerk.

To turn downwind for anchoring, first of all get onto a course less than close-hauled (full-and-by) and lower the mainsail, being prepared for an emergency hoist. Bear away again and approach your chosen anchorage at reduced speed under jib alone.

If the wind is fresh lower the jib early on, although in light winds you keep it up almost until the boat has turned to her anchor. The ideal speed to be making at this moment is about one knot.

After the anchor is down, pay out more chain liberally, having a care for the paintwork.

When the required amount of chain has been lowered the helmsman can help the boat to swing round by luffing to where the chain grows. If the boat has fairleads on either side of the bow, you should have pre-selected which side to use. When there is only one fairlead, or a roller fitting at the centre of the bow, the man on the foredeck indicates to the helmsman which way to turn until the chain has run right out. The helmsman begins to turn on the chain as soon as the rattle at the fairlead stops.

Anchoring in a Current

When there is a strong current flowing, anchoring can be complicated in several ways, so first of all make a little tour of inspection:

To check the strength and direction of the current;
To try to estimate how the boat will swing by watching the other craft on their moorings; but accuracy only comes with experience.

Wind and Current in the Same Direction. There is no particular problem even with up to 20° or 30° difference between the two.
Wind at Right Angles to Current. Approach with head to current and wind abeam (under main and jib if necessary), and check on leeway. As soon as you ease sheets the boat will slow up and, as soon as she begins to drop aft, lower the anchor and drop the sails.
Wind and Current in Opposite Directions. Under these conditions (and with a difference of up to 80° between them) difficulties arise and the procedure varies considerably according to your location and the strength of the current in relation to the wind.

Approach downwind under jib only. Once the anchor is down the boat will be stern to wind and if you keep the mainsail up, it will be hard against the shrouds, it will be difficult to get it down and meanwhile the boat will be sailing beyond the anchor.

Occasionally you may have to approach into the wind with way on. The trick here is to get the mainsail down quickly before the boat swings to her anchor on the current and brings the wind astern. Two boats anchored in a current will not necessarily swing in the same pattern even if they have the same windage for it is their draft that counts. Always allow yourself plenty more room than you may need and lash the tiller amidships.

If you are staying aboard, give the boat a bit of sheer away from the next boat by lashing the tiller slightly to one side or the other.

And never forget the boat's behaviour at anchor may be quite different when the tide turns.

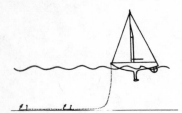

A tandem anchor

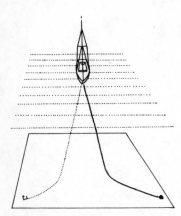

Riding to open hawse

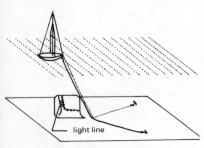

To avoid a foul hawse bind the warp to the chain at level of the bottom

Using More Than One Anchor

Tandem Anchors

This means attaching a smaller anchor to the crown of the bower anchor with a length of chain. It is probably the best way of holding ground in bad weather.

When you attach them, however, you must envisage what will happen when you pull them up. If you join the two anchors with a short chain, you will have to pull up their combined weight and that is tough. It is easier to have a good length of chain ($1\frac{1}{2}$ times depth of water) between the two anchors to allow you to get the bower up first and then haul in the other. Even if you don't have enough chain, it is better to use a short tandem than none at all. It is important that the linking chain should be well stretched out under tension, and this is only possible on a soft bottom. The tandem system is useless on rocky ground.

If you have no chain for joining the two anchors, a length of synthetic rope, of not more than ten feet long, will fill the bill.

Mooring with Open Hawse

This is having two bower anchors on their own lines or chains at an angle somewhere between 40°–180°.

Mooring like this reduces the boat's arc of swing which increases with the size of the boat. It requires good sea room for, with several boats moored side by side, sorting out the tangle of chain can be a fascinating if rather frustrating puzzle.

The angle between the two anchor chains should not be greater than 40° in heavy weather. The weakness of this type of mooring is that the two chains do not bear an equal load. If the wind gets up later, it is usually too late to anchor in tandem because hauling them both up and joining them takes time. So this is the second-best method, although it is always better to have two anchors down rather than one, whichever system you use.

You have to use the dinghy to drop the second anchor. The anchor goes in first and then the warp or chain is piled carefully on top. If the anchor is very large and heavy you can hang it behind or even underneath the tender.

Row away from the boat paying out the warp. When it is all paid out, keeping it as taut as possible, lower the anchor with a light line attached to the crown.

Buoying the second anchor enables you to slip it quickly in an emergency and to recover it later.

When you have to take out anchor and chain in the dinghy, the weight of the chain prevents you from keeping it taut so it is a good idea to attach a 10m line to the bitter end of the chain, making one end of the line fast on board. When you have rowed the anchor out as far as you can go and lowered it, the crew can pull in the line and make the chain fast on the bitts.

When you have to lie to two anchors for any length of time, you have to take precautions to prevent the two chains or the chain and line twisting near the fairleads by seizing them together where you estimate they will hit the bottom; parcel the rope with a piece of sail cloth at the point of seizing to stop it chafing against the chain.

Emergency Second Anchor

When you are riding to your bower anchor and chain and the wind and sea get up, you are unlikely to be able to anchor in tandem, or to lay out a second anchor in the dinghy. Nevertheless, you feel you have to put down a second anchor as a security measure. There are four distinct moves in this order:

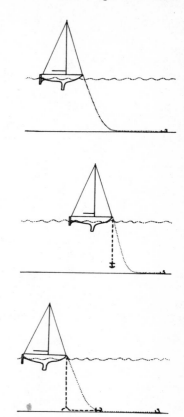

Anchoring

Wait for a relatively calm period and then pull in a fair amount of chain on your main anchor taking care, of course, not to break it out.

Lower the second or kedge anchor onto the bottom, preferably on a chain.

Slack away on the main anchor again and pay out the warp or chain of the kedge at the same time.

Finally, and only after having dropped back from the kedge as above, lower all the chain or line you have on the second anchor onto the bottom.

In this way you avoid lowering the chain of the kedge on top of it in a pile. This is not strictly speaking mooring, but only a precautionary measure, for if the main anchor drags you have extra security in the kedge.

Mooring Fore and Aft

Anchoring fore and aft is a way of mooring in rivers to reduce swing, but it is not particularly efficient, and the boat can swing across wind and tide pulling on both anchors at once. This can be uncomfortable and, indeed, difficult to sort out without slipping one of the chains and buoying it.

There is a similar system which is much better. Both chains are taken over the bow, but one is carried aft and made fast at the stern but in a way that can be easily slipped if the boat swings beam on. When this happens, the stern chain is slipped and the boat swings to open hawse.

Weighing Anchor

Preparation

If the anchor is to be weighed efficiently the boat has to be under control within seconds of the anchor breaking out. This demands almost ritualistic preparation.

As soon as you have decided to set sail the swimmers are called back on board, the fishing lines are brought in and the sails made ready. All this must be done before starting to fiddle with the anchors: the mainsail must be ready to hoist, the jib must be bent on, the sheets free to run and the deck clear.

If you have moored to two anchors, start by getting one in, the heavy one for preference, for the kedge comes up more easily and quickly, when sailing off.

You will probably have to use the dinghy to get in the first anchor – or whichever one has been buoyed – using the tripping line. If you have not fitted a tripping line (and this in itself is an error) you can try paying out a lot of slack and the dinghy is then pulled hand over hand along the warp until it is directly over the anchor which is then broken out.

Once the anchor is on board the dinghy, pull in the slack from the boat, passing the chain straight into the chain locker or coiling the rope on deck or directly into the locker where it is stowed if you want to avoid a snarl up. All the chain or line should be cleared from the deck to make getting up the second anchor a tidy business.

When you are anchored in tandem, the procedure is different. If the two anchors are joined by a short chain, you must break out both at once and pull them up together, and that is heavy work. If you have had the foresight to join the two anchors with a reasonably long length of chain, there are two ways:

The main anchor is brought up on deck by hauling on the chain in the normal way and you are then held by the second, but not too securely because its chain will be almost straight up and down. In this case the sails should be hoisted before breaking out the first anchor because you must now get under way without delay.

If you have put a tripping line on the second anchor, you can get this up with the dinghy, unshackle it from its chain and bring it back on board. Then you can easily haul up the main anchor, the short length of chain trailing from its crown.

Getting the Chain on Board

This is done in several stages and everyone should be clear about them.

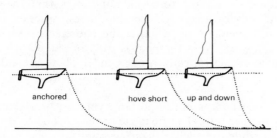

A boat is said to be **properly anchored** when she is lying to an anchor of the right weight and with enough chain out to ensure it does not drag.

A boat is *hove short* (short stay) when some of the chain has been raised but there is still enough out for the anchor to hold well in the prevailing conditions. The 'safety margin' has been removed but, by paying out chain again, you can easily return to it.

The chain is *up-and-down* when her bow is almost directly over the anchor and the chain is more or less perpendicular. The anchor holds on the bottom but will break out under any strain. It all depends on the nature of the bottom: if it is good holding ground, the anchor's resistance will be all the greater. The up-and-down position is essentially temporary and you do not stay long in it (if necessary you can always drop back on your anchor again by letting out more chain but you have to be quick or the anchor will drag or foul). You can get under way as soon as the boat is over the anchor – even slightly earlier because the crew will only too easily call 'anchor aweigh' long after it has already broken out and the boat is already falling astern.

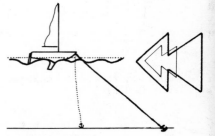

In a strong wind the anchor is ready to break out long before the chain is straight up and down

Getting Under Way

All is ready but the sails have yet to be hoisted and everyone is at his post. The skipper has decided which tack he will leave on: port, starboard or whichever way the boat is more likely to go of her

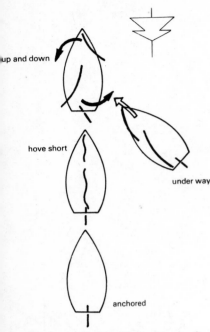

up and down

hove short

under way

anchored

To be sure of bearing away on the desired tack, back jib and main and reverse the tiller

own accord; everyone should understand what is going to happen.

The sails should be hoisted when the boat is nearly over her anchor. The skipper (who should have his eye everywhere at once, directing operations and giving a hand where necessary) should check that the boat is not already dragging by taking a transit on the shore.

The sails flap; the helm is amidships. The boat is slowly pulled up to her anchor.

When the man on the foredeck announces that the chain is straight up-and-down, the skipper has a few seconds to decide what to do, depending on whether the chosen tack seems to be viable (as many as five if the boat is truly over the anchor, much less if it has, in fact, already broken out)! There are still several courses of action:

If the chosen tack is not important, you can break out anchor without further ado. The boat may then bear away to port or starboard while the anchor is pulled right up.

If the boat is bearing away on the chosen tack, break out the anchor and, at the same time, help the boat to keep on its (let us assume) starboard tack as follows: the jib is backed to starboard; the boom is pushed out to port so that the mainsail is filled aback; the tiller is put hard over to port. The boat drops astern. The combined action of the sails pushing aft and the tiller being reversed puts the boat decisively onto the starboard tack.

If the boat is keeping head-to-wind, use the same procedure but much more vigorously.

If the boat falls away onto the wrong (in this case, port) tack there should be no hestitation: let go the anchor again immediately.

In light winds a small cruiser or day sailer can be put onto the appropriate tack by using the way made as you pull in on your anchor. As the boat is moving forward, the rudder will act normally. If you wish to get onto the starboard tack, put the tiller to port and the boat turns away to starboard, it is checked and swings sharply to port as the anchor breaks out. This will work even in a slight breeze.

If the wind and tide are extremely light or the boat small, the anchor can be broken out in one, hauling steadily away without pausing at the intermediate positions or trying to make the boat turn to one side or the other. The anchor is broken out 'on the run' and you then take advantage of the way created by pulling up the anchor to turn away onto either tack. The chain should be brought in steadily and not too quickly, otherwise the boat will pick up too much way and you won't be able to pull in the rest of the chain quickly enough, with the result that the boat will pass over the anchor without breaking it out; and she will be brought up sharply to a halt. A misfire!

If the anchorage is crowded you cannot afford the mistake of leaving on the wrong tack. It may be politic to 'dredge' the anchor: reach a position where the anchor is on the point of breaking out, and then let her drag gently backwards to clearer waters; this plan is not recommended in a port, where there is any danger of fouling other chains or cables on the bottom. In any event, you should not adopt it unless the anchor is buoyed.

Don't be too proud to use a sculling oar if you have one (having first checked that you are able to make up against wind and current). You can then move to a more open spot before you hoist sail. In the last resort you will not lose face if you start the engine. That is better than creating chaos.

Weighing Anchor When the Tide is Running

When you have to weigh anchor in a tide, consider carefully what is going to happen. Firstly, you are probably not going to be able to choose which tack you leave on, for this is only possible when wind and current are in the same direction. Secondly, as soon as the anchor has broken out, the boat will be at the mercy of the tidal stream if there is not enough wind.

You must first decide what tack you are going to be forced on to and what possibilities this offers you. Next hoist the sails before breaking out the anchor to see if you can sail against the stream.

Remember that a boat anchored in a tidal stream has a certain amount of manoeuvrability because the water is flowing over the surface of the rudder. She can therefore be veered to enable the sails to be hoisted. You can also help the foredeck crew to pull up the anchor because the bow can be turned to one side or the other in order as they require. Also, when the anchor is broken out the boat is under complete control at once thanks again to the action of the rudder.

One last point: as soon as the anchor has broken out, the apparent wind is different from the true wind which you felt when anchored; in the worst case when wind and current are in the same direction and the same strength, the wind will effectively drop as soon as the

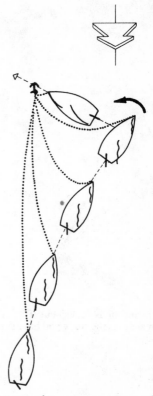

You can also get some way on by heaving in fast, then snubbing her round short on to the desired tack just before breaking the anchor

This anchor is fouled but if its ring can slide up the stock you have some chance

boat is carried on the current. These are the two most common instances.

Wind and Current in the Same Direction. If they are within 45° of each other, the current will hold the boat so that the wind comes over the bows enabling the sails to be hoisted. It is even possible to make the sails draw as the anchor chain is being hauled up increasing your popularity with the foredeck crew.

Wind and Current in Opposite Directions. If you are not able to turn the boat when it is on its anchor to bring the wind at least on the beam, you cannot hoist the mainsail. You have to get under way under jib alone. The prudent mariner will check before leaving that he can sail against the stream under the jib.

If wind and tide are favourable and there is plenty of room down current, you can leave under bare poles. Having broken out the anchor, the jib is hoisted as the boat is carried on the current and, coming up into the wind, the mainsail is also put up. This is a leisurely and stylish way of doing it.

Fouled Anchor

At last the tripping line pays off! It is usually enough to haul on the tripping line and a fouled anchor will break out. There are, however, two occasions when the tripping line will not help: when it is tangled in the anchor chain and when another anchor lies over it.

If you have not got a tripping line, you can try turning the anchor by tugging sharply at 45° and then at 90° to the original direction of the chain; finally try 120°. If you have no luck on one tack, try the other.

If your anchor is of the stockless type with a sliding ring on the shank, you can bring in the chain until you only have a length slightly more than the height of water, then scull up into wind or motor and, when you pass over the anchor, the ring should slide up the shank enabling you to pull the anchor out backwards (but if you succeed, you deserve a medal).

If none of this avails there is only one, desperate, solution: go down and have a look. With a large rock under his arm (in order to get down more quickly), someone slides down the chain which has, of course, been hauled hard in. Give him a little slack chain as soon as he is on the bottom, to help him manipulate. It is a good idea to lay out a second anchor while this is going on (and don't forget to buoy it). With good fortune you will never have to take this extreme measure.

Moorings

Mooring gear is attached either to a pick-up buoy or a mooring buoy. In the case of a mooring buoy the chain rises directly from the bottom to the buoy and is fastened to it by a shackle. In the case of a pick-up buoy, the chain remains on the bottom and a light line joins it to the buoy on the surface. A pick-up buoy is thus generally smaller and lighter than a mooring buoy, because the latter has to support the weight of its chain; it also gives as good as it gets when it comes to exchanging blows with the stem of a boat...

Picking up a Mooring

Picking up a mooring, of either type, is a demanding exercise. You have no margin of error as you had when anchoring, for the boat's way must be judged precisely if she is not to stop too soon or too late: in the one case you flounder like a plaintive figurehead with boathook outstretched in vain; in the other you pick up the buoy, either bringing the boat up so sharply that you may go overboard, buoy and all, or the boat veers wildly and starts off on a frisky semi-circle downwind to the attendant shouts of the crew. Heads start popping out of hatchways all around, and fenders are put out. The peace of the day is shattered.

Nevertheless, it is better to have a little too much speed than too little. You can travel two or three yards ahead after picking up the buoy, and the extra way can be used, in the case of a pick-up buoy, to haul the riding line, which goes to the chain on the bottom, quickly on board.

The Approach

The approach is for preference made full-and-by, with the jib lowered if possible to keep the foredeck clear. Many boats can sail quite well without a jib on this point of sailing, slowing down or picking up speed at will, with little leeway. If they cannot do this, the jib should be kept up.

Luff up when between about a half and one boat's length from

It is better to slip a line through the ring on the buoy, first

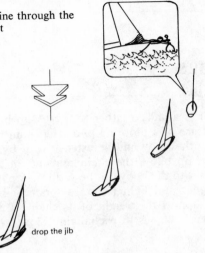

drop the jib

the buoy. You should then have enough speed for the rudder to bite on the water, but only just enough, for the boat must not travel too far or too quickly. The sheets should be slacked right off so that the sails don't fill with wind if the boat turns to one side or the other.

Tidal streams and eddies can obviously make the operation more tricky. All the factors that affect anchoring in a tidal stream apply but more so. Once again it is when the wind is against current that things get complicated, not forgetting leeway. But take heart; the man who has never failed to pick up a mooring has yet to be born.

Mooring

As soon as you have got the buoy, lower sails and make fast.

Mooring on a pick-up buoy is easy. Never tie up with the rider: that is not its job. Bring it all on board until you reach the heavier mooring chain and make this fast to the bitts with at least three turns and no knots or hitches; the turns are secured by making the rider fast to the mast or a cleat.

When you are using a mooring buoy, get a line ready with one end made fast to the bitts. Pass the free end of this line through the ring on top of the buoy and make it also fast to the bitts. The line must be of a size that it can run easily through the ring. This is only a temporary mooring.

If you are staying for any length of time leave the line in place, because it will be useful when you leave. Shackle your anchor chain to the ring (if you merely pass the chain through the ring and bring it back on board, the sharp turn will not do your chain any good). In bad weather or for a long stay, you should shackle your chain onto the rising chain (use a large shackle and see that it is moused). The ring on the buoy is usually not as strong as the rising chain.

If the anchorage is sheltered, you can hang the buoy from the bow (particularly if it is a small one and the yacht is big enough) to prevent the boat hitting it and denting her stem. If the sea is choppy, you should ride to a fairly long chain.

When you moor in a strong tidal stream, do not leave the boat without lashing the tiller amidships, or she will veer wildly in the current.

Lastly, whether there is a current or not, you should not leave your boat on a mooring buoy for long without knowing about the ground tackle. Appearances can be deceptive and it is worthwhile asking the harbourmaster.

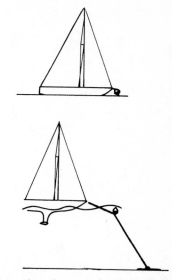

Leaving Moorings

This is very like weighing anchor for you have to get the boat onto the required tack, but it is easier and quicker to slip your mooring in a moment than haul up the anchor.

Protecting the stem head: in light weather hang the buoy from it; in rough weather keep your distance

Leaving a Mooring Buoy

Start by unshackling your chain; the boat stays moored by a short line through the ring. Pass the line through this ring and bring both ends back on board on port or starboard according to the chosen tack. If, for example, you decide to leave full-and-by on the port tack, the line should be made fast on the port side near the shrouds; if you want to leave on a broad reach you should take it still further aft.

When the sails are hoisted and everyone is ready, slip the mooring line and the boat will bear away under the pull of the line. Slip it a little before the boat is heading in the right direction because she will continue to bear away as she has no forward speed.

In a small boat under light conditions, the line is not necessary and the boat is made to bear away by carrying the mooring buoy itself towards the stern.

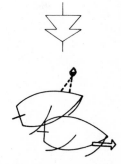

Dropping a Pick-up Buoy

This is not quite so simple. In light conditions you can carry the mooring chain to the side and hold onto it while the boat turns on

By making the mooring line fast at the appropriate place you can get under way on the desired tack

to the right tack. If the mooring line or the rope is strong enough, it can be taken aft before the chain is cast off. But this line is not always stout enough for a heavy strain and, if there is any wind, it is best to trim sails as if you were leaving from an anchor.

It is easier to leave a mooring in a tidal stream than to weigh anchor. You can turn the boat easily by pulling on the chain of a pick-up buoy or on a line passed through its ring and you can usually take your choice of tack.

But when the wind and current are contrary, it is not always possible to turn the boat enough to let the mainsail be hoisted, and you have to leave under jib only.

Jetty and Dockside

It is often sensible to turn on the engine or scull in a crowded port, but don't miss the satisfaction of sailing whenever you can. For one thing, even if you use the engine, sails are the essential stand-by if it fails and it is important to be practised in using them in restricted space. For another, this kind of boat handling, more than any other, leads to mastery of the finer points of seamanship: your boat's capricious ways in fresh winds, her lowest speed for full control, her balance under way, and the manner in which she loses or keeps up her way. Perfect performance under sail in a port, with crew and boat working as one, is the ultimate pleasure of sailing.

Never take chances. Go slowly rather than fast, giving good clearance to jetties and all obstacles fixed or moving. Be prepared for the unexpected round the corner of every harbour wall: a power boat may suddenly appear at speed. You must be able to change course in an instant, even stop, and your kedge anchor may even come in handy.

The way you approach will depend on the direction of the wind and what lies in your way; also on the tide and the space you have for manoeuvre. The suggestions we make here must necessarily be somewhat academic and do not take the unexpected into account. They cater for normal conditions. For the unexpected you have to improvise.

Coming alongside a quay is convenient because it is then easy to embark and disembark crew and gear (at least at high tide). But you need plenty of room and you have to tend your warps as the tide rises and falls.

Tying up in a marina pontoon or to another boat (a big one preferably) is the easiest berth of all.

In some harbours you are required to moor stern or bow to the quay.

Alongside a Quay

The Approach

You must work out what the wind is doing. You want the wind forward of the beam; if it is aft of the beam it will be impossible to stop.

Try to arrive on a close reach with the jib lowered (provided the boat remains under control without it), and the mainsail should be sufficiently sheeted to give enough speed. Above all do not arrive at right angles to the quay; if you arrive at an oblique angle the boat can be more easily turned alongside.

When there is plenty of room, there should be no problem: you finish parallel to the quay, mainsheet completely eased, and with hardly any way. Should you come in too fast the boat will still answer the helm so you can turn away and start over again, knowing what your speed should be; if you stop too soon, allow the boat to fall away and pick up speed for another go.

With practice it is possible to arrive without any sails hoisted, the mainsail having been lowered a few seconds before, so that you reach the quayside under your own way (too little rather than too much, provided you are ready to scull for the last few yards). As soon as you arrive alongside, one of the crew should jump ashore and make fast the mooring lines, bow rope first. If you make fast aft first, there is a risk that the boat will bear away and catch the wind in her sails if any sails are still up. If you arrive too fast, it is once again the bow rope that acts as a brake, and you surge it out to avoid pulling the boat right up against the quayside. Lower sails as quickly as possible.

Lack of room alongside often compels you to approach on an angle. If it is a question of fitting in between two boats, you can come alongside one of them as a temporary measure and the boat can be warped round alongside the quay later.

Wind Parallel to the Quayside. Come alongside upwind exactly as though you were picking up a mooring.

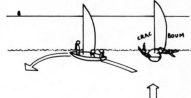

The quay should not be approached at right angles

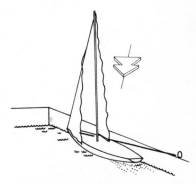

As a general rule you stop the boat by first making fast the warp forward. When the wind blows off the quay this is essential, for otherwise the sails may fill again

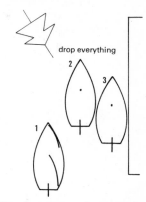

The elegant way: 1. approach close-hauled; 2. drop everything; 3. the wind should then bring the boat alongside

Wind onto the Quayside. This is slightly more tricky, and it is better to go elsewhere if possible.

If there is no other choice, you should come into the wind at an appropriate position, lower the mainsail (when you are alongside the quay you will not be able to ease off the boom) and approach under jib or, better still, under bare poles as the boat falls gently off to leeward.

This method, of course, doesn't allow for mistakes; you are powerless once the sails are down. The careful man drops an anchor as he approaches (on a warp rather than a chain); the approach is continued normally under the jib only, paying out slack on the anchor as you go. You might also anchor just upwind of the quay and then to fall back to where you wish to tie up, checking way on the anchor as you go. If you do this, keep an eye on everything at the after end of the boat: rudder, boom, stern rail, ensign staff, log, etc.

Coming Alongside with the Tidal Stream. The current always runs parallel to the quay. With wind and current in the same direction, come alongside head to wind. If the current and wind are contrary, you must make a choice.

As a general rule you should come in head to current with the wind aft, under the jib; but you may have to use the genoa to make enough way. If the genoa is not enough on its own, it will at least give you fair control as you drift sideways to the quayside aided with the help of the oar or a touch of engine, if necessary.

The wind may be strong enough to beat the tide, even under bare poles; in that case you can come in head to wind, but with care because, when the boat is no longer moving over the ground, the current will act on the rudder as it would do if you were going astern under power – disconcerting if you don't remember. For this reason alone it is usually preferable to approach against the current.

Berthing alongside a pier or pontoon with a cross-tide can be nerve-racking but, fortunately, you rarely have to do it.

Tying Up

Tying up in a basin, to another boat or in a marina is straightforward. Make your lines as tight as you like to keep the boat from moving, using the winch where necessary.

Make your *bow* and *stern lines* fast as far as possible from the boat.

If you cannot secure them far enough aft and forward use *springs* instead: the stern spring is taken forward to the quay and the line from the bow is carried aft so that they cross. *Breast ropes* should also be rigged to keep the boat close to the quay.

You cannot secure the boat so firmly in a tidal harbour. To restrict fore and aft movement, carry the bow and stern lines as far forward and aft as possible, and not onto the top of the quay but lower down, to the rungs of a ladder or a ring at about mid-tide level. If you make them fast on a bollard you have to adjust them as the tide rises and falls, and at high water there would be a lot of slack. By making them fast at mid-tide level you only have appreciable slack at half-tide, none at low or high water.

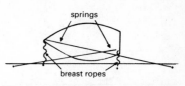

Warps secured half-way up quay wall: no slack at high and low water; but you will have to use bowlines with a long bight if you want to leave at high water

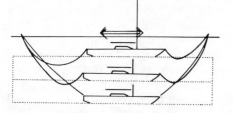

Mooring at a quay: these warps have too much play at half tide and at high water

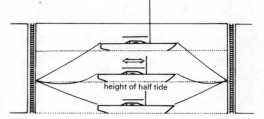

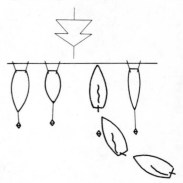

Another elegant way: luff up in front of your slot and reach the quay with no way on. It is prudent to pick up the buoy beforehand

Tying up Bow or Stern On

In this case the boat is held between the quay and a buoy or your anchor. This is the usual system in ports which are subject to swell and tying up alongside is not practicable. It is often the rule in modern yacht harbours where as many boats as possible have to be fitted in.

Making your approach under sail in such busy ports is usually not possible unless you are sailing into a light wind; but sculling or the engine is usually called for.

The Approach

Wind from the Quay. Come in full-and-by with the jib down and as slowly as possible. Luff up towards your chosen berth, so that your way just brings you to the quayside or, better still, just up to one of the boats which will be alongside you. Plenty of fenders and good boat control are what makes for happy relations with the boats already alongside.

Correct use of Warps

You take the end of the warp onto the quay, allowing just enough to tie up with – no more. If you dump a whole coil on the quay you are not just cluttering up the place, you are a nuisance to all and sundry. A disingenuous passer-by might even think you had rope to spare and were wanting to get rid of some!

It is generally a good idea to make a large loop (about 1.5m in circumference) at the end of the warp. When it is taken ashore it can then easily be dropped over a bollard or put under a ring (temporarily in the latter case).

Always adjust warps from the boat end.

When you attach a warp to the rung of a ladder or a ring on the quay, always give it a round turn to stop chafing and consequent wear.

When letting go a double warp you must cast off:
– the leeward length if it has been passed round a bollard;
– the lower length if it has been passed round the rung of a ladder – all this to prevent jamming.

Take a line onto the quay. If there is no mooring buoy at the other end, you will have to take out an anchor (and buoy it) in the dinghy. As the chain will have to be taut, the anchor will have to be taken well out if it is not to drag. A chain is better than a warp because it will lie nearer the bottom and not interfere with passing boats or be cut.

Wind onto the Quay. You should anchor well out from the quay and straight upwind of your berth. When you have anchored, lower sails and allow the boat to fall back on the anchor to the quay.

Marinas have so many pontoons in narrow rows that it is hardly possible to work your way in under sail. Motor in, but keep an eye open for warps under the surface. If your boat is a small one scull in to the first easily accessible place and then warp into your final berth. The only alternative is to take a tow from the harbour launch.

Tying Up

All warps should be taut to prevent bumping the boats on either side of you and, above all, be quite fast fore and aft – particularly important if a swell is felt inside. If too much movement is allowed, the boat is bound to chafe as she is drawn to and fro between slack anchor and shorelines. As she approaches the quay, she is pulled up by the anchor and then moves away from the quay only to snub again, this time, on the quay warp. If this is allowed to continue, the boat is under unnecessary stress.

Prevent this movement from the start. As the anchor always has a certain amount of give, it is the line to the quay that should take up the slack. Have two lines to the quay in a V shape, as wide as possible which give some elasticity to counteract the slack on the anchor. The whole mooring should keep taut.

This tautness can be maintained even in a tidal basin (provided the boat is not too near the quayside), because the distance between the quay and the anchor remains more or less constant, whatever the state of the tide is.

When there is room enough, you tie up stern to quay with long warps. This takes more space but you are better situated for you do not have to adjust the warps for the tide before going ashore. This is also the best way to moor a dinghy to the quay.

A final precaution when tying up to a quay, either alongside or stern on, is to check what the depth will be at low water and you can take precautions if you are going to take the ground.

A long mooring line stays taut at all states of the tide

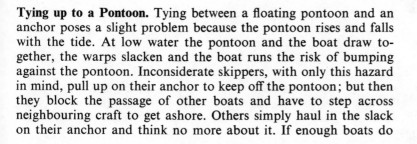

Tying up to a Pontoon. Tying between a floating pontoon and an anchor poses a slight problem because the pontoon rises and falls with the tide. At low water the pontoon and the boat draw together, the warps slacken and the boat runs the risk of bumping against the pontoon. Inconsiderate skippers, with only this hazard in mind, pull up on their anchor to keep off the pontoon; but then they block the passage of other boats and have to step across neighbouring craft to get ashore. Others simply haul in the slack on their anchor and think no more about it. If enough boats do

Proper use of Warps

1. Making fast

To prepare the warp you uncoil it, not from the boat end but from the end you wish to make fast.

To cast the warp ashore:
- take the end and coil it clockwise in the left hand, taking out enough length for the purpose;
- then take part in your right hand (three to five turns depending on the thickness of the warp);
- cast it with your right hand, keeping your left hand open so that the turns will uncoil as needed.

2. Hauling off

When the point to which you are made fast is moving, then you are being hauled or towed, but to haul yourself off, you heave in on the boat end of the warp.
- Hauling yourself off from the bow, pull the boat towards the point where you have taken a turn with the warp.
- On hauling yourself off you can get way on the boat, even enough to make steering possible.

When you wish to get under way, the warp is made double and you let go the short end and heave in on the other.

this and the tide starts to rise, trouble starts for in spite of its heavy moorings, the pontoon can drag. And the man who is shaking his fist outside the harbour office and shouting is the harbourmaster himself!

Marinas avoid this hazard by having a main pontoon with smaller pontoons attached at right angles and boats tie alongside these simply and comfortably. Tighten the warps on a winch, or the boat may suffer in these circumstances.

Leaving the Quayside

It is easy to leave a quayside when the wind is tending to blow the boat out but it must be forward of the beam if you are to hoist the mainsail. If the wind is aft, you can usually leave under the jib; if the mainsail is needed, you will first have to turn the boat round in order to produce one of the positions shown in the sectors in the diagram.

White Sector. The wind blows off the quay and departure is easy as you can hoist jib and mainsail. The boat is held by the forward warp which is doubled round a bollard, ready to slip. Leave just as if you were dropping a mooring, with the added advantage that you can use your stern line as a spring to help the boat to turn.

Lined Sector. The wind is blowing slightly towards the quay, but

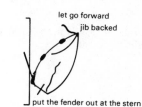

back the jib

let go forward

let go forward
jib backed

put the fender out at the stern

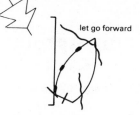

let go aft

sheet in

let go aft
underway

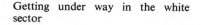

Getting under way in the white sector

Getting under way in the narrow sector to the right of the white sector

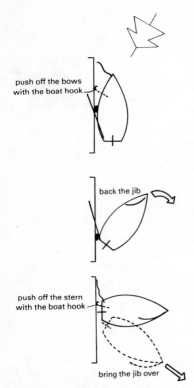

push off the bows
with the boat hook

back the jib

push off the stern
with the boat hook

bring the jib over

Getting under way in the sector next
to the black one

it is still possible to hoist the mainsail without the boom being
forced against the harbour wall.

The boat is held by the forward warp and the stern spring, both
doubled and ready to slip. Put out fenders, particularly aft, because
the topsides can be bruised as the bow is forced around.

Slip the forward line and push the bow off, making it pass
through the eye of the wind. The boat will pivot on the spring and,
as soon as she has the wind properly on the quayward side, sheets
can be hardened and the spring slipped.

Grey Sector. The wind is blowing clearly towards the quay, and
you cannot hoist the main; so you leave under the jib.

Slip the bow line and push the bow of the boat hard away until
it passes through the eye of the wind, when you can hoist the jib
and sheet it aback. The boat will bear away, pivoting against the
sea wall on its after fenders. When the wind is abeam, let draw the
jib and take in the spring. As the boat will move off more or less
sideways, you need plenty of room to leeward.

Black Sector. The wind is blowing hard onto the quay wall and
it is impossible to leave under sail.

In this and any case, when you cannot leave under sail (especially
in a crowded port), you must obviously scull, warp or power off
to where you can kedge or drift safely while you make sail.

Going Aground

This is done intentionally as well as by accident.

If the boat is put aground on purpose, either in a port which dries
out at low water or to scrub her, she is said to be *taking the
ground*.

If it happens by mistake owing to bad navigation or bad steering
and you hit a shoal or a rock, it is called *running aground*.

Taking the Ground

Taking the Ground Alongside

When a boat is to take the ground to dry out alongside a harbour wall, make sure that she leans inwards.

First of all test the bottom to make sure that the keel will be on solid ground. Next, heel the boat some two to three degrees towards the wall, no more. When the boat actually takes the ground, the fenders will compress and slightly increase the heel. Do not heel so much that the shrouds press against the quay wall.

For better leverage, the boat should be made fast from the side away from the quay, using bow and stern lines, breast-ropes and a line from the masthead.

All lines should be hardened just before you touch for the boat must be leaning against the quay at the moment she takes the ground.

This is the best way of drying out. You can get ashore without wading through mud, and you do not have to bother with legs. The alternatives are either to put out legs or let the boat dry out, lying over on her side.

Legs

Legs are designed only to hold the boat upright on her keel. Neither the legs themselves nor their fittings can support the full weight of the boat. Consequently you can only use legs if the bottom is reasonably level and firm, because the boat must not be allowed to heel.

Before deciding to dry out on legs, you must investigate the bottom by sounding all round with the boat hook. If there are rocks the bottom is rarely level. Mud is rarely firm enough and it can conceal a rock under the surface which could mean that the boat would lie heavily on one leg or the other.

Sand or shingle is the best bottom for legs. If the bottom slopes one way (as on a beach) the boat should face with her bow pointing up the slope. Across the slope, she will heel; pointing downward, the bow will drop too low.

Drying Out on Her Side

When a boat is allowed to dry right out on her side, life aboard is fairly chaotic; but this is by far the most natural position for a boat to dry out in, provided you remember that the mast will lean a long way over. It is also the only way that is safe in mud or rocky ground.

In deep mud the boat will settle happily as a hippo in perfect comfort. On rock, you must protect the hull as best you can by putting out fenders, coils of rope and, in the last resort, mattresses.

Don't forget that the fenders will be compressed. The shrouds must not bear against the quay

Drying Out for Scrubbing

Legs

You can take advantage of low water in a port to scrub, but harbours can be filthy and it may be better to go to a beach and dry out in more salubrious conditions. In addition, depending on the slope, you can work out exactly when to arrive to stay as briefly as possible: at the latest when the tide still has to fall at least as much as the boat's draught (or a little earlier if you want to be certain).

Before planning to dry out on a beach, make sure about these three conditions:

That the bottom is even and there are no rocks.
That it is not liable ground swell without warning.
That the weather is set fair.

Drying Out. Anchor from the stern as you approach the beach, and fairly far out to be able to haul yourself off without the anchor dragging. Use a rope as an anchor line because it is lighter, handier and almost certainly longer than your chain.

Take the bottom at about one knot, so that the boat stops at once. Take an anchor ashore (usually the main anchor, with chain) to hold fast forward.

Next put the legs in position. If the water is going down quickly, it might be wise to bolt them in beforehand, but keep them up during the approach or you will foul up the exercise.

Moving Off. You do not have to wait for the boat to be fully afloat before you raise the legs, and get them in early if there is any swell. You can, in fact, raise them very early as soon as the water reaches the tops of the keel.

If you allow a boat to pound on her legs, she will age ten years in ten minutes.

Drying Out Alongside, or on Your Side

These two methods suffer from the same inconvenience: you cannot always finish the scrubbing on one tide. If the boat dries out alongside a quay it is often difficult to reach the side against the quay.

The legs can be removed as soon as the keel is covered. There is no risk then of the hull hitting the bottom

You may either have to heel the boat slightly outwards when she becomes buoyant and work from the dinghy, or turn her and dry out a second time facing the other way.

Drying out, lying over on open sand is the best method for boats with broad beam and shallow draught. The scrubbing is made much easier because you don't have to work under the turn of the bilges as you have to do if you dry out on legs. The drawback is that you need one tide for each side.

Scrubbing Afloat: Careening

You can scrub a light boat without drying out by laying her on her side while she is still afloat. This is particularly appropriate in non-tidal waters where the only real alternative is to have the boat slipped or lifted out, at some expense.

The boat has to be heeled over (careened) until she lies on her side. This is done by hauling on a line attached to the masthead from the dinghy. You can use the jib halyard, provided it runs through a block and not in a sheave cage inside the mast, and that there is a shroud at the right height to take the strain. The boat will heel over more easily if someone is hoisted up the mast, *but make sure that his weight acts from the hounds or you risk breaking the mast.*

When the boat is floating on her side, it makes life easier if the keel can be slid over a jetty or a pontoon, to keep her lying over and you can then work in comfort. Otherwise you need two dinghies: one for the crew holding down the mast and the other for those scrubbing the bottom. If the boat is small enough (6.5m overall) three people will be needed to heel her over but two can keep her over and a third can scrub. It is quite practicable to careen the boat at low tide off a beach in about two foot of water.

When one side is clean, the boat is allowed to right herself gently and the whole operation begins again on the other. Remember to stow the dishes and other breakables safely.

Running Aground

If the boat goes on gently in calm weather and a rising tide, running

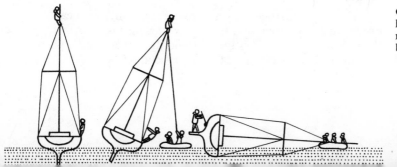

Careening by hauling over: the man hanging on to the stroud sets the movement off and there he is with his brush standing on the keel

aground is nothing to worry about. You just wait patiently for the tide to float her off.

But with a falling tide or in bad weather, you must act quickly. The following measures can be tried, in order of increasing likelihood of success.

Try to push the boat off with a boat hook or an oar.

If sea conditions permit, get the heaviest and strongest members of the crew over the side to lighten the boat and, hopefully, to push her off.

Lay out an anchor with the dinghy and haul her off; this is the action most likely to bring success but you must waste no time about it.

All these measures will work more effectively if you also heel the boat over as much as possible to reduce her draught. Someone going up the mast will be far more effective (as soon as the boat starts heeling at all) than two or three leaning over the side. Standing on the foredeck helps by lifting the keel slightly at the stern.

If you don't succeed on one side, try the other. If that fails, do not immediately rush into putting down legs – if you have them – without knowing the nature of the bottom and taking time to test it carefully. Legs can be the surest way of losing the boat if the conditions are not right. *It is always less dangerous to let the boat dry out on her side.*

After that you can only wait. If you are in a hurry, don't go aground at high water during spring tides: the next high water may not rise enough to float you off.

The Dinghy

This section would be incomplete without a few words on that maid-of-all work, the dinghy. A faithful servant, sometimes with a fickle reputation, has to be endowed with all the qualities and yet has to keep out of the way when she is not needed.

Throughout this section the dinghy has often been called upon to help, but not yet for towing. Now it is time to consider the role it is really designed for – fetching and carrying between ship and shore.

These trips are sometimes hazardous. The dinghy is nearly always overloaded with crew and their gear in a mistaken wish to reduce the number of trips. Firstly, overloading makes it difficult to control and, secondly no one can row or scull efficiently in a cramped space. The principal danger is being carried away by wind or current.

You can spot a good seaman by the way he uses his dinghy. If wind or current is very strong, he won't hestitate to carry or tow it to a point where wind or tide can work to his advantage. When rowing against the wind, he uses sharp, choppy strokes. When he arrives alongside his yacht, he does so head-to-wind or current. You can come alongside downwind or with the tide (unseamanlike however) but whatever you do don't hit the hull with a thump, at right angles, as if you were a pirate's boarding party.

Within its limits a dinghy has the same qualities as the boat it serves. It should be unsinkable; it should have an anchor or grapnel of 5 or 6lb weight with a light line of some 100ft; if it is to be rowed, it should have a spare oar on board; two paddles can come in useful and you should wear life jackets.

A dinghy can be either rigid (usually fibreglass) or inflatable. Our own preference is for the latter, which is much safer and it takes up less room.

On shore, the dinghy must not be left to bump against the jetty or harbour wall. Best of all, it should be pulled up the slipway.

What with gusty winds, tricky currents, shoals, difficult channels, deep mud and boats everywhere, a landfall is fraught with uncertainty. A good seaman is never doctrinaire and is always ready to improvise and adapt to a new situation. He must be able to handle his boat effortlessly and be on the alert. The elements are not always against you. You can use the gusts and lulls intelligently; a current can be helpful; even other boats are not always a disadvantage, as we have tried to show. This chapter would be seriously incomplete without mention of a very important element in arrival and departure in boats. It is not technically an aspect of seamanship but it is nevertheless one of the delights of sailing.

This is, quite simply, the welcome you get in any port. Obviously you must not depend on it too much, but it would be boorish to ignore it. There will be onlookers on the quay, always ready to give a hand and to take or cast off a mooring line. People in boats Ports are worlds on their own, slightly divorced from the town and protected from the hazards of the open sea; the atmosphere is relaxed and bad manners leave an even uglier stain than an oil slick. People in close proximity usually find a *modus vivendi*. This relationship begins anew each time you steer towards an unknown boat to tie up and a welcoming hand takes your line. This is the true brotherhood of the sea.

11. Changing Sail

In earlier chapters we have discussed procedures for changing sail to meet the requirements of weather, points of sailing or in waters – restricted or otherwise – when boat control is important. These drills are all part of boat handling in its broadest sense and must be carried out smoothly and quickly. The business of sail changing and reefing take a little time and slow up the boat; while hoisting or lowering a spinnaker should not affect normal progress. If each drill is performed competently, with meticulous care to detail, all goes smoothly; but, if not, confusion reigns.

It is a question of doing everything the right way and minor carelessness can create major trouble.

Sail changes often have to be made under arduous conditions, when the fate of a sail can depend on the proverbial thread: a jib blows overboard because someone has forgotten to snap a hank on to the lifeline, or a mainsail tears because a reefpoint has been overlooked.

Sail changes involve lowering, hoisting, tightening the luff, hardening sheets. If they are not properly done these routine operations can, in themselves, give rise to problems: something jams, possibly bringing the boat to a grinding halt.

This chapter describes how to change sails and aims to show how to get the best out of them. It will examine exhaustively (not, we hope, exhaustingly) all you can do to reach high efficiency and to conserve your sails.

Except for the spinnaker, dinghies are not usually concerned with sail changes on the move (when the wind is too strong, you come in). But, no matter what kind of boat you are sailing, there are certain principles to be observed.

1 Work out procedures that leave the boat without canvas for as short a time as possible. With practice, a really good crew can learn to change a sail or take in a reef in less than a minute, and can set a spinnaker in ten seconds. But do not rush at it, and be prepared, or a jib will come out of its bag wrong way up and be hoisted that way or a reef will be tied round the lifeline and the spinnaker turned into a trawl.

2 As soon as a sea gets up, the crew should wear safety harness and hook on. The old saw, 'one hand for the boat and one for yourself' no longer applies. Now you can have both hands for the boat, the job is quicker and there is no more danger of falling overboard. This is important because picking up a man overboard while changing sail is specially difficult because the boat is not easy to handle.

3 Choose time and place carefully. Close-hauled particularly, a boat loses power when she is robbed of canvas, slows up and makes leeway; you must have plenty of sea room down to leeward.

4 Each job should be done according to a strict routine, familiar to everyone. And never start until everyone is ready.

One lifeline for yourself and two hands for the boat

The Jib

Modern sailing boats usually have several jibs, each with its particular use. There should be one to suit all conditions.

A jib can be hoisted or lowered on all points of sailing, but it is done most easily on a reach, when the foredeck is not cluttered up with thrashing headsails or murderous clews, and it is a simple matter to get the new sheets trimmed.

Procedures depend on the yacht's rig. Some cruising boats have everything duplicated: forestays, halyards, sheets. This is all rather elaborate and it is worth examining the *pros* and *cons*.

Not only is it not necessary to have two forestays, it is positively better to have only one. Two forestays are not practical because the hanks jam between the two stays, and neither stay can be made sufficiently taut. That is enough to condemn the whole system.

Two tack positions are convenient and certainly make for efficiency.

Two halyards are acceptable, although they can cause confusion.

It is useful to have two sets of sheets.

In practice, speed is seldom achieved with the aid of complicated equipment. A foredeck as clear and open as a dance floor is the best guarantee of quick and accurate work up in front.

Changing Jibs

Preparing the New Jib

If you are handling a fairly small jib, bring it up on deck in its bag and make the bag fast roughly where the clew of the sail will be when it is hoisted. If the sail has been bagged up properly, its tack will be on top and ready to hand.

If the jib is large, it should have been rolled in a long sausage before being put away, and it is brought up as it is and laid along the deck by the lifeline.

To hank it on, take the tack forward and fasten it in position (if there is only one tack position fasten the lowest hank to the stay).

Undo the lowest hank of the jib which is to come off; hank the new sail onto the stay, to windward of the old one and between its tack and second hank. Now for the sheets.

Preparing the Sheets

There are several ways.

The new jib has its own sheets and they run through special fairleads, and they can be immediately rove through.

The same sheets are used for both jibs, running through the same fairleads: nothing need be altered.

The same sheets are used for the two jibs but with different fairleads. The weather sheet must then be taken and brought round to leeward and passed through the fairlead for the new jib.

The new jib has its own sheets but they use the same fairleads as the sheets which are about to come off. This time you cannot reeve the new sheets before the old jib has been taken down.

The jib about to be hoisted has been hanked on

To save time, the windward sheet is passed through the fairlead that will serve the new jib

Proper Use of Winches

Nearly all winches turn clockwise (when a winch turns the other way, it is usually because the pawls have been put in back to front), and the rope that is to be hauled in is put round the winch drum in the same clockwise direction.

In general, the more turns you have on the drum the less strain there will be on the tail which you hold in your hand. But if there are too many turns, they will ride up: a lower turn will climb up onto the next one and cause a jam (riding turn) which is extremely difficult to clear.

Proper winch drill, therefore, must take account of this hazard which can prove to be very awkward; the basic rule is never to put more turns on the drum than is necessary.

Sheet Winches

Start by hauling in most of the slack by hand, without using the winch.

When nearly all the slack is in, put a single turn on the drum and continue to haul.

At the first sign of any real strain on the sheet, put on a second turn; don't use the winch handle until you can pull in no further by hand.

When the rope on the drum and the winch turns without winding in the sheet, put on one more turn.

Continue in this way, until you have four or even five turns on the drum if necessary.

As soon as you see any likelihood of the bottom turn riding up, allow all the turns to slip by winching without hauling in and the riding turn will disappear.

To cast a sheet off the winch, simply lift the rope upwards directly above the drum. Even with top action winches the handle can be left in place during this movement provided that it fits well.

Halyard Winches

Hoist first without the winch.

Put one or two turns onto the winch towards the end, and then add turns each time the strain becomes too much, as with a sheet. If the final haul of the halyard falls between the clicks of two pawls on the winch, to engage the next pawl allow the turns to slip very slightly on the drum while continuing winding. A

Fouling a sheet on the winch. This is what is called 'a riding turn': the bottom turn is riding up over the one above and the sheet can no longer be released

Freeing a riding turn. The only way is to keep the free end from catching round the drum. It is kept clear with the left hand and pulled straight up with the right, without making the slightest rotary movement

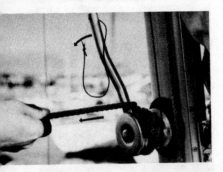

Clearing a halyard winch. This time you pull horizontally. The handle can stay in as it does not hinder the operation in the slightest

You can lend a hand in front of the fairlead but never between fairlead and winch for the sheet reaches the drum at a bad angle and the turns ride over

A little too much slack has been left in the halyard when it was being transferred from one jib to the other. It seems to be rolled round the stay but when you hoist away the turns will unwind

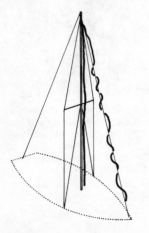

halyard is taken off a winch in the same way as a sheet.

General Precautions

Never haul on a line in front of a winch. This is the best way to get a riding turn without noticing it (particularly at night) and, if you have to make a sudden tack or get the sail down, you are jammed, baulked, betrayed and helpless.

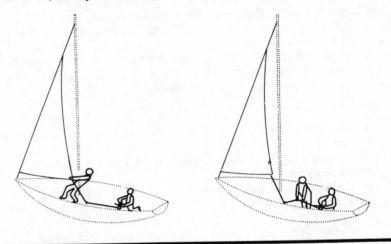

Lowering Sail

If you are reaching or running when the jib is lowered, the sheet should be hauled in at the same time to prevent the sail falling into the water; but if you are close-hauled, you should ease the sheet slightly to allow the hanks to run free on the forestay.

Changeover of Head, Tack and Clew

As soon as the old jib is down, make fast the fall of the halyard on a cleat; lay the heads of both sails side by side and transfer the halyard from one to the other.

Take great care here, particularly at night. If the halyard is allowed to be too slack, it can only too easily foul itself in the rigging; if you delay transferring it from one jib to the other, there is a risk that it will get a wrap round the forestay.

Unhank the old jib off the stay. If you put an arm between the halyard and the forestay, there is less risk of undoing the hanks of the new jib by mistake. Before changing over tacks of the two sails (when you only have one tack point) snap one or two hanks of the old jib onto the lifeline to stop it taking flight.

Change sheets from one jib to the other or reeve the leeward sheet of the new jib through the fairlead.

Hoist, Stretch, Trim

The jib should be hoisted quickly and as soon as it is up, sheet in slightly, just enough to stop the clew flapping. Now stretch the luff fully and do not sheet fully in until the halyard is made fast.

The jib has been dropped on the one you are about to hoist. Which hanks belong to which jib? Putting an arm between the forestay and halyard makes things clearer

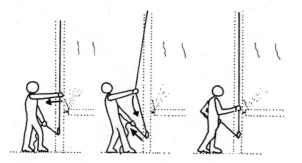

Tidying Up

Reeve the weather sheet through the fairlead if necessary, then stow the old jib. Small jibs are stowed in a bag by putting the clew in first, then the head, so that the tack shall always be on top.

Large jibs should be remade up into a sausage on deck and held together with ti-ers, and then taken below clew first (either into a bag or directly into the sail locker) with the tack uppermost ready for use.

Sweating up. Some yachtsmen make like plucking a harp string rather than really sweating on the halyard. This is how to go about it. When the sail has been hoisted tight, take a turn with the fall of the halyard under the cleat and keep it tight with the left hand. Put your foot against the mast, hold the halyard with the right hand, shoulder-high and fall back to tauten it. Then let it come back to the mast, pulling down hard at the same time and taking in the slack with the left hand

The Mainsail

The mainsail is generally a more difficult sail than the jib. You cannot hoist or lower it on every point of sailing; the helmsman will find that keeping the boat sailing when the mainsail is not filled poses problems; when the wind blows up and you must reduce canvas, instead of changing mainsails (you are unlikely to have two and, in any case, the exercise takes time) you reduce its area by tying in reefs or rolling the boom. Although it is not complicated, it is also an operation to be done in a set routine and we shall look at it in detail later, after considering the general principles.

Hoisting, Lowering

The wind must be forward of the beam. The sail must be able to flap freely if it is to slide smoothly up and down the mast, without bearing against the rigging. This cannot be done unless the wind is somewhere between dead ahead and a close reach. Even with a beam wind, the bolt rope or slides are pressed over tightly and move reluctantly.

If there is need, you can drop sail even on a reach: if the jib is slightly sheeted in, the mainsail luff is back winded and it will slide down easily

The jib can assist in the operation: if you sheet it in rather more than is necessary, it backwinds the mainsail and enables it to be hoisted with the wind abeam even if the topmast shrouds are fixed to the deck aft of the mast.

The boom should be eased, particularly when you finish hoisting and when you start to lower, otherwise the cloth will be stretched on the bias and the bolt rope will be strained at the entrance to the groove or at the first slide. This will quickly stretch the sail out of shape and there is also a risk of ripping off the bolt rope, a slide or even the track.

The boom is eased up by taking the weight on the topping lift. On small boats without topping lifts, the outer end of the boom is held up. This can only be done when you are sailing close-hauled. *Whoever lifts it should be to leeward and not too near the end of the boom:* he cannot get a good purchase anywhere else.

Ways of Reducing Sail

There is a choice of two systems: reef points or roller reefing. Reef points are the traditional way of reducing canvas on a mainsail. Reef bands are sewn into the sail in rows at different heights. Onto these reinforcing patches, on each side of the sail are sewn short lengths of line: the reef points. When you want to reduce sail, the mainsail between the foot and the first or second row of reef points is folded up and laced tightly with the reef points.

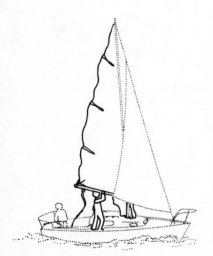

Lift the boom before sweating up or lowering. Otherwise the boltrope jams at the foot of the mast groove

For roller reefing, the boom can be rotated and the mainsail is thus rolled round it – like a blind.

The roller-reefing system is convenient and quick, its basic advantages being that the sail can be reduced as much or as little as is wanted, and it can be used even when the boat is not close-hauled.

In practice it has some disadvantages: it is more expensive and can go wrong; if the main sheet is attached anywhere but to the outer end of the boom, travelling jaws have to be used. They are the weak link in the system and are not recommended for long cruises. Lastly and not least, the roller system does not allow the sail to set so well because it is difficult to keep the tension even along the foot, and the sail loses its shape rapidly.

Reef points have one drawback: the sail can be reduced only by set amounts, sometimes more than is wanted. But they do allow the sail to set well. If the reefing is well done, it will have a good flow and run no risk of stretching badly; the operation is simple and, not being mechanical, there is nothing to go wrong. As the boom does not rotate, the sheet can be attached at the most practical place.

Although roller reefing has become popular, reef points are the more reliable method and you should be familiar with it. Even on sails that have a rotating boom, it is a wise precaution to have one row of reef points, for if the roller reefing gear breaks down, the weather is inevitably bad.

Reefing

If reefing is to be done efficiently, the right working conditions must be arranged.

The whole length of the boom must be accessible, and the sail must not be full. You should therefore be sailing to windward, full-and-by.

If you sail more free than that, with the mainsail flapping, the boom is out of reach. Do not be on a more close-hauled course because the boat will stop and fall off onto a reach: the mainsail then fills again, the boat heels, comes back on the wind, slows and bears away again. And while this goes on your crew are growing frantic! It is equally difficult to work properly by heaving to (with the jib backed to windward) as is sometimes recommended, because you cannot maintain this position without the mainsail sheeted home lightly and filled.

However, the sail should not be filled during the whole operation or tying in the reefs carefully will be gratuitously hard.

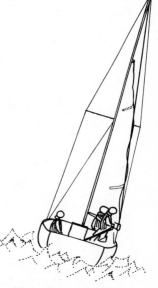

Provided the mainsheet is well secured, the boom provides good support when you are reefing

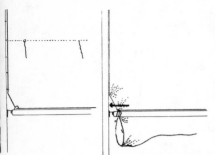

The boltrope is at an angle at the tack but quite straight at the level of the reefing points. It must be possible to hook on the new tack nearer to the mast than the normal tack

Equally, the sail should not be allowed to flap wildly nor for too long. This will damage it, stretching the leech in particular; the battens, too, can break and tear the sail. This is one of the reasons why everything must be done quickly. If the sail shakes violently while a reef is being taken in, it is often because it is under too much tension. The remedy is to haul up a little on the topping lift, or lower the halyard slightly.

Finally, the boom must be held steady. If it is swinging about, it is just about as easy to thread a row of pearls sitting on a bucking bronco as to take in a reef. The boom should be held at a convenient height by the topping lift and the sheet, and athwartships by the crew leaning against it as they work. If there is no topping lift, the outer end of the boom is lowered to the deck and held fast by the sheet.

In both cases the sheet should always be made fast on its cleat. If it is held by hand, it may slip, accompanied by the characteristic splash of someone falling in the water.

Making the Sail Set Well

A well set mainsail, no matter how much it is reefed down, is invaluable in fresh winds. As we have seen, this is the main advantage of reefing points, because if the tack and clew pendants are properly secured and the reef points carefully tied, the sail can set perfectly.

The tack cringle should be made fast down on the boom and as near the mast as possible – nearer even than the normal tack, where the sailmaker will almost certainly have finished off the lower part of the luff at an angle as in the diagram which is not possible at the cringle. If the new tack is too far aft, the sail will have creases and, more seriously, the bolt rope at the entrance to the groove or at the first slide will be strained.

On many boats, the boom has a special hook to which the new tack cringle is attached. Nevertheless, you should know how to lash it down, which is also the only remedy when roller-reefing jams. It is not easy, and the lashing must not interfere with the movement of the goose neck which would cut through it.

The clew cringle should also be secured hard down on the boom,

Making fast the tack reefing pendant
A. Make the line fast to the reefing cringle with a bowline, pass it under the boom and back through the cringle . . .
B. . . . then round the mast and through the cringle again . . .
C. . . . finish off with two half-hitches round the part of the line going round the mast

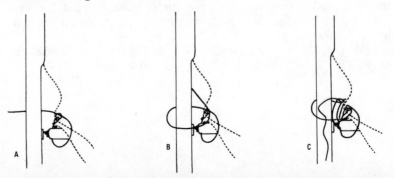

otherwise the aftermost reef point could give. But it should not be pulled too hard aft, and it is important to put just the right amount of tension on the foot for several reasons: if it is stretched too much, the sail will be out of shape along the line of the reef; if it is stretched too little, it is the reef points which will carry the load and might tear the sail. Above all, it is the tension along the foot which determines the shape of the sail and it must be right.

The clew is held by one or two pendants, and they can be secured in several ways to make reefing quick and to achieve even tension along the foot.

The reef points hold down the bunched part of the sail. If the foot runs on a track, the reef pendants are knotted between the sail and the boom; this keeps even tension along the foot. If the foot bolt rope runs in a groove, you have to tie the pendants round the boom, the bunched sail can slip then to the side and, with the wind aft, it may chafe between the boom and the shroud (another good reason for making a figure of eight knot in the sheet to stop it in the block just before the boom reaches the shroud).

On sails of low aspect ratio (where the boom is relatively long) the reef points pull on the sail rather like slides, causing strain on the cloth. Instead of reef points, you can use continuous lacing which allows tension to be spread out evenly, but it is a lengthy operation. In sails of high aspect ratio, the foot does not have to be kept so taut and a shockcord can be used purely to hold in the bunched cloth.

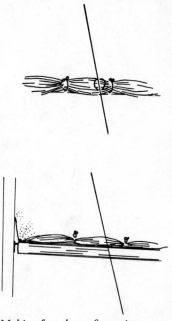

Making fast the reefing points
If knotted round the boom they let the canvas slip and it can be nipped between boom and shroud when running. Knotted between boom and sail the canvas is held better

Taking in a Reef

The simplest method, which does not need special equipment, and the one that is normally used on small boats, is also the one to use if your roller reefing jams. This is how it is done.

Securing the Reef Pendants

You can use one line or two. The single pendant can be attached permanently on the sail, but the double pendant is likely to get fouled.

The single pendant can be made fast to the reef cringle with a bowline, rove through the end of the boom, then taken once again through the cringle and finished off by two loose half hitches at the normal clew if the line is long enough, or else on the reef cringle.

This allows you to be ready well in advance, but no matter how light it is, it is better not to have it on permanently because it will chafe the sail a little.

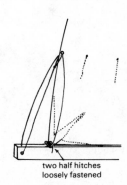

two half hitches
loosely fastened

Single clew pendant rove and ready for use

It is generally best to use a line of about 9–10ft even if there is going to be quite a lot of slack after the reef has been taken in, for it is handier to lash.

Lowering the Sail

Sail full-and-by and take the strain of the main boom on the topping lift. Lower a fair amount of canvas (enough for two reefs when you are taking in one) so that you can bring the boom easily towards the centre of the boat as the sail is not filling. If the luff runs on a track, take off at least one slide too many, not forgetting to turn back the stop to prevent the lot from falling out.

Make fast the halyard as soon as you have lowered as much sail as you want.

If the crew is tired and you want to make the work easier, you can lower the whole mainsail; but remember that the boat will be under-canvassed and liable to roll. There is also the danger of mixing up the reef points of two different rows, and the odd line, sheet, preventers or safety line has been known to get tied in by mistake. In any case, letting the mainsail right down is only really practical when the boat has the wind somewhere near the beam.

Reefing

The boom must be held absolutely steady, then bowse down the reefed tack cringle to the tack shackle or make it fast with a lashing.

At the clew, follow the diagram if you are using a single reef line. Stretch the foot by means of the pendant, take a turn round the boom with losing tautness, finish off with a half hitch around the two after parts of the pendant and then tuck the loop and the free end of the pendant into the slack of the sail.

If you are using double pendants, they should be rove as shown in the diagram.

The longer pendant passes through the end of the boom, back through the cringle and then, after the foot has been stretched, it is made fast with a half hitch around its own running parts, close to the cringle.

The shorter pendant is taken once or twice round the boom and

Reeving a single clew pendant

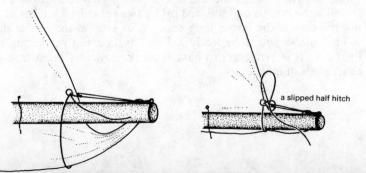

a slipped half hitch

then made fast by a half hitch on the cringle or in the same way as the longer pendant.

Whether you use one or two pendants, you should not have to apply great strength. If you have to use force to bring the new clew down into position, something is wrong:

You are sailing too free, or have been trying to sail too close to the wind and the boat keeps slowing and bearing away too far from the wind.
You have not lowered enough sail and you will be impeded by the sail flapping.

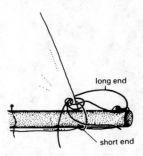
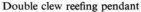

Double clew reefing pendant

Point to Remember

Reefing pendants tend to ensnare anything within sight! The points to watch are the mainsheet, the stern rail, the life lines, life buoys and suchlike.

Reefing pendants should always be made fast by only one thumb knot, using a large loop and tied hard up against the cringle to keep the running parts tight. Any extra knot is dangerous, because it will not untie easily and a reef pendant must be capable of being released quickly.

Hoist, Harden and Trim

Take up the weight of the boom on the topping lift. When hoisting do not replace the slide that you took off when you lowered, for it will almost certainly pull at the luff and damage the sail.

When the halyard is hard up and made fast, ease the topping lift, sheet in the sail and start sailing again.

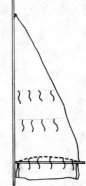

Foot not stretched enough

Examine the Sail

If the reef makes a marked curve away from the boom, the foot has not been pulled right out. Equally, it has been pulled too much if the row of reefing points lies hard up above the boom. As a guide, the curve of the reef in relation to the boom should be between 3 and 5 per cent of the length of the foot.

It is possible, but not easy, to slacken off the foot; and quite impossible to stretch it without again lowering the sail.

Tying the Reef Points

Sail close-hauled so that all of the foot can be reached, then pull all the slack canvas to windward and fold it up tightly. The reef point

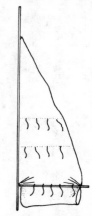

Foot stretched too much

should be tied round the folded sail with a bow.

If it is essential to sail on any point other than close-hauled, you can delay tying the reef points without any harm.

All that remains to be done is to tighten the kicking strap and the job is finished. The whole operation takes longer to describe than to carry out. In practice, with a well trained crew, the boat need not be much more than a minute without her mainsail.

One last point. If the wind blows up strongly, you may have to take in two reefs straight away. If you have enough time (and enough sea room to leeward), it is better to take them in one at a time. Otherwise, if you want to increase sail slightly, you have to shake out both reefs and then take in the first one again.

Shaking Out a Reef

This is simple and quick, but great precaution is needed over the first step of the operation: *all* reef points must be undone. It should be one person's responsibility and a second should check that none has been overlooked. If the former takes umbrage, more fool he for this kind of mistake can happen all too easily, and in any case it is better to offend one man than to tear a sail which upsets the whole crew.

You will have come into the wind. You now only have to:

Take up the weight of the boom on the topping lift.
Undo the half hitch on the clew pendant; release the tack.
Lower some sail so that you can fit the slides on the mast track.
Hoist, stretch the luff, bear away on course.
Stow the reef pendants.

If you have no topping lift, you must remember to hold up the boom as you release the clew pendant or it will fall heavily on the deck.

Roller Reefing

There is one essential difference between tying in a reef and roller reefing: the latter can be done while there is wind in the mainsail. You only need to ease the sheet just enough to let the luff lift and allow the slides to move on the mast track. You can reef down when you are sailing more freely than full-and-by, provided the slides will slip down the track.

The two main points to watch are: rolling the boltrope of the luff correctly and stretching the foot evenly.

Winding the Boom

Rolling the Boltrope. This is easier if the boom is bevelled at the mast end in order to allow for the extra thickness of the boltope as it is rolled up. In any case, for a neat job you should:

> Keep the luff under tension as you roll by easing the halyard slowly as the boom turns.
> Take care that nothing gets caught in the roller gear (boltrope, slides, a fold of canvas).
> Don't let the slides get wound under the rolls of the sail.

Keeping the foot taut. This is the snag, for the only way of keeping the foot tight is to pull aft on the leech as you roll. Rather than a continuous pull, it is better to tug it back vigorously at regular intervals. Whatever you do, a good result cannot be guaranteed. To roll down properly, you need three hands:

> One on the halyard to ease off as required.
> One on the reefing handle, to roll down with one hand and guide the boltrope with the other.
> One to pull aft on the leech.

Shaking Out Roller Reefing

There is no difficulty here unless you only want to shake out some of the reef. That can be horribly tricky, for somehow you have to maintain constant tension on the luff rope as you unroll. If the two operations are not synchronised, the foot goes baggy and forms a nasty pocket near the tack.

If you are shaking out the whole reef, take up on the topping lift before unrolling and it will be easy to slip the slides back on the mast track.

Changing Mainsails

This takes a long time, easily twenty minutes in fresh conditions, even if the sail is not very big.

To lower and to hoist you must come into the wind but, once the sail has been lowered, there is obviously nothing to prevent you sailing more free.

Furling a mainsail

The main problem is keeping a clear head. It is advisable to take the first sail below before bringing up the second. It is equally advisable to have the new sail conveniently folded when it is brought on deck.

The best way to fold up a mainsail is to stretch out the foot and then flake down the sail by the luff and leech backwards and forwards onto it, and that is a job that can only properly be done in the calm of a port; at sea, the wind has a way of wreaking havoc on such orderliness.

You must thus think of something else. Make a deep fold along the foot, equal to the depth of one short reef, and push the rest of the sail into it as evenly as possible. Close the fold around the sail and tie it together.

If you are leaving the sail on the boom when you are in port, this is a neat, seamanlike method.

The Spinnaker

The spinnaker (kite or chute for *afficionados*) was designed as a racing sail and its whole style reflects its origin. A bit of an aristocrat, it is a sail that requires a lot of equipment, and is very impatient: it expects to be trimmed as soon as it is hoisted (or it will play you up). The envious call it a capricous sail, but it is not unreasonably demanding; it only dislikes half measures. Like a sensitive woman, it is liable to swoon, to the consternation of its admirers.

We have already examined spinnaker trim when on course and its control during the gybe. Hoisting and lowering deserve more attention because most of the tribulations of using it (for beginners at least), are encountered during these two operations.

The Sail

The first spinnakers used for racing looked like twin staysails sewn together down the luff. Over the years the sides of the sail have been rounded and it has been given more belly, to the point where we now have the curved and full breasted triangle which is vertically symmetrical.

The apex of the sail (which is usually about 180°) is where the

halyard is attached or the head. The two lower corners are identical (and make angles of about 135°), and act either as the tack or the clew according to whether they are to windward or leeward. The side of the sail to windward becomes the luff and the leeward side the leech. The third side is the foot.

Spinnakers come in all sizes and are made of light or heavy cloth for winds of varying forces. Each has a different shape adapted to its function. The reaching spinnaker, which can be carried with the wind forward of the beam, is flatter than a running spinnaker, and cruising spinnakers are usually flatter and stronger than racing spinnakers.

Gear

The basic gear is:

A *halyard*, that passes through a block on the mast above the forestay, and has a swivel snap shackle at the upper end.

Two sheets to control the angle and trim of the sail. One is fixed to the tack and the other to the clew and they change names according to the tack the boat is on: the windward line is the *guy*, the one to leeward is the *sheet*. Both sheet and guy pass through fairleads or blocks usually sited as far aft as possible, and they are hauled in on winches. On some large boats these lines are duplicated so that each side of the spinnaker has a guy (often wire) *and* a sheet.

A *spinnaker pole*, which holds out the tack. On small boats the spinnaker pole is nearly always *double-ended* or symmetrical so that either end can be fastened to the mast or the sail. It is usually *single-ended* on large boats, which also often have a track to raise or lower the pole or its *cup* on the mast.

A *spinnaker pole topping lift* supports the pole and allows it to be raised to a required angle. It is made fast to the pole either at the middle (small boats) or its outer end (large boats).

A *spinnaker pole downhaul* stops the pole from skying. On small boats it is usually fastened to the centre of the pole and brought back to the foot of the mast, so that the pole can be moved horizontally without having to adjust the downhaul. On large boats it is usually taken to a fairlead at the bow and has to be fastened to the end of the pole. You cannot then move the position of the pole without adjusting the downhaul.

Even on a cruising boat, it is convenient to have all these ropes controlled in the cockpit to let you trim the sail without having to send a hand up to the foredeck.

Dinghy Spinnakers

How you hoist and lower a spinnaker in a dinghy is governed by the dictates of balance. Although it is possible, with practice, to hoist to leeward, it is usual to hoist and lower to windward. All crews work hard at developing technique and gear to cut down seconds and flip the sail up and down under the most difficult conditions. We are only going to consider here standard methods and standard equipment.

Preparing the Spinnaker

A spinnaker should set completely outside all rigging, forward of the forestay and outside the shrouds. In a dinghy there is no question of setting up the rigging under sail. All has to be prepared on shore. For simplification we are going to assume that the exercise will take place on the starboard tack.

The sail is got ready on the starboard side, flaked so that it will go up in good order. The halyard, guy and sheet are snapped onto the sail and all pass from the cockpit forward of the starboard shroud; they are held in jam cleats near the shrouds so that they do not get caught and pull the sail out. Each has to be properly rove and must not get in the way of the jib.

The *spinnaker* itself is stowed in a chute or turtle where there is not too much risk of it falling overboard if you capsize. Start by pushing in the middle of the foot until you reach the two lower corners, which should be set one on each side. Continue by folding in the two luffs through your hand to ensure that the sail is not twisted, put all this in with the head on top of the pile.

The *halyard* comes down beside the starboard shroud, passes underneath the jib sheet, in front of the shroud, back into the boat and the other end is attached to the head, usually with a bowline.

The *guy* (in this case the starboard line), which is fixed to the spinnaker tack, comes out forward of the starboard shroud, passes underneath the jib sheet, and thence to its fairlead aft and then into the cockpit.

The *sheet* (port line) goes forward of the starboard shroud and underneath the jib sheets, then round the front of the forestay, outside the port shroud, and thence to the fairlead aft and into the cockpit.

The *topping lift* and *downhaul* are usually permanent fittings on the mast. The topping lift is often a simple piece of shock-cord, running alongside a preventer to stop the pole from dropping too low. The downhaul is led to the foot of the mast and from there runs aft to the helmsman.

The *spinnaker pole* is double-ended and has a fixing device in the middle (e.g. jam cleat) for the topping lift and downhaul. The pole is usually fastened to the spinnaker tack just before hoisting.

Hoisting

A spinnaker is usually hoisted with the wind aft. It can, in fact, be an advantage to come slightly onto a broad reach, to reduce roll and keep the jib firmly to leeward out of the way. When the spinnaker is hoisted, the mainsail sheet should be eased right off until its figure of eight knot catches in the block.

A. and B. The helmsman stands up, tiller between his legs, to control lateral balance, and sufficiently aft to compensate for the crew's weight forward; he holds sheet and guy in his hands

The crew stands near the mast and puts the windward jib sheet behind his back so that the spinnaker doesn't catch on it

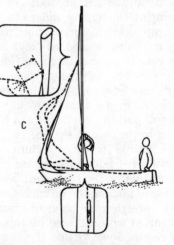

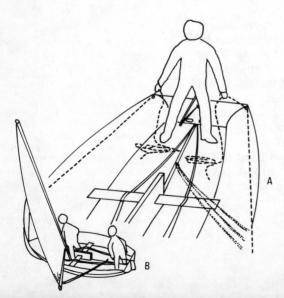

C. The crew hoists quickly, helping the spinnaker up and out and guiding it to prevent it catching on the spreaders and forestay; he sweats it up tight (a knot will have been made, if necessary, on the halyard so that the head stops a few centimetres from the mast). He belays the halyard

The helmsman pulls in the sheet as the spinnaker rises to bring the clew round the forestay, then he adjusts guy and sheet to let the sail unfurl

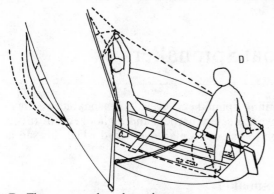

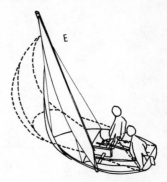

D. The crew pushes the pole out, hooking on the topping lift and downhaul, hooks the pole to the mast and adjusts its height

The helmsman helps the pole to go out by adjusting the guy and then adjusts the spinnaker

E. The crew takes control of the spinnaker; he cleats the guy and sits out to windward, holding the sheet in his hand

Lowering

A spinnaker comes down most easily on a broad reach. In this way the sail is conveniently blanketed by the mainsail. Always lower to windward; if you have to hoist again a little later, remember that you can only do so from the side where you lowered.

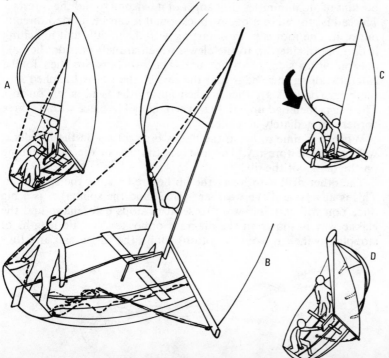

A. The crew stands near the mast with the windward jib sheet behind his head so that the spinnaker comes in underneath it. The helmsman stands as he did during hoisting and takes hold of sheet and guy
B. The crew unhooks the pole from the mast and brings it in behind him, taking off at the same time the topping lift and downhaul. Then he releases the pole from the tack. The helmsman lets go the guy
C. The crew pulls on the tack to bring the whole spinnaker over to windward. The helmsman releases the guy
D. The crew releases the halyard and brings in the sail, tack first and then the luff up to the headboard (the clew must come in last so that the spinnaker doesn't fill again during the operation)

The helmsman adjusts the centreplate, holding the jib sheet, and puts the boat back on course

The crew stows the spinnaker carefully, the three corners sticking up free; he jams halyard, guy and sheet in their cleats; he adjusts and cleats the halyard, gets back in position and takes over the jib sheet

Cruising Boat Spinnakers

When you are handling spinnakers, even in reasonable weather, you should always wear a safety harness and be hooked on. It is a long and difficult job to fish out a man overboard when this sail is up.

Preparing the Spinnaker

All the spinnaker gear, guy, sheet and downhaul are permanently rigged on the boat, but the sail is only brought on deck when it is to be hoisted.

The Sail

The sail should be made ready in the relative calm of the cabin (no smoking and no cooking while it is going on). The time spent on preparation obviously varies according to your system for hoisting.

Normally it is practical to hoist when the jib is up. The various steps that have to be taken need your full concentration and the following drill prevents the sail going up too early and, most important of all, minimises the danger of it twisting round the forestay. The sail is stowed in a bag or bucket and it can be hoisted directly out of it. The foot is put in, starting with the middle and bunching it in on both sides up to the clews, which are left outside the bag, one on either side, ready for use. The two luffs are then folded carefully along their edge and the rest of the sail is bunched into the bag. The luffs are then pushed in and the head is left on top. The bag is then tied up lightly to keep the sail in place with its three corners immediately accessible.

When it is time to hoist, the bag is brought up on the foredeck, well aft of the forestay. This reduces the risk of the sail catching on the hanks of the jib.

The other drill is to lower the jib before hoisting the spinnaker. This is advisable if the weather is fresh and the spinnaker is a big one. You will certainly want to set it in stops beforehand and the classic way is shown in the diagram opposite. You tie lengths of stopping twine (in wool or cotton) round the furled sail and they

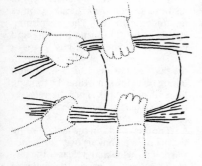

Furling the spinnaker: the two edges are brought together by taking in folds of the sail without rolling it up, then one edge is wrapped round the whole sail (as for furling a mainsail).

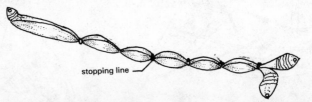

stopping line

break easily when pulled. These are the 'stops'. The first is tied at least six feet from the head (otherwise it may not break) and the rest are tied closer together as they reach the foot.

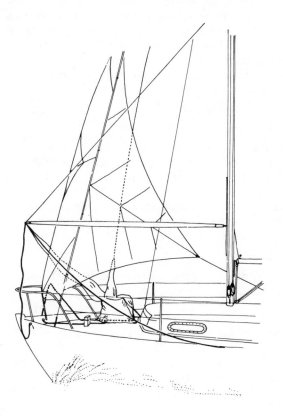

What the skipper has to check

To windward: the tack of the spinnaker is in front of the forestay, the guy comes aft outside everything, and the downhaul passes between the pulpit stanchions
To leeward: the halyard is clear from top to bottom on the lee side, the sheet passes over the guardrails and outside everything, and the downhaul passes over the pulpit and then between its stanchions

The spinnaker bag is placed well aft of the forestay. Everything can run clear

Hoisting

Broad Reach

Particularly in strong winds you want to bear away to let the sail go up in the lee of the mainsail.

Never hoist with the wind dead aft because the disturbed air behind the mainsail will prevent the spinnaker setting well; in medium weather get onto a reach, and in fresh weather on a broad reach.

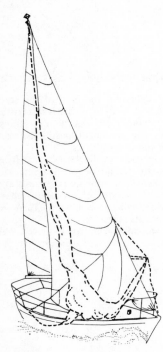

The spinnaker should be set in the lee of the jib to prevent it catching on the hanks

Spinnaker net

Hoisting

The boom should lie fore and aft, right up against the forestay, and the sheet must be completely free. This is a precaution to stop the spinnaker filling too soon.

Then hoist quickly. In strong winds it is best to take a turn on a winch for if you hoist directly by hand, the man on the job might literally take off if the spinnaker filled too soon, in spite of the above precautions.

If you are hoisting without stops, the crew on the foredeck lets the luff run out of the bag through his hands to windward, while the rest of the sail goes up to leeward.

Trimming the Guy

As soon as the head is within a few inches of its block at the top, make the halyard fast and fill the sail as quickly as possible, by pulling aft on the spinnaker pole until it is at right angles to the apparent wind.

If the sail gets into a tangle the reason usually is that the tack and the clew have been reversed. All you can do is to lower and begin all over again.

Trimming the Sheet

As soon as the pole has been squared and braced, harden the sheet until the spinnaker is filling nicely.

Sail Trim

You can now get back on course and adjust the sails' trim to your course.

It is usually possible to keep up the jib as well when you are reaching, and can give extra thrust; but you may prefer to replace it with a spinnaker staysail, big boy or tallboy, which are cut for the purpose.

But on a broad reach or a dead run the jib can get in the way while the spinnaker goes up, and it is wise to lower it. To stop the spinnaker wrapping round the forestay, some advocate the use of a *spinnaker net*, but opinions are divided. To be really efficient, the size of mesh should be about one sixth of the height of the luff. Do not use snap hooks or piston hanks for the net as they catch in the spinnaker. Fasten it to the forestay with bow knots. If you have the misfortune to wrap up spinnaker and net, watch out!

You may decide not to use anything at all, but whatever you do *never leave the jib halyard running down the forestay* because if the spinnaker collapses, it may get caught between the two in a monumental tangle.

Lowering

Hoisting the Jib First

Spinnaker gear (pole, topping lift and downhaul) permitting, it is a good idea to hoist the jib just before lowering the spinnaker as this will help it to spill the wind more quickly and prevent it tangling round the forestay.

However, think at least twice before lowering the spinnaker and avoid any confusion on the foredeck.

The Correct Point of Sailing

The same principle applies to lowering and hoisting: the spinnaker should be lowered in the lee of the mainsail.

The best point of sailing for lowering is a broad reach, but don't have the wind too far aft, especially if there is any sort of sea running, for fear of gybing.

It is possible to lower on a beam reach, although there is less protection from the lee of the mainsail. This can even be a good way provided the crew is well drilled and the weather is light. It often happens that the decision to lower the spinnaker has to be taken on a beam reach if the wind is lightening and the sail flops, but your course does not allow you to bear away.

Ease the Main Sheet

At the moment of lowering, get maximum protection from the lee of the mainsail by easing the main sheet. If the mainsail is bearing against the lee shroud, there is the added advantage that the spinnaker will not wrap itself round the end of the spreaders as it comes down.

Warning

No smoking.

Release the Tack

Ease the guy until the tack can be reached and let go. On small boats, when the guy is spliced to the sail, release it completely.

The spinnaker will then fly away like a flag in the lee of the main.

In the interests of peace on the foredeck the spinnaker is taken straight below

Lowering

The halyard should be lowered just fast enough to let the sail be pulled steadily in. One or two hands should gather it in from the clew and pull it down below. Never take hold of the edges or the wind will fill it again and lead you quite a dance.

The spinnaker can be lowered straight onto the deck, but it may still have some life in it. You can slip on it and tear the cloth. It is best to bring it under the boom, outside the shrouds and down the main hatch.

Make Fast the Halyard

As soon as the halyard is taken off, make the end fast in its usual place. A rope halyard can be clipped on the pulpit (although it adds to windage), but a wire halyard must be made fast aft or it will get fouled on the hanks of the jib. It should really always be made up at the foot of the mast, and always take it back on the same side of the forestay to prevent confusion later. If the sail has been brought down on the opposite side, always take the halyard right round the forestay before attaching it to its usual place.

Tidying Up

Stow the spinnaker pole in its usual place. The guy and downhaul are made fast to the pulpit, and the slack taken up aft before being tied to the side of the deck with stopping twine to prevent them shifting. When everything has been cleared away, hoist the jib if you have not ventured to do so before lowering the spinnaker. And that's that.

When not in use guy and downhaul are made fast to the stanchions

Which Sail to Use?

Perfect sail drill comes with practice but only experience can enable you to take the right decision about when to change sail and which to hoist. The choice of sail can never be reduced to a simple rule of thumb such as: 'take in the first reef at Force 4'. The possible combinations are almost infinite, depending on the boat and the conditions prevailing, so only general indications can be given along the lines of what has been said in earlier chapters.

A boat's behaviour is formed at birth by her lines, weight, beam and sail plan. She can be either *stiff* or *tender*, capable of carrying more or less sail in a given wind strength. In fresh conditions, she can carry more or less weather helm and be more or less steady on reaching courses. In the first case heel, and in the second yawing, will soon show when action is needed.

When you are considering changes, you should always bear in mind that the shape and belly of the sails are as important as their area. As they are full in light conditions, they should be made gradually flatter and flatter as the wind increases. In gusty conditions, it is usually best to have the jib flat which will pull the boat along well in gusts, with a fairly full mainsail which will keep the boat moving in the lulls.

You must also consider the state of the sea: in a given force of wind you may carry full canvas in sheltered waters, but be obliged to reduce considerably in a lumpy sea.

There are other, less precise factors that will influence your decision, such as the experience of the crew and the kind of sailing you are doing. When racing (or if you just have a keen and enterprising crew) you want to lose as little speed as possible, so sail changes must be quick and fast; but if you have a crew of beginners, you should take every opportunity for practice: it's a question of trying out everything and learning the drill for each. When you are cruising, on the other hand, and if the crew is not practised, you should always take the safe course; sail is reduced earlier than necessary, knowing that the work becomes more difficult as the wind gets up; equally, think twice before putting on more canvas or hoisting the spinnaker.

There is no hard and fast rule. Nevertheless, there are basic principles: whatever you do you must have the boat under control, with a balanced sail plan that gives you sufficient thrust. Even if you are not racing, speed is important, for it makes for safety and pleasure. A boat under-canvassed is no better than one with too much sail: the one pitches up and down, the other wallows on her side; neither is very happy.

12. Heavy Weather Sailing

When do you decide the weather is bad? Without a doubt as soon as the wind and the sea stop you doing exactly what you want with the boat. Everything therefore depends on the boat, the crew and the skipper. The bad weather threshold is quickly reached by beginners; with experience the dividing line recedes.

It is probably true to say that the recent greatly increased popularity of sailing has drawn new attention to the whole question of bad weather with development in technique and materials, and to a new attitude as a result of offshore racing. We know now that even small boats can withstand extremely heavy weather without disaster; we are now used to making passages in conditions which, not so long ago, would have made us turn tail or at least heave to. It is also true that this more spartan attitude is accompanied by a far greater awareness of safety precautions.

Bad weather tests your personal stamina: you can no longer rely only on your equipment, and first of all you must know exactly how to use it.

We are not going to consider sailing dinghies in this chapter because in anything like bad weather they should not be at sea, even in well supervised waters; but all other boats, from daysailers to offshore cruisers, are, sooner or later, bound to be confronted with bad weather.

This possibility should always be kept in mind, well before the first warning cirrus appears in the sky. In bad weather, everything, or nearly everything, is a matter of foresight, both long and short term. The best safety measures and equipment will be of no avail on a boat with an ill prepared crew. We shall be emphasising the need for preparation, for it is the only subject on which one must lay down the law.

We shall discuss bad weather under three categories: *manageable* conditions, in which the boat can continue on her course, albeit seriously hampered; *barely manageable* conditions, when you are forced off your planned course, either heaving to or running before the storm; finally *unmanageable* conditions, when the boat is tossed about by the elements and all you can do is to survive as best you can. Obviously, the dividing line between the three degrees is variable. Your plan of action depends upon your assessment of the situation and the risks that may have to be run.

Preparing for Heavy Weather

Until you have experienced it, no one can imagine what bad weather can be like. Photographs and books by the great solo circum-navigators have described it all very well but, even so, only by going through it yourself can you appreciate what it is like to move and carry out even the simplest operations under storm conditions. Your state of mind is important and is an imponderable factor. The boat's violent pitching and the shrieking of the wind as it roars, at what seems to be hurricane force, can make you both frightened and apathetic, even if you are not seasick.

Long-term Precautions

Bad weather precautions must be easy to implement and be thoroughly understood by the whole crew.

Your equipment is vital. It must all be strong and easy to handle be it heavy weather sails, safety harnesses, hanks or shackles. Above all, make sure from time to time that they are in working order. You have to overcome a psychological reluctance to think about really bad weather and the equipment tends to be stowed in the remotest corners of the boat and left severely alone, as if, even to talk about it, let alone bring it on deck, might lay a powder trail which could lead to an explosion; but when you are about to bend on the trysail it is too late to realise that it needs repairing, or to start learning how to hoist it.

Improvisation is no good in bad weather. The sails should have been tried out at least once in boisterous conditions. This is the only way to find out if the equipment is equal to its task, and it will also give you some idea of how the boat will behave in really bad weather.

All special gear on board should be experimented with, such as sea anchor and warps for trailing astern. This will give some indication of their effectiveness and you may even find that a particular piece of equipment is not suitable for your boat and you can dispose of it and have more space for something useful.

Disaster can result from failure to attend to detail, and you must make a real effort, at least once, to visualise everything that might happen. This is not indulging in morbid pessimism; on the contrary, it is the way to reduce your fear of bad weather, which can haunt the happiest cruise.

Short-term Precautions

A sudden bad weather forecast, a disturbed sky or rapidly falling barometric pressure all call for various preparations, at short notice. These of course only relate to boats that are already at sea. *The best precaution when bad weather threatens and you are at a sheltered anchorage is to double up the mooring lines.* In such conditions there are *never* any valid reasons for putting to sea, least of all the need to keep an appointment or to get back to work. The latter is particularly stupid because a *force majeure* is a rare occurrence in our day and age but bad weather is just that and all sensible people accept it. But at sea you must act promptly when the outlook is black: your decision depends on where you are and the practical steps you must take to safeguard boat and crew.

Tactics

Run for Shelter. If you are near a sheltered coast there should be no hesitation: make for port. There are one or two conditions:

> The harbour must be easily recognisable. Visibility drops considerably in bad weather, and nothing looks more like one grey coastline than another grey coastline.
> Entrance to the chosen harbour should be easy under all conditions. Bad weather sometimes sets up a bar at the entrance of some well sheltered ports, making entry difficult or even impossible at certain states of the tide.

Whenever possible aim for shelter to windward rather than to leeward because, as you approach the shore, the *fetch* is reduced (fetch is the distance that the wind blows uninterrupted over the water).

Give Yourself Sea Room. When it looks as though you cannot run for shelter with reasonable safety, and the wind is blowing onshore, keep well out and never close to the land. This advice goes against all instincts of the landsman, but it is a long established fact that the seas are more regular in deep water and therefore less dangerous; and a missed tack or any setback will have less serious consequences well out to sea than when you are near a lee shore.

Get Clear of Dangerous Waters. Whatever you decide to do, you obviously keep well away from known hazards, such as shoals or narrow channels where contrary wind and currents make the seas break still more violently.

In shoal conditions, violent waves grow bigger and break. Breaking waves are probably the greatest danger in bad weather. A normal wave is merely water rising and falling vertically, without release of energy; the crest of one that breaks moves laterally, releasing enormous energy.

In narrow channels, when tide and wind are in the same direction, the swell lengthens but the waves do not break. But with wind against current, the swell is shortened and the waves break; it is this kind of condition which creates notorious disturbances like the Portland Race off the English south coast which can be formidable although a few miles offshore the sea is tolerable.

Considerations like this must be taken into account when you decide what to do. But there are always imponderables such as the strength of wind, how long the bad weather will last and the possibility of rigging or sails giving. In any event, prepare the boat and the crew for a seige, for that's what it is.

The Boat

Comfort in the Cabin. In storm conditions the cabin should be a kind of haven where you can get all-important rest. This depends to a large extent on how you have coped with two major problems: disorder and damp.

Everything must be stowed firmly in place. Stores, the medicine chest and the galley equipment must not fall about. If they spill all over the cabin and into the bilges, the result can have a disastrous effect even on the strongest stomachs and in a gale this can become a drama and life below becomes hellish.

It is never easy to keep the cabin absolutely dry. Start by pumping out the bilges, and this is a good check that the pumps are working.

Then turn the cabin into a kind of strong point, and ensure that all doors and hatches and ventilators are water-tight. Even stop up the hawse pipe. If the boat has a coach roof with large ports or windows, you should already have on board wooden panels which can be screwed on inside as reinforcements if the glass breaks (to repeat: it is too late to start making them under storm conditions; they should be ready, holes drilled, screws chosen and the screw driver available).

It is, of course, too much to expect complete waterproofing. For one thing, you'll have from time to time to open the main hatch to go out or come in. You should therefore stow in a safe place, carefully wrapped in plastic bags, everything that must be kept dry, matches in particular (it is always better to have several small boxes of matches rather than one or two big ones and at least one should be kept in a water-tight tin).

On Deck. You should clear everything off the deck that might get in the way. That means anything that is not indispensable to working the ship. Check the lashings of safety equipment (dinghy, life raft, life buoy, etc.). Lash all equipment firmly: spinnaker pole, boat hook, anchor. Make sure that everything is stowed in a way that makes for least resistance to wind and sea.

The Crew

Your first concern is sea sickness. This is a problem which can have serious results for everyone; it is only a joke in the music hall. Pass round the sea sick pills before the sea or stomachs begin to heave.

It is almost certain too that no one will be able to stay long in the galley so prepare some hot drinks and put them in vacuum flasks. Stow in a handy place food that is easy to eat (crackers, biscuits, dried fruit, chocolate). Next put on safety harnesses, which should be as strong and as effective as a parachutist's. They should fit really tightly.

Safety lines should be suited to the crew's duties: the helmsman and anyone who stays in the cockpit should have short ones so they cannot be swept overboard; the foredeck hands need more freedom of movement, but nevertheless their lines should not be more than six or seven feet long; they should never be hooked to the life rail but to a shroud or something equally strong or, best of all, special life-lines running the length of the deck from which the clip need never be taken off.

The harness may inhibit you at first and that is why you should get used to it before it becomes essential: in gale conditions this

discipline must never be relaxed for a single instant. You should not unhook until you are in the cabin; you should hook on before you leave it. It is just when you come up on deck that you are vulnerable. That may be the very moment when a monster wave breaks green over the boat.

Seamanship

All these precautions should be acted on according to a precise and unchanging plan. It is no exaggeration to say that your success in riding out a gale depends almost entirely on this.

It is difficult to be specific about seamanship – so much depends on circumstances. In this chapter, we work up to full gale force but in practice you can never foretell exactly what is going to happen. The gale can take an unexpected turn, and every decision must be reached in the light of the same foresight which dictated our early precautions: what is happening at any given moment is less important than what may happen a little later.

Within that context, we lay down two basic principles:

All decisions should be made in good time – before they must be carried into effect. Changing headsails can become as difficult • and dangerous as a high-wire act, whereas it might have been relatively easy five minutes earlier.

While there is still a choice of action, you should never be content with compromise. The crime is accepting developments passively: a boat heaving up and down for hours on end soon exhausts her crew, and the effort expended on a quick change of headsails or altering course, for instance, can make everything much more comfortable.

Adherence to these basic principles is important for the physical and moral well-being of the crew, and that is a skipper's prime concern.

Maintain Course

It is not often that gales arrive out of the blue with theatrical suddenness. Usually they can be seen coming and, initially, you can maintain course either to reach shelter or to gain sea-room.

Whether you are beating to windward or running free, the principles for each point of sailing still hold good, but everything becomes more difficult.

Beating to Windward

Rather than repeat all we have said about reducing sail in Chapter 8 we only re-state briefly that to work to windward in strong winds:

> You must balance the boat properly under her canvas.
> The fullness of the sails is at least as important as their size.
> You must keep a certain thrust, to ensure that the boat continues to handle properly.

Close-hauled in heavy weather: raise the tack of the jib and bend on a second sheet

A close-hauled course has certain advantages in bad weather. First of all the strength of the wind or, indeed, changes in its force, are not likely to take you by surprise. The boat herself indicates quite clearly by the way she handles whether she is happy under the canvas that is set. Also, she presents her strongest part, the bow, to the elements. Aft, in the cockpit, you are relatively sheltered.

Nevertheless, it is an uncomfortable point of sailing for the boat slams into the waves, pitches violently and as most of the crew will be feeling off colour and conditions in the cabin may be rather unpleasant. To make reasonable headway in steep seas, you have to work your waves by luffing into each one to reduce the slam, and by bearing away down the farther side to pick up speed again. This is all very well in theory, but usually difficult in practice, particularly at night.

The boat, of course, is undergoing all the while terrific strain. It is only self-deluders who try to maintain a precise course close-hauled: drag, heel and waves rule that out. You have to steer just a little free.

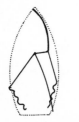

By backing the headsail slightly, speed is reduced and the boat is under less strain

The main risks you run are damage to the rigging – a torn sail, a sheet giving or a broken mast. If you have to make a long leg to windward, it is as well to hoist the jib a little higher than usual at the tack to save the foot of the sail from picking up too much water; it is also wise to reeve a second headsail sheet, either with the weather sheet passed down to leeward and through a different fairlead and made fast to a cleat, or with an extra line made fast to the clew (a precaution that can equally well be taken in ordinary weather, if you have to stay for many hours on the same tack).

You must be aware the moment the boat requires a let-up. A first step is to reduce speed by backing the headsail slightly by tightening the weather sheet slightly – the first step, in fact, to heaving-to.

With the Wind Free

The main advantage of sailing with the wind free is always the same: you are travelling with wind and sea, and life aboard is fairly comfortable, but only relatively because, although the boat is not hitting the waves, she will be rolling heavily. All the hazards, too, of sailing with the wind aft, in bad weather are accentuated.

The wind seems less strong than it is and you are not so aware of changes in the weather.
The boat becomes extremely unstable, and broaching to or gybing can be extremely dangerous.
The boat presents her most vulnerable part, the stern, to the seas.

If, initially, it seems desirable to keep on a fair amount of canvas to reach shelter quickly, you must be quite certain what you are doing and of being able to take in sail promptly should it be necessary. You must do this without delay as soon as you feel the boat pulling hard on the tiller and that she wants to luff up more than ever.

As the wind gets up, it is a sensible precaution to take down the mainsail to avoid the risk of gybing. You will travel fast enough through the water under headsail alone and, in these circumstances, it can be moderately large.

Safety Measures

Heaving-to

Heaving-to is the classic method of marking time until the wind and sea moderate sufficiently for you to get back on a close-hauled course.

The reefed mainsail is sheeted in normally and the headsail is sheeted aback, with the tiller lashed to leeward. The mainsail tends to make the boat luff up into the wind and the headsail makes her bear away: the result is that the boat makes a little headway, and lots of leeway.

That is the general principle. For each individual boat you have to find the correct balance by trial and error. Sloops and cutters

A cutter hove-to: jib sheeted normally, staysail backed

generally heave-to happily with the mainsail reefed right down and storm jib; a boat with very strong weather helm might heave-to under storm jib alone with the tiller down to leeward; another might do better with her tiller lashed amidships or even to windward. With the sail plan of a ketch or yawl, it is usually possible to balance the craft under mizzen and storm jib. In any event, it is only by experiment you can learn what works.

Heaving-to is useful. It allows you to wait, holding fairly well up into the wind, off a coast which offers no shelter; it is also reasonably comfortable. The boat is under no strain; the leeway that she makes creates some turbulence in the water to windward of the hull and that helps to temper the waves; when balance has been achieved it is not necessary for anyone to be at the tiller, and everyone can rest and keep warm. At the same time, the boat is rigged ready to set off again at a moment's notice and even if a man falls overboard, there is a very reasonable chance of picking him up.

But there are limitations. Should the sea get up even more, the boat is at the mercy of the occasional very steep wave which can sweep over the deck, laying the boat well over and all the spars come under great strain. Sheltered in the troughs and laid over on the crests is more than the boat can take for long.

It is now blowing up to a storm and things begin to be serious. If you cannot run before it, one way out is to stream a sea anchor.

Streaming a Sea Anchor

This takes place under bare poles, and there are many variations, carefully planned or improvised, to slow up the boat.

The traditional gear, pioneered by Captain Voss, is a pyramid-shaped canvas bag with its mouth held open by a metal hoop or crossbars, rigged with a bridle and line. It is weighted to make it ride well below the surface and has a tripping line so that it can be brought back on board, peak first.

It is a fairly cumbersome piece of equipment. Sea anchors have been successful on some boats in certain cirumstances, but they have drawbacks:

They are difficult to rig.
The boat has to retain a sail aft, because experience has shown that without it the boat cannot stay head to wind. This is no problem for a ketch or a yawl, but on a sloop you have to try to rig a small jib on the backstay, with the clew held forward; that is not easy.

Lastly, there is a tendency to make sternway, which subjects the rudder to stresses that may break it. Special precautions have to be taken to immobilise the helm.

In general, a sea anchor only appears to be successful in moderately bad weather. In a storm this braking device can become dangerous. Many experienced seamen prefer to run under bare poles, about which we will speak shortly.

It should be mentioned, however, that inflatable life rafts use sea anchors shaped in the form of a parachute which serve well on this type of craft.

Running Before the Gale

There is no basic difference between running free and running before the gale, but the former implies that you are maintaining your original course; when you run before a storm, you abandon your original objective and turn your stern to the gale, allowing the wind and sea to carry you where they will. The initiative is out of your hands.

It is, of course, only possible to run before the gale if you have plenty of sea-room ahead. It is much more comfortable than being close-hauled, but it entails all the hazards of downwind sailing: somebody must be always at the helm, and a man overboard will have little chance of being saved.

In the early stages, you will probably have hoisted a headsail but, if the wind blows up more, you go under bare poles; and there is always the risk of a violent yaw. The boat can be steadied by trailing a bight of heavy warp over the stern of a length that seems to serve, some twenty feet may be adequate.

But if the boat is still going too fast, or if there is a danger of reaching shallows, you must take other steps.

Trailing Warps

It can be dangerous to make a sea anchor fast to the stern: the boat is held back too much, and the stern is not able to ride the waves in a natural manner.

You should trail very thick warps, either two single ones or one looped back to the other quarter. If you attach a weight the warps will sink lower in the water and they will be more effective.

The warps help. The boat moves more comfortably and the waves do not break so readily over the stern. But you have no control over your course.

There are ways of improving your situation: the boat might handle better if, for instance, a storm jib is set; it will keep the stern from being square on to the wind and the warps can be made fast on one quarter or another for instance. Once again, there are no hard and fast rules, and you must experiment cautiously by trial and error; it is a matter of establishing the best speed for the boat in relation to the speed of the waves.

If the shore looms up, however, all that matters is slowing down at all costs. Anything or everything should be trailed, including sails, buckets, planks and the sea anchor itself.

Anything which is trailed will help to keep down the sea but, in practice, the risk of a wave breaking over the stern is extremely serious. No one should be allowed to come up or down the main hatch, which should be kept firmly closed and, if necessary, reinforced.

The warps are made fast forward, pass over the stemhead and outside the shrouds and are cleated aft. When the time comes, you need only free them from the cleats. You will then ride to them and they can be brought in easily

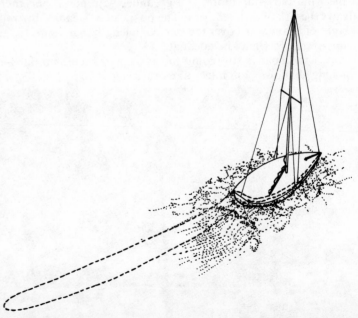

The warps should be taken forward from the stern, passed outside the shrouds and made fast again at the bow. This allows you to turn into the wind when the time comes to take them in, for otherwise it would be extremely difficult to get them in, particularly if the wind is still strong.

Endurance

Finally, tempests must be mentioned. Hurricane force winds are not necessarily the prerogative of the Roaring Forties and they do, from time to time and generally entirely unexpectedly, appear around our coasts.

What can we say? There are hurricanes which are beyond description, except by sailors who have been through them and survived. There are only tales to be told, facts to be stated. (It is not possible to speak of extreme weather conditions without referring to *Heavy Weather Sailing* by K. Adlard Coles. This is the definitive work on the subject and draws lessons from several extraordinary gales and storms experienced by the author or researched by him. It analyses in depth, but never tries to lay down hard and fast rules. In our view, the author's inimitable mixture of calmness and modesty marks him out as a great writer on the sea as well as a great sailor.)

Now there is no longer any question of maintaining control. The initiative has been lost and all you can do is to hold on, and survive, hoping for the best.

It is now impossible to stay on deck. The boat is under bare poles (if there has not been time to take down all sails, the only solution is to take an Irish reef – with a knife . . .). Safety measures are now more than ever important and everyone should go below except the helmsman. A last precaution is to criss-cross the cockpit with safety lines, made very fast, at thigh height.

What can be done? Which point of sailing is best? Adlard Coles says he has frequently lain a-hull – beam on, often heeling over acutely. In that position the boat offers less resistance to the sea, she makes a lot of leeway, establishing eddies to windward which help slightly to modify the force of the waves. The cabin will hardly be comfortable and the knowledge of feeling at the mercy of the elements will be frightening.

In a full hurricane sea and wind may not always keep the boat lying a-hull like this and the principal danger is capsizing. Even if everyone is down below, one man should be ready, with harness hooked on, to leap for the helm to turn the boat back before the wind if that danger seems imminent or if the situation is becoming intolerable.

What about releasing oil onto troubled waters? This sort of action is really only practicable for large ships, with big oil tanks; tankers are an obvious example. On a small boat which is making a lot of leeway fast, the most likely consequence would be turning the deck into a skating rink – not particularly helpful under the circumstances.

According to most accounts, it seems that running before the storm is the usual practice. Oddly enough it is apparently of little use to try to slow down the boat by trailing warps in really severe conditions. This practice seems to work up to certain levels of bad weather, but beyond these points it becomes dangerous, because warps do not allow the boat to 'give' under the onslaught of particularly large waves. The French circumnavigator, Bernard Moitessier, for example, adopted an unhindered run downwind. By keeping the wind at fifteen or twenty degrees on his weather quarter, he did not run the risk of burying his bows in the wave in front and *pitchpoling* or capsizing bow first. Inevitably, the boat attains a terrifying speed like this, with a continual danger of wild broaching.

Further advice on this point seems excessive. We can only tiptoe away from the subject feeling slightly queasy.

Anchoring

Your last chance may be anchoring. Smaller boats may be forced to try this course of action, if it becomes impossible to maintain control in heavy seas, and if the gale is driving them inexorably towards the shore.

It must be carried out coolly and deliberately. To stand any chance of success, you must put your mooring gear to the best possible use; if you have several anchors, attach them one behind the other and have ready all the chain or line you have. When you drop the anchor, pay out the whole chain immediately because, if the anchors begin by dragging, they may very well never bite on the bottom.

As far as possible, pick a spot with a good holding bottom in a reasonable depth of water. You must anticipate that the anchors may not hold, so choose a place where you can be driven ashore with the least possible danger.

Being Driven Ashore

If the anchors do not hold, or the chain parts, that is it. There is nothing to be done, and you are in danger.

Worst of all is being driven ashore onto rocks. The boat will soon start to break up. It is also very difficult to remain on board, when the boat is slamming on the rocks and splinters of wood or fibreglass can wound seriously; and, if you abandon ship, you yourself may be broken on the rocks.

You are in less danger if you are driven ashore on rocks covered with seaweed (this generally means at low tide) for it calms the sea down a little and landing on it is somewhat less hazardous.

A sandy shore gives you a slightly better chance, although it will break up the boat just as quickly. As you reach the shore there is a risk of being overturned by the rollers, and it is very difficult for the crew to keep on the surface because the water is full of air bubbles and lacks density. Some kind of buoyancy is needed to ride over breaking waves and that means a life raft or a rubber dinghy.

If you are lucky enough to land on mud, the dangers are much less. The boat may stand up to the seas and you can stay on board and await help.

Bad visibility, noise, shock and the slam of the boat, dampness and inevitable disorder are the background to a gale. What you do must depend above all on the crew's morale. Sea sickness, fear and fatigue can quickly make a situation which is merely difficult into a gratuitous tragedy.

This is where the skipper comes in. It is his job to lead and carry the crew with him by inspiring confidence. He must never lose his calmness, prudence and good humour.

13. Oars, Engine, Towing

Now that we have dealt with gales and foul weather, it is an agreeable change to turn to flat calms. The manuals are usually all too ready with instructions on how to get out of them, but we shall not evade the truth that what you do in the 'doldrums' is your decision and yours alone.

When the sails hang limp it is either a question of oars or sweeps or starting the engine; and it is not only when there is no wind that they are useful. They can help correct any errors of boat handling, allow you to manoeuvre in a crowded anchorage or get you out of a difficult situation. When even they, for any reason, can't do the job, the last resort is a tow. This may seem simple enough but it is not all that easy.

Sculling

Sculling is a real art, and the mastering of it is one of the most impressive accomplishments of the would-be mariner. The sculling sweep is unbeatably efficient and it is economical in its simplicity.

The General Principle

Like all such expertise, sculling is not easily described. To say that a scull is just a kind of variable-pitch propeller is a superficial explanation. Even the most elaborate account is inadequate and you can only learn by practising it. Written instructions make it sound impossibly difficult, an art that is only given to few.

Anyway, first attempts should be made in a heavy dinghy, when there is not a breath of wind and in a flat calm. You may prefer to go it on your own. The sculler stands in the boat, facing aft, legs apart and body upright, holding the end of the skull in both hands, palms downwards, at shoulder level. The blade should be right under water, pointing well downwards, with the scull so balanced that its weight presses on the rowlock or the notch in the transom.

If the blade is absolutely flat in the water, and moved from side to side, there will be no resistance and no movement of the boat; but if the blade is perpendicular to the surface, resistance will be great but results small: if the boat moves at all, it will only be due to the turbulence acting on the stern.

The blade should be given a certain degree of slant; tilt it to the left and pull the oar across to the right; then tilt the blade to the right and draw the oar across to your left. Simple enough. The upper surface of the blade, instead of pushing hard into the water, slips through it, all the while keeping up a gentle pressure. No doubt we should be describing this phenomenon in terms of physics and hydrodynamics, but let us simply say that you have to acquire the knack.

In practice, the difficulty lies in reversing the blade angle at the end of each stroke. *The hands should not be allowed to slip on the handle of the oar; you rotate it from left to right by using your wrists only.* The upper face of the blade should never stop pushing against the water, otherwise the oar will jump out of the rowlock; this is what usually happens with beginners.

You just have to persevere until you keep the oar in place. Have patience and, after a time, it will be only a question of improving your technique. To turn, the blade is inclined slightly more to one side than the other. When you stop, the blade should be kept vertical, like a rudder, or it will jump out of the rowlock.

You will need a few hours of practice before you achieve the ultimate satisfaction of perfection: sculling with one hand (with the other in your pocket), in a flat calm, the harbour jetty crowded with spectators, making steady progress and your mind, apparently, preoccupied with higher things.

The Advantages

One of the principal advantages of sculling is that you can get going without delay, ready to lend a hand at a moment's notice to help out in minor emergencies – if the boat has failed to go about, for example. It can equally be useful for boat handling in confined

The sculler always sees the same side of the oar blade. You can also go astern sculling. Body in the same position as for going forward; dip in the edge of the oar blade at an angle of about 45°, lay the shaft of the oar over one shoulder, grasping it lower down with both hands, and describe a reverse figure of eight motion while maintaining the oar at the same angle. Keep the hips steady. The manoeuvre demands concentration from the sculler but it is useful if you want to go astern for two or three metres in a straight line without fuss

waters. The advantages over an engine are all too obvious: it is harmless; it does not make a noise; it does not smell; it does not make a mess; it is reassuring and it never breaks down or gets tangled in mooring lines.

But, of course, sculling has its limitations: it is not fast, even with the most muscular man on the oar; it can lack the power to carry you against even a feeble current or a stiffish breeze. If you do not have an engine, however, sculling a boat of any size is much more efficient than using a pair of oars which may only thrash the water.

Although sculling is a noble art, it has not yet been given its final recognition: so far no fanatic (preferably one armed) has yet used it for crossing the Atlantic. That will come, no doubt.

Paddling

We must not overlook the paddle, which is generally used in light or inflatable dinghies. Its advantage in a dinghy is that it takes up little room and can be used without any extra equipment (such as notches in the transom or rowlocks). Even if it is possible to scull a rubber dinghy, paddles are essential as soon as you have to contend with a stiff breeze or choppy waters.

There is no secret in paddling and, unlike sculling, success does not depend on any special knack; you can even make progress by paddling badly. The purists paddle with straight arms, plunging the blade straight downwards well forward and pulling without bending the elbows, getting power from the chest.

If you are paddling solo, you keep to one side without switching from side to side. Settle in the stern, to leeward, if there is any wind. If you are on the starboard side, the first stroke will tend to push the boat to port; at the end of the movement, therefore, you must use the blade like a rudder to get back on course, even slightly to starboard so that it will not veer too much to port on the next stroke. If the boat has a centreboard, it helps to lower it to reduce this yawing.

The good paddler never bends his arms

The Auxiliary Engine

Its Role

Not so long ago cruising boat owners were divided into two camps: one believed in auxiliary engines and spent hours in trying to wheedle the brutes from their sullen silence; the other, the purists, simply mistrusted all mechanical devices.

This traditional mistrust, based as it was on rather pseudo-philosophical arguments, no longer has any real foundation. For one thing, modern engines start readily – although we would be the last to suggest they are infallible; and nowadays they are almost indispensable, particularly if you wish to enter (and not everybody does) ports where it is not possible, often indeed not permitted, to enter under sail.

An engine has, of course, lots of advantages. It enables you to return home on time if the wind drops, it can help you through narrow straits, it can come to the rescue if there is trouble with the rigging, and it is a great help in picking up a man overboard provided that it is powerful enough in heavy weather; but never forget the danger of a turning propeller for somebody in the water.

It is extremely dangerous to place too much reliance on it.

It is important to state its precise role in the scheme of things. An auxiliary engine should never be regarded as a safety factor; in other words, you should always sail as though you had no motor. If you get into the habit of relying on it, you will eventually be tempted to take one short cut too many to explore waters where the boat would be in considerable danger either from a flat calm or from a sudden squall. You should never do this. The engine is there as *an extra*. If it works, so much the better; if it does not work, you should not be in danger.

Its Potentials

To begin with, we must assume that you have chosen an engine that is powerful enough for the weight and windage of the boat. Even with a suitable engine, however, the handling qualities of the boat are very different and this depends on whether you can control the direction of the propeller's thrust.

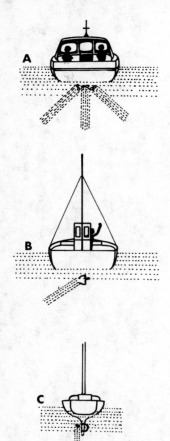

Various degrees of manoeuvrability
A. The propeller can swivel: the boat is highly manoeuvrable, even when stationary
B. The propeller is fixed but directs its jet on to the rudder: still good manoeuvrability even when stationary.
C. The propeller does not direct its jet onto the rudder: the boat is only manoeuvrable when under way

Propeller Thrust

There are three possibilities:

The propeller can be pivoted, as you can do with an outboard motor. Control is good because the direction of the propeller thrust can be directed while full power is maintained. Even with the bow made fast against a marina pontoon it is still possible to move the stern to port or starboard by turning the engine.

The propeller is fixed but its thrust flows across the surface of the rudder. Movement of the helm thus deflects the thrust and the boat can still be manoeuvred when it is moored.

The propeller is so fitted that its thrust is not deflected by the rudder. This is unfortunately often the case with auxiliary engines. The boat can only be turned, as under sail, when it is under way.

In some boats the propeller is not even fitted in alignment with the keel.

Going Astern

An auxiliary engine gives less control when you are going astern than ahead. This is because:

The propeller is not designed to give maximum efficiency turning astern, it has less power in that direction; also, it is sited badly in relation to the underwater lines of the hull.

The propeller thrust does not pass over the rudder and therefore cannot be deflected to help turning unless you have an outboard motor that can be put into reverse.

The rudder itself is badly placed for maximum efficiency.

In fact, the principal advantage of a reverse gear is its use as a brake. It takes way off the boat and that is an advantage.

Effect of the Wind

You must always allow for the wind, even under power. Windage has a considerable influence, for the wind on the coach roof and rigging swings the boat into its natural position, beam to wind. It is therefore only too easy to get into this position, whether you start with the wind ahead or astern; and it can be difficult to get yourself out of it, particularly in a fresh breeze, either by luffing or bearing away. To manoeuvre easily, therefore, the fresher the wind

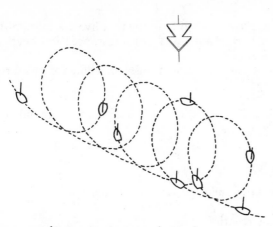

Under power, a boat comes easily into a wind-abeam position and has some difficulty in coming out of it. It cannot maintain station in the same circle

the more you need reserve power and speed.

In practice, the wind takes on a different character when you are under power. It is not the same wind that was recently filling your sails! Obviously, though, there are certain similarities: for example, when you want to stop under motor, you should come head-to-wind; with the wind aft, your speed increases commensurately. But, generally speaking, the ratio of boat speed and wind speed is radically modified. The stronger the wind, the greater the difficulty of manoeuvring; and in light conditions you may well find that you have too much power. The nice counteraction of wind and speed under sail is lost.

As a general rule, when you start the engine in a sailing boat, you are subjected to new laws, which can be disconcerting, and the helmsman can be thrown off his stride. Manoeuvring under power is not a matter of improvisation, and you will be wise to practise, at least once, in a fairly deserted stretch of water: come alongside, pick up a mooring, get under way, learn the ways of your boat and how quickly she loses way, and then you will be prepared when the time comes.

Boat Licences

In the original French edition details are given that do not apply in Great Britain and in the United States of America. In France no licence is required for boats if they are primarily sailing boats; but if a boat is classed as a power boat and it has an engine of 10hp or more, a permit is needed. There are three classes:

Permit A allows you to cruise within five sea miles of the coast.
Permit B allows unlimited cruising ranges for boats of under twenty-five tons.
Permit C allows unlimited ranges of sailing for pleasure boats of all tonnage.

In the United States and Great Britain licences are only required if boats carry paying passengers.

Passage Making

Passage making under power is restricted:

By wind strength.
By the amount of fuel available. This is normally not enough on a sailing boat for a long passage, specially if you have to contend with contrary winds or rough seas.

The motor is usually started in a flat calm, and therefore when the sails are down.

However, if you want to go to windward with the motor, it is not as efficient to lower everything and motor straight upwind as it is to sail close-hauled with engine and mainsail; lowering the jib allows you to point higher without increasing leeway. We should note here rule 14 of the International Regulations for Preventing Collisions at Sea: 'A vessel proceeding under sail, when also being propelled by machinery, shall carry in the daytime forward, where it can best be seen, one black conical shape, point downwards, not less than two feet in diameter at its base.'

It is obviously useful to keep the jib up with the wind free. And do not waste fuel by using the engine if it does not, in fact, increase speed. It is quite useless if the boat is already moving under sail alone at the maximum speed which the engine could achieve in a flat calm.

Do not forget that a boat under power has to abide by collision rules which are different from those of a sailing vessel (see chapter 14).

Handling in Port

So many different situations can arise that it is not possible to detail them here. In practice, a sailing boat proceeding under power is still basically a sailing vessel, and most of the advice already given for handling under sail in port remains valid: approach the sea wall at an angle and not head on, make allowances for the wind in case it blows you up against something hard – and so on.

Proceeding under power has some advantages: there is no longer any need to tack as you can go dead into the wind; one man has, in his hands, the power to go ahead, to turn or to slow down. But it is not always as easy as you might think.

Under power a boat is often easier to turn one way than the other. You therefore need more speed to turn to port than to starboard (or *vice versa*) and that has to be remembered.

A propeller in a port is like a fly hovering over a cobweb: it tends to get tangled in every line and rope which it can find, in mooring lines in particular. This must be borne constantly in mind, so avoid passing near mooring buoys, go under the stern of boats which are at anchor rather than under their bows, and take care not to strangle the engine by trailing your own sheets and mooring lines overboard.

A boat under power should be able to park just like a vehicle – only witness the serried ranks of the average marina. In practice, mooring buoys and other lines around the harbour are often so numerous that you sometimes have to chop the motor quickly and get out the humble sweeps, or warp yourself into position having somehow got your lines onto the quay. In any event, it is a bold man who decides to go in stern first, unless he is certain of his own abilities and has favourable wind conditions.

Towing

Towing must be considered from points of view of the tug and the towed – both in radically different positions although closely linked!

As far as towing is concerned, we shall only consider here a sailing boat with an auxiliary engine. Being towed often boils down to the experience of being killed by kindness. Good intentions of infinite variety must be guarded against.

The Tug

Generally speaking it is the tug who should pass the tow line and not the other way round. It is easier that way and we shall see shortly that it has certain advantages for the towed.

The tow line will almost certainly be subjected to sudden strains. You must use the strongest line you have – a really stout warp, and the longer it is the better it is for the job.

It should be made fast on the towing boat at a strong point well forward of the propeller; if it is made fast at the stern, the towing vessel will not be able to manoeuvre easily. Try to make the tow-rope fast as near as possible to the vessel's centre of lateral resistance – i.e. the base of the mast.

You must be careful about how you arrange the tow line across your own deck: it should pass to windward of the main sheet and of the back stay (or between the two backstays if needs must) to allow you to luff up to windward.

It should be coiled carefully on the deck, so that it can run out quickly as the slack is taken up.

Normally, the tow will start under power, and the sails on the towing boat will be hoisted when all is nicely under way.

Passing Over the Tow Line

The boat giving the tow always places itself to windward of the other as it is much easier to throw the line downwind. It is easier to use a *heaving line* – a light line with one end weighted with a piece of fancy ropework such as a monkey's fist. This makes it

If the towing boat is to maintain manoeuvrability, the tow rope must not be made fast at the stern but forward

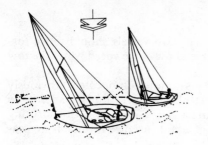

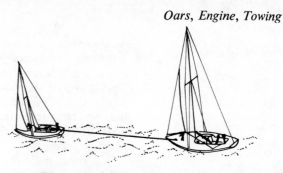

simpler to throw it accurately over a fair distance. The end of the tow rope is made fast to the heaving line and the former is then made fast on the boat that is to be towed.

There are several different kinds of towing:

Taking a drifting boat in tow. This is the easiest kind. Approach as slowly as possible, to windward, very close and very slowly, in order to throw the tow line, and then allow yourself to drift gently in front while the tow line is made fast on the other boat.

Taking in tow a boat with sails up and under way. This operation is more or less the same. Catch up slowly and position yourself to

The towing boat goes to windward of the boat being picked up so as to be able to throw the line. It frees its main sheet to slow down while the tow rope is made fast on the other boat

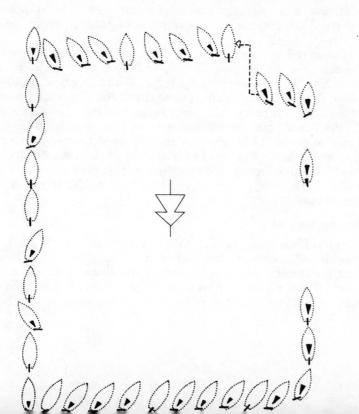

A simple exercise in good powerboat handling

To turn without going forward the golden rule is to put the helm over first and then open the throttle. Starting from top right:

Phase 1. Try to move from right to left, keeping head-to-wind all the time. Whenever you fall away too much you correct by putting the tiller hard to port and opening up the throttle as required (as indicated by the size of the triangles)

Phase 2. Let yourself drop astern, trying to keep ahead to wind. Whenever you fall away, put the tiller over in that direction and open throttle. Never go into reverse

Phase 3. As for phase 1 but this time from left to right.

Phase 4. Go upwind and do it again

When you have succeeded in making a perfect square, you may tell yourself you have mastered boat-handling

windward to pass the tow line. The two vessels should move forward together as nearly as possible at the same speed while the tow line is made fast.

Taking an anchored boat in tow. This is more complicated. Obviously the best solution would be to get him to break out his anchor so that he starts to drift; you would then be dealing with a drifting boat. But this is not always possible, for instance if there is no searoom to leeward.

The main difficulty for the towing boat is remaining head-to-wind without moving over the ground, while the boat to be towed makes fast the line and breaks out his anchor. If the wind is strong enough to counteract the engine going slow ahead, it is simple enough. But if the wind is light, you will have to be constantly adjusting the controls and this will be difficult unless you have an engine of the outboard type with a propeller that turns with the rudder, or have a propeller with a thrust that flows past the rudder. If you master this technique you will find it useful in circumstances other than towing. To stay still you have to go into neutral when the wind is dead ahead; as soon as the boat bears away, to starboard for example, put the helm hard down to starboard and engage gear; go back into neutral when the boat comes back head-to-wind, and so on. Never go into reverse gear to bring the boat back into the wind, because this is a sure way of putting yourself beam on.

If your rudder is not situated in the propeller wash, the whole manoeuvre is much more difficult, because you cannot stop and everything has to be done on the move. The towing boat positions herself fairly far aft of the boat to be towed and approaches slowly while all is made ready. As she passes the boat that is in difficulties, the tow line is passed across and she continues straight upwind, as slowly as possible but with just enough speed to ensure that she answers the helm. The tow line is allowed to run right out its full length. The tow rope should be as long as possible and some of the towed boat's anchor chain should have been hauled in before the line was passed.

Starting the Tow

To start off smoothly, take up the slack of the tow line as gently as possible and, as soon as it is under tension, accelerate hard. If you open the throttle at the right moment, the line will stay taut and the two boats will pick up speed at the same time. It should be remembered that the taut tow line tends to make the towing boat

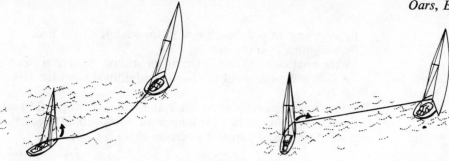

bear away. The helmsman should forestall this by starting off slightly closer to the wind than would otherwise be necessary.

As soon as the tow has got under way, the towing boat should adjust the length of the tow rope. This should be long enough to be never fully taut, and always be in the water. In practice, even with a very long tow line, it is difficult to avoid jerking the line, specially with the wind aft when the two boats will rarely be moving at the same speed.

When the tow rope slackens, the boat being towed moves sharply off course, to prevent the tow rope snatching when it goes taut again

Watching the Tow Line

Minimising the violence of the tugging on the tow line is a matter of boat control. When the line goes slack:

The towing boat should slow down, and accelerate just when it tightens up again.

The boat being towed should alter course so that, when the tow line goes taut again, the bows will be pulled back on course instead of the whole being pulled forward violently.

You can also give some flexibility to the tow line:

Three ways of damping down the snatch on a tow rope

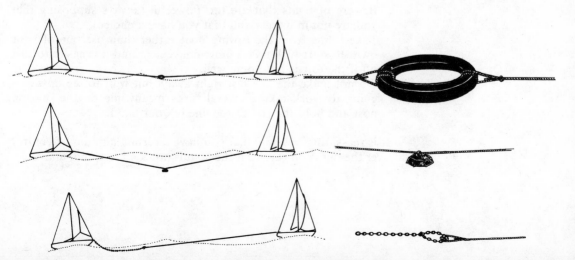

By coupling an old motor tyre in the middle of the line.
By weighting it in the middle.
By the boat being towed fastening its anchor chain to the end of the line and paying out ten to fifteen fathoms from the bow.

The tow rope is also liable to chafe and may part at the fairleads. If the tow is going to last for long both boats should check their ends of the line and parcel it wherever chafe can occur.

Being Towed

Making Fast

First of all, the boat being towed must make the line properly fast by securing it to the most solid part of the boat. The best place is the bitts, or round the mast. If it is rough and the towing boat is powerful, it may even be better to take the line right round the hull.

When making fast, you should only use knots that can be untied and do not tighten under load: either a bowline, or tugman's hitch (several round turns on the bitts or samson post and then a bight of the free end taken under the standing part and half hitched over the top). Never use a clove hitch.

Snags

Trouble starts for the boat being towed as soon as the tow line has been made fast, and usually for one reason: the towing boat nearly always goes too fast. For the boat behind the results are unpleasant to say the least, and it can't always cast itself adrift.

The skipper who has experienced this once will have plenty of time to work out precautions for the next occasion:

Beware of boats that are too powerful (always supposing that you are not in danger and that you have a choice).
Take a line from the towing boat rather than use one of your own; to start with this is more convenient and it is easier to cast off if the tow is not going well.
Do not make the line fast right away, but wait to see how it is going to work taking several turns meanwhile on the samson post and hold the end of the line in your hand.

It is reassuring to know that you have a certain amount of control over the tug. You can see if the boat is not too large and, above all,

It may be wise to secure the tow rope right round the hull. When you are already in a bad state any extra damage is to be avoided

notice if the skipper has made the tow line fast right aft in his boat. If, for example, you want him to go to port, it should be enough to put your helm hard over to starboard for him to follow.

When you are being towed, it is best to keep slightly to windward of the towing boat's wake; this is particularly important with the wind free, when you can run the risk of colliding if you are swept forward by the waves. This kind of accident is fairly common, particularly if the boat being towed is larger than the other.

It is to be hoped that, at the end of the journey, the towing skipper will remember that you cannot go astern and that he will pull up head-to-wind.

Towing by Dinghy

There is one economical solution of the problem of the auxiliary engine: fit one to the dinghy rather than to the boat herself. Such an engine, from two to six horse power, and not so large as would have been necessary for the boat herself, obviously will not give the same results; but it will nevertheless allow you some freedom of manoeuvre, not to mention the ease and speed of going to and from the boat.

Pushing

You can move the parent boat with the dinghy either by pulling or pushing. Pushing is better, but it is only practicable with the inflatable type of dinghy.

Bring the nose of the dinghy up to the stern and push on the centreline (or to one side if the rudder is hung on the transom). You get better control if you tie up very short: if the dinghy pushes firmly to starboard, the boat will turn rapidly to port and *vice versa*.

Used in this way an inflatable is quite safe, even when you are well offshore in a choppy sea. You can have it ready in plenty of time before your arrival; moored to the stern with someone on board, it is ready the moment you need auxiliary power.

Pulling

You can also tow the boat with a dinghy, whether it is an inflatable or rigid one. But this really only works in a flat calm or in a well sheltered anchorage. You are liable to ship too much water if it is rough.

The tow line should be made fast to the bow of the dinghy and at worst amidships, awkward as that is for the helmsman; if it is made fast aft, you cannot manoeuvre.

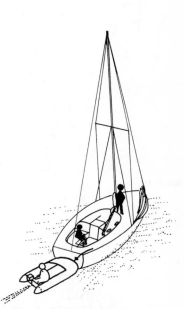

Pushing the boat with the dinghy may not be the first solution that springs to mind but it is nevertheless the most effective

Towing: the tow rope must be made fast right at the bow of the dinghy

The helmsman should move the line from one side of the engine to the other when he has to turn. Incidentally, it is possible to steer quite conveniently by only using the tow line like this: if it is shifted to port, the dinghy will go to port and *vice versa*. This is due to the great difference in weight of the dinghy and the tow.

Another method is making the dinghy fast alongside the boat. This can only be done when it is very calm and, even when you go very slowly, the man in the dinghy is likely to get wet through.

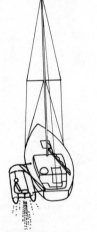

Towing alongside: the dinghy must be tied as near to the stern as possible for maximum manoeuvrability. It is the spring not the breast ropes that is doing the work

Hundreds of miles of salt water will flow under your keel before you achieve complete mastery of your boat, and this is only to be expected when you have chosen to throw yourself on the mercy of inconstant elements like the sea and the wind. You will only be able, little by little, to take your place in this restless world which is for ever changing, day by day and hour by hour. Eventually the spirit of sailing and the sea will permeate you, body and soul. In a dinghy you will eventually sail instinctively – through the seat of your pants. In a larger boat, you gradually pick up the balance and rhythm of the long distance sailor who is not able to walk steadily when he first returns to *terra firma*. Once you have reached that stage and morale on board gets better and better, it is probable that you are getting a better and better performance out of the boat.

In conclusion we must stress this maxim: half measures are no good under sail. Discipline at sea is demanding and nothing makeshift will do. In the course of learning you will have countless opportunities to realise that a hurried or skimped job can start a chain of dire reactions: the boat gets dangerously out of control and, in trying to regain it, things only become worse; the most unfortunate consequences follow one on the other, all leading to total confusion. The law of cause and effect rules with immediate results. Finally, it is not too much to say that, if you handle your boat badly, you are constantly in danger and the fact that you may have an engine makes little difference. If you are determined to sail, common sense requires you never to depend on your engine but to learn to manage under canvas alone.

Unfortunately, the reverse is becoming common practice, more and more, particularly as many marinas refuse to allow entry under sail. This kind of regulation seems to us to encourage accidents rather than safety, because it is pandering to mediocrity and incompetence. It is hardly likely that people who cannot handle a boat in port will be able to do so offshore in heavy weather, let alone cope with unforeseen crises. If the increasing number of boats makes restrictions on movement necessary in ports and marinas, it seems to us that it should be possible to organise special areas which can be reached under sail and from where the boat can move onto its allotted place by other means. Surely this would be a better solution for all concerned, and more in line with a sports vocation.

In practice, absolute safety is no easy matter; but it is part and parcel of your ultimate objective, and should not militate against it. If you have decided to sail, it follows that you are prepared to face up to the risks, not by seeking out danger but not hiding from it either, should it arise. Safety consists in observing the rules of the game and, among these, precise boathandling is paramount. Having once recognised these rules you will wish to play the game to the full, taking everything as it comes, the good with the bad.

Part 3. The Crew

Having discussed the boat and its handling, we come next to the subject of life at sea. We shall return briefly to dinghies and on what the beginner can do about safety when sailing them. Then, we shall go onto the more adventurous business of cruising.

After mentioning adventure, it may seem pusillanimous to begin by counselling prudence and giving tips for comfort on board. But the need for safety precautions and organising life on board, as we shall discuss them in the following chapters, are just as important as all the practical subjects we have been analysing. We must now consider the human aspects of sailing: a cruise is first and foremost an enterprise undertaken by a few people who have, for a week or two, a common goal and they make up what is called a crew. They may be excellent navigators, splendid 'hands', first-class technicians: all that talent alone will not guarantee success. The key question is: will they succeed in living happily and safely together for a week or a fortnight in the close confines of a boat?

The concern for safety is not the antithesis of the spirit of adventure, but confirmation of serious intention. It is easy to risk one's own life and that of others; less easy to prepare carefully, to train, and to organise for success in crises that may well be imposed by the elements (and it is quite as much a matter of morale as of physique, when everyone may have to call on all his resources, to make headway against tides, do without sleep, suffer seasickness, find your way through fog and, perhaps, finish up by battling to bring boat and crew safely into harbour).

Part of the adventure of sailing is building up a crew who do not suffer from capricious prejudices, with the common bond of solidarity that springs from life at sea. The fundamental rule is mutual tolerance. The cohesion of the group depends of course on the good will of each individual; but some practical matters are also important and they must be thought through in detail.

The following pages are based on our own experience. Certain requirements and some of our views may come as a surprise, but they are the outcome of running a cruising school and we did not think it right to exclude them. Not everyone will agree with all our tenets, but no one will deny that a crew cannot live (much less survive) without observing certain rules – rules made in the interests of happy solidarity and to allow each person to be at his best and to feel at ease in a small society where the phoney is quickly exposed.

14. Safety

Like so many others, the whole question of safety has changed within a few years. The emergence of new materials, new concepts of design, a growing awareness of everything pertaining to the sea and sailing and improved rules – all have made much age-old practice and traditional wisdom outmoded. Dangerous boats have become rare. Hulls are sounder, rigging is stronger, and one can often go on sailing in wind strengths that, not so long ago, would have compelled one to turn tail and make for harbour.

These developments, although they eliminate some dangers, have nevertheless increased others. Sailing in harder weather in boats faster than they used to be adds to the hazards of falling overboard. Sailing throughout the year when the water is icy increases the risk of hypothermia. The high quality of boats and safety equipment can induce carelessness.

But basically safety at sea is unchanged. It depends above all on a full knowledge of and respect for the sea, and on how to make the best use of the equipment at one's disposal when faced with foul weather. Safety is the constant preoccupation and no apology is needed for speaking of it time and again in this book. In the first place, it presupposes full awareness of the dangers one runs, how and why they arise and how to forestall them or minimise their consequences. That is the subject of this chapter.

Safety in Dinghies

All the principles we gave in Chapter 1 for beginners remain valid for experienced sailors, particularly the essential equipment: an unsinkable boat in good condition, with all the necessary fittings – anchor and rope, fairlead on the stemhead, oar or paddles, bailer; and each member of the crew wearing a life jacket at all times.

That said, a few extra details must be added here. The beginner makes his first outings some tens of yards from the beach, under the eye of an instructor, always ready to step in if need be. Later, when the tyro has the boat under good control and is capable of righting it and setting off again if he capsizes, clearly he can venture a little further and is inclined to think he can manage on his own – roaming free.

In fact, in a dinghy, one has only a semblance of freedom. Even Olympic medallists can never be sure of always returning to land on their own, unaided. When difficulties arise, someone has to be called in. Realisation of this need alone puts dinghy sailing in its true perspective.

The Place, The Weather

French legislation states that racing dinghies (and racing keel boats) must not go more than two miles from a point on the coast where they can easily find refuge, except when they are watched over by an appropriate escort.

Two miles is already far out and this distance limit is only a minimal precaution; it gives a fair guarantee of speedy rescue. But if this limitation is to be effective two other conditions must be fulfilled: first, that the sailing area is under observation; second, that the weather is suitable.

To sail without supervision on a stretch of empty water is in any case, and even in very fine weather, imprudent. On a well frequented stretch of water, it is less risky: if you capsize, you will (perhaps) be noticed by boats nearby – but you must realise that they cannot do much. In reality, when one has no appropriate escort available, the only solution is to have a look-out on land, someone experienced, who knows *how* to look, and knows where he can go for immediate help if need arises. For this supervision to be effective, clearly the crew of the dinghy must keep to a pre-arranged plan and not, for instance, go off behind rocks where they can no longer be seen. To minimise risks, the crew must also know the stretch of water on which they are sailing. It is useful to look at a chart (a chart rather than a land map), to learn the local dangers – an unmarked rock, a current, a shallow where, even in good weather, there could be a choppy sea too heavy for a dinghy.

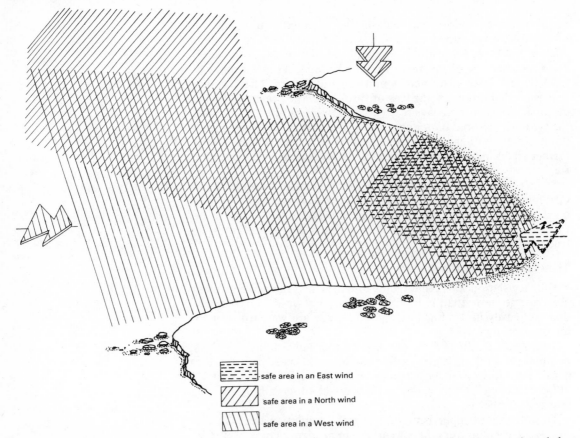

safe area in an East wind

safe area in a North wind

safe area in a West wind

The area in which it is safe for a dinghy to sail in safety varies according to the direction of the wind and the nature of the coast: whatever the situation is the helmsman must keep within limits that allow him to return home with a free wind

As to weather, the answer is simple. You must be convinced that taking out a dinghy in a strong wind is stupid, and that a wind of force 4–5 with squalls up to 6 is much too strong at sea for the majority of crews. You are practically certain to capsize, you cannot be sure of being able to right the boat and material damage is probable; rescue can be difficult in a rough sea; and you compel others to run gratuitous dangers.

Effective supervision and the right weather are the necessary conditions, but you need more. There is one last important factor – the length of the trip. When you set out in a dinghy you have a store of physical strength, which is gradually spent without being restored: for no one can hope to rest and recuperate on a boat whose stability is only maintained by unremitting effort and concentration, conscious and unconscious. You must keep the duration of a sail within the limits of your strength: as exhaustion sets in the more risk there is of capsizing and the less chance of being able to right the boat. Any one in charge of a sailing group must make the recall signal the moment capsizing becomes marked. In any case it is wise to stop the sailing well before sunset: if a capsize occurs at dusk, the chances of finding the boat are reduced.

There is one major difference, as far as safety is concerned, between an experienced and beginners' crew: the former goes further afield without being so closely supervised and may have to wait some time for help. Then, cold and exhaustion beome the real dangers, and it is important to recognise the symptoms and consequences.

Cold and Fatigue

If the water temperature is above 20°C, a healthy person can stay in it for several hours without growing seriously cold. But it must be remembered that the average temperature of the sea in the North Atlantic is well below 20°C (certainly in British waters and most of the eastern seaboard of America): in general 17°C in summer and 10°C in winter, but, especially in winter and in inland waters, it can be much lower.

Prolonged immersion in water at a low temperature brings on progressive exhaustion through loss of calories. Research has defined the average time before loss of consciousness occurs (in the majority of cases, this is followed by death) as twenty to sixty minutes in water of 10°C, two to three hours in water of 17°C. Those figures apply to people in good health, not too old, normally clothed, in calm water and not exerting any physical effort.

To these rough statistics two important points must be added: the length of time of survival is divided into two stages: during the first the subject is still active, and can help in his own rescue; during the second, although still conscious, he can no longer help his rescuers. The lower the temperature of the water, the shorter the first period becomes.

Although intense physical effort, especially if it is exerted for some time, initially contributes for a while to the production of heat in the body, energy reserves are exhausted and the chances of survival are reduced.

From these facts the following conclusions can be drawn.

One must be well clothed. Clothing, and especially woollen clothing, helps to delay loss of heat. (And, although this is strictly speaking on another subject, it is a good idea always to have a knife for you can be caught in a sheet when you capsize and not be able to free yourself, and that has happened.)

When you are sailing in cold waters, the best precaution of all is to wear a wet suit; this prolongs by three or four times the stage of consciousness.

It is important not to lose heat through the head: choose a life jacket that keeps the head above water without effort.

All intense muscular effort must be avoided, as soon as it is clearly impossible to right the boat. If you cannot climb onto the hull, cling onto the boat, tie yourself on if possible and do not move.

Decisions to be Taken

A hull can be seen, a swimmer cannot

When you cannot right the boat and rescue is problematical, two questions arise: anchor or abandon the boat?

If the wind or tide is bearing you out to sea, there is no doubt – you should anchor. If the boat is drifting towards the coast most of the time, it is preferable to be carried along and to wait until you are quite close to land before anchoring. It all depends on the circumstances; above all, it is important not to make a snap decision, but to make very sure first in which direction you are drifting.

Not leaving the boat is nearly always the correct course. If you succeed in hoisting yourself onto the hull, you are sure to be found sooner or later. Even if you can only manage to cling to the boat, that is better than trying to swim to the shore. To swim three hundred metres, fully dressed, in waves, and even supported by your lifejacket, is a feat beyond the ability of the average swimmer. Besides, it is only too easy to underestimate your distance from the coast. Even when you are quite near, remember the tidal streams: it is impossible to make headway against a foul one, even if it is not strong.

So, stay attached to the boat. If there are exceptions to this rule, they are exceedingly rare. We ourselves only know of one justified case. In the cataclysmic storm of 6 July 1969, the crewman who capsized in a light dinghy left the boat: he was found, exhausted but alive, on a rock. The helmsman remained clinging to the hull and was drowned. That day the sea was so wild that rescue was out of the question, and to keep holding onto a hull no doubt impossible.

The circumstances were quite exceptional, but, as it happened, attention must be drawn to it, although in no way can a general rule be drawn from it.

To conclude: a boat in first class condition, fine weather, a crew in good physical shape, effective supervision, these are the basic safety requirements for dinghy sailing. If you consider that a dinghy is a proper boat (and you must if you are not racing), it is imperative that the crew behave like proper sailors. Realise that you should not go out if the wind is too strong or, simply, if you do not feel in top form; know when to come in, well before you are too tired and well before nightfall: these are the real safety criteria. Abiding by them proves you know the limits imposed by the sea and have a true awareness of your own limitations. This last point is very important for, finally, when all is said and done, the real public enemy Number One in this kind of sailing is vanity.

Safety on a Cruiser

A cruising boat carries its own built-in safety. The crew is fully responsible: they know that most probably they can only depend on their own rescue measures. So it is up to them to be prepared, and to have prepared their boat to withstand hard knocks, and to get out of trouble should it occur.

Safety precautions on a cruiser are quite a complicated business, and on several levels. First of all there are the self-evident needs: a boat in good condition and a competent crew. Then there are the more imponderable factors: choosing a suitable cruising area, taking into particular account the kind of sailing that is suitable for the boat; finding a contact ashore who is competent, experienced, who knows when not to get worried if there is no news and when to call for help. And last but not least, everyone must know what to do in crises such as man overboard, collision, fire, explosion – accidents in general. They must also have taken into account the ultimate dangers: shipwreck, and the new kind of sailing experience that then follows.

The Different Kinds of Sailing

Although regulations vary from country to country, the French ones may be of some interest to American and British yachtsmen.

You cannot go anywhere you like in any old boat. A maximum limit of operation has been laid down for each type of boat. Racing dinghies must not operate more than two miles from a port of reference. All other boats are assigned to five clearly defined categories according to their characteristics and the safety equipment they carry.

Category 5. The boat must not move more than five miles from shelter. In this category are: pleasure fishing boats, excursion boats and 'camp-cruising' boats such as the Marauder. With such boats the longest passage allowed is therefore ten miles. That allows longish trips along the coast and an escape to the nearest islands, provided they offer safe shelter: you can go from Concarneau to Les Glénans, for instance, or from Granville to the Iles Chausey; but not to the Channel Islands.

Category 4. The boat must not go more than twenty miles from shelter. This is the category of 'coast hoppers' and small coastal cruisers. Their limits are quite extensive. A Corsaire for instance can cruise along the French coast from Dunkirk to the Gironde.

Sailing limits
Category 5: there are many coastal areas where you are always less than five miles from shelter
Category 4: the most common cruising areas (95% of boats are in this category); there are splendid possibilities except in a few areas where there is no shelter within twenty miles – the coasts of Landes (SW France) and two short stretches of the Corsican coast
Category 3: this is the domaine of deep water cruising

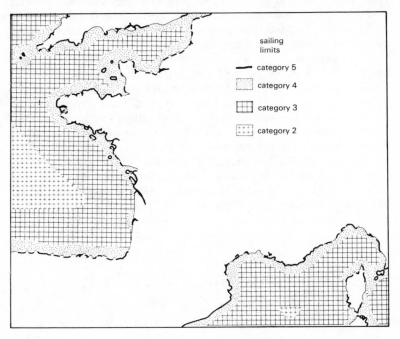

sailing
limits

——— category 5

category 4

category 3

category 2

But there she must stop since shelter is too widely spaced out along the coast of the Landes. She can also coast sail all along the English south coast, on condition that the Channel crossing has been made at the Straits of Dover (or on a car ferry).

Category 3. The boat must not go more than a hundred miles from shelter. This category covers long distance coastal cruising, which includes the Musketeer. It allows one to cruise from one end of Europe to the other without, however, undertaking passages such as Ushant–Finisterre, or Scotland–Norway.

Category 2. The boat is not allowed further than two hundred miles from shelter. This is the class of the Galiot and Nautilus. You can make a passage anywhere except across the great oceans.

Category 1. Worldwide: America, the three capes, and circumnavigation in any direction.

These rules have seemed restrictive to a number of yachtsmen; but we believe that they are liberal and well adapted to the realities of cruising. On the whole, boats are assigned to a category which is a reasonable indication of their maximum cruising range in the hands of a well trained crew.

In addition, the cases of highly qualified sailors wishing to make long passages on small craft have been foreseen: a boat can be authorised to sail in a category higher than her own for the duration of one passage or a race. Authorisation must be sought from the national Safety Commission (Marine Marchande, Bureau de la Plaisance, Place Fontenay, Paris VIIe). It is obviously only granted to someone capable of proving his competence (if he can bring as witness for instance the Commodore of his Club).

It is clear, finally, that when it comes to planning a cruise, the category of the boat is a basic factor, but very insufficient in itself. Within the limits defined for such and such a category many extremely different cruises can be carried out. It is then that the tastes and the capabilities of each individual must decide.

The Shore Link

When you set off on a cruise, do not cut all links with civilisation. It is important that the skipper should arrange for a friend on shore whom he undertakes to keep informed of his movements. The friend will call out the rescue forces if there is a long silence. He should be experienced enough to be able to imagine what is going on at sea, to follow the weather reports and capable of understanding whether the absence of a telephone call or a delay in arriving are serious or not.

When one sets out for a day's sail, returning to the same port, the role of the man on shore is quite simple. He is on the spot, he can observe the weather and the state of the sea for himself. If the boat has not returned by the agreed time, he must make a calm appreciation of the situation. A flat calm might be the reason; the skipper and 'friend' should have agreed on the procedure to be followed in just such a case. Equally, if the skipper anticipates a deterioration in the weather, he must telephone his friend, putting in specially somewhere, it need be, to prevent his raising the alarm quite needlessly. Finally, if the boat doesn't come back because 'we are all having a good time', then the 'friend' has every reason to throw up his hands and tell the skipper to find another, longer-suffering guardian.

When you set off on a cruise your shore contact should be a fairly experienced yachtsman capable of following the development of a weather pattern, and of imagining skipper's reactions in a given situation, which he will be the better able to do if he knows the skipper well, for his role requires a fairly intimate understanding of character.

The contact must know the name and port of registration of the vessel, its class, the colour of the hull, and of the sails and the number on the sail. He must also know the names and addresses of all members of the crew.

All these details are essential if a search is to be made, and if the crew's families have to be kept informed.

The friend must also have full particulars of the general intentions on the cruise and the likely ports of call. *This means that the skipper should telephone or telegraph* (the post obviously is too slow) *whenever he puts in* to say where he is, what his plans are for the next day and approximately when he next expects to call.

If the skipper reports his intentions clearly and regularly, and sticks to the programme; if the friend binds himself to follow the boat's progress with a sense of responsibility, then real progress has been made in the cause of safety. In case of a serious accident or shipwreck, the crew will know that too long a silence will alert the shore contact and that a search will be organised immediately and directed to the right area. There is no better way of insuring against the greatest danger run when you are faced with the loss of your ship – succumbing to despair.

But your friend on shore cannot provide all the answers. There are hazards that can arise at sea for which you must be prepared and fight alone, with whatever means are available on board.

Man Overboard

A man falling overboard is the most common accident at sea and it is as well to have your mind quite clear about it:

– In very bad weather it is almost always impossible to save him.
– At night, whatever the weather may be, it is often impossible to find him.
– As often as not it is the skipper who falls overboard for skippers tend to be casual about securing themselves to the boat. The accident is then often fatal because the crew may well be incapable of taking the necessary quick action to save him.

It must be realised that the danger of falling overboard is always with you. As soon as the weather ceases to be calm (even well before a first reef is taken in) the risk is there. It lurks in wait not just for those who are working on deck, but for everyone. On board the *Ark*, a Glénans boat, a member of the crew was literally pulled out of the cabin by a loop of the main sheet during a gybe, and found himself in the water. Another crewman, on board the *Glénan*, was just putting his head out of the hatch to take a bearing when a squall laid the boat flat and the navigator was only able to hold onto the lifelines where he had been thrown by the violence of the heel.

Whatever the weather this accident is particularly likely when you are running before the wind. A gybe, caused by yawing, can lie in wait for the best helmsman: a man is hit by the boom and goes overboard. To make matters worse the spinnaker is usually up on this point of sailing, and it is a long time before the vessel is under full control and can return to where the man went over.

However, provided a minimum number of precautions are taken, the risk of falling into the sea can be guarded against. First of all we shall list the counter-measures that can be taken: they depend on having available the appropriate equipment. We will then consider what should be done if the accident nevertheless happens.

Prevention

Lifelines and pulpits, individual belaying points are basic safety measures against falling overboard.

If you are not hooked on and fall over, your lifejacket and the lifebuoys thrown from the boat, at least keep you on the surface.

A whistle, a flashing light or a self-igniting flare show where you are.

Lifelines and Pulpits

We have already mentioned pulpits, lifelines and their stanchions in chapter 5. We only need to make it clear here that, according to all normal regulations they must all be strong enough to withstand the sudden impact, at any point whatsoever, of a person weighing at least 75kg.

The Full Equipment: Lifeline, Carbine Hook, Safety Harness

The lifelines in this case are cables fixed flat on the deck, one on each side, from one end of the boat to the other. You fix your carbine hook onto it the moment you leave the cabin and you can then move anywhere without ever having to unhook.

The carbine hook must be in perfect condition; neither oxidised nor dirty in case it jams.

The line should be No. 10 nylon and must be perfectly spliced or sewn on.

Finally, the harness itself must be designed like a parachutist's. It must have a strap going between the legs, so that it cannot possibly slip off. It should be attached at the nape of the neck: a man who has fallen into the water and is being dragged along by the boat is then able to keep his head above water.

The component parts of this gear (beginning with the fastenings of the lifelines on the deck) must each tolerate a pull of 1,500 kilos; we demand 2,000 kilos on board our boats, so that it can all stand some wear before being renewed.

The ideal is to use a line short enough to prevent the deck hands from falling into the water. That is possible when they are working mostly at a fixed place, such as the mast or a stay. It is more difficult

Fully kitted out for sea

when they have to move about on small boats when fixing lifelines is in any case something of a problem. In fact, you really need a short and a long belaying line. Some people attach two lines and two spring clips onto their harness: this is somewhat cumbersome, but to be recommended as it allows these to change belaying points without ever being unhooked. Others use a long line with a loop in it into which they attach the clip when they need a short line; a convenient solution but not as safe as two lines.

Every man should get used as soon as possible to wearing a harness, at first in fine weather. You will soon discover that the whole arrangement, provided you know how to use it, is of practical help in handling the boat and that, perhaps surprisingly, it gives you genuine freedom of movement.

One must hook on systematically:
– at night, whatever the weather;
– under spinnaker, whatever the weather and time of day;
– by day, as soon as the weather freshens, and as soon as any job (changing a foresail, taking in a reef) puts you at risk, however slender it may be, of falling into the water.

Lifejacket

The lifejacket must be of an approved pattern. There are all kinds in existence. The ideal is one with a harness incorporated: this simplifies putting it on and taking it off.

A whistle should be attached to the jacket, for the man in the water to make known his whereabouts; and at night, a watertight torch (really watertight, like a diver's lamp, for instance).

Lifebuoys

Buoys are useless unless they can be thrown into the water in one simple movement; if one has to begin by undoing straps or lines, the person in distress will be a long way behind in the wake by the time the buoy is thrown to him. They must be kept in place by

In France approved lifejackets must have a number prefixed with the letters GS for those approved for boats of under two tons, and by the letters BS for boats of over two tons
The horse-shoe lifebelt is simply kept in a fabric holder from which it can be pulled out in one movement. Its electric buoy-light is kept in place by two clips

shock cords or in a special fitment, within reach of the helmsman.

The round buoy is perfect if its diameter is big enough for a man to slip easily into it, but it is very cumbersome and difficult to stow on board. A horse shoe buoy is preferable to a round buoy that is too small. It is kept in a canvas pouch, from which it can be pulled out in one moment.

Self-igniting Flare

An obligatory accompaniment to the buoy, attached by a thin line a few metres long, is a self-igniting flare. It is a cylindrical metal can containing calcium carbide. It is fixed to the boat by two soldered clips. As soon as the buoy is thrown the can is pulled off and thrown into the water. The water penetrates into it through two holes uncovered when it is torn from its clip. The carbide gives off acetylene which catches alight on contact with a capsule of calcium phosphate, itself heated on contact with the water. It gives a light, visible for several miles by day as well as by night, for about an hour.

The man overboard, if he has succeeded in seizing the buoy, must keep well clear of the flare, for it can give him a bad burn; that is why the line between buoy and flare must be at least six yards long. The flare will light instantaneously if it is rough but not necessarily in calm water. In that case the man overboard must splash the can and go on doing so if the wind puts out the flame.

The condition of the self-igniting flare must be regularly checked. You can be sure it will not ignite if the clips are beginning to pull away.

On many boats, the self-igniting flare has been replaced by electric lights. These miniature battery-lit buoys light up automatically when they are in an upright, floating position. On board, they are stowed head-down in an appropriate fixing, usually a pocket in the lifebuoy pouch from which they can be extracted in one movement, after the buoy itself.

Reserve Manoeuvres

When someone falls overboard and is not hooked on, his life depends on the crew's cool-headedness and competence.

There are many examples of disastrously impulsive action: the helmsman tries to turn back when the boat is under spinnaker, immediately putting it into inextricable confusion; a member of the crew jumps into the water to help his companion, adding to the disarray.

To be successful, every move must be made to an exact plan. The procedure we suggest is not to be followed slavishly; it will vary according to the boat, the ability of the crew, the weather and the circumstances. What matters is that there is a procedure, familiar to everybody which has been practised beforehand. Everyone must know his part, and the skipper must have nominated the member of the crew who is to take over if he himself has gone overboard.

The Search

The moment it happens, the helmsman shouts 'man overboard!'

He throws the buoy and the flare into the water.

He notes the time, to the nearest minute, or the log reading.

Then he stays at the helm. Eye glued to the compass, he keeps strictly on course, while he waits for the crew to get ready.

If there is any sea, no one comes on deck until they have fastened on lifejackets and harness. This is not the time to lose anyone else.

To take a simple case: the boat is under full control, it is daylight, fine weather, the man so designated has not taken his eyes off the man overboard. The helmsman manoeuvres quickly to come straight back in the opposite direction as if he were going to pick up a mooring.

Then a difficult case: the boat cannot turn back at once, being under spinnaker or mizzen stay sail and the rest of the crew are asleep; or it is dark. More than ever, every move must be methodical: the only chance of finding the man is by precise navigation. The helmsman, more than ever, must keep rigorously on course until everyone is ready.

If you are sailing close-hauled or with the wind abeam, it is simple enough. When everyone is ready, all you have to do is to turn through 180° to be able to head straight back to the man.

If you are running under spinnaker, it is quite a different matter. Under spinnaker you have little chance of being able to turn back within five minutes; if you are sailing at six knots the man overboard is already about half a mile behind before you are at last ready to head towards him.

While the spinnaker is being handed, one man must 'do the navigation'. On the chart or on a sheet of squared paper, he marks

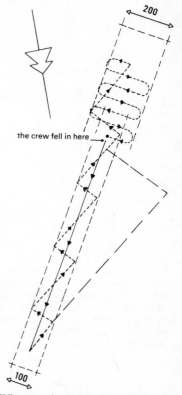

the crew fell in here

Whoever is navigating must be rigorously systematic and not improvise on the spur of the moment. To transfer the track to the squared paper or to the chart (which at that moment is nothing but a piece of squared paper) you must have chosen:

– a scale: the most convenient is 1cm a knot

– a direction system, normally the compass course provided there is no deviation

The moment you turn back there are these alternatives: either return in a 'corridor' 100m wide (the maximum distance to be sure of seeing a man overboard), or make two tacks leading directly to the spot. When you have passed the point where it is assumed the man fell overboard, you return systematically sweeping an area 200m wide

the place, time and course when the man went overboard. He also notes the boat's speed. He can then calculate, the moment the boat turns back, the distance to be covered.

The whole manoeuvre must be ruled by the watch. You sail back, making short tacks to either side of the track, each tack lasting the same number of seconds.

If you draw a blank and are certain you have passed the spot, you quarter the zone in the opposite direction, still navigating meticulously all the time.

Coming Alongside

When you have found the man, you must be able to come alongside at a reduced speed. For that, you must heave-to upwind of him: foresail backed, helm down, and drift. If you arrive close-hauled, try to pick him up as soon as you reach him. If you fail at the first attempt, carry out the classic 'man overboard drill', as it is described in the left-hand drawing opposite. But you must realise that all boats do not react in the same way, and you may have to proceed as shown in the right-hand drawing. The essential is clearly to have trained for such an eventuality, and to have perfected the drill best suited to your own boat.

You can also, without any special manoeuvre, stop the boat sailing as close as possible to the man, and throw him a buoy tied to a rope with the other end fastened inboard (preferably at the

How to come alongside a man overboard. On the left, the procedure for larger boats like *La Sereine* or the Glénans cutters; on the right for smaller boats of the Nautile or Galiote type (of chapter 2)

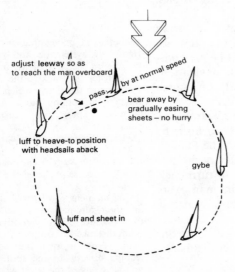

adjust leeway so as to reach the man overboard

pass by at normal speed

bear away by gradually easing sheets – no hurry

luff to heave-to position with headsails aback

gybe

luff and sheet in

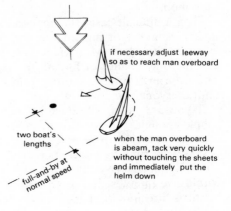

if necessary adjust leeway so as to reach man overboard

two boat's lengths

full-and-by at normal speed

when the man overboard is abeam, tack very quickly without touching the sheets and immediately put the helm down

bow). The lead line can be used as the rope.

It often happens that when the man overboard sees help coming he suddenly gives up the struggle. Many people, after putting up a long fight, have drowned at this very moment – just when they were about to be rescued. It can be a safeguard if someone, properly tied onto a good long line, goes in to help. Alternatively, you can go out to him in the dinghy or the liferaft. It is important then to tie a line round the man and bring him alongside.

Getting the Man on Board

Hoisting him on board is usually no easy task.

The boat must be stopped. If it is hard to keep her hove to, you must drop all sails and lash the helm down.

If the topsides are not high, the man has still some strength in him and the crew are Herculean it is possible that the man will find himself back in the cockpit in a twinkling. But that doesn't happen very often. Usually he must be helped inboard by some method or other. We recommend three: ladder, mainsail, and purchase.

To be used as a tackle, the kicking straps tackle must have easy-to-release carbine hooks at either end; the line must be long enough for the tackle to be extended to at least 4m

– A boarding ladder is simple and effective. It must be made in such a way that it can easily be hooked on quickly to any point of the boat, and weighted at the bottom to prevent it floating up. This is only practicable when the man in the water still has enough strength to grasp it. If not, use another method.
– Drop the mainsail, free it completely from the mast and let it sink into the water, to make a sort of hammock for him to lie in, or be laid in. Then hoist.
– You can also use a tackle (with a minimum of three parts). Each block should have a carbine hook. Hook one of them onto the eye of a halyard, the other onto the man's harness. Haul on the halyard to lengthen the purchase, then cleat it. All you have to do now is to haul on the tackle to hoist the man on board.

The mainsail kicking strap can be used as a tackle, if it has adequate carbine hooks. Remember that a regular block and tackle can only be used quickly if it is properly stowed; either fully stretched with the parts kept together with stopping twine every few inches; or with the tackle choc-a-bloc and the rope coiled up.

A man weighing 100 kilos is hoisted effortlessly . . . and swings over the lifelines without difficulty

The man is now on board. If he is still in good shape, there is relief all round.

If he is badly shaken, we shall not lower morale by mentioning at this point the attention he must be given if he looks nearly drowned or frozen to the marrow. You will find all the relevant instructions at the end of the chapter.

Collisions

The prevention of collision at sea demands that everyone respects the same rules. These rules are strict and flexible at the same time because they are based, not upon rights, but on the responsibility of all concerned. *It is not laid down that such and such a boat has priority over another. It is much more conditional and more realistic than that: one boat must keep out of the way of the other (which must stick to her course), unless the first one has not seen her.* You have to adopt quite a different attitude – not to be compared with those found on the roads today. The official text of *Rules for the Prevention of Collision at Sea* is a compulsory item on the inventory of boats of any size. It is included in all good nautical almanacs and a copy should be on board any boat going more than five miles from port. We will go into this in detail in the chapter on 'Navigation', but meanwhile it is enough to say that even the smallest cruising yacht should have a copy on board or at least a concise version of the rules.

You should learn the text of the rules by heart, whatever the size of your boat, and above all try to master the essentials, and be able to refer to them if you are in doubt.

We will stick here to the principal rules for steering and course.

Under Sail

Keep out of the way of:

– all boats you are overtaking;
– when you are on starboard tack, of all boats also on starboard tack and under your lee;
– when you are on port tack, of all boats on starboard tack; of all boats also on port tack and under your lee.

In principle therefore, you never have to change course when close-hauled on starboard tack. 'He who is close-hauled on starboard is king of the sea', used to be an old saw. But nowadays, on board a yacht, you are king without a realm. Clearly, even on this point of sailing, you change course if the crew of the other boat has

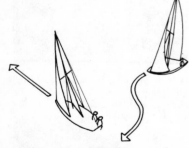

The boat to windward must keep clear

not seen you or if it has no steerage way.

Finally, keep clear by day, of all vessels with cones, half-cones, spheres or baskets hoisted; and by night, of all vessels with lights one above the other, white or coloured, on the same mast. Once you are well clear, you can look up in your almanac what sort of vessel it was and what it was up to.

Under Power

Keep clear:

– of all vessels you overtake;
– of sailing vessels, and all vessels with cones, half-cones, spheres, baskets hoisted, or with lights one above the other on the same mast;
– of all other vessels under engine seen on the starboard bow (to be exact in a sector of 112°5', the arc of visibility of port and starboard navigation lights).

Finally, when two vessels under engine are head on they both alter course slightly so as to pass port to port.

The boat on the right is under power (indicated by the cone hoisted point down); it must keep clear of the boat on the left that is under sail only

When two power-driven vessels are meeting end on, or nearly end on, each shall alter course to starboard so that each may pass on the port side of the other

Under power, keep clear of all other vessels under power seen on the starboard bow

In a Channel

Navigation regulations on the open sea no longer apply in channels, where the essential rule is to keep to the right.

But it must be appreciated that navigating in a channel is a very delicate operation for a vessel of large tonnage: she often has no room to manoeuvre, and if she slows down too much risks losing all steerage way. In a channel therefore, on board a yacht, you must not only keep to the right, but do nothing that might hamper, in any way whatsoever, the movements of large ships. In any case yachts can usually keep slightly outside the limits of the channel.

Collision Risks

By day. Two vessels are on collision courses when the bearing of one in relation to the other does not vary. On sighting a ship the first action therefore is to take its bearing, by reading off the angle between your own heading and the position of the approaching boat. You can avoid any calculations by taking a reference point; you can for instance take a sight on the vessel over the top of a particular stanchion. If the vessel stays in line with this stanchion (i.e. if the relative bearing does not vary), then both vessels are on a collision course; you must alter course accordingly.

By night. Ships' lights indicate their course. Every vessel carries a green light to starboard and a red light to port, the lit sector being ten points on each side (i.e. 112°5′). It may also carry a certain number of white lights; your almanac will tell you their meaning.

Let us simply note that coloured lights are much less visible than white lights (two miles instead of ten miles); it is therefore the masthead lights which first give an indication of the ship's course. You must know that on large ships the after light is higher than the

The boat's bearing is not changing: LOOK OUT

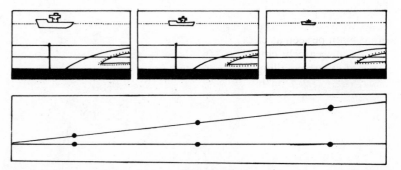

forward light and the superstructures. When these lights are one above the other, then the vessel is bearing straight down on you.

The coloured navigation lights beome visible when the ship draws nearer (7×50 binoculars are very useful for recognising them). There is no risk of collision when you see the other ship's red light in the sector of your red light, or his green light in the sector of your green one. *Red to red; safe water ahead; green to green, safe water between.*

When you are on a collision course with a large vessel whose responsibility it is to keep clear, you must immediately ask yourself 'Have I been seen?' If you are not certain, it is only sensible to get out of the way yourself, and in good time. In practice:

– a large ship cannot always manoeuvre in time, because of its speed and slow reactions;
– on the open sea (especially at meal times) some cargo ships are frequently switched onto their automatic pilots alone, with no one on the bridge;
– at night, too, it is practically impossible to see the lights of a sailing ship from the bridge of a cargo ship.

Changing course is not always enough to avoid a collision. You may have to do everything in your power to signal your presence: shine a powerful lamp (if you have one powerful enough) onto the bridge of the vessel; or, if collision is still imminent, fire flares in the direction of the bridge, using preferably white or green ones.

Radar reflector

In Thick Weather

The rules of helmsmanship and of the road do not change, but it becomes difficult, if not impossible, to know if you are on a collision course with another ship. To avoid each other, sailors have two means at their disposal: radar and sound signals.

Merchant ships, warships, and large fishing vessels are equipped with radar. To have some chance of being picked up on this equipment, yachts must carry a radar reflector at the masthead if possible. This is only efficient if it is large enough and if its faces are at the correct angles to each other. A radar reflector must be at least 20cm across the diagonal. If it can be placed high enough (between 5 and 10m), it can be seen as clearly on a radar screen as a 10m metal hull.

You can scarcely count on sound signals. Your own can only be heard by other sailing boats: on small motor boats, engine noise drowns them, and on big ships the door of the wheelhouse shuts them out.

The signals put out by other boats will reveal their presence but not their course or their distance off. Down below in a sailing boat, the engines of ships and the noise of their propellers can be heard clearly even when they are a long way off. But that does not tell you much.

In thick weather, prudence dictates that you should keep well clear of busy shipping lanes whenever you can. If they cannot be avoided one must at least cut straight across at right angles to minimise the danger period.

Accidents on Board

There is no space to catalogue here all the minor accidents that can happen on board. Many of them arise from untidiness or carelessness: slipping on spilled noodle soup, getting entangled in a jib left untidy, putting your foot through a half-closed hatch – all these can cause serious accidents, and some splendid fractures. Accidents also happen in working the boat: you can easily crush a finger by holding a sheet too close to the winch, or an anchor chain too close to the fairlead; you can easily break one or more if you put your thumb the other way round to your fingers when turning the engine crank handle or fending off a quay – to mention a few examples. It is not difficult to climb the mast without help; but you should use a bosun's chair. The list of careless things you can do on board is endless. A French proverb, typical of the sea, puts it in a nutshell: 'If a damned silly thing can be done, it has been done; when it can't, it will be.'

So we shall confine ourselves to serious accidents which can affect the boat and endanger the crew: damage to the rigging, leaks, fire, explosion.

Damage to the Rigging

The best counter-measure is to have rigging in good condition on setting out, and checking it periodically. On a cruising boat you should make a detailed inspection every week or fortnight, by climbing into the rigging and checking the state of the shrouds, talurit splices, split pins, clevis pins, bolts, halyards, wear on the blocks, etc. As a matter of routine you should cast a critical eye over it every day (the glasses enable you to do this without too much trouble). This is a good habit to cultivate, for you can then notice the slightest change. This survey can be done systematically at daybreak, and that allows you, at the same time, to pick up any mistakes made in securing the halyards the previous night.

These precautions should save you from nasty shocks. But nothing is perfect; neither the men, who forget to renew rigging in time, nor the material itself. A shroud or a mast fitment can break without warning, a talurit splice can crack – many things can break or work loose.

If a shroud breaks, the normal routine is that you must immediately go about; if the forestay suddenly snaps, come onto a broad reach; if the backstay breaks, get wind abeam. It's logical. If the mast has stayed standing, a running repair is always possible provided you have a length of cable on board and some Bulldog grips. Get to work at once.

But one mustn't cherish too many illusions: more often than not, you haven't the time to do anything: down comes the mast, and happy is the man who doesn't get it on his head!

At a stroke you are in a very tricky position: the mast, dangling, still attached to the shrouds and the sail, can make a hole in the hull; the boat is not in control.

You must get hold of the mast straightaway and secure it on deck, or if that is not possible, get rid of it as quickly as possible by cutting through the shrouds (hence the need for wire-cutters on board).

Next you must think how you can get the boat to a safe anchorage. As a general rule, you will have chosen a course which affords shelter to leeward (see chapter 21). The engine, a jury rig or the sweep may enable you to reach it, or even the very action of the wind itself: it is always possible to make a good course of 30° either side of a following wind, even without any means of propulsion.

After a dismasting in the English Channel

Leaks

We are not going to discuss leaks in hulls in bad condition: the best ending for old boats in hopeless repair is to doze away the rest of their days in a mud berth.

But leaks can be sprung even on a well maintained sound boat. Water may only be seeping in slightly, but however small the leak may be, it is not to be neglected, even if it is only making life on board uncomfortable: it must be pinpointed and stopped.

A leak is only serious if it has been caused by an accident: the hull stove in on a rock or a wreck, or the coachroof damaged by a spar breaking or by capsizing.

Dual action is called for: at one and the same time the breach must be filled, and the water expelled.

The hole can be blocked temporarily with a mattress, a pillow or clothing; next a piece of plywood is prepared for an emergency repair. A few pieces of plywood always come in handy. If you have none you will have to use the cabin table or locker door, or a plank from the cabin sole.

If water is running in fast the pump is usually inadequate: buckets must be used. It is only after the hole has been blocked (as well as may be) and most of the water bailed out that the pump can keep the level down while course is being made to the nearest shelter.

This pump must be firmly installed where it can be used in comfort: the work can go on for hours.

Diaphragm pumps with a simple action are best. The body must be easily dismantled for cleaning out. The suction pipe must be corrugated or otherwise rigid so as not to collapse under the effect of the suction; it must have a filter at the bilge end, which can be easily reached and cleaned out. The discharge pipe must be fitted securely from inside to discharge outside the hull or, if there is no other way into the cockpit if it is self-draining.

Fire and Explosion

The causes of fire on board are principally the inflammable substances that have been brought on board, particularly petrol. Obviously it would be desirable not to have such dangerous stuff on board, *but it should always be stowed with care where there is no danger of it seeping into the bilges.*

Our views on petrol/gasoline engines have been given in chapter 6. We ourselves have taken out inboard petrol engines from all our cruising boats, and we only use petrol for outboard engines on open boats.

When these outboards are being used, no tanks must be filled whilst they are running; and no naked light of any sort is allowed: no cooking, no smoking.

Methylated spirit also ignites very easily: it must not be poured onto a stove or lamp until it is completely out. We now use Meta tablets.

Fire spreads very quickly on a fibreglass boat; much less quickly on a wooden one and not at all (with the exception of fitments) in a concrete or metal hull.

The ways and means of extinguishing fire are adequately described in nautical almanacs and manuals and you should be familiar with them. The location of the extinguisher must be carefully considered: it must be readily accessible, wherever fire may break out. Everyone on board must know exactly how it works, and the skipper must not fail to explain this to everyone on board.

Explosions occur on boats where petrol or gas is used. Let us leave petrol (or gas) for the moment and consider *butane gas* (Gaz).

Butane gas stoves are very convenient, clean and easy to maintain, but they are not the safest type. A leaky joint or a loose tap lets the gas escape, and it drops into the bilges. No one knows it has happened until a spark or a match makes it explode. If Butane is used, certain precautions must be taken:

For preference, use a stove with a burner that screws directly into the container or canister.

Every time a canister is changed, plunge the whole thing (burner and canister) into water: everyone knows it ought to be done, no one does it; and yet it is the only way of knowing for certain if it is not leaking.

Keep a close eye on two-burner stoves. They are the ones that leak most. Renew the joints frequently.

Always put the cap back on empty containers; there is always a little gas left in them, and they may leak as soon as you unscrew the cap or burner.

As long as there are bubbles, the stove must be treated as if it were a time bomb

The rigging is a good lightning conductor provided each part is earthed

Do not hestitate to throw away the whole stove as soon as it seems to be in anything but perfect condition.

A gas refrigerator is never to be used. The reason is clear: if the flame goes out no one notices it. The French ship, *Marie-Grillon*, whose burned out remains were found in 1970 near the Minquiers rocks, off Brittany, was equipped with a butane refrigerator.

To be safe with gas or petrol on board, you should install a *gas detector*, and it is no longer expensive. It must be checked daily to ensure it is working by holding a butane gas lighter, open but not lit, close to the filament; if it does not react, the filament must be changed. The detector must be fitted low down in the boat and kept water-tight; if it gets wet it is useless.

Lightning

Lightning can be catastrophic; it can literally blow a boat up or, at the very least set it on fire. The mast and shrouds make good lightning conductors, provided they are 'earthed' – connected to the water, either by the chain plates if they are long enough, or by the anchor chain hung in loops around the boat and connecting the shrouds and stays to the water.

Survival after Shipwreck

After serious accidents such as collisions, explosions or a serious leak, a boat may be unmanageable or sink unless it has built in buoyancy.

Then the crew must survive by keeping themselves afloat or preferably out of the water altogether until help comes. This is when the role of the shore contact is vital. It is he who will give the alarm. How soon? All shipwrecked sailors are haunted by that question: 'When will they begin the search? Shall we be able to hold out until they arrive?' You must have the means to survive, perhaps for several days, without succumbing to cold, fatigue, thirst and despair.

When you are actually shipwrecked you must remember that you still have many means at your disposal: if the boat is unsinkable you can hang on for a very long time, and possibly even continue to sail. If you have to take to the liferaft, you are still in a dependable boat, capable of crossing the Atlantic if necessary: Doctor Bombard did it.

Being Unsinkable

It is quite feasible to make a boat unsinkable, at least if they are of small tonnage. The Muskateer is made unsinkable with the help of 800 to 900 litres of expanded polystyrene; some 2,000 litres are needed to do the same for the Nautile. Obviously this material takes up space on board; you must choose your priorities.

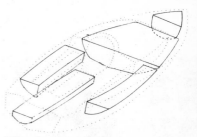

Why the Mousquetarie is unsinkable

The built-in buoyancy of some production cruising boats has been certified by the French Merchant Marine. If you want to test your boat, you remove every bit of gear and replace the weight on board (including that of the crew) with pig iron, and fill it with fresh water!

An unsinkable boat is a comforting guarantee of safety. The crew can stay on board, eat (at least canned food), drink fresh water and have all their safety and navigational equipment. A Musketeer, even when it is full of water, can make one or two knots, and shelter can be reached through your own efforts.

There is little comfort on board: the deck is only a few inches above water; if there is the slightest sea it is constantly swept by waves; the crew cannot rest and are sopping wet all the time. Their situation may become untenable in a rough sea.

But abandoning ship is a grave decision. The liferaft is got ready but, even so, remain on board as long as possible.

The Liferaft

In France we use three types of inflatable safety rafts. With rafts of class IV you can sail up to 200 miles from a port in boats of a maximum length of 10 metres. Boats of more than 10 metres with rafts of class II may cruise between 20 and 200 miles from harbour. Class I rafts are compulsory for boats going more than 200 miles out.

Class IV Rafts

It serves as the tender, and as your liferaft. It can be inflated either by a bellows or, in emergency, by bottles of compressed gas fitted to it (inflation then takes less than a minute).

In harbour it is a convenient tender as all the crew can get into it. In case of shipwreck, it is all the better as a liferaft because everyone is used to its ways. It has a survival kit on board with a tent-like cover and useful equipment like flares, waterproof torch, etc.

Class IV life raft

Class II life raft

The raft behaves quite well at sea. If you can rig a sail you can make way, with wind astern or on a broad reach, at about two knots.

Class II Raft

This is designed for survival only. It is kept in a bag or a rigid container, from which it is only removed in emergency or for its annual check. It has a self-erecting roof and a full survival kit, often contained in a second container attached to the other by a line.

Most of the rafts in this class are round, rather like igloos. Their shape rules out any possibility of making way, and in any case the sea anchor incorporated in their design makes them pretty static. They drift with the wind and all the crew can do is to be patient.

These round dinghies, which are liferafts pure and simple, are specially suitable for merchant ships and fishing boats. The latter are in frequent radio contact with the shore and the other boats; they can usually signal their distress and give their position; help arrives quickly and the less the raft moves away from the original spot, the better.

Let us now imagine a yacht that has been wrecked on the first day of a passage across the Bay of Biscay, as a result of an explosion for instance. Provided the weather is fine, our shore contact will not worry for four or five days, and when the search does begin it will have to scout the whole of the sea area. On a static raft the crew may have to wait in this case, inactive and patient for five days and perhaps longer.

It seems to us that certain class II rafts, which have an oblong shape and dagger boards that enable you to sail, are infinitely preferable. We use them on our bigger boats. They can sail at 1 or 2 knots, within 70° of the wind. In the instance above, the crew in this type of raft might have reached the shore even before a search had been organised, or at least got close enough to be seen by a boat and be picked up.

The ability to sail in some direction is of the first importance; particularly from the psychological point of view: the crew is doing something about their own survival. They lose heart much less quickly than if they had nothing to do.

Class I Raft

Obligatory in France for sailing beyond 200 miles from harbour, this raft has some improvements that make it superior to the class

II type: double bottom, double entrance, better buoyancy, etc.

It is a good tip never to buy a rubber dinghy without seeing it inflated, or at least laid out unfolded. Never miss a chance (and the numerous boat shows afford plenty) of examining these dinghies closely, feeling and inspecting their quality. It is also well worth while to take part in safety exercises and attend demonstrations. At Glénans we practise safety drill at the beginning of each cruise, simulating as much as possible real emergency conditions. When the raft has to be used in earnest, every one then knows that to do; that is the way to avoid panic.

Living in a Liferaft

When the decision is taken to abandon ship, panic must be avoided at all costs. Everything must be done systematically and coolly.

The liferaft is not inflated on the deck (unless it is the tender, well known to be slow and tedious to inflate). It is thrown in the water with the extra container if you have one, and is inflated automatically.

Get aboard in an orderly way without rushing. First one or two people, then all the gear (water, food, lots of clothing, charts, etc.), then the rest of the crew. The gear is carefully tied in. Cast off the painter, and all that remains to be done is to settle down aboard in as little discomfort as possible, by drying out the inside of the raft and wringing out any wet clothing.

A new cruise is beginning. The skipper decides on an unambitious navigation plan which usually pleases everyone: to head for land. A routine is then organised, and many questions arise: what is to be done about resisting hunger, thirst, cold and boredom?

Eating

We tend to forget nowadays that you can quite easily live for several days without eating. In the liferaft's equipment there is food enough, often in tubes: it is not for the delectation of gastronomes, but it is all perfectly edible.

You can also start fishing, for you have the equipment you need and, for once, you are travelling at just the right speed.

Drinking

You can easily skip a few meals but it is imperative to drink.

A plan is made for rationing water and, as the container only holes a small amount, it is as well to have foreseen this and to have brought a jerrican, only three quarters full so that it will float. It should be fastened to the other container.

It has now been established, thanks to the experiment made by Dr Bombard and confirmed by the work of Dr Aury, that drinking sea water does not have the dire consequences, as was once believed. Sea water is too salty, but drinking it is better than depriving the body of all fluid.

It must be drunk as soon as the fresh water runs out; drink little and often – about two mouthfuls eight or ten times a day. At this rate, there will be no serious results for the first ten days.

Bombard has also shown that fish flesh contains about 200 to 250 grams of fresh water per kilo. It can be extracted by pressure or, more simply, by making large incisions in the flesh.

Finally, rain can solve the problem and every possible container is put to use to collect the water as it runs off the sail and cover.

Keeping Warm

This is one of the shipwrecked mariner's main concerns. There are only makeshift ways of keeping out the cold: wring out wet clothing thoroughly, shelter from the wind, insulate the floor of the raft by spreading clothes on it, huddle up close to one another. Special blankets, lined with aluminium, are being made now which retain heat remarkably well.

Distractions

Inactivity is the bugbear of shipwrecked sailors. Life is less irksome when the raft can be kept going for there is navigation to be done, and a course to be kept as best you can. In a static raft there is little to be done and it isn't frivolous to throw in a pack of cards before you abandon ship.

But there is always a watch to be kept continuously. If a ship appears on the horizon, approaches fairly near but only to pass without seeing you, the morale of the crew is knocked hard. Everything must be done to signal to shipping.

Signalling for Help

There are small distress transmitter sets which, when switched on, automatically send out the statutory signals SOS in morse (it is 'Mayday' on radio telephone). These sets still cost a good deal, but manufacturers are trying to produce less expensive models for yachts.

In addition, have ready day and night signals: flares, smoke flares, rockets, torches and mirrors. You must be able to use them at short notice, so keep open the box they are in, and be sure to have read the 'directions for use'. All the crew must know exactly how to use them.

It must be emphasised they are not to be used irresponsibly. Firing off flares at random is wanton and they must be saved for the moment when it is practically certain they will be seen. Ordinary flares only stay in the air briefly. Parachute flares have much more chance of being spotted. The most effective of all signals is undoubtedly the orange-coloured smoke signal. Its smoke spreads out for miles and takes a long time to disperse.

When a ship passes at last and is seen to change course towards the raft, calmness is, as ever, important while getting organised for going aboard it. Only when everyone is safely aboard is it permitted to collapse into the arms of the captain.

Try as we have done in this chapter, the descriptions of the disasters and the measures to be taken to cope with them and to avoid them are nevertheless still somewhat hypothetical. In reality, two accidents are never alike; the circumstances are always different, and countless points of detail will modify the events and the steps to be taken.

Full recognition of this will, however, bring home the importance of high standards of safety precautions. The boat must be in perfect condition and thoroughly well equipped (remember that the strength of a chain is that of its weakest link). Complete safety equipment must be on board and you must know how to use it. But safety is only achieved if it is always in the forefront of your mind – a personal concern for crew, boat and the way it is sailed. Training is needed, as well as imagination: sometimes swift action is called for, sometimes it is better to move slowly. What is of the utmost importance, in short, is a brand of safety-mindedness, compounded of something like a wild animal's instinct and a growing knowledge of an environment and a way of life that makes its own, special demands. You are only safe when you are perfectly adapted to the environment in which you live. An understanding of the true meaning and philosophy of sailing is more important than all the rules and regulations in the world.

First Aid at Sea

These short notes do not claim to replace first-aid manuals (there are some excellent ones around). Their aim is to give you some impression, as simply as possible, of the different kinds of accident that can happen on board, of what can be done and, perhaps especially, of what must not be done.

Drowning

There are two types of drowning: by shock and by asphyxia.

Shock is due to a difference of temperature between the body and the water. It can happen when you bathe after exposing yourself for a long time to the sun, or when you go overboard and the water is very cold. It is characterised by a very sudden loss of consciousness, with cardiac arrest; the asphyxia comes afterwards.

Drowning by asphyxia is due to exhaustion. The drowning man can no longer keep himself up in the water and sinks; cardiac arrest follows rapidly on respiratory failure.

The precautions to be taken are well known. To avoid shock you must not bathe after prolonged exposure to the sun (all the more if this exposure has been coupled with strenuous exercise), or after heavy eating and drinking. Avoid plunging too quickly into the water, begin by splashing the nape of the neck and abdomen. There are often warnings of shock; irritation of the skin, a feeling of abnormal fatigue, cramps, internal upset. Then you must come out of the water immediately.

When you are sailing in cold waters, as we have already said, a wet suit is really essential.

If you are to avoid drowning by asphyxia after falling overboard, expend as little energy as possible while you are waiting to be picked up. Every moment burns up calories and therefore exhausts you.

First Aid for the Drowned

Every second counts when you are reviving the patient; the slightest loss of time can have disastrous consequences. All members of the crew should have attended a resuscitation demonstration (on a model) and should be able to apply the *mouth-to-mouth* method, which is the simplest and most effective of all. It is not in the least silly for the skipper to teach it to his crew at the beginning of a cruise. If you have been trained to do it no time is lost. No matter how suddenly you are faced with a drowned person, resuscitation must begin immediately and you must test for cardiac arrest: feel the pulse, not at the wrist but on the femoral arteries, in the groin. If the heart has stopped beating, respiratory and cardiac resuscitation must be applied simultaneously.

If the head is horizontal, the upper respiratory tracts are obstructed by the tongue

Treatment of Respiratory Failure

The mouth-to-mouth method is carried out as follows:

Stretch the man out flat on his back and put his head on one side to extract dentures and any mucus and extraneous matter from his mouth and throat – all at double speed.

Take the head in both hands and tip it backwards. This is essential to ensure an airway. If the neck is extended, the head pressed backwards, the tongue moves forwards, thus opening the air passages. It helps to place clothes under his shoulders as a support.

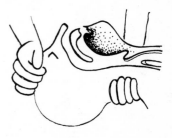

To keep the tracts clear, the head must be pulled well back (in hyper-extension).

Place one hand on his brow and with the other, fingers crooked, pull down the lower jaw to open the mouth wide.

Press your lips round the mouth of the subject, at the same time blocking his nostrils to prevent air coming out through them. Blow strongly. The chest of the subject should be seen to expand. If it does not, the reason is probably that the head has not been tipped back enough.

Move aside slightly to let expiration take place, then blow in again, and continue doing this, following his rhythm (about 12 to 15 times a minute).

Blowing in

A few special cases:

If the drowned man is in convulsion and you cannot open his mouth, use the mouth-to-nose method instead with the head in the same position; with one hand, press on his brow, with the other close his mouth by putting your thumb on his lips. Blow in, taking care not to obstruct the nostrils. Then open his lips to allow expiration; and continue the process.

Exhaling

If the drowned person is a small child, close your lips around his mouth and nose at the same time. Stop blowing in as soon as the chest expands. Follow a rather faster rhythm than for an adult (about 20 times a minute).

Treatment of Cardiac Arrest

If the heart has stopped, you must try to get it beating again, while continuing to practise mouth-to-mouth. If you are alone, apply five cardiac massages between each mouth-to-mouth breath, as follows:

Put the heel of the left hand on the lower half of the breastbone, well in the *middle* of the chest, and put your right hand on the left.

With arms stretched, lean forward and apply all your weight. Operate in a series of two short energetic pressures, but the forward movement should be quicker than the recovery movement. Repeat this massage about 60 times a minute.

Special care must be taken if the subject is an old person or a child; too energetic massage can fracture a rib. In such cases massage with only one hand; with two fingers for a baby.

You must persevere when treating respiratory failure and cardiac arrest. If there are several of you, it can be done in relays. Once the subject has revived he should be taken quickly to port so that treatment can be continued in hospital.

Treatment for Hypothermia

If the man overboard has become very cold in the water, even if he has not lost consciousness, he must be treated with as much care as if he had nearly drowned. Do not follow the dangerous and outmoded practice of undressing the victim, rubbing him down or giving him alcohol.

Research on hypothermia has shown that the cold that penetrates the body sets off a defence mechanism which is characterised by constriction of the blood vessels, first in the *peripheral* zone, then in a so-called *intermediate* zone, the blood flowing back gradually into the zone of the *vital centres* (heart, brain) to try to preserve their heat. If the cold reaches the vital centres, the patient will almost certainly die.

On no account undress the patient but insulate him as quickly as possible from the air outside, the ideal being to plunge him into a large plastic bag or, failing that, into a sleeping bag, two or three people huddling against him.

Also, he should not be warmed superficially by rubbing or giving him alcohol: the dilation of the blood vessels in the peripheral zone causes a rush of blood into an area which is still relatively cold, and that can provoke an additional fall in temperature in the vital centres, as the cold blood circulates there and in greater quantity.

Generally speaking, the best treatment for hypothermia is plunging the victim into a bath at a temperature at least equal to 45°C (the temperature that an elbow dipped into the water can bear). But you are hardly likely to be able to do this on board. But, once the victim has been encapsulated, he can take in very hot drinks, which will induce heating from inside. As with drowning cases, contact a doctor as soon as possible.

As with cases of drowning (and to repeat), treatment of respiratory failure and cardiac arrest must be kept up tirelessly. If there are several of you, then it can be done by rota. Once the patient has been revived, he must be rushed ashore for treatment in hospital.

Health Problems

Minor nuisances like a touch of the sun, or a mild burn that has not been properly treated, can spoil the pleasantest cruise. A little common sense and a little knowledge of elementary first aid are all that is needed to avoid them. In cases of serious accidents (serious burns, deep wounds, fractures), you must above all know what not to do and to be able to assess the urgency of treatment.

We shall consider first the common troubles, for which there are remedies on board, then the serious cases.

Common Complaints

A Touch of the Sun

It is folly to set about systematically roasting yourself in the sun on the very first day of the holidays: the sun's rays can be dangerous because the burn that results can often be very extensive. The roasted victim begins to complain of being very tired, he vomits, develops a temperature and cannot sleep.

Prevention is simply taking care to expose your lily-white body very gradually to the sun and applying a cream that screens you from ultra violet rays.

First aid is the same as for burns – and we will come to them later.

Over-exposure to Light

You have had your eyes fixed too long on the spinnaker; you have taken a sun shot with the sextant; the reflection is intense: your eyes have been over-exposed and the effects can be serious, weakening your sight and even causing temporary blindness; a relatively minor consequence is conjunctivitis, producing a burning sensation in the eyes.

Wearing a peaked cap or dark glasses protects you from it and an eye-wash is soothing.

Sunstroke, Dehydration

A man with sunstroke sweats profusely, his skin is burning, he is feverish, has a headache and is very thirsty. He must be put in a cool, airy spot, sheltered from the sun, with a wet cloth on his head. Give him strong coffee, salt tablets and soft drinks (not alcohol).

The prevention of sunstroke, as with dehydration, is keeping out of the sun and drinking plenty of fresh water, fruit juice and tea regularly between meals.

Infections

A whitlow or a boil are horribly painful and they are the two most common causes of infection.

The whitlow is an abscess in the finger, sometimes called a gathering. It can be caused by an insect bite, or a small neglected cut. The finger becomes rigid, swells up; a high temperature and insomnia make you feel wretched.

Lancing a whitlow should only be done by a doctor. Meanwhile it should be bathed five or six times a day in a warm antiseptic solution. Cover it with a bandage soaked in the same fluid.

If the whitlow continues to be painful, consult a doctor as soon as possible and he will no doubt prescribe an antibiotic. If no doctor is available, it is just as well to have a broad spectrum antibiotic on board, but in Britain it is only supplied on prescription.

Boils are an infection caused by *staphylococcus bacterium*. It is a dangerous infection because it can spread.

A boil must never be squeezed between the fingers, or pierced with a pin. Dressing too must be avoided. Apply an antiseptic ointment and consult a doctor soon.

Diarrhoea

This is the *commonest* of common complaints. It can be the result of a chill or food poisoning (tinned food, fish) or a diet you are not used to: too many dairy products, fruit, fatty foods, certain local dishes (Italian fresh pasta, for instance, should be eaten the day they are made).

There are many different treatments. The simplest is to go on a starvation diet: carrot soup or rice water for the first day, unseasoned rice for the next two days. Avoid orgies for a few days more.

There are various medicines:

Kaolin mixture is the standard remedy; drink a lot of water.

Take care; prolonged diarrhoea, badly treated, can bring on a state of serious malnutrition and dehydration.

Tonsillitis

A frequent occurrence at sea, it is accompanied by a fever. It is helped by sucking antiseptic pastilles and gargling warm sea water.

Toothache

No one should go off on a cruise with bad teeth: you spoil your own pleasure and others' as well. See your dentist before you leave. If in spite of everything you get toothache, some relief can be found:

If it is decay (the pain usually starts at night), by putting a cotton wad soaked in oil of cloves into the tooth;
If it is an abscess, use an antiseptic mouth wash. An antibiotic is still better if you have it.

Burns

You can only too easily burn yourself cooking or attending to the engine. Such burns are usually slight but, if you should be seriously burned by a butane gas or petrol explosion, be aware of the following:

A burn is usually sterile, for the burning liquid or flame will have sterilised the flesh;

A burn can be serious in two ways, according to its extent and depth.

If extensive it is dangerous to life, first through shock and then through infection and loss of fluid. If it is very deep it can leave dreadful, disfiguring scars which can contract and impede the movement of a joint.

Less Extensive Burns

Burns are considered to be extensive when they cover over 10% of the body (less in the case of a child). But a burn which is not extensive can still be deep.

Generally speaking, this is the procedure:

Take care not to infect a wound which is in itself clean; therefore wash your hands carefully; clean the skin around the wound without touching the wound itself.

Apply a patent sterilised gauze or an antibiotic ointment.

Apply a sterile compress and a pad of cotton wool, then an elastic dressing strip, quite tight to begin with to stop the loss of plasma.

If the skin is burned in the hollow of a joint, make sure the dressing is big enough to prevent the two burned surfaces sticking together. If two adjacent fingers are burned, make a separate dressing for each finger.

Do not touch the dressing subsequently, except to loosen the outer strip a little if it is found to be too tight.

The table below summarises the treatment for different degrees of burn.

Severity	Indications	Most frequent causes	Remedies	Prevention
1st degree	redness, burning pain	spilling boiling liquid	patent gauze, ointment	as soon as the sea is rough the cook must wear boots with oilskin trousers over them
2nd degree	redness, pain, blisters	as for 1st degree, plus handling hot engine	same remedies don't pierce blisters before 3rd day	wait until the engine is cold before undertaking a repair
3rd degree	blackish, greyish, yellow patch, insensitive to touch	immersion in boiling liquid, clothes catching alight	a dressing, wrap up, hospital	

Extensive Burns

An extensive burn is a matter of the utmost urgency. It is the life of the victim that is at stake.

Do not undress the victim; simply remove rings, belt, shoes.
Wrap him in a blanket, lay him down with his head lower than his feet, and keep him warm with hot water bottles which have been covered to prevent burning.
Give plenty of fluids (adding 5 grams of salt to each litre of water). On no account any alcohol.
Avoid speaking and coughing in front of him.
Take him with all speed to a medical burns unit, by air if possible.

It is essential in the case of all but the slightest burns to seek medical advice at the first port of call, particularly if they affect the face or any vital area.

The Medicine Chest

Medicine or first-aid boxes can be bought in varying sizes and completeness. Painkillers and disinfectants and other drugs are of course not always available without a doctor's prescription and he should be consulted if your box lacks items you personally feel you ought to have. In addition to such things the following are essential items:

Thermometer
Scissors, dissecting tweezers
surgical spirit
safety pins
1 wide-necked bottle
sterile compresses, 1 box
cotton wool, 1 100g pack
gauze 5cm and 10cm wide
seasick remedy
antiseptic cream

crêpe bandages, 5cm and 10cm
Elastoplast, 8cm, 1 roll
Band-aid strips
aspirin or (better) Paracetamol
eye-wash (conjunctivitis)
Brolene eye drops
medicine for diarrhoea
medicine for constipation
throat pastilles

This list is the absolute minimum. It can all be kept easily in a metal tin. Fix the lid on with adhesive tape to keep the pharmaceutical products from the damp.

Wounds

The treatment depends on the severity of the wound. Small wounds need only be cleaned carefully in tepid soapy water with a little ammonium hydroxide. Foreign bodies are removed from the wound with tweezers or scissors dipped in surgical spirit. Dab the wound with disinfectant and cover with a dressing.

Serious wounds often seem worse than burns, but are generally less dangerous. There are three things to be done: stop the bleeding, disinfect, cover the wound.

Stopping Bleeding

A tourniquet should never be applied except in the last resort: if not tight enough, it makes the bleeding worse; too tight and kept in place for more than an hour and a half, it can damage the limb for life. A tourniquet is only used when nothing else stops the haemorrhage. If a tourniquet is put on, it must be loosened every hour by the clock.

Haemorrhage is usually stopped by pressure with the finger or fist over the wound, then a dressing: sterile compresses, plenty of cotton wool, finally bind tightly with a crêpe bandage and keep the limb raised.

Antisepsis

Clean the wound and the surrounding area, if the skin is dirty, with a disinfectant; if not apply an antiseptic like ammonium hydroxide.

Closing the Wound

If there is a doctor on board, he will put in some stitches. If there isn't one, the wound can often be closed in the following way: dry the skin around the wound carefully; after disinfecting, apply adhesive plaster directly on the wound (without a dressing), bring the lips of the wound together and stick down on the other side.

Fractures

All fractures clearly require hospitalisation as quickly as possible. The procedure to be followed meanwhile varies:

Fracture of a Limb

The essential is to immobilise the fractured limb in the correct position.

The splint must immobilise the joint above the fracture and the one below, the elbow and the wrist for instance for a fracture of the forearm.

The limb must be in a functional position, ie for the arm, elbow bent at 90°. The opposite is the case for a leg; the limb must be stretched out, with the foot at right angles. This ensures that the limb remains serviceable even if it has to stay in this position.

Sedatives and a sleeping tablet are given to the injured person, and one makes rapidly for harbour.

In the case of a compound fracture (when the broken bone pierces the flesh), one must:

put a sterile dressing on the wound;
immobilise with a splint;
give an antibiotic, if it is available on board;
return to port as fast as possible or ask for help.

Other Fractures

If injury to the spinal column is suspected, the injured person must only be moved if it cannot be avoided and with extreme care: it is important to move him exactly in the position in which he is found, without changing the shape of the spinal column. It is advisable to put him on a plank (of a bunk for instance), which also will make it easier to move him subsequently.

In the case of a neck injury, the subject's neck must be kept strictly in line with the body, settle the man flat on his back with head back and wedge him firmly in place in his bunk until you get to port.

Any heavy knock on the head should be x-rayed.

If ribs are fractured (the injured person feels sharp pain and breathes with difficulty) a chest bandage must be applied or, better still, an elastic bandage (very effective also for sprains) to ease the pain.

Appendicitis

Abdominal pains, accompanied by high fever, vomiting and intestinal discomfort, are possible symptoms of appendicitis and you must return to port quickly.

Do not forget finally that, when a sick man has to be taken to port, every means are to be used: signal a passing boat with red flares, hoping it is a fast one with a radio transmitter, be it a passenger ferry or even an aircraft carrier.

Here's hoping you will never have to do this.

15. Life on Board

On a cruising yacht people have to live together, cook, eat, idle, sleep, do the occasional odd job and even sail. Some novices may wonder how it is that life in such a restricted space is possible, much less enjoyable. The cabin is an awkward kind of hutch for him at first, heaving and restless, hardly ever at peace and, as often as not, outside it he is exposed to horrible weather.

At sea everything is different from living on land, with entirely new standards. The strange purpose of it all, sleeping half by day and half by night, the day's work and the close relationships of the crew give it such a novel flavour that it is like being in a completely new world; and on a longish cruise, a self-sufficient world with its own laws and rituals, private jokes and even a degree of anguish. A social climate prevails that no one who has not experienced it can imagine. It is an enclosed society of the crew's own making, a delicate one that a misfit can destroy. What makes a cruise successful? No one can say precisely. It is the happy conjunction between a small boat, a handful of humankind and the unspoken recognition of comradeship as precious as a shared secret. If this can be created spontaneously, the cruise will be more than happy, it will be unforgettable.

In this short chapter we shall not attempt to penetrate the mysteries that combine to create success. We can only give a few pointers which may help you to avoid blunders. There are many things that make for discord: untidiness, not knowing when to be silent, misunderstandings and, of course, the purely material matters of cold, weariness and hunger. They can separately and together spoil the efficiency of the crew, and if seasickness is added for good measure, what might have been your small heaven is turned into living hell. We want to analyse what it is that creates harmony

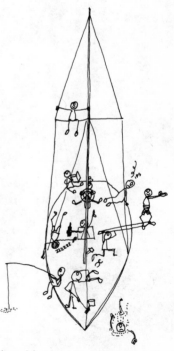

A cruising boat is not just for sailing, it is also a place for living

among human beings and why everyday things and duties, although known by the same words on land, are utterly different at sea and have to be re-defined.

The Men

The term 'men' is used here in its fullest sense: *homo sapiens*, 'the most highly adaptable species in the animal kingdom'. Women, we recognise, belong to the same species. On board we distinguish two sub-species: the skipper, male or female, and the crew.

The Skipper

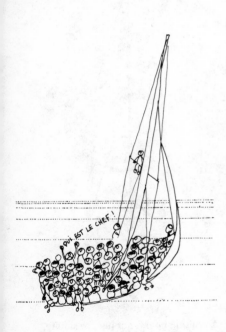

The free man who loves the sea hopes to live in his chosen world with no restraint, subject to no authority. So he can, if he sails alone. Once there are others on board, he must renounce his total freedom: a skipper there must be.

Centuries of experience have confirmed this, and those who think otherwise are in for a rude awakening. No doubt on a day's trip, or cruising in short hops from port to port, and given good weather, a skipper may be dispensed with; all may go pleasantly enough, though maintenance may be left to chance. But in the event of an emergency – the wind freshening, fog coming down, something breaking – confusion arises as to what is to be done and who is to do what: dissension sets in, as miserable as it is dangerous.

It will soon be appreciated that a good life on board is inconceivable without constant, albeit unobtrusive, coordination, whether it be boat handling, navigation, maintenance, safety, the tempo of life or the general concept of the cruise. For this a man is needed who is capable of keeping in view a continuous assessment of these various factors and allocating the work judiciously. Only the skipper can fulfil this multiple role, and clearly he should be the most competent member of the crew. Should everyone be equally competent, still one must be picked, who may yield place to another for a following cruise. But from the moment of departure till the final celebratory drink, the skipper's word is law.

His role is onerous. To begin with he is responsible for his crew's life, which is more than enough for one man. He must know every corner of his ship and keep constant watch on any weak spots; he must have satisfied himself that all the crew are familiar with the safety precautions and that each individual knows what to do in an emergency. He is responsible for getting the best out of his ship, from the setting of sails to navigation. It is for him to allocate duties and to organise a watch system that keeps everyone content. It is up to him, day after day, to determine, taking account of the weather and overall conditions, whether the planned objective is still within the capabilities of boat and crew. This responsibility is heavy, for sometimes there are painful decisions to be taken.

If he is to fulfil this role, with its constant demand on him to keep in view the total situation, he must keep himself a little apart, the better to deploy his own capabilities. He will, for instance, reduce his watch duty to a minimum; he will avoid becoming absorbed in any particular task at crucial moments; for example, he should not be at the helm while the boat is getting under way, but keep himself free to direct the whole manoeuvre, to move anywhere and watch everything that is going on, giving a hand where it is needed.

He must have the art of delegating responsibility, contenting himself with checking what has been done. For he, being only human, must sleep from time to time.

Yet he is never off duty even when he is sleeping, for he will have issued instructions to everyone on watch: wake me up if the wind shifts by 20°, if sail has to be shortened, if visibility deteriorates. Or again, if a large ship is sighted, when any light is seen, at daybreak or when anything significant happens.

Keeping in good shape and retaining his capacity for clear thinking, the skipper is a reserve of moral and physical strength for the whole crew. He is always there when the unexpected happens. In fine weather his days are quiet and his command benevolent. In bad weather, he bears the full brunt of fatigue, lack of sleep and far-reaching decisions.

Nevertheless, this paragon of a man must not be silent nor withdrawn, but share fully in life on board. The atmosphere largely depends on him: he must keep the crew interested in what is going on, explaining the reasoning behind his decisions and showing by example how things should be done. In short, he sees to it that everyone takes an interest in the sailing of the boat and the details of the cruise, captain not only in name, and ship's mentor not only on a training ship, but on every cruising yacht; for it is only right that he should pass on his knowledge as it was passed onto him.

To sum up, a good skipper must be everywhere at once, have eyes in the back of his head, sound judgement, unshakable morale and be a light sleeper. Let us hope, too, that his reserves of good humour are unlimited, for, though he must take his role seriously and show he can be firm when necessary, a sound sense of proportion should prevent his taking himself too seriously.

The Crew

Be it for racing or ocean-going, we aim at getting together an integrated crew with mixed abilities, strong to endure, and ready for anything.

For an ordinary cruise the crew, let's face it, is as likely as not a mixed bag, recruited on the basis of relationship, friendship or by chance. You will have some idea, even by hearsay, of the capabilities of relatives and friends, but what chance will turn up is in the lap of the Gods. In any case, when the crew consists of mutual strangers, a trial sail is essential – a trial which will include every possible manoeuvre to test everyone's seamanship. Otherwise there will be no way of knowing if the proposed cruise is viable. No one sets off from Brittany for Ireland with a bunch of greenhorns: there should at least be an experienced second-in-command and a good watch keeper. Without the right crew there is nothing for it but to change the programme.

Nor is it just technical competence which makes a good cruising companion. The ideal crew is a someone who is easy-going, cheerful, adaptable and makes light work of whatever comes to hand. Moreover, someone resilient enough to be counted on during the hours of a long, hard trick. Unhappily, these qualities sometimes take time to come out: the true merits of a newcomer may only be appreciated by the end of the cruise.

Right away, clear up misunderstandings and introduce the newcomer to the requirements of life on board. Left in ignorance, your new crew may look sour when confronted with obscure tasks, be they to do with maintenance or cooking. Another, over-keen, may mistakenly take the initiative, throw himself into action and make some appalling move in working the ship or steering a wrong course. At sea you are not always steering or working the ship, but engaged in all sorts of tedious duties, varied according to the skipper's will, and the sooner the lesson is learnt the better.

Everyone, as they hump their gear aboard, should have made up their mind to put up with a degree of discomfort and to tolerate living cheek-by-jowl in confined quarters.

The sea, they say, reveals the worth of a man. Put it another way: the sea offers everyone a chance to prove their own worth. They will find themselves mysteriously changed from the moment they set foot on deck, seeing everything with a fresh eye, finding themselves unrecognisable simply because they are becoming their true selves. A ship may return to port carrying a different crew from the one that left. Such is the mystery of the empathy between the ocean and the most highly adapted species in the animal kingdom.

Comfort and Order

This section deals with the everyday things that make life possible for frail human beings who were not designed by nature for life at sea: the things which protect us from everything that undermines our stamina – cold, hunger, exhaustion and disorder. On a boat, as at home, we need clothes, a bed, a kitchen and places to keep belongings, but the affinity ends there, for each one of them has to be adapted for a quite different environment and must answer very particular demands.

Some of the domestic appliances, like lavatories or lighting, that pose technical problems, have already been discussed in Chapter 6.

Clothing

The story goes that a very celebrated sailor used to go on watch in a bowler hat. And why not, if he felt comfortable in it? There is only one criterion for dress at sea – personal comfort; if the garment answers your needs, nothing else matters. What cannot be joked about are oilskins.

Whatever your personal whims may be, a lot of clothing is needed, even in summer. So, for retaining heat: underclothes and skin suits; to protect you from wind and damp: classic seaman's jerseys in wool and heavy cotton, heavy canvas smocks, or light but warm nylon jackets.

But oilskins are most important of all, and they come in all shapes and sizes: coats, one piece suits, jackets and trousers. On a small cruiser, jacket and trousers are most practical.

To be really waterproof, the jacket must have a double flap with buttons or a zip fastener, the outer flap secured over the inner one in the opposite direction and jersey cuffs and pockets with velcro flaps that stick shut. The trousers must come well up under the jacket, with braces (suspenders), without fly or side openings and should cover your boots, preferably secured round them. Wear boots, if the weather is at all chilly, on top of woollen socks (always first class for comfort and warmth). Boots are as important as oilskins. Should they be lined? Canvas wet with sea water is difficult to dry. Unlined, boots are unhealthy. At least choose a pair with white soles, for black rubber makes marks on the deck that are very difficult to remove.

When it is fine, wear canvas shoes with non-slip soles. Tennis shoes and even those frightful plastic sandals (that never slip even on a deck covered in fuel oil) are quite suitable. It is strongly recommended that no one goes barefoot: toes are too precious to risk leaving to the mercy of the hundreds of snags lying in wait for them on the deck of a boat.

A woollen cap is comforting in chilly weather. Rain doesn't keep the brain fresh and, although an oilskin hood has the disadvantage of stopping up your ears, those useful organs, it has advantages. But the classic sou'wester is easily the best headgear. The only way to stop water trickling down your neck is to use a towel as a scarf: take plenty.

If it is cold enough for gloves, wool or plastic ones are better than leather which deteriorates quickly.

In spite of oilskins, clothes still get wet and spare dry clothing is essential. Keep in reserve, if possible, one complete warm set to change into for the rare occasions when a long spell off duty is feasible.

Remember that clothes soaked in salt water must be rinsed out in fresh water, otherwise they never get really dry: the salt encrusted on them attracts damp. Lastly, the great quality of wool is that it is the only material that remains warm, even when wet, if worn next to the skin.

Bunks

In harbour, you sleep royally in a bunk 60cm wide. At sea, it is impossible to sleep a wink in it: it is too wide for you to be able to wedge yourself in comfortably. The sailor who spends his nights clinging to his mattress has ample time to compare his lot with that of wretched mountaineers bivouacking on the North face of the Eiger!

To sleep well at sea, an adjustable berth is needed, a cheap enough luxury if canvas *lee boards* are fitted. These are rectangles of strong canvas, laced to the inside edge of the berth and passed under the mattress and raised towards the saloon deckhead. The upper edge usually has a wide hem through which a rod is slipped; the rod is attached by ropes to hooks fixed in the deckhead. The canvas must rise at least 2ft so that the sleeper is well clear of the rod; and the nearer the canvas is to the deckhead, the more he is shielded from the light.

The berth can be narrowed simply by tightening the lacing. This is done when the boat is running free and rolling. The mattress is then half suspended, in a concave shape, and keeps the occupant firmly wedged in. When the boat is sailing steadily, close-hauled for example, the lacing is slackened and the sleeper wedges himself in the hull side or canvas side.

The mattress itself should not be too thick or it accentuates the jerks and bumps of the boat's motion. A foam rubber mattress, inside a removable plastic cover is the best kind for it dries out well.

For the same reason, sleeping bags must be made of synthetic material. The silk and wool types, used by mountaineers, are useless. At sea damp is the menace; as long as you are nice and dry, you aren't cold.

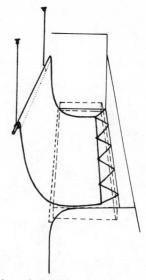

Fixing a leeboard

The Galley

The galley competes with the chart table for the most stable and airy place in the boat. The commonest location is as near as possible to God's air, to starboard or port of the companionway.

There are galleys of incredible luxury on some boats. Our modest definition is that the galley is the place where the stove is and we shall concentrate on that.

A good stove must have three qualities: develop good heat, burn a safe fuel and be easy to light.

The British often used to have small coal stoves with the double function of heating and cooking which suit the temperature of the sea round their coasts. But they require a large boat built around

On board the *Iroise*

them. And it takes time to learn how to light and keep them going.

Petrol or gasoline stoves are strictly proscribed, as with engines, and for the same reasons: stowage and handling dangers.

Paraffin stoves are good, in spite of an often stubborn nature. Lighting them and cleaning them calls for patience, even determination. But they give excellent heat and are quite safe.

Methylated spirit stoves are in the same class. They are easier to light than paraffin ones, but are less hot and more expensive to run.

Butane gas stoves are undoubtedly the cleanest and easiest to maintain. However, they are not so hot as the paraffin types and, above all, they do not provide the same degree of safety. The very real dangers of gas on board have been mentioned in the preceding chapter as well as the precautions to be taken. We need only repeat here that the danger of leaks at the joints must be carefully watched, and that it is as well to have a gas detector on board.

Whatever stove is chosen, it must be capable of providing stability for the kettle and saucepans. Ideally it should swing on gimbals or, at the very least, be mounted to swing at right angles to the fore and aft axis of the boat. To damp down swing, the pivot should be a little higher than the bottom of the saucepan (in principle at the level of the centre of gravity of the liquid inside it).

Whatever the system adopted, however, the fuller the pans the more the liquid rolls and spills and the only remedy is to use pots with wide bottoms (which anyway boil more quickly), high sides, and only partially filled. In bad weather, only kettles and pressure cookers with light lids are practicable.

The cook must have enough elbow room in front of the stove and pans. He has to use both hands so he must preferably be able to sit down or, at least, if he works standing, be able to wedge himself in position. All the utensils and provisions must be within easy reach so fit the galley with enough shelves and cuphooks designed and placed to prevent anything falling out. Cupboards and drawers with enough provisions for one or two days within arm's length of the galley are a great boon and they can be restocked from other lockers and stowage places.

Some galleys have sinks. These are a convenience as long as they are deep and narrow enough to stop water and dishes slopping about. A sink can be connected with a pump to the water tank, if it is large enough for such lavish use. An extra refinement is a second pump for using sea water.

The Chart Table

The chart table is usually opposite the galley whenever there is enough space for it. On larger boats the navigator is more privileged and has a quiet corner to himself with a table wide enough for the largest charts to be spread out on: all his instruments are to hand or visible from where he sits and reference books neatly stowed on a shelf.

Small boats have not enough space for such a lavish area and the navigator must usually be content with a large portfolio for keeping his charts in which also serves as a chart table. It isn't a bad solution. If you always sail in the same area, an equally good solution is to stick the chart normally in use onto a sheet of plywood, and give it a coat of varnish or have it laminated. This process doubles the cost of the chart but makes it last ten times longer.

Then there is the cabin table, for which there is usually no room in smaller boats. It must be reasonably solid to take not just the dishes but the elbows of the diners as well, and it should be expected to bear the full weight of anyone thrown onto it if the boat rolls abruptly – something that is bound to happen.

But we are getting away from essentials. There is, last and certainly not least, the all important matter of stowage space.

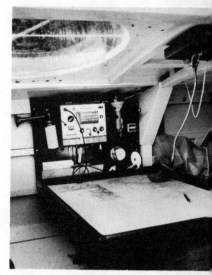

Stowage

The narrow confines of a sailing boat make any untidiness unbearable. Every single thing must have its place, only taken out to be used, and then immediately put back. This applies to everything on board, from the hand bearing compass to the bottle of vinegar, from the spare sweater to the reefing pendants. This implies something obvious: stowage space should be planned for every article.

Gear

Sails are traditionally stowed in the foc's'le. The trouble is that the fore-hatch cannot be opened in bad weather and the sails have to be carried right through the boat, both ways.

Carrying a wet sail is awkward and unpleasant. A good arrangement is to keep the sails in two lots: the fine weather ones forward, and the heavy weather ones in the stern – in the cockpit lockers for instance.

Each sail must have a bag of a different colour or clearly marked with the name of the sail. This bag must be big enough for the sail to be easily stuffed into it, even when it is wet. The bags can be hung on hooks, the bottoms held fast by a shock cord to stop them rubbing on the hull.

The foc's'l'e is also the logical place for spare rigging.

Whatever may be needed at short notice such as tools, sail repair material, chandlery (shackles, thimbles, jib hanks, etc) should all be together in *one* place, known to all and easily accessible, so that when they are required, frantic searching does not fray tempers.

Stores

The stowage space round the galley holds everything immediately necessary, but the main victuals must be stored under the bunks and in the bilges.

This distributes weight evenly over the boat and the heaviest things should be stowed in the centre and as low down as possible. It must be remembered that in a modern boat the crew, baggage and stores make up a large percentage of the total displacement.

It is only logical to store tinned goods in the bilges, where there is every chance of them getting wet. Before leaving on a long cruise, it is better to take the labels off before the bilge water does it for you, and mark them indelibly so as to avoid opening a can of rich paté for breakfast. (In France cans are numbered and you at least know that two cans with the same number contain the same thing.)

On small boats fresh water is stored in jerricans, which makes provisioning easy. Several small jerricans are better than one large one.

Some bigger boats have neoprene tanks, usually in the bilges, fitted tightly to prevent wear and consequent leaks. There must be at least one jerrican, always kept full for topping up the tank at sea.

Everything must have a place of its own, specially the hurricane lamp

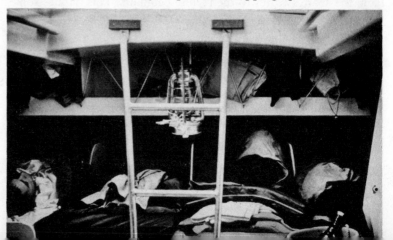

It is also an essential reserve in case the tank water is contaminated.

Clothing and Personal Effects

When all the demands of the boat have been met and the provisions stowed, what space remains has to be used to the best advantage: that means that personal stowage is determined by the length of the waterline and the size of the crew.

On a small boat, a kitbag is a good place for personal effects. Nets fitted in the angle between deck and hull can also be used. These stretch conveniently and are dry, but do not exactly improve the appearance of the cabin.

When space allows, each member of the crew should have a locker for his personal gear.

Wherever it is stowed, each garment should be kept in a waterproof bag (the plastic bags sold in rolls are just right). This is the only way of always having dry clothes.

General stowage for boots and oilskins is acceptable for not more than four people. Above that number, it is infinitely preferable to have a separate space (13 litres in volume) for each person (boots and oilskins well rolled up take surprisingly little room). This avoids a lot of clutter, untidiness and discord. Obviously nothing dries but it doesn't in the hanging locker either. Lifejackets however are all the better for being stowed in one place, if they are all identical.

Smart shore-going outfits deserve a hanging locker. It need not be wider than a coat hanger nor deeper than a dress. If it is tightly packed the clothes swing about less and possibly keep in better shape.

Lastly, have a shelf with a high fiddle above each bunk for personal odds and ends like lighters, tobacco, cameras and wallets.

The Pattern of Life

A handful of men, a few crude fittings on a stout seaworthy boat, and now – 'Make for the open sea!' (Ardizzone).

If the first leg is short everyone stays on deck, shares in the ship's handling and spends the whole day together. But a boat's life goes on twenty-four hours out of twenty-four and organisation there must be. The hours must be divided into set periods. The rhythm of life afloat is very different from that ashore.

On a coastal cruise when you moor each night the whole crew can sleep at the same time. Even so, contingencies may arise which will stretch the day from sixteen or eighteen hours to the full twenty-four. You may have to get under way in the middle of the night or drop downstream to a temporary mooring to take advantage of the tide. Or someone may have to be up at 1 am to check that the berth is not drying out. These don't need the entire crew; and if everyone gets up they are apt to sleep in the next morning, thus spoiling a full day's sail.

Once serious sailing begins a system of watches is indispensable: the crew is divided into groups who work in rotation to ensure the working of the ship and the fulfilment of other duties.

Watches

The organisation of watches varies according to the type of cruise, the time of year, the number of crew, their strength and competence. It is rare to come across a man who is equally good at everything: one can set sails but is no navigator; another can keep watch better than he can helm. Every watch should be manned by crew who share between them all the necessary aptitudes.

Apart from this there is no absolute rule. The length of the watches can vary, usually from three to four hours. Some crews prefer a rotation which lasts for the duration of the cruise. Others opt for a change of shift every two or three days.

The size of the watch obviously depends on the size of the boat. Some prefer fixed teams; others are happy to change a member in the middle of a watch. But when the timetable overlaps, at night especially, the result is a constant to-ing and fro-ing.

It is not for us to lay down specific guidelines. Everyone works the watch system which, by trial and error, has proved the best for him. We only indicate on the table opposite a few examples of rotation.

Whatever the chosen pattern it should allow everyone to take a hand at everything, navigation, cooking, cleaning, maintenance. And this pattern must be strictly adhered to. Those relieving the

Watch Systems

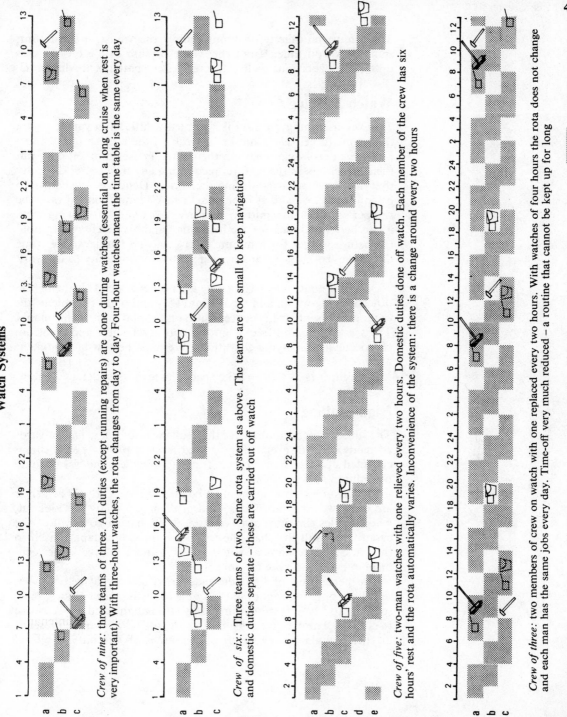

Crew of nine: three teams of three. All duties (except running repairs) are done during watches (essential on a long cruise when rest is very important). With three-hour watches, the rota changes from day to day. Four-hour watches mean the time table is the same every day

Crew of six: Three teams of two. Same rota system as above. The teams are too small to keep navigation and domestic duties separate – these are carried out off watch

Crew of five: two-man watches with one relieved every two hours. Domestic duties done off watch. Each member of the crew has six hours' rest and the rota automatically varies. Inconvenience of the system: there is a change around every two hours

Crew of three: two members of crew on watch with one replaced every two hours. With watches of four hours the rota does not change and each man has the same jobs every day. Time-off very much reduced – a routine that cannot be kept up for long

washing-up   cooking   maintenance   cleaning   watches

469

watch must be exactly on time; equally they must, in their turn, stand down on time. If not the whole rhythm of life on board is upset, work gets done badly, the crew's sleep patterns are disrupted.

Watch Keeping

The watch coming on duty is wakened a little in advance, giving them time to get ready and be on deck on the hour, a punctiliousness which everyone repays in their turn. Those going off duty put their successors in the picture, recounting any incident or difficulty that may have occurred during their trick. Details of the course to be followed are handed over, marks in view are pointed out, the skipper's orders transmitted. In a heavy sea and a following wind it can be a good idea for the helmsman and his relief crew to hold the helm together for a minute or two, giving the newcomer time to get the feel of it. Changing watch is an opportunity to do work that needs two teams.

On small boats only two people are needed: one at the helm, the other keeping watch and navigating. Day and night the role of the lookout is essential: his concentration must match the helmsman's. The sea 'so fine and free' is not without its dangers and collisions can occur in stupefying conditions. We must be constantly on the alert.

At night it is as well to take special precautions, detailed below.

Night Sailing

The sunset watch should leave the deck in good order. The halyards correctly cleated, everything secured, and in place, useless things collected up. The night favours frightful muddles, and risks should be reduced to a minimum.

People on watch at night must be able to see clearly. When their are only two, they are faced by a problem, specially the lookout, who doubles the duty of navigator. As he has to go down to the cabin to consult the chart, he will need time to readapt himself to the darkness. Perhaps it would be useful here to give some technical information about night vision.

The perception of light depends on two sorts of cells: *cones*, sensitised only by bright light but able to distinguish colours; *rods*, sensitive to weak light but blinded by strong light, and not sensitive to colours. The extreme sensitivity of the rods is due to the presence in their cellular structure of a derivative of vitamin A, retinal purple, knocked out by bright light but restored by darkness. This takes about twenty minutes. It is unaffected by red light.

In the centre of the retina there are only cones; on the periphery cones and rods. Consequently:

> The central sector which serves in daylight to distinguish colours and shapes is practically useless in a weak light.
>
> The peripheral sector, useful in daytime for registering a generalised perception of the environment, is most useful at night. It registers the weakest gleam of light, though without distinguishing its shapes or colours. That is, as long as the purple rods are not put out of action by too bright a light. Therefore:

The night watch should only be relieved when the new crew has had at least ten minutes to get used to the darkness.

As red light doesn't destroy retinal purple, paint the bulbs of compass and chart table with red nail varnish.

Torches should on no account be flashed carelessly in the eyes of those who have got used to darkness.

> When identifying an object avoid fixing the eye directly on it but look slightly to one side of it.
>
> Remember that colours can't be reliably identified.

That said, don't make a meal out of night sailing. In clear weather the eyes soon adapt themselves to darkness and one is often surprised by buoys and unlighted rocks turning up before you expect to see them. Long hours on the alert, cold and fatigue can be tough-going. But it is a fascinating experience, even if you wait impatiently for daybreak to make all things plain and clear.

Cooking

The range of cooking that can be done on board is obviously limited by the space and amenities on board. On a very small cabin cruiser hot meals are seldom possible except in fine weather. When it is fresh, the best one can do is prepare hot drinks in vacuum flasks before setting out. The trips are in any case quite short.

On larger boats, cooking is almost always possible, except when it is really rough. But, whatever the conditions are, an obliging person is needed! Everyone is capable of changing a jib in a heavy sea, and there are those who positively find it satisfying and bracing;

Breakfast is an important meal

but volunteers for the role of cook are rare birds even if they are of the marine variety.

This is why work in the galley must be taken in turns and never handed over exclusively to the women on board who, after all, are also on holiday (and not necessarily better cooks).

Cooking in a blow calls for a strong stomach and for the chef to have a position as steady as his determination is firm. All sorts of dodges can be used, including wearing safety harness. The cook must have boots on and oilskin trousers over them – an elementary precaution against the risk of burns when the boat pitches.

As for food and drink, let us just say (at the risk of offending the balanced diet fanatics): eat and drink what you like – in moderation! Breakfast is an important meal and should contain about a third of the day's calorie intake. The midday meal can be a snack; usually there is more opportunity and time to cook in the evening. And the night watches are often the occasion for delicious dishes reminiscent of a clandestine dormitory 'feast' (that last sausage devoured when the others sleep has a special surreptitious flavour). There should always be a 'watch box' with dried fruit, biscuits and chocolate, for the odd snack, easily accessible from the cockpit. That keeps insatiable appetites at bay.

Cleaning, Maintenance

Tidying and washing up must be done three times a day. Otherwise unappetising smells and muddle make life intolerable and a whole day has to be spent cleaning ship at the end of the cruise. It is of course not necessary to clean the boat daily from masthead to bilges; only the deck and the cabin sole, particularly round the table, need such favoured treatment. One way is to divide the boat into well defined sections and clean them, one at a time, each day.

It cannot be over-stressed that order on a boat is imperative. The galley and the foc's'le are the areas where dirt and untidiness breed as the spectre of seasickness stalks there. Stowage of utensils, tools, sails and navigation instruments must always be meticulous if good humour and concern for safety are to be maintained.

In this respect cruising is a good general education: every thoughtless act, every mistake committed is punished, not by parent or pedagogue, but by the sea itself; everything which is not put away falls out and breaks, upsets, is slipped on, gets wet or disappears. Everything that disappears into the bilges rusts, rots or is not retrieved until the boat is laid up.

At washing up time there is the question of what is to be done with the rubbish. On the open sea, anything that the fish will eat, that will sink or disintegrate may be thrown overboard. Everything else – plastic bottles in particular – must be dumped in an appropriate bag to wait for the garbage cans at the next port of call.

Maintenance is principally needed on the rigging, the sails and the topsides: there is always a halyard to be end for ended, a sheave to be greased, something to be whipped or a seam to be resewn. A good crew will spot what needs doing and do it whenever he has the unforgiving minute to fill. All this apart, once in port there is scrubbing the bottom, re-varnishing, chipping off rust and a hundred other jobs to keep the crew occupied.

The Sweet Agony

He who goes to sea for pleasure
Would go to Hell to pass the time.

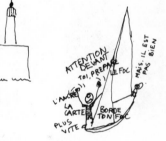

So said the old sea-dogs when the first yachtsmen came on the scene. No wonder they were astonished to see these fellows voluntarily exposing themselves to fatigue, cold, damp, hunger. . . We have learnt that these discomforts can often be overcome by simple and efficient remedies. However, they are to be dreaded, since they open the way to a scourge that spreads alarm and despondency if not sheer terror, respects no one, chooses its hour to strike, saps stamina and will power, and, in its many depressing forms, is often resistant to cure or even alleviation: sea-sickness.

Sea-Sickness

. . . Retchings twist and tie me,
Old fat, good meals, brown gobbets up I throw . . . (Rupert Brooke).

Dreaded by beginners afraid of being laughed at, accepted philosophically by seasoned sailors, sea-sickness is as common as it is disagreeable. Watch this hale and hearty young man, full of enthusiasm and the joy of life, leaping from anchor chain to mainsail halyard, and from there to the foresail halyard – see him, reduced to a limp, corpse-coloured rag, ready to give ten years of his life to

get back to port.

A few privileged ones are totally exempt – but they are a rarity. The gravity and persistence of sea-sickness varies greatly. Happily, it is seldom acute for long, disappearing after a few hours at sea, leaving but a bad memory soon forgotten. But it can last longer.

Clinical Description

The first indications are an increasing *malaise* which weakens the limbs, dulls the brain, destroys the will. Nausea and cold sweats follow, succeeded by vomiting which may give temporary relief. Alas! It is but a short remission: part-digested food is vomited, then bile, finally dry, painful retching. Frequency and intensity indicate the degree of severity. Most people, only moderately affected, can manage to do something between bouts. Others, prostrated in their bunks, are good for nothing.

Sea-sick sufferers do not always present these classic symptoms. Often the signs are insidious but not obvious, so that they may not be recognised by the victims. It may take the form of a migraine, but persistent and not alleviated by the usual treatment. More often a kind of sleepiness overcomes the patient, accompanied by a mental stickiness that slows down thinking as though he had had a stroke.

Sometimes all that is needed is for a man to be 'shaken out of it'. But to do this the skipper himself must be in a fit state.

If the skipper falls ill, it's more serious: he dithers over an urgent decision; his orders are vague and expressed in the conditional tense: 'We ought to take in a reef . . . That sheet isn't strong enough, it should be changed . . . We really ought to check our course . . .' He's on the slippery slope.

Sea-sickness comes on in diverse circumstances. Sometimes almost before you've weighed anchor, or after a mile or so, when the sea isn't really rough. This can afflict beginners or those who haven't yet got their sea legs at the start of the season or a cruise. Sometimes in mid-cruise, a man who has apparently got his sea legs suddenly succumbs. There can be several causes: his resistance may have been lowered by fatigue, cold, sleeplessness, or hunger. A rest, a good meal, and the *malaise* is gone. More often it is due to a change or a worsening of sailing conditions: a wind or a sea of Force 6 or 7 will be the downfall of many a stalwart seafarer. Everyone has his own threshold beyond which he will be prey to the malady.

Causes of the Malady

The chief feature being nausea, it is commonly attributed to digestive troubles. Many a man has been heard, after morose consideration, cursing something he ate the previous night.

An illusion – for though some food is more easily digested than others, well-seasoned sailors don't incontinently throw up a delicious meal carefully concocted by the cook on duty.

Sea-sickness is said to originate in a disturbance of the semicircular canal in the inner ear which controls our sense of balance. The sight of moving objects aggravates the *malaise*, and there are hypersensitive people who are upset by films like the famous *Kon-Tiki*.

It seems blindingly obvious, therefore, that it is the movement of the boat that causes sea-sickness. In calm weather no one on board gets sick, even at the beginning of a cruise. There are, however, factors which can influence the tendency. First your position: you are less likely to be sick on deck than in the cabin, because of the fresh air; also perhaps because on deck you can follow the boat's movements, learn to let yourself go with them and foresee them. This is easiest when you are at the helm; a helmsman doesn't get sick, and sometimes taking over the tiller will nip sea-sickness in the bud.

The cabin should be well ventilated. The victim should lie flat. The worst position is sitting up, which explains the difficulty of cooking or navigating, dressing or undressing.

Personal feelings play their part: anxiety is a prime cause, either the fear of sea-sickness itself, or a lack of self-confidence, or of confidence in the skipper. That is when good conversation, funny stories and songs, and, most of all, sunshine, can allay anxiety.

As for true fear, it will most likely cure sea-sickness – and hiccups.

Treatment

There are a number of sea-sick remedies, no one better than another. Each man should find one that suits him and use it according to the directions. These pills should be taken at least an hour before sailing (and in the case of long-lasting drugs, begun the night before).

There are the traditional recipes: a small glass of seawater (Slocum); a slice of stale bread (Breton fishermen); chewing-gum.

Physical fitness is important. Cold, damp and insomnia, the forerunners of sea-sickness, are to be avoided. Clearly this is something everyone has to work out for himself: the advice of old hands is ignored, and the zealous novice, ill-clad against the wind, pro-

There are many remedies for sea-sickness

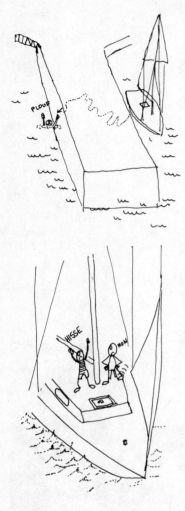

longs his watch unnecessarily, swaggers about in a fine careless rapture, just up to the moment of being laid low. His next cruise finds him booted, helmeted, well covered and getting in his beauty sleep. Nourishment is important but not easy if appetite is lacking: vegetables, fruit, cheese, taken little and often, break the vicious circle: lack of appetite, exhaustion, sea-sickness, no appetite. Salt bouillon is good, and Vichy or some such bottled spa water, because the sick man is short of salt.

If sea-sickness spares few, at least it hardly ever lasts more than forty-eight hours, and it is only the severest cases suffering from dehydration due to constant vomiting, that should be put on shore.

There is also the phenomenon of land-sickness. People who have become accustomed to the sea's movement on a long cruise, will step on shore only to be overcome by a degree of giddiness, which seems to affect the legs. Beginners can even enjoy the sensation, proud proof of their being landlubbers no longer, and in any case it soon passes.

Discord and Misunderstanding

One of the most boring and lowering aspects of sea-going can be the business of living together.

No specific pill exists to cure discord. In this small confined world the slightest quirks and mannerisms take on a dramatic significance. Once a bad atmosphere sets in, the most trivial incident gets blown up: it's hell.

Here we can offer no very useful advice. Obviously some people are intrinsically 'impossible'; the combination of certain temperaments results in an explosive mixture, and there isn't much you can do about it.

Some causes of disharmony can be foreseen and coped with:

A lack of leadership, either because there is no skipper or because the chosen man is not a good leader.
Fundamental differences between people, moral rather than intellectual: skiving, unpunctuality, looking disgruntled – it stands to reason that these shortcomings will destroy the harmony of the whole.
The cruise being unsuited to the crew. We have already referred to this fundamental question. A ship launched without much forethought on an undertaking beyond the crew's capacity is bound to founder in the long run. The limits of a cruise will de-

pend, in the last resort, on the limits of the skipper himself. The better his capacity for sizing up his crew, the richer will be his experience in dealing with more and more variable and taxing situations. But let the skipper once be overcome by events, let him but misjudge the staying powers of one or another of the crew, and doubt and despondency will set in. Miscalculations of this sort have landed the most brilliantly planned cruises on the rocks.

Well-being

Reading this one chapter, it may seem that a pleasure cruise is by no means pleasant, and that there is something to be said for the not altogether unfriendly head-shakings of the aforesaid old sea-dogs. But certain essentials have to be emphasised, and apparent strictures have as their sole aim the truest freedom for everyone.

Not only do the necessary duties that we have outlined, leave time for other things – fishing, lazing, dreaming, and a good deal of laughter – the very spirit in which they are carried out prevents them seeming burdensome. Every moment of life at sea, given a 'happy ship', is full of an inexplicable well-being. Perhaps because, in a world reduced to essentials, everything we do recovers its true value.

You have only to go and find out. At sea one feels good all the time, in storm and sunshine; during peaceful evenings, long nights, and freezing early mornings. Well-being comes from the certainty of having a clean boat that sails well, from taking the weather as it comes, from the outcome of accurate navigation making a successful landfall. And the fun of arriving in port.

From our own experience we would say that the greatest source of good feeling is the unique opportunity, when cruising, of opening our hearts to the free interchange of ideas and experience. In a cruising school, members of a crew won't have met before, and come from diverse backgrounds, each with his own experience. With the passing days comes an astonishing mutual discovery, forever renewed, revealing fruitful divergencies, deep affinities. This is true friendship, of all the joys of life at sea the purest and the most enduring.

Part 4.
Meteorology

At sea, tomorrow's weather is a matter of the utmost importance for us; unfortunately we are quite incapable of predicting it ourselves. Not so long ago, speculation still went on about the colour of the sky, the behaviour of the cat or the captain's rheumatism. The predictions drawn from them were not necessarily wrong. We don't know how to do that any more, but thanks to the meteorological services, we now have access to information about the weather that old sailors could never have dreamed of imagining. It is entirely due to these services that nowadays we can have a pretty clear view of what lies ahead.

Meteorology has for long been denied due recognition. The meteorologists have a difficult role to play. They are working on complicated and problematical information, the evidence of which can be interrupted in more than one way by each forecaster. They work on a scale that is far beyond the needs of most of us, and this often leads to bitter disappointment and gives the impression that forecasting is a guessing game. The truth is that the real users of meteorological information – notably sailors and airmen who have very precise reasons to be interested in the forecasts – know that the reports are very reliable. The use of radar and satellites for exploring the sky, computers for sifting and assessing the information received, as well as the radical advance in the methods of deduction, all contribute to the increasing accuracy of forecasts.

If weather forecasts are still somewhat suspect, it is probably because there is a tendency to look on them as if they were consumer products to be swallowed whole. It has to be realised first of all that a minimum of knowledge is needed for a full understanding of forecasts. Next, that they cover very wide areas and cannot take into account the variations in weather at any one particular point. Some of the work therefore remains to be done by the yachtsman himself. For amateur sailors, as for everyone else, a correct forecast of the weather is subject to two conditions: a correct interpretation of the bulletins; an ability to deduce from them, with the help of one's own observations, the shape the weather will take in the locality where one is sailing.

To get a clear picture of the situation broadcast, it is not enough to know vaguely what is meant by the words *depression, anticyclone,* or *cold front*. We might as well admit it: we can understand nothing of meteorology without taking the trouble to read up the subject and acquire more than a superficial knowledge of the principal atmospheric phenomena, their causes and what the overall pattern suggests. There is no doubt that this has to be done, and that is why we have included a whole chapter to study the subject in general. A rather dry chapter which is nothing else than an account of our research, and which is somewhat outside the mainstream of this book. Boats are scarcely mentioned, and we even take off up into the mountains, where it might well be said we have no business. But the mountains are the very place to study pragmatically the behaviour of the air, before tackling the great spaces themselves, the clouds, the masses of air, the invisible slopes which exist in the sky and along which the wind flows. At this point we can already see the specialists raising their eyebrows: is this going to be a superficial re-hash of the subject? We are open to the charge; but an attempt to treat such a vast subject in a few pages is a calculated gamble and when forced to choose between clarity and exactness (although it is reprehensible to separate these two qualities) we have opted for clarity. We confess we feel passionately on the subject. That is not an excuse, but may go some way to explain why we have not always confined ourselves to professional terms.

The second chapter tries to summarise what is needed for the second part of the study – forecasting on a local scale, starting from personal observation, which can only be useful if one knows exactly the characteristics of the weather in the area as a whole, the *types of weather* which are most common there and the special characteristics likely to be met. We shall attempt therefore to define, at least in broad terms, *oceanic* weather and Mediterranean weather, two very different types which we hope will have some practical bearing on conditions in many parts of the world. We conclude with a few considerations about forecasting itself.

Such as they are, these two chapters can only open a very small window onto a vast scene. It is for the reader himself to pursue

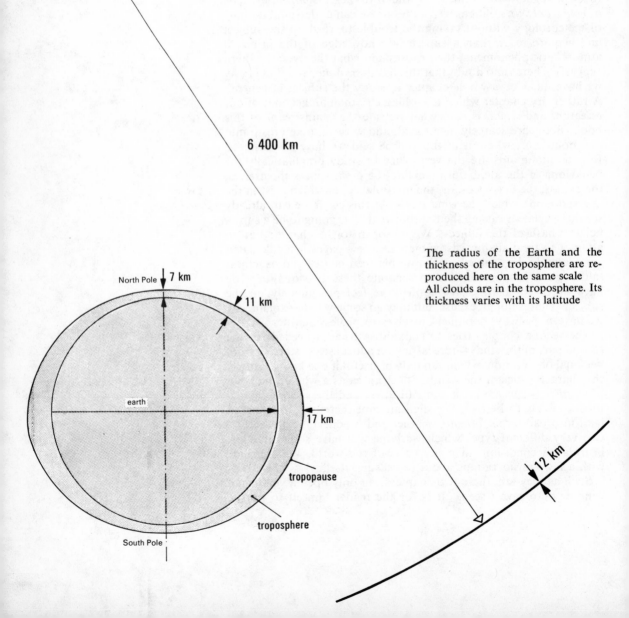

centre of the earth

the research by reading the works quoted in the bibliography (and on which we have drawn generously), and by adopting the habit of observing the sky, by becoming familiar with a fabulous 'world' whose splendour cannot be dulled, even by the most austere analyses.

6 400 km

North Pole ↓ 7 km

↙ 11 km

earth

17 km

tropopause

troposphere

South Pole

The radius of the Earth and the thickness of the troposphere are reproduced here on the same scale
All clouds are in the troposphere. Its thickness varies with its latitude

↓ 12 km

16. The Life of
   the Atmosphere

Meteorology is an esteemed science, mainly because it tries to answer honestly the questions of persistent children. The sun warms the Earth – as everyone knows. But why does the air grow colder and colder with increase in altitude, although the sun is getting nearer and nearer? Why is it hot at the equator and cold at the poles? Why does that cloud stay still on the top of the mountain, although the wind is so violent? And why are there clouds? And wind? Where do they come from and where are they going?

We wave goodbye to the experts and those blessed with good memories, who can smile at such questions. Let us proceed gradually, step by step.

The sun radiates energy towards the Earth, a sphere surrounded by atmosphere. Part of this energy is reflected back towards space as the solar beams approach our planet, and has no effect on it. Another, quite small, part is absorbed by the atmosphere itself, which is slightly warmed by it (a light ray absorbed by an obstacle is in fact changed into heat). Another part is finally absorbed by the Earth's surface and warms it considerably.

Let it be appreciated from the start that, if the transfer of energy went in one way only, the temperature of the Earth would go on increasing and we would not be here to speak about it. But the Earth, like any heated body, radiates in its turn. Globally – that is the word – it radiates as much energy as it receives and a balance is established.

The first important point to be made is that in any one period of time, the ground absorbs about three times more energy than the atmosphere above it. The ground is therefore, on average, hotter than the atmosphere and begins to heat it from below. This heating process is felt to a height of about 12km. From the Earth's

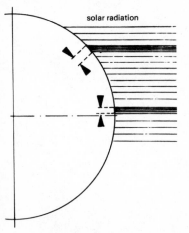

solar radiation

Solar radiation is uniform but in high latitudes it is spread over a greater surface than at the Equator

surface up to 12km, the temperature therefore decreases with the altitude. This is the principal characteristic of this low stratum of the atmosphere, called the troposphere: the changing sphere. The thickness of this layer varies, according to the latitude (12km is only an average: it is much thicker at the equator than the poles); it varies too from one day to the next, and in the process creates the weather. Its upper limit is called the *tropopause*. Above that, and up to 50km, is the *stratosphere*, where the temperature increases slightly with height and in the lower part can be very turbulent. The higher regions are outside our scope.

Compared with the 6,400km radius of the terrestrial globe, the troposphere, with its altitude of 12km may be relatively as thin as tissue paper around an orange; but this skin nevertheless contains 80% of the total mass of air, and 90% of the atmosphere's moisture; it is the core of what concerns us here – where all the clouds appear, and the majority of the phenomena that affect us.

The next question is: why is it cold at the poles and hot at the equator?

The sun's rays are parallel (or for our purposes can be considered to be), but the Earth is a sphere. The polar regions consequently get less heat because they receive less insulation per unit area of surface than the equatorial regions, which are far more exposed.

This simple answer is apparently satisfying, but it is in fact misleading, leading as it does to another difficult question. The calculation of the quantities of energy absorbed respectively by the equator and the poles reveals an enormous imbalance between the two regions that should result in a far greater difference of temperature than is in fact the case. It would appear that the equatorial regions should be terribly hot and the polar regions terribly cold, both of them equally uninhabitable. As this is not so, and if the temperature is, give or take a few pullovers, bearable almost everywhere, the reason is, obviously, that an atmospheric change occurs between the equator and the poles. This raises a new question: how does this change come about? The answer, this time, is more complicated and is the real purpose of meteorology.

Physics tells us that any body heated at a particular spot tends to spread out the heat through its entire mass. This dispersal is carried out through *conduction*, that is to say by contact, little by little, to the interior of the mass itself. But this does not happen on the planet Earth, for the ground is a bad conductor of heat. The process can also be effected through *radiation*. But the radiation of the Earth is almost entirely lost in space. Only a small part is reflected back by the clouds (which explains why the nights are not so cold when the sky is clouded over as when it is clear), but that is far from being sufficient to establish an equilibrium between the equator and the poles, for great quantities of heat have to be transferred.

Conduction and radiation are the only means of exchange on the Moon, for instance. And temperatures of 200°C are registered there in sunny areas, and −100°C in areas in shade.

But the Earth has its atmosphere and oceans. Air and water are in themselves bad conductors of heat, but they can move. The air can also carry water, abstracted by evaporation from the wet parts of the planet. Can these two mobile elements, which seem to be constantly mixing, not contribute to equalising temperatures on the surface of the globe? And could this equalisation of temperatures not be, precisely, the reason why they move? This is really what the meteorologists have made clear: on the planet Earth, thermal exchanges happen essentially through the movement of huge fluid masses, some towards the poles, others from the poles towards the equator. The exchanges occur by *convection*.

There are also warm ocean currents, such as the Gulf Stream, that carry the heat of the tropical seas towards the north, and cold ocean currents, such as the Labrador current flowing down in the opposite direction. These currents, however, move very slowly and only account for a small part of the exchange. Most is done by the atmosphere: the masses of warm equatorial air tend to move towards the poles and the masses of cold polar air to drift towards the equator.

As a result of this scheme of things, it might seem that, from now on, an explanation of the winds should be easy. One is entitled

Principal currents in the North Atlantic

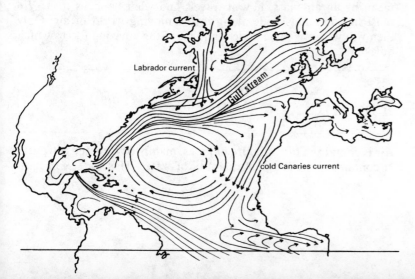

Labrador current

Gulf stream

cold Canaries current

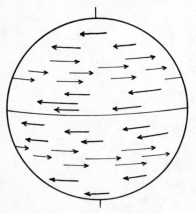

Average winds at ground level

to expect the principal winds in the atmosphere to be north and south winds. But, if the standard patterns of the winds on the globe's surface, as they have been recorded by observations carried out over many years, are considered, one must think again. Those from the north and south don't figure in them (on balance, they cancel each other out); the normal winds are east and west: east winds in the equatorial and polar regions, west winds in the temperate regions. Apparently, again, the winds are, on average, very weak: hardly four miles per hour, but we know some blow far more strongly.

Here the children's questions begin to be provoking. One might answer them peremptorily and briefly thus: 'The Earth rotates on itself. As it is full of bumps and hollows, this rotary movement creates eddies in the air. Some of them turn in one direction, some in another; some point upwards, some down. Again, the oceans and continents heat up and cool down at different rhythms: their disparity of temperature creates other eddies, which appear and disappear periodically. The masses of warm air and the masses of cold air which try to ensure the exchanges between the equator and the poles are dragged into all these movements and thereafter go in unexpected directions. Moreover, when a mass of warm air and a mass of cold air meet, they absolutely refuse to mix: they clash with each other, and that in turn creates still more eddies, in which the wind is strong, and which move between the original great eddies. It's a little like a complex of cogwheels.'

No one need know more than this. But if you want to get to the heart of the matter, summon up all your patience, get right down to it, put on a thinking cap and examine the subject from the very beginning. Learn first of all what this air is, that we are speaking about (and which we breath as well); next define precisely what we mean by an air mass, how it travels and what happens to it. We must in our minds glide along in the moving world of air. Only then will we have some understanding of the amazing forces which quicken it.

The Air

Air is composed of a mixture of gases, mainly oxygen and nitrogen. It contains as well a great quantity of water. This water can itself be in the gaseous form of water vapour, which is invisible; or else in liquid and visible form as clouds.

A point to be stressed is that the air contains a lot of water. Solar radiation, by heating the oceans and other moist parts of the Earth, causes great quantities of water to evaporate. It has been estimated that the sun, on good days, sucks up an amount equal to one glass full of water per hour per square metre of ocean. There are therefore thousands of millions of tons of water suspended in the air.

Air already weighs something. The ground therefore is under pressure from the atmosphere. The *atmospheric pressure*, at a given point on the surface of the globe, is equal to the weight of the column of air which rises above the spot. The pressure diminishes, naturally enough, with the altitude, but more gradually as it rises: the air is, in fact compressible, and this compression is noticeable in its lower layers. Pressure and height are, in any case, closely related, and height is calculated by measuring the pressure. The altimeters used in aircraft are in fact aneroid barometers. Yachtsmen also use aneroid barometers. In meteorology the unit of pressure used is the *millibar* (mb) with the average pressure at 0 altitude, or sea level, a trifle over 1,000mb.

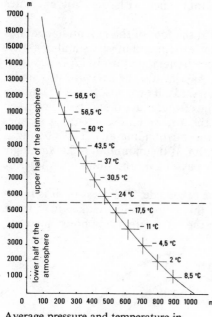

Average pressure and temperature in relation to altitude

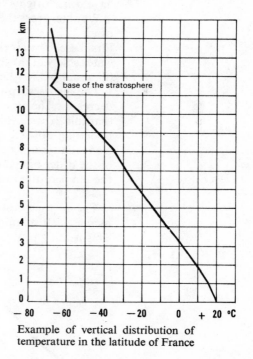

Example of vertical distribution of temperature in the latitude of France

The air, as we know, has a certain temperature, and in the troposphere this diminishes with altitude. The *vertical thermal lapse rate* or environmental lapse rate, which is the rate at which temperature decreases between the Earth's surface and the tropopause, is on average 6°C per kilometre.

In short, any motionless parcel of air at a given point in the troposphere, is defined by the three coordinates: temperature, pressure and humidity.

But a parcel of air is rarely motionless; and its characteristics are modified as soon as it moves. Moving air (the subject of our study) thus undergoes changes which can be justifiably referred to as different 'states'. It is important to analyse these states closely; that is the key to all that follows.

States of the Air

Let us take the example of a wind arriving at the foot of a mountain, and compelled to rise to get over it. This is a somewhat special case in that the movement of the air is imposed here by the surface (*orographic* movement), while the movements in a free atmosphere have other origins. But it is illuminating.

We shall cross the mountain four times, with four different states of air.

First case. The air that arrives at the foot of the mountain contains water solely in the form of water vapour and in very small quantity. (diagram below) Let us suppose its temperature is 17°C.

The air rises up the slopes. As a result, the pressure it is under decreases. The air is less 'compressed'; it expands. It will be realised that this *expansion* has a cooling effect (a fact that is easily checked by letting down a cycle tyre: the air, which expands as it escapes from the tyre, is colder than the surrounding air). This cooling is of the order of 1°C for each 100m. If the mountain is 2,000m high, the temperature of the air as it passes over the summit is therefore −3°C.

The air then descends on the other side. The pressure it is under increases. It compresses, and this compression makes it warmer. This heating process occurs at the same rate as the preceding cool-

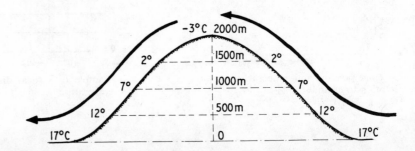

ing: 1°C per 100m. At the foot of the mountain, the air has recovered its former temperature: 17°C.

Three principles must be remembered from this example:

As it rises the air has cooled, but it regains its original temperature at the end of its descent. The changes it has suffered have been counteractive: no loss or gain of heat. The variations of temperature of the moving air go on in *adiabatic* fashion, that is to say without heat exchange with the surrounding environment. The rate of variation of temperature of the moving air is 1°C per 100m, if this air only contains water in the vapour form. It is called the adiabatic gradient of unsaturated air, or more simply *dry adiabatic lapse rate* (DALR).

It is seen that the vertical lapse rate of the moving air is clearly different from the vertical lapse rate of motionless air: 10°C per km instead of 6°C per km.

Second case. The air has the same temperature as in the preceding case: 17°C. It is still clear but this time it contains more water vapour.

As it rises it cools. At a certain height (let us say for instance, at 1,000m, where the temperature of the air is 7°C), suddenly something happens: everything becomes murky. We are witnessing the birth of a cloud. Why?

Because the air can only retain a limited amount of water in the form of vapour, and the colder it is the less it can hold. The relationship between the quantity of water vapour that the air actually contains and the maximum amount it can contain for the same temperature, defines its *relative humidity*. This is expressed as a percentage. In our example, the quantity of water vapour that the air easily accepted at 17°C, becomes its maximum amount at 7°C. Its relative humidity is then in the order of 100%. *Saturation* is reached. Should the air cool still further, the excess water vapour is transformed into microscopic droplets, kept in the air by the wind. There is then *condensation* (the change from the gaseous to the liquid state) which takes the form of cloud. Note that this condensation frequently occurs only after some delay during which

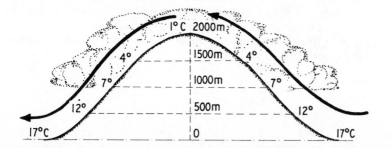

the air is in a state of *supersaturation*.

As its water vapour condenses, the air continues nevertheless to rise up the mountain. But, from the moment when the condensation occurs, its temperature decreases less quickly with the height. The condensation, in fact, frees heat (the same heat which had formerly brought about the evaporation of the water over the ocean; it is called *latent heat*). The variations in temperature now take place according to a different lapse rate, which is the saturated *pseudo-adiabatic lapse rate* (pseudo, because there is an exchange of heat between the air and the water droplets or the ice crystals contained in the cloud) and which henceforward we shall call *saturated adiabatic lapse rate* (SALR). This rate can vary between 0.5°C and 0.8°C per 100m. We shall take it here as 0.6°C.

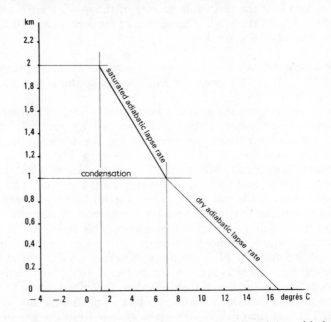

A mass of rising air cools less quickly when its water vapour condenses

At the top of the mountain, the air is therefore less cold than in the first case. It is at 1°C. As it descends, it is compressed, and heats up at a rate of 0.6°C per 100m. As it warms, the water droplets evaporate. At 1,000m altitude, the evaporation is complete and the air is again clear; in the ensuing descent, the temperature increases according to the dry adiabatic lapse rate. At the foot of the mountain, the air is again at 17°C.

Conclusions from this example:

Condensation is due to the cooling of the air.
As it rises, saturated air cools less quickly than clear air.

It should be noted at this point that the condensation of water vapour can occur as a result of cooling which does not only originate from the rising of the air. Cooling can be caused by radiation (as happens at night: the air radiates its heat and this radiation is no longer compensated for by the sun's rays); and by contact with a cold surface (the bottle one takes out of the ice box is covered with mist). But in a free atmosphere, the most frequent cause of cooling, and therefore of condensation, is the expansion of the rising air we have just been describing.

Taking an overall view of the mountain, it is clear that the cloud which covers its summit has a very clear cut base, at 1,000m altitude. It does not move, although the wind is moving through it. In fact, it is never the same cloud; the water droplets which compose it are constantly being renewed.

The clouds which originate in free atmosphere have similar characteristics. Their base is often horizontal; in a given situation, clouds of the same origin all have their bases at the same height. And it can already be guessed that a cloud, even when it drifts with the wind, is not a stable, simple ball of cottonwool, but rather an agglomerate in a constant state of renewing its particles that are rising and falling, some condensing, others evaporating.

Third case. The air which approaches the mountain has still the same temperature, but this time it contains still more water vapour. The condensation of the latter occurs very quickly, at an altitude of 200m, for example and at a temperature therefore of 15°C. At the summit, the air is at 4.2°C.

But, in the course of the rise, another change has taken place: there has been *precipitation*. It has rained. Despite appearances, rain is a very complicated phenomenon, which we shall not even try to explain. If it has rained, the air has lost some of its water content – we shall leave it at that.

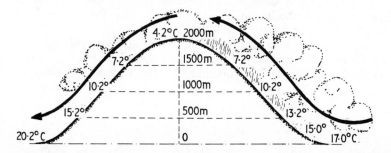

When it descends on the far slope, the air warms up according to the saturated adiabatic lapse rate. But it contains less water than before and there is a smaller number of droplets to evaporate. After 1,000m fall, for example, the temperature being 10.2°C, evaporation is complete. The heating process then continues according to the dry adiabatic lapse rate, at 1°C per 100m. At the foot of the mountain, the air is at 20.2°C. In other words, after its passage over the mountain, the air is warmer than it was before (this phenomenon is known to meteorologists as *Föhn effect*). The heat freed by the condensation is only partially reabsorbed by the evaporation; the 'excess' contributes to increasing the temperature of the air. The simple conclusion is that by losing water, the air has warmed up.

Fourth case. In the preceding examples, the wind was hot. Let us now imagine it is much colder. The air approaching the mountain is at 6°C.

Condensation occurs, for example, at a height of 300m. The air is then at 3°C. Its temperature, decreasing subsequently according to the saturated adiabatic lapse rate, is at 0° at 800m. One might then expect the water droplets composing the cloud were going to change into ice; but this is not always the case. It is often found that this change takes place in phases, and is only completed at a temperature around −40°C. The droplets of water that remain thus in a liquid state below 0°C are said to be in a state of *supercooling*.

This can be disconcerting. A motorist crossing the mountain, when he arrives at an altitude where the temperature is below 0°C, is annoyed when his windscreen frosts over. In fact a slight impact or the presence of impurities in the air is enough to change the supercooled droplets instantly into ice; this is the sole cause of freezing fog.

To complete our survey of the possible air changes, we repeat that when it is very cold its water vapour content is changed directly into ice, without passing through the liquid state (*deposition*); similarly and conversely, it changes directly from the solid state to the gaseous one. This phenomenon is called *sublimation*.

Clouds composed of ice crystals appear at high altitude (usually above 6,000m). They are easily recognisable by their silky, dazzling-white appearance. Clouds composed of water droplets are greyer, nor are they so high, but it is known now that they can exist at heights with temperatures well below 0°C.

Now that we have acquired these basic facts we shall leave the mountains. This account of the changes that occur in air as it rises and falls has supplied the fundamental facts for understanding the other part of the story, which is an infinitely more complicated and tortuous one, about the air masses that circulate in free atmosphere, and whose twists and turns create weather.

The Air Masses

The principal characteristics of the atmosphere is unquestionably its sensitivity to influences. When, for example, parcels of air have remained for a time on one geographic area, they finally acquire similar characteristics: the same humidity and temperature. They can form a homogenous whole or *air mass*. So it is that we can speak of warm air masses and cold air masses, damp air masses and dry air masses, tropical air masses and polar air masses. The volume of these masses is very variable: they can extend over a few hundreds or over several thousands of kilometres and be several hundreds or some thousands of metres thick.

An air mass is characterised in the first place by its place of origin. But as we have said, air masses travel and it follows that in the course of their journey they are influenced by the regions they cross, and that their characteristics change with conditions. They can be transformed.

To put a recognisable label on these air masses, two concepts must be grasped. One concerns their temperature: what do we call a warm air mass, a cold air mass, what do we mean by 'heat' and 'cold'? The other is about what is best described as their temperament. There are masses of stable and unstable air. What is the difference? When one goes sailing, one soon finds out.

Warm Air, Cold Air

The sensations of hot and cold, as we experience them, are relative and the terms 'hotter' and 'colder', even more so. In fact, the human body is rather insensitive to small changes in temperature, but much more so to variations in the relative humidity of the air. So, when a mass of very damp air arrives, there can be an impression of cold, even when the temperature is in fact rising, for damp air takes more calories out of us than dry air.

In any case, when it comes to determining the temperature of the air mass invading our immediate environment, our sensory impressions, even when correct, prove to be inadequate; the idea of hot and cold, in meteorological terms, is on quite another scale.

To understand this, let us return for a moment to the first case in our recent example – air passing, without condensation, over the mountain. If two parcels of this air are compared, taken at different altitudes, one at 400m, for instance, as it rises, the other at 1,500m as it descends, they are found not to have the same temperature; one is at 13 °C, the other at 2 °C. However, we know that the air, after crossing the mountain, returns to the temperature it had when it approached its foot. Can it be that one of these parcels is hotter than the other? In fact, in order to compare them effectively, we must, by calculation (taking into account the adiabatic process) bring them both to the same pressure. It is only then their temperature is the same.

It is the same with the second case we cited, when condensation occurred. By contrast, in the third case where the air loses part of its moisture on the way, if two particles of air are compared, one before precipitation, the other after, it will be found that they are different: under the same pressure, one is actually hotter than the other.

In short, when warm air rises it can reach a very low temperature but nevertheless it remains warm air. The arrival of a warm air mass can thus be forecast (as often happens) by the appearance of clouds solely composed of ice crystals.

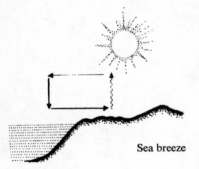

Sea breeze

Observations taken vertically through the atmosphere reveal the temperature and moisture content of the air at given altitudes. Through bringing, by calculation, different particles of air to the same pressure, the so-called *reference pressure* (conventionally 1,000mb), meteorologists can know what sort of air masses they are dealing with.

Land and Sea Breezes

The behaviour of warm air and cold air in relation to each other depends essentially on their different densities. Warm air is lighter, cold air heavier. The warm air tends to rise, the cold air to descend and spread out.

A typical example of their relationship is provided by the phenomenon of land and sea breezes, frequently to be observed on the coast during periods of fine weather.

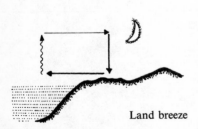

Land breeze

This phenomenon is bound to a fundamental fact: the land and the sea have very different thermal properties. The land warms and cools very quickly; the sea, in contrast, is subject to slow variations of temperature.

In the day time, the land warms under the heat of the sun, heats the air above it, and this warm air tends to rise. The colder air over the sea tends to spread and fill the vacuum left by the warm air. The wind then blows from the sea towards the land.

At night, the land cools. The sea is warmer (or less cold). The wind now blows from the land towards the sea.

Warm air and cold air, in brief, organise themselves into a kind of vertical circuit: the warm air rises, the cold air takes its place and is heated in turn. The warm air, which has risen, cools and comes down again to take the place abandoned by the cold air. This is the principle of convection of which we have already spoken.

It is important to know that, owing to their different densities, warm air and cold air mix no better than oil and water. The behaviour of coastal breezes is on the whole better organised; but, on quite another scale: when warm air and cold air masses meet, it doesn't happen without a clash, as we shall see.

Stable and Unstable Air

Vertical movements can occur in the very heart of an air mass as a result of influences around it. Sometimes these movements are quickly subdued and the air mass is designated *stable*. In other cases the influence is considerable and the air mass is then *unstable*.

Take a mass of clear air with a vertical thermal environmental lapse rate (the rate of decrease of temprature with height) of 0.5°C per 100m, that is to say less than the dry adiabatic lapse rate. Under the effect of some impulse, a parcel of this mass gains 100m in height. Its temperature decreases according to the dry adiabatic lapse rate of 1°C. It is colder, therefore heavier than the surrounding air and it tends to fall. In the same conditions, a parcel of air falling by 100m is warmer, therefore lighter than the surrounding air and it tends to rise again. The air mass under consideration is stable.

If it is a saturated air mass, the variations of temperature occur according to the saturated adiabatic lapse rate, but the result is the same.

Let us now take an air mass with a greater vertical thermal environmental lapse rate of 1.2°C for instance. A parcel of air rising 100m cools by only 1°C: it is then warmer than the surrounding air and it has therefore a tendency to continue rising. On the con-

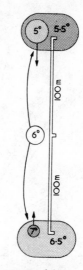

The environmental lapse rate of the air mass (0.5°C per 100m) is less than the adiabatic lapse rate: the air is stable

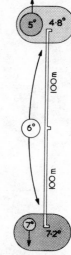

The environmental lapse rate of the air mass (1.2°C per 100m) is higher than the adiabatic lapse rate: the air is unstable

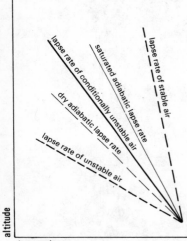

The vertical temperature lapse rate of an air mass determines its degree of stability or instability

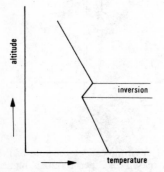

Warmed from above or cooled from below, the air becomes stable

trary, a parcel falling by 100m is colder than the surrounding air: it tends to continue falling. The air mass is traversed by vertical movements which make its interior remarkably turbulent. It is therefore unstable.

It is seen therefore that the degree of stability or instability of an air mass depends on the relationship between the vertical thermal environmental lapse rate of the air in question and the adiabatic lapse rates. Two particular cases must be considered:

The environmental lapse rate of the air mass is equal to the adiabatic lapse rate (dry in the case of a mass of clear air, saturated in the case of a mass of saturated air): this air mass is in *neutral equilibrium*.

The vertical thermal environmental lapse rate lies between the two adiabatic lapse rates. As long as the air remains clear, the air mass is stable. But if, for any reason (total rise of the mass, for instance), condensation occurs, the air mass becomes unstable. This type of air mass is termed *conditionally unstable*.

From these different observations, it can be deduced:

Everything which tends to increase the vertical thermal environmental lapse rate of an air mass (heating from below, or cooling from above) tends to render that air mass unstable.
Everything tending to reduce its vertical thermal environmental lapse rate (cooling from below, heating from above) tends to make it stable.

Naturally, if the temperature increases with the altitude instead of decreasing, the environmental lapse rate being inverted, there is total stability. This is the case in the stratosphere. These *temperature inversions* also occur in the troposphere, when a mass of warm air passes over the top of a mass of cold air. The layer where the inversion occurs blocks off all rising movements, as if it were a tight lid closing off all vertical exchanges.

At our level, the stability or instability of an air mass is given concrete form by the sort of wind that springs from it. A mass of stable air gives winds that can be strong but steady. In a mass of unstable air, on the contrary, the wind is variable, often blowing in gusty squalls. That is the time to keep your weather eye open.

But there exists a much more precise method of identifying the air masses. All one needs do is to lift the eyes and look up at the

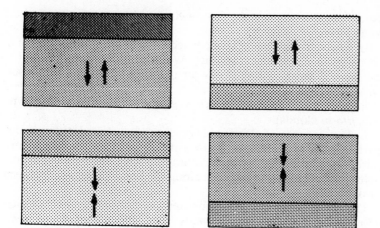

Cooled from above or warmed from below, the air becomes unstable

sky. The air movements are revealed, in the clearest possible way, by the clouds.

Clouds

A mass of unstable air is shown up by rounded masses of cloud heaped on each other. Generally well separated from each other, sometimes with marked vertical development, these clouds demonstrate intense convective activity in the atmosphere. They are *cumulus* or *cumuliform* clouds.

Often they can be seen climbing into the sky, during fine weather at the hottest hour of the day. They sometimes form up in line, over the coast, reproducing its outline exactly (revealing, at sea, the presence of a distant island). The appearance of these cumuli is comparable with the routine of land and sea breezes, mentioned above. It reveals the existence of rising currents above overheated land; the air cools as it rises, condenses and forms these clouds, separated from one another by stretches of blue sky which conceal descending currents. Very often the sky is heavy over the coast, while it is perfectly clear at sea. The air above the land is unstable, the air above the sea is stable. If you want to take advantage of the sun, now is the time to get under way (but if you want to profit from it to the very last ray, you will come home with the wind on your nose).

In a mass of stable air, these convection movements do not occur; this type of cloud never appears. When condensation occurs it is due to a general cooling of the air mass. The clouds which result spread out in a uniform layer, never very thick, which often covers a larger area. They are generally grey and are the *stratus* type (*stratiform* clouds).

Both categories of clouds are sometimes associated, the cumulus gather in groups, in round or rocklike shapes that rise like mountainous towers according to the altitude. Such clouds usually denote some instability and turbulence along the demarcation line between two different air masses.

Of course clouds defy, in hundreds of minor ways, this rather rough classification. It is usually very difficult to know their precise significance. Familiarity with clouds takes as long to acquire as familiarity with the wind that drives our boats along. It takes patient study, done in a mood of contemplation and a distrust of categorical assertions. Some would call it daydreaming, being unaware how fruitful daydreaming can be!

Officially, clouds are divided into ten different *types*. This classification takes into account both their shape and the height at which they appear. The troposphere, the region of the clouds, is then divided into three layers. A cloud's name indicates both its structure and the layer where it lies:

The cirrus, cirrocumulus and cirrostratus belong to the upper layer; they appear between altitudes of 6 and 13km in northern latitudes, and are composed of ice crystals.
The altocumulus and altostratus are the middle layer clouds (between 2 and 7km high). They are composed mainly of water droplets.
The stratocumulus and stratus are found in the lowest layer between the Earth's surface and a height of 2km.

But this classification is a little too precise: three types of cloud lie outside it. These are the clouds with vertical development which can occupy several layers at the same time: nimbostratus, cumulus, and especially the enormous cumulonimbus.

To describe the ten cloud types, we will keep to our original three classifications: clouds of instability, of limited instability and of stability – taking into account the concept of layers.

Clouds of Instability

Cumulus (Cu). Clouds separated from each other, with clear outlines, with quite considerable vertical development. Their base is often horizontal and their summits often take the form of protuberances in the shape of towers and domes, sometimes burgeoning not unlike cauliflower curds.

Cumulus form in all sizes. The smallest ones are often the result of a very localised warming of the ground: a cumulus can even form over a cornfield, which is clearly hotter than a small copse nearby. This is the cumulus *humilis*, the little clouds typically seen scattered along the coast. This is the outstanding fine weather cloud. It means no rain.

Larger cumulus, cumulus *mediocris*, or cumulus *congestus*, invades large areas of sky and can indicate the arrival of a mass of cold air, which heats on contacting the land and therefore becomes unstable. The base of heavy cumulus is usually dark with summits blinding white in the sun. A cumulus *congestus* can be several kilometres in diameter and as thick as 5,000m. The tall towers it

Cumulus (humilis)

Cumulonimbus

thrusts up into the sky characterise it clearly. It sometimes brings showers but specially violent squalls of wind.

Cumulonimbus (Cb). King of the clouds, the cumulonimbus is a cumulus congestus which has grown out of all proportion. Its depth varies from 5 to 12,000m. Its top is made up of ice crystals and often spreads out in the form of an anvil, to the limit of the stratosphere. It marks the existence of extremely powerful, ascending air currents, and produces violent showers of rain, hail or snow, and thunder storms. Below such a cloud, the wind blows at gale force, in unpredictable directions.

Clouds of Limited Instability

Cirrocumulus (Cc). Small clouds of the upper layer, very white and shiny, without shadow. They assemble in banks or ridges, regularly distributed like fish scales (hence the term 'mackerel sky') usually against a very blue sky. Each unit has a width apparently less than 1° (ie it is concealed behind a little finger held at arm's length).

Altocumulus (Ac). Clouds of the middle layer, with the same kind of organisation pattern as the cirrocumulus, but with larger components (three fingers are needed to cover them). They are composed of rounded masses with a wavy appearance, white or grey, or both white and grey at the same time. They are fairly thick and more or less fused together. The sun can often be seen through them. They are the clouds of the French proverb: a mackerel sky, and a powdered woman don't last long.

The alto cumulus are very frequently seen. They can be observed forming simultaneously at different levels (between 1,500 and 5,000m). When they have a stormy character, they can become very thick and yet remain quite clear.

Stratocumulus (Sc). Clouds of the lowest layer, which arise in banks or sheets. They are grey or whitish, or both, at the same time and almost always have dark parts. Their components look like broad slabs or pebbles and have often a thick wavy appearance. They can fuse together and cover the whole sky overhead, their wavy forms only revealed by shades of grey. They bring drizzle rather than rain.

Clouds of Stability

Cirrus (Ci). Clouds of the upper layer, the cirrus are quite different from the other clouds in a stable weather pattern. They are isolated clouds, white threads or 'mares' tails' like claw marks on the sky.

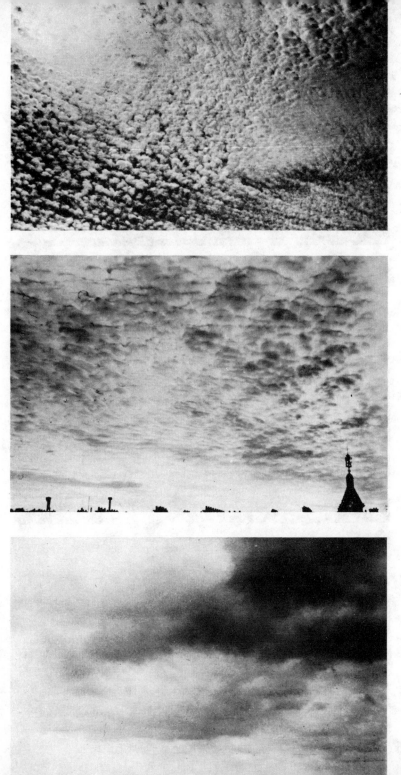

Cirrocumulus

Altocumulus

Stratocumulus

Cirrus

Cirrostratus

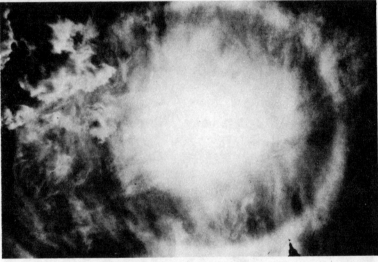

Altostratus

Composed solely of ice crystals, they are shiny, have neither a shadow of their own nor a projected shadow. The forms they take often denote the presence of strong wind at high altitude.

Cirrostratus (Cs) is a thin, transparent cloud that forms a veil over the sky. Smooth or fibrous, it often succeeds the cirrus. The blue of the sky pales, but the sun shines virtually as brightly. So tenuous is the cloud that it is often only disclosed by the sight of the haloes that it produces round the sun or moon. A halo 22° wide is said to be measurable by holding your hand straight out at arm's length towards the sun so that it is at your finger tips.

Altostratus (As) has a thicker veil-like appearance and appears lower down than the cirrostratus, to which it often succeeds. It is a greyish or bluish colour, furrowed or smooth, and covers the sky partially or entirely. The sun still penetrates it as if it were shining through frosted glass. It all looks innocent enough but at sea it can still burn you very badly.

The altostratus can thicken, become very grey and bring a few drops of rain.

Nimbostratus (Ns) is a thick cloudy grey layer, often very dark, which spreads over the whole sky, and usually follows a thick veil of altostratus. Its outlines are blurred by continual precipitations. Often, small black ragged clouds run beneath it.

It darkens the sky and lights must be turned on. The nimbostratus is the cloud that brings interminable rain (or snow). It can be 5,000m thick and extend over hundreds of miles.

Stratus (st). A very low cloud, of uniform grey, it is often quite clear. Sometimes the outline of the sun can be seen clearly through it. It can cover the whole sky or else trail over the sea in jagged banks. It is often the result of fog which has risen slightly up from the ground. It can produce drizzle, hail or granulated snow.

The succession, cirrus, cirrostratus, altostratus, nimbostratus, stratocumulus (and sometimes stratus), is a classic one in northern latitudes. It heralds, as we shall see in the next chapter, the arrival of a warm air mass, like the advance guard rattling along the heights while the main body of the troops follow at sea level.

Stratus

Fogs

The meteorologists speak of *fog* when visibility at ground level is below 1km; of *mist* when it is between 1 and 2km. Sailors refer to fog, whatever visibility it allows. There is some terminological inexactitude in weather descriptions.

The fog and mists met with at sea are closely associated with the phenomena of advection and radiation.

Advection fog is the most common type at sea. Advection – in contrast with convection – is displacement of air horizontally. Advection fog arises from condensation occurring in a mass of warm, damp air passing over a cold surface. This sort of fog is almost permanent over the Newfoundland Banks where the air, warmed and saturated with humidity over the Gulf Stream, meets the cold Labrador current. Generally speaking, the higher the latitude, the colder the sea, and the more frequently is this type of fog met. It is commoner in winter than in summer. In France, it is particularly prevalent in areas with strong currents, like the Raz de Sein, the Four channel on the North West coast and the Raz Blanchard for instance. The turbulence that occurs in a swift tidal stream brings cold water up to the surface.

Radiation fog is essentially a land fog that occurs in clear, calm weather. During the night, the Earth loses its heat by radiation, the air in contact with it cools and the water vapour it contains condenses. This fog is particularly dense at first light, the coldest hour. It lingers sometimes for a long time on low ground where the cold air tends to gather. It occurs in estuaries and sometimes spills over a little out to sea, obscuring the coastal lights.

Nimbostratus

Classification of the Air Masses

With practice, one succeeds in identifying the various cloud types at a glance. But the precise identification of the air mass in which it lies needs the application of other senses than sight – touch and smell itself because the air masses can pick up the smells of the regions they have passed through.

We know for a fact that air masses are characterised by their origins and their journeyings. This is how air masses from the Arctic, the North Pole, the tropics or the equator, be they maritime or continental, can be distinguished.

Arctic air. Coming from the Polar icecap, Arctic air is, at the outset, cold, dry, and stable. Moving towards more temperate latitudes, it becomes laden with moisture over the sea and heated from below and becomes unstable. Sometimes, around Iceland, it finds a path down which it tracks straight down to North West Europe. The weather is then very cold, and the sky is a pale, very characteristic, emerald green, with many cumulus and cumulonimbus. Thunderstorms are frequent, squalls violent, winds strong. Between squalls, visibility is excellent.

Polar air. The Polar maritime air is usually Arctic air which has not succeeded in escaping, and which has hung around a long time in the sub-polar regions (between 60° and 70° latitude). It has absorbed its moisture gradually, and has become progressively warm. When it arrives in the English Channel area, as it commonly does, this Polar maritime air is unstable, but less so than the Arctic air. The cumuliform clouds are not so numerous, the squalls not so violent. Visibility is still excellent.

The Polar continental air is Arctic air which has made a detour over the continents. Its characteristics vary according to the seasons, and the nature of the ground it has passed over. It is stable in winter, sometimes unstable in summer. When it arrives in western Europe from Russia, it gives dry cold weather with a cloudless sky in winter; in summer, fine, rather cloudy weather.

Tropical air. Tropical maritime air, coming out of the sub-tropical regions (between 30° and 40° latitude), is warm and laden with moisture, unstable from the outset. As it reaches temperate latitudes, it is cooled from the base and tends to become stable. Its arrival in western Europe is often signalled by the famous succession of stratiform clouds which we have mentioned above. Sometimes this maritime tropical air is still unstable on arrival and this is characterised by severe thunderstorms.

Tropical continental air, originating in North Africa or the Near East, is very dry and very stable when it sets out, and cannot create clouds. But as it passes over the Mediterranean or the Atlantic, it becomes laden with moisture. Its arrival in Europe, in summer, brings very hot weather and violent storms over high ground.

Equatorial air is very hot, very damp and very unstable. It contributes to the formation of Tropical cyclones. It rarely reaches France and the United Kingdom but when it does arrive it gives rise to very violent disturbances.

The air masses have not always got the clear-cut characteristics we have just given and, in any case, there is no consistently uniform air mass, be it Polar or Tropical, but many and varied masses of air have a Polar or Tropical origin. They develop and circulate at different rates; they warm up, cool down, become moist or dry, or more stable or less stable, as their wanderings take them. The essential fact to grasp is that when two air masses of different temperature (and therefore of different density) meet, they do not mix: they clash. The area where the confrontation takes place is called the *frontal zone* and its track over the ground a *front*.

The principal fronts are:

The Arctic front, separating the masses of Arctic air from the masses of Polar air;

The Polar front, separating the masses of Polar air from the masses of Tropical air;

The inter-Tropical front, a zone of convergences for the winds of the two hemispheres.

We shall have good reasons for reverting to the Polar front in the next chapter.

Wind

Our study of the behaviour of moving air and of the different types of air masses travelling over the globe eventually drew attention to the wind and some of its local manifestations. It is now time to examine winds without attempting to get involved too deeply in scientific phenomena. What is wind? Why does it blow in one direction rather than another? Why does it vary in strength?

The answer lies first in a reconsideration of atmospheric pressure, that has just been referred to in connection with the phenomenon of expansion. It has been made clear that atmospheric pressure is closely connected with temperature, cold air being heavier than warm air and the weight of an air column at a given spot depending on the temperature of the air itself. In addition to the thermal factor there are the dynamic ones – the rotation of the Earth and movements of air masses. It has also become clear that pressure can vary considerably from hour to hour within the same area, and it follows logically enough that it varies from one place to another.

The comparison of pressures taken at different points on the Earth's surface is one of the keys to meteorology. To make this comparison, all measurements are first of all reduced to the same reference point, which is sea level. The results obtained are then charted and all points with equal pressure are joined together. These lines of equal pressure are called *isobars*. Drawn usually at intervals of 5 millibars, they disclose the equivalent of a relief map of the atmosphere, just as contour lines on survey maps show land contours, and surroundings on charts indicate least depth.

The outlines of the isobars outline various shapes on the maps – the so-called isobaric shapes – which illustrate the characteristic movements of the air masses. It will be noticed that in certain areas the isobars are circular and fit more or less regularly into one another. When the height of the isobars decreases towards the centre of the shape, in the outline of a bowl, there is an *area of low pressure*, or a *depression*. Conversely, when the height of the isobars increases as they approach the centre, forming a 'hill' there is an *area of high pressure*, or *anti-cyclone*.

There are also other shapes outlined on the weather charts:

'Valleys' that extend the depressions between areas of high pressure are known as *troughs*;
'Promontories', projecting the anticyclones into a depression are *ridges*;
Areas of relatively low pressure, connecting two depressions (or two highs), are *cols*;
Finally areas with contours showing pressures not much different

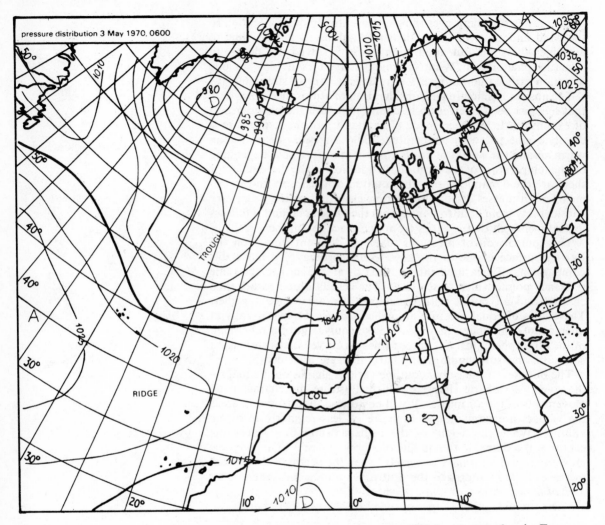

pressure distribution 3 May 1970, 0600

from the average pressure are called *barometric fens* in France.

Winds result from the differences in atmospheric pressures shown on the map. It would all be much easier if a simple definition were possible. Wind is air moving from high pressure towards low pressure areas, like air escaping from a tyre or a ball rolling down a slope. Unfortunately, that is only a half-truth.

Direction of the Wind

A ball, released at the top of a hill, rolls in the direction of the steepest slope. One might think it would be the same with air and that the wind direction would be at right angles to the isobars. This would no doubt be the case if the Earth were motionless, and if it were a perfectly smooth globe. But the Earth turns perpetually and is, moreover, not upright.

Because the Earth is rotating, all moving bodies on its surface are exposed to a deflecting force, called the *Coriolis Force*, which acts at right angles to the direction of the movement. Observation shows that, in the Northern hemisphere, all trajectories are deflected to the right, whatever their direction, and that they are deflected to the left in the Southern hemisphere.* Thus, the Gulf Stream, as it moves North, curves away towards the East; the Labrador current, descending in the opposite direction, is flattened against the American continental barrier.

On land, on very busy railway tracks, a micrometer demonstrates that the right hand rail is always more worn that the left hand one. Fortunately the Coriolis Force is very weak and is not felt by human beings when they move, but it has as much influence on the wind as the pressure force.

In anticyclones, air tends to move outwards from the centre towards the circumference. Deflected to the right, it therefore moves in a clockwise direction. But in depressions, the air tends to move from the circumference towards the centre and, still deflected to the right, it therefore moves in an anti-clockwise direction.

A practical observation follows from this law (*The law of Buys-Ballot*), that an observer facing the wind always has low pressure on his right and high pressure on his left.

That is the main principle, but there are important variations because the wind blows in different directions high up and at ground level.

At heights, two forces determine direction: the pressure force, directed from high towards low pressure, and the Coriolis Force which deflects the air towards the right. They balance each other out in such a way that the wind blows parallel to the isobars.

*This is a fundamental fact, and it can be stated once and for all that all movements of atmosphere in the Southern hemisphere go in the opposite direction to the Northern one. We shall only speak here of the Northern hemisphere.

For the convenience of the reader who adventures into Southern waters and who will read this chapter upside down.

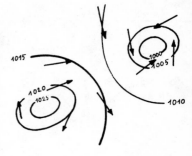

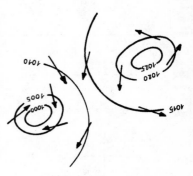

northern hemisphere

Buys-Ballot's law

southern hemisphere

Buys-Ballot himself

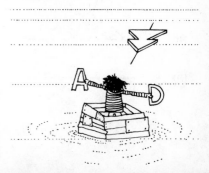

Near the ground, friction intervenes. Its action is proportional to the unevenness of the surface. It modifies the relationship of the forces in such a way that the air, at ground level, is deflected less towards the right than it is high up. So it can be said that the wind has a tendency to 'move out' of anticyclones, and to 'move into' depressions. At sea, the angle it makes with the isobars is, on average, of the order of 30°.

The difference of direction between wind at height and wind on ground level explains a phenomenon which can be often observed at sea, in squally weather. When an observer, standing facing the wind, sees a squall coming straight at him, he eventually remarks that the squall passes to his left. But it is the squall coming a little from his right that he ought to keep an eye on.

Let us suppose that the wind is constant, ie that the parcels of air are all moving at a constant speed. In this case, the forces acting on these parcels are balanced.

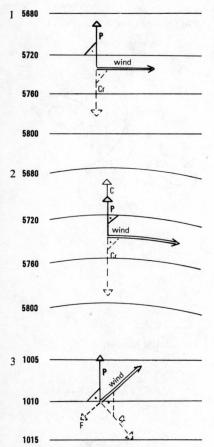

1 *High altitude wind (more than 2,000m) parallel straight isobars.* If there is to be a balance of forces, Cr (Coriolis Force), which is at right angles to the wind, must be equal and opposite to P (pressure force) which is also at right angles to the isobars and the further apart they are, the gentler the wind. This is the *Geostrophic Wind*; its scale is given on met maps and allows an evaluation of the ground wind speed to be made.

2 *High altitude wind, curved isobars.* For a balance of forces, Cr which is at right angles to the wind must be equal:
to P+C (centrifugal force) in an anticyclone;
to P−C in a depression.
P is at right angles to the isobars.
C is at right angles to the wind, therefore parallel to P; concurrent with P in an anticyclone, opposed to P in a depression. This wind is called the *gradient wind*.

3 *Ground wind, straight isobars.* The three forces must balance out. P is at right angles to the isobars. Cr is at right angles to the wind. F (friction) is opposed to the wind (or at right angles to Cr). The greater F is, the more the wind will approach the direction of P. This wind is equal to about 0.8 × the geostrophic wind.

4–5 *Ground wind, curved isobars*. The four forces must balance. P is at right angles to the isobars. Cr is at right angles to the wind. C is at right angles to the wind. F is opposed to the wind (or at right angles to Cr). This wind is also equal to $0.8 \times$ the geostrophic wind.

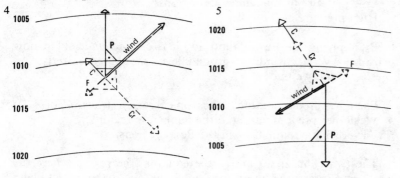

Wind Speed

The speed of the wind is directly linked to the *pressure gradient*, represented on the maps by the spacing of the isobars. The closer the isobars are together, the steeper the gradient, the stronger the wind. In our latitudes, isobars spaced out at some 100km apart indicate winds of approximately 100km an hour.

It will be noticed that the isobars in anticyclones are usually well spaced out: the winds are weak. Around depressions on the contrary, the isobars are often very close together and therefore indicate violent winds.

Let us note finally that, because of friction, wind at ground level is considerably less strong than at heights. Even a few metres from the ground, the difference is perceptible (in the order of 10% for the first ten metres). This percentage mounts increasingly the higher up the wind is blowing.

General Circulation

Normal weather maps, which give the average pressures on the globe's surface in winter and summer, bring out the fact that, be-

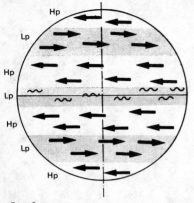

Lp: low pressure
Hp: high pressure

tween equator and the Poles in both hemispheres, there is an alternation of high pressure and low pressure zones.

Low pressure at the Equator;
High pressure in the Tropics;
Low pressure in the temperate regions;
High pressure at the Poles.

By applying the Buys-Ballot law, it is easy to understand now why the average winds at ground level should be easterly and westerly, and we find:

Easterlies predominating in the tropical regions (the *trade-winds*);
Westerlies predominating in the temperate regions;
Easterlies predominating in the Polar regions.

The two calm zones are at the equator (the region where the gradient of pressure is weak – the *doldrums*) and in the tropics (calm sunny zones of high pressure).

This pattern is not absolutely regular. The uneven heating of the oceans and continents, seasonal variations and the appearance of 'disturbances' in the temperate zones all contribute to variations and the breaking up of these pressure belts. The winds come as a consequence of them.

A concrete picture of the average circulation of air streams in summer and winter is given on the maps opposite.

A number of eddies (vortices) will be immediately noticeable. They correspond to anticyclones and depressions of a permanent or semi-permanent type which are called *action centres*.

The large swirls which appear in the Pacific and the Atlantic (their distribution is impressively symmetrical) are anticyclones of dynamic origin which is a symptom of the rotation of the Earth. From one season to the next, they only move slightly and their configuration does not change. They are *permanent* action centres. The North Atlantic anticyclone, the one which particularly interests us, is called the *Azores anticyclone*. This is the one which pushes the masses of Tropical maritime air (Tm) towards our latitudes.

More difficult to distinguish, but no less important, are the depressions situated between 60° and 70° North, between the east winds of the Polar ice cap and the west winds of the temperate regions: to the north of the Aleutians, to the west of Greenland, to the south of Iceland. These too are also permanent centres of action

A. Normal wind directions and action centres in July

B. Normal wind directions and action centres in January

of dynamic origin. It will be noticed besides how much these anti-cyclones and depressions are linked: the Aleutian depression is situated to the north-east of the North Pacific anticyclone; the Icelandic depression to the north-east of the Azores anticyclone. This Icelandic depression, it will again be noticed, is more accentuated in winter than in summer and many yachtsmen exploit this as an argument for staying indoors at this time of the year.

On continents, variations are much more clear-cut from one season to the next. They are linked to the great temperature variations which the land is subject to. The case of the Asian continent is particularly noteworthy. In winter with the ground cooling, high pressure areas are established and an anticyclone is formed: the winds move outwards towards the oceans. In summer, the ground is overheated and the anticyclone is replaced by a vast zone of

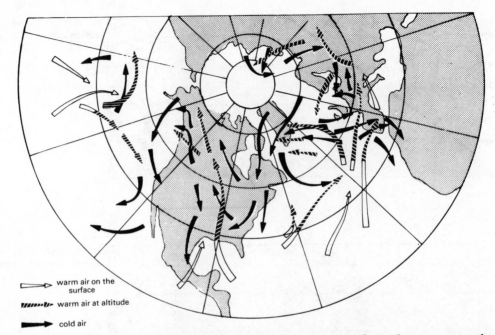

warm air on the surface

warm air at altitude

cold air

Example of the general circulation of air masses between the Tropics and the Polar regions (7 May 1933)

low pressure. The winds then move inland from the oceans to the interior and the rainy season begins. This phenomenon is familiar the world over as the *Monsoon*. The anticyclones and depressions which are formed in this way on the continents therefore have a thermal origin. They are *seasonal action centres* of which Eurasian anticyclones are typical.

This general picture of the circulation of air masses does not exactly explain how heat transfers occur between the Equator and the Poles, and an explanation has still to be found. An examination of *synoptic* charts (which give an overall picture) shows that air masses become detached from time to time from the Polar ice cap and make their way towards the Equator. To compensate for this movement, warm air masses leave the Equator for the north. The Coriolis Force deviates all the movements towards the right and it is likely that none of them ever reach their destination and that the heat transfer takes place in stages. A mass of equatorial air, for instance, that arrives at latitude 45°, continues to be subject to the Coriolis Force, and so tends to return southwards. But at the top of its curve this air mass has lost heat and it has therefore become a cooling agent on its return to the hot areas where it originated.

The same process may well be repeated from one area to another. Perhaps this is how it happens – or there may be some other explanation.

No doubt the disturbances which take place inside these great air movements (extra-tropical depressions, tropical cyclones, waterspouts, thunderstorms and tornadoes) also play a part in establishing the Earth's thermal balance but there are too many unknown factors for it to be possible to be certain of their role in the system.

The Wind and the Sea

The similarity between atmosphere circulation and oceanic surface currents may seem remarkable but it is natural enough as the same influences are at work in air and sea movements. We have already drawn attention earlier in this chapter to the activity of the great ocean streams which influence the thermal exchanges between the Equator and the Poles. An examination of an ocean current chart makes it clear that the similarity is very extensive. The direction of the rotation of the Gulf Stream corresponds exactly to the rotation of the winds around the Azores anticyclone; and the Labrador or the Aleutian cold currents to the currents of cold air coming from the Poles. In some areas seasonal currents set in rhythm with the monsoons.

To these so-called *density* currents must be added *drift* currents which are caused by the wind and which behave in exactly the same way as the wind itself.

This is not the book to cover all the essential points of the foregoing description of the ocean currents for it would be too detailed to be of any practical use for yachtsmen. The great atmospheric migrations are a different matter since they run after us and create our daily weather, while we, who sail over relatively tiny areas of sea, do not need an overall picture of ocean currents to plan tomorrow's cruise.

What is of enormous interest, though, is a particular point in the relationships between the atmosphere and the oceans: how wind and sea react when they meet in the area where we are sailing and the adjacent areas; what happens when the two elements are at their extremes, especially when the wind is strong.

Waves

When the wind blows over a calm sea, the friction of the air raises ripples on the water. These can be quite transitory, but if the wind continues, undulations or wavelets form, then waves running over the water in the direction of the wind.

With rather less violence, the wind has the same effect on the sea as a paving stone thrown in to a pond: it makes a series of waves, and it is to be remembered that it is the waves that move, not the water itself. The liquid particles merely move orbitally, without changing position appreciably, as each undulation rolls by. The principle of this movement is demonstrated by watching a cork bobbing about on the water; when the wave arrives, the cork rises on the slope and moves a little forward; then, once the crest has passed, it moves downwards and backwards until it finally returns almost to its point of departure. Something of this movement is felt on board a boat running before the waves, when these are large enough: the boat accelerates on the forward slope of the wave, then seems, quite perceptibly, to be braked on the rear slope. Waves do not in reality correspond to the horizontal movement of the water which the eye seems to see.

In spite of appearances, the water does not move: the cork returns to the same spot in relation to the bottom after the wave has passed

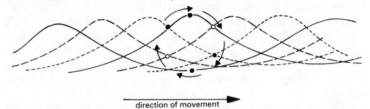

direction of movement

A wave can be defined first of all by its dimensions: its *height*, the vertical distance between the top of the crest and the bottom of the trough; its *length*, the distance between two troughs or between two crests (it is quite precise to talk of wave length). The relationship between a wave's height and length is its curve or steepness. A wave is always much longer than it is high; its steepness becomes critical when the ratio between height and length is in the order of 1/13. If the height increases any further, the waves *break* and then there really is a displacement of water in a horizontal direction.

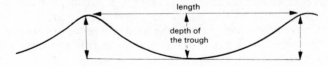

length

depth of
the trough

A wave is also defined by the *depth* to which its movement penetrates. Its depth is believed to be equal to its length, but in fact the movement is already very reduced at a depth equal to 1/9 of its length.

A wave, in fact, moves as part of a system of waves, which has its own rhythm, characterised by its frequency – the time which elapses between the passage of two crests at a given spot – and by its velocity, or the distance covered by a wave in a given time.

Clearly there exists a direct relationship between the length of the waves and the characteristics of the system of waves. This length (L) is equal to the product of the frequency (F) multiplied by the velocity (V): $L = FV$.

These definitions may be a little dry (and they are the only dry thing about them), but we shall see them come to life in the description of the principal characteristics the sea can assume wherever one happens to be.

We speak of a sea or sea condition to define any pattern of waves arising locally owing to the actual wind. We speak of *swell* when, in contrast, we see waves appearing, coming from a long way off, as a result of a wind which has blown (or is still blowing) somewhere else.

How Waves Originate

Let us suppose that the wind begins to blow, on a calm sea, in an area where you happen to be. The size of the waves which are going to develop depends on three factors:

– the strength of the wind
– how long it blows
– its *fetch*, that is the distance over which the wind can exert its effect without meeting any obstacles, or without changing direction itself.

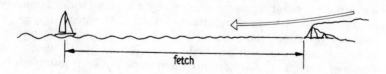

fetch

The developing waves gradually gain height. At first they have a very steep curve as their velocity is still low in proportion to the speed of the wind. If the wind continues, they gradually get longer.

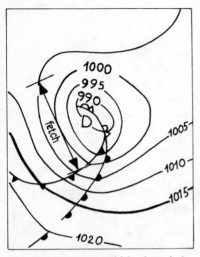

The distance over which the wind blows, its 'fetch', can alter

Height, length, frequency and velocity increase progressively to their maximum, according to the strength of the wind. It can then go on blowing for days, but, if its strength does not change, neither will the character of the waves it has created alter.

But if the fetch is too short, they cannot reach their optimum shape. When the first waves that developed, where the wind began to blow, reach the end of the fetch (at the coast for instance), a balance is set up. Here again, the duration of the wind is of no importance, provided it continues to blow at the same strength. It follows that the shorter the fetch, the less chance the waves have of becoming big. It does not follow that sailing is necessarily any pleasanter in a small enclosed sea than right out in the ocean, for the waves cannot space out, but remain short and steep and the boat pounds harder than on a well formed sea.

It will also be noticed that the wind is never perfectly regular either in strength or direction, so that the waves in this kind of sea are seldom consistent; some are shorter than others and they cross each other's tracks. When the wind changes direction, the first wave system only decreases slowly and another system forms and combines with it. The different vintages meet and mingle with each other. The sea becomes chaotic and the waves don't hesitate to climb aboard.

Swell

Sometimes, in this type of chaotic sea, a slower, deeper rhythm can be felt coming from a direction that is quite different from that of the actual wind, apparently with a life of its own. On some calm days, the swell appears in great splendour: the sea is smooth and huge regular rollers undulate over its surface. They can be very high, but, above all, they are very long, with as much as two or three hundred metres between them. Waves have become swell by the time they leave the turbulent battlefield where the wind has stirred them into existence or, to speak more scientifically, when they leave their generating basin. Caused by a distant wind, far away in the North Atlantic for instance, which has since stopped or changed direction, these waves have gained considerable power, and they only diminish gradually. The shorter waves disappear first and a regular, harmonious movement is slowly established. The height of the waves gradually lessens while their length increases.

The swell created like this can roll for hundreds, even thousands of miles. The longer the waves are the further it will persist and it can sometimes be seen reaching the coast, when the weather is fine, the wind light or non-existent, and the sun blazing. It breaks white on the rocks along the shore – the sea is 'working'. You can be sure that somewhere, far out on the open sea, the wind has blown hard yesterday or two days ago. According to the height and frequency of the waves, you can even make an approximate calculation of the strength of the wind and how far away it was blowing.

This kind of swell is sometimes a forerunner of bad weather, for the waves themselves can travel faster than the wind that created them. The wind acts upon the liquid particles and their orbital movement is less than the velocity of the series of waves set in motion. A wind of 10 miles an hour can thus very easily supply enough power to waves to give them a velocity of 12 miles. This disparity becomes noticeable after a certain time, as the waves get well ahead of the wind. Very often therefore the swell precedes the disturbance which has created it and it is as well to be on the lookout in calm weather when the ground swell begins to make itself felt.

Wave Obstructions

The state of the sea varies greatly as a result of any obstruction the waves encounter. One of the most spectacular changes takes place when waves (and the wind which drives them) clash with an opposing tidal stream. They are then braked, strangled as it were, between wind and current, their length is reduced, their height increased, their steepness can become excessive and they break. When wind is against tide you often therefore have a broken, very steep sea which can be dangerous. But, when wind and tide are in the same direction, the waves lengthen, become smoother and there is less likelihood of their breaking.

The nature of the sea bottom will also affect the waves. If the bottom rises abruptly, they are suddenly braked, as they are when

they meet a contrary current and their height increases and they break. These are the characteristic *breakers* of shoal water. The areas with strong tidal streams are often shallow (the races, for instance) and it is easily understood why memorable seas are encountered in them.

As they approach the coast, other phenomena can occur. When the rise in the sea bottom is not progressive but sudden, the waves will all for certain break in the same place, which is called a *bar*. On some coasts, this bar can be seen a long way off. On others it is very localised, forming at the mouth an estuary where an accumulation of sediment brought down by the river creates a shoal which the waves cannot cross without breaking.

Another factor is that the swell can change direction considerably when it approaches an island or a headland. Then the phenomenon of 'diffraction' can be seen (dramatically in aerial photographs) and it is analogous to those which affect sound and light waves. The swell passes on either side of the island and re-forms beyond it. The interference of the two lines of swell often brings about a confused sea for some distance. A swell can pass round a headland or a mere jetty, and often makes an anchorage dangerous which you had assumed to be safe.

Eventually all waves die away. When they reach shallow water, the movement of the water particles becomes elliptical, and flattens. Braked by the bottom, the waves slow down but increase in height. At the last moment, owing to friction, the bottom of the wave is retarded and the crest carries on, overspills and breaks.

As the depth of waves is related to their length, the longest waves – that is the oldest – touch the bottom very soon and can, as a result, increase enormously before reaching the shore. It is the longest and slowest swell which produces the strongest surf. It is a splendid sight to see waves rearing up in the air when the sun is dazzlingly bright, regaining their youthful vigour before they die in a myriad flashing lights. On coasts that shelve very gradually they can run on for a long time just on the point of breaking. It is then, that, balanced on a simple board, on the crest of a wave, you can experience for a few moments the unparalleled glory of surfing before crashing in a burst of foam on the hot sand.

17. The Weather

Now that the principal atmospheric phenomena have been concisely explained in the last chapter, it is time to see how they work for yachtsmen. We shall concentrate on the areas we know – the North Atlantic, the English Channel and the Western Mediterranean. But these regions illustrate weather in general and Americans will know what allowances to make.

To speak of 'average weather' in any one area is to make even more unreliable statements than to describe the atmosphere in the same terms. You can sketch out the vast overall atmospheric movements without much risk of error, but establishing patterns for daily weather is a chancy business. So as not to lose our way, we shall keep closely, for the moment, to what can be observed. The approach of oceanic weather, in particular, can, it seems to us, be effectively foreseen by looking for characteristic skies. The identification of typical or significant skies may appear complicated as the sky is the most changeable landscape in the world, but it is worthwhile although all predictions must be qualified. Provided allowance is made for the unforeseen, the principal weather patterns which appear throughout the year can be interpreted, at least in the Atlantic areas. In the Mediterranean, the patterns are much less trustworthy. All kinds of local anomalies have to be taken into consideration and predictions are more speculative.

There is an amusing reference to 'knocking the skies into shape' in a well known song about 'Professor Nimbus' by Georges Brassens, the celebrated French poet and singer who has won international fame but, thank God, we haven't yet reached the stage of controlling the weather. At the end of the chapter, when we go beyond present to future weather, it is principally to give the reader the basic elements of a field of research which is never finished.

Maritime Weather

The north west Atlantic region is a transit area where air masses meet, exchange places and pass through. The weather is in fact very varied. However, it is possible to sketch out a simple overall picture of it, even if it has to be modified later.

The weather there is influenced principally by the great centres of activity – the Azores anticyclone and the Icelandic depression. Their respective positions and strengths determine the latitude at which the Polar and Tropical air masses meet – i.e. the latitude of the Polar front.

In winter, the anticyclone remains in low latitudes; it hardly ever comes further north than the 40th parallel. The Icelandic depression makes ground southwards and the Polar front comes into our latitudes. The clash of these air masses creates disturbances which are carried along in the general west–east stream of the temperate regions and frequently reach the British Isles and France. We then speak of *unsettled westerly weather*.

Unsettled

In summer, the Azores anticyclone extends towards the north and the Icelandic depression remains in very high latitudes. The disturbances associated with the Polar front are pushed beyond the 60th parallel and they move from Greenland to Scandinavia without reaching us. We are then in *anticyclonic conditions.*

Of course this pattern is susceptible to all kinds of variations and not only in spring and autumn. It isn't always fine in summer! The Azores anticyclone is usually very stable at its western edge but much less so at its eastern limit where it breaks down periodically and creates disturbances. Some summers, for reasons not yet understood, the anticyclone does not come up as high as usual. We then speak of a 'wretched season' for the Polar front is still with us.

In the same way, the winter season is not one long continuous westerly gale. The Siberian anticyclone sometimes extends to our regions and diverts the disturbance to the south or the north, bringing dry, cold weather.

All these very general data bring out one basic fact and its practical importance cannot escape anyone: the weather experienced on the Atlantic coasts and in the English Channel depends entirely on whether the disturbances of the Polar front do or do not pass our way. These disturbances are a vital influence which is now our immediate concern.

Disturbances of the Polar Front

A mass of warm air originating in the tropics moves around the Azores anticyclone and makes its way towards the NE. A mass of cold air coming from the Pole moves around the Icelandic depression and makes its way SW. These two masses of air meet somewhere off Newfoundland. The boundary between them is called a *frontal zone* and the line where it intersects the surface is called a *front*.

This frontal zone is not necessarily disturbed. When the two air masses are not moving at great speed, and their temperature and humidity are not very different, the convergence can be tranquil.

Sometimes the warm air mass pushes the cold air mass back to the north, but in doing so, as it is lighter than the cold air, it is forced to rise over it. The new frontal zone inclines therefore up towards the Pole almost horizontal to the surface (the slope is about 1/100 to 1/1000) and results in what is called a *warm front*.

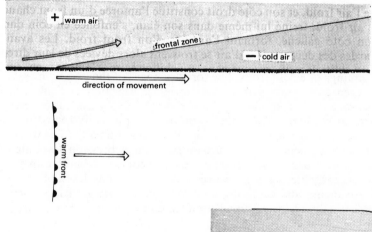

Warm front: the warm air pushes back the cold air, at the same time rising above it

Cold front: the cold air mass edges under the base of the warm air mass and pushes it back vigorously

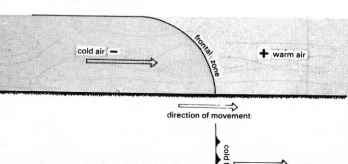

Sometimes it happens the other way round and it is the cold air mass that pushes the warm air mass before it. The heavier cold air undercuts the warm air, and forces it to rise, forming a *cold front*. The frontal zone also slopes up towards the north, but it is much steeper than in the case of a warm front (in the order of 1/50).

When the temperature differences between the air masses are slight, the fronts are not very active, even weak as, for instance, when the flows of cold and warm air are moving parallel to one another or almost so. The Polar front then takes on, alternatively, the characteristics of a warm front and a cold front, without any notable disturbances. The front is then said to be *stationary*.

But this kind of situation rarely lasts long. Most of the time the warm air masses and the cold air masses, which leave their places of origin for unpredictable reasons, travel at different speeds and with very distinctly different characteristics. Then they clash. The edge of the Polar front becomes very clear cut, and it is then that there is, scientifically speaking, *frontogenesis*. The Polar front, under pressure by the air masses, is distorted and develops undulations, each one of which can create a disturbance.

Clash of the Air Masses

The warm air mass making towards the NE tends to repulse the cold air mass coming from the opposite direction and at the same time rising above it. A wedge of warm air, in consequence, advances over the cold air; and its right-hand side forms an embryo warm front. The cold air, checked in its forward thrust, in turn makes an inroad with its left side into the warm air, and forms the beginnings of a cold front. The forward edges of the two air masses are then turned away from their original direction and an anti-clockwise movement begins, called *cyclogenesis*. A depression then forms at the extremity of the warm air and this eddy (or vortex), once it has taken shape starts on a sort of life of its own. The whole of this phenomenon (the disturbance and the depression associated with it) then usually set off on an easterly course, towards Europe.

In its early life the disturbance consists, at ground level, of warm air advancing and replacing cold air (i.e. a *warm front*), a *warm sector* (the tip of the warm air itself) and of cold air, as it advances,

Birth of a disturbance

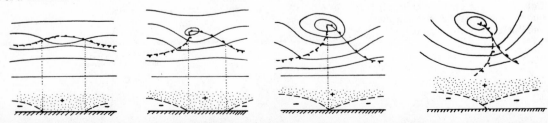

replacing warm air (i.e. a *cold front*). The cold air surrounding the warm sector is sometimes referred to as the cold sector.

Once under way the disturbance gradually extends, covering hundreds sometimes even thousands of miles. All this time its depressionary characteristics are becoming accentuated and its structure is evolving. As the cold front moves more quickly than the warm front, it gradually catches up on the latter. The warm sector separating them is compressed and the warm air is slowly driven upwards by the thrust of the cold air behind the cold front. Finally the cold front catches up the warm front, and an *occlusion* occurs. This occlusion begins in the narrowest part of the warm sector and gradually extends over the whole of the front, until there is only one *occluded front*, which in turn is driven upwards. The characteristics of this front depend eventually on the temperature difference of the cold air ahead and behind it. If the air behind the occlusion is not so cold as the air which precedes it, it rises over the latter: this is an occlusion with warm front characteristics; but if the cold air behind the occlusion is the colder of the two, it penetrates below the preceding cold air and there is an occlusion with cold front characteristics.

From this moment on the disturbance begins to run down, the depression is closed up or occluded and the whole occluded front gradually weakens and finally disappears. This is *frontolysis*. The disturbance has now died, after having lasted only a few days, perhaps a week. The path it has followed has varied according to the shape of the field of pressure it has crossed. If an anticyclone was protecting the Atlantic, it would be diverted towards the north to die away on the coast of Scandinavia. Had the anticyclone been situated over the British Isles, it might have been diverted towards the south and lost itself in the Mediterranean.

But all is not over yet. We have already seen that when the Polar front was distorted under the thrust of the air masses, several wave movements were formed and each one of them gave

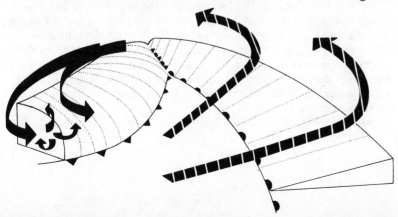

Movements of air masses in a disturbance

rise to a disturbance. The first disturbance is therefore followed by all the rest of the group. This *family of disturbances* numbers on average four to six members advancing in order of age: the eldest go in front, more or less occluded, followed by the younger ones which still have some impetus and often travel further south than older ones.

Eventually, after the last disturbance has gone, the Polar air arrives for the final grand 'sweep up'. As this is rarely uniform, we can still suffer some *cold secondary fronts*, which often have violent effects. But peace returns at last. The invasion of cold air brings with it a general rise in the pressure and finally what the average tourist calls 'fine weather' and meteorologists, in their more guarded language call simply *an interval*.

A family of disturbances

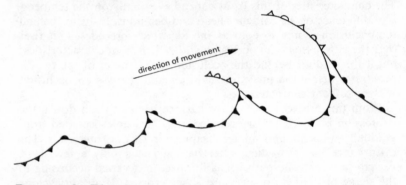

direction of movement

Passage of a Disturbance

This description of the birth and development of a family of disturbance is obviously rudimentary and rather theoretical. In reality each disturbance, like every living creature, has its own character, formed by the nature of the confrontation that originated it; it is also changed throughout the whole of its existence under all sorts of influences. A disturbance can take on all kinds of shapes. Once it is launched on the highways of the sky, it does not necessarily follow a straight and predictable path. Disturbances can be seen to speed up or slow down suddenly, or even stop for a while. Some change direction, split in two or interfere with other disturbances that have originated elsewhere. The depression accompanying them can deepen suddenly and quite unpredictably, or fill earlier than can be foreseen. With such individual 'meteorological types' anything can be expected.

Such differences must not however be allowed to obscure the

fundamental similarity in the basic structure of each. Generally speaking the passage of a disturbance over the area where one is sailing is marked by a series of phenomena which follow each other in an order, which reveals precise organisation. These phenomena come about essentially through marked variations in temperature, pressure, wind and the look of the sky.

Temperature. People have to bear alternately the consequences of the passage of cold Polar air, warm Tropical air and then cold air again. The variations cause chills and the pharmaceutical industry reaps the harvest.

Pressure and Wind. The pressure variations are clearly illustrated in the diagram below. When the warm air mass makes progress, pressure drops. It is at its lowest when the warm air mass has

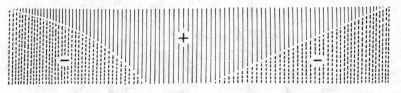

As a warm front approaches, the dense cold air is gradually replaced by warm, lighter air: the barometer falls. On the arrival of the cold front, the warm air is in its turn replaced by cold air: the barometer rises

invaded the whole of the sky; that is the moment the warm front and the warm sector are passing by. It rises rapidly thereafter with the arrival of denser cold air.

We know too that, around a depression, the wind turns in an anti-clockwise direction and that it strengthens as the depression deepens. Anyone on the line of the depression's advance can observe (and the weather map will confirm) that the wind comes first from the SE or south, veers gradually to SW and from there to NW at the end of the depression. A subsequent examination of the map gives an accurate appreciation of what has been observed on the ground: the direction of the wind quite clearly changes with the passage of the warm front (shown cutting across the isobars) stays in the same quarter while the warm sector moves across

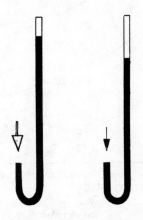

Torricelli's experiment: the mercury in the tube rises more or less according to the weight of the air outside. Cold air: high pressures. Warm air: low pressures

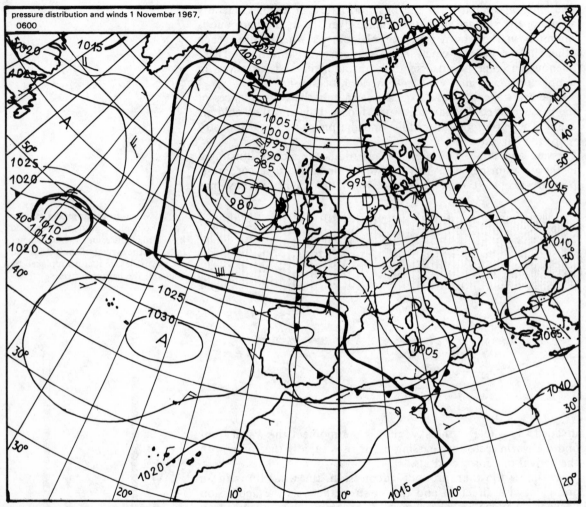

pressure distribution and winds 1 November 1967,
0600

Conventional signs for wind on
meteorological charts

NW wind 5 knots

E wind 10 knots

SW wind 50 knots

West wind 35 knots

(shown by the straight isobars) and veers again with the passage of
the cold front. The spacing of the isobars allows an estimate to be
made of wind strength at any given point in the depression. It is
usually observed that the strongest winds are in the southern part
of the depression, at some distance from the centre (50 to 200
miles) and immediately after the cold front passes on.

These variations of wind strength and direction produce big changes in the state of the sea. The strength of the wind increases the size of the waves, but its rotation in particular sets up differing wave systems, the first coming from the south or SW, the last from NW or North. The interference patterns of these wave systems often stirs up a lumpy sea both on the arrival of the cold front and during the invasion of Polar air that follows it. When several disturbances follow each other, we are finally left with many wave systems which clash with each other, producing a confused sea.

The Appearance of the Sky. As you would suspect, the great confusion to which the air masses are being subjected encourages the growth of significant cloud formations, but there is a new factor: these cloud formations do not wander at will across the sky, but, on the contrary, their distribution in space and sequence in time are so distinctive that they constitute a *cloud system*, an ordered grouping, covering several different areas giving the whole sky classic characteristics.

There are cloud sequences, as we shall see. The one accompanying a disturbance of the Polar front (known in full as 'moving extra-Tropical depressionary cloud sequence') is the most characteristic of all. Each of these zones corresponds to an exact moment of the disturbance and gives it its name. An observer stationed in the line of advance of the disturbance will see, passing in succession, the *head* (the area in front of the depression), the *body* (the area at the centre of the depression), the warm sector and the *wake* (the area behind the depression). An observer situated a little further north will only see the *cold edge*; situated a little further south he will only pick out the *warm edge* and eventually the *boundary zone* which links this disturbance to the one that follows it.

The disclosing of such a cloud sequence is particularly valuable for us. Knowing the different faces of the sky makes it possible to see that a disturbance is on its way, to assess one's position in relation to it, and to follow the different stages of its development. We shall therefore base our detailed analysis on the description of the principal *patterns of sky* which characterise this development.

The Sky During a Depression

It is already clear that any definition of a sky type must not be taken too literally. The cloud sequences vary greatly from one depression to another, according to their age and the time of year. The really typical sequences only occur, for the most part, in winter. In summer, the time which most interests us, we have to deal usually with *weakened* sequences which have rather different characteristics. There are all sorts of variants to take into account, even if that makes for complications.

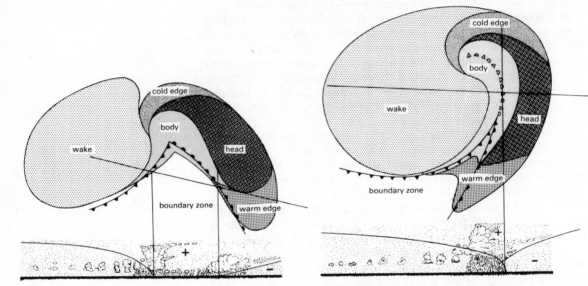

Cloud system in a young disturbance   Cloud system in an occluded disturbance

Head

The head of the cloud sequence is characterised by a sky of well ordered cirrus, progressively invading the sky, accompanied by a thin veil of cirrostratus or altostratus. The pressure drops slowly. The wind tends to back southerly and freshen.

The head of the system corresponds to the arrival of warm, damp air at altitude. It begins a long way from the central part of the disturbance – usually several hundreds of miles.

The warm air rises slowly above the cold air and expands; when it has reached a height of six or seven kilometres, its water vapour is changed into ice crystals. The first clouds to appear are therefore cirrus, of the type *uncinus* (in the shape of commas or hooks), or *fibratus* (of fibrous appearance). They are also called 'messengers' since they announce the approach of a disturbance. They come from a well determined quarter of the horizon (usually west or SW), where they appear very dense.

The sky remains clear and fine weather cumulus can still be seen. However it will be seen to flatten and this flattening is due to a lessening of the convection, limited by the warm air high up.

The light is often very clear during these first hours and visibility is very good. 'Tood good', say the coastal observers who have noticed this abnormal visibility the day before and have deduced an imminent change in the weather.

The light grows gradually dimmer. Following the cirrus and coming from the same direction, cirrostratus drifts in and soon covers the whole sky, bringing with it those halos that form round the sun and moon. In reality the appearance of cirrus and cirrostratus does not mean with absolute certainty that you are in the head of a disturbance. They appear too, as we shall see, on the cold edge where everything clears up quickly. The fact that the barometer begins to drop and that the wind backs SE is not conclusive either. But the sky's ceiling begins to lower slowly. The warm air mass makes further progress and after the cirrostratus we soon have altostratus, a middle layer cloud, covering the sky. This altostratus is still quite thin, it is the *translucidus* type, first slightly bluish, then changing to grey. This cloud intimates the end of the head and the beginning of the body of the disturbance.

In summer, when we are in a weakened system, the head sky is not necessarily characteristic: the cirrus are less regularly organised and are rarely followed by cirrostratus. It even happens that no cirrus is observed and that the only clouds composing the head are altocumulus. These are laid out like an enormous pavement Head sky

through which the blue of the sky can still be made out (alto-cumulus stratiformis perlucidus) or they take on a cylindrical or boulder-like form (undulatus) or even suggest cuttle fish bones (lenticularis).

Here too the expert can be mistaken and think that he is on the warm edge of the system, which is characterised by the presence of extensive, numerous altocumulus.

The Body. The body of the sequence is characterised by the appearance of a continuous layer of altostratus or nimbostratus, frequently coupled with low ragged clouds and it all generally leads to steady rain. The pressure drops still further and reaches its lowest point with the arrival of the warm front. The wind that has gone on strengthening veers from the south to SW or to west.

The warm air mass now spreads into the lower layers of the sky. The altostratus translucidus is followed by thicker and thicker altostratus opacus and the clouds drop lower and lower. It may have already begun to rain. Usually visibility is still quite good, right up to the moment when the 'rack' appears – small black clouds scudding under the grey vault, cumulus fractus foreshadowing heavy rain. These little clouds precede the arrival of the enormous nimbostratus. It rains then without stopping, often for hours. Visibility becomes poor and even plain bad as the lowest part of the nimbostratus passes over, with the arrival of the warm front. At this stage the warm air mass occupies all the sky, the thermometer rises, the barometer is at its lowest point and the wind veers quite noticeably (between 20 to 40°) to SW or west.

The newly arrived warm air is usually stable, but it can be

Body sky

unstable, and cumulus convectus or cumulonimbus can develop above the altostratus or the nimbostratus. They are not seen but their presence is disclosed by more irregular rain, sometimes thunder with violent squalls.

In a weakened system, the nimbostratus can be absent, and the altostratus itself has a structure like that of altocumulus, accompanied sometimes by ragged clouds and giving lighter and intermittent rain.

At this stage of the description distinctions must be made between new and old disturbances. In the case of a newly formed disturbance, a warm sector succeeds the warm front. After this we are in the 'second part' of the body associated with the passage of the cold front. This is the case we are going to study here. When we are in the middle of a more developed disturbance, the cold front follows hard upon the warm front, without the intermediary sector being noticed. Occluded disturbances are different again and will be examined towards the end of this chapter.

Warm Sector

In a warm sector, the sky is generally very low and covered by an often continuous layer of stratocumulus, sometimes accompanied by fog. There is a light drizzle. Barometric pressure and wind remain almost constant until the arrival of the cold front.

The warm air mass from now on occupies the whole sky. Normally, during the passage of a warm sector, the rain stops, the ceiling tends to rise a bit and is composed of fairly compact stratocumulus and there may be drizzle near hills and coasts. The appearance of

Warm sector sky

this type of cloud is connected with the turbulence caused by the friction of the air at sea level.

A little to the south of the disturbance, in the zone which links it to the next disturbance, known as the boundary zone, visibility is sometimes bad, with stratus low overhead, at least during winter.

In summer, the warm sector and the boundary zone are usually not so cloudy.

As the cold front approaches, the sky may become dark again or, in winter, the overcast is strengthened. This is where the body of the disturbance is found.

The cold front itself is made up of a quite formidable sort of barrier. The cold posterior air is pushing back violently on the rear of the warm air mass. This warm is then driven suddenly upwards and becomes unstable. Cumulus congestus and cumulonimbus, often huge, loom up and create a *line squall* along which blow fierce gusts of wind and there are violent showers, sometimes thunderstorms. When this cold front arrives, the wind frequently backs briefly to SW, then veers sharply NW and suddenly there is sunshine again; but it is colder.

Wake

This last part of the disturbance is characterised by a variable sky, with alternating bright periods and cloudy stretches producing showers, squalls or thunderstorms. The barometer begins to rise rapidly. The wind settles in the NW and often freshens again.

The sky in the wake is one of the loveliest. Cold air then reigns supreme and, as soon as it appears, the thermometer falls considerably while the barometer rises. This cold air, warmed through

Wake sky

its base being in contact with the sea, becomes unstable. As a result, the wake sky has burgeoning clouds, cumulonimbus generating violent squalls, and cumulus congestus with strong vertical development, sometimes producing showers and almost always strengthening wind. In the bright periods, visibility is excellent. The sky is an intense blue or sometimes takes on the pale green tint peculiar to Polar air. The wind is often very strong and, above all, irregular. For yachtsmen the wake is often the most dangerous part of the disturbance.

In summer, this wake does not always have its classic characteristics. The cumulonimbus are often absent, and there is always cumulus and the somewhat menacing cumulus congestus. They are sometimes accompanied by altostratus and banks of stratocumulus.

The wake of a disturbance can be very broad. It can extend over a thousand kilometres or more and its passage can last for over twenty-four hours. Very often, in a wake sky, the first cirrus of the following disturbance begin to appear. When there is no other disturbance to come, the weather gradually calms down, the wind veers north and the big clouds disappear. Soon all that is left in the sky are a few cumulus *Humilis* – by far the best type of cumulus.

Cold Edge

An observer situated a little to the north of a disturbance's line of advance sees the passage of cold edge of the sequence. He remains in the Polar air and does not experience the passage of any front. In reality, disturbance usually circulate too far North for cold-edge skies to be seen at all frequently in our latitudes. It can nevertheless happen, especially in winter, and it is worth knowing their characteristics for they can easily be mistaken for a head sky. In fact the

Cold edge sky

cold edge of this cloud sequence is characterised by a veil of cirrostratus, either partial or complete, sometimes following cirrus. Pressure drops and the wind turns SE. It is only too easy to be misled.

However this veil of cirrostratus, instead of thickening, gradually disperses and soon other clouds belonging to other types of sky begin to appear. Pressure rises and the wind, instead of veering south, backs though east gradually to north.

Warm Edge

Much more frequently one is situated a little to the south of a disturbance, on the track of the warm edge and the boundary zone which follows it.

The warm-edge sky is characterised by isolated banks of altocumulus, spread in an irregular pattern, not very extensive, often lenticular in shape and in a state of change. These clouds are preceded generally by cirrus and sometimes accompanied by cirrocumulus.

The frequent presence of altocumulus lenticularis, of cirrocumulus (early in the morning) and especially the continuously changing sky are the clearest proofs that you are in this warm edge, where variations of pressure and wind are otherwise very slow.

The sky is never completely covered. The cloudiness of the altocumulus, once its attains its maximum, decreases. On land and principally in summer, a sky associated with a ridge of high pressure (which we shall examine later) often returns then and the effects of the disturbance are not felt. On the sea, banks of stratus and stratocumulus may appear and you then have an overcast sky which is associated with a boundary zone and the disturbance that follows.

Warm edge sky

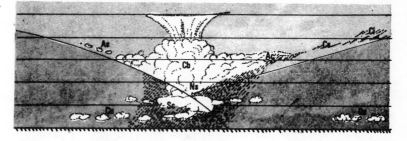

An occluded front is often characterised by dense cloud cover

A frequent occurrence: passage of a family of disturbances at 50°N

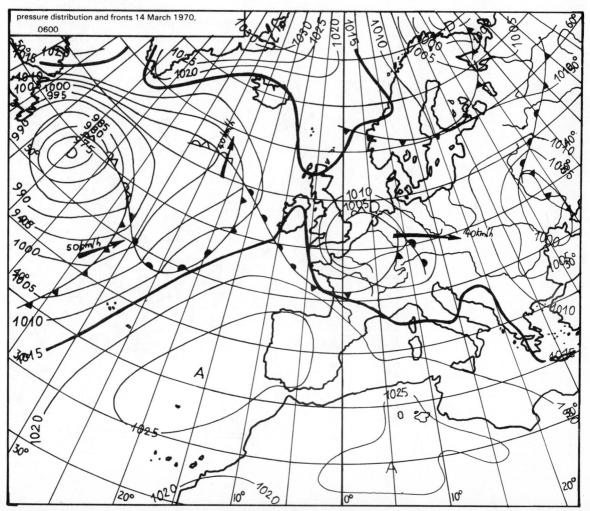

pressure distribution and fronts 14 March 1970, 0600

Occluded Front

The arrival of an occluded disturbance is heralded by a quite normal head sky. But the body of the disturbance has particular characteristics as it is only made up of one front, the cold front having caught up with the warm one. The occluded front usually looks at first almost like a warm front, but the line of cumulonimbus of the old cold front follows immediately, or even appears to be fused with the nimbostratus (or the altostratus if the warm air mass has already been driven to some height).

In fact, the bases of all these clouds are very much alike. But precipitation changes the pattern, showers succeeding continuous rain; the veer of the wind is considerable, the barometer rises rapidly and the temperature drops. All these signs indicate that we are dealing with an occluded front. It will also be noticed that this occluded front is often remarkable for the amount of cloud present (much stratocumulus, stratus fractus or cumulus fractus) and partial superimposition of the different cloud layers often brings on heavy rain.

Cloud system corresponding to the situation on the previous page

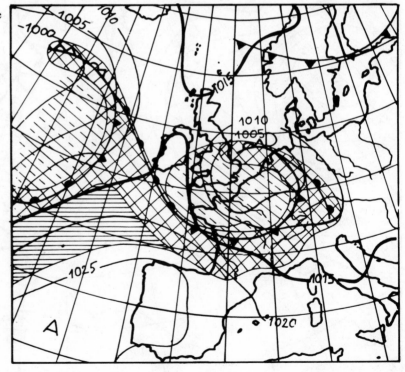

wake

body

boundary
zone

Fine weather skies

The term fine weather is ambiguous, and normally meteorologists are careful not to use it. Yet fine weather exists, as we know by experience, and it would be a shame to camouflage it under a scientific name which would, to coin a metaphor, cast a shadow on it. All that is required is to agree about what the term means.

For a sailor, fine weather isn't necessarily sunny weather, nor should it be too calm for we need wind to sail. What we want most is well established, clear weather that we can rely on. In meteorological terms, this is weather associated with a passing ridge of high pressure, characterised by the absence of disturbance on the Polar front or stormy formations. The sky patterns associated with this weather are outside all organised cloud sequences. Three principal skies of this type can be recognised: the one associated with a ridge of high pressure, a stratiform sky and the sky of instability.

Sky Associated with a Ridge of High Pressure

This is a clear sky, or with some cumulus not greatly developed vertically, and sometimes a few isolated banks of cloud in the middle and upper layers.

This type can be seen in all latitudes and at all times of the year. But it is in particular the classical fine-weather summer sky. Its appearance means that we are in a unified, stable mass of air, sometimes without enough moisture for clouds to form.

This kind of sky is called 'clear or partly cloudy' when the amount of cloud is nil or below 3 octas*. It is 'cloudy or partly cloudy' when the amount of cloud is for a time between 3 and 8 octas. These two categories of sky can alternate in the course of a single day; the cumulus composing it usually develops considerably over the coast during the day. Over the sea, convection occurs mainly at night. If the convection stops the cumulus always decrease, and then disappear.

In addition to the cumulus the following can also be encountered in a sky associated with a ridge of high pressure:

stratus, sometimes masking the upper sky, particularly over the land and in estuaries;

*Meteorologists evaluate cloud cover in eighths or 'octas': 8 octas means the sky is completely covered.

isolated banks of stratocumulus or even altocumulus, especially in the evening, because these clouds result from the development of the cumulus by day;
dense cirrus (spissatus), but in no organised fashion.

This weather is also often characterised by:
- slight mists which hardly hamper visibility but give the sky the 'washed blue' colour, typical of fine anticyclonic weather;
- advection fogs which can cover all the English Channel, for instance, in spring and in NE winds;
- the appearance of dew even before the sun has set: towards the end of the afternoon the deck is often wet (with fresh water), and it remains wet all night and only dries in the sun next morning.

Land and Sea Breezes

This type of sky, with little cloud, is characteristic of a shallow pressure gradient. It encourages land and sea breezes, which happily take over from an often weak synoptic wind (the synoptic wind being the normal wind connected with the pressure gradient).

We have analysed the principle behind these breezes in the preceding chapter: a sea breeze blows during the day and is 'drawn in' by the rising air over the heated land; a land breeze blows at night when the land has cooled and the sea is now warmer than it is. The strength of these breezes is therefore bound up during the day with the strength of the sunlight and the cooling of the earth by radiation at night.

This 'play' of land and sea breezes happens at various points along the coast, but the conditions in which it becomes established vary from one place to another. These breezes are not always alternating, and they follow, to some extent, the movement of the sun (this is why they are often called *solar breezes*): a NE breeze in the morning, turning east then SE and dying away usually before midday, to pick up again from the SW in the afternoon and to come round to NW or north in the evening. It disappears again and picks up from the NE in the latter half of the night.

When the synoptic wind is weak or non-existent, these breezes predominate. When it has some strength, they may well combine with it, modifying its direction, either reinforcing or reducing it. Here are some typical consequences of a NE synoptic wind: in South Brittany, a fresh or even very fresh NE wind at night and a weak NE wind, calm, or a weak SW breeze during the day; in North Brittany on the other hand, a fresh NE wind by day, and a

In a NE synoptic wind: offshore wind strong in South Brittany at night, slight in North Brittany; sea breeze slight in South Brittany by day, strong in North Brittany

weak NE wind, calm or a SW breeze at night.

The distance to which the breezes are felt at sea is very variable. It usually extends about 5 or 10 miles offshore, and sometimes, but very rarely, up to 20 miles.

Turbulent Sky

A stratiform sky, composed of stratocumulus in a continuous layer, and sometimes stratus. There is normally no precipitation or, if there is any, very weak (in the form of drizzle, granular snow or ice needles).

This definition is enough for we are dealing now essentially with fine winter weather, those peaceful grey days when a great cloak of stratocumulus stratiformis, capable sometimes of covering the whole of Europe, spreads far and wide.

This type of sky (known as anticyclonic gloom) can, however, be met with at all times of the year and in any latitude, in areas of high pressure or at their edges.

On land, it is usually the result of the turbulence caused by the friction of the air over the Earth's surface. Stratocumulus which cover the sky can last for several days consecutively in the same area. Temporary lifting of the cloud layer can occur at the warmest times of day.

This type of sky is rare in summer, but then it discloses a very clear daytime development: the stratocumulus form during the night and are reabsorbed quite quickly in the course of the morning.

At sea, a stratus sky often forms in the lower layers of warm damp air that arrive over colder waters (the Newfoundland fogs). This type of sky often marks the boundary zone of a series of disturbances.

It is to be remembered that a stratiform sky, usually very low, may be hiding another sky type that is developing above it.

Sky of Instability

A cumuliform sky is composed of cumulus congestus which can develop into cumulonimbus and be accompanied by showers and sometimes thunderstorms.

This type of sky indicates fairly strong vertical instability in the heart of a large air mass. It is very much like the wake sky (the area behind a depression), but it is always outside any organised cloud system.

It is uncommon in northern latitudes, where great masses of warm, damp unstable air do not often occur. But it can come

Unstable sky

across in the Mediterranean at night, for instance. It arises then from a very marked development of a sky associated with a ridge of high pressure: the cumulus reach and pass the stage of cumulus congestus to become cumulonimbus, causing storms at night, although during the day the weather is calm and the sky clear. On land, it happens in reverse: the development takes place during the day and the storms break towards the end of the afternoon.

An alternation of unstable skies and skies associated with a ridge of high pressure can be observed several days running without the least change in the air mass or the approach of a cloud sequence.

Thunder Storm Skies

The concept of thundery weather is not necessarily any easier to define than fine weather. Apart from the more spectacular features, we may be dealing with unsettled weather, strangely 'disordered' without any clear-cut characteristics. You can't always be sure about it.

Two kinds of thundery weather of different origins can be observed. The first is the result of the development of a sky of relative fine weather, when the convection, at night at sea, by day on land, is sufficiently strong to change inoffensive cumulus into cumulus congestus or cumulonimbus. This type of thunder storm is born in a unified mass of air which, having been heated strongly from below, has become unstable. In our latitudes, this development only happens during summer, and usually in barometric 'fens'.

It is in its turn clearly influenced by local conditions: the nature of the land and sea surface, hills and undulations, wind and any other factor that influences the temperature and humidity of the lower layers of the atmosphere.

The other type of thunder storm appears in Polar front disturbances. We have already spoken of them in describing the warm and cold fronts of such disturbances. Here the storms do not result from local conditions, but solely from the confrontation of air

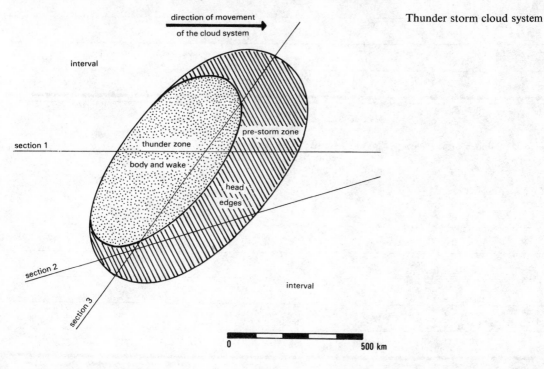

Thunder storm cloud system

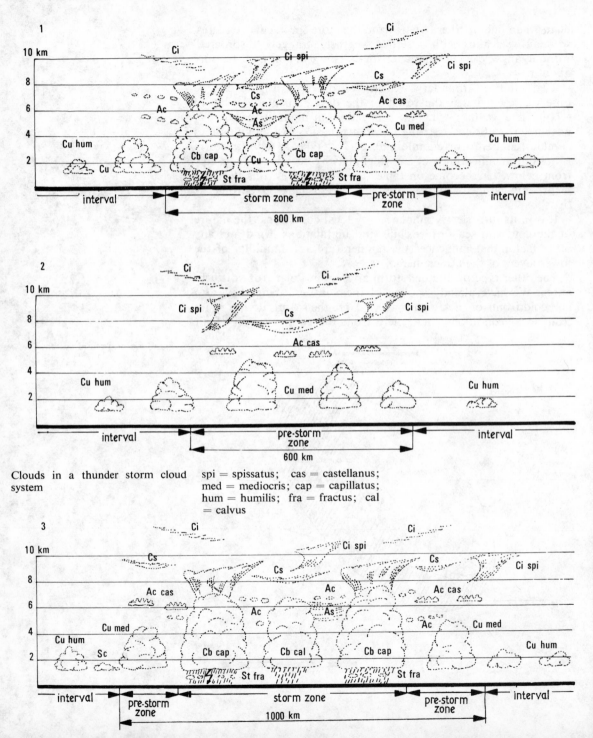

Clouds in a thunder storm cloud system

spi = spissatus; cas = castellanus; med = mediocris; cap = capillatus; hum = humilis; fra = fractus; cal = calvus

masses and their violence varies according to the degree of instability and humidity of the warm air mass.

Originating through the phenomenon of convection or linked to frontal instability, the thunder storms give rise to sufficiently characteristic cloud formations to be described as distinct cloud sequences. It is quite impossible to analyse the structure of these sequences as precisely as the cloud sequences of depressions, but we can at least distinguish two kinds of sky: the *pre-thunder storm sky (head sky and edge sky) and the stormy sky (body sky and wake sky).*

Pre-Thunder Storm Sky

This sky is characterised by dense cirrus and a thick partial veil of cirrostratus, accompanied with banks of altocumulus and occasionally cumulus.

These clouds, moving slowly, are in the van and on the edge of the storm system proper, and are at one and the same time, its head and its edges. The altocumulus castellanus or floccus, appear as long as five or six hours before the storms; they are generally preceded or accompanied by quite dense cirrus, very varied in form: cirrus uncinus or spissatus in the shape of frothy flakes, fern leaves, vertebrae, tufts and suchlike. These cirrus are often the residue, brought by the wind, of old cumulonimbus anvils. Sheets of thick cirrostratus may also appear and, lower down, stratocumulus, or cumulus whose development in daytime is conspicuous.

This sky persists and extends as long as the general conditions,

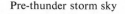

Pre-thunder storm sky

in particular the temperature and humidity in the lower layers, do not vary. It can happen that the storm does not break, but usually it is not far off.

Thunder Clouds

This is a sky characterised by an overcast, chaotic, heavy, motionless appearance, with cloud elements of many different forms at all heights. It is usually accompanied by precipitation in the form of showers.

Thunder clouds normally follow the pre-thunder clouds but it can also result, and especially in summer, from:

– the change taking place in the body and wake of a depressionary cloud sequence that arrives in an area where the barometric gradient is slight;
– from the rapid development of cumulus congestus to the stage of cumulonimbus when, in areas where the convection was already very strong, conditions of instability occur in the middle and upper layers of the sky.

The stormy sky is characterised by the presence of convection clouds with much vertical development. In particular the budding of the upper part of these clouds, developing with startling rapidity, is noticeable. Cumulus congestus develop in all directions and change rapidly into formidable cumulonimbus. The latter, after a limited journey (usually less than 100 miles) during which they create squalls and violent gusts of wind, gradually disintegrate, leaving cloud banks or veils in the sky at different levels: cirrus and cirrostratus, altocumulus and stratocumulus of the most diverse

Thunder storm sky

shapes. Other cumulonimbus form in their turn, then disintegrate a little later, and the cycle begins again.

This disintegration of the cumulonimbus is the reason why one can see, in a thundery sky, such a great diversity of clouds at all levels. It is also for this reason that it is impossible to differentiate with any precision between the body sky and the wake sky.

In the relatively clear periods separating the storm centres, one often sees altocumulus castellanus or floccus. Layers of strato-cumulus opacus, or undulatus appear nearer the storm centres.

The extraordinary spectacle offered by a thundery sky can last for a few hours or several days. Sometimes, too, just when you think it is all over it begins again, with renewed fury.

Types of Weather

The concept of weather types may seem unsatisfactory. In practice two exactly similar meteorological situations are seldom identical. However, analyses carried out over many years have established certain constants, certain 'models' of weather that occur sufficiently regularly and last long enough to give us reasonable hope that we shall encounter them again. A type of weather is a type of atmos-pheric circulation, linked generally to a particular season when it reappears frequently, and persists for several days, even for several weeks. This question of duration is important: when we speak of 'squally weather', for instance, or 'thick weather', we must realise that we are not dealing with a type of weather, but only with a particular phase of a much more general type of weather.

The prototypes of weather are based essentially on a study of the characteristic distribution of pressure on the Earth's surface and its day-to-day development. When weather begins to resemble one of these types, reproducing the overall conditions and develop-ing in the same way, then we can accept that we are experiencing recognised patterns of weather.

It must be realised, however, that surface conditions may not be associated with the corresponding pressure fields at altitude. To recognise a weather pattern with certainty, we ought to consider at the same time the surface maps, and the upper air maps of the average atmosphere (in this context the surface is at 500m). This comparison can only be made by the professional meteorologist. We shall only deal here with the surface map which allows a good enough analysis of the situation to be made, and we shall restrict ourselves to describing the most common types of weather encountered in the eastern Atlantic.

Disturbed Patterns

Disturbed Westerly Air-Stream in High Latitudes

A quite frequent situation in summer. The disturbances circulate up to the latitudes of the British Isles. The 1015 isobar (line of average pressure) passes to the north of the English Channel. The pressure is rather high in the Channel and in the Bay of Biscay.

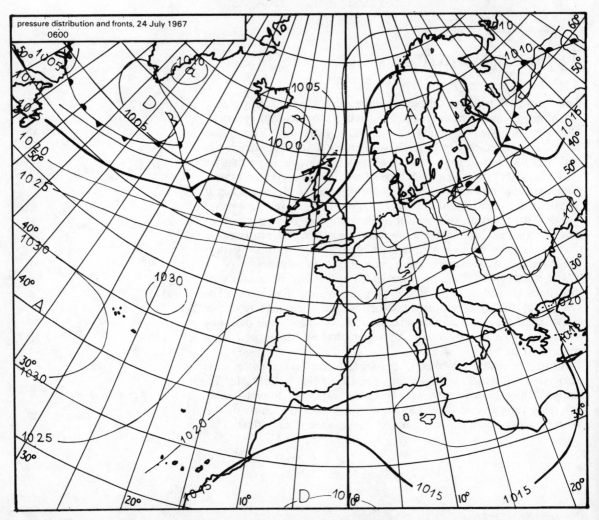

pressure distribution and fronts, 24 July 1967
0600

The weather is only slightly disturbed over Brittany and in the Channel. Rain slight or nil. Fine clear periods and rapid improvement.

Wind mainly from the west, quite regular, Force 3 to 5, with some squalls as disturbances pass by.

Sea rough in the Channel, moderate swell.

Skies varied: alternating between sky associated with a ridge of high pressure, warm edge, boundary zone, sometimes wake.

Visibility generally good, reduced by mist on the edges, and by stratus in the boundary zones.

Outlook. This situation can develop as:

Unfavourable, if the Azores anticyclone weakens: the pressure drops, and formidable secondary depressions can then circulate round the main centres of low pressure;

Favourable, if the anticyclone extends: the 1020 isobar coming a little higher in latitude, we then find ourselves in skies associated with ridges of high pressure and the winds are moderate.

Disturbed Westerly Airstream in Middle Latitudes

A common situation at all times of year.

The disturbances cross France.

The 1015 isobar is situated almost on the 45th parallel. The pressure is below average in the Channel and in the Bay of Biscay.

Classic disturbed weather. The disturbances follow each other every 36 or 48 hours bringing heavy rain as the fronts pass through. Some of these disturbances can be very active, even in summer. The weather changes quickly.

Wind veers from SW to NW as the disturbances pass through; Force 4 to 6 generally, with increases on the arrival of the fronts.

Sea heavy for a short time, with broken swell.

Skies head, body, warm sector, wake, the cirrus of the following disturbance often appearing in the wake sky.

Visibility moderate in the body and warm sector skies.

Outlook. This situation can develop as:

Unfavourable, if the disturbances which follow one another become deeper and deeper, with fronts and wakes more and more unmistakable;

Favourable, when all the group of disturbances has passed: we have the grand 'clean up' of the northwesterly wind and the appearance of a wake sky more vigorous than the others, bringing an improvement and contributing to the formation of a ridge of high pressure (anticyclonic) over the east Atlantic.

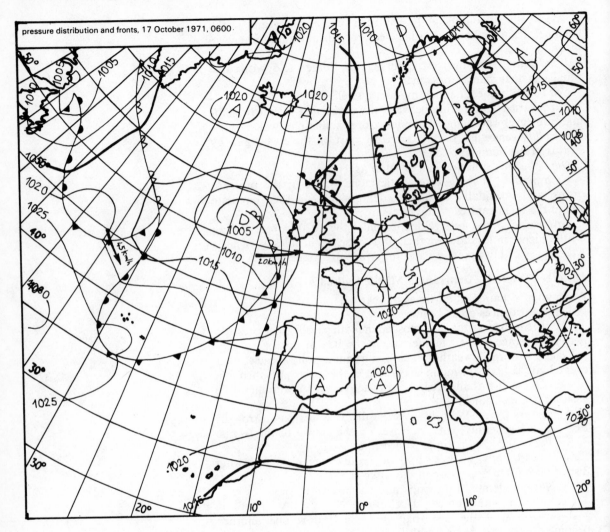

pressure distribution and fronts, 17 October 1971, 0600

Disturbed Westerly Airstream in Low Latitudes

A very frequent situation at the end of winter, rare in summer.

A depression is centred to the NW of the British Isles; a vast area of low pressure extends over the whole of Europe and the Mediterranean. The 1015 isobar is pushed to the south of Spain, pressure is particularly low and only suffers minor variations as the disturbances pass through. The pressure gradient still remains quite steep.

The weather is very disturbed, with long periods of rain and heavy weather on the open sea. The temperature is higher than normal for winter.

Wind mainly from the westerly sector, with the usual veering as the disturbances pass through; Force 4 to 6, reaching 7 and even more for short periods.

Sea heavy, sometimes very heavy, with westerly swell in all coastal areas.

Skies the classic skies of depressionary systems, with vigorous wakes.

Visibility very variable, sometimes nil in the warm sectors, very good in the wakes.

Outlook. This situation can develop as:

unfavourable, if the 1015 isobar moves into a higher latitude: the pressure gradient increases, and violent winds occur;

favourable, if the depression fills: the gradient lessens, the wind abates. But the swell still persists for a long time.

Disturbed North-Westerly Airstream

A frequent situation in summer, especially during July. The Azores anticyclone extends off the Bay of Biscay, a stream of disturbances circulates to the north of the anticyclone. The 1015 isobar runs through the British Isles. Pressure is relatively high and varies little with the passage of the disturbances.

Fine weather at sea, cooler than normal on the coasts, with frequent showers, especially in the Channel.

Wind mainly NW, very gusty. Turbulence and squalls.

Sea smooth with moderate swell from the NW.

Skies, warm edge, body and above all wake, the cold fronts or occlusions with cold front characteristics being dominant in this type of disturbance. Ridge-of-high-pressure skies between disturbances.

Visibility mainly good, less in squalls and showers. Fog rare.

Outlook. This situation can develop as:

unfavourable if the ridge that extends towards the Alps breaks down, allowing the disturbances to drop to lower latitudes (an infrequent occurrence); but if the gradient increases between the anticyclone and the depressionary area, we may expect strong winds from the NW to N in the Channel and over Brittany (a frequent occurrence);

favourable, if the anticyclone moves into higher latitudes: the disturbances are then pushed back towards the Baltic. The NW wind becomes moderate, under ridge-of-high-pressure skies.

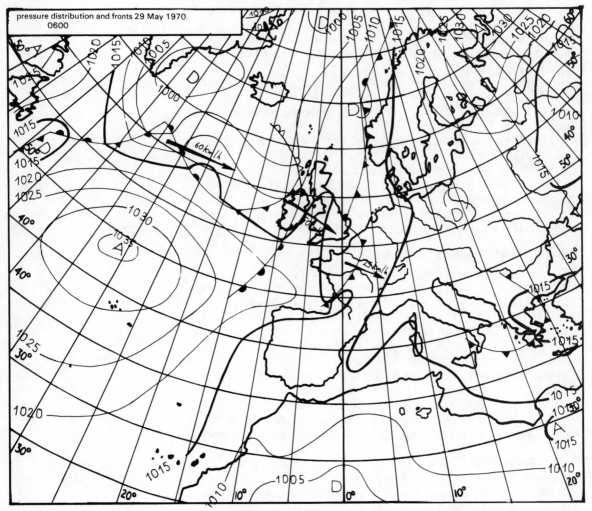

pressure distribution and fronts 29 May 1970.
0600

Unsettled South-Westerly Weather

A very frequent situation in winter (from November to March); very rare in summer.

A depression is centred between Iceland and Scotland, a vast area of low pressure extending as far as Brittany and Normandy.

The 1015 isobar passes over the Vendée and curves up towards Denmark. Pressure remains average over Brittany and Normandy, but the gradient is steep.

A strong SW airstream passes over the east Atlantic, bringing warmer weather than normal (for instance 18° at Brest in February), but also drizzle and heavy, continuous rain. Heavy squalls of SW wind at sea.

Wind mainly SW, pouring into the Channel area.

High sea with heavy SW swell off Ireland, strong SW swell in the Channel.

Skies, head, body, and above all strong warm sectors. The wakes are not very marked.

Visibility often below one mile in nimbostratus, stratus or fog.

Outlook. This situation can develop as:

unfavourable, if the pressure gradient increases: squalls of wind

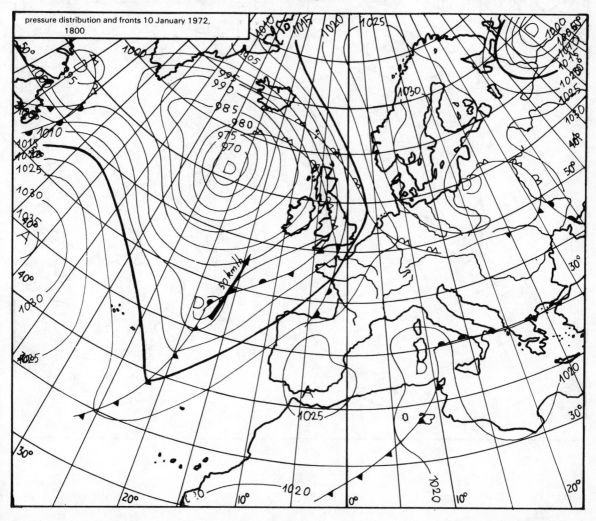

pressure distribution and fronts 10 January 1972, 1800

are to be expected; but, if small secondary depressions develop and circulate to the area of the Channel, local violent, brief storms can develop;

favourable, if the SW airstream shifts north; the wind abates and can even become very weak. This is 'the calm after the storm'.

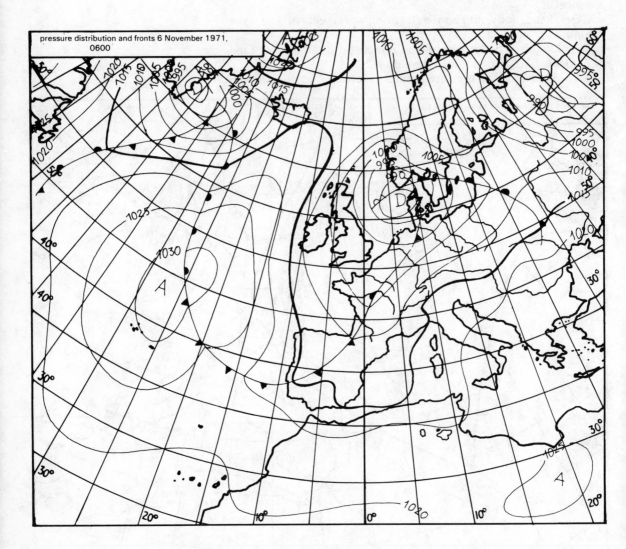

pressure distribution and fronts 6 November 1971, 0600

Disturbed Westerly Airstream with Trough

A quite common occurrence in spring, repeated at the end of summer and becoming very frequent in autumn.

In a westerly airstream, a fairly deep trough of low pressure crosses France.

The 1015 isobar is bent steeply south, pressure is very variable, without the gradient becoming steep.

The weather can be bad for short periods, with showers and stormy squalls. It develops quite slowly (average length of a depression is three days).

Wind turning from SSW to NNW and freshening as the disturbances move through; moderate between them.

Sea not at all rough usually, with SW or NW swells, rarely broken.

Skies, head, body and wake. The wakes can develop stormy characteristics, if the pressure gradient decreases appreciably; then pre-storm or even storm skies may appear.

Visibility limited under the cumulo stratus, without the weather being really thick.

Outlook. This situation can develop as:

Unfavourable, if it takes a stormy turn, or if a direct Polar air stream comes and reactivates a current disturbance;

Favourable, if the Azores anticyclone moves north, the weather improves.

Disturbed Airstream in a Col

A very frequent situation towards the end of spring and at the beginning of summer.

An area of relatively low pressures joining two depressions stretches from west to east at the latitude of the British Isles.

The 1015 isobar passes on either side of this line. Pressure is below average to the west of Brittany and in the Channel, but it is not subject to much variation.

Small moving depressions run from west to east in the col, giving rain for short periods. Weather colder than normal to the north of the col is noted; weather warmer than normal, quite dry and with little cloud to the south.

Wind well established in the western sector veering as the disturbances pass through, usually without any noteworthy increases in strength.

Sea moderate to rough with westerly swell.

Skies, ridge-of-high-pressure or boundary zone.

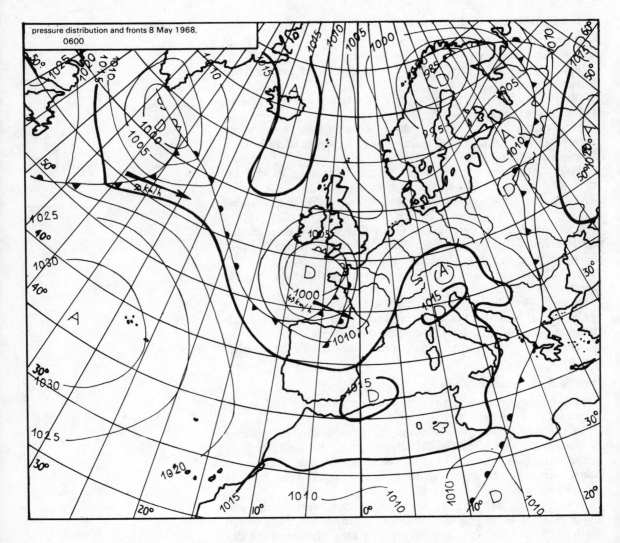

pressure distribution and fronts 8 May 1968, 0600

Visibility reduced for a time in boundary zones and as warm fronts move through.

Outlook. This situation can develop as:

unfavourable, if the pressure gradient increases and the depressions moving through deepen;

favourable, if an anticyclonic ridge settles in place of the col and drives the stream of disturbances north. But this ridge is often fragile; a head sky appearing in its western part heralds another worsening in the weather.

Anticyclonic Patterns

High Pressures in the West of Europe

A frequent situation in May, June and sometimes July.

An anticyclone is centred over the British Isles and there are no disturbances in sight.

The 1015 isobar is well to the north. Pressure is high in the Channel and over Brittany.

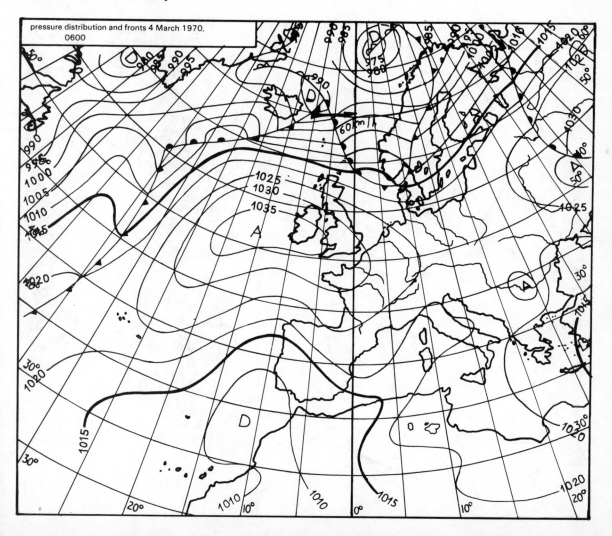

pressure distribution and fronts 4 March 1970, 0600

It is fine, slightly misty weather.

Wind mainly easterly, quite steady, from Force 2 to 3. Some coastal breezes that can produce a strong NE wind at night in Southern Brittany (Force 6 is not uncommon).

Sea flat-calm to calm.

Skies, associated with a ridge of high pressure, with altocumulus over the sea; convective clouds along the coast.

Visibility good, but slight haze on the horizon.

Outlook. This situation can develop as:

unfavourable, if the pressure gradient increases: the wind can then freshen near the coasts, in the Channel or in Ireland, and reach Force 6 during squalls; and if the anticyclone shifts east: disturb-

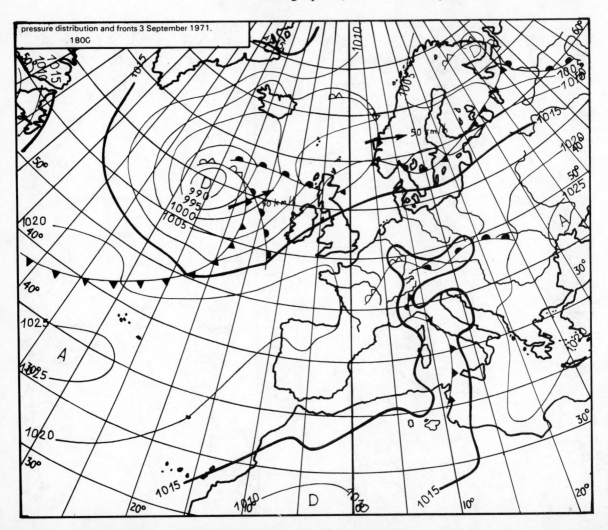

pressure distribution and fronts 3 September 1971. 1800

ances will reappear along its western slope;

favourable if, quite simply, the anticyclone lasts longer than foreseen (which does happen as they only move slowly).

Ridge of High Pressure Lying in an East-West Direction

A characteristic situation at the end of summer (September).

An anticyclonic ridge becomes established up Channel. There are no organised disturbances.

The 1015 isobar is a very long way from the Bay of Biscay, pressure is high, and its gradient slight.

Dry, slightly misty weather over the sea, cool at night and quite warm during the day.

Wind light easterly; calm in the Channel, some solar breezes.

Sea flat-calm to calm.

Skies, associated with a ridge of high pressure.

Visibility good, but possibly some fog in the morning near coasts.

Outlook. This situation can develop as:

unfavourable, if the ridge breaks down: disturbances will then cross the British Isles from north to south, often accompanied by heavy squalls;

favourable, if the gradient increases a little, bringing a wind of Force 3 to 4, clearly more pleasant for sailing.

Ridge of High Pressure Lying North-South

A frequent situation from May to the end of July.

An anticyclonic ridge covers the British Isles, the north of France and Spain. The disturbances pass by out in the Atlantic, and only their very much weakened edges reach the west of France.

The 1015 isobar outlines the ridge, which is very fragile (often 1018mb). The pressure gradient is therefore very slight, or we find ourselves in an area of almost uniform pressure.

Warm dry weather, calm at sea, but stormy depressions can appear in the Bay of Biscay.

Wind calm or light, from the southern sector in Brittany. Calm in the Channel. Local breezes set in.

Sea calm; a SW swell may reach the coasts.

Skies, associated with a high-pressure ridge at sea. On land, a sky of instability, cloud with stormy development daily: 'heat storms'. Skies pre-stormy and stormy (frontal thunderstorms) when cool gusts of oceanic air pass over the very warm land.

Visibility generally good, limited during squalls.

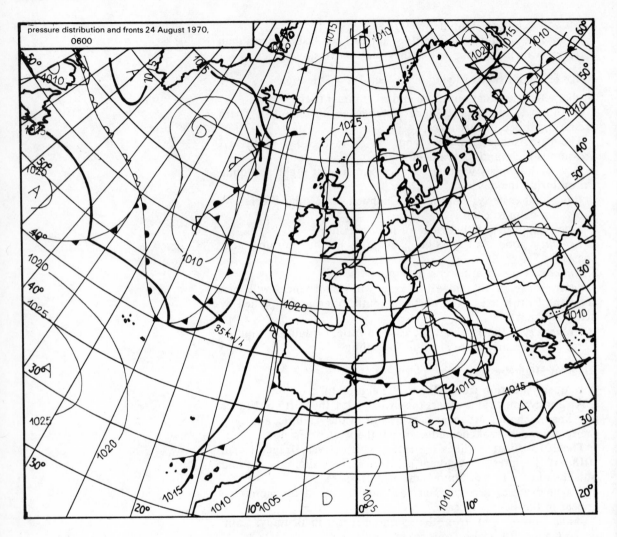

pressure distribution and fronts 24 August 1970, 0600

Outlook. This situation can develop as:

unfavourable, if the ridge breaks down: disturbances once more cross the British Isles; they are generally weakened, but their front edge is often composed of unstable warm air (cumulonimbus on the warm front);

favourable, if the ridge strengthens: the gradient increases, the wind freshens, the storm trend disappears.

Stable centres of activity, regular wind patterns, characteristic skies, well defined types of weather: it can be said that oceanic weather is above all a dependable kind of weather, without treacherous unexpected change for anyone who knows how to interpret it. Sometimes, but only rarely, it can let all hell loose, with one of those cataclysmic storms (there was a memorable one on 6 July 1969) which result from the sudden deepening of a small depression, and which play havoc locally. However, as we shall see at the end of this chapter, when we deal with forecasting, even these exceptional phenomena can be detected a few hours in advance by watching the barometer and the sky.

Generally speaking, the types of weather that appear over the Atlantic are sufficiently typical for average long-term forecasts of about a week to be valid. So it is possible to plan a cruise with some confidence. According to the position of the centres of activity, their development and the pattern and strength of the disturbances that can happen, you can work out your route. With a little flair the whole cruise can be achieved with free winds – or only going to windward in light weather. This may seem to be a timid approach but, in practice, it makes for sailing for pleasure and that is the most agreeable kind of cruise.

Mediterranean Weather

The Mediterranean has a reputation of being an area apart, where the weather does not stick to the rules. The yachtsman familiar with the Atlantic coasts, expert in observing the indications there that usually precede changes, can feel let down by the sky. In the Gulf of Lions on the French south coast, for instance, he meets gales that no cloud has foreshadowed, or when a front of good-natured appearance, stationary for days, suddenly wakes up and becomes very active.

He would be wrong however to deduce from this that he ought to forget all his previous knowledge and revise all his theories. In fact, the meteorology of the Mediterranean is not all that different and all the fundamental laws given in the preceding chapter remain valid there and in all parts of the world. The phenomena which

The Mediterranean is a real reservoir of heat for two reasons: the height of the surrounding mountains and the shallowness of the Straits of Gibraltar (450m)

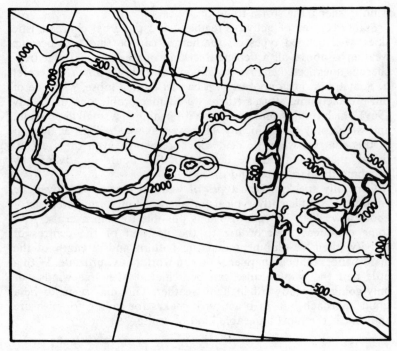

Limits of the Mediterranean climate

occur are not peculiar. If they sometimes take a rather surprising turn it is entirely due to the following natural causes:

The Mediterranean is an enclosed area with its own waters and its own sky – a character that outside influences never succeed in eliminating completely.

All round this sea, the contrasts in temperature are considerable and they make the circulating air masses very changeable.

Last and not least, along the coasts the land height is very varied. This causes the very special local phenomena that mask the overall situation.

To understand Mediterranean weather, particular attention must be given to its peculiarities and it is important first of all to see them in their context. We will first make a quick survey of the overall conditions: the air masses and the centres of activity controlling them, and the general patterns that emerge at different seasons. Then we will go into the detail of the western end which is of immediate interest to most yachtsmen in these waters.

The General Picture

First, one basic fact: the waters of the Mediterranean and the Atlantic are very different, particularly from the thermal point of view. The water temperature of the vast Atlantic depths is in the order of 0° to 12°C, and in the Mediterranean between 10° and 13°C. This accounts, to a great extent, for the way in which the air masses, which arrive over the Mediterranean, develop.

Air Masses

These air masses originate in widely different areas and are influenced by the conditions they have passed through: masses of cold air coming down from the Poles and of warm air coming up from the Tropics have different characteristics according to whether they have been over oceans or continents. When they pause over the Mediterranean, they are modified still more as a result of local conditions, and so much so that we must add a new type to our list: the Mediterranean air masses.

The occurrence and behaviour of all of them vary from one season to the next.

In Winter

Some of the *maritime Polar air masses* which reach the Mediterranean have first come down from Greenland to the Azores, and in the course of the journey have been well heated and loaded with humidity; others, also originating in the neighbourhood of Greenland, have taken a short cut across France and are, therefore, less warm and moist. Some, less commonly, come directly from the Arctic. They have all come very quickly and are still very cold when they arrive. In all cases, these air masses, warmed from below by the ocean, are already unstable and become more so, in varying degrees, when they approach the warmer Mediterranean. Their arrival is often announced by the cumuliform clouds forming over the coast line.

The *continental Polar air masses*, which cover vast stretches of land in winter (from Scandinavia to the Balkans and the plateaux of Asia Minor), are originally stable but they also become unstable when they enter the Mediterranean area; nevertheless they are not very humid and do not generally create large cloud formations.

The characteristics of *Mediterranean air masses* depend on the temperature of the surface waters; this is in the order of 13°C to

16°C, from November to March. The sea, being warmer than the lower layers of the atmosphere, the latter are warmed and become heavy with humidity. It follows that air masses over the Mediterranean are unstable, and favourable to the development of cumuliform clouds. They are very much like the air masses of the tropical regions of the Atlantic.

In Summer

Maritime Polar air masses reach the Mediterranean less frequently. When they do arrive, having been well warmed on their journey, they have a noticeably unstable character which systematically triggers off stormy conditions.

The *continental Polar air masses* remain stationary over the extreme north of Eurasia. Nevertheless, the pressure distribution is such that a regular airstream is established from the Polar regions to the central and eastern Mediterranean: these are the *Etesian winds*. The cold air, passing over the extremely hot plains of Eurasia, becomes very hot and dry. Reaching the much cooler surface of the sea, an inversion of temperature occurs and produces great stability to the lower layers. There is fine, stable weather.

The *maritime Tropical air masses* reach the Mediterranean in a highly developed state. They only occur at the western end and can be compared with warm maritime Polar air. They are unstable.

All these types of air masses are now familiar to us, but we shall describe in a little more detail the *continental Tropical air masses* (Saharan air). They do not occur in winter but they appear over the sea specially in spring. This is very hot, very dry air, loaded with dust; as a result of cooling from below there is an inversion of temperature and therefore great stability in the lower layers.

It is hot Saharan air that produces the steadiest and long-lasting winds, good for sailing, but accompanied by rather disagreeable cloudy conditions if the influx of hot air is great.

The clouds characteristic of this hot air are:

- altocumulus floccus and castellanus, at the beginning;
- stormy altocumulus at several levels follow;
- sometimes high cumulonimbus;
- stratus and fog at night and in the morning.

In summer, this Saharan type of air (which also originates in Asia Minor, the Balkans and even Spain) is present over almost all areas bordering the Mediterranean, but extends only a little out to sea for several reasons:

- A strong monsoon airstream is established towards the centre of Africa and then air flows from the Mediterranean Sahara-wards.
- The same phenomenon occurs, but on a larger scale, with the Asian zone. The winds flowing from the sea towards the deserts being the selfsame Etesian winds already mentioned.
- The 'Saharan' air originating in the Balkans or Turkey is caught up in the Etesian airflow and mixed with air, a little less warm, of continental Polar origin.
- The 'Saharan' air which forms over the Iberian peninsula is an isolated nucleus which only persists if there is a general flow from the south, and it then tends to spread over western Europe rather than the Mediterranean. If the general flow is NW, the warm continental Iberian air is pushed rapidly upwards.

As in spring, when these very unstable air masses enter the Mediterranean (which happens most frequently at the end of summer and occur at the eastern rather than the western end) they become very stable in the lower layers. They then produce fog and stratus on the coasts of Libya and as far east as Malta. However, they pick up moisture at altitude and remain very unstable; if Polar air comes in at the same time, there is a systematic series of violent storms, sometimes with very high cloud bases.

The *Mediterranean air masses* have almost the same characteristics in summer and winter: they are unstable in the lower layers. But in summer, if they have passed over the continent before stagnating over the Mediterranean, temperature inversion takes place in the lower layers (because the sea is not as warm as the land) which prevents any convection movement starting. On uneven levels of the coast, on the other hand, cumuliform formations are often more conspicuous than in winter.

Action Centres

Over the Atlantic areas, the pressure field appears on the whole to be well organised. The lines of equal pressure surround, in clear patterns, the depressions and anticyclones and centres of activity which cover vast areas. In the Mediterranean, nothing is quite so clear. There is no permanent anticyclone, like the one over the Azores. The activity centres are greatly reduced and are often only transitory. The analysis of the pressure field becomes therefore generally much more complex. Nevertheless, the principal activity centres which govern the weather over the Atlantic are also playing an important part.

In Winter

The Azores anticyclone does not go further north than the 40th parallel and the area of depressions off Iceland comes down to very low latitudes. The Siberian anticyclone stretches over the continent, a ridge extending it towards the west as far as the Alps. This ridge frequently disappears when the disturbances of the Polar front penetrate as far as the Mediterranean.

A depression becomes established over the Tyrrhenian sea (between Italy and Sardinia) resulting from other depressions of both local and Atlantic origin (but an anticyclone can replace them from time to time). Other small depressions occur in classic fashion in particular parts of the Mediterranean: the Balearic Islands, Gulf of Genoa and the Aegean Sea.

The Siberian anticyclone is the only stable centre of activity. The other contours of the average winter isobar patterns are associated with other, very varied, conditions.

The weather is variable over the western Mediterranean basin, with dominating NW airstreams over the Gulf of Lions, westerly airstreams between Corsica and Tunisia, and southerly airstreams between the Gulf of Sidra (off Libya) and the Aegean.

Over the Adriatic there is somewhat less variable weather, owing to the predominance of a cold NE airstream.

Average isobar situation in winter

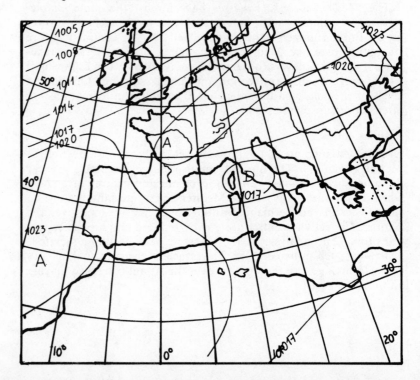

In Summer

The Azores anticyclone develops northwards. However its eastern part collapses from time to time, letting in disturbances of Atlantic origin, which can, although weakened, reach the Mediterranean.

The result for the western Mediterranean is a variable pattern, subject to disturbances from the Polar front, the dominating flow being NW and weak, which does not rule out violent tempests from all directions.

At the same time there is over eastern Europe a barometrically flat area, which is also subject to disturbances from the Polar front.

A vast depression links the Asian and African sub-Tropical regions. The appearance of this depression in summer is systematic and long-lasting. The lowest pressures are situated in the Persian Gulf area. The result, over the eastern end of the Mediterranean, is the very regular and permanent N and NE flow of the Etesian winds (this flow is linked with the summer monsoon of the Indian Ocean, which is itself governed by the central-Asian depression, and behaves with the same regularity). The stormy disturbances of the European barometric flat area do not overflow much into the stream of Etesian winds, where there are excellent sailing conditions. In the middle of summer, this flow can affect both the Adriatic and the Tyrrhenian seas.

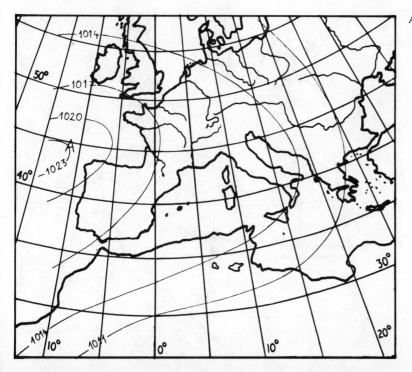

Average isobar situation in summer

Disturbed Patterns

Disturbed weather patterns generally become established in the Mediterranean in the winter months; but there are exceptions, principally in the north of the western end (the Gulf of Lions, the Ligurian Sea, the Tyrrhenian Sea).

The disturbances coming from the Polar front, as has just been mentioned, reach the western end mainly in winter and spring. They are not uncommon in summer, but they are slight and it is their wake (NW squalls of wind) that is noticeable. In winter they can be very active, as the Mediterranean air masses revive the warm fronts. The disturbances can last for several days at a stretch, bringing heavy winter rains and often NW gales. The incursions of cold air that follow them give rise, at all seasons, to the Mistral and the Tramontana, famous winds of which we shall have more to say later.

Sometimes there are other disturbances that come from the Azores and the shores of Morocco. They particularly affect the African coastline, then the eastern Mediterranean. They do not lead to storms, unless they interfere with the disturbances that originate from the North Atlantic; but they almost always precipitate a lot of rain. Their normal season is December, January and February.

Principal tracks of disturbance and areas of cyclogenesis

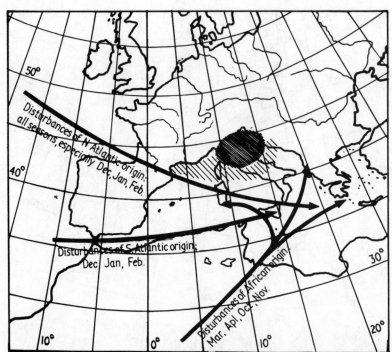

The disturbances of African origin are born on the edges of the Saharan area, when there is a depression over it and when there is an incursion of cold air after the passing of an Atlantic disturbance. These conditions arise in spring when the Sahara is already very hot, or in autumn when it is still very hot. These disturbances move slowly and unpredictably and their activity is moderate. They can affect any area of the Mediterranean but mainly its central and eastern regions.

Finally these 'areas of cyclogenesis' are noted at all times of the year for the small depressions they tend to form and which invite disturbances from elsewhere, the most common being the area that extends from the Gulf of Genoa to the Tyrrhenian Sea and to the north of the Adriatic. In these areas the pressure gradient is usually steeper, and consequently the winds are more violent, than elsewhere.

Anticyclonic Patterns

Anticyclonic patterns become established:
– In summer, when the Azores anticyclone spills over into Europe and the western Mediterranean.
– In winter, when a continuous band of high pressure extends from the Azores to the Sahara and Eurasian anticyclone areas. The

Stable anticyclonic situation in summer

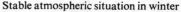
Stable atmospheric situation in winter

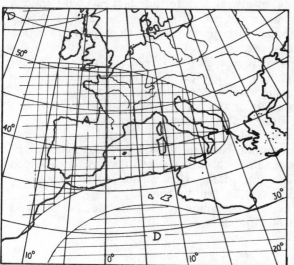

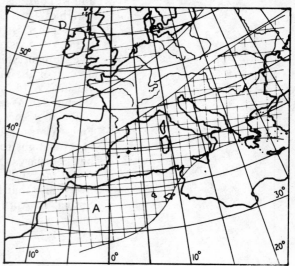

The Weather Throughout the Year
According to Popular Tradition

For lack of statistics linking the weather patterns to the different times of year, we are going to trust to the traditional indications, which form a fair guide. It must be used with caution, popular belief being probably ready to accept heavenly phenomena but not meticulous enough about dates. To use the main features of this guide discrepancies of up to three weeks must be allowed for and heavy weather may only amount to a local storm. But with all its deficiencies it gives useful indications. It only covers the western Mediterranean.

Early Summer. The summer gradually sets in from May on. The NW storms become less and less frequent and do not last, but they remain frequent until mid-June.

High Summer: mid-June to mid-August. The weather is fine, the storms are anomalies which make people comment: 'It's a wretched summer'.

The Mistral occurs infrequently and does not last long but can still be very strong.

The End of Summer. It begins with the 'mid-August' storm, which has the reputation of being violent. A disturbed period follows, almost cold, lasting for a week to a fortnight. It rains, the wind is variable. Then 'summer returns'. It is not so hot as in July, but the weather is reputed to be more stable. The winds at sea are slight, the coastal breezes consistent.

The Autumn Storm. It is reputed to take place at the end of September or the beginning of October and it is said to begin with a violent SW blow; 'the weather goes haywire' for several weeks.

Winter Bad Weather. It occurs between mid-November and mid-January. A succession of classic storms, often violent.

Fine Winter Weather. There is always a reputed stable period, of a fortnight to a month, between mid-January and mid-March; but February is said to have at least one bad ten-day patch, which sometimes spills over into March. Here we are concerned with the lively days that February has lent to March.

Spring. In April and the beginning of May, the weather becomes mild again, but it often rains.

situation is then stable and lasts for several days.
– In any season (and frequently in summer at the western end) when moving ridges cross the Mediterranean region. These ridges settle behind incursions of cold air, in between disturbances.

All these situations, as in the Atlantic, are characterised by fine weather, with little or no wind. But in contrast to what happens in the Atlantic, fogs and low cloud are infrequent, except along the African coastline and in the northern Adriatic.

Conditions vary within the various parts of the anticyclone:
– In its eastern part, the winds are slight and in the NW sector, on the open sea, not very good for sailing. In contrast, the coastal breezes are quite strong and have their own characteristics which we shall discuss later on.
– In its central part the weather is less agreeable. The sun is often hidden by nearly continuous layers of stable clouds (suspended stratocumulus), especially at sea. There is virtually no wind, but near the coasts the breezes, although faint, are regular.

The western end is the region of the SE, South and SW winds at sea. On the coasts, the breezes are light or non-existent. The weather is warm and sunny. At sea, the wind is light or moderate but, the sea not being disturbed, you have easy conditions for sailing and you can make good progress.

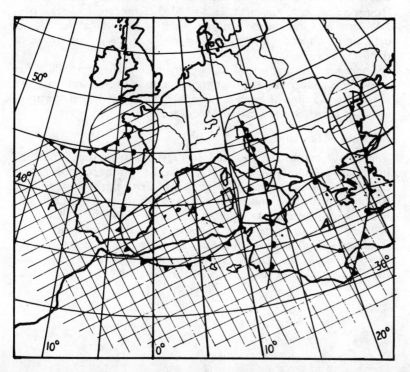

Moving anticyclonic ridge

When the anticyclonic situation is the result of a moving ridge, one must never forget that bad weather is never very far away. Besides, it is often heralded by its 'ambassador', cirrus, that we have already seen in other skies.

Regional Winds

In the course of this general analysis, some of the peculiarities of Mediterranean weather have cropped up: rapid change due to the presence of very diverse air masses, great variety of pressure, unpredictable centres of activity and complicated wind patterns. The essential feature, however, remains to be described – the winds that appear not so much complex as plain anarchical to yachtsmen accustomed to regular Atlantic patterns.

In fact, the different airstreams which approach the Mediterranean are not unusual in themselves; if they become so it is because of the very patchy and steep coastline which borders the greater part of it. Forced to rise above the mountain masses or to whistle down the valleys, the winds take on quite different characteristics from one place to the next. In the Mediterranean, to speak of a NW or SW wind means nothing: each wind has its own name, defining its direction and its character. There are several dozen of them.

There are too many to discuss even if we knew them all. After a few facts concerning the topography and its overall influence, we shall just examine the main regional winds and the patterns of coastal breezes in the western Mediterranean.

Influence of the Topography

The Mediterranean is isolated from the surrounding areas by important mountain masses: in the west the various Spanish ranges and the Pyrenees; in the north the Massif Central, the Alps and the Balkans; in the east, the plateau of Asia Minor and the Lebanon; in the south, the chains of the Atlas and the Saharan plateau.

There are four narrow entrances through these mountains: the Straits of Gibraltar to the Atlantic, the Lauragais shelf towards the Bay of Biscay, the Rhône–Saône corridor towards Europe, and the Dardanelles–Bosphorus corridor towards the Black Sea.

Elsewhere, from Tunis to Alexandra, the flat coast opens directly on to the African deserts.

In the middle of this region we find still more mountains, the Apennines, which stretch along the whole length of Italy and mark the limits of the western and the eastern Mediterranean.

Behaviour of the Cold Air

All these mountains masses, even the lowest, form important barriers to the movement of the lower layers of the atmosphere. They do not interfere very much with the warm air masses which usually circulate high up, but they stop or impede the cold air masses, especially (and this frequently happens) when the latter are not very thick. The following reaction then occurs: the cold air, forced to rise up the slopes, cools by expansion. If it is moist, it causes heavy precipitation on the windward slopes; then, having lost some of its humidity, it warms rapidly while it descends the leeward slope, and arrives at the foot of the mountain considerably warmer. This is the classic Föhn effect which we analysed in detail in the preceding chapter to illustrate the different states of the air.

This Föhn effect occurs over the western end of the Mediterranean on each incursion of maritime Polar air. The cold air does not necessarily become very warm, nor is the sky necessarily clear, but nevertheless the reputation of the Côte d'Azur for its blue sky and mildness is largely due to this occurrence. In short, the nature of the land which allows the warm air masses to penetrate and limits the effects of the cold air masses, is the physical background of the privileged climate the region enjoys.

But it is a privileged climate only to a certain extent, for the four entrances we have mentioned above must be taken into account. Far from being obstacles to the cold air, it pours through them, and its action is increased by a 'corridor effect' between the mountains. This is why Gibraltar, the Dardenelles and especially the Gulf of Lions are areas of violent winds and frequent storms.

Typical Föhn wind effect

All these influences are found again on a local scale. In detail, the terrain that borders the coast is broken up by valleys alternating with mountains. The cold air finds an outlet in each one of these valleys. Thus all along the coast there are very special winds which have only remote connections with the synoptic wind. Their general flow is very turbulent and they blow irregularly in squalls, sometimes with up and down currents.

The ground surface does not need to be very high for these aberrant winds to rise, nor for the corridors to be very distinct for them to become violent. They can happen along the north coasts of Corsica or any small, mountainous island.

Between each small valley is a col down which the wind rushes furiously (there is even a considerable difference in pressure between its two slopes). If the air is sufficiently unstable, whirlwinds can even set off spectacular waterspouts, interesting enough to watch if you are not too near. Off the coast between the corridors that the wind blows down, the air is practically still. It goes without saying that one can hardly imagine worse sailing conditions.

Finally, these winds seem to be all the more sudden and violent the more local they are: the big Mistral, coming out of the Rhône–Saône corridor, is certainly easier to cope with than the 'raggiaturi' of Cape Corsica. In the same way, an influx of cold air that is limited to the very lowest layers is more dangerous than a vast movement, whose air flow is large enough to become regular in spite of the lie of the land.

Indications of Cold Air

In summer, as incursions of cold air are always linked to overall movements, they are predictable and are effectively foreseen by the meteorological services. But in winter they can occur very suddenly, even in very fine weather, and prediction is almost impossible. The cumulus, the cold air type of cloud, do not act as a warning system because, when they appear, the cold air influx has already begun. There can be invasions of cold air without any cloud, when it is dry.

It can be said, however, that the appearance along crests or ridges and, to lee of them, of jagged cumulus, lying in long roller formations, is a sure sign of a cold, fluky and dangerous airstream: it is safer then not to go too near the coast.

The appearance of altocumulus *lenticularis* can also be regarded as indicating the arrival of cold air; but it is very rare that such an incursion occurs when middle layer clouds other than these altocumulus are in the sky.

To conclude this analysis of the relationship between the cold air and the nature of the Mediterranean land surface, it is as well to call attention to yet another phenomenon that occurs on coasts exposed to influxes of warm air, in winter, when there is snow on the mountains. A cap of cold, stable air forms over the snowy surfaces and establishes a regular airstream in its lower layers towards the sea. As the cold air is very dense in comparison with the warm air, the latter cannot reach the coasts near these snow surfaces. The warm SW to SE winds are then stopped two or three miles from the coasts and a light wind blows from the land in their

Principal local winds

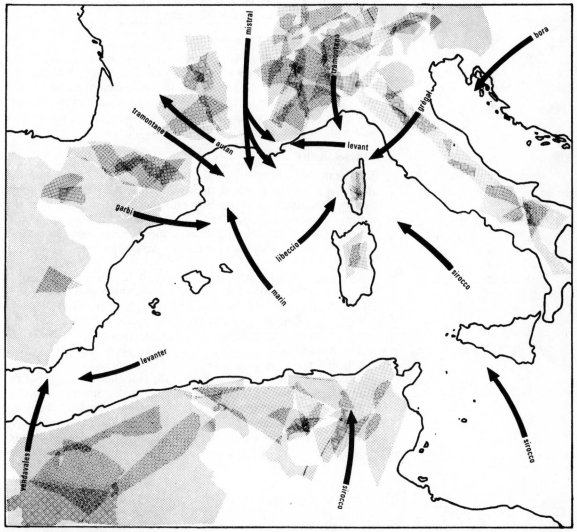

place. This is an important phenomenon in the interplay of coastal breezes.

After this analysis, it is pretty clear that there is a great variety of winds in the Mediterranean, and that each wind has its own characteristics. It follows that at least the more important ones must be studied individually.

Mediterranean folklore provides a unique collection of names for them. Each is quite precise, taking into account not only the area where the wind occurs, but also its direction, speed, sometimes even the characteristics of its turbulence and the effects it produces. The terminology has been largely adopted by the meteorological services and it is used in their forecasts.

The Mistral and the Tramontana

These names from the folklore of Provence and Languedoc, Mistral and Tramontana crop up in the forecasts for the Gulf of Lions, the Gulf of Genoa and the Ligurian sea, all areas where these two winds often blow. They are undoubtedly the most typical of winds and, as the yachtsman has every chance of encountering them, we shall deal with them at greater length than the others.

Characteristics

The coming of the Mistral and the Tramontana is linked with the arrival of a cool maritime airstream from the Atlantic, more rarely with cold continental air coming into the Mediterranean over the Laurageais shelf and down the Rhône–Saône corridor.

In short, we have a stream of cold air strengthened at these entrances: the analysis made in the last paragraph is also applicable here.

This wind is called the Tramontana in Languedoc, Mistral in Provence and the Côte d'Azur, but it is the same wind, sometimes under other names, that occurs in the whole of the Gulf of Lions as far as the Balearics, in the Ligurian sea, in Corsica and to the north of Sardinia. It reaches its maximum strength as it comes out of the Rhône–Saône corridor. But it can be particularly violent locally at Cape Corsica or in the Strait of Bonifaccio, for instance; and the sea is liable to be rougher off the Roussillon coast (near the Spanish frontier) than off the Camargue, further north.

The Mistral (as we shall call it from now on) blows from the north or NW on the Côte d'Azur, Provence and Languedoc. In Corsica, it blows more from the west and only its cold-wind characteristics allows it to be differentiated from the Libeccio, a hot

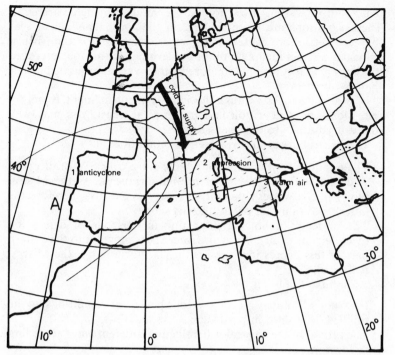

The four conditions for the appearance of the Mistral

violent wind which also blows from the west. There are also many confused areas: in Bastia, for instance, where a marked Foehn effect takes place on the heights of the Balagne and Cape Corsica, the Libeccio is blamed for storm conditions when the Mistral is really responsible.

The Mistral is often more violent than the synoptic wind. A strength reaching 40 knots, with squalls of 60 knots, are not uncommon. It usually lasts for three to six consecutive days. But it can blow for only a few hours or, on the other hand, for 15 days on end. This last duration usually occurs during the cold season and it coincides with a disturbed NW pattern extending over the whole of western Europe. The temporary calm periods which are sometimes associated with the areas under the influence of these conditions do not, however, affect the Mediterranean: the Mistral continues to blow unceasingly.

The Mistral is normally stronger by day than at night (the

maximum day strength is double the minimum night strength). These variations are more evident on the coast than out at sea; they are even more evident if the sky is clear, and if the Mistral coincides with an incursion of air colder than the air that preceded it. They are in fact recognised more by their variations in turbulence than by their force.

It is as well to know that the improvement at night is only a remission, and that if you find it along the coast, you may well lose it if you take to the open sea.

The Mistral arises under these four conditions:

– The establishment of an anticyclonic ridge over SW France.
– A depression over the western Mediterranean. As the Mistral blows in the western part of this depression, it is therefore the latter's position that determines its scope.
– The presence of hot air stagnating in the zone of depression (Mediterranean air). If hot air from Africa moves into the eastern part of this depression, the weather is shocking but the Mistral is limited.
– An influx of cold air.

It is not absolutely necessary for these four conditions to be fulfilled. The third in particular is 'optional'.

The arrival of the Mistral is heralded in different ways according to location:

The Mistral gives a quite different warning of its approach east and west of the 6°E meridian

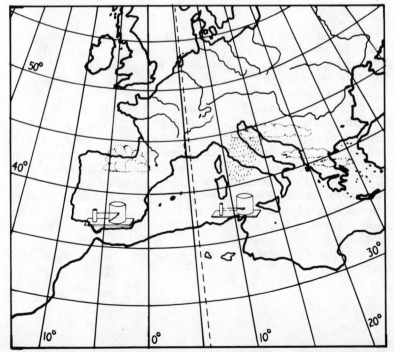

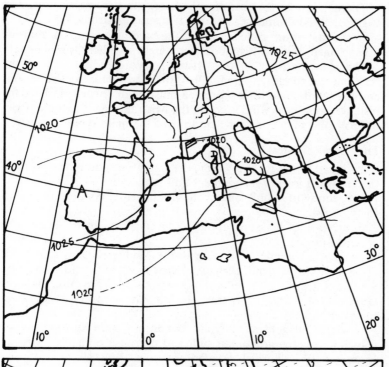

Two isobar situations conducive to the local Mistral
Above: increase of pressure over SW France
Below: anticyclone and cold air over Central Europe

– To the west of the meridian 6° East: the barometer rises, rain stops, cloud diminishes and the temperature drops.
– To the east of the same meridian: the barometer drops, it rains or it has rained, the wind is moderate or light but there is a big swell.

The characteristics of the Mistral vary according to how the fundamental conditions are fulfilled; there are all kinds of variations and the opinions of long-shoremen must be distrusted: in Nice for instance every cold wind is called the Mistral, even if it comes from the SW. We shall consider here four of the main types of Mistral.

The 'Local' Mistral

It is limited to the Rhône Valley, the Camargue and to the north of the Gulf of Lions. Very frequent and moderate.

It is enough for only one of the fundamental conditions to exist for it to rise:
– an increase of pressure, even if not very great, from Gascony to central France;
– or again a thermal depression in the Mediterranean, a frequent occurrence with an undisturbed pattern: a vast anticyclone covering western Europe, with only slight lowering of pressure over the Gulf of Genoa and the Tyrrhenian Sea. The Mistral then blows in the afternoon;
– in winter, in cold anticyclonic conditions over Europe, the air cooled locally by radiation is sufficient to trigger off a local Mistral, characterised by hardish squalls.

The 'White' Mistral

The Mistral is 'white' when it isn't accompanied by cloud and precipitation. This happens when the cold air is dry and stable – of continental origin. It also occurs when the Mistral arises behind a typical disturbance. The required conditions are all fulfilled, the considerable increase in pressure following the cold front gives a violent Mistral and a clear sky. This is the origin of the reputation the Mistral has of clearing the sky. This is a frequent and spectacular occurrence but it is not systematic.

The 'Black' Mistral

When cold air of maritime Polar origin is moist and unstable the Mistral is 'black', as it is accompanied by a sky covered with low clouds, often backed with cumulonimbus bringing squalls. In winter it can snow.

The black Mistral occurs whenever there is no very great increase

White Mistral

Black Mistral

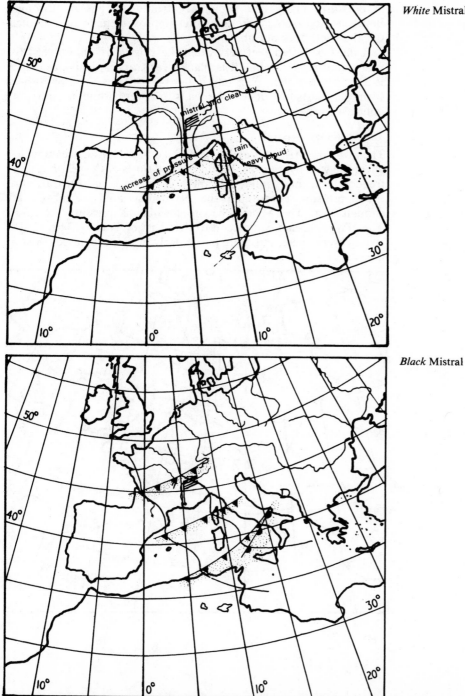

in pressure; many cold secondary fronts are passing through. Between each front, there is a brief improvement in the weather, but the wind does not abate.

It must be noted that very often the Mistral is white over Provence and the sea, while it is black over Corsica. This peculiarity is due to the Föhn effect and it can persist for several days. Seen from the coasts of Corsica, the sea is then very luminous, in strong contrast to the sky.

The Ordinary Mistral

The ordinary Mistral is associated with a vast NW airstream which affects all western Europe. It occurs at all times of the year but most frequently in mid-winter, and there is then a black Mistral, until the depression controlling the NW airstream has moved far enough east. The Mistral becomes white as pressure increases. The NW airstream can extend to the coast of Tunisia. The wind is strong everywhere, but more particularly in the recognised 'Mistral areas'.

The ordinary Mistral

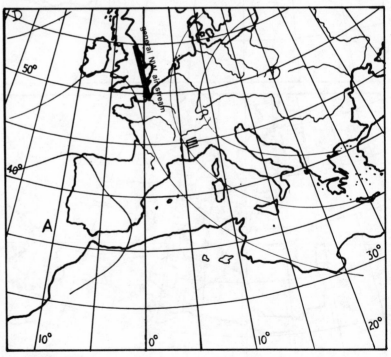

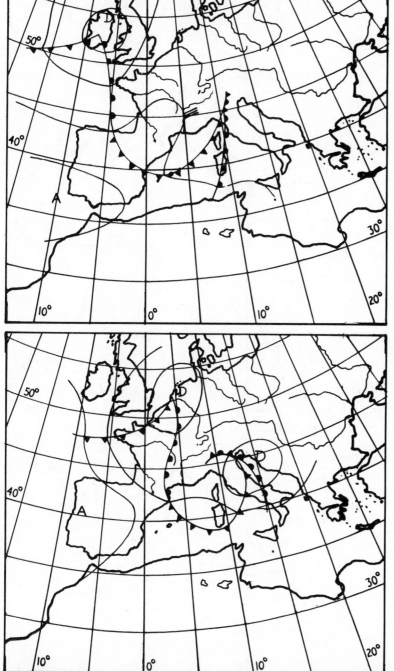

An *anticyclone ridge* forms behind a disturbance; the Mistral blows

A second disturbance arrives: the Mistral stops but there is only a brief respite

The last disturbance of a family has passed: the Mistral blows

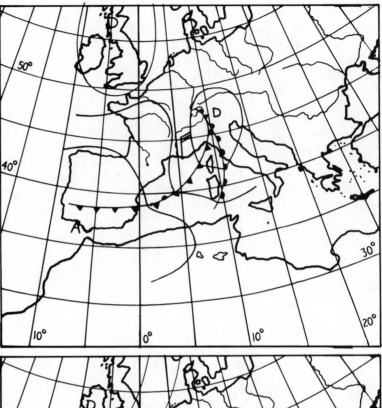

The anticyclone develops: the Mistral gradually dies down, for good this time

The End of the Mistral

The Mistral dies down or stops altogether when the four fundamental conditions are waning. This can happen in different ways; we shall only mention the two classic cases.

The Gascony anticyclonic ridge collapses and a group of disturbances of Atlantic origin moves down towards the Mediterranean. After the passage of the first disturbance, the anticyclonic ridge appears and the Mistral blows. The arrival of the second disturbance interrupts the influx of cold air. Pressure falls and the temperature becomes milder; cirrus spreads over the sky, followed by middle layer clouds; the wind abates and tends to blow in a westerly or SW direction.

The end of the Mistral is accompanied by a rapid and clear improvement in the weather, but it does not last long. A new disturbance follows: first rain and SW winds, then the Mistral returns after the second cold front has passed through.

It is in these conditions that the local saying holds good: 'a short Mistral does not bring back fine weather'.

The Extension of the Anticyclone towards the Mediterranean

The high pressures of western Europe extend towards the south. The depression of the Gulf of Genoa and the Tyrrhenian Sea fills up or moves east. There are the beginnings of an anticyclonic pattern, and the Mistral weakens.

Note that such a situation is favourable for making a passage from Marseilles to Corsica or Sardinia: a good north wind to start with, turning to NW then west, and weakening throughout the passage. And fine weather to follow. A Mistral which persists and only abates slowly brings back fine weather.

Out of a hundred cases of the Mistral blowing at over 25 knots at sea, thirty-eight developments of the first type have been noted and sixty-two of the second type. A yachtsman cooped up in harbour by bad weather can look on the arrival of the Mistral as a happy event: he will not be frustrated much longer.

The Tramontana

It arises in the Gulf of Genoa – Tyrrhenian Sea area. The Tramontana is a north to NE wind affecting the west coast of Italy and the Tuscan archipelago, but it can also reach and even go further than Corsica.

It often follows a Mistral. After the influx of cold air over the west Mediterranean, an anticyclonic pattern sets in with the

The Tramontana blows up after the
Mistral

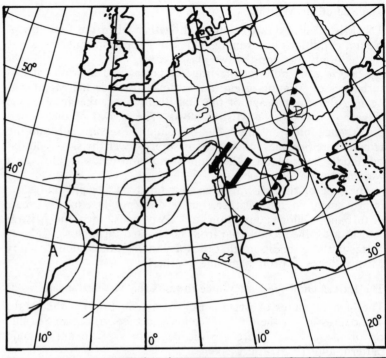

The Tramontana in winter

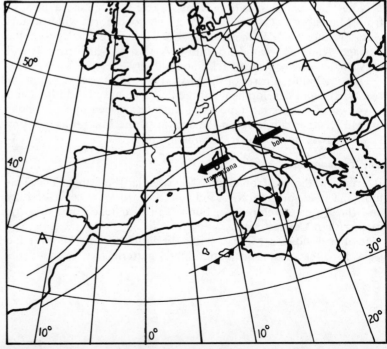

formation of a ridge of high pressure as far as the plain of the Po, while low pressures have become established and persist over southern Italy.

Rarely very violent, the Tramontana is however quite strong off Cape Corsica, when it follows hard on the Mistral. It usually affords pleasant sailing in a good breeze.

In winter, the Tramontana is often a prolongation of the *Bora*, a seasonal wind blowing over the Adriatic. It is then extremely turbulent. The pressure gradient in the lower layers is steep, an anticyclone being well established over central Europe with extension over the Alps. The cold air of Balkan origin is very dry and arrives in the Mediterranean after crossing the Apennines, without there being any Föhn effect (dry air, no precipitation). If the airstream is strong enough, it reaches and crosses the Corsican mountains. This orographic rising disorganises the stream more than it checks it, and the cold air arrives in short, violent squalls, interrupted by periods of calm. These gusts are often very localised and can be overlooked by the meteorological forecasts.

The Marin

The Marin is a mild or warm, damp wind, accompanied by rain which blows from the SE, South or SW over the Gulf of Lions and the neighbouring coasts.

It has no particular meteorological characteristics, as it corre-

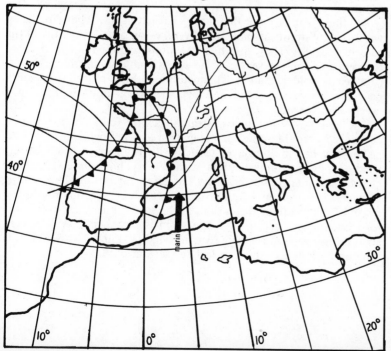

The mild and damp Marin wind is to the Mediterranean what the south-westerly is to the Atlantic

sponds to the very classic case of the rainy wind that generally occurs in advance of a warm front. It merits a special mention however since it is the opposite and almost hostile to the Mistral. Although not so strong as the latter, it raises quite a sea along the coasts of Provence, as its fetch is so long. On the coasts of Languedoc, it is allied to the *Autan*, a warm local wind.

We can recall and clarify here a remark we have already made. In winter, when conditions favour a local Mistral (cold air on land, the mountains of the Cevennes and of Provence being snow-covered), the Marin cannot reach the coast. A curious spectacle then takes place: the sky is covered with the typical clouds of a warm front, it rains, and yet the Mistral, although quite weak, blows several miles out from the coasts. Go a little further out and everything changes: the wind is southerly and clearly much warmer. This is the 'lost' Marin.

The Sirocco

The Sirocco, and the other hot winds of the same family (*leveche, chili, ghibli, khamsin*) come from Africa or Asia and spread over the Mediterranean when a strong south-north airstream is established between a depression centred on the Mediterranean and a ridge of high pressure situated to the east of it. Such winds only affect clearly one part of the Mediterranean at a time. The chosen time is spring (April or May), but they are equally common in autumn.

All these winds have the same characteristics. They are laden with dust: visibility is bad, the sky takes on a yellowish tinge, the sun is blurred. They are hot in comparison with the average temperature for the season. The air is stable in the lower layers (the sea is colder than it is), unstable at high altitude. It is dry near the coasts of Africa and becomes very moist in the lower layers as it spreads over the sea.

The result is fog and low stratus, lasting for a long time and certainly as troublesome for navigation as Channel fogs in winter.

The sky has middle layer clouds with thunderstorm characteristics, or even cumulonimbus with a very high base. Electrical charges are intense but not very dangerous at ground level. Short showers of warm muddy rain may occur, more commonly in the north of the Mediterranean than in the south, but never lasting for long and never very heavy. The wind is strong but seldom very strong. The swell is very big (for the Mediterranean) as the fetch is long and winds like this can last for several days.

The Sirocco blows at the east or west end of the Mediterranean according to the positions of the action centres

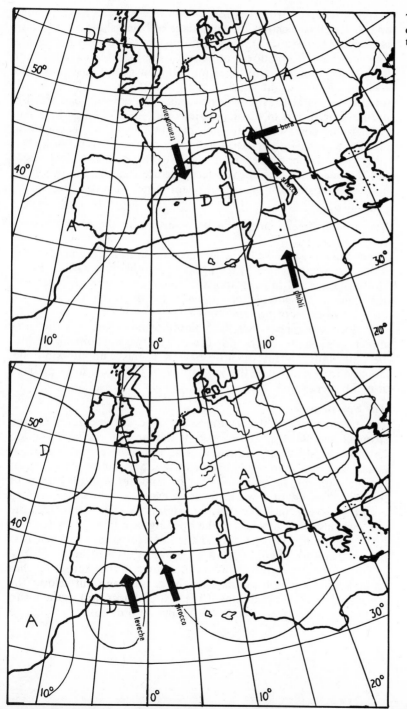

In short, apart from the fog (which doesn't occur everywhere) and the swell (which has the advantage of being short, as it usually is in the Mediterranean), the conditions are quite good for sailing. The drawback is one does not benefit from the Mediterranean sun (and this is not the only occasion). If you go off eastwards, the weather improves, but you lose the wind. If you go off westwards (or the activity centres move eastwards), you get very bad weather in the western part of the depression: rain and violent storms.

There are some other regional, or rather local, winds which do not have sufficiently generalised characteristics to be described here. We will refer to them later when we recapitulate the features of the different areas of the western Mediterranean. But we must first consider one last important phenomenon: coastal breezes.

Coastal Breezes

The coastal breezes are particularly strong on the Mediterranean for two reasons:
– they are linked, as we know, to sunshine, and that is considerable;
– they are strengthened by the proximity of the mountains, where a similar pattern of breezes appears: a *valley* (or *anabatic*) breeze in the daytime, a *mountain* (or *katabatic*) breeze at night.

The two types of breezes combine.

It does not appear that the synoptic wind, when it is the same direction as the breeze is added to it. The two phenomena seem to be quite independent: in little bays it is the synoptic wind that dominates (even if it is the less strong of the two); in large bays, it is the breeze that takes over.

The Sea Breeze

The mechanics are always the same. The sea breeze is all the stronger and starts all the sooner, as the air over the land is more unstable. Seen out at sea, cumulus appearing over the land mass give hopes of a favourable breeze to take you landwards, even if, for the moment, the wind is weak or contrary. But an arrival of stable air (ahead of a warm front) prevents the breeze setting in even if it is very fine. The synoptic wind itself, if it blows from the sea, can find itself blocked at the opening of a bay surrounded by high mountains. This calm near the coast in summer, when it is fine, is therefore often a sign of a change in the weather.

The sea breeze starts up two to four hours after sunrise, reaches its maximum strength a little after the passage of the sun over the meridian. In good conditions it reaches 20 knots, more often 8 to 12 knots; it dies away one or two hours before sunset.

The Land Breeze

The land breeze is usually not so strong as the sea breeze, but it is more regular and sustained. It is capable of driving up a fairly strong synoptic wind in opposition to itself. In winter, when there is snow on the mountains, it is particularly steady and strong.

If the air over the sea is warm and unstable enough, stratocumulus and cumulus appear near the coast when a land breeze sets in.

It occurs immediately after sunset, sometimes a little before; it reaches 6 to 8 knots, sometimes 10 knots towards the end of the night; it disappears with the dawn or a little later.

Even more than with the sea breeze, the absence of a land breeze when it is fine is a sure sign of an approaching disturbance. Its absence indicates an equalisation of temperature over land and sea.

After the passage of a warm front, when the rain stops and the sky clears, even partially, the breeze reappears. But it can die during the wake's passage when the air is equally cold over sea and land.

The Extensive Area of the Breezes

It is customary to assume that the breezes only affect a coastal band twenty miles deep. This can indeed be taken as the extreme limit; it must be reckoned from the average shore line and not from headlands. The sea breeze does not often get that far but the land breeze usually does towards the end of the night.

Naturally the play of breezes varies greatly according to the indentations of the coastline. Each little bay, inside a much larger gulf, has its own wind pattern, at least at the time when the breezes set in. When they have gathered strength these very localised winds become part of the breeze blowing along the whole coastline. This is particularly true for the land breeze which, at the beginning of the night, takes as many directions as there are small bays and valleys, and only finds a regular pattern and strength as the night goes on.

These breezes are characteristic of fine weather, and very favourable for dinghy sailing off the coast. When cruising, you know that you can count on a land breeze to leave harbour and reach open water towards the end of the night. By the same token you can take maximum advantage of the sea breeze to make a landfall on a broad reach in the early afternoon.

West Mediterranean by Areas

We shall assemble here a number of tips on the sailing conditions to be found at different points in the western Mediterranean. These are only the very classic indications that give the basic knowledge that will lead you to make your own discoveries.

Languedoc, Provence, Gulf of Lions, North Balearics

When we have said this is the zone of the Mistral, we have said all. However a few particular points call for attention.

– The NE wind is sometimes violent (if the Tramontana); it is called the *Gregale* in Provence, the *Levanter* in Catalonia and the Balearics. It is not common.
– The summer sea breeze is steady and sustained (without exceeding Force 4); it almost always becomes the predominant wind on the shore line, even when the Mistral is blowing. The latter comes again at night, out to sea.
– The land breeze often becomes integrated with the Mistral, and together they usually prevent the sailor from reaching land.

Out of a hundred cases of wind of 30 knots or more at sea, the following distribution has been recorded:

Mistral-Tramontana: 88
Marin   3
Gregale   9

This area is where the strongest winds in the Mediterranean are recorded. At Marseilles, on average, a hundred days' Mistral a year are recorded.

South Balearics and Alboran

An area with a very Mediterranean character on the whole. In particular, it has a regular and systematic pattern of breezes on the coasts in summer but less regular in the cold season.

In winter when there is a disturbed situation with a depression centred over Oran, the wind that blows from the east and brings rain, is called the *Solano*.

The area east of Gibraltar is where the Atlantic and Mediterranean influences confront each other, and result in two winds:

– the *Levanter*, an east Mediterranean wind, mild but often irregular;
– the *Vendavales*, a SW Atlantic wind, cool damp, steady. It is often accompanied by showers.

One of the characteristics of this area is that one passes suddenly from one wind to the other.

The Ligurian Sea and Around Corsica

The dominant wind is the *Libeccio*, but its name does not correspond to a wind with precise characteristics. One thing is certain: it is a west to SW wind, moderate to strong, hot or mild, never excessive. It foreshadows, or is accompanied by, bad weather.

We have seen that in Corsica the Mistral blows usually from the west (or WSW), as it reaches Corsica when the depression, which is its partial origin, has moved towards the Gulf of Genoa or the Tyrrhenian Sea. The only difference between the Mistral and the Libeccio is that the arrival of the first coincides with a lowering of the temperature and often to a clearing of the sky, while the second brings mild, rainy weather. In a Mistral, one is in Polar air or cold maritime Arctic air; in the Libeccio, in warm maritime Polar air or Mediterranean air.

But when the wind is from the NW and brings rain, it is also called the Mistral (really the black Mistral).

At this stage it is worth analysing in a little more detail the winds around Corsica.

Cape Corsica and the North of the Island

West winds dominate all the year round with maximum frequency in summer. The strong winds (70% are westerly), caused by the frequent cyclogenisis over the Gulf of Genoa, raise a steep sea over the coast between the Gulf of Galeria (to the south of Calvi) and the extremity of Cape Corsica. In certain cases, owing to the orographic effect of the land surface of Corsica, these dominantly west winds reach Force 7 to 9 to the north of Cape Corsica over a strip of water running in a north-south direction, some ten miles wide.

East Coast

During west winds of Force 6 to 7, the wind is light on the east coast, but between Cape Corsica and Bastia (on the lee coast) and in valley openings, it can gain strength.

As a general rule when one is sailing near this coast, watch out for violent squalls coming off the mountains, even if the west wind is only moderate.

The strength of the Mistral and the Libeccio is much weaker to the south of Bastia, between this port and Porto-Vecchio.

In summer the sea is relatively calm. East winds are rare. But when they do blow, the swell usually precedes them by a few hours.

The South Coast, Bouches de Bonifaccio

The Bouches de Bonifaccio are remarkable. Between the high rocky shores of Corsica and Sardinia, they make a passage where the wind is almost always violent. Legend has it that the monsters, Scylla and Charybdis haunted these waters, which will hardly surprise yachtsmen who wait in the excellent port of Bonifaccio for along enough calm period to get through the strait.

Without over-simplifying, it can be said that in these Bouches, the wind is either west or east, that it blows either at less than 10 knots or above 40 knots. A speed of 45 knots is quite usual, even when it is very fine elsewhere.

The West Coast

As one goes northwards up the coast, the predominant winds are roughly NW. The change is very sharp at the northern limit of the sector towards the Island of Cargalo to the north of the Gulf of Porto.

Perhaps the most important conclusion this study brings us to is this: in the western Mediterranean most winds (thanks principally to the Mistral and the Tramontana) are accompanied by clear skies. The yachtsman gets no warnings and this is all the more irksome as the wind can sometimes rise in a matter of minutes and is immediately violent. Moreover, at any moment, it can change and strengthen suddenly by more than one Force. One must always be ready to change plans and be carried away east when you intended to go west or *vice versa*. Unless there is no alternative one doesn't argue with the Mistral. It raises a horrible sea, with short very hollow waves, which cut down the speed of the boat and the morale of the crew. Do not cruise against the run of the weather.

In fact, perhaps one of the delights of sailing in this sea is following and using to the best advantage the meteorological situation without trying, at all costs, to pursue a precise plan. By not hesitating to change the itinerary and to make unforeseen stops, a cruise in these waters is almost always pleasant.

A good preparation for cruising in the Mediterranean is to read Homer. When the winds are not favourable, the best course is undoubtedly to do as Ulysses did: wait patiently. But like him, one must also know how to be wily and seize an opportunity as soon as Aeolus, who was given power over the winds by Zeus, seems to be in good humour.

The Weather to Come

Yesterday's weather has been experienced and recorded, enjoyed or suffered but it is not of much use today, although it may show trends. What really matters is tomorrow's weather, a somewhat unknown quantity, but which must be foreseen if a sensible course has to be worked out – tactics if and when bad weather comes.

Knowledge of weather past is clearly very useful for the prediction of weather to come as it allows certain constants to be established which can be collated with the characteristic developments that are predicted. However, when it comes to determining the general picture of the weather for the next few days, you certainly cannot depend solely on personal observations, however experienced one is. The preceding analyses have demonstrated that the weather at any particular spot, is only one aspect of an overall situation which lies far beyond the horizon of the observer; it is often the result of what was happening the day before, hundreds or thousands of miles away; its subsequent development depends therefore above all on how the general situation develops. This information can only be supplied by the meteorological services, whose observation network covers the world.

Personal observation comes next and it is a matter of comparing the local weather with the overall situation and trying to see, from the barometer, the sky and the state of the sea if the forecast matches up with local conditions or if the situation is developing faster or slower than was expected in the forecast or if one is heading towards worsening or improving weather.

Defined thus, the role of observation seems very modest. In practice, only years of experience enable you to reach conclusions of your own. That is also why not much advice can be given on forecasting the weather. It only comes, as we said at the beginning, from a good understanding of the weather forecasts and from immersing yourself in studying the subject. No other person can help you.

Weather Forecasts

All the essential information that concerns yachtsmen is given in

A classic disturbance photographed by the meteorological satellite, ESSA 8. This kind of observing gives fundamental information for forecasting. The warm front just reaching the coasts of Europe is shown very clearly; the cold front is still a long way out to sea, the beginning of the occlusion where the fronts join; and the vortex, marking the centre of the depression on the extreme left, are all clearly visible. Iceland and Scandinavia are covered in snow

the weather forecasts broadcast on the radio and (if one wants to go in deeper) by the daily information that are published by most of the national meteorological services.

Marine almanacs give the stations and times of the regular shipping weather forecasts. Wherever they are broadcast they give, with some variation in detail, but in the same order, the following information:
– Warnings of possible storms, then the overall picture: characteristics of the pressure fields, locations of activity centres, the track of disturbances and the position and speed of movement of fronts.
– Area forecasts.
– General trends of the weather.
– Summary of observations taken at the different coastal stations.

All this information gives a good overall picture, in the area where one is sailing, of the general situation and of what is likely to happen in the short term. But it is important to realise the limitations.

First, there is an inevitable delay between the time when the observations have been made and when the forecasts are broadcast. A forecast broadcast at 0900, for instance, is drawn up as a result of observations made at 0100. Usually this delay is not serious but it can be if there are very rapid developments. It is worth remembering that the summaries of observations made by coastal stations given at the end of the forecast are usually more recent than the overall analysis (summaries at 0700 for the 0900 bulletin). These summaries deserve to be listened to with particular attention because they sometimes reveal anomalies not mentioned in the general situation report and give more exact information on what developments can take place.

Again (and this is the main limitation of the general forecast already mentioned) the information given covers enormous areas. It does not give exact information on the intensity which a particular

France I, one of the two frigates of the French Meteorological Services

METEOROLOGIE NATIONALE
CEMS LANNION
Montage des photographies reçues d'ESSA 8
le 26 Mars 1971 entre 11 h 30 et 14 h 00.

phenomenon can take locally nor its exact timing. The intensification and weakening of a front, for instance, might not be indicated and, for a very localised area, this might greatly modify the forecast as far as you are concerned. Moreover, and especially in summer, these forecasts often have to give a variety of possibilities from which a choice must be made.

It is here, therefore, that personal observation comes in, and above all the use of the only meteorological instrument that is indispensable on board: the barometer.

The Barometer

The sorcerer, as it was called by sailors of days gone by, sits quietly in its corner, with its highs and lows giving a faithful account of the comings and goings in the atmosphere.

The pressures it shows have however one significant limitation. One can easily believe that there is an anticyclonic situation if the needle reaches and goes higher than 1,020 mb, or that there is a rather depressionary area when it goes below 1,010mb (the figure for a very strong depression can be 960mb, in its centre). But it is also possible to experience bad weather with pressures in the region of 1,015mb. In any case it is a good thing for the barometer to be adjusted (calibrated) so that it indicates true pressures. We shall see that this is particularly important for forecasting dangerous conditions.

But what is of the utmost importance to watch are, in practice, the variations of the needle, which indicate *tendency*.

This term, tendency, is used by meteorologists to define changes of pressure (higher or lower) during a period of three hours.

The barograph is the ideal for following changes in pressure. But it can be disconcerting

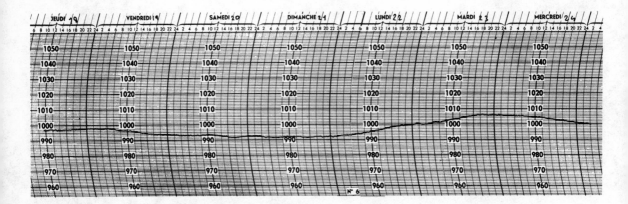

This is very important. Besides, in the daily weather reports (DWR) there is a map of tendencies, on which are marked lines of equal pressure change (*isallobars*). These isallobars usually take the form of ellipses merging into each other and forming centres of pressure change which generally go in couples (a centre of lowering pressure, a centre of rising pressure). Evidence of these is one of the chief concerns of weather forecasters.

For the isolated observer, this tendency is also the fundamental piece of information, for it can indicate, in the most precise fashion, a development in the weather. Generally speaking, a drop of 2 to 3mb in the space of three hours must lead one to think seriously of the possibility of worsening weather; a drop of 3 to 5mb indicates the approach of a strong disturbance; and if the drop is more than 5mb, then something quite out of the ordinary is going to happen.

But these statements need some qualifying. A tendency does not give an absolute indication; the violence of a disturbance is not exactly proportional to the negative tendency which indicates it. There can even be storms with a completely positive tendency, in a cold air stream from the NW to NE sector for instance. Most of the time, nevertheless, it is important to watch this tendency, and see if observation confirms it: a negative tendency and the appearance of a head sky usually indicate that things are going to get worse. The barometric tendency is even, sometimes, the one available fact, particularly for foreseeing dangerous conditions which slip through the meshes of the meteorological network.

Forecasting Dangerous Conditions

At sea, the dangerous conditions are the unexpected ones, those that surprise by their suddenness.

Among these phenomena, the one to fear most is clearly the cataclysmic freak storm, usually produced by a small harmless looking depression, which suddenly deepens near the coast and does enormous damage even before the meteorological services have been able to announce the danger.

This sort of storm is fortunately rare, but not exceptional: six have been recorded in twenty years in Brittany. Two of them have taken place in summer, the one on 6 July 1969 being the deadliest of all since it caused the death of thirteen yachtsmen.

The speed with which such hurricanes develop clearly make their forecasting very difficult. They move too quickly for the swell to precede them. The state of the sky certainly makes one think that

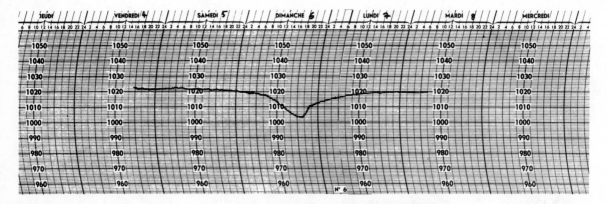

| JEUDI | VENDREDI 4 | SAMEDI 5 | DIMANCHE 6 | LUNDI 7 | MARDI 8 | MERCREDI |

A typical drop recorded at Dinard at the time of the great storm of 6 July 1960

bad weather might be on the way but gives no reason to anticipate its intensity. Only the barometer can give some warning of their approach, at least a few hours in advance.

In practice, one can conclude that something serious is going to happen when one or several of the following incidents are noticed:

– The barometer falls rapidly, the tendency being more than 5mb in three hours.

– Much sooner than predicted, the pressure it indicates approaches or becomes lower than was announced by the last forecast as the centre of the depression. This means either that the depression has speeded up, or that it has deepened – or both at once.

– The pressure drops very low while the wind remains stubbornly in a SE direction, suggesting that the centre of the depression is still a long way off.

One sees here how important it is to have a calibrated barometer, because it is only by comparing the pressure given in the forecast with the one observed that it is possible to be alerted in time. It is obviously necessary to note the position of the centre of the depression, as well as its forecasted direction and speed.

It is important not to be deceived by the calm which usually settles close to the centre of a depression. During the course of the freak storm of 6 July 1969, it was observed that the wind changed a few minutes from calm to Force 12. In general we know too that the cold front of a depression is more formidable than its warm front and this was certainly the case here.

Other conditions can be dangerous in spite of being less violent. The danger with them is due not to a lack of forecasts but rather to yachtsmen not paying sufficient attention. This is especially the case for *secondary cold fronts*, against which one is not on one's guard, although they are in fact more violent than the main cold front. You must therefore be on the look out when the forecasts mention these minor fronts, and also when you notice, after a normal cold front has gone through, that the wind does not go northerly (and all the more so when it has a tendency to back slightly south, in spite of a wake sky persisting). Finally, watching the sky ought to allow one to make preparations in time, as the arrival of each one of these fronts is marked by a line of squalls consisting of cumulus congestus and cumulonimbus.

Following through the same line of thought, you must also watch out for the squalls which occur in very unstable air and which sometimes bring a much stronger wind than was expected. It is not uncommon for an average wind of Force 5 to reach Force 6 or 7 in gusts.

You must be particularly on your guard in thundery conditions. Here anything can happen. For instance, the wind is weak, Force 1 to 2, heavy clouds pass over without any appreciable increase in wind and, suddenly, when you least expect it, you are in a squall of Force 6 and more. . .

As in many other fields, direct experience helps to sharpen your nose – 'once bitten, twice shy'. A good fright with a lucky outcome is worth volumes of bookish knowledge if you want to be a good weather forecaster.

Glénans, 6 July, 1969. With a fetch of some 500m, the seas rise and break in a matter of moments; the almost ubiquitious streaks of foam follow the direction of the wind. There is spray everywhere. The wind reaches Force 10.

Observation

Knowing how to watch the sky and interpret it only comes after long apprenticeship. The honest observer, who is not satisfied to simulate knowledge by throwing off technical jargon, has a long haul up a steep mountain to a fount of real expertise. Only when he has drunk at it will he know how to qualify his assertions and not stand by them in the face of new developments. He will, as a matter of course:

– take out a subscription to a meteorological journal or at least study the daily weather maps published in some newspapers.
– listen to the weather forecasts morning and evening, look at the sky at least four times a day, and at the barometer too, then draw a forecast for the next day and
– the next day, compare his forecast with what actually happened and analyse the discrepancies.

He will practise this exercise for several months, at different seasons.

He will then find there is really no reason to stop. If he stops, he must not in any case wait until the day before leaving on a cruise to take up his studies again. One must get back into the swing of things several days before by listening to the forecasts, consulting the maps and making contact with a coastal station to get the middle range forecasts.

Once at sea again, forecasting is based on constant observation. This is the fundamental discipline. Keep it up, day after day, and you get the habit of 'living' the weather. Unconsciously, the variations of temperature, the gradations of light and the beat of the wind are noticed and recorded. A new sixth sense is acquired which helps you on the road to reliable forecasting and you will have mastered the theory and be putting it into practice with instinctive sensitivity of the old salts.

Part 5.
Navigation

Navigation is the art of conducting a ship from one place to another using all available methods of position finding to check that the chosen course is being followed.

This definition does not imply that it is confined to vessels on the high seas. It begins from the moment when, being some distance from the shore, you turn round to see how far off you are – the distance you have covered over the ground. It hardly arises on board a dinghy – except perhaps in a few special cases when you want to know the best tack to take between one buoy and the next. When out for a day, sailing or fishing, some basic knowledge is required: how to use landmarks along the coast, taking account of tides and eddies, reading a chart and using a compass. But for coastal cruising this is not enough: you must then learn to use more complicated methods and instruments; how to make a fix, how to set course and how to keep it. This is already true navigation. We shall deal first with coastal cruising by outlining what you must know to sail a small cruising boat like the *Mousquetaire*, which can be used both for inshore pilotage and offshore sailing.

We have two main points to make.

The first is to make clear the enormous difference there is between theory and practice in navigation, especially when the practice takes place in the cabin of a small boat. It is easy to grasp the principles on *terra firma*; but the art of navigation has not been acquired until it has been put successfully to the test in a confined space when the sea gives you no rest. So we shall as far as possible concentrate on simple methods and ways of avoiding dangerous mistakes. There will be a few refinements thrown in which can be used only in fine weather. They are of no use at other times.

The second point is to use non-technical terms to explain the theory and to illustrate it with concrete examples which will sometimes even take the place of theory. The techniques used in navigation are really a special way of looking, reasoning and reacting that is peculiar to being at sea. It is this faculty that has to be acquired. All the examples will only be fully understood if it is appreciated that navigation is, in the long run, an art which demands both discipline and intuition, caution and boldness (a boldness that is a sort of superior caution), modesty and persistence. For some it is an all-absorbing passion, a sort of comprehensive discipline in which mathematical reasoning and poetic insight assume their real unity in the pursuit, not only of the right course but of that 'sea-sense' which the right course will entail.

18. What You Need to Know

Landmarks, Charts and Sailing Instructions

Too many people go out in boats with a picnic lunch, some beer and nothing else. And of course that is not enough if you are not to lose your way. First, you must know how to recognise and use the various landmarks along the coast: by day, the beacons and buoys and, by night, the lights; and in fog, the foghorns and whistles. With their help you can both check on your position and keep your distance from the coast. Equally importantly, you must be able to calculate the distance between your keel and the bottom. So you must know about tides: the height of water at any hour of the day and how the tidal streams vary at each stage of the tide. All this information is given in books, such as the *Admiralty List of Lights and Tide Tables*. Study them in conjunction with the chart and Pilot books.

In this chapter we shall deal with land and sea marks and the works of reference. First of all there are *Reed's Nautical Almanac* and the Admiralty Pilots published in Britain and the *Coast Pilots of the Oceanographic Office* in the United States; and in France, *Renseignements relatifs aux documents nautiques et à la Navigation*, known as SH 1. This chapter, it must be emphasised, is not meant to replace these essential publications but simply to guide you through them.

Landmarks

Our forebears had good eyes and noses. The only marks they had to locate their position at sea by were on the coast itself. A high point peculiar to a stretch of shore or on the hinterland a distinctive tower or spire, a tumulus, fort, a particular rock or just a

604

No shortage of landmarks on this part of the coast; and next year there will be still more

clump of trees was all they had to find out where they were and to get back to their home port.

In our days, landmarks, the fixed and clearly visible points on the coast, are still precious. You must however take into account that they change more quickly than they used to do. A steeple, a factory chimney or a water tower, whose prime function is not to help the navigator, can be masked from one day to the next by the progress of civilisation, or more uncommonly alas, by vegetation. The only safe landmarks are the official ones – a whitened rock, a lighthouse or a daymark which are described in the pilot books and carefully maintained and protected against the 'developers'.

The Buoyage System

The buoyage system is organised for the use of mariners in Britain by Trinity House and other bodies. It includes buoys and all types of beacons and marks.

How to Recognise a Mark

Each buoy and mark has a precise meaning, shown by its shape, colour and topmark.

The shapes are can, conical, spar (or pillar) and spherical.

The colours are red, black, green and yellow. Rust colour only means that the mark is badly maintained, but that is fairly rare.

The topmark (can, cone, sphere, cross or T) removes all doubts about their meaning as it repeats the indications given by the colour, sometimes with additional information.

The buoyage system is divided into two:

- one is used to mark both sides of a channel (entry into a harbour, estuary etc.): this is the *lateral system*;
- the other marks dangers where there is no definite channel: this is the *cardinal system*.

The Lateral System

This is international and is found at the entrance to channels and ports virtually throughout the world.

It is designed for ships coming in from the open sea. Therefore when you are leaving port the directions are reversed. The lateral marks are basically either black or red and, very simply: all marks painted black and with a conical topmark pointing upwards (and possibly with a green or white light) should be left to starboard.

All red marks topped with a red can shape (with red or white light) should be left to port.

These marks are numbered from seawards. Red marks have even numbers and black ones odd numbers.

It is convenient that the colour of the lights corresponds to ships' navigation lights – red to port, green to starboard.

In some estuaries the marks are painted with 'dayglow' paint – very conspicuous in the beam of a light (but the cones of the starboard marks are painted dark green).

The lateral system also includes marks showing where different channels join or separate. These marks are painted in black or red horizontal stripes on a white background. The course to follow is clearly indicated by the topmark crowning it. You do not, however, have to learn all of these topmarks by heart (unless you are taking an examination) as you have on board reference books giving their description. If you are in the slightest doubt, refer to them.

Sometimes the colours in the lateral system are chequered. This has no significance and is to make a mark more conspicuous when it might blend into a background.

The Cardinal System

Until recently this system has been used only in French waters

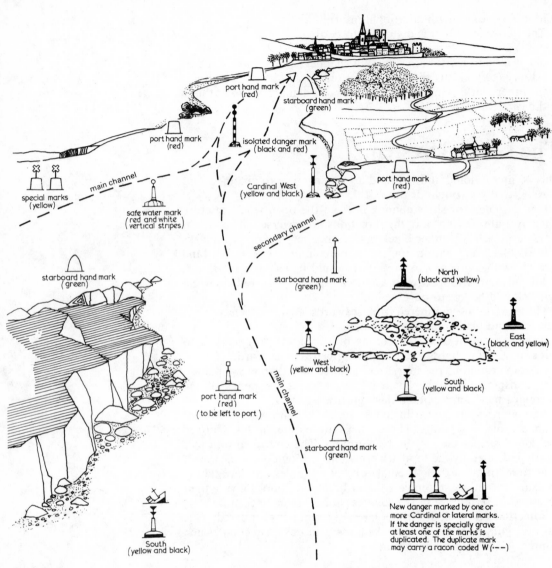

port hand mark
(red)

starboard hand mark
(green)

port hand mark
(red)

isolated danger mark
(black and red)

Cardinal West
(yellow and black)

port hand mark
(red)

special marks
(yellow)

main channel

safe water mark
(red and white
vertical stripes)

secondary channel

starboard hand mark
(green)

North
(black and yellow)

starboard hand mark
(green)

East
(black and yellow)

West
(yellow and black)

port hand mark
(red)
(to be left to port)

main channel

South
(yellow and black)

starboard hand mark
(green)

New danger marked by one or
more Cardinal or lateral marks.
If the danger is specially grave
at least one of the marks is
duplicated. The duplicate mark
may carry a racon coded W (·——)

South
(yellow and black)

IALA Combined Cardinal/Lateral Buoyage System

and serves to mark both coastal and offshore dangers. The system is very simple in that each of the marks has its own quadrantal position defined in relation to the danger. For example, a south mark is placed to the S of the danger and we must therefore pass to the S of the mark.

A mark can be recognised from a distance by its colour and closer to by its topmark. North and west marks are black, south and east are red.

As for the topmarks, two cones point upwards to the N and, very logically, two cones point downwards to the S. In order to remember east and west marks, study the diagrams. A Cardinal mark covers a precise compass quadrant so a west mark indicates that an area free from danger is to be found between NW and SW of it.

Other Marks

Transition Mark. The transition mark indicates that when you are approaching a port, for instance, you are moving from the cardinal system to the lateral system.

This mark is painted in oblique bands, red or black, on a white background, and surmounted by a papal cross (like a cross of Lorraine, but with the two arms the same length). It will have, according to the circumstances, a topmark of either system.

North cardinal: indicates the top of the chart

South cardinal: indicates the bottom of the chart

West cardinal: by tilting your head you can see a W in it

East cardinal: you can see an E in it

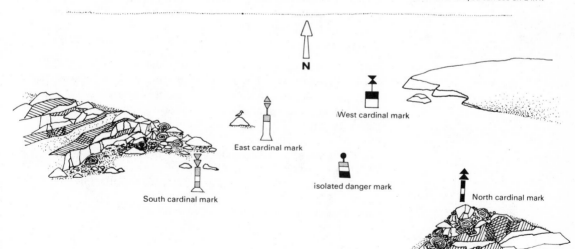

N

West cardinal mark

East cardinal mark

isolated danger mark

South cardinal mark

North cardinal mark

Cardinal marks indicate the side that is free of dangers

Isolated Danger Mark. This mark indicates a danger of limited extent and it is moored on top of it. It is generally spherical, or in any cause surmounted by a sphere, which indicates that it can be left on either hand. It is painted in broad red and black bands, sometimes separated by narrow white bands.

Landfall Mark. This mark indicates the approach of land to vessels coming from the open sea. Painted in vertical red stripes (more unusually black) it has a cross topmark and a flashing light.

Wreck Marks. Wreck marks are green, including their topmark and, if they have one, their light. They sometimes carry the letter W in white or the word Wreck. These marks can belong to the lateral system (with cone, cylinder or sphere) or to the cardinal system; in the latter case, only the east and west marks are used.

The IALA 'A' System

Starting in 1977, the IALA 'A' system of buoyage will be progressively introduced in North-European waters. The system has the simplicity of combining the use of Lateral and Cardinal marks and it introduces Safe Water marks and Special marks.

Lateral Marks

Lateral marks are used to mark the sides of a well defined channel.

Porthand Marks are red and can or spar shaped, often with a single red can topmark. Its light will be red with any rhythm.

Starboard Hand Marks are green and conical or spar shaped. If there is a topmark it will be a single green cone, pointing upwards. Its light will be green, with any rhythm.

Cardinal Marks

Cardinal marks are used to indicate the safe side of a danger on which to pass, the deepest water in an area or to draw attention to a bend, junction or fork in a channel. The buoys are normally pillar but may be spar, black and yellow, always with black cone topmarks, and lights are always white, flashing, and marks and rhythms are as follows:

North Quadrant – yellow base, black pillar, very quick flashing (VQkFl) or quick flashing (QkFl).

East Quadrant – yellow and black base, black pillar, light – VQkFl (3) every 5 seconds or QkFl(3) every ten seconds.

South Quadrant – black base, yellow pillar, light VQkFl(6) + LFl every 10 seconds, or QkFl(6) + LFl every 15 seconds.

West Quadrant – black and yellow base, yellow pillar, light VQkFl(9) every 10 seconds or QkFl(9) every 15 seconds.

Other Marks

Isolated Danger Marks mark a small isolated danger with safe water all round. Colour – black with one or more horizontal red bands; topmark – 2 black spheres; shape – pillar or spar; light – white, gp fl (2).

Safe Water Marks indicate mid-channel or landfall. Colour – red and white vertical stripes; shape – spherical, pillar or spar with spherical topmark; light – white, isophase, occulting or 1 long flash every 10 seconds.

Special Marks are not to assist navigation. Their purpose may be determined from the chart. Colour – yellow; shape – optional, not conflicting with navigational marks; topmark (if any) – single yellow X; light – yellow, rhythm not conflicting with white navigational lights.

Remarks on the Uniform Buoyage System in British Waters

Until recently all marks were lateral and formed part of an imaginary channel running in the general direction of the flood tide.

These British marks, at first sight, often look slightly odd but, close to, they have no fundamental difference from marks anywhere else, except in one particular: the cylinder of the porthand marks is replaced by a section of a cone.

Lights

Lights are shown by lighthouses, lightships, beacons and buoys. At night, they give a simple and remarkably clear outline of the coast, so much so that landfalls are usually easier to make out at night than by day.

The characteristics and positions of lights are given in detail in lists of lights, and on charts they are marked in magenta and described in abbreviations.

Each light has its own distinguishing colour, characteristics, phase and period.

Colour. White, green, red. Other colours are sometimes used, but only in ports and rivers.

Characteristics. These are mainly fixed, flashing, occulting, isophase and quick flashing:

Lenses for group flashing two flashes Light visible all round. In contrast to the one above, it does not turn: the phase is obtained by switching on and off. A flashing, occulting, fixed, quick-flashing or isophase pattern can be achieved

Revictualling and inspection of the Armen light house

– fixed light: a continuous steady light.
– flashing: the light periods, called the 'flashes', are much shorter than the periods of darkness.
– occulting: the periods of darkness, called the 'occultations', are much shorter than the periods of light.
– isophase: a light showing equal intervals of light and darkness.
– quick flashing: an isophase light with a very fast rhythm (more than 40 flashes a minute).

Rhythm. The periods of light and darkness give the rhythm of the light.

In occulting lights, for instance, three sorts of rhythm are found:
– the periods of light between each occultation are always of the same length and the light is called regular, that is a light with one occultation, e.g. Basse-Bilien in the light rhythm diagram;
– the occultations, separated by short periods of light, are grouped in two, three or four, a much longer period of light separating each group, e.g. Les Moutons which has two occultations (see light rhythm diagram);
– the occultations are in mixed groups such as the Trévignon light with only a short period of light between the three and a longer period of light separating them from the one occultation.

The principle is the same for flashing lights.

Period. The period of a light is the time occupied in exhibiting one complete sequence. The Trévignon light, for instance, has a period of twelve seconds from the first occultation of the group of three until the first occultation of the next group of three.

PHARE D'ARMEN.
Ravitaillement et Inspection du Phare.

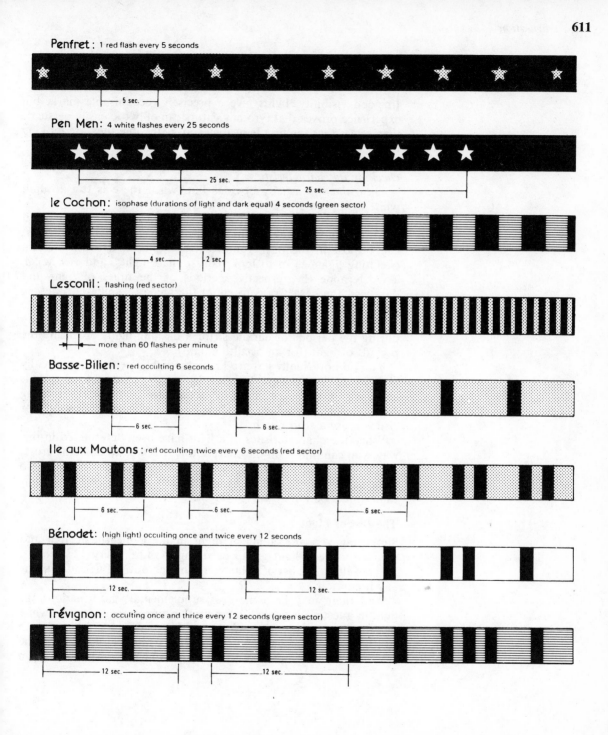

Penfret : 1 red flash every 5 seconds

5 sec.

Pen Men : 4 white flashes every 25 seconds

25 sec. 25 sec.

le Cochon : isophase (durations of light and dark equal) 4 seconds (green sector)

4 sec. 2 sec.

Lesconil : flashing (red sector)

more than 60 flashes per minute

Basse-Bilien : red occulting 6 seconds

6 sec. 6 sec.

Ile aux Moutons : red occulting twice every 6 seconds (red sector)

6 sec. 6 sec. 6 sec.

Bénodet : (high light) occulting once and twice every 12 seconds

12 sec. 12 sec.

Trévignon : occulting once and thrice every 12 seconds (green sector)

12 sec. 12 sec.

How to Recognise a Light

In good visibility, lights give a precisely recognisable mark, but experience proves that tyro navigators can only too easily persuade themselves that the first light they spot is the one they are looking for.

To identify a light, you must make no assumptions, start by calmly checking its characteristics.

The *colour* is usually obvious but, when there is fog around, white lights can appear reddish.

The *characteristics* of the light appear without any doubt when it is a flashing or quick flashing light. Some fixed lights, however, can be lost in the background of the lights of a town. Certain occulting lights seem to look like isophase lights, and *vice versa*. To determine the respective periods of the times of light and darkness, the best way is to count the seconds regularly (one *and* two, *and* three *and* four, etc. is one way of doing it).

The rhythm of the light is discovered by counting in the same way during the periods of darkness (for a flashing light) or during the periods of light (for an occulting light).

You do not usually have to know the light's period for normally all lights in one area are different. If there is any doubt the cycle is again measured by counting in seconds (as above or by reciting A1, A2, A3, etc., which usually gives a sufficient indication), or else you use a stop watch.

When the characteristics of a light have been determined in this way, you can find it on the chart and it is as well to do some cross-checking on its position in relation to other lights or bearings, so as to be absolutely sure. All this demands practice and no opportunity must be missed for getting it.

The List of Lights

Supposing you are sailing at night in the Concarneau area and you see a green light group occulting 1 and 3 every 12 seconds. By consulting the list of lights you can pick out Trévignon without any hesitation.

And there may be a mass of supplementary information: the light in question is green but from other directions it may be white or red. That means it is a *light with sectors*. The colour of each sector has different meanings. Often, the white sector indicates the safe zone (an entrance channel for instance) while the red and green sectors cover dangers. But this is not always so and only a scrutiny of the chart will tell you precisely what they indicate.

A light's intensity varies with the colour: white is the most brilliant (all the landfall lighthouses have white lights), then red, then green.

- In the adjoining column of the list, you find the height of the light: say, 11m above M.H.W.S.
- Next you find the light's range of visibility in its different sectors. This is its luminous range when meteorological visibility is 10 miles according to the standard of the International Association of Lighthouse Authorities. In some countries the IALA definition of range is not used and the list of lights does not take these differences into account.
- The visibility of the Trévignon light, white sector, on the light diagram, is 9 miles. The *geographical range* of the light, or the maximum distance at which the light can be seen above the apparent horizon, is sometimes indicated but only when it is less than the visible range on charts previous to 1972.

The list then gives a description of the structure carrying the light, and its height above ground level. This is very useful for lighthouses are good landmarks by day. And it also obviates a frantic search for a tower when the light is tucked away in a house on a hill.

- In the last column come the details. The intervals between the different aspects of the phase are often complex and may only confuse you. You do not have to read them. The description of the sectors and their limits is, on the other hand, very important. Here we learn that the Trévignon light has six sectors: two red, one obscured, two white, one green. The green sector covers 34°: from 051° to 085°. Be warned: the sector bearings are given *from seawards*; that is, they are the bearings a navigator would take. The green sector of Trévignon therefore covers an area to the WSW of the lighthouse (and not to the ENE, where there are herds of cows and the chapel of Saint Philibert, an architectural jewel of the XVI century).
- The last column also gives, when applicable, information on fog signals, radio beacons, and manning of the lights. Note that buoys are not manned either (except by occasional cormorants). It must not be forgotten either that a buoy light can fail and, especially in bad weather, may not be put right for some time.

The bearings of light sectors are given from seawards. The sector shown (346° to 11°) sweeps an area to the south of the light.

614

Number	Name and Position	Latitude and Longitude	Characteristics and Intensity	Elevation in metres	Luminous range - sea miles
0936	— Le Cochon	47 51.5 / 3 55.5	Iso WRG 4s	9	W10 R 7 G 6
0940	Baie de Pouldohan	47 51.0 / 3 53.7	F G	6	5
0944	TREVIGNON — Breakwater	47 47.6 / 3 51.3	GpOcc(1+3)WRG 12s	11	W9 R6 G5
0945	Mole . Head	47 47.7 / 3 51.3	Fl G 4s	..	7
0946	PORT MANECH — Pointe de Beg-ar-Vechen	47 48.0 / 3 44.4	GpOcc(4)WRG 12s	38	W10 R 7 G 6
0950	Brigneau. Mole. Head	47 46.9 / 3 40.2	GpOcc(2)WRG 6s	7	W9 R6 G5
0952	Merrien	47 47.1 / 3 39.0	QkFl W	26	11

Extracts from pages 43–44 of the
Admiralty List of Lights (Vol D, 1976).

Description and height in metres	Remarks: phase sectors, arcs of visibility. Minor lights
Black tower, white diagonal stripes 13	G048°–205°(157°),R205°–352°(147°)' W352°–048°(56°)
White square tower, green top 6	Vis 053°–065°(12°)
White square tower, green top 7	ec 1, lt 3, ec 1, lt 1, ec 1, lt 1, ec1, lt 3. W004°–051°(47°), G051°–085°(34°), W085°–092°(7°), R092°–127°(35°), R322°–351°(29°)
	fl 1
White round tower, red top 8	ec 1, lt 1, ec 1, lt 1, ec 1, lt 1, ec 1, lt 5. W(unintens) 050°–140°(90°), W140°–296°(156°), G296°–303°(7°), W303°–311°(8°), R311°–328°(17°) over Les Verres, W328°–050°(82°). Obscured by Pointe de Beg-Morg when bearing less than 299°
White column, red top 6	ec 1, lt 1, ec 1, lt 3. G280°–329°(49°), W329°–339°(10°),R339°–034°(55°))
White square tower, red top 7	Vis 004°–009°(5°)

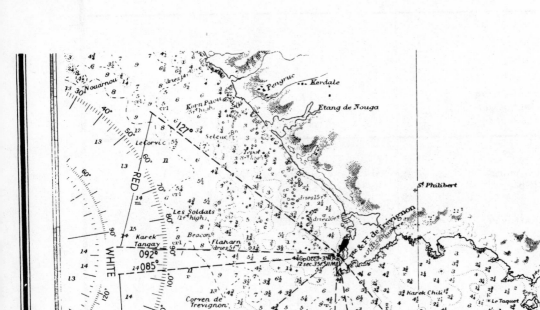

Trévignon light and its sectors
(Admiralty Chart 2352)

Other Publications

There are many good nautical almanacs and sailing guides which summarise the information given in the various official works.

The Chart. Coastal navigation charts can only give a brief resumé of all this vital information. Light sectors are shown and their characteristics given in abbreviations – Gp.Occ.(4)WRG. 12 sec. 125ft 15. 10. 9m (see Beg-ar-Vechen light, page 614). This indicates a group occulting light, occulting every twelve seconds with white, red and green sectors visible respectively at fifteen, ten and nine miles from a height of 125ft. Note that there is often a discrepancy between the ranges of lights given on charts and those given in the list of lights. This is due to the fact that until 1972 the geographical range of a light was inserted on charts unless the luminous range was less than the geographical range. New editions of charts issued after that date and the Admiralty List of Lights only show the luminous or nominal range.

When the colour of a light is not indicated, then it is a white light that is shown.

Be sure, however, that the information on the chart is treated with the greatest circumspection, in case it has not been kept strictly up to date. The same is true for the list of lights. Modifications are carried out quite frequently. One of the tasks of a good navigator is to keep his charts and reference books up to date with all the latest corrections. Like the punishment of Sisyphus, it is a never-ending task.

Corrections

Corrections to the list of lights are broadcast in 'Urgent notices to Mariners' at the end of the weather forecasts from coastal stations. The names of lights which are out, and those brought back into service are announced. These corrections are also given in the *Notices to Mariners* published by the Hydrographic Departments. They are issued weekly and published as an Annual Summary. You must have the latest of these notices (it cancels all preceding ones) and consult it at the same time as the list.

If, on the chart opposite, for instance, you had checked the Trévignon light you would have noticed that a green flashing light (every 4 secs) has been added at the end of the breakwater and that therefore the chart needs correction.

Special Lights

Besides the ordinary lights already mentioned, there are some special lights. Among them are:
Directional Lights. They have a narrow sector in one direction

System of lenses for an intensified sector light. It is brighter at the centre than at the edges

only and act as a single leading light. Within the sector the light is very much brighter than on either side.

Auxiliary Lights. On the same structure as the main light of a harbour, covering a particular danger or indicating a passage. These lights are weak so as only to be seen from close to.

Alternating Lights. A continuous steady light which shows changes of colour on the same bearing.

Air Obstruction Lights. These are charted as aero and listed as obstruction. They are often occasional and usually send out a Morse letter. Finally, some sector lights, which do not change colour from one sector to another, but change pattern. One of the most noteworthy is undoubtedly the Cape Corrubedo light, not far from Cape Finisterre, which shows 3 red flashes in one sector, then 3 + 2 red flashes in the next sector. You really have to be wide awake to make out such lights.

Fog Signals

When buoys and lights disappear in the fog, sound signals take over. Old hands still remember the gun shots which used to be heard around the Stiff, on the NW corner of France, on these occasions. Guns are seldom, if ever, used any more, and the signals today are, in decreasing order of power:

- diaphones, with a very deep note (Le Creac'h at Ushant, Le Guéveur on the Ile de Sein, off the Brittany coast have them);
- sirens, usually on lighthouses;
- fog horns, at the end of harbour jetties;
- bells and whistles, on buoys.

Lighthouse sirens usually have the same pattern as the light, with a longer period (if it has 3 flashes every 20 seconds the siren gives 3 blasts every minute). The bells and whistles on buoys being powered by the motion of the sea, follow its rhythm. The characteristics of fog signals are given in the lists of lights.

All these signals do what they can, but in many cases you cannot hope for precise information from them, especially concerning their position. Fog distorts sounds to the extent that you can hear the signal faintly when it is quite near, and even seem to hear it on the left when it is on the right.

That said, sound signals can nevertheless be very useful, as a group of Mousquetaire yachts from Glénans Centre at Baltimore in Ireland discovered: they were able to go right round the Fastnet rock in a peasouper of a night without having seen the light once. The essential, in cases like this, is to check the information given by the signals by tireless use of the lead or echosounder. Radio bearings, of which we shall speak later, are also a help.

It is worth mentioning underwater signals, as yet little used, but they may be very effective.

The Tides

The tide is the more or less regular movement of the rise and fall of the sea, resulting from the pull of the moon and sun on the huge water masses on the Earth. Further explanations can be found in *Reed's Almanac* and the preface to Admiralty and other tide tables.

This movement is not the same in all parts of the world. In some oceans, the cycle of the tide extends over a whole day. On the coasts of western Europe – the only ones we shall treat here – this cycle extends over little more than twelve hours: the tides are semi-diurnal. There are also places where tides scarcely exist (in the Mediterranean for instance).

High Tide, Low Tide

By drawing on a graph the different heights of water observed during the course of a day at a given spot (which never dries) a tidal curve is obtained roughly in the shape of a sine curve.

The tide rises for six hours, twelve minutes on average: this is the *rising* tide or *flood* tide. At the top of the flood, the level remains constant for a short time: this is *high water slack tide*. Then the movement reverses and the sea falls, again for six hours, twelve minutes on average: this is *falling or ebb tide* until the *low water slack*. And the cycle begins again.

The duration of a cycle is, therefore, on average 12hr. 25. The times of high and low water are some fifty minutes later each day.

Spring Tides, Neap Tides

If a curve of the tide is plotted for a whole month, it is found that the difference in height between high water and low water varies from day to day. Tidal movements vary and the *tidal range* varies.

The variations in movement are related to the relative positions of the Earth, moon and sun. When the moon and sun are in conjunction or in opposition (*syzygy*), the range is at its maximum: this is the period of *spring tides*. Spring tides therefore occur around the times of full moon and new moon. Subsequently, the movement diminishes and the tides become less. When the sun and moon are out of line (*quadrature*), the range is at its minimum: this is the period of small or *neap tides*. The neap tides correspond with the first and last quarters of the moon. Then the movement increases again and the tides increase, until the next spring tides. The complete cycle lasts about fourteen and a half days.

Lastly, the range of the tide varies from one moon to the next, the greatest ranges being experienced at the time of the spring and autumn equinoxes (equinoctial tides). The range of the equinoctial tides itself varies from year to year.

Graph showing a period of increasing tides. The range of the evening tide is greater than the morning tide

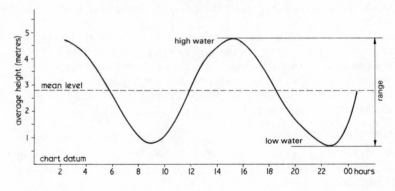

Heights

The pattern of the tide has some regularity and fairly accurate predictions can be made of its characteristics in any given area for every day of the year.

Coefficient. The coefficient is a standard, used in France, indicating the size of the tide in relation to the position of the heavenly bodies. This coefficient is in hundredths and the reference coefficients are:

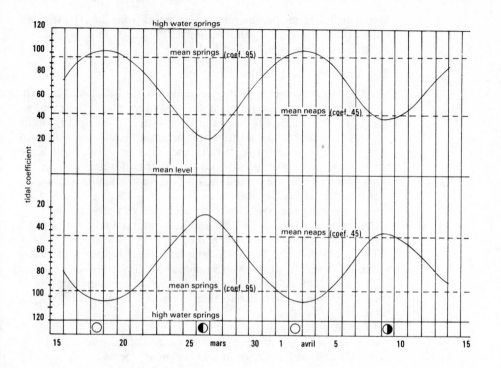

C = 120 for the biggest known tide (maximum astronomical tide);

C = 95 for average spring tides;

C = 70 for an average tide;

C = 45 for average neap tides;

C = 20 for the smallest tide known (minimum astronomical tide).

Tidal coefficients vary from one day to the next

Range. The range of the tide varies considerably from one point to another, depending on the bottom and the shape of the coastline. So that on the same day (and therefore for the same coefficient) the range can be 11.2m at Saint-Malo and 4.6m at Lorient.

However, it must be noted that:

– in every place, the ratio of the ranges is equal to the ratio of the coefficients: the range at maximum spring tide is six times greater than the range at maximum neap tide;

– *whatever the range is at a given spot the level of the sea is always the same at half tide.* This half tide level is called the *mean level*; it is an invaluable reference, as we shall see.

Times. In NW Europe, the tidal wave comes from the Atlantic and moves from south to north. It follows, therefore, that high tide is at different times at Brest and Calais.

The Admiralty Tide Tables

The relative movements of the heavenly bodies being well known, it is possible to predict, for each day and every place, the range of tide, and the times of high and low water. The hydrographic services' computers are set to work, and the results are published each year in the form of Admiralty and other tide tables which are reproduced in many publications – in France for instance in the *Almanach du marin breton* and the English *Reed's Nautical Almanac*.

In French tide tables we find:
- a table giving the coefficients for each tide of the year;
- the times and heights of high and low water at standard ports;
- the tidal differences for *secondary ports*.

They also give the heights of the tide, hour by hour, at places where the tide is 'distorted' (in France at Le Havre and St Malo for instance), a table allowing tide calculations to be made, and finally the corrections to be made to tide levels as a result of barometric pressure.

In most other countries' tide tables we find:
- the times and heights of high water at standard ports;
- the Mean Level at standard and secondary ports;
- time and height differences for secondary ports;
- tables to help the mariner extrapolate the hourly state of the tide in any port.

Times

It is most important to establish just what time system is operating in relation to the tide tables you are using.

Heights are expressed in metres nowadays relating to a datum which is not necessarily the same in all countries.

Certain countries – amongst them France – have chosen the level of the lowest astronomical tide, and we think, on the whole, this is a wise principle for, exceptional cases apart, the depth of water at a given spot is never lower than the depth given in the books.

For other countries, the reference level is *Mean Low Water Springs* (MLWS). When you calculate low water depth of above-average spring tides, you will have heights which will be less than datum.

Tidal Calculations

When you are sailing near the coast, you have many reasons to be interested in the variations of depths. Your wish to keep, at all costs, a decent distance between keel and sea bottom is no doubt your main concern. But you can also calculate height of tide in order to visualise the appearance of the approaching coastline, which rocks will be above or below the surface and for exact points of reference which will define a safe sailing area. Finally, sometimes, and particularly in fog, the combined use of the lead line and tidal calculations will give an answer to the question that gnaws at your mind: Where on earth am I?

In practice, it is a matter of finding, for a given place:
– either the depth of water at a given time, or
– the time when there will be a certain depth of water.

The facts needed to work out these calculations are: the times and heights of high and low water and, in some cases, the coefficient.

When you are near a standard port, there is no difficulty: the tide tables give you the precise facts for the port in question, for every tide of the year.

When you are elsewhere, first you must find from the tide tables the tidal difference (time and height) between the secondary port you are near and its neighbouring standard port. As often as not, in the majority of cases these differences are negligible. You only start making corrections if you find a difference of more than 10 minutes, or more than 0.30 metres.

In the tide tables, you notice that the differences vary according to whether there are spring or neap tides. The difference given is valid for mean spring tides (coefficient 95) and mean neap tides (coefficient 45). If you want to know the precise corrections corresponding to the day's coefficient, you must either interpolate or extrapolate. But often this calculation only brings out minor differences (except in the case of estuaries). Normally, all that is needed is to apply the corrections for spring to tides with a coefficient above 70, and the corrections for neap tides to the others.

You can get an idea of how inexact the calculations are by comparing the difference between the differences for springs and neaps.

Supplied with this basic information, we can now look at the problems in a practical fashion by citing the following example.

It is 9 July 1975 and we are sailing somewhere around Saint-

TIDAL COEFFICIENTS
COEFFICIENTS DE LA MAREE

GMT + 1h
Heures T.U. + 1 h.

H.W at BREST — in hundredths
Heure de la pleine mer à BREST - Coefficient en centièmes

JUILLET 1975			AOUT 1975			SEPTEMBRE 1975			OCTOBRE 1975			NOVEMBRE 1975			DÉCEMBRE 1975		
	h. m.	Coef.		h. m.	Coef.		h. m.	Coef.		h. m.	Coef.		h. m.	Coef.		h. m.	Coef.
8 MA	4 05	76	8 V	5 18	102	8 L	6 23	115	8 ME	6 43	103	8 S	7 52	72	8 L	8 16	66
	16 28	81		17 40	106		18 44	111		19 04	96		20 16	65		20 38	61
9 ME	4 50	86	9 S	6 02	109	9 MA	7 05	106	9 J	7 26	88	9 D	8 41	58	9 MA	9 01	56
	17 12	90		18 24	110		19 26	99		19 49	80		21 07	52		21 26	52
10 J	5 34	93	10 D	6 45	109	10 ME	7 48	91	10 V	8 12	71	10 L	9 37	47	10 ME	9 53	48
	17 56	96		19 06	107		20 10	83		20 36	63		22 10	44		22 22	45
11 V	6 19	98	11 L	7 28	103	11 J	8 34	74	11 S	9 03	55	11 MA	10 46	41	11 J	10 54	43
	18 41	98		19 50	98		20 58	65		21 34	65		23 24	40		23 27	42

CHERBOURG

HRS AND HEIGHTS OF H.W AND L.W
HEURES ET HAUTEURS DES PLEINES ET BASSES MERS

GMT + 1h
Heures T.U. + 1 h.

Lat. 49° 39' N.
Long. 1° 38' W.

JUILLET 1975

Heures h. m.	Haut. m.	Heures h. m.	Haut. m.
8 2 23	1,6	23 3 22	1,4.
8 03	5,7.	8 59	5,8
MA 14 46	1,5	ME 15 42	1,5
20 26	6,0.	PL 21 18	6,0.
9 3 10	1,3	24 4 01	1,3.
8 48	6,0	9 37	5,9
ME 15 32	1,3	J 16 19	1,4
NL 21 10	6,2.	21 55	6,1
10 3 54	1,1	25 4 37	1,3
9 33	6,2	10 12	5,9
J 16 17	1,1	V 16 53	1,4
21 55	6,4.	22 28	6,1
11 4 39	0,9.	26 5 09	1,4
10 17	6,3	10 45	5,9
V 17 01	1,0.	S 17 26	1,4.
22 39	6,5	23 00	6,0

AOUT 1975

Heures h. m.	Haut. m.	Heures h. m.	Haut. m.
8 3 38	0,9	23 4 13	1,2.
9 16	6,4	9 48	6,0
V 16 01	0,8.	S 16 28	1,3
21 39	6,7	22 03	6,1.
9 4 23	0,7	24 4 43	1,2.
10 01	6,5.	10 17	6,0
S 16 45	0,7.	D 16 57	1,3.
22 22	6,7.	22 32	6,1
10 5 06	0,6.	25 5 12	1,3
10 43	6,5.	11 04	5,9.
D 17 27	0,7.	L 17 27	1,4
23 04	6,7	23 01	6,0
11 5 48	0,7.	26 6 15	1,4.
11 25	6,4	11 15	5,8.
L 18 10	0,9.	MA 17 56	1,5.
23 46	6,4.	23 29	5,8

SEPTEMBRE 1975

Heures h. m.	Haut. m.	Heures h. m.	Haut. m.
8 4 44	0,5	23 4 43	1,3
10 21	6,7.	10 16	6,1
L 17 05	0,6.	MA 16 57	1,3.
22 42	6,8	22 31	6,0.
9 5 26	0,7	24 5 12	1,4
11 03	6,5.	10 46	6,0
MA 17 47	0,9	ME 17 27	1,5
23 23	6,5	23 01	5,9
10 6 08	1,0.	25 5 42	1,6
11 44	6,2	11 16	5,8
ME 18 30	1,3	J 17 57	1,7
		23 32	5,7
11 0 05	6,0.	26 6 14	1,8.
6 51	1,5	11 49	5,6
J 12 29	5,8	V 18 32	2,0
19 16	1,7.		

HRS. AT CHERBOURG — HEIGHTS AT CHERBOURG

NOM DU PORT	LAT. N o '	LONG. o '	Mean level Niveau Moyen m	HEURES AU PORT DE RÉFÉRENCE				HAUTEURS AU PORT DE RÉFÉRENCE			
				H.W Pleines mers		L.W Basses mers		H.W Pleines mers		L.W Basses mers	
				Sp V.E. h.m.	Np M.E. h.m.	Sp V.E. h.m.	Np M.E. h.m.	Sp V.E. m	Np M.E. m	Sp V.E. m	Np M.E. m
CHERBOURG pages : 67-71	49 39	1 38W	3,78	9 51 / 21 51	3 26 / 15 26	4 24 / 16 24	10 01 / 22 01	6,3.	5,0.	1,1.	2,5.
Saint-Vaast-la-Hougue	49 34	1 16	3,80	+0 53	+1 08	+1 20	+0 58	+0,2.	+0,3.	−0,2.	−0,2.
Barfleur	49 40	1 15	3,79	+0 51	+1 00	+0 48	+0 35	+0,0.	+0,2	−0,1	−0,1
Omonville	49 43	1 52	3,76	−0 09	−0 14	−0 18	−0 26	−0,1.	−0,0.	0,0	+0,1

Vaast-la-Hougue, on the east coast of the Cotentin peninsula. This is a good illustration for us because Saint-Vaast is a secondary port, where the range and times of the tides are very different from its neighbouring standard port, Cherbourg, This will allow us to examine every aspect of the problem.

We want to know the times and heights of high water for the following night and, in particular:
– what will the depth be at Saint-Vaast at 23.30;
– when will there be 4m of water.

The first thing to be done is to look for the basic details of the tide at Saint-Vaast.

High and Low Water at a Secondary Port

We look in the tide tables for the three facts we need:
– tides at Cherbourg on 9 July;
– correction to be made for Saint-Vaast;
– the day's coefficient.

We find that the coefficient is 90. The corrections to be made are therefore the ones for springs.

Which give us:

High Water Cherbourg	21.10	6.2m
Corrections	+ 53	+0.2m
High Water Saint-Vaast	22.03	6.4m
Low Water Cherbourg	03.54	1.1m
Corrections	+ 1.20	−0.2m
Low Water Saint-Vaast	05.14	0.9m

Depth of Water at a Given Time

There is no lack of ways and means of calculating depth. There is one for every circumstance and to suit all tastes. Some navigators are allergic to using pencils and others cannot count up to twelve. So we shall propose enough methods to please most types (and especially those who find tidal calculations fascinating). It is just as well to be warned beforehand however that it isn't always necessary to go in for very precise calculations; very often you must

626

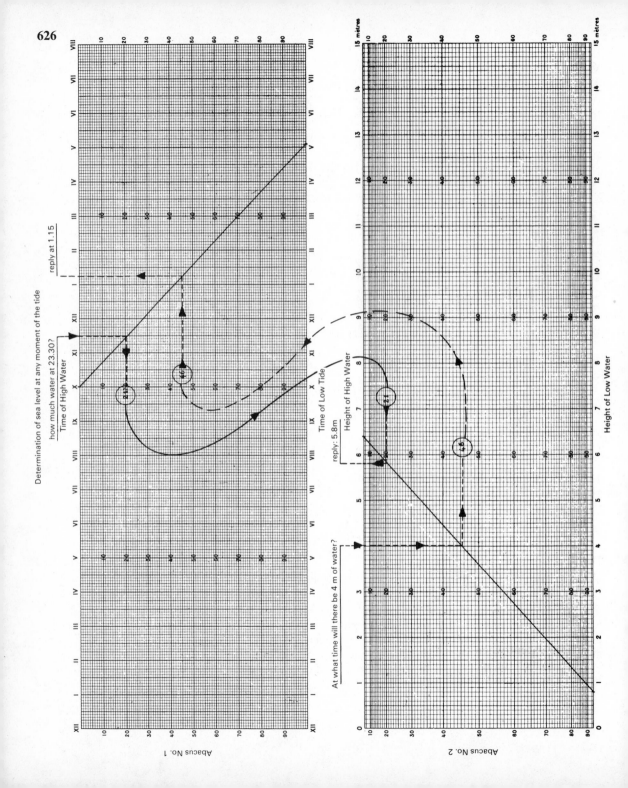

Determination of sea level at any moment of the tide

how much water at 23.30?

reply at 1.15

Time of High Water

Time of Low Tide

Height of High Water

reply: 5.8m

At what time will there be 4 m of water?

Abacus No. 1

Height of High Water

Height of Low Water

Abacus No. 2

metres

metres

be content with simple estimates, as we shall see after we have gone through the methods.

The Hundreds Method

The hydrographic departments in France have two methods based on dividing the tide into hundredths.

The SH4 Plotter is, without any doubt, the easiest considering that there isn't the slightest calculation to be made. Starting with chronometer time you measure directly the depth or *vice versa*.

The SH4 has two graphs, one for time and the other for heights. The only thing to be done is draw a straight line on each graph: one to join the time of high water to the time of low water, the other to join the depth of water at high water to the depth of water at low water.

At 2330 hours, the depth is 5.8m.

The 4m level is reached at 0120 hours.

The Tables in the Tide Tables. Based on the same principles, the tables at the end of the tide tables are a little more complicated to use. First of all, a calculation has to be made of the range of the tide and the period of time between each. They give as the difference in level or period of time in relation to the depths or times of high or low water.

The Twelfths Method

The twelfths method is based on a simple fact: the tidal curve is very like a sine curve. From one slack water to the next, the sea rises or descends by:

1/12 of its range in the 1st hour,
2/12   ,,   2nd hour,
3/12   ,,   3rd hour,
3/12   ,,   4th hour,
2/12   ,,   5th hour,
1/12   ,,   6th hour.

This is what is called the *rule of twelfths*.

The range being divided by 12 and the time interval between two slack waters being divided by six, it becomes very easy to know the depth of water from hour to hour. It must be noted, however, that the interval being, on average, longer than six hours, the *tide time* is different from clock time. However, no notice is taken of this difference except when the time interval is very different from the average (which happens in the English Channel, for instance, where time intervals can be less than 5 hours, or more than 7

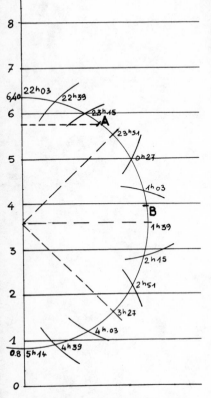

To divide the semi-circle into twelve: three radii are marked, one at right angles to the vertical, the others at 45°: with the compasses, adjusted to the initial radius, you mark out, from the five radii which you now have, the required intersections (the last two are obtained from the intersections which are on either side of the horizontal radius)

hours); practically speaking, one does not make the corrections unless the time interval is less the 5hr 30min or more than 6hr 30min. The rule of twelfths can be used either by calculation or graphically.

The Calculation

First question: what will be the depth of water at 2330?

1. Calculation of a 12th $\left(\dfrac{\text{range}}{12}\right)$

$$\frac{6.4\text{m} - 0.9\text{m}}{12} = \frac{5.5\text{m}}{12} \simeq 0.47\text{m}.$$

2. Calculation of an hour's tide $\left(\dfrac{\text{time interval}}{6}\right)$

$$\frac{(2400-2203) + 5\text{h }14}{6} = \frac{7\text{h }11\text{min}}{6} \simeq 72\text{min}.$$

3. At 2330, the tide has been going down for 1h 30m, that is 90 minutes by the clock, which must be converted into tide-minutes by using a rule of three: $\dfrac{90 \times 60}{72} = 75\text{min}$ tide, that is $1\frac{1}{4}$ tide hours.

The tide has therefore gone down by approx 1.5/12ths, that is: 0.70m. At 2330 the depth of water at Saint-Vaast will be:

$$6.4\text{m} - 0.70\text{m} = 5.7\text{m}.$$

Second question: At what time will the depth be 4m?
When the level has reached 4m, the sea will have dropped by:

6.4m − 4m = 2.4m, that is a little more than 5/12 $\left(\dfrac{2.4}{0.47} = 5.1\right)$

The sea goes down by $\frac{5}{12}$ in $2\frac{3}{4}$ hours tide, that is 165 tide minutes. A rule of three allows us to change these tide minutes into clock minutes: $\dfrac{165 \times 72}{60} = 198$, i.e. 3h 18min. The level will be 4m at:

$$2203 + 3\text{h }18\text{min} = 0121 \text{ hours}.$$

The Semi Circle. On a vertical scale graduated in metres, a semi-circle is drawn with a diameter equal to the range of the tide, taking care to make low water and high water fall at the required depth. The half circumference is divided into 6 or, better still, into 12 equal parts, corresponding to each hour of half-hour of tide.

FALLING TIDE
SAINT-VAAST-LA-HOUGUE. — MARÉE DESCENDANTE 27

12	13	14	15	16	17	18	19	20	21	22	23	HEURES P. M. BREST	H.W at BREST
16 56	17 54	18 52	19 52	20 52	21 52	22 50	23 51	0 53	1 57	2 58	4 00	HEURES P. M. ST-VAAST-LA-HOUGUE	H.W at ST VAAST

HEIGHTS OF H·W AT BREST — I AFTER H.W

HAUTEURS DE LA P. M. À BREST — APRÈS P. M.

5,2.	5,5	5,7.	6,0	6,2.	6,5	6,7.	7,0	7,2.	7,5	7,7.	8,0	8,2.	Sᵗ V. La HOUGUE min.	h.
4,7.	5,0	5,2.	5,5	5,7	5,9	6,1	6,3	6,4.	6,6.	6,8	7,0	7,2	0	
4,7.	5,0	5,2.	5,4.	5,7	5,8.	6,0.	6,2.	6,4	6,6	6,7.	6,9.	7,1.	15	0
4,7.	4,9.	5,2	5,4	5,6.	5,8.	6,0	6,2	6,3.	6,5.	6,7	6,8.	7,1	30	
4,7	4,9	5,1.	5,3.	5,6	5,7.	5,9.	6,1	6,2.	6,4.	6,6	6,7.	7,0	45	
4,6.	4,8.	5,1	5,3	5,5	5,7	5,8.	6,0.	6,2	6,3.	6,5	6,6.	6,8.	0	
4,6	4,8	5,0.	5,2.	5,4.	5,6.	5,8	5,9.	6,1	6,2.	6,4	6,5.	6,7	15	1
4,5	4,7.	4,9.	5, .	5,4	5,5.	5,7	5,8.	6,0	6,1.	6,3	6,4	6,5.	30	
4,4.	4,6.	4,9	5 1	5,3	5,4.	5,6	5,8	5,9	6,0.	6,1.	6,3	6,4	45	
4,3.	4,5.	4,8	5,0	5,2	5,3.	5,5	5,6.	5,8	5,9	6,0.	6,1.	6,2.	0	
4,2.	4,4.	4,7	4,9	5,1	5,2.	5,4	5,5.	5,6.	5,7.	5,8	5,9.	6,0.	15	2
4,1.	4,3.	4,6	4,8	5,0	5,1.	5,2.	5,4	5,5	5,6	5,7	5,8	5,8.	30	
4,0.	4,2.	4,4.	4,6.	4,8.	5,0	5,1	5,2	5,3	5,4	5,5	5,6	5,7	45	
3,9.	4,1	4,3	4,5	4,6.	4,8	4,9	5,0	5,1	5,2	5,3	5,4	5,5	0	
3,8	3,9.	4,1	4,2.	4,4	4,5.	4,6.	4,7.	4,8	4,9.	5,0	5,1	5,1.	15	3
3,7	3,8	3,9	4,0	4,1	4,2	4,3	4,4	4,4.	4,5.	4,6	4,7	4,7.	30	
3,6	3,6.	3,7	3,7	3,8	3,8.	3,9	4,0	4,0.	4,1	4,1.	4,2	4,3	45	
3,8.	4,0	4,1.	4,2.	4,3	4,3.	4,4	4,4.	4,4.	4,4.	4,5	4,5	4,5	45	
3,8	3,9.	4,0.	4,1	4,1.	4,1.	4,1.	4,2	4,1	4,1	4,1	4,0.	4,0	30	

Depth of water at 2330: point A at 2330 on the semi-circle is on the horizontal 5.75m.

The time when there is 4m water: on the horizontal 4m, at the point B, we read 0120.

To be readable, this graph must be drawn on squared paper.

Tidal heights

Table of Water Depths

It is important to know that the French hydrographic services publish a Table of Water Depths (ref. Nos 580A and 580B), drawn up as a result of observations, and takes into account any peculiarities of the tide at each place. Giving, in a simple way, the depths of water every quarter hour, this table is clearly very useful when you are are sailing is waters where the tide is distorted. When you have it, you no longer need the tide tables. In France, for example, all you need is the annual supplement to the 580 tables, which is an annual tide table for Brest. Brest is in fact the reference port for the 84 ports in the table.

With this table (page 629), the problems we have at Saint-Vaast are resolved as follows:

1 Calculation of high water at Saint-Vaast-la-Hougue

High water at Brest on 9 July is at 1712.

High water at Brest being 12 minutes after 1700, high water at Saint-Vaast will take place 12 minutes after 2152, that is: 2152 + 12min = 2204.

2 Depth of water at 2330.

Depth at high water at Brest is 7.3m.

At 2330, the sea has been going down for 1h 26min. On the line 1h 30min, in the column 7.2, we read: 6.0m.

3 The time when the depth reaches 4m.

We look for 4m in the column 7.2. On the line 4m we find the indication: 3h 45min after high water at Saint-Vaast.

The level 4m is reached at:

2204 + 3h 45min = 0149.

Special Tables

Certain places on the English Channel have a very particular tidal pattern, such as, in France, in the bay of Saint Malo and the Bay of the Seine, and in England on the Solent, between the Isle of Wight and the mainland. In the tide tables, there are found special tables giving the depth of water hourly at Saint Malo and Le Havre. For the Solent *Reed's Nautical Almanac* gives all the information necessary.

Notes on the British Reference Books

The British reference books on tides differ from the French.

They give the times and depths of high water for the standard ports and the necessary differences for secondary ports, but you have to calculate for yourself the times and depths of low water, from the information given on the mean level and duration of mean rise.

To find the time of low water, you subtract from the appropriate highwater time the duration of mean rise. To find the height of low water you subtract from the height of the appropriate high water twice the Mean Level. For example: It is Wednesday 9 July 1975 and we are bound for St. Vaast la Hougue and we want to know times and heights of High and Low water. The standard port for the St. Vaast is Cherbourg so first we must consult the appropriate table then add or subtract the differences for St. Vaast:

HW Cherbourg	21.10	6.2m
Corrections	+ 0.48	+0.5m
HW St. Vaast	21.58	6.7m

To calculate time and height of low water we now find the Mean Level (ML) and Duration of Mean Rise (DMR) in the table of tidal differences for Cherbourg. For St. Vaast these are; ML 3.9 and DMR 5.18 hours, so:

Time of HW St. Vaast	21.58
less DMR	5.18
Time of LW St. Vaast	16.40
2 × 3.9m (2 × ML)	7.8m
Height of HW St. Vaast	6.7m
Height of LW St. Vaast	1.1m

To find height of water at any time between HW and LW one can either use the twelfths method or the simple conversion table that almanacs such as *Reed's* provide.

Until 1974 the depths were given in *feet* (0.305m). They are now given in metres. They still often refer to the average level of low water spring tides (MLWS). However, gradually the international system is being adopted where chart datum corresponds to the level of the lowest tides known (LAT-Lowest Astronomical Tide).

Warning: there are still lots of charts around where the depths are given in feet or fathoms!

Calculations and Reality

Whatever method is used to calculate the depth of water, you must remind yourself that the results are approximate. In the example for St. Vaast, it will have been noticed, for example, that the results vary according to the method. When the tide is shown by a sine

632

Tidal terms in French and English

HW	*High water*	pleine mer
LW	*Low water*	basse mer
Sp	*Spring*	vives-eaux
Np	*Neap*	mortes-eaux
ML	*Mean level*	niveau moyen
MHWS	*Mean high water springs*	pleine mer moyenne de VE
MHWN	*Mean high water neaps*	pleine mer moyenne de ME
MHW	*Mean high water*	pleine mer moyenne
MLWS	*Mean low water springs*	basse mer moyenne de VE
MLWN	*Mean low water neaps*	basse mer moyenne de ME
MLW	*Mean low water*	basse mer moyenne
LAT	*Lowest astronomical tide*	plus basse mer connue
CD	*Chart datum*	zéro des cartes
Ft	*foot, feet*	pied, pieds
	Rise	montée
	Duration of mean rise	durée moyenne de la montée
	Height difference	différence de hauteur
	Time	heure
	Time difference	différence d'heure
GMT	*Greenwich mean time*	temps universel
BST	*British standard time*	heure Europe centrale (heure en usage en France).

curve, the 4m level is reached a quarter of an hour before half tide. In the table of depths it is reached a quarter of an hour after half tide; and the results are different again according to whether the calculations are made from high water or low water (10min difference). If it is also noticed that the tide tables indicate a mean level of 3.80m for Saint-Vaast, there is really good reason for meticulous minds to despair.

Generally, it is the table of depths of water which give the most accurate results, but the compilers of this table themselves estimate that the inaccuracy (especially around half tide) can be between plus or minus 0.30m and plus or minus 0.40m.

Other factors can aggravate the inaccuracy. One often forgets, for instance, to consult the last page of the tide tables where the necessary corrections for atmospheric pressure are given. The effect of the wind itself, which cannot be exactly calculated, can be quite considerable (plus or minus 20cm to plus or minus 50cm).

In general, in high pressures and with a wind off the land, the depth of water is likely to be lower than that given by calculations; higher when the pressure is low and the wind blows from the sea.

All this amounts to the conclusion that one can do without making very complicated tide calculations. And you get seasick doing it, which increases the danger of mistakes! Except in special circumstances, common sense decrees that it is better to stick to a simple estimation around the mean level; caution suggests that one increases it by a certain margin which is called 'pilot's extra foot'.

Mean Level and the Pilot's Foot

The mean level of the tide being constant for a given spot, we have therefore always available a valid point of reference. This mean level is indicated in the tide tables for every port, standard or secondary.

According to the rule of twelfths, the sea level varies by a quarter of its range during the hour preceding half tide; and another quarter during the hour following it. All that is needed is to calculate this quarter (in our example: $\dfrac{5.6m}{4} = 1.4m$) to have, based on the mean level, two other interesting levels:

one hour before half tide: 3.80 + 1.40 = 5.20m
one hour after half tide: 3.80 − 1.40 = 2.40m

This 'rule of fourths' seems sufficient in most cases, especially if a comfortable pilot's foot is added to the results.

A foot is about 30cm, but it often happens that, as the pilot gets older, so his foot grows longer. Experience makes for caution, and one soon learns that it is pleasant to sail without having to worry continually about whether or not there is enough water. In this spirit it seems to us that the rule of fourths, plus a pilot's foot equal to half the range, ensure complete relaxation (let those who have never gone aground be the first to cast stones at us – if they dare). It is only when circumstances compel one to go below this safety margin that more exact calculations need to be done.

In certain cases, one may be compelled to do with very little water. Let us say that the pilot's foot can reasonably be reduced to less than 30cm if the weather is calm, the bottom sand, and the tide is rising.

Never lose an opportunity to check calculations by direct observation whenever it is possible. A rock, the height of which is shown on the chart, gives a very exact measurement the moment it breaks water. In some ports, too, tide gauges are equally useful.

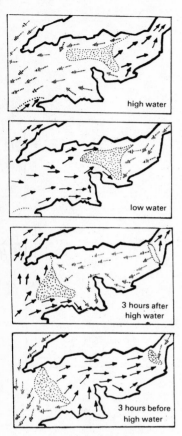

high water

low water

3 hours after
high water

3 hours before
high water

Dover or Boulogne tides

ebb

slack

flood

Tidal Streams

The rise and fall of the tide produces streams, which are obviously periodic and whose cycle is linked to that of the tide.

The stream due to the rising tide is called the *flood*, when it is caused by the falling tide, the *ebb*. These definitions are left vague on purpose since, according to its location, the cycle of the stream does not necessarily follow that of the tide: near the coasts, the slack of the stream usually coincides with high or low water, but, a little further out to sea, this turn can take place at a different time and even at half tide.

The speed of the stream is in proportion to the range of the tide, but it varies greatly from place to place. In the English Channel the currents are swift: 4 to 5 knots on average. They reach even greater speeds in certain narrows: 10 knots in the Raz Blanchard, 8 knots in Le Fromveur. They are weaker in the Atlantic, to the south of Audierne (0.5 to 1 knots) and are only felt near the coast, strengthening (1 to 2.5 knots) at the mouths of rivers, behind certain islands (Glénans, Noirmoutier, Ré) and reaching 6 to 8 knots at the entrance to the Gulf of Morbihan.

The direction of these currents is extremely variable, depending on the shape of the sea bottom and the coastline. Even when it is known that the main tidal stream is eastward, and the ebb stream westward, you are by no means fully informed. To get more exact information, once more we must delve into books.

The Reference Books

All kinds of general and detailed information on the streams is found in the nautical Almanacs and Pilots. Many charts have *insets* in which the speed and direction of the stream are shown, area by area, and hour by hour.

There are tidal atlases for most areas with local tidal streams and currents. For the English Channel, for instance, there is the *Pocket Tidal Streams Atlas*, published by the Hydrographic Dept. This last is very useful when crossing the English Channel but it is less accurate for the coastal areas (except for the Solent and the Channel Isles, which have special sections). It nevertheless shows the times of the turn of the tide for any given spot and this is normally enough.

It must be emphasised again that all the information given by these publications is approximate. Account must be taken of the

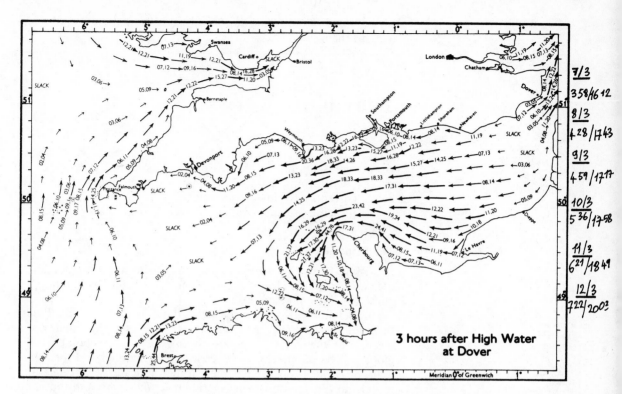

3 hours after High Water
at Dover

caprices of local conditions and of the whims of the wind in particular. A fresh wind, blowing for several days in the same direction, can by itself create a current of 1 to 1.5 knots; it can also strengthen or reduce a normal current by the same amount.

It is also obvious that charts and books cannot describe in detail what is going on at every indentation of the coastline. One must learn to find out for oneself the directions of small local currents. There are indications in plenty: smooth upwellings of water, the movement of seaweed on the bottom, the rippling of the water against the buoy, the angle of a moored lobster pot, patches of turbulence or streaks of foam.

There is no doubt that these currents and eddies are among the more complicated influences at work on the sea but they are not to be ignored. In some channels they can become impassable obstacles. When the wind is against them, the sea becomes broken, very unpleasant, even unsafe for a small boat. It follows that

A page from the *Pocket Tidal Streams Atlas*, English and Bristol Channels. In the margin the navigator has noted for the next six days the times of day when these tidal conditions will recur

currents add to the complications of navigation and we shall come back to them later.

The Chart

The chart is the navigator's basic tool. It gives a very precise visual representation of the sea and coasts and also provides, in abbreviated form, a mass of information about landmarks, buoys, lights, currents and much else besides.

The principles of cartography are well known to all good school children but we will go over them briefly all the same.

The Principles

Realising the size of the world and anxious to find his place on it, man conceived the idea of a simple reference system by dividing the globe's surface into squares.

Parallel lines are drawn between the Equator and the Poles: these are the *parallels*; then lines at right angles to the equator and meeting at the Poles: these are the *meridians*. Any point on the globe can be pinpointed by referring to its parallel and meridian.

Its position in relation to the parallel indicates its *latitude* and its position in relation to its meridian its *longitude*. Latitude and longitude are measured in angles, expressed in degrees and minutes.*

Latitude. The axis of the Poles forms an angle of 90° with the plane of the Equator. The latitude 0° has been assigned to the Equator, latitude 90° (north or south) to the Poles. All latitudes are therefore included between 0° and 90° north or south and are measured in relation to the Equator. Thus, the latitude of the Ile de Penfret (47° 43′N) corresponds to the angle which the plane of the Equator makes with the imaginary straight line joining Penfret to the centre of the Earth.

This angle corresponds to a distance on the surface of the globe. A minute of latitude is equivalent to 1,852m†. This distance has been retained as a unit of measure: the *nautical mile*.

1 minute of latitude = 1 nautical mile = 1,852m.

The Ile de Penfret is therefore 2,863 sea miles from the Equator.

Longitude. There is no argument about the meridian system. Meridian zero passes through Greenwich, in England. The globe

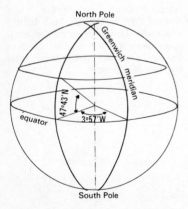

The Penfret light is at 47°43′ N, 3° 57′ W

*The Earth not being a perfect sphere, the minute of latitude is, in fact, subject to variation. It is 1,842.78m at the Equator, and 1,861.55m at a latitude of 85°.

†By international convention, the abbreviations of the cardinal points are: N, S, E and W. It will be guessed that it is the English abbreviations which have been retained.

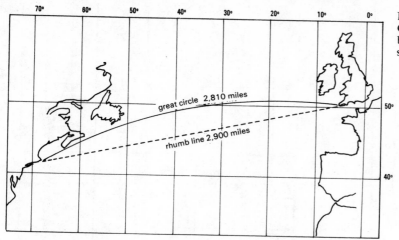

The figure labels: 70°, 60°, 50°, 40°, 30°, 20°, 10°, 0° across top; great circle 2,810 miles; rhumb line 2,900 miles; 50°, 40° on right side.

In spite of appearances, the Great Circle route is the shorter. This can be checked by stretching a piece of string across the Atlantic on a globe

being divided into 360°, longitude is reckoned from the Greenwich meridian, 180° towards the west, 180° towards the east.

The longitude of Penfret is: 3° 57′W.

Distances cannot be measured by longitude as the meridians are not parallel to each other.

Mercator's Projection. On a chart, however, the meridians are well and truly parallel to each other. The reason is that a convex surface cannot be reproduced on a plane without distortion. Something must be given up, either a precise representation of the angles, or an exact representation of distances. As the measurement of angles is indispensable in navigation, charts are normally drawn on Mercator's projection. On the chart the angles correspond to fact. The distances, on the contrary, are only exact at the Equator: the further from the Equator, the more the representation is exaggerated. Around the Poles the distortion is considerable: Greenland, on a planisphere, seems as big as Africa, whereas it is, in fact, fourteen times smaller.

From this distortion it follows that, on the chart, the shortest distance from one point to another does not correspond to a straight line. If you stretch a string over a terrestrial globe between two points on the same parallel, you realise that the string naturally follows an *arc of a great circle* (a circle whose centre is the same as that of the centre of the Earth): the shortest course does not follow the parallel. Now, on the chart, the parallels are straight lines. The navigator who wants to go straight must therefore

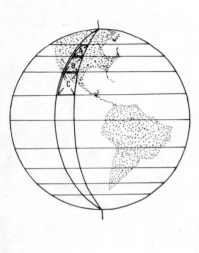

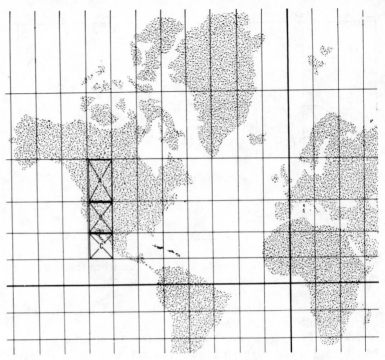

The principle of Mercator's Projection is that an angle on the globe must be represented by the same angle on the chart. For this principle to be fulfilled the scale, ie the ratio between the distances on the globe and the distances on the chart, must be the same in all directions. On the globe the distance between the meridians lessens the further they are from the Equator. On the map this distance remains constant and this means that the scale on the parallels increases with the latitude. The scale must therefore be increased in the same proportions on the meridians

gradually change course. The straight course is called the *orthodromic, or great circle course;* the course by the chart, the *loxodromic, or rhumb line course.* Let it be stated right away that there is no need to take this peculiarity into account on coastal cruises or even on long passages when the distances covered are not great enough for the difference between the great circle and rhumb line courses to make any significant difference in the miles travelled.

Reading the Chart

Reading charts needs practice and great care must be taken as the old fathom chart is slowly being replaced by the metric chart. Their information is often given in conventional signs and abbreviations that must be recognised and understood without mistake. We shall only give a brief summary of them here, for they can be found on Admiralty chart number 5011 which is now published in book form.

Scales

The north and south sides of a chart (north being, as it should, at the top) show the longitude scale, allowing one's position to be related to the Greenwich meridian. You rarely need it.

The west and east sides show the latitude scale which, apart from giving your latitude, is used to measure distances.

The scale of latitudes is variable, as we know, the representation of a minute of latitude increasing as the Poles are reached. If this increase is not always obvious to the naked eye on the scale of coastal navigation charts, it is none the less real and must be taken into account. To find the distance between two points, the distance must be measured at the level of the two points in question.

Depths and Heights

The three zones on the charts are quite distinct:
- the sea, where there is always water, in white or blue;
- the land, *terra firma*, where there is never any water, in an even grey area, bounded by a continuous black line (yellow on metric charts);
- the foreshore, the intermediate area, which is sometimes under water, sometimes dry, in a zone shaded according to the nature the bottom (green on metric charts).

The underwater contours are drawn in fine firm lines which are called *depth contours*, and by *soundings*. The depth of water is measured in metres and decimetres or in fathoms and feet (4_2 means 4.2m or 4fm 2ft for example), so check on your chart.

On metric charts soundings are based on the lowest known depths at low water (coefficient 120). This level is known as the *chart datum*.

All countries do not use the same datum. On fathom charts, for instance, it is the level of mean low water springs which is used.

Every time one uses a new chart, one must therefore check in its title to see which reference level is used.

The *drying heights* are also expressed in metres and decimetres or in feet as appropriate, using the same datum. But on the chart the height uncovered at low water is underlined. *3.5* indicates a point emerging 3.5m at low water.

Heights are also expressed in metres or feet, but relate to mean

The distances are measured on the latitude scale. The distance from the Bodic light to Les Heaux light is six miles (*Admiralty Chart 2668*)

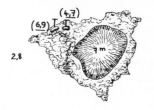

Different datum levels are used for soundings and heights

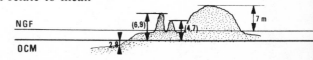

The title of the chart must be carefully read, particularly for the datum levels and whether it is a metric or fathom chart (*Admiralty Chart 1598*). Different datum levels are used for soundings and heights

high water springs, or mean sea level. Brackets are used whenever the figure expressing height is necessarily set apart from the object. To avoid any confusion with soundings, the figures are followed by the letter *m*.

The Landscape

The scales and levels give basic facts, but the chart has many other bits of information which, together, provide a picture of the landscape which is suited to the peculiar needs of navigators. On the chart, the land looks bare, merely an area for landmarks: it consists only of high points, conspicuous buildings and its stateliest trees. The world is not a reality until we meet the sharply defined edge of the land. It is a curving, uneven region of blank areas between particular features. The most modest buoy has the significance of a village. The magenta marks showing lights catch the eye, much as the lights themselves do at night. In fact the seascape is remarkably faithfully portrayed by the chart, which even gives a hint too of the actual environment.

There is only one way to learn how to read a chart: look at it for a long time, and orientate it with the area it describes. We shall leave it at that and you will find enough to keep you interested in the fold-out chart of Glénans that faces page 656. But you must also look at others on winter evenings. A few good charts are worth all the TV channels rolled into one.

Corrections and Care of Charts

Depth contours are subject to change by shifting gravel and sand banks, and the buoyage system in some areas is subject to frequent modification; hence the necessity to keep the charts up to date. We have already spoken of the *Notices to Mariners* published by the Hydrographic Dept. that notify these changes. These notices are also reproduced in periodicals and yachting association bulletins. They must be consulted, but be on your guard for corrections cannot be published immediately.

Corrections should be made on the chart in indelible ink, preferably magenta, and in the left-hand bottom margin the number of the corrections is entered, with the date. You will then know how up to date the chart is.

Charts are fragile and expensive. The only satisfactory way not to damage them on board is to have a table the same size as the charts (even if you have to trim them slightly round the edges). On a small boat, where space is short, a portfolio secured at each corner seems to us a good alternative: it serves as a container as well as a chart table.

If charts are kept rolled up they are difficult to use. Folded in two or in four, it is soon impossible to read along the folds and they wear out quickly. If they must be folded, turn the printed side inwards.

To repair a chart, line the torn place with a piece of old chart, stuck on with a good glue. Be wary of sticky tapes: unless they are of exceptional quality, they stretch when the chart is folded and make it wrinkle.

Charts can also be coated with plastic and in our experience they have a long life, but it is no longer possible to make corrections.

On this chart the last correction is shown by the figure 1100, the reference number in *Notices to Mariners*

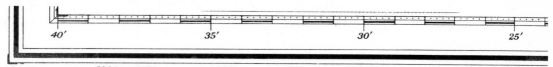

Small corrections 1969-281-1970-462-463-1436-1971-47-189-368-1972-962-1973-1064-1150-2466-1974-295-1241-2133
1975-1949-1976-258-419-567-956-957-2056-1977-1054-1100

To work on a chart with minimum damage, use an **HB** pencil and a soft rubber. Chinograph pencils work well enough on plastic coatings. Lastly, each chart has a serial number, which minimises mistakes and Pilot Books and most volumes of sailing directions list the chart numbers for the areas they cover.

Pilot Books and Sailing Directions

Sailing directions are the fruit of the experience of centuries. They are the sum total of observations made, in every latitude, by generations of sailors. They are constantly being checked, amplified and re-published. They are invaluable. They should be used in conjunction with the charts: they are, in practice, a very detailed companion to them. Originally drawn up for merchant ships, they obviously see everything from a high level, but information for yachtsmen is creeping in, and this tendency will no doubt increase. In any case, although the information is primarily for large vessels, it is useful, provided the effort is made to adapt it for smaller craft.

Each volume of the Pilot Books is divided into two parts. The first is devoted to general information on the area it covers: meteorology, oceanography, geography, regulations, traffic lanes, courses at sea and landfalls. The second is a detailed description of the coast, with its dangers, its landmarks, the buoyage system (by day), the tides, currents, channels, anchorage, ports and their resources. This information is complemented by sketches and panoramic outlines of the coast.

The official Pilot Books have regular correction supplements and new editions appear that cancel all others. Keep your collection up to date.

The vast amount of work entailed in the continual publication of these reference works is done with great accuracy. Considering the amount of information given in them, errors and omissions are extremely rare. Hydrographic departments invite sailors to call their attention to errors and omissions, and this should be done.

All in all, Pilot Books and other sailing directions do more than enable you to find your way. They give you very detailed knowledge of the area in general.

19. Coastal Navigation

Now we can set out. The facts laid out in the previous chapter will begin to have practical use. The landmarks will be used as leading marks for navigating close to the coast. When we are a little further out, we shall take bearings to fix our position accurately on the chart. On the chart, taking into account factors such as leeway and tide, we shall set a course to steer by.

Pilotage, fix and choice of course are the preoccupations of the navigator in sight of land. Further offshore, navigation is clearly a different problem.

Pilotage

In good visibility when there are plenty of landmarks, one can navigate by them, checking your progress as you pass them by: this is pilotage.

The reference works are: firstly, the chart; and secondly, the Pilot, tide tables and the list of lights. An essential tool is a piece of string – as you will learn in the next chapter.

Although the pilot's tools are simple, pilotage is an exacting technique, calling for a strictly methodical discipline. Approximations may be enough when you are sailing in a completely clear area, without immediate dangers: going by relative positions gives an adequate approximation of where you are, and that is often enough. But it is a very different matter when you approach land, to enter into a narrow channel or sail along a coast strewn with reefs. Trusting to flair or the accuracy of vision becomes dangerously hit-or-miss and for a very good reason: at sea, it is impossible to judge distances absolutely correctly by eye. Something more than guesswork is needed. Pilotage consists essentially in taking reference points, and making them work for you by a simple system: leading marks or transits.

Leading Marks or Transits

When two landmarks stand exactly one behind the other, they are in transit. This supplies the invaluable information that the boat is somewhere along an extension of the alignment of the two marks.

What you want, is to have clear transits on the chart which you can recognise easily on the land. Then the coast is yours. With good leading marks ahead, you can enter the narrowest channels confidently. When you have them to port and starboard you can move safely among dangers. With two transit lines you can fix your position precisely for you are at the intersection of the two lines when they are extended. By taking a transit, as we have seen in the first chapter, you can observe the boat's leeway and know how she is making against the tide. In short, for the experienced pilot gazing at his chart, each rock is a potential point for projected pencil lines joining it to other rocks. Used in this way, they can pilot you through the most treacherous channels into harbour.

But the transit marks must be unmistakable, so we shall begin with good landmarks.

A buoy is not a good mark, in spite of its exact outline: it moves a little in wind and tide, and that is enough to eliminate it. The same applies to a moored boat. Permanently fixed marks are needed.

Landmarks must be as clear-cut as possible: a hill without a clearly marked top is not a good mark. Neither is a house too close to you, but its chimney might be. Lighthouses and beacons are perfect marks, and all the more so as they are easily identifiable.

Rocks are less identifiable, but they are often all you have. They must be scrutinised on the chart. Note their size, height and shape (which all change with the depth of water). A rock lost among a mass of others of the same height (or hidden behind a bigger!) is useless. A very large rock, an islet or a headland can only be useful if you pick out their profiles, but remember that the state of the tide can lengthen or shorten their slopes and mislead you.

What you can use for marks would make an endless list. Generally speaking, transit marks are more precise the further apart they are and the narrower and the higher they are.

Landmarks on either side of the observer are in no way to be considered as transit marks, except by sea birds because they have eyes on each side of their heads.

On the other hand, two marks slightly out of line can serve as perfectly valid transit marks on occasion. One mark can be 'open' of another. Rock W, for instance, open to the right of beacon X;

lighthouse Y open 2 widths to the left of tower Z. This sort of transit is used, either because nothing better can be found or because a danger is just on the transit of the two marks; all that is needed then is for the leading line to remain 'open' for the danger to be avoided.

When a course has to be plotted in a rock strewn area, the choice of transit marks must be carefully thought out. The surroundings, in a manner of speaking, must be exploited for your use and natural features have not exactly been created for that purpose. The art of pilotage is using even potential hazards to your advantage.

The pilot must be methodical. Everything must be foreseen on the chart: the course, the leading marks and the means of recognising marks on the ground. Nothing must be vague or obscure. Reasoning must be pursued to the bitter end. Doubt is tantamount to error. Even if everything seems plain sailing, have alternative plans. Once you are committed to a course, do not invent a variation on the spur of the minute, as this is always liable to lead to a dilemma. Do not allow yourself to be distracted: find the marks first, admire the scenery afterwards.

These rules of the game are simple, human reasoning less so. Much depends on the particular circumstances. Theorising in general is not the equal of a good practical example, and we are going to describe one, set in the Glénans group of islands, which is an area particularly suited to this sort of exercise.

To follow the pilot's reasoning, you must have the same equipment as he has: a length of whipping twine and a chart of the Glénans islands. The leading marks are shown on the first fold-out chart facing page 656.

How the Navigator's Mind Works

This is what might go on in the mind of a sailor on the Ile de Groix, some twenty-five miles SE of the Glénans islands: I want to visit my girl friend, Sophie, who is on a sailing course on the Ile de Fort Cigogne, an island in the archipelago (cf. fold-out chart, centre). The wind is WSW and I'm raring to go.

The Entrance

I've looked at the Pilot book and the chart. 'This group of islands is littered with rocks, and there isn't much water between them. To help people move among them, the Pilot book points out some splendid landmarks: on Penfret Island a lighthouse to the north and a signal station to the south; there is another small lighthouse on a rock, le Huic; the fort and tower of Cigogne (will Sophie be on the ramparts?); a landmark on Guiautec Island; a factory chimney on the Ile du Loch; and a white house on St Nicholas Island.

My boat draws 1m. The tide is rising. A quick calculation tells me that there will be about 2.50m water when I arrive.

In front of me, Penfret Island, very recognisable with its two hills, the lighthouse on the one on the right and the signal station on the left. On which side shall I pass?

It is tempting to go in from the south: the chart indicates the wide Brilimec Channel, with a leading mark straight to Cigogne. But to get to this channel I shall have to go round some not very conspicuous dangers in the SE, and I don't like the look of that.

Better to go in from the north. I shall pass close to Penfret; its rocky northern point, Pen a Men, is *sheer*. There is no foreshore.

Once past Pen a Men, there is a very easy entrance between Penfret and an islet called Guiriden, which dries (*8.8*) above chart datum which seems to be highest point of a sand bank, which dries (*4*) above chart datum. Between Penfret and Guiriden, there is enough water. Only one snag: a little rocky plateau, marked (*1.8*), right on my course. When I arrive it will not be visible. I shall therefore have to keep close to Penfret for a while to avoid this bit of trouble (which I shall learn later is called the *Deadman's Head* – some of the people at the sailing centre seem to know it intimately).

Once this danger is cleared, everything is plain sailing as far as Cigogne. There is a (*0.1*) rock in my path, but I have enough water to clear it.

My problem therefore is to find safe leading marks to get round the *Deadman's Head*. I shall first need a line in an approximately north-south direction to avoid going too far west as I sail in; then an east-west line showing me the moment when, having passed the rock, I can cross the barrier represented by my first leading line.

Transit les Méaban by Guiautec

The chart shows an entrance transit. This is splendid but, as it is right into the wind, I can't use it (I shall find out later anyway that this transit is not easily seen from the deck of a small boat). Another way must be found. Ile Guiautec, to the south of the channel, is surely a good landmark as the Pilot mentions its beacon. It remains to find another landmark to line up with it.

I take my whipping twine. I put one end on the beacon and I sweep the stretch of water between the *Deadman's Head* and Penfret; I find nothing. To the south of the beacon there is also nothing (besides, owing to its height, I shall not be able to see anything behind it). Perhaps I shall have better luck along Ile Guiautec itself. West side, no; east side, yes; in a little group of rocks called the Méaban, I find a rock *9.4* above datum whose western edge can line up with the eastern edge of Guiautec. This *9.4* rock suits me well, since it is clearly higher than all the neighbouring ones, and makes a perfect transit for avoiding the *Deadman's Head*: OK at high water, it is even more so at low water, as the transit of Guiautec's foreshore keeps me even further off the danger.

However, even if Guiautec is easily picked out, how am I going to identify my (*9.4*) mark among the rocks round it?

First I must know in what order the rocks will emerge as I arrive. I put one end of my string on Pen a Men and I sweep the channel between Guiautec and Penfret, from west to east. The first thing I come across is Penfret itself: on a level with the lighthouse keeper's house, there is a foreshore which will be covered when I arrive. Then, in the distance low rocks (*3.9*), (*4.4*); then some quite high rocks (*7*), (*7.1*) and, in front of them, sticking out of Penfret, a rock (*5*) above datum which might possibly obscure them partially. It is only when I am a little past Pen a Men that I shall be able to see my (*9.4*) mark and no doubt it will be more or less fused into the mass of other rocks. But, if I believe my string, this (*9.4*) rock has a stretch of clear water immediately beyond it, before two perfectly sheer rocks, one (*6.4*) the other, height not marked, which will merge with each other. I recap: my (*9.4*) rock is the highest and on the left of the Méaban rocks, with water to its left. It seems to me that this is quite clear.

Transit Le Huic by Bananec (6.3)

Now I need an east-west line, leaving the *Deadman's Head* to the north. On the chart, the transit of the summit of St Nicholas through the summit of Bananec seems splendid: it lies right on the path of the danger. I could only use it as an 'open' transit. But I'm

View from point A. Right to left: Guiautec and its beacon, les Méaban, the (*7.1*) rock then the (*5*) one attached to it, the (*9.4*) rock and, further off, the (*6.4*) one – finally Penfret

suspicious. Those 12m and 9m summits aren't Alpine peaks, there must be something round there, and two round summits in transit hardly make a straight leading line. Let's drop it.

To the NW of St Nicholas, there is the Le Huic lighthouse. I like lighthouses, they're clear and sharp, easily identifiable. There are no others around, so I'll try to use it. Put my string on Le Huic, stretched towards the *Deadman's Head*. What I need comes up right away: a (*6.3*) rock at the top of the northern foreshore of Bananec. There is nothing better in the area. But how am I going to identify it?

Only one solution: take the string again and sweep the upper part of the archipelago, from north to south. The first rocks to appear are the Pierres Noires, and Basse Cren, a rather vague collection of rocks. Then Le Huic, just between a rock, Le Buquet, and the first island, Brunec. Then more rocks in the distance. Next, in the foreground, lies the Guiriden sand bank, which dries *8.8* above datum. And then I notice that my (*6.3*) mark on Bananec is right behind the Guiriden peak. I shall not be able to see it when I arrive. Going a little further north, I ought to be able to see it immediately to the right of Guiriden. But this is not certain: the shingle bank to the NW of Guiriden may be just high enough to hide it from me.

I must try something else. By putting my string on Le Huic and by sweeping the stretch of water between Guiriden and Guiautec, I see that Le Huic will be momentarily masked by Brunec, then it will appear to its left: the first rock then to come up before Le Huic is my (*6.3*) Bananec mark. This time there can be no mistake. In any case, if I don't find it at the right time, I can go back and begin again.

I have drawn in my leading lines on the chart and noted the list of marks in my notebook, according to the order in which I must look for them:

le Huic

– Le Huic
– Brunec
– The Guiautec beacon
– The (*9.4*) mark on the Meaban
– The (*6.3*) Bananec mark

View from point B. Le Huic has just appeared to the left of Brunec. The first rock on its left is the (*6.3*) one we are looking for. The slightly lighter rocks are in the background

I am ready. Soon the *Deadman's Head* will be behind me, I shall make some quite short tacks without going too near Vieux Glénan (no older than the rest, surely!), and I shall drop anchor finally, in triumph, beneath the ramparts of Fort-Cigogne.

Exit Route

Sophie wasn't on the ramparts. She must be more interested in her bearded companions than in me. I'm off. Sitting round the fire in the evening beneath the vaults of Fort-Cigogne, I heard tell of a tight little channel between Le Huic and Le Gluet, and I'll choose that. Looking for leading marks will disperse my gloomy thoughts.

This morning, the wind is ESE. The passage seems possible: I shall have the wind free most of the time. To the NW of St Nicholas I shall have to go NE for a while and the wind may be a little too much on my nose, but it seems to me that there is room enough up there for me to make a short tack if necessary.

When I am ready, the tide will be low. There will be about 1m of water. So there is no question of going between Drenec and St Nicholas. I shall have to go south of Drenec.

Between Drenec and Cigogne one can get through. The (*3*) rock on the west point of Cigogne is clearly visible. But the (*1*) rock in the middle of the channel less so. I notice that this (*1*) rock is just in line with the (*8.8*) mark of Guiriden and the (*4.5*) one on the E point of Bananec. All I will have to do, therefore, to avoid the (*1*) rock is to keep this line open, that is, have the summit of Guiriden always to the right of the (*4.5*) Bananec rock. I can easily identify these two leading marks from my anchorage.

So, I shall get under way by taking a wide sweep to the north, as there isn't much water near Cigogne; I shall follow the open leading line I have just found and, when I am abreast of the (3) Cigogne rock, I shall bend my course a little south.

Transit Guiautec by La Bombe

Now I need a line along the south coast of Drenec. There is a channel with enough water between this coast and a (2.5) rock. I put my string in the channel and I immediately find splendid leading marks behind me: the Guiautec beacon and La Bombe. I know the beacon well by now. I saw La Bombe yesterday evening when I arrived and, besides, I can still see it from the anchorage. It is a completely isolated, sheer rock which I shall easily find again south of Cigogne.

The Way Out

I use quite a long string to find my marks, and today I am glad it can stretch from the Guiautec beacon to the west margin of my chart, and I notice that my line Guiautec – La Bombe has another great virtue: it allows me to get straight out of the archipelago westwards if I happen not to pick up my leading marks to go up northwards to Le Huic (you never know, I'm weary and I slept badly). There is only an annoying little (1) rock to the south of the Broc'h beacon. To avoid it, I must stick closely on my leading marks – the Guiautec beacon in transit with the north edge of La Bombe is perfect; all the more so since it makes my passage to the south of Drenec safer still by keeping me clear of the (2.5) rock.

Transit le Gluet by Le Bondiliguet (8.2)

Up to now it has been quite easy. But I next need a line to go northward after clearing Drenec. Among the clutter of rocks I see on the chart, Le Gluet attracts me: it is big, it is high and it must be of some use. I find a good transit – Le Gluet and the (8.2) rock, Le Bondiliguet. But it may not be so easy to pick it up.

The W. edge of Drenec seems to be sheer enough. I'll use it as I used Pen a Men yesterday evening. I put the end of my string on this edge and swing it from west to north. I should see, one after the other: the Broc'h beacon, the only one in the area. Then, in almost uninterrupted succession, a whole chain of high rocks: Castel-Bras, Karek Christophe, Castel-Bihan. Castel-Bihan must be recognisable. It is (10) above datum and is quite sheer on the NE, whilst immediately to its right there is quite a wide channel. Then, in the distance, the two peaks of the Run. After that, it gets very complicated. In the distance the Run, Le Gluet, Le Huic; nearer the Bondiliguet group. I may be able to see Le Gluet, but I can't be sure.

All things considered, it will probably be better for me to use Le Huic again as my mark. Starting from Le Huic, and coming backwards, I must pick them out, one after the other: the (5) rock which lies well off the west point of St Nicholas and hides the exit channel from me; after that (5) rock there is the (9.2) Bondiliguet; then I may see a (6.4) rock and, right in the background, the mass of Le Gluet. The first rock to the left of Le Gluet is the (8.2) rock I am looking for.

I must remember that the leading line, Le Huic – W edge of Drenec gives me the (8.2) rock off Le Bondiliguet, just to the left of Le Gluet.

This means I have a lot of things to identify at the same time. I shall have to keep a sharp look out as I turn round Drenec. And it would be a good thing to take an extra precaution. On the chart, I measure the distance between the transit marks Huic – W. edge of Drenec and the Gluet – the (8.2) rock off Le Bondiliguet. It is 200m. With a following wind, and this fine breeze, I shall be making at least 5–6 knots. Roughly, I shall be across these 200m in a minute. If at the end of a minute and a half I haven't found anything, then I must go back on my tracks. Besides, I have a final mark: Rocher Job, a big isolated rock almost dead ahead of me and which I should be able to identify in the distance. If I begin to make out limpets coming into transit on Rocher Job, then I really will have missed my turn by a good way.

Room to Move

All this is not absolutely clear. I think it would be wise to allow for a little space to manoeuvre to the SW of Drenec to let me turn around for a while until I have found the marks I am looking for. I define this field of manoeuvre by three simple transit marks, two of which are already known:
– Guiautec – La Bombe, which protects me to the north;
– Le Huic – W. edge of Drenec which protects me to the east;
– finally, le Broc'h – Rocher Job, which completes the triangle nicely.

I shall therefore be able to turn around inside it as long as I like. And in the end I *will* see the (8.2) rock off Le Bondiliguet.

I will then follow the leading line Gluet – (8.2) rock almost up to the latter, and there I must turn right to avoid the last two (*6.4*) and (*9.2*) rocks which separate me from the exit. On the chart, it seems ridiculously unnecessary to want a transit to make a little turn like that, but that's the sort of reasoning which lost me my last boat, *Sophie VII*. Besides, to make the turn I have to make a tack, and I run a risk of being really caught out without leading marks.

Another Exit Channel

I note in passing, that if I've really had enough by then I can run clear out to the west by leaving the Broc'h beacon to my left. I shall then leave by the royal highroad of the Bluiners channel. But I'm obstinate and I'm set on going out the way I've chosen.

Buquet and (9.6) and (11) Rocks

I put my string between le Bondiliguet and Roc'h ar C'haor (a very evocative name for those who speak Breton), in a SW–NE axis: the N. edge of Brunec, or more precisely of le Buquet which is just behind it, comes up between two rocks, very close to each other, (*9.6*) and (*11*) which must be easily visible as they are so adjacent.

If I need to make a short tack, I can do it safely by using the line: the N. edge of le Buquet just visible to the right of the (*9.2*) rock will be my northern limit; the same edge obscured the (*11*) rock will be my southern limit.

How shall I recognise all this?

Roc'h ar C'haor must be visible immediately I have passed the transit line le Huic – W. edge of Drenec: it's the first rock of any size to the right of le Huic.

Then, when I am following the leading line Gluet – (*8.2*) Bondiliguet rock, I shall keep a close eye on the territory to my right; once past Drenec, I shall see Cigogne, then the Penfret signal station; at that moment exactly, my two old friends, the (*9.6*) and the (*11*) rocks will be plumb behind Roc'h ar C'haor. I shall see them therefore a moment later. And in the background, to their right, Brunec. No problem.

Leading Line Fournou Loch – Drenec

I need one more north-south line to get me through the channel between le Huic and le Gluet, since there is an awkward (*0.3*) rock in the way.

To find anything useful, I am forced to look a long way off, to the south of Drenec, where there is a group of rocks, Fournou

View from point C. Between l'Ile du Loch on the left and l'Ile de Quignenec on the right, there is only one significant mass of rocks – Fournou Loch. The biggest one on the right is the (9) one – a necessary mark for taking the Huic channel

le Broc'h   le Huic

View from point D. Here the following can be picked out: behind le Broch'h – Castel Bras and then in this order – Castel Bihan, le Run, le Bondiliguet, the (8.2) rock and then, in the back ground, le Gluet. There can be no mistake as the two big rocks (6.4) and 9.2) and a flat bank of rocks (5) are still to be seen between there and le Huic

tombée N du Buquet

View from point E. The (9.6) and (11) rocks frame the north side of le Buquet. The 11m one is hard to make out against Brunec but it can be picked out when the bearing changes since back and middle grounds are quite far apart

View from point F. The (9) Fournou Loch rock can be identified clearly: it can been seen isolated in the background between downward slopes W of Drenec and E of Quignenec respectively. Right on the exit transits

Loch, to the west of the Ile du Loch. These are narrow, quite high rocks *(6.3)*, *(6.8)*, *(8.6)*. But wait a moment: there is a *(9)* rock on the western edge of the group that must be the most easily recognisable. It is just visible to the right of the W. edge of Drenec and is perfect. But it is a long way off and if I want to find it I must locate it very early on, when I pass to the south of Drenec. In fact, I notice that I must almost be heading for Fournou Loch when I'm going south between Cigogne and Drenec. It's the group of rocks just to the right of the Ile du Loch, and the *(9)* rock is the right hand one. Later, when I am near the exit, I shall see the other Fournou Loch rocks disappear one by one behind the W. edge of Drenec and only the *(9)* rock will remain visible between Drenec and Quignenec. And if by chance I miss it (it isn't serious, I have enough water), the line E. edge of Quignenec – W. edge of Drenec will tell me. All I shall need to do is bear away for it to reappear.

Now what I must do is take a careful note of my leading marks, and the order in which I must look for them.

At anchorage:	*(4.5)* rock of Bananec
	(8.8) Guiriden
	La Bombe
Going south:	*(9)* Fournou Loch
On the alignment Guiautec–La Bombe:	Rocher Job
	Le Broc'h
	Castel Bihan
	Le Run
	Le Gluet?
	Bondiliguet?
	Le Huic
	Le Gluet
	(8.2) Bondiliguet
	Roc'h ar C'haor
On the leading line Gluet–Bondiliguet:	The Penfret signal station
	(9.6) and *(11)*
	Brunec, Buquet
On the leading line Buquet *(9.6)*–*(11)* rocks	Fournou Loch

After all that, I can lay course for Loctudy to have my headache cured by Josephine. PS added a few days later: in preparing my leading marks, there is one thing I had not foreseen: the passage is fantastically beautiful, and that is distracting.

Taking a Fix

A little way out off the coast, most landmarks become indistinct against the background. Soon all that remains are a few outstanding points, scattered on the horizon. Leading marks become scarce, one can no longer reasonably hope to find two at the same time to check the course.

Without leading marks the only recourse is bearings. The pilot's string is replaced by more complicated apparatus: the hand-bearing compass and the protractor or a pair of parallel rules. Arithmetic is replaced by geometry and we begin more serious work: we make a fix.

Fixing a position means:
- taking bearings;
- correcting them by the amount of variation;
- plotting them on the chart;
- checking the result.

Taking a Bearing

Taking the bearing of a landmark, means measuring the angle at which one sees it in relation to North.

The measurement is made with a hand-bearing compass, one you can hold in your hand. It has a sight and a prism. A sight is taken on the mark and the bearing shown on the compass card is read through the prism.

It must be appreciated right away that this measurement is not very accurate, specially when it is taken from the deck of a small boat. The further off the mark is and the rougher the sea, the more inaccurate your bearing becomes. One must allow for an error of 1° in flat calm, 2° in normal weather, and easily 5° in heavy weather.

If this margin of error is to be kept to a minimum, practice is needed in the correct use of a hand-bearing compass. The main thing is not to tire yourself out to no purpose. If you first bring the sight of the instrument up to your eye and then sweep the horizon to find a landmark, you will only make your arms ache. It is

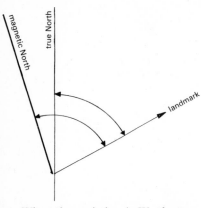

When the variation is W, the true bearing is smaller than the magnetic bearing

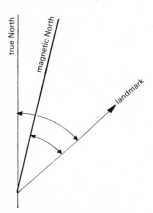

When the variation is E, the true bearing is greater than the magnetic bearing

better to proceed in the following order: find the mark; bring the compass up to the level of your chin and wait for the card to settle; look steadily at the mark, then bring the sight up to your eye and read off the bearing on the card.

It is important not to stand where there is a risk of the compass being deflected by the proximity of metal such as the engine. We shall come back to this later when we deal with the compass itself.

Correcting the Bearing

The compass shows *Magnetic North*, and we know that this does not coincide with *True North* (the direction of the meridians). Before plotting a bearing on the chart, we must first take into account the *variation*, that is, the angle that Magnetic North makes with True North. This angle clearly varies according to where one is. It varies also with time, since Magnetic North is not fixed: it changes very slightly year by year.

According to where one is, the variation is east or west. It is marked on the chart, as well as the annual increase or decrease. In the area of Les Glénans, for instance, the variation was 10° 50′ W in 1945; decreasing by 8 seconds each year, it was only 7° 20′ W in 1971, and it goes on decreasing.

When the variation is east, it must be added to the compass reading. When it is west it must be subtracted. In this way a Magnetic bearing is adjusted to a True bearing.

To remember how to make the correction, mathematicians will recall the formula:

$$T = M + V$$
V positive if it is east
V negative if it is west

– the less mathematically minded may be helped by the doggerel lines:

Variation East Compass least,
Variation West Compass best.

– realists will consult the diagram in the margin.

In any case it's as well to have a trick to know for sure if the variation has to be added or subtracted. What seems perfectly clear when you are comfortably settled in your armchair becomes much less obvious at sea, when the boat is tossing about and a vague queasiness on top of indigestion foreshadows seasickness.

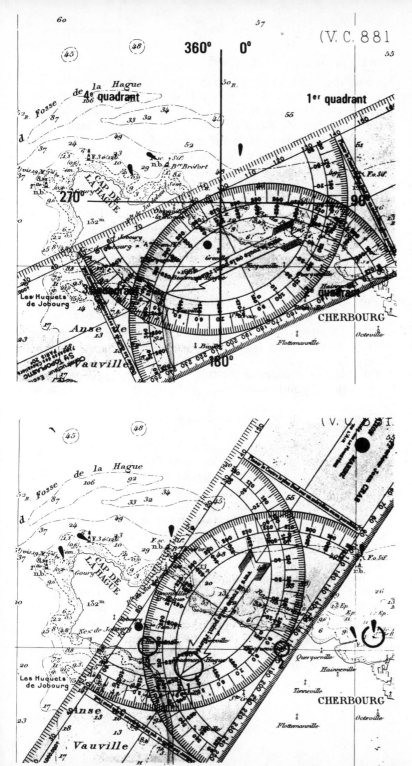

How to use the Cras protractor

A navigator is in the vicinity of the Cap de la Hague. He takes a bearing on the Basse Bréfort buoy at 213° T and wants to plot it on the chart

1. He places the protractor on the chart so that the arrow points in the direction of the bearing taken. The 213° bearing lies in the third quadrant

2. He next brings the edge of the rule on to the mark, then tries to make the southerly centre point of the protractor coincide with a meridian or parallel. Here a parallel is used (the bearing must therefore be read on the inner scale). The protractor is now in place: the arrow (1) is pointing in the direction of the mark; the southerly centre point (2) is on the parallel; the bearing 213 (3) is on the same parallel. To plot the bearing it only remains to draw a line starting from the mark. The boat is somewhere along this position line

Plotting the Bearing on the Chart

To plot the bearing on the chart you need a protractor-plotter (Règle Cras) to transfer the angle from the meridian or parallel. Or parallel rules when using a chart which has a compass rose. Many variations of protractor and set square are also used depending on the yachtsman's taste and nationality.

On the Cras ruler (see diag. p 657) there are two protractor graduations, which allow an angle to be measured from a parallel as well as from a meridian. An arrow indicates the direction in which the ruler must be set, and that is all.

The extreme simplicity of this instrument is at first disconcerting, especially for anyone who hates using figures. But as you move this ruler over the chart you will quickly understand the principle. To plot a bearing, you proceed by stages:

1. Place the chart as straight as possible in front of you, north to the top.
2. Put the ruler on the chart so that the arrow roughly points in the direction of the mark on which you have taken the bearing. This assumes that you know automatically the *quadrant* in which the mark is: a mark on a bearing of 213°, for instance, is in the 3rd quadrant.
3. Put one of the edges of the ruler on the mark. It is convenient to put a pencil point on the mark and to push the ruler up against it.
4. Slide and pivot the ruler at the same time so as to bring at the same time:
   - the most southerly centre (marked by a small circle on the protractor) on to a meridian or a parallel;
   - onto this same meridian or parallel line up the figure corresponding to the bearing taken. There is no need to twist your neck to read it: the figures that are upright are the valid ones. You will realise that of the two scales on each protractor, it is the outside one that applies when you are using a meridian and the inner one when you are using a parallel.

The only problem is to succeed in placing the ruler exactly in relation to its three reference points: the mark, the meridian (or the parallel) and the figures. When the boat is heaving about, this can be something of an acrobatic feat. But when you have succeeded, all that remains to do is to make a mark (or if you prefer, draw a straight line) from the mark to where you are in relation to it. You now have a position line and know that the boat is somewhere along that line, or near enough to it.

If the chart incorporates a compass rose a pair of parallel rules are very convenient. To plot a bearing you lay the rules across the centre of the compass rose and line it up with the appropriate figure on its circumference. The parallel rules are then 'walked' across the chart until one edge is lined up with the mark which you have taken a bearing of and so gives you a position line. If the chart is a recent edition you can use the Magnetic Rose directly. This will make the purist shudder but a tired navigator heaving about in a small yacht will, more often than not, make greater errors in computing Variation and Deviation than in taking this short cut. Anyway, a bearing taken on a HB compass in such circumstances is rarely accurate to within 5°.

A Fix. Of course at least two bearings are needed for a fix. If it is to be good, it is important that the two landmarks should not be too close together. The ideal is to have two bearings at right angles to each other. The diagram shows that inaccuracy in bearings gives rise to a 'quadrilateral of uncertainty' which becomes bigger the nearer the bearings are to each other. This quadrilateral gets even bigger if the marks are far off and the boat is pitching.

A Three Point Fix. A fix by two bearings is seldom accurate. It is usually necessary to take three bearings to achieve some accuracy. If at all possible, these bearings should be about 60° apart.

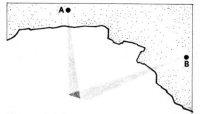

Two-point fix

When you plot these bearings on the chart, you get a triangle, a *cocked hat*, within which, in principle, you ought to be. The size of this 'hat' gives an initial, very approximate indication of the value of your fix. If the 'hat' is huge, there is error somewhere, either in the identification of the landmarks or in the bearings themselves. If it is small, one may at most assume that no glaring mistake has been made, but it is still only an approximation. And if by chance there is no 'hat', if the three bearings cut at the same point, do not exult for, barring a miracle, it's too good to be true. Usually a fourth bearing brings you back to reality.

A Fix by Two Bearings and a Transit Line. Nevertheless from time to time one comes across a transit line. The moment one passes over this transit line is a good time to get a fix: all one needs to do then is to take two bearings and on the chart one gets not a 'hat', but a simple segment delineated by the two bearings on the transit line. One has therefore a more exact fix.

Checking the Fix

When you have plotted the bearings on the chart and have got not too ridiculous a cocked hat, the fix must now be scrutinised and, if

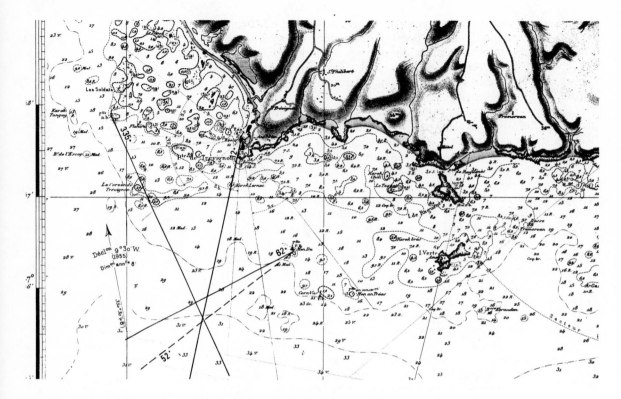

Three-point fix (*Admiralty chart 2352*).

possible, improved. This is done by orientating the chart with the surroundings. Starting from your fix the most notable features you see should have the same bearing as on the chart.

As we are just passing in sight of Trévignon point, let's use it as an example.

The weather is fine and we have landmarks quite close-to and conveniently placed: on the left there is the Soldats beacon, in the middle the Trévignon lighthouse, and on the right the Men-Du beacon.

We take bearings: Les Soldats is 342°
the lighthouse 19°
Men-Du 69°

The corrections for variation must be included as shown on the chart: 9° 30′ in 1955, with an annual decrease of 8′ = 7° 22′ in 1971 (let's say 7°).

That makes: Les Soldats 335°
              the lighthouse 12°
              Men-Du 62°

The three bearings make a respectable cocked hat. Now we must check immediately how close it is to reality. The chart does correspond: Trévignon chateau is to the right of the lighthouse; the tower of Men-Du to the left of Raguénès; the Corn-Vas buoy to the right of the Ile Verte.

As Men-Du is the nearest mark, its bearing is probably the most accurate of the three; it is therefore likely that we are in the north of the cocked hat. There could be still more accuracy if 'the angle of uncertainty' of each bearing were plotted by adding or subtracting 2° for instance, as in the diagram. In principle we ought to be in the darkest area.

In practice, it isn't necessary to push the checking so far: consider yourself to be in the middle of the cocked hat, but without completely eliminating the possibility that you might be outside it. A mistake is easily made: suppose that the bearing of Men-Du had been read as 59° on the compass instead of 69° (i.e. 52° True); the hat would be quite different – very small; but that is out of the question. And yet, we do have Trévignon chateau to the right of the lighthouse, and Men-Du to the left of Raguénès. There is only one chance of tracing your mistake: on the chart, Corn-Vas is almost in line with the Ile Verte, whereas you see it is clearly to the right. That ought to make you smell a rat.

A Fix Using Horizontal Sextant Angles (Position circles)

The method of fixing position by three bearings is the classic method and the one most commonly used. However, its inaccuracy makes it quite useless when the only available bearings are very close to each other. You then have recourse to another method of getting your fix by using Horizontal Sextant Angles.

This is no longer a matter of measuring the angle between the direction of the landmark and north, but the angle between the directions of two landmarks. For this you must have a sextant, but it isn't worth using a valuable instrument in such cases – a plastic sextant is quite accurate enough.

To measure the angle, the sextant must be held flat and the images of the two marks brought into line, one above the other. You first set the instrument roughly, steady your arm and adjust the coincidence (superposition) with the micrometer.

The advantage of this method is that you only need the two

images of the marks to coincide for a moment for the measurement to be accurate – even very accurate. This cannot be done with a hand-bearing compass because the card is never quite steady.

But now we have to make these measurements effective on the chart, and that is not so easy. Like it or not, we have to embark on pure geometry.

The Principle

The geometrical position from which one can see two points A and B at an angle a, is an arc of a circle passing through A and B.

In plain English that means that, having taken the angle subtended by A and B at the observer, from this angle a circle passing through the two marks can be constructed and one can be certain of being somewhere on this circle.

Taking in the same way the angle subtended by B and that of another landmark C, a second circle can be constructed, passing through B and C, and this circle cuts the preceding one at a point which is the exact position of the observer.

The Practice

We are approaching Jersey, coming from the SW, and we identify three landmarks not very far from each other: A, the lighthouse on Point Noirmont; B, the lighthouse of La Corbière; C, the lighthouse of Point Gros-Nez.
- We measure with the sextant the angle between A and B: 17° (angle a); then the angle between B and C 22° (angle β).
- We draw a straight joining A to B.
- From A we draw another line making with AB an angle of $(90°-a)$.
- The same from B.
  The intersection of these two lines is the centre c1 of the circle passing through A and B.
- We do the same with B and C, to obtain the circle c2 passing through B and C.
- The two circles cut at point M: this is the position of the boat. If you do not have a pair of compasses, or if the arcs of the circle to be drawn are too big for the compasses you have, it is possible to get your result in another way:
- Through B, draw the line making with AB the angle $(90° - a)$.
- Through A draw the perpendicular to AB.
- The two lines cut at a point d1.
- In the same way, draw through B the line making with BC the

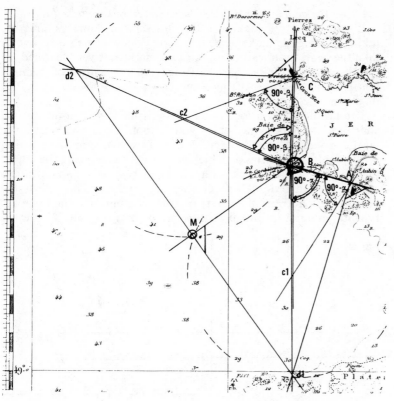

Fix, using position circles. The lighter lines are contructed using compasses; the heavy lines by using erpendiculars

angle $(90° - \beta)$, and through C the perpendicular to BC. You get d2.
- Draw a straight line joining d1 and d2.
- The perpendicular to the segment d1–d2, drawn from B, gives the position M of the boat.

Finding New Landmarks

However good they may be, all landmarks have one defect: they soon cease to be effective. The boat moves forward and new landmarks have to be picked up ahead as the next links in the chain. When you are sailing in an unknown area (and that is an experience we hope that everyone will have), the search can be arduous and demands a methodical approach.

It is a good principle always to check the identity of each new mark on the chart, even if you believe you have recognised it.

When you have identified two or three landmarks and are taking bearings to make a fix, it is good policy at the same time to take the bearings ahead of one or two marks not yet identified.

Subsequently, on the chart, starting from the position of the boat, you plot the bearings of these unknown marks to see what they might be.

The problem can arise the other way round: you notice on the chart a useful landmark, which you cannot identify with certainty on the ground. You must then plot on the chart, from the position of the boat, the bearing on which you ought to be seeing the mark; then look for it on deck with the hand-bearing compass in the appropriate direction. But remember: you must first adjust the bearing taken from the chart (a true bearing) into a compass bearing, making the required correction for variation. Where the

Coming from Cherbourg, you want to make a landfall on Durlston Head in order to enter Poole Harbour. You catch sight of the coast in the haze but nothing can be identified except a fairly sheer headland on the left. Its bearing is 315° true. By moving the rules over the chart, you see it can only be St Alban's Head. You are further west than you expected (*Admiralty Chart 2615*).

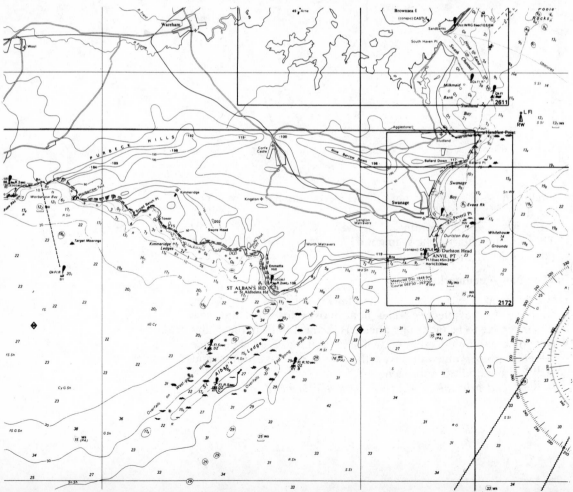

variation is West, the degree of variation must, it will be remembered, be added to the True bearing.

In this rigmarole of corrections, you just have to remember that, *as long as the magnetic variation remains West:*
- as you bring the compass bearing *down* to the chart, it must be *decreased* by the amount of variation;
- as you bring the chart bearing *up* to the compass, it must be *increased* by the amount of variation.

No matter how meticulous you are, you can never be completely confident about not making a glaring mistake and, as always, common sense is the final check. If the fix indicates, for instance, that you have covered twelve miles in an hour, you have some cause for doubt. The same applies if the fix indicates that you have 15° of leeway to windward. The 'improbable' is always a wrong.

A Course for the Helmsman

To steer by sight, or laying course for a visible objective, is very pleasant, but it isn't always possible. You don't necessarily have a landmark ahead. Visibility can be reduced and you often have to reckon with drift due to wind or current. In such cases you have to follow a compass course.

To give the helmsman his course, the navigator must change the true course he has measured on the chart to a compass course.
1. To lay the true course. This is easily done in the following way: Place a ruler on the course to be followed, then slide the Cras ruler along this ruler until you make the most southerly centre of the protractor coincide with a meridian or a parallel. The true bearing is read on the meridian or on the parallel chosen. With the parallel rules one just slides them across to the compass rose. Then read off the course to be steered.
2. To convert the true course into a compass course. You have to take into account the magnetic variation and, the compass *deviation*, (the compass deviation card having already been established). The sum of variation and deviation is termed 'compass error'. If this is East it is deducted from the true course, if it is West it is added.

Giving the helmsman a course is a simple enough job, at least when it leads straight to a destination and leeway and tide can be ignored. As soon as the wind ceases to be free, the boat makes

Swinging the Compass

Choosing the right position on board and making proper compensation (see chapter 6) are usually sufficient to eliminate all compass deviation, at least on wooden, plastic or aluminium boats. If there is still some deviation, then the amount must be known by swinging the compass.

The simplest method is to compare the ship's compass with the hand-bearing compass. This check should be made daily, when out of sight of land, and it is, strictly speaking, advisable to do it on each change of course.

For a more exact check, the boat must be anchored at a precise spot (ideally moored to a buoy), that is, shown on the chart with landmarks in plenty. The boat is turned by oar and the heading noted every time a landmark whose bearing can be measured on the chart lies in its axis (either ahead or astern). Comparison of chart and compass bearings gives the variation, from which the deviation can easily be deduced.

This check should also be made every time one is sailing along leading marks.

If this adjustment is to be valid, all loose metal objects near the compass must first (and for good!) be removed. Nothing must be overlooked, in particular tins, pocket knives, photo-electric cells, transistors and loud hailers. And don't forget to look under the cockpit sole where much that causes interference is dumped.

more or less leeway. If there is a tide running that is one more factor. Now we must consider these disrupting factors and how to take them into account when plotting a course.

Estimating Leeway and Current

Estimating leeway comes from experience and familiarity with your boat. You have to watch out for it, and note how it varies on different points of sailing and with different sail combinations, and wind strengths. Near land, it is easy enough to make these observations. If you are passing very close to a buoy, for instance, you keep an eye glued on its bearing in relation to your course away from it. At the end of ten minutes or so, take an accurate bearing of it and

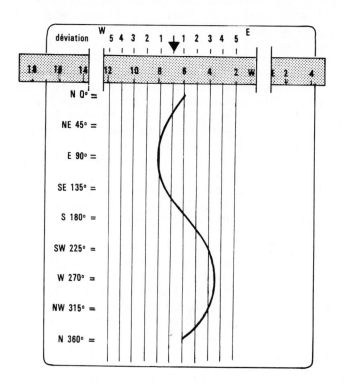

This table is easy to make and allows the compass error to be obtained without calculation. First, the compass deviation curve is drawn as discovered from swinging the compass. The table shows, for instance, that on a heading of NW (315°) the deviation is 3°E. The small sliding ruler is graduated on the same scale as the one used for deviation. The variation for one's position is set under the arrow (here 7°W). The compass error for each heading is then read off directly: on 315° it is 4°W

the comparison between the course being sailed and the compass bearing will give your amount of leeway. Another way is to make a fix, then follow a precise heading, make another fix a little later and measure the angle of leeway on the chart.

Estimating the stream is usually more difficult. It is the whole sea that is moving in one direction or another, taking everything floating (and whatever is not anchored to the bottom) with it. All one can do mostly is to trust the tidal information in the Tidal Stream Atlas and on the insets on the charts which, if the area described demands it, give the strength and direction of the stream hour by hour, If they state, for instance, that between 6 hours and 5 hours before high water the stream is 1.5 knots in a direction of 306°, it must be realised that, whatever the course that is being sailed on the surface by the boat, it will be carried over that period by 1.5 miles over the ground in a direction of 306°.

This is the distinction that has to be made between *course through the water* and *course made good over the ground*. The course made good over the ground, the only one that counts in the long run, is equal to the course through the water made by the boat (as measured by the log), plus the 'course made by the sea' during the same period. The course made good over the ground can therefore be very different from the course through the water, especially if there are streams varying in speed and direction to be contended with. Laying a course in circumstances like this takes some working out.

The following examples show the kind of difficulties facing a navigator of North Brittany whose favourite passage is from the NW buoy of the Minquiers (the 'Minkies' of Hammond Innes' *The Mary Deare*) to the Grand Léjon lighthouse.

First Voyage: No Leeway

Today, the wind is north. The boat will be on a broad reach on the starboard tack. There is no problem of leeway owing to the wind direction. It is neap tides – their effect can be ignored.

The true course on the chart is 224°. Our navigator increases it by the magnetic variation of 7°. His compass is perfectly adjusted.

The compass course is therefore 224° + 7° = 231°.

Second Voyage: With Leeway

This time the wind is WNW. The trip will therefore be done full and bye on the starboard tack; on this point of sailing the boat will make appreciable leeway. The navigator who knows his boat well, estimates his leeway at 5°, to port naturally. To arrive bang on Grand Léjon, he must therefore aim 5° further to starboard, that is, add 5° to the course. The calculation then is:

True course	224°
Correction for variation	+ 7°
Correction for leeway	+ 5°
Compass course	236°

If the wind were SSE, the boat would be full and bye on the

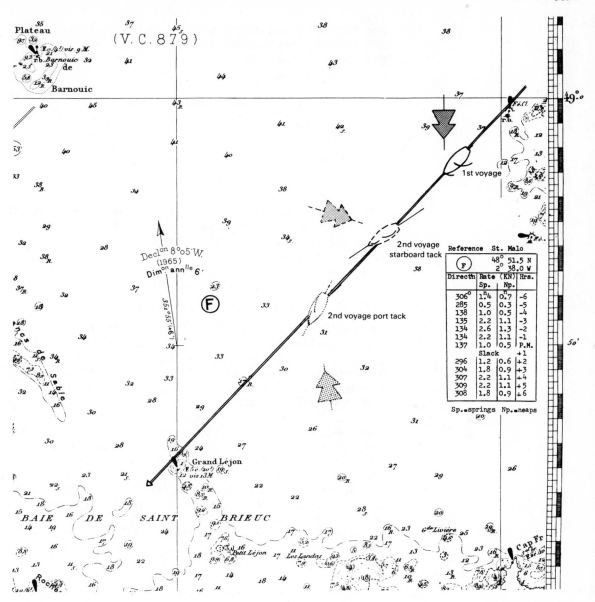

Heading of the boat in relation to the
true course as a result of leeway due
to the wind

port tack and would therefore have 5° leeway to starboard. This time the navigator would have to aim 5° further to port, that is take 5° from the bearing. Thus:

True bearing	224°
Correction for variation	+ 7°
Correction for leeway	− 5°
Compass course	226°

If the wind were SSW, it would be necessary to beat. In that case there is no point in giving a course to the helmsman. You might just as well cover up the compass: the helmsman must not attempt to keep on a compass course but concentrate on making his best possible course to windward. It is then up to the navigator to check frequently the course that is being averaged.

Third Voyage: With a Constant Tidal Stream

The wind is weak NE and tides are neap. We are leaving the NW buoy of the Minquiers three hours after high water (HW + 3).

First thing: what will be the speed of the boat? This can only be a personal estimate and our navigator thinks it will be 5 knots. The distance to be covered is 19.5 miles so the trip should take approximately four hours.

In area F, during the four hours following HW + 3, the chart inset indicates the direction of the current as varying between 304° and 309°; its speed between 1.8 and 2.2 knots at springs, 0.9 and 1.1) knots at neaps. As we are at neap tides, we can reckon with a constant current of 1.5 knots, bearing 307°.

To lay the right course we shift the departure point on the chart for the distance and direction the tide will take the boat off course during one hour's sailing.

1. We plot the direct course NW Minquiers-Grand Léjon.
2. From the NW Minquiers buoy, we plot a line representing an hour's current: that gives us point A, 1.5 miles at 307° true from the buoy.
3. Taking point A for centre, we mark with compasses an arc of a circle of 5 miles radius (speed of the boat through the water). This arc cuts the direct course at point B.
4. Draw the line AB and measure the angle it makes with North: 206°. This is the true heading. Now it remains to calculate the

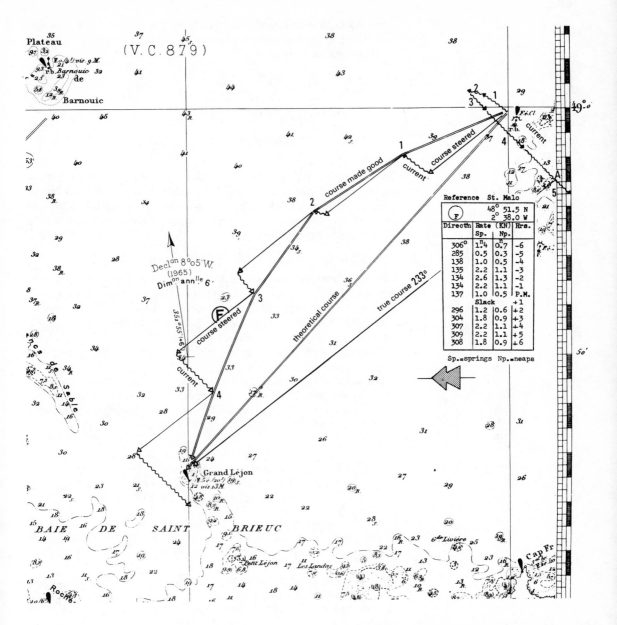

(V.C.879)

Reference St. Malo

| | 48° 51.5 N |
| | 2° 38.0 W |

Direct'n	Rate (KN)		Hrs.
	Sp.	Np.	
306°	1.4	0.7	-6
285	0.5	0.3	-5
138	1.0	0.5	-4
135	2.2	1.1	-3
134	2.6	1.3	-2
134	2.2	1.1	-1
137	1.0	0.5	P.M.
	Slack		+1
296	1.2	0.6	+2
304	1.8	0.9	+3
307	2.2	1.1	+4
309	2.2	1.1	+5
308	1.8	0.9	+6

Sp.=springs Np.=neaps

Heading of the boat in relation to the
true course in a constant current

compass course. Since the wind is NE, the boat will be running free: there is no leeway.

Therefore we have:

True course	206°
Correction for variation	+ 7°
Compass course	213°

The tide is slightly against us. *The speed over the ground is therefore not as great as the speed through the water*. It is represented by the length of the vector NW Minquiers – point B, i.e. 4.8 knots instead of 5. It will therefore take a little longer to reach Grand Léjon than if there were no tide.

Fourth Voyage: With a Variable Tidal Stream

We are at springs, and we are leaving the NW Minquiers buoy at HW – 6. This time it is all too obvious that the chart inset shows there will be considerable tidal variations in the hours to come.

We shall have to shift our departure point to compensate for all tidal changes during the whole trip.

First of all we must estimate how long the passage is likely to take.

The wind is East, therefore free, but weak. The boat will probably travel at 4 knots. It is possible to make the trip in four hours?

To find out, we 'shift' the departure point taking into account the tidal variations in the next four hours:

1st hour:	1.4kn at 306°
2nd hour:	0.5kn at 285°
3rd hour:	1.0kn at 138°
4th hour:	2.2kn at 135°

From the theoretical point 4 we measure the distance of Grand Léjon: 18.8 miles, the actual distance to be covered through the water. Four hours is therefore a bit short. Add another hour of tide: 2.6 at 134°.

From point 5 the distance is 19.3 miles. Five hours is then more than we need, so we place our theoretical departure point (A) between points 4 and 5. From there, we plot the line to Grand Léjon and measure the true course 233°.

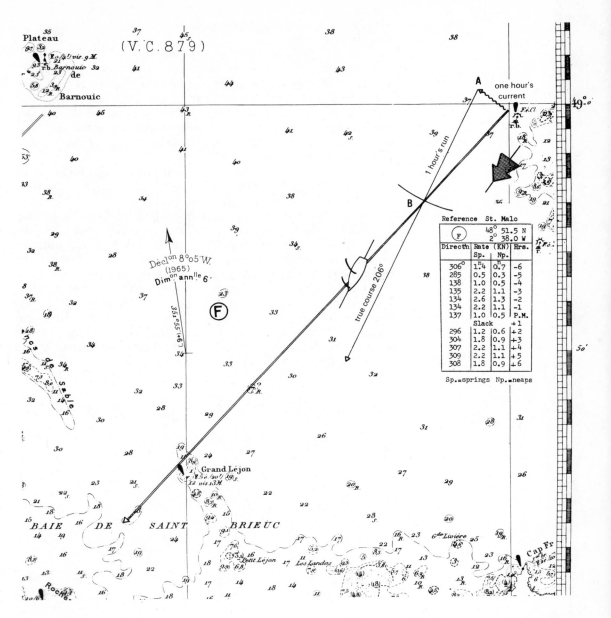

Plateau

de

Barnouic

(V.C. 879)

A

one hour's current

1 hour's run

B

true course 206°

Déclᵒⁿ 8°·05′W.
(1965)
Dimᵒⁿ annᵉˡˡᵉ 6′

351°·55′(+6′)

F

49°·0

50′

		Reference	St. Malo	
	F	48° 51.5 N		
		2° 38.0 W		
Directn	Rate (KN)		Hrs.	
	Sp.	Np.		
306°	1.4ⁿ	0.7ⁿ	−6	
285°	0.5	0.3	−5	
138°	1.0	0.5	−4	
135°	2.2	1.1	−3	
134°	2.6	1.3	−2	
134°	2.2	1.1	−1	
137°	1.0	0.5	P.M.	
	Slack		+1	
296°	1.2	0.6	+2	
304°	1.8	0.9	+3	
307°	2.2	1.1	+4	
309°	2.2	1.1	+5	
308°	1.8	0.9	+6	

Sp.=springs Np.=neaps

Grand Léjon

BAIE   DE   SAINT   BRIEUC

Petit Léjon   Les Landas

Roche

Cap Fr.

Gᵈᵉ Livière

Estimating the course with a variable current

As there is no leeway the compass course is:

$$233° + 7° = 240°$$

The boat will then follow the course over the ground shown on the chart. It is some way off the direct course, but, tides being what they are, *it is unquestionably the shortest to be found: in fact, the boat sailing on a constant heading, will make the trip in a straight line on the water.* She will have travelled 20.5 miles over the ground, and only 19.3 miles through the water.

If, in a case like this, the area is cluttered up with rocks on all sides, it is often wise to trace your course along a ruler to check exactly what, if anything, may lie on it.

Also if the direction of the wind makes it seem likely that tacking may be necessary, the route calculations we have just explained must on no account be omitted: it might very well turn out that the 'compulsory detour' imposed by the tide will allow you to make the passage full and by, without having to tack at all!

All these problems need not, however, make life too difficult. We have been assuming that the speed of the boat remained constant. In practice it varies a lot, as a result of meteorological conditions, for instance, and that complicates everything. Theory must be constantly adapted to circumstances and this will be the subject of the chapter on choosing your course.

20. Navigation Offshore

Dick Sand, apprentice on board the brigantine *Pilgrim* making passage from Auckland to Valparaiso, is promoted captain as a result of dramatic events that resulted in the officers and almost all the crew perishing. Near to despair but full of spirit, the boy is determined to bring his ship safe into harbour. Not knowing how to take an astronomical fix, he has to depend on dead reckoning only, that is, an estimate of the course travelled each day according to the compass and the log readings. Unfortunately, there is a blackguard on board and he has managed to secrete a piece of iron under the compass. This gives it a deviation of 45° East. He also arranges for the log line to break. Thereupon a terrific storm springs up which drives the boat SE, then NE, at a speed that is impossible to estimate. The upshot is that Dick Sand, having passed Cape Horn without seeing it and mistaking Tristan da Cunha for Easter Island, finally runs aground on the shores of Angola, believing he had arrived in Bolivia. Such a colossal mistake in dead reckoning is without precedent in the annals of the sea; but that is the tale told by Jules Verne in *A Fifteen-Year-Old Captain*, one of the most gloriously botched-up novels of all time. But it is a parable about a basic truth: the proudest captain can do nothing with a dead reckoning that is right out from the start.

Nevertheless, provided there are no blackguards on board, dead reckoning is the most accurate way of locating your position when out of sight of land, and it is the method we shall analyse in detail in this chapter. As crossing the Pacific or even the Atlantic is not yet common practice for us we shall not go into celestial navigation, which is only really useful when it comes to trans-oceanic passages. On long cruises it can be practised for pleasure, but it would, in our view, be gratuitous to describe the rules of a game which is, after all, rather complicated for us at this stage. There are excellent books on the subject which you would in any case have to consult and they are included in the bibliography.

After studying dead reckoning, we shall consider the different techniques for finding your position accurately when you are approaching land. The only real difficulty about navigation offshore boils down to making a landfall. And you don't have to have made a long passage for this problem to arise: you only have to be caught in fog a few cables from shore or after dark along a badly lit coast. The methods of dead reckoning must be known even if you have no intention of venturing offshore: losing sight of land is undoubtedly the dream of all would-be sailors, but it is also a risk they take every time they set out for a sail.

Dead Reckoning

Dead reckoning is a matter of calculating from the course followed, the distance run, estimated leeway and tidal stream, the track made good by the boat from its last known position.

To transfer dead reckoning on to the chart, what is called *plotting the course made good* is a simple enough operation in itself. It consists of:
- correcting the compass course by the amount of the variation deviation and leeway to get the true course;
- from the true course, plot the course made good through the water and mark on it the distance run;
- finally, should it be relevant, adjust the position arrived at by the amount of tidal stream the boat has been subjected to to obtain course made good over the ground or track.

It is, in short, the reverse operation to what was done when the course was laid. When laying the course, the navigator was thinking ahead and reckoning on possibilities. When plotting the course made good, he has to think in terms of what has in fact happened and of the conditions and circumstances under which the boat has been sailing, and these are never as simple or as predictable as foreseen. Correct assessment of the facts of dead reckoning is the heart of the job and it presupposes unflagging attention and a highly developed sense of the sea and life afloat.

This is the time when the personality of the navigator comes into its own. On the job he must be a reserved kind of type but at the same time be constantly on the alert. His kingdom is the chart table (the ship's nerve centre), but nothing that goes on on board escapes his notice. He sees everything, records everything and says little about it. He establishes facts but passes no judgments. Psychologist as well as technician, he has summed up every helmsman and knows what to expect from the boat's performance at a given speed under such or such sails. The state of the sea, changes in the wind and the weather that can be expected – everything interests him. It is as if he were conducting a perpetual enquiry and considering every incident from a view point all his own. At table, when a sudden lurch sends the crockery flying, he draws different conclusions from the rest of the crew and when he urinates leaning out between the shrouds he uses the opportunity to observe the second bow wave. Back in his bunk, he still listens and ponders. Finally, when the moment arrives, summing up all his observations and calculations, he puts the point of his pencil on the chart and says 'We are here'.

How has he arrived at this decision? It is obviously not just a matter of checking off the thousand and one details which account for the accuracy of a dead reckoning position. Science is learned in books but a good navigator has to be something of an inspired artist as well. All we can do here is to lay out some of the principles to guide the tyro navigator.

Appraisal of the Information Available

Having a very accurate 'last known position' available is the important factor for arriving at a valid dead reckoning or estimated position. Make a mistake with the first button and, no matter how careful you are with the rest, you will finish with your trousers badly done up.

Even when there is no intention of losing sight of land, the navigator is always on the alert. Its useless to be feverishly making a fix every twenty minutes when visibility is perfect and the forecast announces, for instance, cool, changeable weather; but if there is any likelihood of fog, it is sound to fix your position at least once an hour, and whenever the course is changed.

Is the Boat being kept on Course?

Is the helmsman steering a good course? That is the navigator's preoccupation. From the cabin a discreet eye can be kept on a compass be it a repeater or the hand-bearing compass. One helmsman doesn't like having the wind dead astern and always tends to come on to a broad reach: note any disparity. Another, sailing close-hauled, gets too close to the wind: leeway will be excessive. Still another, a novice, always steers 5° too much to starboard, so give him a course 5° more to port – and so on. If the boat is yawing too much the sails will have to be trimmed to make the helmsman's job easier.

When the boat is close-hauled, don't give a strict course to follow; it does not help dead reckoning in spite of appearances. If you are on a compass course and the wind is fairly variable, how in any case can leeway be estimated? If you are content to steer as the wind dictates, the leeway remains constant and that is what counts. What really matters on this point of sailing as on all others, is that the helmsman should know and say honestly the average heading he has followed. False pride ends with experience.

Leeway

Strength of wind, point of sailing, the state of the sea, the tuning of the boat, and the skill of the man at the tiller: all add up to so many degrees of leeway, more or less. Do not fail to check on this leeway at every opportunity. But don't tell the helmsman that you are doing so for he would only concentrate on keeping on course during the check and it would then be valueless. It is not what the helmsman can do that matters but what he does do.

Distance run

You can trust the log, provided that its weaknesses and limitations are known: certain logs are optimistic, others pessimistic and many are unreliable at low speeds.

The vane of a patent log has to be carefully watched. It might have suffered a knock since it was last used and turn faster (or slower) than it should. It can also catch up seaweed and, quite simply, jam. An eye must therefore be kept on the dial and readings taken very regularly – every hour for instance. Always be estimating the speed of the boat in your mind, in order to be able to assess the distance run if the log breaks down.

The Tidal Stream

Tidal stream predictions are all very well but personal observation is better. The information given on tides is not very accurate and, as is well known, the wind can upset the calculations. Passing a lobster pot or a buoy is a gift: the exact direction of the tidal stream and its approximate strength are disclosed. When an exact position is required, in the fog near land for instance, getting close to any fixed object is well worth a detour.

Sometimes, with no land in sight, it is difficult to determine in which direction the boat is being moved. The lead line can then be usefully employed or better still a fishing line with a heavy weight. The lead is dropped giving plenty of slack to the line. The angle the line makes (with the stern) when it taughtens gives a fair indication of the direction of movement in relation to the bottom.

The Log Book

All the entries on the ship's log are a kind of Ariadne's thread which the navigator can follow, step by step, back over the course run. *Everything relevant to navigation must be regularly entered in it*: courses (the one chosen and the one actually followed), the log readings, wind strength and direction state of the sea, name of the helmsman. All changes such as going about, sail changes, changes in the weather, fixes taken (and how they were made) and any ships met. No event is too insignificant to be recorded.

Only the Bare Facts Should be Listed: compass course and not true course, readings taken from the log and not estimations of the distance run – and suchlike. If each individual adds his own small personal interpretation in the log book, the risks of mistakes are multiplied by the number of people on board and the record will be completely unreliable.

The Ship's log must always be kept up to date, even when no dead reckoning is expected to be made. It may well become necessary. Also, if there is an accident or damage caused, the ship's log is invaluable evidence for an appreciation of what happened.

In France it is compulsory for sailing boats in the third category and above to keep logs. But it is sound policy for smaller boats to do it too.

Uncertainty

No matter how great the navigator's flair and the precision may be, dead reckoning can seldom give an exact position. There is a degree

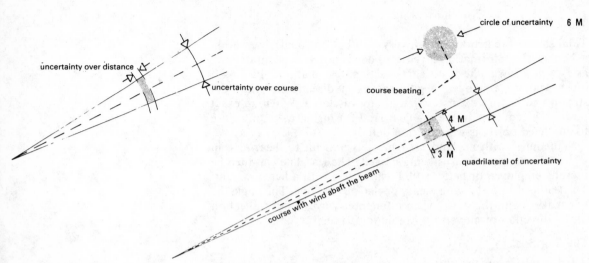

uncertainty over distance

uncertainty over course

circle of uncertainty   6 M

course beating

4 M

3 M

quadrilateral of uncertainty

course with wind abaft the beam

Estimating the area of uncertainty

of error in each one of the facts, and when a fix is made the sum total of these errors is disclosed.

They can be substantial for so much depends on the conditions at the time. Sailing in an area with little or no tides (or where the tidal streams are precisely known), and running free with a steady, moderate wind, on a calm sea, one can reckon that the margin of error is reduced to approximately 4% of the distance run. On the other hand, if tacks have had to be made in light weather and over little known tidal streams, or if you have had to heave to in bad weather the margin of error is bound to be large and can amount to or exceed 10%.

When a passage has been made in a straight line, the area of uncertainty can be marked on the chart with some precision: it is a quadrilateral, longer than it is broad if there is more doubt about the distance run than the course followed or, wider than it is long if steering has been difficult. But if tacks have had to be made, the zone of imprecision can only be marked with a circle, whose diameter shows the maximum amount of possible error. It has to be assumed one is in the middle of the circle.

The longer the distance run, the greater the circle of possible error becomes. No opportunity must be lost to check the DR, especially when making a landfall. Running fixes and running a line of soundings are good and old-fashioned, but effective, and a radio direction finder can also help to restore confidence. Chance encounters with other boats can also play their part. All the methods that we are about to analyse make for greater accuracy in dead reckoning. It cannot be over-emphasised that the value of this supplementary information given can only be useful if each calculation of the dead reckoning itself is well done. DR is the basis for all navigation.

Transferred Position Line

The position line is any bearing, position circle, azimuth, or even depth contour which contributes to the establishment of our position.

The principle of the transfer is very simple. We know at least two places must be recognised if a fix is to be made: where their bearings cross gives our position. But if there is only one bearing available, it can very well be kept in reserve, until another is found. The first position line is then transferred according to the course run: it cuts the second and the job is done but only on condition that the dead reckoning has been correctly kept up.

A fix can be made with transferred position lines on two landmarks. At 0800 for instance, lighthouse A is seen at 120°. At midday lighthouse A is out of sight but we see lighthouse B on a bearing of 60°. By dead reckoning we have run 18 miles at 40°. At 0800 the boat was somewhere on the line Ac. To transfer this line the simplest thing to do is to transfer the landmark A 18 miles in a direction of 40°. From there draw a line parallel to Ac. The transferred position line cuts the line Bd at point F and that is the position of the boat at noon. It is possible by starting from F to

Running fix on two landmarks

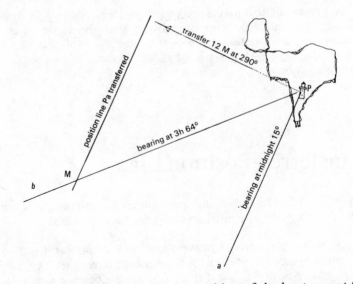

go backwards and find what the position of the boat was at 0800: point E. This is a useful check on the accuracy of the transfer. This calculation can be done with less data, by making a fix with successive bearings on the same landmark – *making a running fix*. At midnight, we have lighthouse P at 15°. Three hours later, we still only have this lighthouse P as a mark but this time its bearing is 64°. By dead reckoning we have covered 12 miles at 290° during these three hours. The bearing Pa, shifted by the 12 miles of the reckoning, cuts the bearing Pb at point M, and that is the boat's position at 0300.

This method of transferring the position line on the chart has great potential. There is nothing to stop us from transferring the same position line several times in succession, making it 'tack' with the boat and using it in several different positions. A detailed example will show the kind of reasoning to be gone through to make a landfall using this method.

Qui voit Groix voit sa joie (see chart 2 of Groix facing p 657)

It is a June dawn. Fog has come down towards the end of the night and is still hanging about in broad patches that the sun is beginning to penetrate here and there. We have come from Belle-Ile and are aiming for Lorient. The wind is NNE. Because the visibility is bad it is better to go round the west end of Groix and be able to make landfall on an open, easily recognisable coast: the point of Pen-Men.

We are making a course of 330° true. At 0500 we catch sight of Groix through the haze, but cannot identify anything precisely. It is time to plot our dead reckoning on the chart. We estimate the margin of error at 6 or 7% which gives us, taking into account the distance run since Belle-Ile, a circle about 2 miles in diameter. This circle is drawn and in its centre (the estimated position of the boat) the time of the fix 0500 and the log reading 53.2 is entered.

At 0512, in a clear period, the lighthouse of Pen-Men is glimpsed for a moment. We immediately take its bearing: 50° true. This is bearing I. When this position line is plotted on the chart, it shows that the estimated position (EP) was somewhat optimistic: we have not covered as much ground as we thought. The area of uncertainty is no longer the circle we drew but only a sector of it as wide as the bearing is reliable. The boat is assumed to be at point A; but it is safer to reckon on being in the most unfavourable position, that is, at point B. To clear Pen-Men from point B, we calculate that we still have 1.3 miles to go on a bearing of 330° before going about. We shall therefore go about when the log reads 55. This margin will be good enough to avoid any risk of hitting the point, but let us pass close enough to have a chance of seeing it.

At 0525 we go about and settle on a heading of 70° on the port tack.

The minutes pass. Now, we must be near the point and everyone is screwing up their eyes. Gradually, in the sunny greyness, a darker mass looms up. It is the coast. And there is the lighthouse. We take its bearing at 145° true. This is bearing II. It is 0548, log 56.7.

Since going about we have run 1.7 miles at 70°. We must now transfer bearing I by the amount of the course run. So we move the lighthouse itself 1.3 miles at 330° then 1.7 miles at 70° and, from the new point (P1), we draw a line parallel to bearing I. This line cuts the bearing II at C. This is the boat's position.

As we can still see the coast quite clearly, it is a good idea to take a third bearing to get a proper fix. We wait for a little while: the bigger the angle between the last two bearings, the more accurate the fix will be. The lighthouse is soon out of sight but the point itself is still visible. We take its bearing just before it disappears, at 205°. It is 0555, log 57.3. We have covered 0.6 miles from point C.

We plot a new bearing, bearing III. Then we shift 0.6 miles the two bearings that have given us fix C (P2 and P3). In short, we obtain a cocked hat D and the boat probably lies inside it.

For curiosity's sake we can amuse ourselves by retracing from the middle of the hat the track that we have in fact covered. This shows that when we saw Pen Men for the first time at 0512, we were in fact at point E.

And that at 0500, when we drew the circle in the middle of which we thought we were, we were in fact at point F, at the very limit of the margin of error.

Navigation by Soundings

When everything disappears in the fog, one reference remains unshakably reliable: the bottom. The sea bottom is a well defined stretch of ground with its plains and valleys, different crops and deeper channels: it provides information of all kinds, but it has a particularly and specially useful characteristic of rising towards the surface when land is near: it gives you warning. We therefore have, in the last resort, when there is no visibility, this aid for making landfall: go by dead reckoning to an area where you know you will find, according to the chart, easily identifiable bottoms, and then take soundings.

The procedure to follow varies according to the nature of the bottom: sometimes there is a line of soundings outside all dangers off the coast and all that needs to be done is follow it to arrive in harbour. Sometimes you may have to get an accurate position by 'running a line of soundings'. But everything depends on the available depth-finding equipment.

The Echo Sounder and the Lead Line

The echo sounder and the lead line are clearly not to be compared. The echo sounder can take soundings at great depth and gives accurate and continuous readings. The lead line is really only accurate in shallow water (less than 15m) and only gives periodical information from time to time. Beyond 20m, the most one can know is which depth marks lie around you. It is therefore not possible to use a lead and a depth finder in the same way. The one allows you, sometimes, to locate yourself with great accuracy. The other registers the approach of dangers.

Another significant difference is that using the echo sounder needs no special expertise or patience on the part of the operator. But the correct use of the lead calls for technique that has to be learned.

When an exact depth must be taken in shallow water, the procedure is as follows. The line is got ready in a bucket or laid down loose on the deck. The man throwing the lead stands usually on the lee side, about amidships. He holds the line in his leeward hand, the lead on a level with the water. He tries to swing the lead like a pendulum and throw it as far forward as possible to give it time to hit the bottom before the boat overtakes it. The faster the boat is going, the further forward he must throw the lead. Some champions can throw it 15m. Male chauvinists claim that some women drive the whole crew below deck when they take to swinging the lead. This is nonsense of course, but it's best to watch out.

As it strikes the water the lead makes a splash which leaves a visible ripple on the surface. When you come up to this ripple the line is held straight up and down to mark the depth.

As soon as it gets fairly deep the lead line is unsatisfactory, since the boat has often passed before the lead has touched bottom. If it is vital to get an exact sounding, then the boat must be stopped or at any rate slowed down a lot.

Up to 20m the lead line is particularly useful for finding the depth contours. The technique is then somewhat different. If you want to know, for instance, when you will cross the 20m line, you first make ready the required length of lead line, that means 20m plus the depth of water above the chart datum for that hour of the tide, plus the freeboard of the vessel and the height of the stern rail to which the line is fastened. One of the crew throws the lead from the bows of the boat, as far forward as possible. The line must be vertical when you pass on a level with the ripple (if it isn't, you are going too fast). Once the ripple is passed, the line is hauled in and the tallow smeared on the base of the lead will show whether it has touched bottom or not.

Sounding in Deep Water

To be of any real use in deep water cruising, an echo sounder must be capable of registering depths up at least to 100m. If it can do that, it can supply all kinds of precious information far offshore. When crossing the Channel between Torquay and Paimpol, for instance, a dead reckoning position which has become pretty shaky owing to

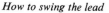

How to swing the lead

1. The leadsman gives it a pendulum motion

2. He throws it as far forward as possible . . .

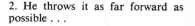

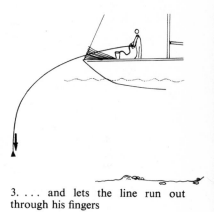

3. . . . and lets the line run out through his fingers

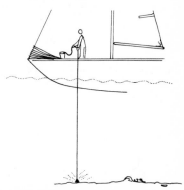

4. The lead must be on the bottom when the boat passes over it

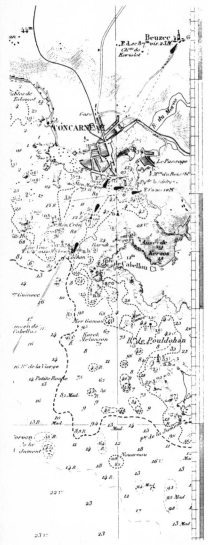

In thick weather the Cochon tower can be reached by following the 10m sounding line

periods of calm and a certain amount of beating can be made reliable when crossing the Hurd Deep where the sounder suddenly shows, for a short distance, depths of over 100m. Coming in from the open sea to make a landfall on Penmarc'h in thick weather, littered as that neck of the woods is with rocks, you know you have nothing to fear as long as the 100m line has not been reached.

Making a landfall on Groix, described in the preceding paragraphs to illustrate the transfer of bearings, could have been achieved in quite a different way by using the echo sounder. The moment you sight the Pen Men light for the first time, a reading of the echo sounder will give an exact position immediately. Thanks to the bearing, we know that the boat is somewhere on the line drawn from the lighthouse, but as the echo sounder gives a reading of 45m, we can only be in the immediate vicinity of point E.

Following a Depth Contour

With an echo sounder, following a depth contour is child's play. But, as we have seen, it is also possible with a lead line. Obviously the boat must not be going too fast, or having to tack. Following a depth contour amounts, in fact, most of the time to trying not to get too far away from it.

Let us take, for the last time, the example of Groix to examine the depth contours around the point of Pen Men. We saw that even if the fog had come down, it was still quite possible to sail round the point in complete safety and without ever seeing it, simply by following, step by step, the 20m line, which is quite clear of all the dangers.

Another example is the entrance to the port of Concarneau. We are caught in the fog 1.5 miles to the south of the Cochon beacon. We take soundings and find less than 10m water, so we immediately set course NW to find the 10m line again, which we follow leaving it always a little to starboard. And so we arrive at the Cochon, and from there we can enter the channel using DR and never crossing the 5m line on either side.

Running a Line of Soundings

We do not always have soundings to serve like a flare path to lead us straight to our goal. On many occasions we must go step by step, trying first of all to reach an unquestionably identifiable spot, which allows our position to be fixed before going further.

To make a fix by using soundings, the dead reckoning must often be made in a special way by running a line of soundings. To do this, take a squared piece of tracing paper which can be moved over the chart parallel to meridians or the parallels. It is in effect a blank chart, with north at the top.

As we approach our landfall, we plot on this paper, in the direction of the boat's movement, the track made good over the ground together with the soundings taken, scrupulously respecting the scale of the chart. All that then need be done is to move the paper over the chart and try to make the soundings on the one coincide with the soundings on the other. You may, if the soundings are very distinctive, succeed in locating yourself straightaway and with astonishing accuracy. But it may not be as clear as that and you must back-track and begin again, never failing to keep the dead reckoning up to date. This is an exercise in perseverance and we are going to give, intentionally, a rather complicated example of the procedure.

Making a Landfall on the Bancs de Sable

(See chart 3 of the Bancs de Sable and the traced line of soundings, chart 4, facing page 657).

We are en route from Granville to Lézardrieux. It is neap tides. At 0430 (HW−6) the navigator makes a fix placing the boat 2.3 miles to the south of the SW Minquiers buoy. The log reads 87. Wind NW Force 4. We are close-hauled on the starboard tack and the heading has averaged 280°.

Fine weather, smooth sea, good visibility. The navigator thinks it isn't necessary to plot the course and goes to bed.

At 0715, he is roused brutally from his berth: fog has come in. A glance outside is enough to show him that, true enough, visibility has fallen to about half a mile. What is to be done? Can we go on and try to make a landfall by soundings, or must we be content to tack around gently until the fog lifts?

First of all let's look at the chart. Is there a possible point on the coast we are making for that would serve as a landfall well away from dangers? Yes: there are the Sand Banks, off Paimol. They are very easily recognisable by sounding: the bottom rises slowly up to a 20m line, then less than 20m for a mile or so, then a sharp drop to 30m. It looks as if we should be able to find this hog's back easily without any possibility of mistake since no other feature, to north or south, has the same characteristics. If we succeed in locating ourselves correctly on the Banks, it will become possible later to pick up the S.E. Basses buoy. From there it will be easy to stand in for the entrance to the Trieux by going from buoy to buoy.

But locating ourselves precisely on the Banks is certainly not so easy. The answer surely is to go backwards and forwards several times over them to get our position more accurately, running a line of soundings all the while. Whatever happens, we run no risk in trying: if we do not find our exact position, it will always be possible to go out to open water again and wait.

So let us get down to it.

Bring Dead Reckoning up to Date

The log book gives the following information on what has happened since 04.30 hrs.

SATURDAY 21 JUNE 1969	Port ST MALO						
		Coeff 50	AM Time	Height	PM Time	Height	
From: GRANVILLE		HW	1047	9.5	2308	9.8	
To: LEZARDRIEUX	Miles run in the day	LW	0522	3.4	1740	3.8	
		Range		6.1		6.0	
		Duration	0525		0528		

Time	Course	Log	Wind Dir.	Strength	Baro.	Cloud	Visib.	
00 00	280	62	NW	4	1033.5	0	5-10	under way from Granville for Le Trieux
0100	280	67.5	NW	4	1034	0	5-10	
0115 0200	280	73	NW	4	1034	0	5-10	South of Chausey
03 00	280	79.5	NW	4	1034.5	0	5-10	about 2 am south of the South Minquiers Buoy.
3-45	280	84	NW	4	1034.5	0	5-10	On the Canal of the W. Buoy of the Minquiers 2-3 m. South
430	280	87	NW	4	1035	0	5-10	
500	280	89.5	NW	4	1035	2/8 MIST	?	misty horizon
06 00	277	95	NW	4	1035	2/8 MIST	?	the wind is tending to head us
700	275	100.5	NW	4	1035.5	2/8 MIST	?	
715	275	102	NW	4	1036	MIST	0	Fog closed in suddenly

With the help of these facts we must first get to know where we are. We make a dead reckoning fix for 0730, log 103.5.

We plot the track through the water, taking into account the variation (7°W) and leeway of 6° to port. That gives us, according to the entries noted in the log:

2.5 miles at 267° true
5.5 miles at 264° true
8.5 miles at 262° true

Next, we plot the track over the ground by moving the fix by the tide movement shown on the chart inset – ie:

HW—6: 0.7 M at 306°
HW—5: 0.3 M at 285°
HW—4: 0.5 M at 138°

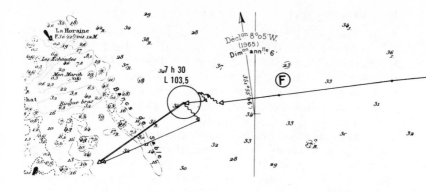

Reference	St. Malo		HW - 6
(F)	48° 51.5 N		4 h 30
	2° 38.0 W		L 87

| Directn | Rate (KN) | | Hrs. |
	Sp.	Np.	
306°	1.4	0.7	-6
285	0.5	0.3	-5
138	1.0	0.5	-4
135	2.2	1.1	-3
134	2.6	1.3	-2
134	2.2	1.1	-1
137	1.0	0.5	P.M.
Slack			+1
296	1.2	0.6	+2
304	1.8	0.9	+3
307	2.2	1.1	+4
309	2.2	1.1	+5
308	1.8	0.9	+6

Sp. = springs   Np. = neaps

Now we must scrutinise the position that gives us.

The boat has done an average of 6.5 knots. The log at this speed under-reads by about 6%. On the distance run (16.5 miles) that makes it about a mile out. Let's move the fix a mile forward on the average course followed: 264°.

The helmsmen assure us they have kept their course within plus or minus 2°, which represents a possible inaccuracy of 7% over the course.

But the estimate of the tidal streams is still more uncertain: we put it at 10% of the distance run.

We are still most uncertain of our position which gives us, around the fix obtained, a circle of potential error 1.7 miles in diameter.

Setting the Course

Now we must get on target. To give ourselves the best chance, we are going to try for a landfall in the middle of the sand banks (Bancs de Sable). The track over the ground is 235°. With the tide that makes a course through the water of 246°, plus 4° for leeway (4° only since we are no longer close-hauled), plus 7° variation. Compass course: 257°.

According to our dead reckoning position at 0730 we were 2.2 miles from the Bancs de Sable. Taking into account the area of possible error, we shall have to begin to take soundings quite soon, let's say when we have covered another 1.5 miles, when the log reads 105. Between then and now, we will make a list of the depths.

Let's get down to it again. If anyone wants to follow our calculations, let him begin by reproducing our plot on tracing paper. Without it he runs a grave risk of losing us on the way.

First Crossing

At 0830 we cross the 20m sounding line, log 105.5. We immediately luff up close-hauled. The bottom continues to rise. Log 106: 10m; at 106.1:8m. Then a sudden drop at 106.2:20m. This is the fall we expected and confirmed on the surface by seeing a few lobster pot markers. The floats are tending to sink, proof that the tide is quite strong. No doubt more than one knot, let's say 1.3 knots. The markers are being tugged in the direction of 150°. We go about.

The navigator has already begun to plot the course on the tracing paper. Taking the compass course and the tide into account, he plots the track made good. The distance measured through the water is first plotted on the course, then transferred to the track together with the tidal stream.

Second Crossing

Immediately after going about, we find the 20m sounding line again, the log reads 106.3. The bottom then stays at between 20 and 10m, without any marked variation until the log reads 107.4 when we have come back to 20m. The navigator plots on his tracing paper the course followed during this second crossing in the same way as he did for the first one. So we are now to the east of the Bancs de Sables and we continue for a moment close-hauled on the port tack so as to compare the trace and the chart and see where we are.

Nothing is very accurate yet. On the first crossing we found less than 20m water for more than half a mile: we have therefore come over quite a wide part of the Bancs de Sable and it is significant we have recorded a depth of 8m. We cannot therefore be further south than the 9.7m and 8.1m depths on the chart, around 48°48′.8. But on reflection that can't be right, since the 8m reading was made just before the drop in the bottom and not in the middle of the banks. It is therefore probable that we have passed a little higher, on the soundings 8.7 situated around 48°49′. This is in any case the most southerly position possible. The most northerly clearly cannot possibly be beyond 48°50′.5. Judging by the soundings on the second crossing, it does indeed seem that the most southerly position is the right one. But by moving the trace about on the chart, we find that there are several other possibilities. It isn't necessarily the one which appears to fit best that is valid. Everything is still too vague. We must go about and try again.

Third Crossing

We go about with the log clocking 108.6. We find the edge of the

Bancs de Sables at log reading 109.3, then record successively:

                        109.8 :10m
                        109.9 : 4m (good!)
                        110   :10m
                  log 110.1 :20m

and the depth plunges again beyond 20m.

This 4m reading is certainly going to help us in our search for an accurate position.

At first sight, it looks as if we have passed over the northern slope of that little shallow marked 4.5 at either end, situated between 48°49′ and 48°50′.3. The trace and the chart indeed fit together very well like that, and as far as the first crossing is concerned the most southerly reading should therefore be the right one.

But we can't yet confirm it. Perhaps we have passed over the southern slope of the shallow: it's quite possible. Perhaps we have passed even lower, over the 4.9 sounding situated at 48°49′.5 (although this last position does not seem very likely, given the course run since our second crossing).

In any case, we must get it just right. We go about again with the log reading 110.4.

Fourth Crossing

The Bancs de Sables continue to turn up on time: we find the 20m line once more when the log reads 111.2. The bottom rises to 10m at 111.6. It is still 10m at 111.8 by the log, then drops again. At 112.2 we get 20m. We are on the other side again; but no: at 112.9 we suddenly find 12m. Then, once more, more than 20m.

What does this isolated reading of 12m correspond to on the chart?

The 11m sounding, shown on the chart to the NE of Basse Bec arm (at 48°51′.7) seems to be the most plausible. The bother is that the trace does not quite coincide with the chart, not at least if we really have passed over the northern slope of the shallow on our third crossing. If we had crossed over the southern slope, the fourth crossing fits better, but it's the first crossing which no longer fits with anything!

There is nothing unusual about all this. Everything points to the possibility of the course plotted on the tracing paper being somewhat extended compared with the probable course on the chart. The most likely explanation is that we must have underestimated the current. It must be running stronger, so the course made good would be less to the north and slower than we thought.

This is probably what has happened. We guess that if we compressed the plot on the trace a little, we would get a much better coincidence, from one end to the other.

If this hypothesis is correct, we shall miss the buoy on the course we are following at the moment. We must go about.

Fifth Crossing

We go about with the log at 114.2. At 114.7 the bottom rises to 20m, then stays between 20 and 10m for a bit. At 115.2 we read 20m again, then the drop. The readings of this fifth crossing coincide quite well with the 11m sounding of the previous crossing. We must go about yet again and soon, in theory, we ought to see the buoy.

Note that not one of these soundings taken has been decisive in itself. But the whole of the reasoning seems to hang together: the different crossings over the Bancs de Sable make a coherent sequence and the possibility of a glaring blunder seems to be completely ruled out.

Now, if we miss the buoy, we can at least say we did what we could, and just tack around in open water without worrying until we can see everything quite clearly.

Radio-navigation

Navigating by radio beacons is absolutely comparable with navigation at night with lights. In both cases it is a question of locating position by picking up 'active marks' with known characteristics. Only the means are different. Instead of using light waves and the eye as an optical receiver, radio waves and a receiver, which turns these into sound are employed.

Radio Beacons and the Consol system are the two most useful radio systems on a small boat.

Radio Beacons

The Transmitter

The active marks used in direction-finding are *radio beacons* (almost always located in important lighthouses) transmitting a very accurate signal, on a predetermined frequency on the long wave band.

To avoid overcrowding the frequencies, radio beacons usually transmit their identification signals three to six times in succession on the same frequency. They transmit in turn and always in the same order. The signal transmitted by each beason lasts one minute in all and consists of:

- the identification signal of the beacon, a group of two or three Morse letters, repeated several times for 22 seconds;
- a long dash, lasting for 25 seconds;
- the identification signal transmitted once or twice for approximately 8 seconds;
- a silent period of at least 5 seconds, after which the next beacon comes in.

The characteristics of the radio beacons are given in the nautical almanacs and the *Admiralty List of Radio Signals*. There are also radio beacon maps which are convenient and adequate for small boats.

The Receiver

The receiver is a radio set with a movable aerial plugged into it called a DF aerial. The aerial used on board small boats is a ferrite rod usually attached to a small HB compass.

When the receiver is tuned into the frequency of a radio beacon* the radio wave transmitted by the beacon induces a current in the DF aerial, with an intensity that varies according to the position of the aerial. This is exactly what happens with an ordinary transistor which must be orientated in relation to the transmitting station if you want your music at full blast. The strength is at its maximum – and consequently the sound itself at a maximum – when the ferrite rod is at right angles to the direction of the transmitter. The strength is minimum, that is you can no longer hear anything, when the rod is end on to the transmitter. It is this null point of the sound that you want to find in order to get the bearing of the radio beacon; it

---

* The handbooks give the *frequency* of the radio beacons in kilohertz (khz); the dial of the receiver is often graduated in metres, that is it indicates the wavelength. To convert from frequency to wavelength apply the formula

$$L \text{ (in metres)} = \frac{300.000}{F \text{ (in khz)}}$$

is more precise than the maximum strength. When the 'nul' (the arc of weakest signal) has some breadth, you rotate the aerial slowly to find the 'edges' of the 'nul', and the bearing of the beacon lies in the middle of this arc.

The magnetic bearing is read directly from the compass; but some aerials are not fitted with a compass, only with a *Pelorus* which, gives the *relative bearing* of the beacon – that is the angle between its direction and the axis of the boat. To obtain the true bearing of the radio beacon, all that needs to be done is to add this relative bearing to the true heading of the boat (if necessary subtracting 360°).

The bearing obtained is accurate 180° either way, that is to say that you do not know at which end of the ferrite rod the beacon lies. Some receivers are fitted with a device which can allay doubt, but unless the circumstances are very exceptional (radio beacon on a light vessel, and dense fog) there is not much doubt about the bearing.

When the boat is a very long way from the radio beacon, another step can be taken: the navigator must apply half convergency correction. This enables him to plot, as a straight line on a Mercator chart, the bearing which lies along an arc of a great circle. In practice, on board a small boat far from the coast, radio bearings soon become inaccurate and, generally speaking, they become unusable by the time you would want to apply half convergency correction to them. It is enough simply to say that 50 miles away from a radio beacon the maximum correction would be of the order of 1.4 miles; at 100 miles 3.7 miles; at 200 miles, 5.3 miles. The correction is nil for north and south bearings because, you will remember, the arcs of a great circle, which make up the meridian, appear as straight lines in Mercator's projection.

The Value of Radio Bearings

For various reasons, a radio bearing is seldom accurate. It can be to do with the way the radio waves diffuse or with the reception itself.

Wave Propagation

Radio waves are not always transmitted in a straight line: they can be deflected by an uneven surface and be refracted when they pass obliquely from the land to the sea; the direct wave can be subject to interference with an indirect wave reflected by the ionosphere (night error).

An error due to refraction can be as much as 5° when the bearing cuts the coast at an angle of less than 30°. The night error is often greater. It is worst at sunrise and sunset, so these are bad times to take radio bearings. The best time is in the middle of the day.

Deflection. Many factors combine to falsify information at the receiving end. In the first place, radio waves can be deflected around the aerial by any magnetic objects on board. This is particularly so in steel or concrete boats. In these cases a fixed aerial must be used and the error has to have been calculated (by making a deviation curve as for fixed compasses). On other boats, a movable aerial can be used, but it must always be kept away from anything magnetic. Beware of loud speakers, earphones and particularly if they are the stethoscope type. If you tend to hold the aerial close to you, the yoke must be held behind the head and not near the chest.

The quality of the receiver also must be taken into account, specially its selectivity: if several transmitters are interfering with each other, reception becomes very poor and very unpleasant too if the set has poor selectivity.

Rough seas can also be a source of major error. In the trough of waves you cannot hear anything, and there is a risk of mistaking an incidental null point for the real one.

In short, the skill of the operator is a determining factor in deciding the accuracy of the bearing. If the bearing is to be correct, constant practice is required as well as enormous powers of concentration, not to mention a very strong stomach.

Eventually it has to be accepted that, even in the best of conditions, it is difficult to give a sound estimate of a bearing's accuracy. If the time is favourable, reception clear, the null zone of the order of 5°, one can reckon on a discrepancy of 2° either way in fine weather or of 5° in a rough sea. If the reception is muzzy and the null zone wide (10° to 20°), one cannot hope really for an accuracy of within 4° in fine weather and 7° to 8° in a rough sea.

When conditions are not propitious the potential degree of error is usually impossible to assess.

To Make a Radio Fix

To get a more or less accurate fix, several bearings must be taken on each radio beacon and then the most likely one is chosen for each (and this is not necessarily the average one). In good conditions three bearings of each beacon are sufficient, but it may be necessary to make five or six to get an accurate fix. All these bearings are not taken in quick succession, but usually at one or two hours' interval, transferring the fix each time by the distance run meanwhile.

As each beacon only transmits every 6 minutes, you have to reckon on taking 30 to 45 minutes to make a fix. That's why concentration and ability to cope with seasickness are important factors in the accuracy of the fix. Concentration is easier if you have earphones, which cut you off to some extent from what is going on on board. But the whole job becomes much quicker and simpler if you have a set with two different receiving circuits; you can then pass from one band to another simply by pressing buttons. On a one-circuit receiver, searching for frequencies is frustrating and time-consuming (a useful tip is to mark the frequencies on the dial with a chinagraph pencil).

In the following example, we do have by good fortune a receiver with a double circuit.

A boat coming from the Fastnet Rock is making for Swansea in South Wales. There is a heavy sea and poorish visibility. As the English coast approaches, a radio fix is considered desirable to make the dead reckoning position on the chart more accurate. This fix has an area of potential error reckoned at 7% of the course covered – or a circle of discrepancy 12.5 miles in diameter.

The radio beacons available are: Tuskar Rock (to the SE of Ireland), Mizen Head (to the SW of Ireland), South Bishop (to the west of Wales), Round Island (on the Isles of Scilly), Lundy Island (in the Bristol Channel), Créac'h (on Ushant).

They are distributed in the following manner (see chart overleaf):

Minutes	Frequency: 308khz	296.6khz
0		Tuskar Rock
1	Mizen Head	
2		South Bishop
3	Round Island	
4		Lundy Island
5	Créac'h	

By tuning the set on the two frequencies, it is possible to pick the beacons up in this order: Mizen Head, South Bishop, Round Island, Lundy Island. Then you can take two minutes rest as there is no point in using Tuskar Rock because it is too far away, nor Créac'h which is also a long way off and Cornwall is in between (the radio waves can be distorted as they pass over land).

In 24 minutes, we get the following bearings:

Mizen Head at: 270°, 275°/277°, 286°/283°/273°
South Bishop: 346°/349°/356°/345°, 348°
Round Island: 198°, 197°/210°/208°, 210°/207°, 206°
Lundy Island: 120°/127°/128°/117°

The bearings of some of the beacons have been picked up twice in the same transmission, except for Lundy Island which is not coming through clear.

Now that these bearings have been taken, a little thought is needed to choose the most likely ones.

Mizen Head: the bearings vary a lot; we choose to take the average 277°), bit without much confidence since there is a difference of 16° between the highest and lowest readings.

South Bishop: we will keep 347° as the 356° bearing seems to be an accident. The average would be 349°.

Round Island: we choose 208°, average of the five figures, since 198° and 197° are probably wrong.

Lundy Island: same proceeding as for Mizen Head; we take the average reading – 123°.

These bearings are plotted on the chart. Now the result must be analysed:

Radio fix at the entrance to the Bristol Channel. According to dead reckoning the boat is in the dotted circle. The radio bearings enable a more exact position to be fixed but these bearings are only to be regarded as an aid to DR itself

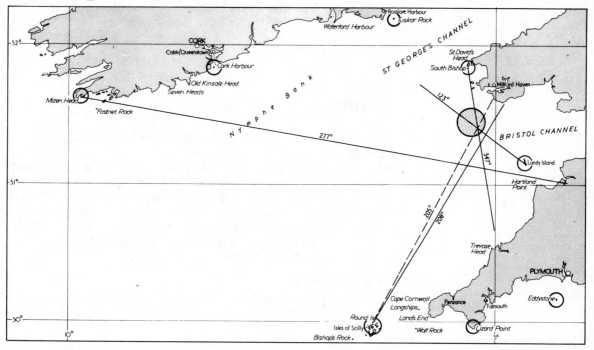

– the bearing of Mizen Head, 277° is certainly wrong. To justify it, we should have to have an error of at least 40° for Lundy Island which is quite near; besides, there is the dead reckoning.

It looks as if we must be to the west of the bearing of Round Island, which would indicate that 198° and 197° were not all that far out. We therefore average out the bearings of Round Island: that gives us 205°. At a first glance the cocked hat formed with the bearing of Lundy and South Bishop is almost too good to be true. But taking the bearing of Round Island into account we may reasonably assume that the boat is a little to the east of the cocked hat, so we have a chance then of seeing the Helwick light vessel sooner than the dead reckoning would have us think.

Homing on a Radio Beacon

When a radio beacon is situated close to the port of destination, or on the course you are following, it is very convenient to use this beacon as your heading.

You must obviously be quite sure that you can home in without running into any dangers on the way. It is, for instance, quite possible to 'home' in on the Roches-Douvres beacon off Brittany if you are coming from the north, but it is not to be recommended if you are coming from the south. One look at the chart will show you why.

Consol

Consol is a long range radio aid intended mainly for aircraft, which can be very useful for offshore sailing.

In the Consol system, the transmitter of the radio beacon sends out a signal which is not the same in all directions. It works on the same principle as a light with sectors, but here the sectors are very numerous and so narrow that they are used as position lines. Merely by listening to the signals you get, thanks to a special chart, the sector where you are located; and a fix can be made once you have two such position lines.

The Transmitter

A Consol beacon has three aerials which are aligned. The accuracy of the signal is at its maximum when you are at right angles to the line passing through the three aerials; it is at a minimum when you are on the extension of this line. There is in fact, at each end of the line, an ambiguous sector of about 50° (rather like dark sectors of a light).

The Consol beacon, after giving its identification signal, transmits a series of dashes followed by dots, or dots followed by dashes, 60 in all. During this transmission, a vague period, called the *equisignal*, separates the dashes from the dots, or *vice-versa*. This equisignal shifts as the transmitter's relative bearing changes, so that the bearing of the beacon is determined by counting the number of dots (or dashes) before the equisignal, the the number of dashes (or dots) that follow. The signals lost during the equisignal are allocated, finally, half to dots, half to dashes: the grand total amounts to 60.

The same combination of dots and dashes is never in areas less than 10° apart. If there is any doubt about your position, it can be checked by taking an RDF bearing of the same beacon or consulting the dead reckoning.

The characteristics of the Consol radio beacons and the list of charts are given in lists of radio signals. The range of these Consol beacons being very great, the coverage of Consol for the whole of Europe, for instance, is provided by only five beacons: Stavanger in Norway, Bushmills in Ireland, Ploneis in France and Lugo in Spain.

Consol charts are ordinary charts overprinted with the bearings of the Consol beacons, with a scale giving the number of dots or dashes emitted on each bearing before the equisignal.

The Receiver

Consol signals can be picked up on any ordinary receiver without a special aerial, provided that its long-wave band extends sufficiently far beyond Radio-Luxembourg.

Nevertheless even with such a receiver, it can be difficult to distinguish between the dashes and the dots as the wave transmitted is not modulated (in technical jargon it is an A1 wave; A2 and A3 waves are modulated and are used for the transmission, one for Morse signals, the other for speech and music). A receiver with a beat frequency oscillator (in jargon: BFO) is needed for clearer reception.

The Accuracy of Consol Bearings

The radio waves of the Consol system are subject to the same limitations as those of ordinary radio beacons. You must always be aware of error caused by ground effect, refraction and interference. The accuracy of Consol bearings varies, too, with distance, and in an unexpected way:

- less than 30 miles from the transmitter, it is nil: for practical purposes one cannot use Consol;
- between 30 and 150 miles it is usually good, whatever the time of day;
- between 150 and 600 miles interference between the direct and the reflected wave can give rise to errors and even make the bearings valueless;
- beyond 600 miles, the reception and the accuracy of the bearings are good again and can remain so up to 1,200 miles by day and 1,500 miles by night.

The lists of radio signals have tables indicating the mean extent of the error, according to the ship's position in relation to the meridian of the line of the aerials. It is as well to consult when listening to a beacon more than 200 miles away.

The Consol system has two great advantages over DF: the accuracy of the bearings does not depend on the quality of the receiver and it is always good whatever the state of the sea.

Making a Consol Fix (see Consol chart 5 p 720)

Let us go back to the passage Granville-Lézardrieux that was the example used in the description of navigating by soundings. The ship's position during this passage can be located by Consol, provided you have Consol chart No L.13 (British Isles) on board, with the bearings of Ploneis and Bushmills and a BFO receiver (Bushmills is inaudible on an ordinary receiver).

On a first reading, Ploneis (identification signal FRQ) gives 44 dashes – 13 dots; the second time 45 dashes – 12 dots. The missing signals being allocated half-and-half give a total of 60, we are therefore approximately on the bearing 46 dashes from Ploneis.

Bushmills (identification signal MWN) gives the first time 16 dots – 51 dashes; the second time 7 dots – 51 dashes. The bearing is therefore: 8 or 9 dots.

So we are at point 1 shown on the chart between Saint-Malo and the Minquiers.

Listening later, Ploneis gives 12 dots – 48 dashes; and Bushmills 57 dashes – 3 dots. We are therefore at point 2. This demonstrates that a Consol fix needs neither calculations nor discussion.

Notice that precious information can be received from Ploneis alone, when one is trying to locate position on the Bancs de Sable, and even with an ordinary transistor. Ploneis is in fact very close to Radio-Luxembourg. When soundings tell us we have reached the Bancs and the bearing of Ploneis (20 dots – 40 dashes) immediately gives us our whereabouts. When we can proceed on an accurate course northward and, when we get 32 dots – 28 dashes from Ploneis, we are for sure, somewhere in the immediate vicinity of the SE Basses buoy.

It follows that the most ordinary transistor can become, provided one has a Consol chart, a considerable aid to navigation. A useful extra bonus is that it allows you to practise in winter, far inland: in Paris, some 500–600km away, you can pick up the signals from Ploneis, and gradually learn to distinguish the dots from the dashes and to recognise the equisignal. And imagine 'the terror, the agony, the nostalgia of the heathen past' (or your bad moments at sea) that are aroused by the sound of Consol at night in a city!

RDF and Consol are precious aids, but it would be dangerous to trust entirely to them.

'*Each of these radio aids –* we read in the *French Instructions Nautiques – must not be taken as supplying the navigator with information which he can trust exclusively and blindly.*

'*It is up to him, taking into account the accuracy he can expect from each one of these aids with respect to his estimated position, to use it in conjunction with all other aids to navigation (radio or not) which he has at his disposal, reaching a considered compromise between the different sources of information available to him.*

'*In particular, radio aids must not exclude a simple recognition and observation of landmarks, wherever that is possible.*'

It could not be expressed better.

Meeting Merchant Ships

To round off this survey of the various ways of establishing your position at sea, we must mention one more method that is unorthodox but very effective: taking the bearings of the courses followed by passing merchant ships. The appearance of a ship on the horizon is

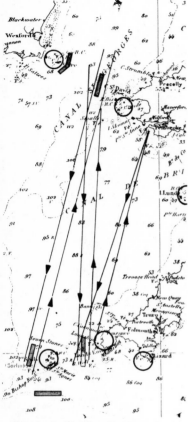

Principal shipping lanes at the entrance to the Bristol Channel

not, after all, unusual or a matter of chance. Shipping follows lanes with an over-all pattern that is as regular as a railway network, with main lines, branch lines and junctions. By taking the bearing of the merchant ship's course one can usually know what its heading is and consequently it provides a valuable indication of one's position.

These traffic lanes for merchant ships are well known: on the east Atlantic Ushant – Cape Finisterre; on the French side of the English Channel, Ushant – the Casquets – la Bassurelle; on the English side: Bishop Rock (Scilly) – Lizard – Start Point – Royal Sovereign. Such lanes all over the world are real highways with traffic diverging at crossroads, which are marked on the charts by pink lines about two miles wide. Less important lanes can easily be deduced from the course of the ship that is met: often all that is needed is to lay the parallel rules on the chart along the course followed. The Pilot books also describe the traffic of ports, and consequently the types of vessel that put in. One quickly learns to distinguish between a banana boat (dazzling white and going to Dieppe), a ship with a cargo of ore (all black perhaps coming from Cardiff) and a warship in its dapper grey, coming and going as it pleases.

The main lanes for merchant vessels passing across the opening to the Bristol Channel between Land's End and South Wales are plotted on the chart section in the margin. One of these tracks goes from Bishop Rock to the Smalls; it is used by ships coming from the south Atlantic. The second, which is the direct route between Cape Finisterre and Liverpool, passes between Wolf Rock and the Seven Stones (which made the unfortunate *Torrey Canyon* notorious). The third, taking the same route, goes to the great oil port of Milford Haven.

In the course of our passage from the Fastnet rock to Swansea, which we described in our discussion of an RDF fix, the crossing of these cargo lanes proved a good moment to check up on the dead reckoning position. If you meet a merchant ship on a heading of 0° true, you can be pretty certain you are on the line Wolf Rock– Smalls; if the ship is heading 15° true, you are probably on the line Wolf Rock – Milford Haven . . . unless you have been slower than you thought and you are only on the line Bishop Rock – Smalls, where all the shipping follows approximately the same heading! But it is 26 miles between the two lanes and the dead reckoning would have to be very badly out for a mistake of that magnitude to be possible. To get an accurate bearing of a merchant ship's course, it is best to wait for the moment when you cross its track and its masts come into line with each other. If you are not crossing its track, a real bearing cannot be taken but at least it can be estimated and that is often good enough.

Landfall

The first member of the crew to sight land has a right to a double Scotch and that is a rule never to be forgotten. But then comes the really important job of making your landfall. The land that has been sighted must be identified and the boat's position fixed in relation to it before continuing on course for harbour.

If you can, within reason, choose the area for it and an ETA, making landfall is clearly easier. The ideal is a sheer coastline, with prominent landmarks or profile, approached over a *shoaling bottom* with characteristic features (like the Bancs de Sable off Paimpol in Brittany.) The ideal time is towards dawn: it is easy to establish position by the powerful lighthouses and enter harbour very early. Even if both these ideal conditions don't obtain, other aids are not lacking: positions can be 'transferred', soundings taken, an RDF or Consol fix made, merchant ships may be seen and, as a last resort, candles to your patron saint can be lit. But the essential is to examine scrupulously all the information that is available, ensuring nothing is contradictory: everything must agree.

In practice, there is no general advice for making a landfall: it is always different and a very special moment, even quite emotional and the degree of satisfaction and excitement depends very much on the sort of passage that has just been made. For the navigator it is the moment of truth; the moment when the validity of his dead reckoning is put to the test and he either gains or loses face with his companions. Up to that time his skill at the chart table has been taken on trust, but who knows some error has not crept in and quietly thrown out all subsequent calculations? The unexpected can happen with landfalls and perhaps that is part of their fascination.

21. Passage Making

Courses at sea have to be carefully planned. The Pilot book and charts, good land or sea marks and your navigational instruments all, in their way, help you to know your position and are the guarantee of the satisfying liberty of being able to go from one place to another on the course of your choice. It is up to each skipper to decide in the light of the circumstances – and his own fancy. There is no argument. Some prefer to dawdle along gently, in no hurry, others think only of their comfort and try to avoid confrontation with the elements at all costs; while for others still the only pleasure is speed. There are the realists and the dreamers, the ancients and the moderns. Your state of mind when cruising undoubtedly influences the choice of course and sets the tone of the trip.

But there are other factors. When the leg to be covered has been chosen and the distance to be run estimated, nothing is yet known about what the passage will be like. It can be short or, on the contrary, well nigh interminable, according to the direction of the wind. No course can be defined in terms of distance, but only in terms of duration. It is a matter of the number of hours and days spent at sea, in constantly changing conditions: tides rising and falling, tidal streams turning, wind freshening, dying, or changing direction; the sea may be disturbed or calm, you may have the sun on your back or in your eyes or the fog may come down when night is coming on.

Whatever your state of mind may be at sea, all these circumstances demand serious reflection before setting off. One has the right to choose a course, but it must be practicable, rational and within your limits, whatever the circumstances; and there must be an alternative plan if need arises. In other words, choosing one's course means in the first place choosing a safe course. Then, and only then, can it be embellished.

Choosing a Course

One rarely comes back from sea without having learned something new, even if the ground has been covered a hundred times before. Every course conceals some element of the unknown or, if you prefer, of risk. Choosing a safe course does not mean eliminating all risks. It is a progress from the known to the unknown that stretches your powers of imagination, first trying to foresee what is going to happen and endeavouring not to be caught unprepared by the unpredictable.

All manner of factors have to be reviewed. Some are immutable and described in detail on the chart and in sailing directions: these are the characteristics of the area you are sailing through; the hazards to be avoided, like shallows, isolated dangers, tricky channels and shipping lanes. Then there are the reference points you can rely on: landmarks, lights and radio beacons. Other factors change but are predictable, depending on the tide: the depth of water, tidal streams which make channels passable or impassable. Others can be anticipated to some extent: the direction of the wind, visibility and the state of the sea in different places. But there is always the unexpected: a violent change in the weather, accidents, misjudgement, the landmark that cannot be picked up or a buoy that is just not there.

Choosing a course means facing up to these facts and seeing how they can be coped with. There is no systematic way of examining them. On one day one factor may predominate, another day what seemed unimportant the day before becomes significant. There is a plethora of choice in choosing courses, and it's a question of temperament: one of them seems to be the obvious one, but a search must be made nevertheless for an alternative. But the tidal stream may rule it out and so on *ad infinitum*.

Enough of theory, here are a few examples.

From la Vilaine to Le Palais (see chart 6 of Quiberon Bay facing p 720). We are at Tréhiguier, of the mouth of the River Vilaine. Our first leg is to Le Palais, on Belle-Ile.

On the direct course, there is a shallow: the Plateau de la Recherche, then a sizeable obstacle: the line of rocks jutting out from

Quiberon Peninsula, with Houat island in the middle. Must we avoid the Plateau de la Recherche or not? Everything will depend on the weather and the course we choose to pass through the reef. There are three channels: la Teignouse, le Béniguet and les Soeurs. There is a fourth solution, which means going south round the Grands-Cardinaux: this is what the sailing directions call the eastern channel, whichever we use, the distance to be run to reach Le palais does not vary much: 28.5M by Le Béniguet, 29.5M by la Teignouse and by Les Soeurs, 30.5M by Les Cardinaux.

First Choice

It is fine. The weather is settled, the wind steady from the NE and visibility is good. Probable speed of the boat is 6 knots. We reckon therefore on a passage of about 5 hours.

With this wind, the sea can't be heavy on the Plateau de la Recherche. We can go over it, provided there is a good metre of water above chart datum.

The course by le Béniguet being the shortest, that is the one we think of first. With these winds, the passage is easy. The only snag is that it isn't lit and we can't go through it at night.

The course through the channel of Les Soeurs seems a little less easy: the marks to use are far off and there is a chance of making a mistake. Here too a night passage is out of the question.

La Teignouse is practicable by day and night and so is the eastern passage.

Must we take tide into account? The currents are relatively strong in all the channels (except the eastern one) so it is preferable to go through on a falling tide. The most favourable time to get under way is at high water. We shall then benefit from a fair tide for the whole passage.

In short we have only too wide a choice but it looks as if there is no catch and, if the unforeseen arises, we can always get to a harbour to our lee: Houat or simply Le Palais. The only precaution to take, perhaps, if we are going through Le Béniguet or La Teignouse is not to run too close to Houat or the Béniguet reef, where we might find ourselves in a nasty situation if there is any kind of mishap.

Second Choice

This time the wind is quite fresh from the west and the visibility uncertain. Close-hauled, at 5 knots (which means a real speed of 3 knots into the wind) we reckon that the passage will last about 10 hours whatever course is chosen. If the wind is in fact dead ahead, taking the tacks to be made into account, the four routes are all much of a muchness in distance.

In this weather, the sea may be heavy on the Plateau de la Recherche – it will be better to avoid it. In the channels through the reef, there is a risk of it being really bad during the whole of the ebb, when it will be wind against tide. Must we go through with the flood? It isn't by any means certain that we will be able to make any headway against the tide when we are beating. The only favourable times seem to be at high or low water slack.

The Pros and Cons of the Different Courses

- La Teignouse: the channel is broad enough for tacks to be made. By taking this route we shall be in the shelter of the line of rocks for a large part of the passage.
- Le Béniguet: the channel is short, but too narrow to allow for beating; if the wind is dead west, we might hope to get through on one tack; but if it backs a bit, no.
- Les Soeurs: if we go through there, we get little shelter from the reef; the channel itself is long, narrow and no doubt the leading marks will be difficult to identify. It certainly isn't the safe way.
- The eastern passage: here the tidal stream is weaker than anywhere else; by passing a good way off the Cardinaux, in a depth of over 30m, we shall no doubt have a quieter sea than in the channels and we can tack at will. The disadvantages: beyond the Grands-Cardinaux, part of the passage will have to be made without any shelter; at night, if the visibility is poorish, there is only one light of any use to us—the one on the Cardinaux.

When must we get under way to get through the reef at the right time? There is no possibility of getting out of La Vilaine during the flood. By setting off at high water, we miss the low water slack at La Teignouse and Le Béniguet. We must therefore set sail near the end of the ebb so as to get through at the high water slack. If we choose to take the eastern passage, the tide factor is simpler: we can no doubt get round at any time by giving a wide berth to the Cardinaux. The most likely plan seems to be to leave Tréhiguier at full tide and to go through the channel at the end of the ebb.

What are our reserve plans in case of trouble? As long as we are in Quiberon Bay, we can always return to the Vilaine. If the unforeseen occurs around La Teignouse, we have on our lee the harbour of Houat, Port Navalo and, at a pinch, La Trinité. On the course for the eastern passage, we can bear away towards la Turballe or le Croisic. All these harbours are open to us at all states of the tide.

If we have to adopt an emergency plan when we come out of La Teignouse or Le Béniguet it could be awkward, as we shall have to be well clear of the channels before we can bear away SE. In fact, we could turn back. It would nevertheless be better to avoid going through Le Béniguet with the last of the daylight as doubling back through it at night in the opposite direction would be most imprudent.

There remains one final question and the decisive one if visibility is bad: what means have we of checking our course? To find the entrance to La Teignouse channel, or even the entrance to Le Béniguet in the murk would surely not be easy. The only reasonable course in all the circumstances must be the one that avoids all the dangers – the eastern one: the whole passage can be made by dead reckoning, and a landfall make on Kerdonis point which is completely free of dangers.

All things considered, in this kind of weather the eastern route is certainly the safest. The course by Les Soeurs, or even by Le Béniguet is risky and La Teignouse is possible only if visibility holds.

But weather can change. If we are, for instance, at the end of a depression, if we consider that the wind might come round to NW and visibility might improve, we might well see things differently. La Teignouse route is shorter, and as soon as we got through the channel we could run straight down to Le Palais. By going round Les Cardinaux we shall, on the contrary, have to spend a good deal of time beating and the course will be less safe because it will be longer and more tiring. On the other hand, if the wind is going to back SW, the eastern passage is no doubt the best answer. We should still have to anticipate when the wind might change and consider whether it might change in strength too, not to mention what the state of the sea might be.

From Concarneau to Royan

From Concarneau to Royan is 85 miles. The passage can be made on a dead straight line, by going outside the island of Groix, Belle-Ile, Noirmoutier, Ré and Oléron. This is a very feasible passage for a coastal cruiser like a *Mousquetaire* for instance: at 5.5 knots in a good following wind, it could do the passage in 34 hours.

But the *Mousquetaire* is not made to face up to high seas. So all along the route, shelter must be at hand and easily accessible should

Choosing a safe route also means having pre-selected bolt holes. If you are making a direct passage from Concarneau to Royan, on board a Mousquetaire for example, first ensure that there is always a safe shelter to leeward in case of an accident or bad westerly weather.

It can be estimated that in front of each port or refuge there is a safe sector approximately 60° wide (a Mousquetaire, even disabled, can almost always sail with the wind about 30° on the weather quarter) extending some 20 miles out (the dark areas offer a potential run for shelter in 4 hours) and at a pinch up to 30 miles (the clear areas offering a run for shelter in 6 hours).

It will be noticed that on the passage Concarneau – Royan there are three 'blank' areas – three points on the voyage when the boat is off an exposed leeshore with no shelter: between Groix and Bell Ile, to windward of Belle Ile and between Chassiron and Royan. Contingency plans must be made for each of these areas, taking every circumstance into account

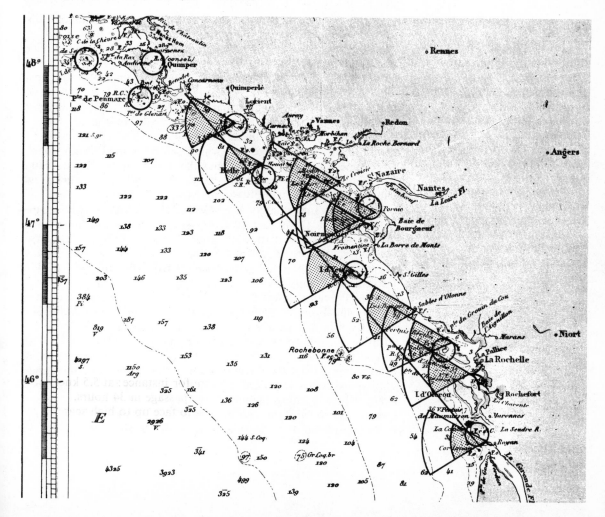

bad weather threaten, or simply if anything unforeseen required the original plan to be abandoned.

With the help of the chart and sailing directions we therefore draw up a list of ports offering the necessary guarantees of safety: they must be easily identifiable, well buoyed, accessible at all states of the tide day and night, and provide good shelter in westerly winds.

From Concarneau onwards we have: Port-Tudy at Groix, Sauzon and Le Palais on Belle-Ile, then Le Croisic, Pornic, Le Bois de la Chaise on Noirmoutier, Port-Joinville on the Ile d'Yeu, les Sables-d'Olonne, Ars-en-Ré; we could also find refuge in le Perthuis d'Antioche (la Rochelle, Ile d'Aix-Chateux d'Oléron) and, finally, Royan.

Is this string of ports to our lee sufficient to guarantee there being an emergency harbour at every stage of the passage?

The problem is like this: from the moment when the Met. Office announces that we are in for it, we must be able to get into harbour within 4 or 6 hours at the most; we must also remember the possibility of something breaking that would make the boat difficult to handle; we allow for the fact that, in the worst case, with a jury rig, it is still possible to sail with the wind some $30°$ on the quarter.

In these conditions, there is, outside each of these ports, a special zone – a safety sector – which can be plotted on the chart. It becomes clear immediately that the direct course Concarneau–Royan is not entirely covered by these safety sectors. There are a few gaps which must be closely examined.

The first is immediately after Groix: between Lorient and Quiberon, the coast is in fact devoid of shelter. If the weather is fine, this obviously is not disturbing, and we can take the direct course without any worry. If it is not so fine, it might be as well to shape our course slightly towards the open sea to be able to come quickly into the next safety sector of Sauzon.

After Poulains Point, there is another gap: we pass quite close to the wild shores of Belle-Ile, very beautiful but not at all hospitable. Even in fine weather, it is a good idea to keep some way off so as to be able to escape to one or the other side of the island should any serious trouble arise. If the forecast is not very good, it is far better to leave the direct route and pass to the lee of the island.

If we passed to windward, we would be outside the safety sectors again before reaching the mouth of the Loire. But this is a rather special case: we are simply some way off from shelter, which is only to be considered if the weather were to turn really threatening.

We can soon be in the safety sector of the Ile d'Yeu, backed up immediately by the one at Les Sables d'Olonne: it becomes very clear that, if the weather is bad, passing to leeward of the Ile d'Yeu would not be a good option, since we would be to windward of a shore with no anchorages.

There remains one last gap, the most serious one of all: between the Pointe de Chassiron and Royan. Here the weather forecasts are critical. If foul weather is predicted, it is much better to relax in le Perthuis d'Antioch and wait for an improvement if the weather is reasonable, it is once again wise to make some offing so as to get into the safety sector of Royan as quickly as possible.

In brief, the plot of the different safety sectors reveals three areas where, in case of trouble, we do not have an easy and completely safe emergency plan: after Groix, to windward of Belle-Ile, and to windward of Oléron. But our plot also throws up an answer that may not be immediately apparent: in the three areas, safety does not lie in coming in close to land but in standing out to sea, which results in a quicker passage into a new safe sector.

Of course, this reasoning is only valid for the type of boat we have chosen – a *Mousquetaire* or a boat in the same category. A smaller boat, a Corsaire for instance, cannot in any case make this passage without a stop and, for it, different problems arise: for making the leg Groix-Belle-Ile in such a boat favourable meteorological conditions are essential; otherwise it must wait. But with a deep-water cruiser safety often lies out to sea, and it can ignore all the 'safe' sectors near the coast.

These few examples are not a complete survey of the business of choosing a course. They are simply meant to give an inkling of the kind of reasoning which sometimes must be pushed much further. That is why we call attention to some of the traps that might arise as a result of an unfortunate combination of weather and coastline.

Some Traps

The lovely bay without shelter when the wind freshens and turns nicely to block the exit: the bay of Porto and the mistral have been polishing this little joke over the centuries. The reef with a tide setting towards it when the wind suddenly drops: to the south of the Chaussée de Sein during the flood tide, this can be an extremely unpleasant experience. The channel with no leading marks (such as the one between the Roches de Saint-Quay and the coast) if one is compelled to beat and night comes on before the ship is through. The Gaine Channel (between les Héaux-de-Bréhat and Tréguier) on lovely sunny summer evenings when you suddenly notice that the leading marks cannot be seen against the light. Some channel or other when the fog drifts in. These are just a few examples. What is important to notice in all this is that there is really nothing baffling or completely unforeseeable about it all. In almost all cases the forecast, a little gumption and a little flair can forestall most surprises.

To sum up, a safe course is one that gives you some offing to play with: offing in relation to the dangers of the coast naturally, but also in relation to bad weather, accidents and weariness; the kind of offing one allows in boat handling by going about well before you have to (especially after a long tack) and by changing sails as soon as necessary. It is the offing of the old French sailor's proverb: 'If you want to live long and hale, give wide berths and reduce your sail'. A safe course is where you have plenty of water to move about in and escape routes. It is also, and perhaps first and foremost, a course that is easy to check and rich in reference points of all kinds. The most thorough study of charts and the most polished and complicated navigational techniques can all be in vain if commonplace seasickness takes control. Tiredness increases the risk of error enormously; but you must always know where you are and it is a comfort to be on a course thronged with unmistakable marks or lights.

Improving on Your Course

Comfort and speed on one and the same course can vary very much. There is little to be said about comfort: when you want to live the easy way you soon learn to avoid confrontations with the sea and to realise that the coast and islands, according to the wind, offer you some areas that are more sheltered than others; also that a course run with the wind free is pleasanter than one that means a long hard beat to windward. It isn't for nothing that we use the expression; 'battling into the teeth of the wind'. Choosing a comfortable route is, in a way, choosing a safe route, as it allows the crew's strength to be conserved.

Opting for the fast route is clearly something to do with an attitude of mind, but a quick passage can also be in the interests of safety. Even if you have settled on taking your time, you should always be in a position to change at any moment to the fastest course to get to a harbour in a hurry should, for instance, bad weather threaten. Going fast can also extend a boat's range. If you gain an hour here and there on a fortnight's cruise, in the long run another, unforeseen port of call may very well be fitted in, and it might turn out to be the best part of the cruise.

But going fast is also, for many, what ocean racing is all about. This is a subject that raises the whole philosophy of sailing and boats and opinions are divided. John Illingworth, the famous ocean racer, writes: 'Sailing a boat in an ocean race means driving it at its maximum speed in all weather encountered'. His compatriot Hilaire Belloc, a poet and rough old salt, too little known to the younger generations, replies: 'From one's boat (at least from one which is a true companion) one must expect rational behaviour. One must say to oneself that, when she is making seven knots, she is doing well, and that when she is making nine, she is upset and will be better for a night's rest.'

There we have the supreme example of the utterly profitless but passionately felt debate. Since we can hardly pursue it here, let us simply advise those who are interested to read both *Offshore* by John Illingworth and *The Cruise of the 'NONA'* by Hilaire Belloc.

Let us just be content to believe for the time being that the day will come when you have had enough of not understanding why people who sail the same boat as you always go faster; why you are always badly placed when the wind changes and you always make that bad tack in a strong tide. The time will come when you want to do better. The search for this goal assumes the fascination of a game. This does not necessarily require you to have the competitive spirit; it is just fascinating in itself. It is the challenge of proving yourself equal to that volatile trio, the sea, the wind and the tide – three forces that make a choice of the fastest course an intriguing puzzle. It is like a maritime knot-garden.

We shall try to give the principal rules and give some guidance on how to discover the finer points.

The Shortest Route

In the first flush the fastest course from A to B might seem to be the shortest. This is indeed often the case, and this is always a possibility to be considered first, even when you know you are capable of shaping more complicated courses. The bee-line at sea still undeniably preserves some of the virtues that have contributed to its success on land.

However it can happen that you can go faster by moving off the direct route when the state of the sea, the direction of the wind, or a tidal stream inhibits the boat from giving of its best. We already know that shallows are best avoided in the interests of safety, but it is also understood that they must be circumvented if you want to sail fast, because the seas you encounter there are liable to be short, steep and choppy; they break and can bring a boat completely to a standstill. You go faster in calm water. You also go faster in deep water. In his book *Deep Sea Racing* Cuthbert Mason has shown that in shallow waters the speed of a heavy displacement boat is limited to S (*in m/s*) $\approx 3\sqrt{D}$ (m/s being metres per second and D being the depth of water expressed in metres): that means that it cannot do more than 4 knots in 2m of water and more than 5 knots in 3m, etc. This factor is more troublesome for large than for small craft but it is convincing evidence why sailing in shallow water is to be avoided.

It can also be good policy to move off the direct course in view of the wind: to side-step calm waters and seek better wind, to find a point of sailing on which the boat goes faster or to get into a position which will give you the benefit from an expected change of wind.

Most frequently you move off the direct course to benefit from a favourable tide, to avoid a contrary one or to make the best of the current you are compelled to cope with. In every case the problem that arises is the following: on the 'detour' you have chosen to make will the increased speed be adequate to let you reach your objective faster than if you had followed the direct course? The answer is always far from being certain and there is also a serious possibility, if you have not done your calculations properly, of losing more than you have gained.

The time gained or lost by avoiding shallows can hardly be reckoned anything like exactly. Each case is a special one and the real game begins when it comes to changing course to get the best wind.

Wind Tactics

It is easy to talk about avoiding areas of calm or areas where the wind is too strong or contrary, but much less easy to put it into practice. When the weather is fair and the breezes fitful the skill lies in being on the alert for puffs of wind and keeping in them at all costs (sometimes the cost entails some very strange detour). This expertise depends principally on acute observation. Close inshore it becomes an even more subtle art and anyone who does not know the area well is often utterly bewildered. In these conditions speculating on the wind is wellnigh tantamount to weighing flies' wings on the scales of a spider's web. Sailing directions are of little help on such occasions. There is nevertheless such a thing as wind psychology, not utterly fanciful, which Jacques Perret, a French specialist in this aspect of navigation has dealt with in his books. He believes that the unity of time is synonymous with the lapse of time but his theory will only mean something to yachtsmen who are familiar with Descartes and there can't be many of them.

Exploiting coastal breezes is the art of using data that are less indeterminate. It is often worthwhile making detours to catch offshore breezes at night and sea breezes that rise up in the afternoon when the winds are generally weak, or in an unfavourable quarter. The problem is to know how far out to go to find them. This depends on the nature of the coastline and what the weather forecast predicts. The distance varies between 5 and 10 miles, sometimes less, rarely more. You also have to think about coming inshore in time.

It is in practice, when the wind is poor, always difficult to know what you will gain by moving off the direct route. Covering twice the distance to get near land at night can be really worthwhile if you are to get the benefit of a good breeze throughout the night instead of being becalmed out to sea. But it is infuriating if, having gone inshore, the wind then rises at sea. How are we to know?

It is only possible to reach rational decisions when the wind has become fairly settled. And nevertheless the wind can still change against the predictions! Before plunging into complicated calculations and navigational geometry, it is as well to keep up-to-date with the weather forecasts and to work out what is to be expected. Whatever plan you make is based on these hypothetical meteorological facts, and this is where the whole thing can become a game of pure chance.

What it amounts to is that what can be gained by gambling with the wind is only really measurable in two principal situations:
- when one moves away from the direct course to get on a faster point of sailing;
- or to benefit from an expected change of wind.

Looked at closely, the second situation is really only a variant of the first so that must be the basis to found our initial reasoning on.

If you are to decide whether you will gain time by sailing faster along a longer course, you must first estimate the length of the detour, and then the anticipated gain in speed that will result. Then do the arithmetic.

Estimating the Longer Course

In the diagram below, it is clear that by moving off the direct route AB by an angle a, then by getting to B at an angle b, the direct route is increased by the distances DC + CE which are arrived at by the value of the angles a and b.

The increase in distance is often not so great as you would imagine

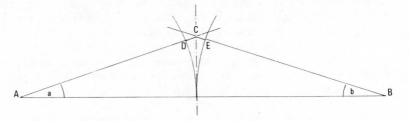

First impressions are rather encouraging: in this case the extra mileage doesn't amount to much; and further calculations made for different values of angles a and b confirm them:

for 5°: 0.4% extra mileage   for 20°: 6% extra mileage
for 10°: 1.5% ,,   ,,   for 25°: 10% ,,   ,,
for 15°: 3.5% ,,   ,,   for 30°: 15% ,,   ,,

In fact it can be reckoned that a shift of 20° from the direct route does not entail an unreasonably longer course. Beyond that, the ratio becomes inequitable and the gamble is against the odds unless a very high increase in speed is going to be ensured.

Moving off the direct course by 10° for 30% of the passage only increases the distance by 7%

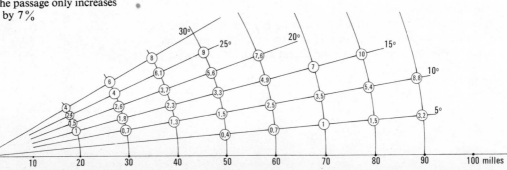

Estimating the Speed Gained

The gain in speed to be expected from a change of direction can only be estimated if you know your boat's capabilities really well on each point of sailing and in different wind strengths. Clearly you can make do with notional estimates, but you can acquire very precise knowledge, for use on an occasion like this, by taking the trouble to measure carefully the speed of the boat on the different points of sailing and drawing diagrams to illustrate how they compare.

Obviously the estimates will only be valid for the boat on which they have been made, and for the wind and sea conditions under which the measurements have been made. The diagram below can clearly only show some examples. They were carried out on a light displacement boat, 8m on the waterline (therefore with a critical

Polar diagrams illustrating the performance of a boat 8m on the waterline (critical speed 6.8 knots). In an 8 knot wind on left, in a 19 knot wind on right
Curve I: under jib
Curve II: under genoa
Curve III: under spinnaker

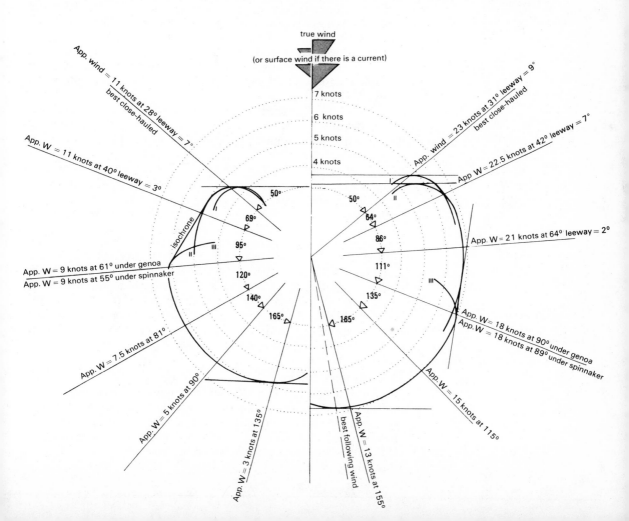

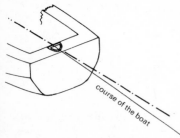

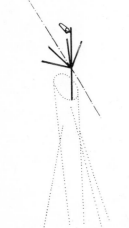

A leeway meter that is easy to make

course of the boat

Airsleeve vane with adjustable arms

Making a Polar Diagram

A polar diagram is the graphic representation, for a given strength of wind, of a boat's capabilities on the different points of sailing.

To draw it, starting from the centre of the diagram mark out sectors of a length proportional to the speed of the boat, according to the headings followed and in relation to the real wind. The diagram (or curve) of speed is the curve joining the ends of all the sectors.

Measuring Apparatus

Some measuring instruments are needed to draw the diagrams, but they don't need to be electronic – much simpler and less costly pieces of apparatus will do the job equally well.

To measure the boat's heading in relation to the real wind, you use the steering compass.

To measure the leeway, you can make yourself a 'drift meter'. Take a schoolboy's protractor with a large radius, say 10cm, fix it to the stern of the boat, the round edge towards the stern and the straight edge at right angles to the axis of the boat. Fix a thin line about 10m long (fishing line will do) in its centre with a 100 to 200 gram lead weight attached to it. The leeway is read off on the protractor.

To measure the speed, the 'ships' log and the patent log (with line and rotor) are perfect for they usually serve the purpose better than electronic logs which are too sensitive to momentary variations in speed.

To measure the speed of the wind, you need an anemometer: a hand anemometer (not expensive) or one on the masthead (expensive). The Ventimeter, which is inexpensive, can do the job quite well; its major drawback is that it is only sensitive to winds of over 6 knots.

To measure the angle between the axis of the boat and the apparent wind, you need a wind vane, which must be at the masthead. It can be a wind sock such as you see at aerodromes or along motorways, or sheet metal arrow such as you have on chimney stacks. To get a good measurement of the angle the support must have two arms on either side, arms which are adjusted at appropriate angles, 60° and 40° to start with. If you are rich, you can allow yourself the luxury of an electronic apparatus which is a wind vane and anemometer all in one.

Making the Diagram

First the real wind must be known. Its direction is found either with wind astern, or by taking the average of the headings followed close-hauled on both tacks. Its speed is measured with wind astern by taking the sum of the apparent wind speed and that of the boat. If the apparent speed is too weak to be measured, don't bother for this can be done later.

Then, for each point of sailing, the speed and course of the boat are measured. The heading is followed on the compass and, if necessary, it is corrected by the amount of leeway to get the true course of the boat. If the diagram is to be realistic, a large number of measurements must be made: every 10 to 15 degrees on a broad reach and a reach; every 5° when reaching the limit of the spinnaker, then between sailing on a close reach and close-hauled.

While this is going on the speed of the wind is checked at least once. If you have a complete set up of equipment, the speed on each heading and the direction of the apparent wind are noted. If you only have a rudimentary wind vane, you note the speed of the apparent wind for the angles where its direction is easily identifiable (90°, 60°, 40°). As the apparent wind is much stronger at these points of sailing than with the wind astern, it's only with a dying wind that the ventimeter becomes inadequate.

You can then check the value of these measurements by making a simple diagram.

Three diagrams are drawn: one with spinnaker, another with genoa, and a third with jib. The three curves obtained for the same strength of wind are all plotted on the same graph which, without hesitation, allows you to choose the best sail plan for a particular point of sailing and the most advantageous heading to steer.

NB. It is worthwhile (but not essential) to note on the diagram the strength and direction of the apparent wind for several points of sailing, since these are the only known factors against which performance can be measured.

When several diagrams have been drawn up for different strengths of wind, the arms of the wind vane can be adjusted for two very distinct points of sailing: for instance the points when the spinnaker can be hoisted and when the genoa must be exchanged for the jib.

Checking the measurements for an angle between the ship's head and the apparent wind of 40°

The available facts are:
True wind: 10 knots
Apparent wind: 11 knots
Speed: 5 knots
Leeway: 3°
You plot the vector for apparent wind (2cm per knot for example), then the vector for heading. By adding the leeway you arrive at the course. The vector that completes the triangle is the true wind. Measure it and you get 8 knots. There is something wrong

apparent wind 11 knots

true wind 8 knots

boat's heading

leeway 3°

boat's course

69°

40°

speed 5 knots

speed of $2.4\sqrt{8} = 6.8$). They are nevertheless worth looking at because they reveal certain constants and characteristics common to most modern boats.

One of the curves was drawn up in fresh weather, the other in light conditions. The first fact to emerge is this: the differences in speed from one point of sailing to another are much more marked in light than in heavy weather. This is fundamental and deserves to be number one in the book of rules:

It is only worth making a detour to go faster in light weather. In heavy weather (if no change of wind is expected) it is better to stay on the direct route.

The curve that emerges in light weather shows significant variations in speed in three sectors: when the wind is ahead, astern and abeam.

Head wind: the gap at the top of the diagram corresponds, naturally enough, to the beating sector.

Wind astern: it appears that the boat goes faster when the wind is slightly on one or other quarter, which suggests that gybe tacking downwind may well be useful.

Wind abeam: the sudden acceleration noticed corresponds to the moment when the spinnaker becomes more beneficial than the genoa.

Between these sectors, the curve has a very regular line because speed does not vary much: from full-and-by to close-reach, from a reach to a broad reach, it is not easy to see how a change in direction could lead to an increase in speed. Quite clearly then, on these points of sailing the direct course is the fastest.

It is a very different matter when we examine the three sectors where the speed varies: there are questions to ask. When the objective lies in a beam wind sector, is time not gained by running some of the distance under spinnaker on a broad reach, then finishing on a close reach? When the objective is just to lee, is it not reached quicker by gybe tacking rather than going straight for it dead downwind?

As far as the head wind sector is concerned, the question is a quite different one: here, in any case, progress can only be made by making detours and it is a matter of knowing if some detours are not better than others.

The diagram in any case allows the gain in speed for a given change of course to be reckoned precisely. It also demonstrates, as we shall see, the gain in time that is achieved by the combination of different points of sailing.

Estimating the Time Gained

Take the case of a head wind. With the help of the adjacent diagram, it is easy to see that the geometrical position of the points which can be reached in the same space of time by beating is a straight line, at right angles to the direction of the wind, and tangental to the upper edges of the diagram on both sides of the beating sector. The tangental points of the straight line and the diagram indicate precisely the best close-hauled course that can be made on either tack.

According to the same principle it is possible to know all the targets which can be reached in the same space of time by 'tacking' on either side of a beam wind or a stern wind. In both cases, all the targets are situated on a straight line tangental to the edges of the diagram. This straight line – called the *isochrone* – therefore allows an exact evaluation to be made of the amount one gains in relation to the course that would have been run by taking the direct route. Its tangental points with the diagram also show which are the best close-reach, the best reach or the best broad reaches to make.

For all points of sailing where the direct route is the fastest, the isochrone naturally merges with the diagram.

It is now high time to see what conclusions all this leads to in practice; first in a steady wind, then when a change in the wind is expected.

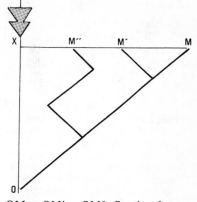

OM = OM′ = OM″. Starting from O, all points that can be reached within the same time by beating are situated on a line at right angles to the direction of the wind

Reaching

You are in the vicinity of the buoy SN 1, off the mouth of the Loire, and you are making for Belle-Ile. The wind is light, from SW. Your boat is doing 5 knots, and you are engaged in pondering that eternal question: 'to spinny or not to spinny'. You do not know your boat very well, you know nothing of racing tactics and, anyway, you have no reason to go to Belle-Ile as fast as you can. You simply have a yen to sail under spinnaker and it does seem to be possible to carry one on the point of sailing you are on. So finally you decide, and you hoist it. But alas! you have made a mistake, your spinnaker doesn't pull well, and the boat does not go any faster.

It is simply sickening that you have done all this work for nothing, and you decide to bear away slightly so that the spinnaker will be of some use.

You therefore bear away 10° and you immediately realise that everything is much better. The spinnaker is pulling correctly, speed mounts to 6 knots. It is very pleasant.

Nevertheless, you take a look at the chart to see where this departure from the straight and narrow is taking you. You notice

gain in speed	angle c
10 %	25°
15 %	30°
20 %	34°
25 %	37°

The moment when one must set course for the objective does not depend on the angle of deviation from the direct course line (angle a) but solely from the gain in speed obtaines. It is evaluated taking into account the bearing of the objective (angle c). The greater the gain in speed, the longer one can wait

	gain in time (in %)			
gain of speed	10 %	15 %	20 %	25 %
angle a 5°	6	9	12	15
10°	3	6	8	11
15°	1,5	3	5	7
20°	1	1,5	3	4,5

Taking into account the angle of deviation from the direct course line (angle a) and the gain in speed obtained along the first part of the passage, one can evaluate the total gain in time (assuming one has laid course for the objective at the right moment and that the speed on the second leg of the passage is equal to what would have been made on the direct course).

that it is not very far off the original course and that you can go on like this without risk for a while. The boat is going quicker so the loss of time will not amount to much in the end.

It is at this moment that, in your softening brain, the idea begins to germinate that in fact your gain in speed is considerable in relation to the longer course. This is quite right, and we now call your attention to this: if you decide to do half the passage under spinnaker, then to head directly for Kerdonis, you have only made your course 1.5 % longer. Your speed has increased by 20 % over the first part of the passage. In fact, you can even do more than half of the trip under spinnaker, and you will still gain. If you want to know the best moment to hand the spinnaker and head for your goal, just refer to the adjacent table. You will sail the last leg of the passage on close reach, a point of sailing on which your speed will be little different from the one you were making on the direct course. You will be at Kerdonis much earlier than you thought.

The forecast announces that the wind is going to back southerly? It may well be possible in that case that you will be able to do the whole of the passage under spinnaker. But if, on the contrary, the forecast is that the wind is going to veer northerly, then you should consider doing the first part of the passage on a close reach. To know the right moment to head straight for Kerdonis under spinnaker, you must first know exactly on which point of sailing your spinnaker becomes effective; then plot on the chart from Kerdonis, a straight line representing your course on this point of sailing; and join this course on a close reach. In fact, if the wind is due to veer, it is better, as you are not very experienced, to give up the idea of the spinnaker and to take the direct course. Prudence counsels you in fact not to move from the direct course unless you are going to profit immediately from it – unless you are very sure of yourself. In any case you ought to know how to assess the significance of the forecasted wind change and when it will happen. If you think that you will be at Belle-Ile before it happens you can chance your luck by running first under spinnaker; you risk however finishing up with the wind dead ahead. It's up to you.

Now you must learn that there are less rough and ready methods than yours. If you are in the vicinity of buoy SN 1 and you see passing you by, head down, a racing yacht which rounds the buoy, breaks out his spinnaker in double quick time and unhesitatingly takes the right course, tell yourself that there is an expert navigator on board who doesn't ask himself metaphysical questions about spinnakers.

Well before getting to buoy SN 1, this navigator has taken out of his archives the speed diagram for today's wind and sea conditions. It was drawn on tracing paper. He has laid it on the chart, the centre of the diagram on buoy SN 1, and has orientated it according to the wind. You may be certain that he has immediately discovered the best heading to follow, what his gain in speed and time is and he is quite satisfied. Each man takes his pleasure where he finds it.

Wind Astern

Here the tactic is very simple, as we know: you go faster by gybe tacking than by running right before the wind.

Going from SN I buoy to Kerdonis in a light SW wind, there are three possibilities: take the direct course, bear away and be able to carry the spinnaker finishing on a close reach, or begin by making the close reach tack and finish under spinnaker
6. From Vilaine to Le Palais
7. From SN I buoy to Kerdonis
8. La Horaine I
9. La Horaine II

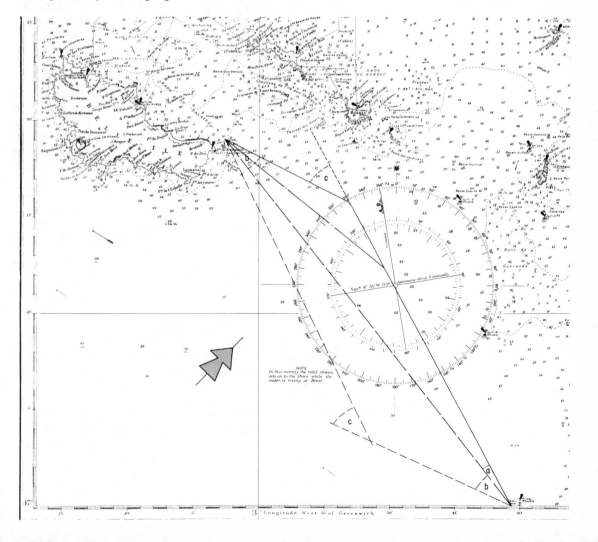

You can be quite satisfied, if you wish, with a rough and ready estimate of the best broad reach which is the point of sailing for getting the maximum speed without moving too far off the direct course. But it is quite possible now to make precise calculations without much effort. When the wind is dead astern (and on this point of sailing only), the real wind and the apparent wind are in the same direction. We know that if your diagram is to be of any use it must show the real wind. All that is needed now is for you to set yourself in the dead downwind position, to log the compass course and the speed, then to luff up gently and slowly, continuing to record the speed every 5°. In a very short time you will know which is the best angle of broad reach for that particular wind strength at least. Even if you don't go so far as to make a diagram, you can note down those things in a corner of the log book.

To make short tacks or long tacks? Everything depends on how the wind is going to blow. If it is not going to change direction, or if we don't know, making short tacks is usually more sensible (although the time lost in gybing is not negligible). If you move too far off the direct course, it only needs a slight shift of wind at the last moment for you to be compelled to run on the last gybe with the wind dead astern, which makes you lose all or part of the benefit you have gained up to that point by gybe tacking. But if you have not moved far off the direct course, a shift of wind either has no effect or is beneficial. Unless it is more than 80° when it compels you to take down the spinnaker. When a change of wind of this magnitude is forecast, you must give up any idea of gybe tacking and immediately get on the course that will be imposed on you before long by the wind veering or backing; in other words, luff up in the direction from which the wind is expected.

With a Head Wind

How can you improve on a course when your destination lies in the direction the wind is coming from? Here questions of tactics take a very particular turn: the boat is beating and it is no longer a matter of asking if a detour will result in a better progress to windward since, by definition, beating is the point of sailing which provides that. Besides, as long as the wind does not shift, the question is answered easily enough.

The Theorem of the Head Wind

Let us take several identical boats, all making 50° to windward. They are spread out irregularly on a line BC and they prepare to beat to

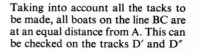

Taking into account all the tacks to be made, all boats on the line BC are at an equal distance from A. This can be checked on the tracks D′ and D″

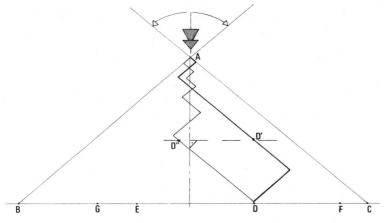

windward to reach point A. The bisector of the angle BAC is the line of the wind and the angle itself is the beating sector – 100°.

The important premise is that the boats on the line BC are, allowing for the tacks to be made, all at an equal distance from A. As can be checked on the sketch, two boats starting from the same point D, and making different tacks, cover exactly the same distance to get to A, and that any point on the passage – for instance half way are D′ and D″ – their progress is identical. Conversely, any boats to the left of B, or to the right of C, are further from the objective and will take longer to get there.

Close-hauled, the shortest course lies within an angle equal to the beating sector whose bisector is the axis of the wind; all courses within this angle are at an equal distance from A.

The Shifting Wind Theorem

But now the wind backs 25° (left), and everything changes. The new beating angle is xAy and the position of each boat projected onto its bisector shows that, from now on, E is nearest to A followed, in order by D, F and C. B is out of it. There is still some doubt about G, which lies outside the beating angle, but slightly to windward of E. The distance GA is only 10° greater than the distance EA. G from now on being able to sail full-and-by, goes faster. This gain in speed may compensate for the longer route.

The distance of the boats in relation to the objective is equally modified except for D. It is 21% less for E, increased 43% for F,

The wind backs 25° and everything is changed. The boat now in the best position is E. The D″ course is reduced by almost half compared with D′. See pull-out chart 7 (pages 720–721)

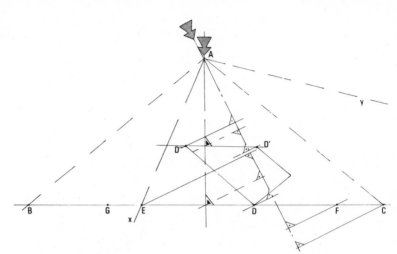

60% for C. It may well be thought that morale too has changed somewhat on board boats D′ and D″: the distance in relation to A is reduced by 10% for D″, and increased by 30% for D′.

All these conclusions lead one to modify somewhat the foregoing theorem. If the wind is not going to shift, tacks can be made effectively in the whole of the triangle BAC, but, in practical terms, it is not wise to pursue that theory because, if the wind shifts, there is more than one chance in two of losing out: either because one finds oneself too far to windward (the case of B), or too far to leeward (the case of D, F and C) in relation to the objective.

Practical experience proves that *when it is not known if the wind is going to change, whether backing or veering, the most prudent plan is tacking within a sector of 10° which has the true wind as its axis.*

It is worth noting in this context that when the objective does not lie exactly in the eye of the wind the question arises of the choice of direction for the first tack. It is an extension of the preceding rule, it can now be seen that the *paying tack is the one which brings the boat closest to the objective.* In our diagram, it is D″ which has made the best tack.

Now if a change of wind is expected, and if its new direction is known, this is no longer valid. Here we must look again at the diagram: when the wind change occurs, it is D′ which has the windward station, yet it is E which wins out. The following rule may be immediately deduced from this:

When a change of wind is expected, you must keep to the side from which the wind is going to come.

The problem is to know just where to go in that direction and which sector of beating you must adopt. To find the answer an attempt must be made to assess, as nearly as possible, the extent of shift of the wind. Generally speaking it can be assumed that: the angle between the direction of the present wind and the windward edge of the new beating sector must not be greater than the difference between the present heading of the boat and the angle of wind shift predicted. If, for example, the boat is making $45°$ into the wind, and a wind shift of $30°$ is predicted, the difference $45° - 30° = 15°$ indicates that the direction to windward of the new beating sector must be between $5°$ and $15°$ off the axis of the present wind, on the side from which the wind is going to come.

This simple bit of arithmetic throws up another rule: *The greater the shift in the wind is expected to be, the less you should move off the axis of the present wind.* If a wind shift of $40°$ is forecast, the calculation $45° - 40° = 5°$ shows that no change must be made.

Now let us return to where we were recently, somewhere between the buoy SN 1 and Belle Ile. Five identical boats are now making for Kerdonis. The wind is NW (head wind) and the forecast announces it is going to veer north.

see chart 7 facing p 721

There is a conference going on on board each boat, trying to reason out what is to be done in view of the forecast.

On board boat A, it is thought that they will have reached Belle-Ile before the wind changes. So they continue to beat within the sector of $10°$ (green sector) on the axis of the present wind.

On board boat B, it is thought that the wind will veer soon and that it will be about $30°$. So the calculation $45° - 30° = 15°$ is made. B makes a long port tack to place himself ready for a beat in the grey sector, between $5°$ and $15°$ from the axis of the present wind.

On board boat C, the extent of the change is not discussed. The more to windward, it is argued, the better. So C sets off on a long tack to the NE, without thinking about when he will go about.

On board boat D, it is thought that the wind will not change much: $45° - 20° = 25°$. D sets off to beat in the pink sector situated between $15°$ and $25°$ from the axis of the present wind.

On board boat E, on the contrary, it is thought that the wind will change considerably: about $40°.45° - 40° = 5°$. So they stay as they are.

So, for diametrically opposite reasons, boat A and boat E stay in the same sector, while all the others try to make up to windward in the same direction from which the new wind will come.

The wind does change, about 20° (green on the chart). Let us count the points. For A and E, the course is shortened by 6%. For B, by 11% but for D by 21%.

C has gone too far off: he is outside the new beating sector. But he is clearly to windward of D and the distance which separates him from the objective is only 9% greater than that of D. Perhaps the increase in speed he gets by being able to sail full-and-by will compensate for the longer course he has made for himself.

It is interesting to see what would have happened if the change in the wind had been more or less.

If the wind shifts 40° (grey area), the passage for A and E is shortened by 22%. B is outside the beating sector but will perhaps make up by his speed on full-and-by on A and E although he has further to go; D and C are no longer in the race: the speed of one would have to increase by 10%, the other's by 18% for them to arrive at the objective at the same time as the others.

If the wind shifts 60° (red area), everyone is outside the new beating sector; A and E are nearest to the objective.

If the wind turns the wrong way by 20° (red area), C's course is lengthened by 16%, D's by 10%; B's does not change; A's and E's is shortened by 6%.

The following conclusions can be drawn from these results:

- *The winner is the boat which has made the best estimate of the degree of wind change.*
- *The boat which chooses the direct course is always well placed. He wins in three cases: if the wind does not change; if it changes a lot, and if it turns the other way.*
- *In every case making a big detour is absolutely useless.*

In several cases, it will have been noticed that boats outside the beating sector, but to windward of their rivals, have some chance of catching up on lost time, as they are heading for the objective full-and-by and are therefore sailing faster than those close-hauled. This leads us to consider a particular case: when the objective being made for can be reached in one tack close-hauled. It can be advisable sometimes to bear away a little to gain speed, if a wind change is expected before the end of the passage: either because the wind heads you by more than half the boat's heading, or because it frees a little.

It is obvious that you work out your plan according to the distance that has to be run and according to the meteorological conditions: the farther away your objective, the more chance you have of seeing the wind change during the passage: if a polar front is active over the area where you are sailing, the choices to be made affect the hours immediately following the decision; in an anticyclonic situation it is more likely a matter of days; and if you are in the region of monsoons, it's a seasonal matter.

Crossing the English Channel

To recapitulate, we shall discuss the policy to be followed for some different kinds of Channel crossings, in a classic meteorological situation: a depression has just passed through, another is forecast, and the wind is NW and is soon going to back.

If you are going from the Isles of Scilly to Bréhat (course 115°), the direct route obliges you to sail with the wind dead astern, always a bad point of sailing. But it would be inadvisable to gybe tack, as you would do if the wind were not going to change. Now there is a risk of it shifting to the point where you would not be able to carry the spinnaker any longer. So it is preferable to luff up a little on the starboard tack and to keep on it; you will then stand a good chance of making the crossing first on a broad reach then on a reach.

From Torquay to Bréhat (course 169°), the direct course is done

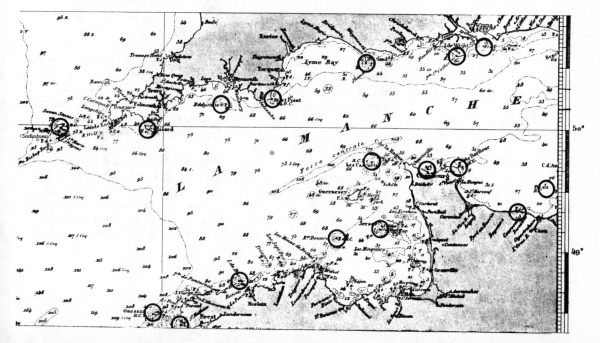

on a broad reach. But for the same reasons as in the preceding example, it is in your best interests to luff up in the direction from which the wind in going to come. If you reckon that the wind is going to change during the first part of the passage, it is as well to luff up by 15° as soon as you have cleared Start Point. You only luff 5° if you think that the wind will only change towards the end of the crossing.

From Plymouth to Ushant (course 199°), you are on a reach on the direct course. Here the choice is difficult and it becomes important to know the latitude over which the forecast depression is going to pass. If it is passing to the north, the wind will perhaps back no further than west: to luff to the spinnaker's limit from the start then becomes the likely plan. If the centre of the depression is going to pass over the Channel, it is probable that the wind will turn south, even perhaps SE. In these conditions, bearing away by 15° in relation to the direct route can be good tactics. But you must be very sure of yourself because this is a bold decision. Finally, if you think that the wind is going to settle in the SW, it is useless looking for difficulties where there are none, and the direct course is the best: it is policy to be as near as possible to Ushant when the wind turns against you.

Tidal Tactics

Finding the fastest course in an area that is criss-crossed by tidal streams is quite a complicated business. All the factors have to be taken into account at the same time: wind, the tidal stream itself and the combined action of wind and tide which creates completely new problems. Here, it must be said, the game begins to resemble a Chinese puzzle; but this is the time when a little thought can lead to rewarding results.

First, it must be appreciated that a tidal stream is seldom consistent: it has its swift areas and its slow areas, and its counter-currents. The tactics therefore are finding the fast area when the current is favourable, and the slow one or counter-current when they are foul. For instance, when you come into the Channel along the English coast, remember that the current is generally weaker out to sea than near the various headlands along your route: Start

Point, Portland Bill, St Albans Head, etc. It is therefore advantageous to keep close to the coast during the flood, and to move out towards the open sea (or to go into the bays) during the ebb. You will in this way make better progress than by following a straight course.

Difficulties begin to arise when you meet a cross current. If it looks as if you can get no advantage from an alternative cross current (which carries the boat just as much in one direction as another), you are likely, in any case, to be at a serious disadvantage if you try to struggle abortively against it. We have already studied this question in the chapter on coastal navigation where we made the distinction between track over the ground and course through the water. If you try to make a straight course over the ground against a tidal stream, the boat sails further through the water (there is more water to pass under the keel, to point out the obvious) and the duration of the passage is therefore longer. The example of a Channel crossing, illustrated in the margin, shows in contrast how, by letting yourself simply be carried by the current, six hours one way and six hours the other, and by keeping a constant heading, the boat follows a sine curve over the bottom while sailing in a straight line through the water. That is certainly the shortest possible route.

To find the shortest course in an alternating cross current, the principle is therefore always the same: *You must count the hours of tide you will meet during the whole passage, then move the point of departure on the chart by the net amount of miles the tide is expected to carry you off course.* Your heading will then be clear and it must be kept during the entire trip.

But now the whole question becomes intriguing because the shortest route arrived at in this way is not necessarily the fastest; it might be worthwhile to take a somewhat longer course in order to go faster!

This involves taking account of a new concept which is the key to subtle navigation in tidal streams: the idea of surface wind.

Surface Wind

When a boat enters a tidal stream, the wind changes. As the boat is travelling in a water mass that is itself moving, the wind it receives from then on is not the true wind, but a combination of the true wind and the wind due to the speed of the current. We call this wind the *surface wind*. It is not a theoretical force for it is the wind that creates waves in tidal races and what you feel on board a boat that is drifting in the tide.

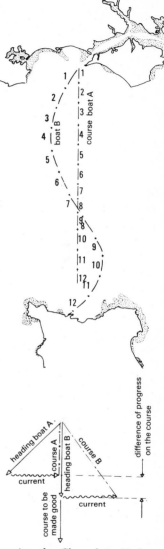

Crossing the Channel in 12 hours. Boat A struggles against current to follow a straight course over ground. Boat B is carried by current following a sine curve over ground but straight on water – despite appearances, the quicker course

When the true wind is strong and the current weak, the surface wind is obviously not of such significance; but in lighter weather the difference between the two winds can become very marked.

When a true wind of 5 knots, for instance, is against a 3 knot current, you will feel a surface wind of 8 knots on board; but if the true wind and the current are both travelling in the same direction, the surface wind is no more than 2 knots. When the true wind and current meet at an angle (and this is of course usually the case) the surface wind differs from the true wind both in strength and direction.

Basic understanding of tidal tactics is appreciating that, as surface wind depends partially on the tidal streams, its characteristics vary according to the variations of the stream. Does it then follow that, as the variations of the tidal stream are predictable, it is not impossible also to predict the variations in the surface wind and take advantage of them?

Geometry

Now we meet the excellent navigator again who, in the chapter on coastal navigation, has already made the passage NW Minquiers buoy – Grand Léjon for us four times. He is making a fifth trip for us today, in conditions very like the fourth – at spring tides, and leaving the NW Minquiers at HW-6. The only difference is the wind which was NE last time and has come round to the west and has freshened a little to Force 3.

Our man reckons he can do the passage in about five hours, if he hasn't to beat. He calculates his course in the same way as he did for the previous trips, moving his point of departure on the chart by the amount of the current he will have under him during these five hours and he works out his true course which he corrects by the variation and leeway to get his compass course.

As it is HW-6, he realises that he can make the heading easily, and that he can get to Grand Léjon full-and-by. But the tide is going to turn in the course of the next few hours: at HW-3 it will be running at 2.2 knots at 135°. So the question arises: when the tide turns, what will it do to the surface wind?

For forecasting the characteristics of the surface wind at HW-3, we must know about its constituents, which are the true wind and the tidal stream that will be running at that time. The tidal movements are known. As for the true wind, we must now make inquiries (we are assuming that it will not change in the next three hours).

Now, when you are sailing in a tidal stream, it is quite impossible to know what the true wind is doing unless you anchor. You can only calculate it from the surface wind and the tide.

You search out the surface wind in the same way as you search for the true wind to establish speed diagrams. As the facts about the tide are known, all that is now needed is a simple bit of geometry on the chart. The surface wind is plotted as a vector (AC), orientated like the wind in question and of a length proportional to its strength (so many knots, so many miles on the chart). At C, you plot the current (vector CD, corresponding to 1.4 knots at 306°). The true wind is then represented by the vector AD.

Anticipating what the surface wind will do. Above: from the present surface wind vector AC and the present current vector CD, one gets the true wind vector AD.

Below: from the true wind A′D′ and the effects of the current D′E at a given time, you arrive at the surface wind speed and direction for the time in question.

It is clear here that the surface wind will drop and head you

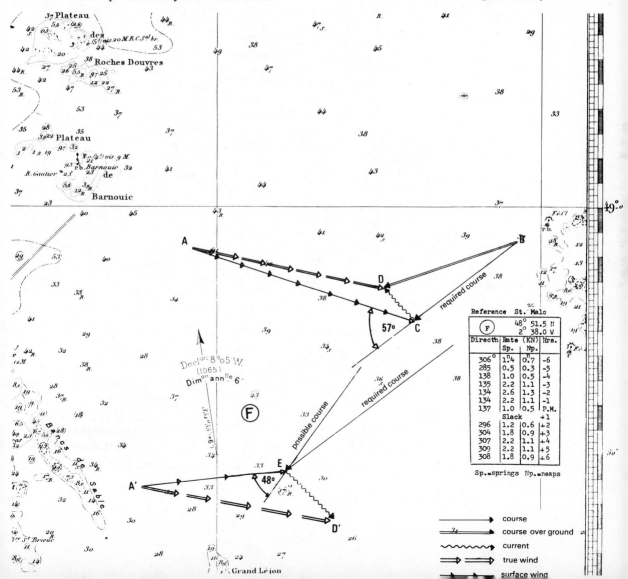

Reference St. Malo		
(F)	48° 51.5 N	2° 38.0 W
Direct.n	Rate (KN)	Hrs.
	Sp. / Np.	
306°	1.4 / 0.7	-6
285	0.5 / 0.3	-5
138	1.0 / 0.5	-4
135	2.2 / 1.1	-3
134	2.6 / 1.3	-2
134	2.2 / 1.1	-1
137	1.0 / 0.5	P.M.
Slack		+1
296	1.2 / 0.6	+2
304	1.8 / 0.9	+3
307	2.2 / 1.1	+4
309	2.2 / 1.1	+5
308	1.8 / 0.9	+6

Sp.=springs Np.=neaps

→→	course
═══→	course over ground
∿∿∿→	current
⇨⇨⇨	true wind
➤➤	surface wind

To find out the surface wind at HW-3, the same sort of geometry must be done the other way round, by starting this time from the true wind A'D', and by plotting from D' the current vector A'E'. Then our navigator immediately realises that his fears were well founded: after the turn of the tide, the wind is going to abate and back quite perceptibly. It will be 34% weaker, and 20° further ahead than it is at present. We shall no longer be able to make the heading we want and we shall have to beat to reach Grand Léjon.

As this is what is going to happen, the navigator immediately takes the necessary decision: instead of following the course he had originally planned and sailing full-and-by on leaving NW Minquiers, he will luff up immediately and sail close-hauled. Then he has some chance of reaching Grand Léjon on the same tack and so saving lots of time. He can see from his first calculation that he can make an excellent tack close-hauled the moment he leaves as the surface wind is not so far ahead and stronger than the true wind. When the boat is pushed towards the wind by the tide it can sail closer to the true wind than if there were no current. It turns out exactly the opposite three hours later.

Our navigator has kindly been giving us a detailed demonstration to show the sort of reasoning which must go on, but most of the time it is not necessary to know every minute detail about the subsequent behaviour of the surface wind. It is important though to know in broad outline how it will develop. The simple geometry we have already done will be very useful for avoiding later confusion. It is enough to scribble them down on a scrap of paper, taking as your basis the only known vector (that represents the tide) and by relating it to the vectors representing (even very approximately) the true wind and the surface wind. It then becomes immediately apparent whether the latter, from one hour to the next, will back, veer, abate or freshen.

'En passant par la Horaine'*

see chart 8 facing p 721

Two identical boats are together at the NW Minquiers buoy and are making, not as you might expect for Grand Léjon, but for la Horaine (distance: 24 miles, true course: 258°) to get to the mouth of the river Trieux. It is springs and the boats pass the NW Minquiers buoy at HW+4. Wind is WSW, therefore a head wind.

On board the first boat, the navigation is being well done, but without any histrionics. The forecast has not said anything about

* A reference to the well known French folk song 'En passant par Lorraine'.

the wind changing for the time being and the navigator is satisfied, after examining the inset and the chart (area F), he knows the tidal movements: he sees that the turn occurs in four hours' time. He settles on setting off on starboard tack; the good one that will bring him close to his objective.

Two hours later he realises that the starboard tack is no longer the right one and that he will have to go about. This decision is all the more sensible because he will be able to take advantage of the end of the ebb to put himself in a position where he will not have to struggle against the flood for the rest of the passage.

So he makes tack to port. An hour and a half later (3h 30), the navigator reckons that the boat is well enough placed, and can go about again. So off he goes again on starboard. But in the course of the fifth hour, the wind begins to head him a bit more, the course is getting less and less than the one he had hoped to make; the flood tide, which has now set in, makes things even worse: he has to go about again. Half an hour later (5h), the boat is once more in a good position and he can go about. But this starboard tack is a disaster. A quarter of an hour later without any hesitation, he knows he must go about. This time he is home and dry; he passes by la Hioraine. The passage has taken six and a half hours.

But when the boat arrives at Loguivy, it is found that the boat that was sailing in company with us at the beginning of the passage is already on a mooring with everything stowed away shipshape and Bristol fashion, and the crew are getting into the dinghy to go ashore. How was it done?

The navigator on the second boat simply asked himself what effect the tidal variations were going to have on the wind. Starting from the facts given in the tide tables for the next six hours, he had the geometry explained above and noticed that the surface wind was going to back progressively south and lighten. At the end of the passage it was going to be 25° further south than the true wind, and 35% weaker.

In these conditions, it was clear from the diagram that the best tack to make was the starboard one for the first three hours of the passage and the port one during the fifth and sixth hours. During the fourth hour, while the current was beginning to change, either tack was equally good. But in this case, if he continued on the starboard tack for the fourth hour, he would have been too far south in relation to his destination. So he went about at the end of the third hour, and passed la Horaine three quarters of an hour ahead of the other boat.

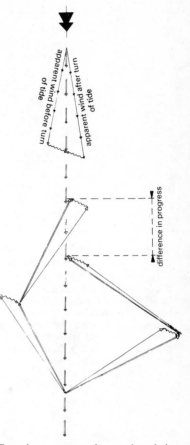

Even in a current the good tack is always the one that is closest to the true wind! It is therefore the tack on which one makes the best close-hauled course (closer than if there were no current). Here it is starboard tack before the turn of tide and port tack after

In choosing his tacks in relation to the surface wind, it must be noted that the navigator in fact chose, each time, the tack which brought him closest to the true wind. Tacks made in relation to the surface wind are not fully effective because it is into the true wind that progress is made and that is what really counts. A rule can therefore be drawn from this example:

When you are sailing close-hauled in a tidal stream with variable strength and direction, the right tack is always the one closest to the true wind. The first boat in our example made three bad tacks: port during the third hour, starboard at the beginning of the fifth and sixth hours.

This same rule is expressed in another way in the diagram below, which tries to demonstrate every eventuality that can arise when you are tacking in a tidal stream. Do not be discouraged by these calculations for the thought needed is not really great and it is just what makes the difference between the performance of two identical boats. As an expert, Alain Gliksman, has said: 'In tacking some are good or at least not bad while others are bad or even worse'.

Choice of the good tack in a current. In all cases in the diagram right the best tack is the one that makes the sharpest angle with the current: a following current is better than a beam current and a beam current better than a head current

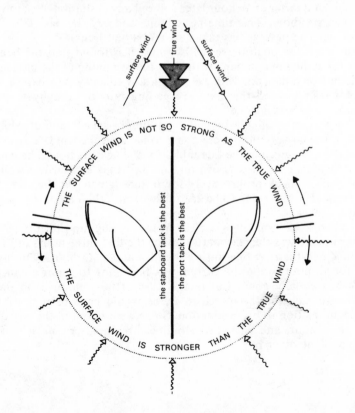

Second Verse

Our two boats are once more at the NW Minquiers, at HW+4 springs and are making for the entrance to the Trieux river, but this time the wind is NNW and light.

See chart 9 on fold-out charts between pages 720–721

On board the first boat, the navigator, who has not yet learned the lesson from the example above, is satisfied with calculating the course in relation to the tide the boat will encounter during the passage: it is 27 miles to the mouth of the river and the estimated speed is 3.5 knots, so the passage will probably take approximately eight hours at a true heading of 258°. Let's be off.

This time everything goes well, even better than had been hoped for, as after four hours the wind frees, and goes north. It is possible to hoist the spinnaker and the speed goes up by a knot. At the end of the sixth hour, it is noticed that the tide is carrying the boat west; we bear away 10°, the speed increases even more and we arrive at the river Trieux going flat out and a good hour earlier than the estimated time.

And yet, in the calm waters of Loguivy harbour, we find the other boat, swinging gently on its mooring and it seems to have been there some time as no one can be seen on board.

Once more, the navigator on this second boat had tried to foresee the development of the surface wind in relation to the tide. With the help of the usual scribbled calculations he realised that the wind was going to free and lighten when the tide turned; he realised too that it would be very likely that it would be right for the spinnaker during the second part of the passage. Indeed, so likely, that the question immediately was: would it not be possible to hoist the spinnaker at the start and do the whole trip under it?

An exact answer to that question admittedly needs a little work. First the point of sailing on which the spinnaker can be carried must be determined and what the boat's speed will be on that point of sailing. Next, what will be the track over the ground if this point of sailing is maintained throughout the passage?

In the event, the spinnaker was hoisted to begin with, just to see. It turned out that it could be carried at 55° to the apparent wind, and that the speed was 4.5 knots.

Starting from these facts, and the tidal information, the navigator did the geometry that gave him the direction and strength of the surface wind for each hour of the passage.

He found that the surface wind was the same for the first two hours. Knowing his speed and heading at the time he could plot, from the wind surface vector and the speed course vector, his

course over the ground vector for these first two hours.

He then plotted on tracing paper the angle between the surface wind and the course–speed vector. Then he moved this tracing paper around on the sketch, so as to make one of the sides of the angle coincide with the surface wind vector for the third hour of the passage. In this way he worked out the vector course–speed, and from there the vector course over the ground for this third hour.

Continuing in the same way for the following hours (gradually shortening the course-speed vectors as the surface wind was easing), all that remained to be done was to place, one after the other on the chart, the vectors he had worked out for course over the ground and he knew where his little wheeze would take him. It was clear he could easily pass by la Horaine and would do the trip in six hours, an hour in front of the first boat. She was so late, not because her navigator had made a detour: on the contrary, he had made the passage straight through the water. But the second boat, by going faster, had been travelling in a foul tide for a shorter time, and had in fact taken a shorter route through the water—1.6 miles less.

The point is that, if speed diagrams are available for the boat, the navigational work is made much simpler. Everything can be predicted before reaching the NW Minquiers, since you know in advance the point of sailing on which the spinnaker can be carried and what the speed of the boat will be. But if you want to be absolutely accurate, then you must take into account that the wind, as it frees, will lighten, and therefore use different diagrams for the beginning of the passage and the last leg.

However, as you can easily imagine, in the middle of the exercise a completely unpredicted change of wind occurs and all the paper work might just as well be thrown to the four winds and the navigator be allowed to come up for a good breath of fresh air.

Envoi

This chapter rounds off the book. It is not intended to be a summary of the foregoing chapters but an explanation of some of the deeper reasons for it being written.

To sail means that you have to know how to navigate and handle a boat, the painstaking maintenance of which will bring out its maximum potential. It means that you must know how to proceed, in the day or at night, all the while avoiding danger, making use of the tides and anticipating the direction and force of the wind and the state of the sea. It means knowing how to live on board in safety and being aware of the importance of the compatibility and skill of the crew.

Sailing also means 'going places' in a very real kind of way. It is not just a matter of moving around in an abstraction of space, force, motion and obstacles. It also means feeling, seeing and understanding 'sea areas'.

We would like, here, to help the reader to understand the concept of a 'sea area', to teach him some methods of approaching it and to give him a practical example of one case among many.

What Do We Mean by a 'Sea Area'?

When an idea is a new one it always seems difficult. Once it has shed new light on things and everyone has got used to it, it seems obvious.

In France, except for a few professionals and some yachtsmen, the idea of a 'sea area' is new and therefore surprising. For the majority of landsmen the sea is just the sea, a great expanse of water, more or less cold depending on whether you go south or north, with waves on it if there is any wind, with rocks and beaches, with ports and fish and gulls. You go down to the sea.

However, this sea—which penetrates deep into the mainland along estuaries or surrounds its off-lying islands, whether it is strewn with rocks or sandbanks or flows freely; subject to a different motion depending on the place, its depths irregular, fringed by a continental shelf of varying extent, heated or cooled by vast currents, the movement of Tropical or Polar water or the upwelling of water from the ocean deeps along the edge of shallower basins – this sea is not everywhere the same.

One must first of all realise that the sea has as many differences as the land. Instead of *the* sea there are many seas, each one with its own numberless separate characteristics. This diversity is neither haphazard nor without a name. There are frontiers and transitional zones and each sea or part of a sea has its clearly defined character. A sea can be defined, understood and recognised by certain constant, permanent features.

It is not just a matter of grasping the fact that the English Channel and the Mediterranean (for example) are different but that within their respective areas (whose main outlines one should be familiar with) there is a whole series of minor areas, some of which have their own name such as the Tyrrhenian Sea, the Ionian Sea, the Aegean Sea. Furthermore there are stretches where, depending on the boat and the season, it would be easy and pleasant to sail (or just the opposite) and this is not just a matter of coastal areas which differ from one another but regions of the high seas themselves. So the Bay of Biscay off the Adour can't be compared to Sole (in the North Atlantic) or to the Trade Wind belt in the latitude of the Canaries.

Maritime nations have a knowledge of such things that goes back a thousand years or more. The Greeks and Romans had already thought of 'The Seven Seas'. The Mediterranean and its areas, especially in its eastern half, are carefully described in the Odyssey. The Norse sagas tell of the Baltic and the North Atlantic which were explored by the Vikings. The voyages of the Phoenicians and Carthaginians opened up several sea regions either side of the Pillars of Hercules (Straits of Gibraltar). The names given by history to oceans and seas, gulfs and bays reveal an attempt to define and qualify certain well-characterised zones. Listen, if you have ears to hear, to sailors and above all to fishermen when they are speaking of sea areas, large or small, rather as countrymen or shepherds or foresters speak of a stretch of country – be it valley, plateau or range of hills – each with its fields, meadows or clearings. You should go out with a fisherman picking up lobster pots ten

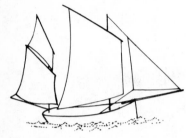

Etaples lugger

miles offshore in the small hours, navigating without a compass for two hours and coming up on the black markers at first go – in order to understand that a stretch of water, so like any other to those who don't know, is in fact so very different either in the colour of the water, the direction of the swell, the nature of the bottom, the aspect of the coast, or just its 'feel'. There's nothing magical about it. Listen to a south Brittany longshoreman: 'I know the waters from Penmarc'h to the Pointe du Talut. In this spot it's always calmer but over there it's often choppy. In this little corner the wind's always contrary. Your anchor will always hold behind that rock over there, but this inlet here isn't safe, in spite of its looks. The swell comes round the point especially when the wind backs nor'west. Over there watch out for the sou'easter – it raises a heavy ground swell. Beyond that I wouldn't know.'

Try to search out old Cape Horners or the skippers of sailing tunnymen or Newfoundland schooners who will tell you in the same vein about the high seas where the differences, although spread out over a wider area, are none the less striking.

One aspect of the passion for understanding sea areas is an interest in the hull form and rig of the many types of boat developed by maritime peoples. Compare the slender craft of the Mediterranean, the crescent shaped caïques of the Aegean, decked but shallow draught with long straight keels; Portuguese sardiners and tunnymen with well rounded counters; heavy 'sinagots' of the Morbihan; the lightly built pinnaces of Andernos and Arcachon descended from types of boat used by the ancient Greek settlers; the powerful pilot boats of the Channel; the broad, heavy, flat-bottomed Dutch 'botters' with their lee boards. In this area the vessel must be able to punch its way through short steep seas, have an enormous sail of light canvas to catch the breezes but capable of being dropped in an instant before a sudden gust of the Mistral. It must also be light enough to be drawn up on the beach as there are few anchorages that are secure from all winds. Here they pull the fish in over the stern. Here the breakers are heavy when you return to the shore and a string of oxen is necessary to drag you up on the beach. On this part of the coast you need a boat that can pass over the shallows. Over on that part you need a deep keeled vessel that will grip on the water so that you can carry all sail in order to punch the tide. Up there you must have boats that can work in heavy seas and strong winds while down along they must be able to smash through a short chop over a shallow bottom and occasionally dry out on a sand bank. A visit to the many little boatyards along the shores of the Atlantic, the English Channel, the North Sea or the Mediterranean or a short chat with a fisherman on the jetty have often taught our members more than any amount of learned lectures. One should therefore try also to understand the why and wherefore of the Chinese junk, the Polynesian outrigger or the North American schooner.

Obviously one must go beyond mere local knowledge but the build up of a detailed understanding of various sea areas has as its final justification the achievement of that particular flair, a mixture of instinct and intelligence, which some seamen have.

We can now give a clearer definition of a sea area: a sea area forms a definite whole, with subsidiary zones whose outlines and the interplay of whose characteristics must be grasped. Understanding them requires intuition, careful observation and systematic reasoning.

Education of the Senses

Intuition (or should we rather call it 'intelligent guesswork') and the five senses should be educated. Much depends on your familiar environment; most of us are better trained to recognise the sound of a moped in the street than the sound of breakers ahead of us. We are more used to the waving of the corn in a breeze than to overfalls caused by wind against tide. At sea such clues combine in a subtle way within the narrow range of a two-dimensional universe. The third dimension, depth of water, is hidden beneath the surface and must be discovered from the chart no matter how far

offshore you happen to be. The bottom is always there but unseen, except when you run aground on a falling tide. It is rather like the training that is needed to be at home in the world of music and to appreciate the balance and rhythm of sounds.

You must learn to look at the land from seawards. The view is sometimes stupendous. If the Corsicans, for instance, together with the bureaucrats responsible for the protection of the environment, had been in the habit of viewing their enchanted isle from the sea, they would straightaway have declared it a national (if not an international) park. Here, at sea, it is rather like being in the front row of the stalls before a stage whose receding background is made up of mountains, woodland and little villages. Elsewhere one comes across a scene which, in contrast, is flatter and more gentle. In yet another spot you are confronted with a menacing wall of cliffs in which you try to find a welcoming gap. Even towns, when seen from the sea, are beautiful.

Venetian topi

You must also understand the line of demarcation between sea and land. The necessity of training is never more obvious than when entering an unknown port for the first time and you are desperately seeking clues in what you see before you. 'It's bad enough trying to identify this church tower, that line of cliffs, those jetties, or this beacon but how am I going to work out how they lie with regard to one another and which course do I choose to get by them?' Who hasn't suffered this agony of indecision when the view in front of you presents an insoluble puzzle (it's worse in the day than at night) and that boat seems to be going like a torpedo.

You must also learn to read the sky which anticipates changes in the sea; to know the difference between the mackerel sky of the western Mediterranean and fair weather clouds, to recognise the various types of cirrus some of which are ominous signs, to judge the speed and direction of a squall, to notice the smooth upwelling or the broken water caused by the tide rushing over a shallow patch and to estimate the limits and strength of a tidal race which can, at times, look like the Rhône in full flood in spring thaws.

Finally, you must understand that a sea area is not just a matter of space, surface and volume as is an area of land. It is not a stable thing but there is a coherence in its movement, a totality of many elements linked to time and tide which perhaps echoes your own internal rhythms of time well spent, time wasted, time to fill, time to run for shelter, a time for standing and for floating off, for fighting a contrary tide, a time of hard-won battle or a triumphal procession. As on land, the light too must play an important role.

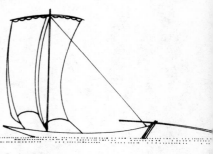

Lake boat

One Approach: The Constants in a Changing Element

This exploration of a new universe, this education of the senses, this acquaintance with the multiple facets of the sea, how can it be done when we know that direct personal experience is the prime factor. Unlike the old shell-backs of the days of sail we cannot spend a long apprenticeship first, as cabin boy then as able seaman, before venturing to take a position of command. Fortunately we have an easier and simpler way out. Knowledge in depth of two or three sea areas, well chosen for the range of differences within them, and a clear understanding of their salient features, together with the judicious use of various pilot books and a little geography, will allow us to extrapolate the characteristics of other sea areas not yet personally experienced.

We know that with a few basic components, each one different in scale and scope, we can build up an infinity of possible combinations. Put the other way round, the endless variety of sea areas can be separated down to a score of primary features or, better still, 'variables'. Of course each area has its own unique, specific character, but a single stretch of sea that is rich in contrasts can provide most of the essentials. Once one or more of such stretches has been thoroughly mastered then we can explore others without an instructor but this is only on condition that we have done our 'homework' properly and that we proceed cautiously ensuring that we have plenty of shelter to run to.

So, rather than exhausting ourselves in never completed studies of innumerable seas and coastlines we must first familiarise ourselves with the basic features of one particular area so that in practice we will recognise them and anticipate their effects. In this way a 'basic framework' of knowledge is built up that can be used as a checklist anywhere side by side with information drawn from the various pilot books and other sources of nautical information. Let us now try this out in theory and look at the results.

Sources of Information

Before defining what we think a basic framework of knowledge ought to consist of and applying it to a particular case, we must, at the risk of repeating what we have already explained in previous chapters, set out the tools needed for the study of a chosen sea area.

We don't place much trust in the various 'yachtsmen's guides' which, however conscientiously or otherwise, try to replace the thorough use of the proper sources of information by a ready-made package. This is not to deny the excellence of many of such works such as the Adlard Coles publications on the Channel ports and the Brittany coast (they have even been quoted in the official 'instructions to mariners' which is a rare honour) or the interesting 'Where to Sail' series in the French magazine *Bateaux* or the Blondel charts for yachtsmen – they provide, however, only an introduction to the art of pilotage and their treatment of the subject is by its very nature piecemeal. One should never forget that at sea things are constantly changing. The maritime authorities are a case in point. They make 'improvements' every year and are continually altering the buoyage system. No private concern, even with the present expansion of the yachting market, can guarantee up-to-date information which even the official services, that are free from purely commercial interests, are hard put to keep abreast of.

If a road map has errors and omissions there's no great problem (you can always find a little side road that will provide an unexpected short cut) but it's a different matter with a chart. The unmarked change of position of a buoy, for instance, can lead to a catastrophe.

We therefore recommend as essential the publications of the various hydrographic services whose admirable and irreplaceable work cannot be praised too highly. We only regret that lack of resources prevents them from making fuller use of their archives from the days of sail that could be so useful to yachtsmen.

Among French publications there are, besides the S H 1 admirable charts, tidal atlases, lists of lights and radio beacons, tide tables and pilot books which are all of fundamental importance.

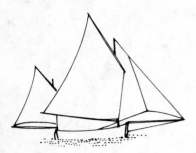

Baie de Seine Picoteux

The preface to the last-named states that its 'aim is to give navigators all the information necessary to them which is not incorporated in the charts or if so, only briefly'. Such works should become the bedside books of every sailor not only for the vast amount of information that they contain but also for the model clarity of their style. To these it would be well to add several atlases containing details of geology and relief maps. Lastly one could choose a number of travelogues on the area where you wish to sail. In this field perhaps the old classics are the best, such as *Sailing Alone Around the World* by the inimitable Slocum, *The Cruise of the Perlette* written by Marthe Oulié (which is still a useful authority for anyone wishing to tackle the Aegean and the Ionian seas), and the logs of Claud Worth whose many passages to Brittany at the turn of the century contributed to the popularity of cruising as we know it today. Many since have told of their voyages. Beware however of overblown and selfconscious writers who seem to imagine that the eyes of the world are on them as they put to sea. Humour, as long as it is not too elephantine and laboured, is a tell-tale sign of the genuine article. The sea does not lend itself to the heroic vein. It's an element full of difficulties, joys and sometimes tragedies. Not all seas, thank God! are the equivalents of the north face of the Eiger.

This varied mass of reading matter can put the beginner off. But, don't worry! The accumulation of a little maritime library and the habit of dipping into it, getting to know charts, preparing the details of future cruises, these are but some of the real joys of sailing. Without this imaginative preparation there is no sense of discovery, either of the sea or of yourself.

The 'Basic Framework' Proposed

Let's get down to first things. What are the questions to be asked before tackling a sea area and where exactly can one find the

Mediterranean tartane

answers to these questions in the publications mentioned above and elsewhere? The questions can be placed in four groups depending on the common ground they cover – an arbitrary method but quite useful:

1. The meteorology of the area in question; the direction, strength and frequency of the winds; visibility, temperature and the incidence of storms.

2. The character of the sea in this area; its fetch, the patterns of swell, the temperature of the water, the importance of tides and tidal streams.

3. The geography of the coast and the seabed; the aspect of the coastal zone and the types of foreshore that result from it, the profile and relief map of the continental shelf, the lie of the coast with respect to the sun, the winds, swell and currents.

4. The human and economic geography of the area; port facilities, visual, aural and radio aids to navigation, shipping lanes, government rules and regulations and the historical and cultural background.

The replies to 1 can be found in the appropriate Pilot book (under the heading Meteorology amidst the general information contained in the beginning of each volume) and they must be studied with the chart before you. A study of the composite charts, drawn up by the Americans, is also recommended, especially to deep water sailors.

For 2 one should consult the Pilot book (under the heading Oceanography in the general information section and the paragraphs headed Tides and Currents in the various chapters), the tide tables, charts and harbour plans.

Answers to 3 will be found in the Pilot book, geological maps which are of great use (especially those which include the sea bed), atlases and charts where the underwater contours revealed by soundings should be examined carefully, all of which should be compared with the system of prevailing winds and the tidal streams. For those particularly interested in geography we would recommend *The Morphology of the Sea Bed and the Shore* by André Guilcher which is old but far from out-of-date.

The answers to 4 are in the *Admiralty List of Lights* and the companion volume on radio signals and also in the Pilot book. For existing facilities, the economy of the region and its past one could consult, with advantage, recent textbooks on its human and economic geography, magazine articles, the publicity hand-outs of yachting centres, tourist guide books and monographs of local studies.

Tartane

Gathering all these answers together can give one a comprehensive knowledge of the area from which much of practical use will, we hope, be drawn.

In justification of our methods we would point out that, logically, having once established the basic framework, we might be expected to carry on and give you the full authoritative details of the chosen area. That, however, is bad teaching. It is better you find out for yourself.

A Case-study: South Brittany

The best thing therefore is straightaway to apply the 'basic framework' to a given area and see what we can get from it.

Let us take the very diverse region between the Raz de Sein and the mouth of the Loire. The area between Sein and Penmarc'h is really a zone of transition from the Iroise area and South Brittany proper starts at Penmarc'h (coming from the north you only have to notice how the swell flattens out and the surface of the sea changes within a few instants, once you have passed the point, to realise that you are in a new sea area). However, as the sea around Sein has a multitude of features essential to our study, we have tacked it onto South Brittany.

Let us arm ourselves with the necessary documentation, in particular the Pilot: *France, North and West Coasts*, together with its booklet of corrections; the *List of Lights:* 'English Channel – East Atlantic Ocean'; large and small-scale charts for the area Sein to the Loire and the geological and physical maps of Brittany. Now let us apply them to the basic framework.

Meteorology

An examination of the section entitled Meteorology on pages 1–42 of the (French) Biscay Pilot (1966, series C volume II) shows that this region of South Brittany which really forms part of the Bay of Biscay, is characterised by prevailing winds from between SW and NW with an important series of winds from between north and NE. We'll take as a point of reference the Pointe de Talut which is in the centre of the area and not Ushant or Brest which are too far north or La Coubre which is too far south. The diagrams in the margin portray the direction and strength of the winds depending on the season, temperature and cloud cover. So, for the month of July (based on an average of four daily observations taken over a period of ten years between 1946 and 1955) north and NE winds make up respectively 10% and 14% of the total. These are mainly land breezes whereas in spring and autumn the winds depend on a wider meteorological situation. SW winds make up 10%, west winds 25%, NW 28% and east 4%, while south and SE winds barely surpass 3%. There is 3% of calms. You should further note that strong winds make up less than 20% and that storms (over Force 8) are rare.

It is as well to remember however that storms are possible and since the last edition of the (French) Biscay Pilot a real mini-cyclone of Force 11 to 12 passed through this very area. It was the result of a meteorological situation that is fortunately rare. Although unexpected it did give warning of its approach by a steep fall in the barometer, an essential instrument that should never be ignored. None the less as the diagrams in the Pilot book show, winds along the South Brittany coast during July are usually moderate.

You will also see that the visibility is good (two days of fog) and the temperature is mild (from 14.5°C to 20.4°C on average, the extremes being 8.2°C and 34.4°C).

Closer attention plus a minimum of practice will teach you that during July the weather is dominated by stable anticyclonic systems which give sea breezes during the day with, sometimes, a calm at the beginning of the afternoon and at night a land breeze, often quite fresh from the north or NE. The more disturbed periods of weather in this month are linked to the trailing edges of depressions passing far to the north which give a brief interval of damp south to SW winds followed by a longer interval of west to NW winds with clear skies but often colder. Such sequences usually come in series. Anyway if the first weather pattern is blissful the second is far from being infernal.

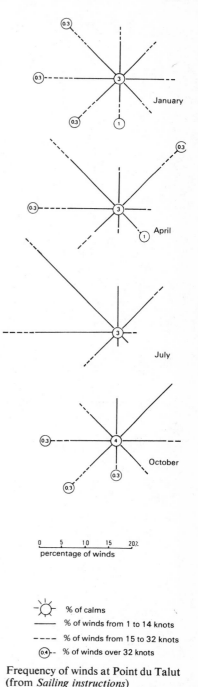

percentage of winds

☀ % of calms

—— % of winds from 1 to 14 knots

---- % of winds from 15 to 32 knots

(0.4)-- % of winds over 32 knots

Frequency of winds at Point du Talut (from *Sailing instructions*)

In short, if you compare conditions during the summer months (and for the whole year) with those that obtain in other areas (such as the Channel, South Biscay or the West Mediterranean) you will see that the weather is very clement in South Brittany and what is more, being stable, it can be forecast easily.

You should also note that, not counting the worst months, November and December, which can present problems, you are at no time prevented from sailing by winds that are strong or unexpected. It is not an area of persistent fogs either. Finally, the air temperatures, even in winter, are very mild compared with those at Dunkirk, for instance, or even those at Socoa, and present no insurmountable difficulties even for night sailing.

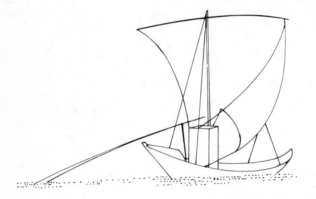

Rabello (wine transporter), Portugal

The Nature of the Sea

To get the basic facts about tides, currents and the patterns of swell you should study the charts of the area, the tidal stream atlas, the general introduction to the (French) Biscay Pilot under the heading Oceanography (pp. 43–65) and the information given in chapters XI, XII and XIII under the heading Tides and Currents. You should also check the tide tables, the standard port for this area being Port Louis (for the centre of the area at least – otherwise use Brest for the north end and St Nazaire for the south).

The range of tide is about 5 or 6 metres at springs (the biggest range being 7.77m at Brest; 5.7m at Port Louis and 6.4m at St Nazaire) and about 2 or 3 metres at Neaps. The prevailing swell comes from the Atlantic being mainly SW or west and doesn't constitute any danger as it does in South Biscay. The tidal streams run parallel to the coast and, in general, are not strong. They form, in part, an offshoot of the Gulf Stream. However at certain spots the tidal streams are strong such as at the mouths of rivers, through narrows and over shallow ground. You should note in particular the strength of the currents around the Raz de Sein, the Pointe de Penmarc'h, the Iles des Glénans, around the Ile de Groix and Belle Ile and at the entrance the Baie de Quiberon (Teignouse and Béniguet). The currents in river estuaries such as the Pont l'Abbé, the Odet, the Pouldohan, the Aven and Belon, the Laïta, the Blavet, the Etel, the Vilaine and the Croisic are considerable and the 'inland sea', the Morbihan, has exceptionally strong tidal streams which require separate attention.

The water temperature is neither too high nor too low, being between 10°C and 17.5°C. This is a point which people don't think about often enough. The water temperature can entail many consequences when, for example, someone has fallen overboard, or if you are living on board during the winter.

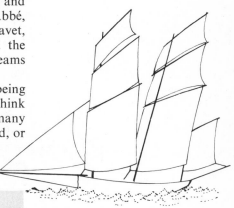

Cancale bisquine

All this lets us know that the sea is both safe and varied in South Brittany. There are tidal streams but their comparative weakness (except in the Morbihan and around the Raz de Sein) and their limited area, enables you to experience them in safety and to avoid them without limiting your itinerary. The seas are seldom heavy.

The Coastline

Following an international conference of the sea in 1970, it is to be hoped that the Bureau of Geological and Mining Technology will take even more initiative in drawing up geological and relief maps of the continental shelf and of the shore line in the Baie de Quiberon. The business world has already brought out a relief map of Brittany (including the offshore sea bed) from the Iles Chausey to Noirmoutier. There is no better tool than this for understanding the interplay of wind, water and land. This kind of presentation would give charts a dimension which we are unused to.

A short study of its geology and physical geography will help us understand this stretch of coast which is oriented WNW to ESE. South Brittany is partly granite, partly schist and partly sedementary rock and the whole area has been in the process of subsiding ever since the beginning of the quartenary period. As a result the lowest levels have become 'drowned' with islands and reefs marking the edge of sunken valleys. The sea penetrates deep inland. The structure of the land is similar to the 'rias' of Southern Ireland, Cornwall, Wales and Galicia. In the case of South Brittany the coast has been further complicated by the more recent upheavals of the Tertiary period which preceded the subsidence and drowning of this area, *viz* André Guilcher:

'The south coast of Brittany between Penmarc'h and the Vendée seems to be like this: the islands and archipelagos follow the *anticlinal alignments*, effects of the Tertiary period, which are interrupted by faults in several places. The same pattern is continued into the hinterland and it has given along the coast a series of parallel depressions in between the raised portions which have become drowned such as the Anse de Pouldon (Port l'Abbé), the Baie de Kerogan (Quimper), Lorient roads, the Etel river, the east part of the Morbihan, Croisic and Brière.'

In making a study of this coast using the various aids, you can make out as you go from north to south the following characteristics: from Sein to Penmarc'h the shoreline, apart from the Audierne gap, is low and straight, there is no protection against the prevailing wind and swell. These last come, unobstructed, all the

Portuguese sardine boat

way from far-off America. There is nothing to stop them and the 100 metre line is not far offshore. There is only shelter from NW through north to SE. During the east and NE winds of spring and autumn you can sail close along the coast or easily find shelter at Audierne or even at Saint Guénolé if you can manage to get in.

From Penmarc'h (Guilvinec onwards) to Lorient you find the first little yachtsman's paradise. The waters are, for the most part, protected from the ocean swell by a string of islands. To the west and NW of the bay stretches the twenty square miles of the Glénans archipelago with an extension to the NW formed by the Ile aux Moutons and its adjacent islets and shallows which reach to the mainland. Eastwards stretch the Basse Jaune reef, the Basse Doun and Ile Verte. At the east end of the bay the Ile de Groix forms a wall six miles long lying east to west. In addition to acting as a breakwater these islands offer refuge. The Glénans enclose a veritable lagoon, protected from most winds especially at low water. All along its northern shore Groix provides a sheltered anchorage and a safe sailing area. The western end of the bay, which is perhaps somewhat overendowed with granite rocks, is oriented in such a way that its creeks and estuaries are protected from most winds and the prevailing swell. Nearly all the ports and harbours (or at least their entrances) are accessible at all states of the tide, which is essential. Several tidal rivers penetrate deep inland. It should be noted however that between Benodet and the entrance to the Baie de la Forêt there are six miles without shelter and that the Pointe de Mousterlin extends quite a long way out to sea. The centre of the bay is less well-endowed but none the less beautiful. Between Pouldohan and the entrance to the Aven the exposed stretch of ten miles only provides two precarious shelters, Trévignon and Raguenès (the latter is free of dangers but is open to the swell).   Douélan

Between this point and Lorient there are a number of havens in the rocky shaly coastline, among which are the rivers Aven and Belon, Brigneau, Merrien and Douélan, all accessible at most states of the tide but whose entrances are exposed to the prevailing winds.

From Lorient to Port-Maria de Quiberon and to Belle Ile there are twenty miles of inhospitable coast apart from one single haven; the river Etel which is wide and beautiful but the entrance has a sand bar and is exposed to the swell and the prevailing winds and is not always accessible. To seawards the Birvideaux plateau forms dangerous shallows.

Beyond Quiberon and between Belle Ile and Le Croisic there is a second yachtsman's paradise wherein is found Belle Ile, Houat, Hoëdic, the Ile aux Cheveaux and the Ile Dumet which, together with the granite Quiberon peninsula, protects the western half of the area including Port Haliguen, La Trinité and the entrance to the Morbihan, from the prevailing winds and swell. The last named is a real inland sea, completely protected from the open sea, with rocky granite shores and strewn with small wooded islets. The river Auray opens out at its entrance.

The eastern part of this region is more difficult. The low coastline of schist, marshy in some places, is exposed to the swell and the prevailing winds. A number of havens exist here, such as Penerf, Keroyal and the estuary of the Vilaine, La Turballe and Le Croisic, but their approaches are less straightforward than those of the western part and few are accessible at all states of the tide as are La Trinité and Port Haliguen. Moreover, long distances separate them; there are about ten miles from the mouth of the Morbihan to Penerf and more than twenty to Le Croisic.

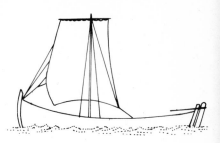

Norwegian boat

Belle Ile, a regular fortress of schist and granite, deserves particular mention. Its northern shore, which is oriented NW–SE from the Pointe des Poulains to the Pointe de Kerdonis, is sheltered from the prevailing winds and swell and boasts two excellent harbours, Sauzon and Le Palais. Its lee provides a wide stretch of calm waters. The wild southern shore is completely exposed.

It should be noted that here again the whole area is rock-infested particularly at the entry to Quiberon bay and off Le Croisic.

Human Affairs

This question is always a basic one. Without specifying South Brittany it must be emphasised that, in France, port facilities and above all the buoyage system together with lighthouses and radio beacons, are very well provided. This cannot be said for many countries, even in Europe, either because of neglect or, as in England, a knowledge of the sea is so taken for granted that a detailed buoyage system is not considered necessary. So, when abroad, don't expect such a well marked coast as in France. We should also emphasise here the matter of shipping, whether it be the massive exodus from or return to the fishing ports morning and evening every day, or fleets of trawlers shooting their nets or the stream of commercial shipping along the sea lanes such as one finds off Ushant or the Lizard. These all present risks of collision that the yachtsman should never lose sight of. Finally, the attitude of the authorities (customs, police, harbour masters), of such or such a country must be taken into account if you wish to avoid trouble. If you have not learned beforehand what is expected of you by the authorities, the attitude and behaviour of such officials will soon let you know.

This said, let us return to the Biscay Pilot and the Lists of Lights and Radiobeacons which will tell us that South Brittany is superbly marked and that, day or night, it is easy to find your bearings there. We shall also learn from the reading of articles that the port facilities are many although mainly concerned with the fishing industry. A certain finesse and courtesy are therefore required if we wish to find acceptance at ports, like Guilvinec, Douélan or La Turballe; but once accepted, what a welcome! Extensive yachting facilities are gradually being provided at several places.

We shall also discover that there is great fishing craft activity especially at times when the main fleet put to sea and return to harbour. This increases the risk of collision. Otherwise South Brittany is outside the main shipping lane leading from Finisterre to Ushant so the coastal cruiser will only meet large cargo vessels beyond the Armen buoy.

For the rest, let us just say that if the Glénans Sailing Centre has been able to attract so many thousands of the young and not so young, it has been mainly due to the great historical interest and geographical variety of the South Brittany coastline and long may the Bretons themselves defend it against the disfigurements of false modernity and the encroaching tide of holiday villas.

To Pastures New

We could end here on a lyrical and, at the same time, a practical note. South Brittany is ideal for sailing and for learning how to sail for it provides all the difficulties that one is likely to encounter at sea but in such small doses that the beginner can rarely come to harm. The region offers sailing what school supplies to the young – experience of the ups and downs of life. Safe anchorages there are in plenty and there is a close succession of harbours. The pattern of wind and tide is regular and therefore foreseeable. An acquaintance with the various sea areas is comparatively easy. Like the country-side inland which is divided into a series of distinct terrains, the coastline is diversified. The divisions are clear cut and the differences obvious.

Now you should go further afield and built up a wider knowledge. So far we have assumed that our reader is new to the sea. These first steps are therefore fundamental; by doing the necessary homework for one narrow stretch of sea, you will establish a basis of reference for future experience. This basis can be strengthened by applying it in other contexts.

The simplest way of doing this is to take another look at South Brittany, using the basic framework of information from the point of view of the visiting yachtsman. What possibilities does this area offer and how does it compare with other such areas? The visitors can be divided into four different categories:

1. Those who only want a stretch of water suitable for a small sailing dinghy or rowing boat near to where they live or spend their holidays. This is not too difficult but certain conditions are a 'must'. Firstly, the situation should be such that the first gale will not blow all the boats out to sea or smash them on the rocks ashore. Secondly, the safety measures (visibility and means of getting to those in distress) should be easily available. Thirdly, the prevailing weather conditions should be fairly equitable with no violent alternation between calms and strong winds. Fourthly, the tides should not be too strong and finally the shore should lend itself to the easy launching and hauling out of boats. Such a sailing area can be big enough for Olympic racing to take place within it or it can be on a much more modest scale. All that is needed is that it should be safe for small boats.

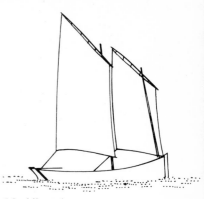

Morbihan sinagot

2. Those who want to combine camping and sailing and so need speedy access to shelter or at least to somewhere where they can haul their boats out of the water. This hauling out of boats is a very ancient practice as we can see from history and legend, especially in the *Iliad* and the *Odyssey*. Modern yachting has not yet rediscovered this practice, mainly owing to the inadequacy of boat design and structure. How much vain laying of concrete mooring blocks could have been avoided if only the right questions had been asked, ie 'how can we haul a boat easily up on land?' instead of 'how can we keep it afloat sheltered from wind and sea?'

Whatever the type, the boat in this case must be comparatively small, a cruising dinghy, capable of short voyages in calm weather or sheltered waters within easy reach of beaches or protected slipways or foreshore where it is safe to dry out. Such places should be close together, not more than two miles apart. A piece of ground suitable for putting up a tent should be close by. Big tides can sometimes be a problem.

3. The coastal cruising man who only rarely sails at night and who wants a safe haven to sleep in. His boat draws between 0.7 metres to 1.30 metres. He doesn't want to spend all his holiday in the same port, setting out in the morning only to return in the evening. He wants to be able to run quickly for shelter when bad weather strikes unexpectedly. He would like to keep within the same area, at least during the holiday period and possibly winter his boat there as it's difficult to transport except by sea. The next season becoming bolder he may move onto another attractive stretch of coast.

This visitor is looking for a cruising area where he can find a choice of major ports with good facilities (where a boat can be safely left, maintained and repaired), small fishing ports and natural harbours where he can stop overnight, open anchorages where the water is calm, in the lee of islands or tucked away in inlets. He must also have ports of refuge to leeward so that he doesn't have to beat against heavy seas, in order to find shelter. It's all a matter of variety and balance.

4. The deep water cruising man for whom a 100 mile trip is normal. He wants to know whether the approaches to the coast are difficult or easy (a matter of rocks, tidal streams, swell, visibility and buoyage) and whether there are any major ports with enough water to allow the entry, at any state of the tide, of boats drawing between 1.5 and 2.3 metres and which have all the necessary equipment and facilities. He would also be interested to know whether there are any suitably sheltered open anchorages.

Now all these things which our four categories of yachtsmen require, are they to be found in the area we have just analysed? Where can they be found in greater abundance or found to be lacking either wholly or in part?

To reply to the second question would take a lifetime, but we can briefly answer the first and at the same time give some hints on the second. So, we will complete our study of South Brittany and fire your imaginations.

Dinghy Sailing Areas

For the lovers of dinghy racing such areas exist without number in South Brittany. Just look at the multitude of sailing clubs and sailing schools that have flourished in a number of places; Loctudy and Benodet, in the Baie de le Forêt, Pouldohan, the Aven, in the Ile de Groix, the NE of Belle Ile, in Quiberon Bay and at Carnac. Other regions may be equally well provided and have wider expanses of water but few have such well sheltered dinghy sailing areas. Compare them, if you will, with the roadsteads of Brest and Cherbourg, the Baie de Bourgneuf, the area to the NE of Ile d'Yeu, the Pertuis Breton, La Rochelle roads, the Lac d'Houstin, the Etang de Thau, Marseille roads under Frioul, the roadsteads of Toulon and Hyères and, in Corsica, the bays of Saint-Florent, Ajaccio, Valinco and Santa Manza.

Sailing and Camping Areas

These too are numerous in South Brittany; in the rivers, in the lee

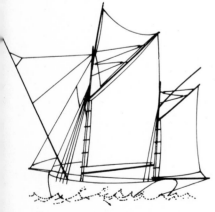

Concarneau tunnyman

of islands, along numerous beaches although the facilities on land are desperately lacking and the expanses of muddy foreshore, although moderate in extent, are nevertheless wide enough, especially at low tide, to discourage those who want to haul their boats out of the water. For the most part it is best to moor in sheltered waters and either sleep on board or wade ashore to set up tent.

In this field Corsica is queen; whether it be in the north around Cape Corsica, in the NW along the Agriates flats, in the west above Carghese, in the SW in the Baie de Cupabia between Cape Muro and Porto-Pollo, in the south and SE from Tizzano to Paloubaggio (with a few interruptions), then eastwards towards the island of Pinarello and after Solenzara the long stretch of beaches bordered by pines reaching to the outskirts of Posetta.

Here there are no mud flats but plenty of beaches and creeks where you can haul your boat out. There are no coastal roads (or not yet, and, we hope, never) and as to climate and water, they are justly famed. The ideal boat for this coast is, however, yet to be invented. The Marauder and its ilk are more suited to Atlantic coasts. In the Mediterranean, if you haven't stayed wide awake, you may have to pile on canvas or use full throttle on the motor in order to reach shelter and a capsize can be fatal. The Cavale, which is ideal for these waters, draws too much and is, above all, too heavy to be hauled out unless you have special gear. At the present moment we are trying to bring out a suitable adaptation of the Caravelle.

If you cannot make Corsica or the Dalmation coast or the east Mediterranean don't dismiss the Atlantic coast or the English Channel. Here the coast-hopping sailor/camper can find plenty of suitable spots bearing always in mind the need for immediate bolt-holes.

Despite extensive sand and mud flats, perhaps even because of them, North Brittany can offer some surprising possibilities.

Cruising Areas

South Brittany is exceptional in its two cruising areas (Penmarc'h to Lorient and Quiberon to Croisic) where everything is beautifully proportioned; distance between ports and havens, choice of anchorages, sheltered areas in which you can make to windward more easily, and weather conditions that can be forecast.

To the north of Le Havre there is nothing like it, and you need courage and patience for cruising between Dunkirk and Fécamp along a coast of low, straight sandy shores or steep cliffs upon seas

Cove in Sormiou

Trabacolo, Adriatic coaster

that are steep on account of the shallow bottom and encumbered to the north by sandbanks. In nigh on 200 miles of coast there are only five ports that one can enter at any state of the tide. Of course, further northward there is Zeeland which forms practically an inland sea and over on the English side there is the Thames estuary.

There are good cruising grounds between Le Havre and Barfleur but you have to check your tide tables because the harbours, with the exception of Le Havre and St Vaast, are only open at high water and their facilities are still insufficient to compensate for the natural advantages of South Brittany. The day will come when the remarkable possibilities of Courseulles, Isigny, Carentan and St Vaast, to mention but a few, will be developed to meet the growing demands of the nearby urban areas. For the present the coastline remains grim (as becomes the theatre of the Normandy landings) and waiting for the tide can be an awful bore.

On the west side of the Cotentin peninsula we come to a region of strong tides exposed to the westerly winds. There are few easily accessible havens (Port Bail, Carteret and Goury) and they require a great deal of skill to enter. Facing this coast is a marvellous but tricky cruising area stretching from Granville to Roscoff and the Ile de Batz and containing the Iles Chaussey and the Channel Islands. This veritable maritime park is characterised by wide sand or mud flats, violent currents, few deep-water anchorages except in the river Trieax and the islands, ports where you have to lock in or where you must moor or anchor to a long scope of warp and chain. In case of mistakes your boat will need legs, unless you prefer living life at an angle of 45°. North Brittany, especially towards its eastern end, has difficulties which far exceed those of the south.

The Iroise, swept by strong currents and strewn with rocks that extend far out to sea and upon which the heavy ocean swell breaks, is a cruising area that is hard and difficult but open. For the yachtsman coming from South Brittany, the sea between Sein and Ushant seems to have a strange, disturbing life of its own. Brest roads, although a preserve of the navy, can nonetheless provide numerous possibilities. Douarnenez, Tréboul, Morgat, Camaret, Aberwrac'h and Aber Ildut, Sein and Molène are also excellent ports of call. If you sail here during the off-season when heavy weather sets in, you will be made to feel very small and wretched by each line of swell as it passes. On returning to South Brittany, once past Penmarc'h, you'll soon appreciate its gentle seas which stay at a reasonable size even in a Force 7.

Between the Loire and the Sables-d'Olonne there are several limited cruising areas; in the Baie de Bourgneuf, under the lee of Noirmoutier or around the Ile d'Yeu. There are not many harbours that are secure in all winds and in rough weather everyone rushes to find refuge in the same few ports.

The last cruising area on the French Atlantic coast lies between La Rochelle and the Gironde. Although less varied than South Brittany it is worthy of remark and in the channels between its islands and the mainland it provides wide stretches of sheltered water.

Short cruises are also possible from Saint-Jean-de-Luz along the Spanish coast.

Obviously there are many cruising areas along the Atlantic coasts of other European countries. The SW coast of England with its marvellous rivers together with the Isles of Scilly, hardly need to be mentioned. We would also mention the SW coast of Ireland from Baltimore to Dingle Bay. The beautiful coastline with its deep, sheltered bays is dominated by rapidly changing winds which makes

Les Héaux de Bréhat

River Trieux

Arcachon pinnace

rounding the headlands tricky. Finally, there is Galicia in NW Spain with its great 'rias' which are little seas in themselves, the Ria de Arosa above all where, in midsummer, the water is colder than at Glénans in springtime.

There are plenty of cruising areas all over the Mediterranean. Each one is a law unto itself for the Mediterranean is a sea of localised weather conditions. Some are a yachtsman's dream, others, like those around the Dalmatian islands, don't have enough wind. We shall only speak here of South Corsica where, from Porto-Vecchio in the east to Figari in the west and as far as Olbia in Sardinia to the south, including Cavallo, the Lavezzi islands, Budelli, La Madalena and Caprera there exists an area comparable to South Brittany. There are times however when the harbours, which although far from perfect, are the best that Corsica and Sardinia can offer, seem too far apart.

We should not forget to mention the North Sea, the west coast of Scotland, Norway and the Baltic with its innumerable twists and turns. Yachts from the Glénans Sailing Centre have sailed these waters as they have the others already described and many more beside. However, we have not yet established bases in these areas and would not set ourselves up as an authority on them. However, as to Corsica, Galicia, Brittany, Southern Ireland and Languedoc, in these places we have established centres (rather like the Hanseatic League in the Middle Ages) whence our boats fan outwards. A few visits to these enable our members to experience other sea areas and to compare them with those bordering on the Glénans archipelago.

Major Ports

There are several of these in South Brittany: Benodet, Concarneau, Lorient and La Trinité to mention only the biggest. There are sheltered deep-water anchorages in many places; rivers, under the lee of islands tucked away inside bays. The approaches from the open sea, although not free from difficulties (rocks, narrow channels, the constant coming and going of fishing craft) are easy as several ports are accessible at nearly all states of the tide, wind and swell are favourable in direction and visibility is usually good.

Estuary sailing boat, Holland

Elsewhere you can find similar conditions such as on the coasts of Devon and Cornwall in England or in the neighbourhood of La Rochelle. Closing with the land in the Iroise area at l'Aberwrac'h, Brest, Camaret and Donarnenez is equally easy as long as a heavy sea doesn't put you off. Things are different in the area from Ile Vierge to Cap La Hague where, except in the river Trieux and in the Channel Islands there are no parts with deep water except behind lock gates. Admittedly there are many good temporary anchorages where you can wait for high water. Here, the strong tidal streams and narrow channels edged with innumerable reefs demand careful navigation. Apart from shipping traffic Le Havre is easy of entry although its tides are peculiar to it and the chop at the mouth of the river Seine is unpleasant. The bay, however, affords little shelter. To the north, Fécamp is almost inaccessible in a fresh west or sou'west wind on account of the surge between the pier heads. The lock gates at Deauville are shut most of the time, Ouistrehan also has a lock and you can only get into Courseules a short while either side of high water. Saint-Vaast-la-Hougue is too far to the west. Cherbourg is the exception among its neighbours. It affords complete shelter, is easy of access and its breakwaters open like welcoming arms to visitors from England.

Tucked away down south in the Bay of Biscay, Bayonne, Saint-Jean-de-Luz and Hendaye are sometimes difficult of access. At Bayonne especially, when the wind is over Force 5 and the rollers that have crossed the Atlantic are breaking on its gravel banks, one may remain harbour bound for quite some time, certainly during winter. The Côte d'Azur has many ports but they are sometimes difficult to beat back into against the Mistral blowing from the north.

You should not therefore conclude, because rough weather rarely

prevents entry into Benodet, Concarneau or Lorient, that all ports are the same any more than you should assume that only South Brittany provides a safe landfall for the deep-water yachtsman. There are areas just as good elsewhere. Nevertheless, rocks or no rocks, anyone coming in from the high seas can count on a warm welcome in South Brittany; and as soon as Penmarc'h heaves into view you can breathe a sigh of relief.

This case study and the brief comparisons that followed it, can only claim to provide a rough guide for those venturing into an unfamiliar sea area. We have only wanted to indicate some of the constants, differences and features that can be found among all sea areas. We shall have succeeded if a beginner, reading this chapter, has realised that the possibility of making a dependable forecast of the weather in South Brittany, is a rare privilege in the Channel, where changes are more rapid, and are completely unknown in the Mediterranean, where you can never be rid of a nagging worry and where there is an extraordinary diversity of local conditions. We hope also that he has understood that the moderate wave system of South Brittany is different from the confused seas around the Channel Islands or the heavy swell of the Iroise; that there is a difference between being able to enter port whenever he wishes and

Maltese gozo

having to wait for high water; that the sea is not necessarily clear once he has passed the coastal dangers and that, as in the North Sea, he may be obliged to thread his way through banks and channels while at his back he can always hear the sound of ships' motors drawing near; in short that nothing is more like and, at the same time, more unlike than one sea area to another and that the widest differences are of often the most subtle.

But now we must allow the reader to escape from this book to go down to the sea, to the joy of discovery, either on the deck of his boat or in studying charts and pilot books. We have done what we could to prepare him, trying to put our experience into simple terms but without covering up the difficulties or providing misleadingly facile introductions.

One day, we hope, he will know more than we do now. In any case, we are going back to the sea ourselves for, on the water, and with the wind, there is no absolute certainty and it is better to check and check again rather than to assume you are right.

Index

Detailed Contents

PART 2: Boat Handling

PART 3: The Crew

PART 4: Meteorology

PART 5: Navigation